THE GOD OF
JESUS CHRIST

THE GOD OF
JESUS CHRIST

Walter Kasper

Translated
by
Matthew J. O'Connell

Crossroad · New York

231
K

1984
The Crossroad Publishing Company
370 Lexington Avenue, New York, N.Y. 10017

Originally published under the title *Der Gott Jesu Christi*
© 1982 Matthias-Grünewald-Verlag, Mainz

English translation copyright © 1984
by The Crossroad Publishing Company

Printed in the United States of America

Library of Congress Cataloging in Publication Data
Kasper, Walter.
   The God of Jesus Christ.

   Translation of: Der Gott Jesu Christi.
   Includes bibliographical references and indexes.
   1. God   2. Trinity.   I. Title.
BT102.K33813   1984   231   84–16991
ISBN 0–8245–0629–4

CONTENTS

Contents

PREFACE

The God-question is the fundamental theological question. The present book is intended as a strong plea to give it that status once again. True enough, there is no lack of publications on the God-question; for the most part, however, these limit themselves to a discussion of modern atheism. The Christian understanding of God, the God of Jesus Christ, and thus the confession of the triune God are usually brought in only as a kind of appendix and without any closer study of the problems involved. Contemporary Protestant theology shows the opposite tendency. On the basis of a *solus Christus* (Christ alone) and a *sola fide* (faith alone) that are interpreted with greater radicalness than they had in the Reformers, an effort is being made to find a standpoint beyond atheism and the theism to which the previous approach leads. In my view, however, both of these standpoints are equally untenable. The only answer to the modern God-question and to the situation of modern atheism is the God of Jesus Christ and the trinitarian confession, which must be brought out of its present existential obscurity and turned into a grammar for theology as a whole.

To this end I have gone back and studied once again the church fathers and the other great doctors of the church. What I have learned from them is not a spiritless traditionalism but a courage – hardly imaginable nowadays – in thinking things out for myself. A renewal of both tradition and speculation is needed, precisely in the present much-deplored stagnation of theology. For a theology which is pastoral, that is, which tackles the question of contemporary man, and which knows what it is about, demands not less but more scientific thoroughness. This triad of ecclesial-mindedness, scientific thoroughness and openness to the times – and not the other things occasionally claimed – are the true Tübingen tradition out of which this book has emerged.

The present book is therefore addressed primarily to students of theology, but it is also meant for all who have a deeper interest in the theological questions connected with the faith: priests and lay-persons in the service of the church; Christians for whom participation in theological discussion has become part of their faith; and the growing number of people, even outside the churches, whom the present crisis of meaning has led to a new interest in the God-question.

Unfortunately there has been a longer delay than planned between my book on christology, which appeared in 1974, and this volume on the doctrine of God and the Trinity. Numerous obligations inside and outside the university and, in no small part, turbulent developments within our university that took their toll on time, energy and nerves, have considerably retarded the work. Above all, however, the difficulty of the subject-matter itself called repeatedly for deeper investigation and reflection.

That the book should finally have appeared at all is due to the selfless efforts of my fellow-workers: my assistants, Giancarlo Collet and Hans Kreidler, who relieved me of a great deal of labour; Miss Martina Lanau and Messrs. Wolfgang Thönissen, Erich Pöschl and Brad Malkovsky, who tirelessly did the detailed technical work and compiled the indexes; my secretaries, Mrs Elli Wolf and Mrs Renata Fischer, who carefully prepared the manuscript; and, finally, the collaborators at the Matthias-Grünewald-Verlag in Mainz.

The book I now offer to the public is far from finished. But, then, who is ever done with the God-question? Even though the book spends so much time winnowing and summarizing the discussion, it is itself intended only as a contribution to the discussion which others will carry on in a critical fashion. If anywhere, then certainly in dealing with the theme of this book, the words of the great Augustine – from whom I have learned so much, even though I have often dared to disagree with him – are applicable: 'Therefore let my reader travel on with me when he shares fully in my convictions; let him search with me when he shares my doubts; let him return to me when he recognizes that he is in error; let him call me back to the right path when he sees that I am the one in error. In this way let us advance along the road of charity toward him of whom it is written: "Seek his face unceasingly" (Ps.104.4)' _(De Trinitate_ 1, 3).

I would like to dedicate this book to the memory of my mother who first taught me to talk of God.

Tübingen,
Feast of Matthew the Apostle, 1982

PART ONE

The God-Question Today

I

God as a Problem

1. The traditional formulation of the problem

The confession of faith which all the great churches of the East and the West have had in common from the early Christian centuries down to our own day begins with the statement: *Credo in unum Deum*, 'I believe in one God.'[1] This opening sentence is also the foundational statement of the entire creed; it contains in an implicit way the whole of the Christian faith. For anyone who believes that God exists and that he will give life to those who seek him is saved (Heb 11.6). In other words, anyone who believes that God is the one God who has revealed himself in the Old and New Testaments as the God who helps and liberates, who is life and gives life – that person is saved. As far as their content is concerned, the other statements of the faith speak of many other things besides God: the beginning and the end of the world; the origin, sin, redemption and fulfillment of the human person; the church, its preaching, sacraments and offices. But these many and varied statements are statements of the faith only to the extent that they are related to God, that is, to the extent that they speak of God's saving action or the mediations of this action.[2] God is therefore the sole and unifying theme of theology.[3] God – who is the salvation of the world and the human race – is as it were the one word spoken in the many words of theology. To this extent theology is accountable speech (*logos*) about God (*theos*), or the science of God, as the ancients called it.[4]

But what does it really mean to say 'God'? This question of Kurt Tucholsky is quite understandable; in fact, it is even necessary. For, as M. Buber says in an often quoted passage, God,

is the most heavy-laden of all human words. None has become so soiled, so mutilated . . . Generations of men have laid the burden of their anxious lives upon this word and weighed it to the ground; it lies in the dust and bears their whole burden. The races of men with their religious factions have torn the word to pieces; they have killed for it and died for it, and it bears their fingermarks and their blood ... They draw caricatures and write 'God' underneath; they murder one another to say 'in God's name' ... We must esteem those who interdict it because they rebel against the injustice and wrong which are so readily referred to 'God' for authorization.[5]

Therefore before we ask 'Does God exist?' and before we answer 'God exists' or claim 'God does not exist', we must know what is at issue when we use the ambiguous word 'God'. Unless we have a clear concept of God or at least some preunderstanding we cannot answer the questions just asked, and any answers given are bound to be empty formulas.

The question, then, is this: how can we arrive at such a preliminary concept of God? How are we to set about theologizing? We certainly cannot begin with a proof of God that supposedly has no presuppositions. Anyone who undertakes a proof of God must already have some idea of what he wants to prove; any meaningful question supposes some pre-understanding of what the questioning is meant to ascertain; so too a proof of God presupposes a provisional concept of God. The principle may be formulated universally: there is no such thing as presupposi-tionless thinking. All human knowing occurs through the medium of language, which always provides us with pre-existent symbols and schemata for interpreting reality. For this reason, the only way to begin theology is by inquiring what the religions and the theological tradition have understood by 'God'. We must investigate the history of talk about God and thus make clear to ourselves the problem that resides in the word 'God'.

We may begin with one of the great masters of theology, Thomas Aquinas (1225–1274). At the start of his theological *Summa* he immediately gives a number of descriptions of what 'all' mean when they speak of God: God is the ultimate, ungrounded Ground of all reality that sustains and moves everything; God is the supreme Good in which all finite goods participate and which is the ground of all these goods; God is the ultimate End that directs and orders all things.[6] For these reasons Anselm of Canterbury (1033–1109), the father of medieval Scholasticism, defined God as *id quo maius cogitari nequit*, 'that than which nothing greater can be thought',[7] and indeed that which is greater than anything that can be thought.[8] This definition is not simply a superlative; it is not saying that God is 'the greatest thing that can be thought'. If this were the case, God would simply be the highest possible realization of the human person. God is, rather, a comparative that can never be matched: he who is always greater and fuller; he who amid all likeness is always more unlike, always other, always more mysterious.

The definition which Luther gives in his *Grosser Katechismus* is quite different in character. It is utterly unphilosophical and expresses, rather, the existential importance of the understanding of God: 'What does it mean to have a God, or: What is God? A God is that from which we should expect every good and to whom we should have recourse in every distress.' 'That . . . to which you attach your heart and on which you rely is in fact your God.'⁹ The necessary *(notwendige)* being of the scholastic definition has become for Luther the one who 'turns afflictions around' *(der Not-wendende)*, who supports and sustains human beings in the distresses of life, the one who is absolutely trustworthy and on whom human beings can base their lives. There is no doubt that Luther has effectively brought into play basic motifs of biblical faith in God.

Various modern definitions attempt to combine the abstract philosophical and the concrete existential dimensions. According to P. Tillich, God is 'what concerns us ultimately'.¹⁰ According to R. Bultmann, he is 'the reality determining all else'.¹¹ G. Ebeling calls God 'the mystery of reality',¹² and K. Rahner speaks of him as 'the holy mystery' which is the term and origin of man and which 'is present in loving freedom' as 'that which is nameless and which is not at our disposal, and at whose complete disposal we exist'.¹³

Despite differences in their details all these definitions make one point clear: the word 'God' is not intended to answer one question among many others. For the tradition, God is not a reality alongside or above the rest of reality. He is not an object of questioning and understanding in the way that other objects are. God is not a given in the way that human beings and things are given. He is rather the answer to the question that is contained in all questions; he is the answer to the question that is contained in the very existence of the human person and the world.¹⁴ God is an answer that includes and transcends all other answers.

The all-inclusive and all-transcending answer given in the word 'God' corresponds exactly to the basic situation of the human person. Man is unlike any other living thing in that he is the one being that is not adapted by sure instinct and therefore unquestioningly to a particular environment. On the contrary, he is the being who is open to the world, as the anthropologists like to say.¹⁵ He does not live in an unforced harmony with himself and his environment; he himself must shape both himself and his environment. He is pregiven to himself but also given to himself as a task to be carried out. He therefore has the power to ask questions, and he is constantly asking them. This ability to ask questions is the source of man's greatness; it is the ground of his transcendence, that is, his being insofar as it reaches above and beyond everything else, and it is the ground of his freedom as well. But his ability to ask questions is also the source of his wretchedness. He is the only being who can be bored, the only one who can be discontented and unhappy. Man, thus open to the world in its entirety, finds fulfillment only if he finds an answer to the meaning of his own existence and to the existence of reality as such.

The religious tradition is convinced that the reality expressed in the word God provides this answer. According to this tradition, therefore, God is not just one reality alongside all the others; he is the reality that comprehends, grounds and determines all other realities, the unconditional in all that is conditioned, man's all in all. To put it differently: the God-question is not a categorical but a transcendental question, in the twofold sense of a question that includes all that is (transcendental, therefore, in the sense the term has in the Scholastic doctrine of the transcendentals) and a question that has to do with the condition for the possibility of all other questions and answers (transcendental, therefore, in the sense this term has in modern transcendental philosophy).

Because God is the question in all questions, he himself can be placed in question. Even classical theology did not develop in a sterile atmosphere in which there were no contradictions or in an idyllic world falsely assumed to be sound and good.[16] In his theological *Summa* Thomas Aquinas introduces his article on the question 'Does God exist?' by stating the two objections which are still fundamental even today. He cites evil in the world as an argument against the affirmation of a God who is infinitely good, and the possibility of explaining the world in a purely immanent way 'if it be supposed that God does not exist'.[17] Thomas thus anticipates the modern explanation of reality 'even if there were no God'.

But in Thomas' discussions with the pagans (the *gentiles*), and especially with Islam, it was not only the existence of God but also the identity of God (who is God?) that was disputed. Otherwise he would not have had to write an entire *Summa contra gentiles*. Even for a medieval thinker like Thomas, then, God is not something self-evident, and talk about God is anything but a peaceful exercise of poetic contemplation. Given the character of reality as we have it, faith in God has always been a questioning and a seeking faith. Human beings have always had to say: 'I believe: help my unbelief!' (Mark 9.24). For this reason, in the classical tradition faith was always a *fides quaerens intellectum*, a faith in search of understanding.

In this formula we have the classical definition of theology or accountable speech about God. Following Augustine, Anselm of Canterbury defines theology as *fides quaerens intellectum*,[18] faith in search of understanding. According to this definition neither the asking nor the understanding is extrinsic to faith. Faith itself is understood as a faith that questions and understands. Faith is an act of the human person (even though from another standpoint it is also an act of sheer grace in which God enlightens man); faith exists only in the medium of human hearing, understanding, assenting and also questioning. Theology therefore prolongs and develops a movement that arises within faith and from faith. In the proper sense of the phrase, theology is a science of faith. The special character of theology as a science consists in the fact that it prolongs, in a methodical and systematic way, the quest for understanding that is inherent in faith, focuses this quest on the problems that arise in each situation, and seeks to satisfy it with the tools made available by the thinking of a given age.[19]

2. The formulation of the problem today

Although God was never something that could be regarded as self-evident, the situation in which and for which there was to be speech about God has changed radically since the beginning of modern times. For the religious person of the past, God or the divine was the only true reality, and the world was in danger of being regarded as a mere appearance and illusion.[20] But in the consciousness of the average person at the end of the twentieth century the situation is just the reverse. The thing that he takes for granted is the reality which the senses apprehend; God, on the other hand, is suspected of being simply a reflection of the world, a purely ideological construct. F. Nietzsche's statement about the death of God is widely regarded as a diagnostic key to modern culture. In like manner, M. Heidegger, following Hölderlin, speaks of the absence of the god,[21] and M. Buber of the eclipse of God in our time.[22] Amid the interior and exterior tribulation of their imprisonment by the Gestapo, the Protestant theologian D. Bonhoeffer[23] and the Jesuit Catholic priest A. Delp[24] saw the approach of a religionless, godless age in which the old religious values would be powerless and unintelligible. So universal has this situation become in the years since then that the real issue has long since been, not the atheism of others, but the atheism in our own hearts. According to the Second Vatican Council atheism has become 'one of the most serious problems of our time';[25] it is one of the 'signs of the times'.

The background for this atheism of the masses – which is a novelty in the history of the human race – is usually summed up in the term 'secularization'. By this is meant the process that had led to an understanding of the world and its spheres of activity (politics, culture, the economy, sciences, and so on), and to a handling of them that at least prescinds from their transcendent ground and thinks of them and deals with them in a purely immanent way.[26]

Contradictory evaluations have been made of this development. In reaction to the liberal programmatic affirmation of secularization, traditional theology could see in modern secularization nothing but an unparalleled great apostasy from God and Christianity and could only think that it is bound to end in catastrophe. It was therefore thought that the program of secularization should be met by an opposite Christian program of restoration. In opposition to this traditionalist view with its emphasis on restoration, a new and more progressive current of thought, the secularization theology, as it was called, of the 1950s and 1960s took a different view: following the lead of Hegel, M. Weber, E. Troeltsch and K. Löwith, it maintained that modern secularization is a consequence of Christianity and even, in a sense, the fulfillment of Christianity within this world (F. Gogarten; J. B. Metz). For it was the biblical distinction between God and the world that opened the way for a wordly conception of the world. According to this view, modern atheism, which has forgotten its Christian origin and is in protest against it, is a possible interpretation of the modern process of secularization but not the only possible one, and is certainly not inevitable. For this reason, these writers sought to distinguish between a legitimate secularization and an illegitimate secularism.

This 'progressive' theory has the advantage over the 'restoration' theory that it makes possible a Christian affirmation of the various modern processes of liberation. On the other hand, it remains at a rather abstract level when compared with the actual course of modern history. For the actual history of the modern age has unfolded largely in opposition to Christianity and against the protests of the churches. The resulting secularized world is not a Christian world but a world that is indifferent to Christianity. This fact cannot be rendered innocuous by attributing it to misunderstanding on both sides.

For this reason H. Blumenberg has criticized the secularization thesis and offered a third explanatory model: the modern age originated as an act of human self-assertion against an overwhelming transcendence that enslaves human beings, as well as against ecclesiastical structures that had become rigid, reactionary and repressive. In this view, the modern age is interpreted as a critical reaction to Christianity and an attempt of the human person to achieve autonomy and find his ground within himself. This theory is certainly more in accord with the actual development of modern history than is the quite abstract secularization thesis. It is unable, however, to do full justice to the valid points of view set forth in the secularization thesis, and to this extent it too does not offer a fully satisfactory theory to explain the modern age.

An adequate judgment on the situation requires us to take into account that the modern age, and especially the atheism of the late modern period, is a many-layered phenomenon that cannot be treated monocausally and derived from a single source.[27] As far as the history of ideas is concerned, we may, like H. Blumenberg, take as our starting point the conflict between autonomy and a crushing theonomy, but we must immediately add various other points of view. For the emancipation from Christianity was itself based on Christian presuppositions. The idea of the freedom and dignity of the individual person is one that entered the world with Christianity.[28] Modern emancipation presupposes this Christian liberation of the person as well as the misunderstanding of Christian freedom in late medieval nominalism and in the rigidified ecclesiastical structure of the confessional era. Thus the human self-assertion against Christianity was itself made possible by Christianity. The return to the humanism of antiquity and the renaissance of the ancient world provided aids for the establishment of a new humanism.[29] The often misunderstood ideas of the Reformation on the freedom of the Christian, the two kingdoms, and the secular calling[30] also played a part.

But in addition to these motifs from the history of ideas account must be taken of the objective historical factors which were closely connected with those motifs: the division of the churches in the sixteenth century and the rise of the modern bourgeoisie.[31] After the Reformation had led to the destruction of the unity of faith and thus of the basis for the unity of society up to that time, the whole social order inevitably fell into disarray. The result was the wars of religion in the sixteenth and seventeenth centuries, which brought society to the brink of destruction. This development made it clear that religion had lost its integrative function. The survival of society demanded that religion be set aside and a new basis be found that would tie everything together and be binding on all. For the sake of peace, religion had to be declared a private matter, and people had to accept as a new basis for social life the reason which all men have in common or, as the case might be, the order of nature which was recognized as rational and which, it was thought, would be unchanged 'even if there were no God' (H. Grotius).[32]

This development was aided and abetted by the rise of the modern bourgeoisie. The bourgeoisie – whose development had started in the twelfth century and was powerfully aided by the Reformation – came into existence as a result of emancipation from traditional political, social and intellectual forces and had as its basis the principle of the autonomy of the individual who makes his way by knowledge, work, achievements and diligence. When life and its meaning are thus given a coherent, autonomous basis in personal insight and personal activity, religion, which sees reality as established and ordered by God, becomes, if not superfluous and meaningless, at least a matter of private morality; it is turned into an answer to the question 'What ought we to do?' and as such is accepted because of its social usefulness among the people. Religion could then easily be distorted into an ideology promoted by the prevailing system wherever ceremonious, though not constitutive use was still made of it.

Finally, we must not forget the development of the modern sciences which made possible a new vision of a world that is independent of any and every transcendent ground and is even contradictory to the vision of things presupposed in the Bible and ecclesiastical tradition.[33]

The emancipation of the public realm from the theological contexts that had previously provided it with its foundations led to a loss of the universality proper to the idea of God. Religion became a purely internal affair and thus lost its connection with reality. Pietism and the various revivalist movements made religion completely a matter of subjective devotion, a religion of the heart. Hegel's description of the situation has never been bettered: 'Religion builds its temples and altars in the heart of the individual. In sighs and prayers he seeks for the God whom he denies to himself in intuition, because of the risk that the intellect will cognize what is intuited as a mere thing, reducing the sacred grove to mere timber.'[34] Hegel realizes that the objectification of reality and the withdrawal of religion into subjectivity leads both to a flattening of reality and an emptying of religion. The world becomes godless; God becomes worldless and – in the proper sense of the term – objectless. Hegel therefore sees in the sentence from a hymn in the Lutheran hymnal 'God Himself is dead', an expression of modern culture and of the feeling 'upon which the religion of more recent times rests'.[35]

The conclusion we may draw from this brief survey is that modern secularization has various roots. Having been made possible by Christianity, it sprang into existence as a reaction, in the name of freedom, against an absolutist image of God. It is inseparable from modern subjectivity, which grounds its autonomy not theonomously but in terms of immanence and even by way of a critique of religion, and therefore also makes its own the humanism of antiquity. Thus many and partially contradictory motifs explain the rise of modern autonomous culture, which is clearly distinguished by its immanentist orientation from the medieval world-picture that had been formed by Augustine and was transcendent in its orientation. In this secularized world God become increasingly superfluous as a hypothesis for explaining phenomena within the world; he loses his function in regard to the world. We must live in the world 'as though there were no God'. Thus faith in God becomes increasingly emptied of its perceptual and experiential elements and increasingly unreal; God himself becomes increasingly unreal. When all is said and done, the statement 'God is dead' could serve as a plausible interpretation of the modern sense of life and reality.

It is not possible, of course, to expunge the reality of God and expect that everything else will go on as before. In the history of the human race the word 'God' stands for the ultimate ground and ultimate goal of man and his world. When God drops out of the picture, the world becomes

without ground and without goal and everything threatens to become
meaningless. For a thing has meaning only when it stands in a larger
context that is inherently meaningful. Then, once the meaning of the whole
has been lost and once the reality of God as that which ordains, governs
and supports the whole has been removed, every individual reality also
becomes ultimately meaningless. Everything descends into an abyss of
nothingness. In other words, as J. Paul, Jacobi, Novalis, Fichte, Schelling
and Hegel already saw, nihilism stands at the term of this development.
Nietzsche was one of the few who had the courage to face up to the nihilistic
consequences of atheism. In *The Gay Science* he follows his message of the
death of God with some questions:

> What were we doing when we unchained this earth from its sun? Whither
> is it moving now? Whither are we moving? Are we not plunging
> continually? Backward, sideward, forward, in all directions? Is there
> still any up or down? Are we not straying as through an infinite nothing?
> Do we not feel the breath of empty space? Has it not become colder? Is
> not night continually closing in on us?[36]

Nietzsche's thinking has become dismayingly to the point today. It is more
relevant than the various plans for an atheistic humanism, more relevant
even than Marxist atheism, which until recently was regarded by many as
the challenge to Christianity. For with the disappearance of the mystery of
God the mystery of man likewise disappears. People look upon the human
person as simply a being with biological needs or as a sum-total of social
relations. When that which is greater than man and his world is no longer
present, it is replaced by an ideology of total adaptation to the sphere of
needs and desires and to social relationships; freedom dies, the human
person retrogresses and becomes a clever animal, and all hunger and thirst
for an unconditional justice disappears as well. The death of God leads to
the death of man. Consequently people today feel a dreadful emptiness, a
loss of meaning and direction, that is the deepest source of the existential
anxieties which many experience. Even more than atheism, the nihilism
that flows from atheism is the real mark of the age.

According to L. Kolakowski,

> along with the self-confidence of faith, the self-confidence of unbelief is
> also shattered. In contrast to the comfortable world of Enlightenment
> atheism, in which a benevolent, friendly Nature extended its protection,
> the godless world of today is perceived as an oppressive, everlasting
> chaos. It is stripped of any meaning, any aim, any directional signal, any
> structure . . . For a hundred years now, ever since Nietzsche announced

the death of God, few cheerful atheists have been visible . . . The absence
of God became a continuously open wound in the European spirit, even
if people managed to narcotize themselves into forgetfulness of it . . .
The collapse of Christianity, which the Enlightenment awaited with glee,
proved (insofar as it occurred) to be almost contemporaneous with
the collapse of the Enlightenment itself. The radiant new order of
anthropocentrism that was to be built where the overthrown God had
stood never arrived.[37]

In this situation, talk of God as the ground and goal of all reality becomes
an urgent task of the theologian for the sake of the human person, in fact
it becomes the most urgent of all his tasks. I began this section with the
statement of M. Buber, the Jewish philosopher of religion, that the word
'God' is 'the most heavy-laden of all human words'; let me end it with this
further statement of his: 'We cannot cleanse the word "God" and we
cannot make it whole; but, defiled and mutilated as it is, we can raise it
from the ground and set it over an hour of great care.'[38]

3. The theological formulation of the problem

The question before us is: given this situation, how are we to speak
intelligibly about God? Certainly we cannot start directly from a faith in
God that is taken more or less as a matter of course and then, in a purely
positivistic manner, begin with the God of biblical revelation. Such a start
directly 'from above' is barred to us today. The reason is that no answer
is intelligible unless people first grasp the question to which it is the answer.
Neither, therefore, can we adopt an (apparently or really) presupposition-
less point of view and try step by step to demonstrate God's existence. This
way 'from below' is also barred to us, because every question already
presupposes a preunderstanding of the reality with which the question is
concerned. If we had never even heard of 'God' we would never get the
idea of talking about him or even of proving his existence. In addition,
proofs of God are usually convincing only to those who already believe in
him. In our talk about God we are therefore forced to turn back to tradition
and to refer to it.[39]

Traditional speech about God is a possible starting point, because this
speech is not simply something traditional. Religious tradition could and
still can remain an abiding force because it is an answer to an abiding
question: the question which is identical with man himself. The human
person can never forget the question of God because it accompanies the
person himself. An atheistic cultural policy and atheistic schooling that are

carried on for a generation or two can of course have far reaching effects. Yet even the propaganda of the godless helps in its own way to keep the problem of God alive. Complete silence about God would require the silencing of those questions which the tradition of the human race has answered by referring to God. For this reason it is probably not simply chance that even totalitarian systems have thus far not succeeded in effecting this complete silence. On the contrary, the *question* of God is at present being revived in a remarkable way throughout the world.

I shall therefore take as my starting point the problem which is recorded in the word 'God' which history has handed down to us. A problem is a preliminary sketch (a *pro-blēma*, 'something thrown forward'), an answer that at the same time contains a question, a pointer showing the direction to be taken in order to reach the goal.

Aristotle already maintains the thesis that the sciences, even and especially metaphysics, must start with problems that have emerged from previous study.[40] With due qualifications this is also of theological science. *Theology* takes as its starting point the talk about God *(theos)* that has been transmitted in the church's confession of faith, and endeavours to justify this talk at the bar of reason *(logos)* in view of the questions of human beings and to understand it more fully. The intention of theology, therefore, is to give an account *(apologia)* of the hope that finds expression in the confession of God, and it does this in response to the challenge of the world's unbelief (I Peter 3.15). To that extent, theology is *fides quaerens intellectum*, faith in God that seeks understanding. In the process, the believer is influenced by the situation of unbelief and of the eclipse of God. The decisive thing is not the atheism of other people but the atheism that makes its home in one's own heart. Thus faith itself becomes a question. The whole purpose of theology is to grasp in a scientifically reflective way the understanding, the seeking *(quaerere)*, and the questioning which are part of faith itself. When theology transforms the question inherent in faith into a scientific problem, it is not constructing something different *(aliud)* from faith but is simply articulating one and the same faith differently *(aliter)* and giving it the form of methodically scientific reflection.

To articulate one and the same faith differently does not mean turning faith into a gnosis. Since the question represented by God is not a particular categorical question but the basic transcendental question, it must be said *a priori* that the goal of theology cannot be a rationalistic comprehension of God. Any such comprehension supposes an all-inclusive standpoint and viewpoint. But since God is the reality that includes all else, he is also *id quo maius cogitari nequit*, that which cannot be conceived in terms of some more inclusive horizon. A theology that has managed to conceive

God has in fact misconceived him; it has stripped him of his divinity and reduced him to the level of a finite idol. A theology that sells out to a rationalism which aims to grasp everything, even God, in its concepts, has no power to dislodge the superstition in claims to be attacking; it is itself the most ignorant kind of superstition.

All this means that for the theological mind God is not a problem comparable to the many other problems which a person can, at least in principle, solve one after the other. God is an abiding problem; he is the problem par excellence which we describe as 'mystery'.[41] The goal of theology, therefore, is not primarily the resolution *(solutio)* of problems nor an advance *(progressio)* from problem to problem, but the reduction of all knowing and questioning to the mystery of God *(reductio in mysterium)*. It cannot be the goal of theology to move beyond faith in God by means of thought, but only to grasp the mystery of God as mystery.

In accordance with all that I have been saying, the only way to carry out this task is by understanding the mystery of God as a response to the mystery of man. Concretely: it can be carried out only amid a conflict regarding the mystery of reality and man and in a debate with the interpretations which present-day forms of atheism offer as projects of meaning and hope. By its whole nature this conflict is not a purely theoretical problem; nor does it touch only the private and personal sphere. The conflict about God, being also a conflict about man, is an eminently practical problem, which also has a political dimension since it concerns man in all his dimensions.

A person who believes in God as the reality that determines all else cannot acquiesce in the bourgeois separation between a secular public sphere and a private sphere in which alone religion is given a place. We can only agree eagerly with the new *political* theology insofar as it calls attention to this baneful separation and bids us relate God to public life as the truth about man and human social life. On the other hand, insofar as this theology turns the political dimension into a programmatic foundation and the all-inclusive framework and horizon of its arguments, it is to be no less decisively rejected. Even in inner-worldly terms, the political is not the quintessence of reality nor, consequently, the framework within which the freedom of the person is to be discussed. The person is indeed social by nature and dependent for its concrete fulfillment on a social order marked by freedom, but it also has inherent rights over against society and is even in its turn the ground or origin, the supporting base, and the goal of all social institutions.[42] The point of departure for our argument is therefore not society as such but the human being who as person has a social dimension, but also transcends this in the direction of a real Whole which he or she always possess only in a pre-apprehension *(Vorgriff)* but never in a concept *(Begriff)* and to which he or she is always on the way as one who seeks, asks, hopes and dares.

Talk of God as the reality that includes and determines everything, as the ground and goal of everything, and as *id quo maius cogitari nequit*, is to be understood as the answer to the question, inseparable from the human being as a person, regarding the whole of reality; moreover, it is only in relation to the most comprehensive of all questions that talk about God can become articulate. Metaphysics is the name given to the science which enquires not about individual beings or realms of being but about being as such and as a whole.[43] Talk about God presupposes the metaphysical question about being and at the same time keeps this question alive. In our present situation, therefore, theology as talk about God also acts as protector and defender of philosophy as the question about being as such. 'The Christian is the person who by virtue of his faith is compelled to philosophize.'[44] This does not imply a choice of one particular philosophy, as, for example, Aristotelian philosophy and metaphysics; it does, however, imply an option for a philosophy that in opposition to every narrowing and obscuring of the human horizon keeps open the question about the meaning of the whole and precisely in this way serves the humanness of humanity. For it is the removal of these limits as well as human openness, transcending reality as given, that sets us free from all reality as given and endows us with freedom and dignity within the existing and any future social order.

If talk about God transcends any and every inner-wordly sphere, including the political, then to preserve the transcendence of God is also to preserve the transcendence of the human person and therefore the freedom and inalienable rights of humanity.[45] For the sake, then, of both God and man 'the return to the sacred' is our essential task today.[46] In view of the many reductionist theological programs now in existence it is unfortunately not a redundancy to say that, especially today, a theological theology is the need of the hour and the only appropriate answer to modern atheism.

II

The Denial of God in Modern Atheism

1. The autonomy of the modern age as the basis for contemporary atheism

Atheism in the strict sense of the word came into existence only in the modern age. Even the word atheism seems to have entered common use only around the end of the sixteenth and beginning of the seventeenth centuries.[1] The content of the concept may not be derived simply from an analysis of the two components of the word itself (theism and alpha privative or the negating particle). It would be both a narrowing and an unwarranted extension of the idea if we were to understand by 'atheism' simply a denial of (monotheistic) theism and therefore to regard even pantheism as a form of atheism. Only that view should be regarded as atheistic which denies any and every divine or absolute that is not simply identical with man and with the world of our empirical experience and with its immanent principles. Atheism, therefore, rejects any and every claim that God or the divine exists. This means that there can be and are not only various forms of the idea of God but also various forms of atheism.

Given this concept of atheism, it can be said that no primitive people is unqualifiedly atheistic, since among all primitive peoples there is some kind of an idea or a worship of a divine reality. Even the high religions of Asia that do not acknowledge a personal absolute (Buddhism, Taoism) are not atheistic, as is often mistakenly claimed. By reason of its conception of the world as numinous, classical antiquity likewise did not have any atheists in the sense described above. From the second century bc on we do indeed find lists of names of *atheoi*, but the term refers to people who disregarded the gods of the state and their public veneration, not to people who simply denied everything divine.[2] It was in this limited sense that even Christians were subsequently execrated and persecuted as *atheoi*. Justin comments:

'We admit that as far as all such false gods are concerned we are atheists, but we are not atheists when it comes to the true God.'[3] It is therefore a kind of fraudulent labelling to make the 'accusation of atheism' against the early Christians the basis for a contemporary Christian atheism.

Atheism in the proper sense, which denies everything divine, became possible only in the modern age. It presupposes Christianity and to that extent is a post-Christian phenomenon.[4] The biblical faith in creation had broken with the numinous conception of the world that was current in antiquity and had effected a denuminization of reality by distinguishing clearly and unambiguously between God the creator and the world as his creation. In so doing, the Bible thought of the world in wordly terms and God in divine terms and of the two as qualitatively distinct in infinite degree. Only when God had been conceived as radically God was it possible also to deny him in a radical way. Only when the transcendence of God had been taken seriously did it become possible to experience the immanence of the world, and only after the world had been acknowledged simply as world could it become the object of objectifying scientific study and technical transformation. The way was being prepared for this kind of autonomous understanding of the world as early as the twelfth and thirteenth centuries. Albertus Magnus and Thomas Aquinas were the most outstanding representatives of this movement. But the autonomy of the world, based as it was on the idea of creation, remained part of a total context that was theonomous; in fact, the autonomy itself was given a theonomous justification.[5] On the other hand, the very emancipation of autonomy from its theonomous context and reference and thus the presupposition for the rise of modern atheism had theological causes. These were provided by late medieval nominalism. Nominalism carried the idea of God's omnipotence and freedom to an extreme, turning him into an absolutist deity who acts in an arbitrary manner. The rebellion against this God who does not liberate human freedom but oppresses it, this God who might well command even what is untrue and unjust, was an act of human self-assertion.

The reaction is especially clear in Descartes (1596–1650). He is tormented by the thought of a *genius malignus*, an evil spirit, 'very powerful and very tricky', who 'bends all his efforts' to deceive him. At last Descartes discovers an unshakable foundation on which to base knowledge of the truth. In triumphant tones he declares: 'Let him deceive me as much as he will, he can never make me be nothing as long as I think that I am something.'[6] Descartes expresses his new insight in the formula: *Cogito ergo sum* ('I think, hence I am').[7] The 'hence' does not point to the conclusion of a syllogism, but is simply a way of expressing an insight given in the very act of thinking: 'I am a thinking being.'[8] In thus starting with the *ego cogitans*, with the subject who grasps himself as subject. Descartes provided an Archimedean fulcrum for the entire modern age that followed; subjectivity was to become the modern mode of thought and intellectual attitude. Kant described this as a Copernican revolution.[9] But subjectivity should not be confused with subjectivism, although this is a mistake constantly made. Subjectivism, which abolutizes the subject's limited position and private interests, is a particularist point of view; modern subjectivity, on the other hand, is a universalist mode of thought, a new approach to the whole of reality.

In a special way, modern subjectivity has consequences for the God-question. Descartes and all the great thinkers of the modern age down to the nineteenth century were anything but atheists. In fact, in his third and fifth meditations Descartes falls back on traditional arguments for the existence of God (the proof that concludes from effect to cause, and the proof that starts with the concept of God). But for Descartes knowledge of God occurs in the medium of human subjectivity. In contrast to the nominalist exaggeration of theonomy autonomy here becomes the norm of judgment. The idea of God is admitted as the ground and means of human autonomy. In this approach, God ultimately becomes a factor in the self-fulfillment of man, although Descartes himself does not yet draw this conclusion.[10]

This new basic attitude which was established by Descartes was henceforth given the name 'autonomy'.[11] Antiquity and the Middle Ages knew this idea only as a political category; autonomy meant the freedom to live according to one's own laws, that is, political self-determination. The concept acquired a broader meaning in the context of the confessional or religious wars of the sixteenth and seventeenth centuries. Unity, freedom and peace could no longer be defended on theonomous grounds; recourse had to be had to natural law, which binds everyone and alone is evident to all, and in terms of which autonomy can be granted to the religious dissenter. Thus the modern doctrine of natural law was formulated by J. Bodin and H. Grotius, under the influence of Stoic ideas. This teaching identifies *lex naturae* with *lex divina*, but grounds it no longer theonomously but autonomously with the help of human understanding 'even if there were no God'.[12] The autonomy of law leads to the autonomy of morality. While in antiquity and the Middle Ages law, custom and morality formed in large measure an inextricably interwoven complex, morality was forced to become conscious of itself now that the state and law had achieved emancipation. The result was an autonomous morality based on interior conviction.[13] It was owing to Kant that this morality was given its philosophical justification. His starting point is the dignity of the human person who can never be made a means to an end but 'exists as an end in himself'.[14] This autonomy has its basis in freedom, which 'can be efficient, independently of foreign causes determining it'.[15] Freedom can therefore only be its own law. But the autonomy enjoyed by freedom is not to be identified with caprice; it had its norm in the freedom of the individual himself as well as in the freedom of everyone else. For this reason Kant's categorical imperative runs as follows: 'I am never to act otherwise than so that I could also will that my maxim should become a universal law.'[16] This principle is only seemingly a formal one, for in fact it bases morality on the dignity of the human person; it grounds an interpersonal (not an individualistic) ethics in a perspective which embraces the entire human race.

The emancipation of law and morality from the theological contexts that had given them their foundations meant a new situation for religion. If religion is no longer the necessary presupposition of order, law and morals in society, then it inevitably becomes a private affair. Once the various secular spheres had been freed of their theonomous connections, religion became increasingly a matter of the interior life. It became a matter of subjective piety, a religion of the heart, with the way being paved by pietism and the various revivalist movements. Hegel recognized that this withdrawal of religion into the subjectivity leads, on the one hand, to a flattening of reality and, on the other, to an emptying of religion itself. The world becomes godless, God worldless and – in the strict sense of the word – objectless. The consequences are atheism and nihilism.[17]

Modern thought has laid the foundations for various forms of atheism. The word 'atheism' is applied to very diverse phenomena that are classified in quite different ways in philosophical and theological literature.[18] Fundamentally, however, atheistic systems may be reduced to two basic types, corresponding to the two possible understandings of autonomy in the modern age. There is, first, the autonomy of nature and the secular spheres (culture, science, art, the economy, politics, and so on), for the understanding and functioning of which there is increasingly less need of the God-hypothesis (naturalistic, materialistic, scientistic, methodical atheism or agnosticism). There is, second, the autonomy of the subject, whose dignity and freedom militate against the acceptance of an omnipotent God (the humanistic atheism of freedom and the political atheism of liberation). To be distinguished from these are the forms of atheism that spring from protest against the wickedness and evil in the world. From an existential point of view wickedness and evil are far more decisive for many people than are theoretical and ideological denials of God. I shall discuss this third kind of atheism in connection with the question of theodicy rather than here.[19]

It would, of course, be absurd to focus attention here solely on the systematic philosophical approaches to atheism and on the major ideologies of the modern age.[20] These, after all, suppose that basic atheistic attitudes are already seen as plausible. To describe this state of affairs K. Rahner has coined the phrase 'troubled atheism'; by this he means the experience of being crushed by a secularized world, the feeling of no longer being able to make the divine real to oneself, the experience of the silence of God, and the fear of the emptiness and meaninglessness of the world.[21] Atheism thus becomes a plausible interpretation of modern secularization. At the same time, troubled atheists, who are frightened by the absence of God and whose hearts are restless, are a pastoral windfall.

In addition, there is an atheism characterized by indifference: a complete unconcern with religious questions, an atheism that, either seemingly or really, is all too much at peace and takes itself for granted, an atheism that represses, no longer raises, or even disparages the great questions asked by the religions. Nietzsche has drawn a sarcastic picture of this 'last man'. The last man only blinks when the great questions are raised (Zarathustra is speaking in this passage):

> 'What is love? What is creation? What is longing? What is a star?' thus asks the last man, and he blinks.
>
> The earth has become small, and on it hops the last man, who makes everything small. His race is as ineradicable as the flea-beetle; the last man lives longest.
>
> 'We have invented happiness,' say the last men, and they blink . . .
>
> One still works, for work is a form of entertainment. But one is careful lest the entertainment be too harrowing. One no longer becomes rich or poor: both require too much exertion. Who still wants to rule? Who obey? Both require too much exertion.
>
> No shepherd and one herd! Everybody wants the same, everybody is the same: whoever feels different goes voluntarily into a madhouse.[22]

What Nietzsche has done here is, of course, to anticipate the consequences of modern atheism. Despite all the humanistic impulses at work in modern atheism, the death of God leads ultimately to the death of man.[23]

2. Atheism in the name of the autonomy of nature

The first great conflict that made a decisive contribution to the rise of modern atheism was the conflict between theology and the new natural sciences of the modern era.[24]

The trial of Galileo, which ended in 1633 with a condemnation of his teaching, was, more than any other incident, of prototypical and epochal significance.[25] As everyone knows, in developing the discoveries made by Copernicus and Kepler, Galileo was led to reject the ancient geocentric picture of the world that is presupposed in the Bible. He advocated the thesis that the sun does not circle the earth but rather the earth circles the sun. The Roman Inquisition on the other hand defended an outdated picture of the world and an unhistorical interpretation of the Bible (in this respect, by the way, it was in agreement with the Reformers). It must be said, however, that there have been few historical events in which the historical reality has been so unrelated to the historical influence it exerted as in the Galileo case, which quickly became a myth. For the issue at the time was not only a claim to the autonomy of the natural sciences, a claim which was quite legitimate from the standpoint of modern theology. The issue was also Galileo's claim that it is for the natural sciences to interpret what the Bible says about creation or, in other words, the claim, in the name of natural science, to determine the scope of theological statements. Both sides went beyond their competency, even allowing for the fact that the Inquisition would have been satisfied if Galileo had presented his thesis as a hypothesis – which is precisely what it is by modern standards. The conflict that marked the Galileo case was unfortunately not an isolated phenomenon. Similar conflicts arose, especially in the nineteenth century, in connection with the disputes over Charles Darwin's theory of evolution; these conflicts have lasted well into our own century, as the debate over Teilhard de Chardin shows. The result was one of the greatest catastrophes in the history of the church: the schism between natural science and theology and even between the church and modern culture.[26] For the modern natural sciences are the hard core of modernity.[27] The modern economy and technology which these sciences made possible provided the foundations for the bourgeois culture in which the modern philosophy of subjectivity could develop and in which the modern immanentist outlook of which I have already spoken could spread abroad. Conversely, the natural sciences have their roots in the modern identification of the human person as subject, for only then could nature become the object of scientific observation and technical mastery. Consequently, if any new talk about God is to be serious and to be taken seriously, it must prove itself by the hard standard of the scientific understanding of reality.

In the Middle Ages nature was an image and symbol of God. In Nikolaus Copernicus and especially in Johannes Kepler such a symbolic view of the cosmos is still present in the background. In his *Mysterium cosmographicum* and his *Harmonices mundi* (World Harmony), Kepler's aim is to capture the creative thought of God himself. As for Copernicus, although his rejection of the old geocentric world-picture expels man from his position at the centre of the cosmos, he keeps man as the spiritual centre and reference point of the universe; man is no longer by his physical nature the centre of the world, but he becomes this centre actively and spiritually by his own efforts.[28] The age had now dawned in which the dominant vision was of a world which man creates for himself scientifically, artistically and philosophically. Central position had given way to central function. For this reason Kant was justified in seeing himself as the one who had completed the Copernican revolution.

In Galileo and Newton this revolutionary new mode of thought bears fruit in a method proper to the natural sciences.[29] The laws of nature are not simply read off, in a purely objectivist way, from nature itself, but emerge rather from the interaction of hypothesis and experience. The natural scientist compels nature, as it were, to give answers to questions which he puts to it. But as early as Newton the danger arises of confusing this way by which knowledge of nature is gained with the way of nature itself; of turning the laws enunciated by the natural sciences into iron laws of nature itself; and of converting the method of the natural sciences into a new metaphysics. The danger becomes acute in the mechanistic approach to the world which Newton developed. In this approach nature is treated like a gigantic clockwork that operates in accordance with minutely determined patterns.

Initially there was a widespread conviction that faith and knowledge were reconcilable. The work of G. W. Leibniz (1646–1716), one of the last universal scholars, was representative of the attempt to find a new synthesis of faith and knowledge. But the more the scientists discovered the regularities of nature, the more they were forced to eliminate God from the world. They needed him now only at the periphery and to fill up lacunas in human knowledge (for example, in the case of Newton, to correct the deflections in the orbits of the planets). In the course of such withdrawal skirmishes God was increasingly pushed off to the periphery of the world and into the hereafter. On the other hand, scientists were more and more convinced that the world is infinite. Did this mean that in the final analysis divine predications must be made of the world itself? that God and world were in fact one? As a result of these developments two possible but contrary ways emerged of defining a new relationship between God and the world: pantheism and deism. Atheism is, by comparison, only a relatively late product of this development.

Pantheism[30] means that in his being and nature God is one with the whole *(pan)* of reality. The concept occurs only in modern times. Factors inclining to pantheism are to be found, however, in all religious cultures, especially in the Asiatic high religions but also in the ancient Stoa, in Neoplatonism and even in the Middle Ages (Amalric of Bena, David of Dinant). But the formation of a pantheistic system is a modern phenomenon.

G. Bruno[31] (1548–1600) is the first in the line of pantheistic thinkers of the modern age. He was stimulated by prototypes in antiquity, but the decisive influence came from the new outlook on the world and life that developed in the Renaissance; he was a man captivated by the beauty of the world. As a result of Copernicus' discoveries he became convinced that the new science and the traditional world picture were in conflict. He dared, therefore, to be the first to think of the world as infinite and consequently of God and world as identical. For him the world is the necessary unfolding of God. For these ideas he was burned at the stake in the Campo dei Fiori at Rome in 1600.

B. Spinoza (1632–1677) developed the most consistent of all pantheistic systems. He drew upon Neoplatonic and Jewish mystical sources, but especially on the ideas of the Renaissance. For Spinoza God is the one, absolutely infinite substance which by a process of immanent causality engenders its own infinite attributes and finite modalities. The basic principle of this pantheism can be formulated as *'Deus sive natura'* (God or nature).[32] But the formula does not assert a downright or undifferentiated identity; God and nature remain, being distinguished as *natura naturans* (nature actively creating itself) and *natura naturata* (the system of what is created).[33] This doctrine exercised an immense influence. Through the offices of Lessing it became the basis for the religious attitude to the world which characterized the age of Goethe; it decisively influenced the young Hölderlin, Schelling and Hegel, as well as F. Schleiermacher in his speeches on religion.[34] The fascination which Spinoza's concept of God can have precisely for natural scientists, even today, can be seen not least in the cosmic religiosity of A. Einstein, who saw God in the harmonious regularity of being but did not believe in a God who involves himself in the destinies and activities of human beings. God does not interfere – he does not play dice![35]

Early on, Jacobi objected to this pantheistic identification of God and the world as being atheistic, since it dissolves God in nature and nature in God.[36] The debate over whether or not Spinozism is a concealed, though refined, form of atheism lasted into the nineteenth century.[37] It is no less possible, of course, to agree with Hegel that Spinozism is a form of acosmism, since according to Spinoza the world is simply a disposition and mode of the one divine substance and not something substantial in itself.[38] Pantheism is thus a profoundly ambiguous system.

The characteristic religious philosophy of the Enlightenment was not, however, pantheism but deism.[39] It started in seventeenth-eighteenth century England (Lord Herbert of Cherbury, T. Hobbes, J. Toland, J. Locke, M. Tindal, A. Collins, and others), became the religious philosophy to which the French Enlightenment gave its allegiance (P. Bayle, Voltaire, D. Diderot, and others), and finally gained entrance into Germany (H. S. Reimarus, and others).

Deism was 'natural religion', or the embodiment of normal religious truth to which everyone has access without any dependence on the supernatural. The authority of supernatural religion had been relativized by the discovery of other religions; in any case, in the confessional conflicts at the beginning of the modern age it could no longer serve as a common bond of union; furthermore, its absolutist claims were challenged by the new knowledge that had been gained by the natural sciences. Thus the natural religion of Deism was in a position to become the modern religious view which all could share and understand. In this view, nature, understood after the manner of the Stoics, became the critical court of appeal and the norm of religion.

Deism's concept of God showed variations ranging from the absolute transcendence of inactive God *(Deus otiosus)* who has formed the world after the manner of a master builder and clockmaker and now allows it to operate in accordance with its own natural laws, to more immanentist and pantheistic notions. Initally, therefore, deism, pantheism and theism were not unambiguously distinguishable either in concept or in content. The clear distinction between deism, pantheism and theism was in fact the work of later dogmatic theology as it developed its classifications. According to this later explanation, deism reduces God to a state of transcendence, in that it fails to recognize his immanence in the world. Commentators frequently, and justifiably, saw this deism as in danger of turning into a subtle atheism.[40] For a God who no longer plays an active role in the world is in the final analysis a dead God. Yet deistic motifs often exert an influence even today, for example, in the discussion of the possibility of miracles, the meaning of petitionary prayer, and faith in divine providence.

Pantheism and deism could not have the last word, for both contained a latent tendency to atheism. The decisive influence in the development of an explicit atheism came from the empirical, sensate and materialistic concept of nature in the natural sciences of the eighteenth and nineteenth centuries.[41] As faith in God found itself compelled more and more to fight rearguard actions in the face of the victorious spread of the Enlightenment, God was increasingly deprived of a place and function. Thus when Napoleon asked Laplace where God fitted into his *Système du monde* (The System of the World), he replied: 'Sire, I no longer have need of that hypothesis.'[42] Lalande, Laplace's contemporary and fellow philosopher, asserted that God's existence cannot be proved, 'because everything can be explained without him'.[43] As a purely immanent explanation of reality became more and more widespread, the way was paved for the return of the materialistic ideas of antiquity (Democritus, Epicurus).[44] We already find these in P. Gassendi, T. Hobbes and R. Descartes. In the French Enlightenment they gained currency especially through the *Encyclopédie* published by D. Diderot in 1751–1780. J. A. de LaMettrie was the first to apply them to the human person in his book *L'homme machine* (Man a Machine). P. H. D. von Holbach and C. A. Helvétius became their propagandists. These views reached their high point or, better, their low point, in the 'popular materialism' of the mid-nineteenth century as seen in the writings of J. Moleschott, L. Büchner and especially E. Haeckel, whose *Die Welträtsel* (The Riddle of the Universe) ran to about 400,000 copies and was translated into twenty five languages. Haeckel could not see God as anything more than a higher mammal, gaseous in nature; he mocked him as 'Doctor of Engineering, first degree'.[45] All this was at about the same level as N. Khrushchev's trick question to the first astronauts: Had they seen God while they were out there in space?

Mechanistic materialism and the scientistic atheism to which it gave rise are regarded today as outmoded.[46] This shift is the result not least of the development of the natural science itself. The theory of relativity (A. Einstein) and quantum physics (N. Bohr and W. Heisenberg) turned upside down the mechanistic picture of the world that had often been deduced from classical natural science. That picture of the world had been rendered possible only by a methodologically irresponsible crossing of the boundaries of the natural sciences. The doctrinaire atheism of the past is replaced today by a 'methodical atheism' (the phrase is from J. Lacroix), which says that the natural scientist as such can and must methodically prescind from the question of the existence of God. The natural scientist's own method allows him only to make statements pertaining to the sciences; as a scientist, therefore, he can neither refute nor positively justify faith in God. Conversely, the theologian's method does not permit him either to dispute or to confirm what is said in the natural sciences. God is by definition not an inner-wordly entity alongside other such entities; neither, therefore, is he a hypothesis that can be reliably tested by empirical methods. Anyone who dismissed as meaningless such assertions as are not empirically verifiable or falsifiable, himself steps outside the realm of empirically verifiable or at least falsifiable assertions. He contradicts himself, since his thesis about meaninglessness cannot itself be empirically tested.[47] He absolutizes and ideologizes a form of knowledge that is legitimate in its own sphere and is inherently conscious of its own limitations, turning it instead into a faith in science (scientism), which can only be a superstition.

Natural science and theology are thus on different levels; this does not mean, however, that they can be indifferent to one another and that they have nothing to do with one another. Modern science that is conscious of its limitations is today running into the question of God in two ways: when in inquires into its own ultimate presuppositions, which themselves are no longer of a scientific kind, and when it inquires into the ethical responsibility of the scientist when faced with the consequences of his research, especially in the nuclear and genetic areas. The basic defect of scientistic atheism, on the one hand, and, on the other, of the ecclesiastical apologetics that was launched against it and sought to harmonize faith and science, was that they tried to put God and the world as it were, on the same level. God and the world became competitors, and it was assumed that anything attributed to God had to be denied to the world, and *vice versa*. But the notion of competition mistakes both the absoluteness of God and the freedom of man. For God, as the reality that encompasses everything, cannot be an entity alongside or above the world, since, if he were, he would be limited by the world and would himself be a limited finite being. It is precisely when God is taken seriously as God that he liberates the world to be the world. The converse is also true: when the world and its laws are made absolutes, the result is a deterministic system in which not only God but man as well is dead, because there is no room left for human freedom. The deplorable thing about mechanistic materialism and the atheism to which it gives rise is that it surrenders the great insight of the modern era, namely, that humanity is the point of reference for the world, and turns human beings into a function of the world and of matter. It is only logical, then, that a further discussion of the God-question should be narrowed down to the question of the relation between theonomy and autonomy, divine absoluteness and human freedom.

3. Atheism in the name of human autonomy

The point of departure for modern thinking is not nature and substance, but subject and freedom. The decision in the God-question is therefore made not in dealing with the problems raised by nature but in the debate over human freedom. Here again, atheism comes on the scene only at the end of the modern development. The great thinkers from Descartes to Hegel held resolutely to the idea of God. On the other hand, the new point of departure altered the concept of God in a decisive way and thus created the presuppositions for the humanistic atheism of the nineteenth and twentieth centuries.

As I indicated earlier, Descartes already introduces the idea of God in order to protect the human ego. In the process the idea of God becomes ambiguous. God is in danger of becoming the means of human self-fulfillment and thus of being reduced to a function. This danger becomes clearer as early as Kant. According to Kant, the idea of God cannot be reached by speculative reason; Kant introduces it, however, as a postulate of practical reason.[48] For man's desire for happiness can be fulfilled only if the desire is in harmony with external nature; but this harmony between spirit or freedom and nature can in turn only be ensured by absolute Spirit and absolute Freedom, that is, by God. Only if God is presupposed, then, can human freedom 'turn out well'. Kant needs God for the sake of man's happiness. God is no longer important 'in himself' but only in his significance 'for us'.

In thinkers after Kant, in Fichte and Schelling, for example, the idea of human autonomy is again the focus of intense interest. The young Schelling, in his *Philosophische Briefe über Dogmatismus und Kritizismus* (Philosophical Letters on Dogmatism and Criticism) already comes quite close to a postulatory atheism. He seems to regard human freedom as incompatible with the idea of an objective God.[49] The conflicts are already evident here which will become acute in the atheism controversy started by Fichte in 1798. In an article entitled 'Concerning the Foundation of Our Belief in the Divine Government of the World',[50] Fichte identified God with the moral order of the world; God is thus the means and mediation of freedom, but he himself is not free. Fichte denied that God is personal, because he was afraid that this would introduce limitation and finiteness into God.[51] What he was trying to say in this misleading manner was that God should not be thought of as existing after the manner of substance, for the concept of substance is derivable from the sensible world and (in Kant, for example) is in the service of human happiness. In Fichte's eyes, such a God would be an idol and not the true God. For him, the true God belongs to the moral sphere, that is, to the dimension of freedom. From this point of view Fichte is close to the late philosophy of Schelling, who repeatedly tries to think of God not as a means of freedom but as absolute freedom in himself.[52]

Hegel in particular grasped the situation and emphasized atheism as the current flowing in the depths of modern thought. He made his point by referring on several occasions to the hymn in the Lutheran hymnal, 'God Himself is dead'.[53] The way was prepared for him here by Pascal and by Jean Paul's address of the dead Christ from out of the universe. Hegel called the sentence 'God himself is dead' an expression of the culture of his age, as 'the feeling upon which the religion of more recent times rests'. With the help of his idea of the 'speculative Good Friday', that is, of the reconciliation of God and death with the help of the idea of absolute freedom that recovers itself in its contrary, he sought to overcome this situation. God must be thought of as a living God, as kenotic freedom, as love that empties itself out in its opposite, namely death, and is thus able to abrogate death.

Despite the sublimity of the ideas involved, Hegel's effort to eliminate atheism dialectically was marked by ambiguity. This is why immediately after Hegel's death (1831) his disciples split up into a right wing and a left wing. While the Right Hegelians, especially P. Marheineke, sought to interpret Hegel in terms of orthodox theism, the Left Hegelians soon charged him with atheism. Typical here was B. Bauer's book *Die Posaune des Jüngsten Gerichts über Hegel den Atheisten und Antichristen* (1841; The Trumpet of the Last

Judgment sounded over Hegel the Atheist and Antichrist). According to Bauer, Hegel acknowledges only the universal World-Spirit that becomes conscious of itself in man. Naîve disciples like Strauss (says Bauer) have regarded this simply as pantheism; but in fact it is the most deliberate atheism, that puts self-consciousness in the place of God.[54] A. Ruge called Hegel a 'messiah of atheism' and a 'Robespierre of theology'.[55] We may leave aside here the question of the true interpretation of Hegel. The only important point in this context is the fact that as far as its historical influence was concerned, Hegel's philosophy turned into the atheism that has shaped our situation down to the present time.[56]

Two thinkers in particular must be mentioned as prophets of the new humanistic atheism: L. Feuerbach and K. Marx. The third thinker with whom I shall deal, F. Nietzsche, already saw the nihilistic consequences both of this atheism and of theism.

(a) Ludwig Feuerbach

L. Feuerbach (1804–1872) was the most influential and successful of those disciples of Hegel who reduced theology to anthropology.[57] Feuerbach himself was converted from theologian to anti-theological philosopher, from Hegelian to the anthropologist of a materialistically understood sensuousness that today is often explained as emancipatory sensuousness.[58] I am interested here only in his criticism of religion. K. Marx was of the opinion that Feuerbach had largely completed the criticism of religion.[59] 'And there is no other way for you to *truth* and *freedom* except that leading *through* the stream of fire [the *Feuer-bach*]. Feuerbach is the *purgatory* of the present time.'[60]

Feuerbach gained this influence through his book *Das Wesen des Christentums* (1841; The Essence of Christianity). In this book Feuerbach reverses Hegel's dialectically understood identification of God and man. His starting point was: 'Religion . . . is consciousness of the infinite.'[61] The consciousness is a necessary element in the consciousness that distinguishes man from the beasts. For this reason Feuerbach can say 'In the consciousness of the infinite, the conscious subject has for his object the infinity of his own nature.'[62] 'The *absolute* to man [i.e. a man's God] is his own nature.'[63] 'God is the manifested inward nature, the expressed self of a man – religion the solemn unveiling of a man's hidden treasures, the revelation of his intimate thoughts, the open confession of his love-secrets.'[64] 'God is the mirror of man.'[65] The mystery of theology is therefore anthropology. In religion, man projects and objectifies his own being.[66]

Feuerbach explains the origin of religion with the aid of his theory of projection. Because man does not find fulfillment in himself, he projects his desire for infinity on to God. 'Man makes a god of what he is not but would like to be.'[67] But in so doing man alienates himself. 'To enrich God, man must become poor; that God may be all, man must be nothing.' 'Man denies to himself only what he attributes to God.'[68] Religion is therefore, 'the disuniting of man from himself . . . God is not what man is – man is not what God is.' This disunity is nothing else than 'a distancing of man with his own nature'.[69]

The religious projection thus leads to alienation and estrangement, to the negation of man. In this perspective atheism is the negation of negation and thus the new higher position. A No to God is a Yes to man. Once the mystery of theology has been shown to be the mystery of anthropology, faith in God becomes the faith in man in himself. 'The beginning, middle and end of religion is MAN.'[70] Anthropology, therefore, is theology that has become conscious of itself. '*Homo homini Deus est*: – this is the great practical principle: – this is the axis on which revolves the history of the world.'[71] Feuerbach's atheism ultimately leads to an apotheosis of the world. 'The profoundest secrets lie in common every-day things.' Water, bread, wine are by their very nature sacraments. Feuerbach concludes: 'Therefore let bread be sacred for us, let wine be sacred, and also let water be sacred. Amen!'[72] The change to a new kind of religion shows even more clearly in this passage: 'Thus do things change. What yesterday was still religion is no longer such to-day, and what to-day is atheism, tomorrow will be religion.'[73]

Later on, Feuerbach further expanded this philosophy. His 'new philosophy' anticipates an I-Thou philosophy[74] and even political theology: 'Man *with* man – *the unity of "I" and "You"* – that is God.'[75] 'The *true* dialectic is *not a monologue of the solitary thinker with himself*; it is a *dialogue between "I" and "You"*.[76] Religion is therefore not replaced by a cult of the individual; religion and the church are replaced by politics, prayer by work.[77] 'The new religion, the religion of the future, is politics.'[78]

'Whatever else it may imply, this anti-theology of Feuerbach represents a question; a question put by him to the theology of his time, and perhaps not only of his time.'[79] But questions in reply are also necessary. With regard to the theory of projection it must be said first, and as a general principle, that projection is part of all human experience and knowledge; there can therefore be no question of denying it as part of religious experience and knowledge. But the fact of projection proves only that there is an inevitable subjective element in our knowledge; it proves nothing about the reality of the object we experience and know. It is indeed possible with the help of the theory of projection to explain to some extent subjective conceptions of God, but the theory as such tells us nothing about the reality of God himself. With regard to Feuerbach's theory of projection in particular it must be said that while human consciousness is indeed infinite in its intention, it is precisely within the horizon of this intentional infinity that its own finitude becomes clear. By reason of his material finitude man can never materially fulfill his formal infinity. For this reason, man cannot in the final analysis endure by his own resources; he is not to be made unconditionally happy by becoming closed in within himself. For this same reason, man can never be man's God. The reduction of theology to anthropology does not solve the problem to which theology seeks an answer. It is true that the intentional infinity of man does not prove that some real transcendence exists to answer the self-transcending of man; but neither does it prove the non-existence of God or the validity of reducing the idea of God to the idea of man. Feuerbach's criticism fails of its purpose. At the very least it leaves the God-question still open.

Feuerbach's anthropological reductions of religion has nonetheless remained a basic part of the criticism of religion down to our own day. This is true not only of Marxism, but also of thinkers who are more bourgeois in their orientation. It lives on in the 'postulatory atheism' of the twentieth century, which denies God for the sake of man and his freedom (N. Hartmann, J.- P. Sartre, Merleau-Ponty, and others). Kant's postulatory proof of God's existence is here turned into its opposite: not the existence but the non-existence of God is postulated by human freedom. Even if God existed, the fact could play no role in man's life.[80] Human autonomy contradicts every kind of theonomy!

Feuerbach's continued relevance could not be more clearly shown than by mentioning the name of Sigmund Freud[81] (1856–1939), whose psycho-analysis of the experience and consciousness (in the broadest sense) of the self has opened up a new dimension and had far-reaching practical consequences, especially for sexual behaviour. Meanwhile psycho-analysis is far more than a medical and therapeutic procedure; it represents a further stage of the Enlightenment and exercises an influence today in the sciences of literature, culture and art as well as in pedagogical theory, ethics, the science of religion and philosophy. It is a new key for the interpretation of reality, including not least the reality of religion. The outcome of Freud's psychoanalytic explanation of religion is very much the same as that of Feuerbach's projection theory, thus making it all the more necessary to come to grips with this latter.

Freud's criticism of religion is part of his entire anthropology and psycho-analytical theory, but it is not possible here to deal with these broad areas. Nor shall I discuss Freud's later derivation of religion in terms of the history of religion and culture; from the historical standpoint this derivation, worked out in *Totem and Taboo* and *Moses and Monotheism*, is questionable, to say the least. I shall restrict myself here to Freud's chief work of religious criticism: *The Future of an Illusion* (1927), which he then carried further in his *Civilization and Its Discontents* (1930).

Freud defines man primarily as a creature of instinct that is nonetheless called upon by external reality and by civilization to renounce his instincts; erroneous or unsuccessful efforts to overcome the conflict lead to neuroses, to a flight from hard reality to surrogate solutions. Freud's decisive step is to recognize an analogy between such neuroses and religious behaviour. According to Freud, religion originates in the effort to find consolation in the face of life's difficulties and the renunciations imposed by civilization, and in this way to make human helplessness tolerable. Religious ideas spring from 'the necessity of defending oneself against the crushingly superior power of nature' and 'the urge to rectify the shortcomings of civilization which make themselves painfully felt'.[82] Religious ideas are therefore 'not precipitates of experience or end-results of thinking: they are illusions, fulfillments of the oldest, strongest and most urgent wishes of mankind'.[83] They are infantile wishful illusions, a 'universal obsessional neurosis', 'a system of wishful illusions together with a disavowal of reality'.[84] To this infantilism Freud opposes an '*education to reality*', which includes the acceptance of the necessities imposed by fate, for against these no science is of any help. But this resignation includes an element of very muted hope: 'By withdrawing their expectations from the other world and concentrating all their liberated energies into their life on earth, they will probably succeed in achieving a state of things in which life will become tolerable for everyone and civilization no longer oppressive to anyone.'[85]

Freud's criticism of religion was meant not only to strengthen the unbelief of unbelievers but also to explain the faith of believers. It is therefore of the greatest importance, both theologically and pastorally. On the other hand, its limitations must also be pointed out. Is it really possible to start in such an unquestioning way with an analogy between religious and psychopathic phenomena (obsessional neurosis, infantile wishful illusions)? The least that must be said is that no identity of nature may be deduced from such analogies. Rather, the religious phenomenon must first be analysed on its terms; it may not be *a priori* reduced to other phenomena. Otherwise the critic opens himself to the suspicion that atheism rather than religion is a wishful illusion. On the basis of a more detailed analysis of the phenomenon of religion as such, other depth psychologists reach a much more positive view of religion than Freud did (C. G. Jung, E. Fromm, V. Frankl and others). In any case, psychology can explain only the psychological reality, the psychic content and the psychic consequences of religion; its methods do not permit it to say anything about the objective reality and truth-content of what is being conveyed by religious representations. This fact brings us once again to the limits of the projection theory and its effectiveness.

(b) Karl Marx

Karl Marx[86] (1818–1883) was born into a Jewish family that was later converted to Protestantism. As a young man he was already familiar with the French Enlightenment; later on, as a member of the Doctors' Club in Berlin (A. Ruge, M. Stirner, M. Hess and others) he adopted the atheism of the Left Hegelians and made Feuerbach's criticism of religion his own. He came to socialism and communism only subsequently, during his years in Paris, where he became acquainted with the ideas of the early socialists (Proudhon, Saint-Simon, Owen, etc.) and became a friend of H. Heine and F. Engels. In 1948 he and Engels composed the *Communist Manifesto* which thenceforth became the basis of the Communist movement. It was likewise Engels who stimulated Marx to study political economy (A. Smith, D. Ricardo, J. S. Mill). While the early 'Paris Manuscripts' (1844) still move in the direction primarily of a philosophical humanism, Marx was becoming increasingly interested in a more realistic humanism. In his principal work, *Capital* (1867), economic analyses occupy the entire foreground. On the other hand, the later dialectical materialism (Diamat) came into existence only as the result of the *Anti-Dühring* (1878) of F. Engels, who turned the doctrine of the historical dialect followed by society into a general view of the world by adopting Darwin's theory of evolution and integrating the historical dialectic into a more encompassing dialectic of nature. Lenin made Diamat the official world-view of the Communist Party. The relation between the early and the late Marx, between Marx and Marxism, is debated. Nowadays, amid all the differences in emphasis, scholars tend to stress more the connections and the continuity.

It was the publication of the Paris Manuscripts in 1932 that led to a discussion of the original Marxism of Marx himself as distinct from the orthodox doctrinaire and totalitarian Marxism found in the ideology of the Communist party and state. The debate led to various anthropological and humanistic interpretations of Marx (Lukács, Korsch, Gramsci, Schaff, Kolakowski, Machovec, Bloch, Sartre, Garaudy, Lefèbvre, Merleau-Ponty and others), which were rejected as revisionist by orthodox Marxism. These new interpretations introduced the idea of a democratic Marxism as well as new possibilities of dialogue with Christianity. The 'Frankfurt School' (M. Horkheimer, T. W. Adorno and others) sought to present Marxism as a continuation of modern enlightenment and to revitalize it as a philosophy of history that has a practical purpose (J. Habermas). The structuralist interpretation of Marx offered by L. Althusser, on the other hand, insists on the very opposite: that is not the individual human being but the totality of relations that is the subject of history. More recent interpretations are once again contending that totalitarian traits are to be found not only in Marxism but in the thinking of K. Marx himself, so that the internal development of Marxism is to be considered not a degeneration but a more or less consistent evolution (A. Glucksmann; C. Jambet; G. Lardreau; B. H. Lévy). From the theological standpoint, the most important question in the interpretation of Marx is whether atheism and the criticism of religion are essential to Marxism or simply historically conditioned and, as such, accidental.

Looked at simply in historical terms, Marx's criticism of religion took as its incontrovertible basis the humanistic atheism of L. Feuerbach. 'The basis of irreligious criticism is this: *man makes religion*; religion does not make man.'[87] As for Feuerbach, so for Marx religion is a projection. And as for Feuerbach, so for Marx atheism is not simply a negation, but a negation of a negation and, to this extent, a positive assertion: the assertion of humanism. Communism presupposes this atheism, but atheism is not yet communism. For Marxist thought the criticism of religion is rather a presupposition for a criticism of the world. 'Thus the criticism of heaven is transformed into the criticism of earth, the *criticism of religion* into the *criticism of law*, and the *criticism of theology* into the *criticism of politics*.'[88] This is the point at which Marx takes a decisive step beyond Feuerbach. Unlike Feuerbach, Marx is bent on understanding man in and through his economic and social conditioning. But 'the essence of man is no abstraction inhering in each single individual. In its actuality it is the ensemble of social relationships.'[89] 'Man is *the human world*, the state, society. This state, this society, produce religion.'[90]

This concrete economic and political view of man has consequences for the new humanism which Marx is seeking. Whereas Feuerbach was bent on unmasking Hegel's pantheism as a form of atheism, Marx wants 'the world's becoming philosophical' in Hegel to be replaced by 'philosophy's becoming wordly'.[91] Hegel reconciled philosophy and the world only in thought, not in reality; philosophy made perfect now stands in contrast to a world that is perverse. Marx wants to fulfill and thus cancel out philosophy; he wants to turn theory into practice. 'The philosophers have only *interpreted* the world in various ways; the point is, to *change* it.'[92] According to Marx, therefore, the chief defect of materialism up to now, including the materialism of Feuerbach, is that it has grasped reality only as an object of perception and not subjectively as human activity and practice.[93] Marx thus moves beyond the previous mechanistic materialism and replaces it with a historical materialism. The latter makes its own the modern idea of subjectivity and is thus able to see itself as the true heir of the Enlightenment and idealism. Marx's materialism is thus at the same time a humanism, according to which man is the supreme being for man.[94] But since there is also the question of the concrete person, this humanism is also a naturalism, that is, the realization of a human world.

This realization in turn presupposes that the products of work, being mediations between man and the world, belong to all in common. For this reason the elimination of private property, or communism, is true humanism.[95] In the final analysis Marx's aim is a radical and universal emancipation, that is, the complete restoration of man, 'a *restoration* of the human world and of human relationships to *man himself*'.[96] The need, therefore, is '*to overthrow all those conditions* in which man is an abased, enslaved, abandoned, contemptible being'.[97]

This practico-political understanding of man necessarily had to modify the criticism of religion that had been taken over from Feuerbach, by expanding it in terms of politics, economics and practice. The classical passage here is in the 'Contribution to the Critique of Hegel's Philosophy of Right' (1843/44). Religion is not inverted self-consciousness but inverted world-consciousness: inverted because it is the expression of an inverted world. Religion is even 'the general theory of this world', 'its moral sanction', 'its general basis of consolation and justification'. 'Religion is the sigh of the oppressed creature, the sentiment of a heartless world, and the soul of soulless conditions. It is the *opium* of the people.'[98]

Several interesting points are made in these passages. First, religion is understood as a projection. But the starting point for the projection is not humanity as such; religion is rather understood (to use a later phraseology) as a superstructure built upon relations. This idea finds expression in what is from the standpoint of the criticism of religion the most important chapter in *Capital*, a chapter that has the significant title: 'The Fetishism of Commodities and the Secret Thereof'. A commodity is, in Marx's eyes, 'a very queer thing', 'abounding in metaphysical subtleties and theological niceties'.[99] The mystical character it possesses and the secret surrounding it are due to the fact that it comes before man as an object and thus reflects back to him his own nature as this produces itself in work. It is thus analogous to 'the mist-enveloped regions of the religious world'.[100] This is why the removal of religious alienation is only a presupposition of true humanism. The philanthropy which is fostered by atheism is only philosophical and abstract; it becomes real only in communism, which eliminates real alienations.[101]

The religious illusion is, secondly, not simply the work of a ruling caste of priests who keep the people in a state of stultification. Marx is far removed from any such primitive explanation. He does not say, as Lenin will later, that religion is an opium *for* the people, a consolation deliberately administered to the people. Marx says rather that it is an opium *of* the people, a consolation which the people administer to themselves because of the wretched conditions in which they live.[102] The religious ideology is not viewed by Marx as something arbitrary but as a kind of necessary natural process. 'Consciousness can never be anything but conscious existence.'[103] 'The ruling ideas are nothing more than the ideal expression of the dominant material relationships.'[104] If these relationships are changed, religion will by itself die out and cease to exist. 'The religious reflex of the real world can, in any case, only finally vanish when the practical relations of everyday life offer to man none but perfectly intelligible and reasonable relations with regard to his fellow-men and to Nature.'[105] Then there will no longer be any need of religion.

The third point to be made is that Marx's judgment on religion is not purely negative. He sees in it not only a function that sanctions and legitimizes existing relations but also a protest and a sigh of the oppressed creature. But religion deals in promises of an illusory happiness, in 'imaginary flowers from the chain'.[106] This illusion must be eliminated, so that man may take control of his own history, 'so that he will think, act and fashion his reality'. Criticism of religion is therefore a presupposition of an earthly, political criticism. 'It is the *task of history*, therefore, once the *other-world of truth* has vanished, to establish the *truth of this world*.'[107]

Is atheism, therefore, an essential presupposition in Marx's judgment, or would he find acceptable a belief in God and a Christianity that do not serve to justify oppression but are in the service of a prophetic criticism against unjust conditions and of the liberation of man?

Opinion is divided in the answer to this question.[108] In the Marxist-Leninist ideology that is officially professed today in the Soviet Union and in other communist countries atheism is undoubtedly regarded as an essential point of doctrine and even as the basis for some of its fundamental theses. But according to theologians like T. Steinbüchel, M. Reding and H. Gollwitzer, the connection is not an unconditionally necessary one. Early on, the representatives of religious socialism (C. F. Blumhardt, H. Kutter, L. Ragaz, the early K. Barth, P. Tillich) maintained that the impulses of Marxism in the direction of justice and peace were compatible with the Christian gospel, and were even in conformity with it. After 1945 came the 'Christian Peace Conference' (J. L. Hromádka, H. Iwand and others); numerous efforts were made to establish communication, especially in Italy and France (G. Girardi; G. Fessard and others); in Germany there were the conferences sponsored by the Paulus-Gesellschaft and, until 1975, the *Internationale Dialog-Zeitschrift* edited by H. Vorgrimler; in Austria, the *Neues Forum*, edited by G. Neuning; and, finally, the Christians for Socialism movement which was begun in Santiago de Chile in 1972. The new political theology, the theology of revolution and liberation theology likewise derived important stimuli from Marxist and Neo-Marxist thinkers, at least as far as the analysis of social relations is concerned.

Official Catholic teaching is likewise not as monolithic as it may seem if one takes into account only the decrees of Pius XII and John XXIII that forbid Catholics to belong to the Communist Party under pain of excommunication. The social encyclical *Quadragesimo anno* of Pius XI (1931) already has important points in common with the Marxist analysis and criticism of capitalism. This criticism of capitalism has persisted down to the very recent social encyclical *Laborem exercens* of John Paul II (1981). In addition, the encyclical *Pacem in terris* of John XXIII (1963), the Pastoral Constitution *Gaudium et spes* and the encyclical *Populorum progressio* of Paul VI (1967) began to make distinctions. This process shows most clearly in the Apostolic Letter *Octogesima adveniens* of Paul VI (1971), where various levels of Marxism are distinguished: Marxism as the active practice of the class struggle; as the exercise of all forms of political and economic power; as an ideology based on historical materialism and the denial of anything beyond the present life; as a scientific method and tool for the investigation of social and political relations. But the Letter is realistic enough to acknowledge the internal links between these various levels.[109]

As a matter of fact, Marx himself always regarded the atheistic criticism of religion as not only a historical but also an essential presupposition of communism; moreover, he was of the opinion that the humanistic impulses present in atheism find their true fulfillment only in communism. For this reason Marx did not attack only an unsocial and socially backward Christianity; he also conducted a vehement onslaught upon a socially committed Christianity that was getting involved in the problem of the workers, as in the case of Bishop Ketteler.[110] Marx's disciples, K. Kautzky and E. Bloch, were the first to discover the social, emancipatory and even revolutionary potential of Christianity. But Bloch reclaims this potential for socialism and atheism, since 'without atheism there is no place for messianism'.[111] In his eyes, therefore, only an atheist can be a good Christian.[112] But even though hope in an absolute future does not exclude a rightly understood commitment to an intra-historical future, but unshackles, motivates and inspires such a commitment,[113] it remains a fact that the this-wordly messianism of Marxism and the eschatological hope of the Christian are evidently incompatible.[114]

The reason for this is to be found in the Marxist picture of man, according to which man or humanity is its own creator and owes its existence only to itself.[115] According to Marx, man is his own redeemer. Every notion of a mediator is excluded from the outset.[116] 'For man, the root is man himself.' Such radical autonomy excludes every form of theonomy. 'The criticism of religion ends with the doctrine that '*man is the supreme being for man.*'[117] V. Gardavski comments: 'Marxism is essentially atheistic. Or to put it another way: it is atheism which provides the radical aspect of the Marxist philosophy of life. Without it, both Marx's plan for a "total man" and his concept of Communism are equally inconceivable.'[118] We must therefore put our cards on the table and admit that not only for orthodox Diamat, but also for Marxism in its original form, atheism is an essential element. The question of whether it is possible to separate this atheism from the socio-political and economic thrust of Marxism is one that can only be put – at best – to a radically revised Marxism that surrenders its (necessarily) totalitarian messianism. But would this then be the original Marxism?

Every theological criticism of Marx must begin with self-criticism. With the exception of a few men like Bishop Ketteler, A. Kolping, F. Hitze and others, nineteenth-century Christianity came much too late to an appreciation of the social question. The General Synod of the Sees of Germany (1971–1975) speaks, not without reason, of a continuing scandal[119] that has its basis in an erroneous mentality, especially in a primarily caritative and insufficiently structural view of the problem. In addition, there has long been a failure to distinguish adequately between the various levels of Marxism and in particular between the Marxist analysis of the social problem and the ideological interpretation then given by Marxism. Even if we formulate fundamental theological objections to the ideological interpretation offered by Marxism, we need not deny that Marxism has developed important and by now indispensable tools for analysing social, economic and political problems. These methods become ideological only if they are turned into universal absolutes, that is, if religious phenomena are *a priori* discussed only in a socio-economic perspective and no longer in themselves.

In addition to this methodical advance, Marxism makes a contribution of a substantive kind: its demonstration of the fundamental importance of work. The encyclical *Laborem exercens* (1981) has adopted this viewpoint, but in a Christian perspective; it sees work as a fundamental form of human self-fulfillment and thereby shows the primacy of man the worker over things, even over capital. The defects of the Marxist interpretation of religion are due, among other things, to the fact that Marx nowhere expressly analyses the phenomenon of religion in itself but *a priori* reduces it to economic and political functions. Since Marx does not himself justify his criticism of religion, but more or less takes this from Feuerbach, the objections against Feuerbach's theory of projection hold against Marx as well. This means that from the fact that ideas of God are influenced by the socio-economic relations of a given time, it does not follow that God is simply a reflection of these relations. If Marx had really investigated the role played by religion in the social process, he would have had to ask himself whether in addition to the influence of socio-economic relations on religious ideas, there is also an influence (shown by M. Weber) of religion on social ideas and social practice.[120] At least by allusions he makes, Marx shows his realization that not only do relations determine ideas, but ideas, in the form of utopias, determine and can revolutionize relations. This means in turn that spirit enjoys at least a relative independence in regard to matter. The end result is that religion is not a function of bad economic and social conditions and that it does not simply die out when these conditions change in a revolutionary degree. This is why religion has still not died out in the communist countries; despite harsh persecution and suppression it not only survives but is even revitalized.

This situation is connected with a second point: communism is still unable to give an answer to the individual person's questions regarding meaning. These questions are asked also and especially in socialist societies, because the latter bring new types of alienation of the individual from society. The question of personal happiness, of a personal destiny, of individual guilt, suffering and death does not accept as adequate the explanation that these are part of the progress toward a classless society. Here is the decisive point. Christianity sees man not simply as an ensemble of social relations but as a person who, no matter how thoroughly integrated he is into society, possesses an inherent value and dignity[121] and is in turn the source, subject and object of all social institutions.[122] Christianity therefore sees evil as taking the form primarily not of structures and institutions but of sin, which has its origin in the heart of man. The dignity of the person is ultimately based on the transcendence of the person.[123] Human autonomy and theonomy are therefore not related to each other as competitors; they increase in direct, not in inverse proportion.[124]

From the Christian view of man and his constitutive relatedness it follows that every form of intra-historical messianism is excluded for Christians. Because of his constitutive relatedness to God, man can never be completely his own master. Neither, therefore, can he completely liberate himself from his history and begin fully anew. Even the revolutionary is caught in the entanglements of history; even he needs forgiveness, redemption and the grace of a new beginning. Finally: revolution can – at best – offer a hope to coming generations. But what about the suffering, the oppressed, the losers of the past and the present? Are they simply a means to the happiness of others? If hope and justice are to be possible for all, even the dead, this can only be if God is lord of life and death and if he is a God who raises the dead.[125] There are doubtless mistaken ways of looking for consolation in the next world, but when every form of consolation in the next world is rejected as an empty promise, then this world, too, is stripped of all consolation.

(c) Friedrich Nietzsche

Even as a student, Friedrich Nietzsche (1844–1900)[126] was alienated by the sentimental and moralistic Christianity he came to know in the close atmosphere of a Protestant parsonage. His argument against Christianity is drawn less from reason than from life. Consequently, Nietzsche is more than a philosopher; he is rather a prophet of the death of God and a witness to the question which modern man addresses to Christians and to the ascetical ideal of Christianity. But Nietzsche is also already aware of the result to which atheism leads, namely, nihilism; he anticipates the twentieth-century crisis of meaning and attempts to overcome it by a new view of the world and of life.

Nietzsche's thought has met with many interpretations and misinterpretations. He was first claimed as an aesthetic thinker by the Stefan George group: then his statements about the morality of masters and about the blond beast were misused for political and nationalistic ends by National Socialism. His influence was at first a more literary kind; in this context we may mention Thomas Mann, Stefan Zweig, Nikos Kazantzakis, André Gide and André Malraux. Because of his aphoristic style and the way his thinking in terms of opposites involves him in numerous contradictions, he was initally refused the rank of a philosopher who is to be taken seriously (W. Windelband; J. Hirschberger); it was not until K. Jaspers and M. Heidegger that he began to exercise a serious influence on philosophy. But Jaspers and Heidegger interpret him rather in terms of what is left unsaid in his thoughts and thus in terms of the direction of their own philosophizing. Nietzsche's importance is probably to be found in the fact that he seeks to overcome the appreciation of history which Christianity introduced, together with its secularized consequences in the modern faith in progress, and to foster a revitalization of the cyclical thinking of antiquity (K. Löwith; E. Fink) and a Heraclitean philosophy of opposites (Müller-Lauter). On the other hand, Nietzsche's keyword is not cosmos but life. It is in this perspective that he formulates his passionate criticism of Christianity, which he interprets as a ressentiment against life. For this reason, Christians generally and theologians in particular initially responded to Nietzsche in a hypersensitive way. Soloviev saw him as precursor of the Antichrist. G. Marcel, H. de Lubac, K. Barth and others see him as prophet of a human race without God and at the same time as a witness to the crisis which this godlessness brings upon the West. More recently, B. Welte, E. Biser and others, despite all the unbridgeable differences of principle between themselves and Nietzsche, have entered into an open dialogue with him.

Nietzsche interprets his own writings as a 'school of suspicion'.[127] All previous values, ideas and ideals are examined in terms of their historical and psychological origin; all truths are identified as approximations, perspectives, prejudices advantageous for life, expressions of the will to power.[128] 'Truth is the kind of error without which a certain species of life could not live. The value for *life* is ultimately decisive.'[129] 'There is *only* a perspective seeing, *only* a perspective knowing'.[130] and this perspectivism is the basic condition of all life.[131] What remains in life, which demands illusion and lives by illusion,[132] and is identical with the will to power.[133] Nietzsche also speaks of this as the 'Dionysian', meaning all that is ecstatic, irrational and even anarchic in contrast to Apollonian clarity.[134] Here Nietzsche parts company with the modern belief in reason, morality and ideals. In the final analysis his intention is to renounce the whole of metaphysics since Plato, and to renounce Christianity as well, since 'Christianity is Platonism for "the people"'.[135] Even science is based on a metaphysical faith.[136] Nietzsche is engaged in a struggle against any ulterior world of truth, goodness, being, or the *Ding an sich*, which would cause life in this world to be depreciated as something unreal.

According to Nietzsche, the illusion of an absolute truth reaches its high point and ultimate concentration in the idea of God. God is our 'most enduring lie',[137] it is 'invention, poetic pretension'[138]; it is the 'counter-concept of life'[139] and an expression of ressentiment against life.[140] Nietzsche was therefore compelled to make the death of God the central content of his thinking. The death of God was, for him, the highest expression of the death of metaphysics.[141] But the reader would be dangerously deceiving himself if he were to think that Nietzsche is concerned only about the death of the god of metaphysics and not the death of the Christian God. Quite the contrary is the case, for Nietzsche considers the Christian conception of God to be 'one of the most corrupt conceptions of God arrived at on earth'. In it God 'degenerated to the *contradiction of life*, instead of being its transfiguration and eternal *Yes!*'[142] 'The god on the cross is a curse on life.'[143] Therefore: '*Dionysus versus the Crucified.*'[144]

Nietzsche's message about the death of God finds its classical expression in *The Gay Science* (1886). Here he offers the parable of the madman who on a bright morning lights a lantern, runs to the market place and cries incessantly: 'I seek God! I seek God!' He jumps in among the laughing crowd, pierces them with his glance, and cries: 'Whither is God? I will tell you. *We have killed him* – you and I. All of us are his murderers.'[145] These words of Nietzsche about the death of God go back to Pascal, Jean Paul and Hegel. But in Nietzsche the message had a new and much more comprehensive meaning. The death of God is 'the greatest recent event'; 'the event itself is far too great, too distant, too remote from the multitude's capacity for comprehension even for the tidings of it to be thought of as having *arrived* as yet. Much less may one suppose that many people know as yet *what* this event really means.'[146] God's shadow is a long one, and we must first conquer this shadow.[147]

The immediate consequences of this event are 'a new and scarcely describable kind of light, happiness, relief, exhilaration, encouragment, dawn'; 'at last the horizon appears free to us again'.[148] But Nietzsche is far removed from this kind of optimistic atheism. He sees the 'long plenitude and sequence of breakdown, destruction, ruin, and cataclysm that is now impending'.[149] Therefore he has his madman say:

> What were we doing when we unchained this earth from its sun? Whither is it moving now? Whither are we moving? Away from all suns? Are we not plunging continually? Backward, sideward, forward, in all directions? Is there still any up or down? Are we not straying as though through an infinite nothing? Do we not feel the breath of empty space? Has it not become colder? Is not night continually closing in on us?[150]

Ultimately, of course, it is not the death of God, that is, unbelief, but faith in God itself that is for Nietzsche the cause of nihilism. This is because God is a No to life. 'In God nothingness [is] deified, the will to nothingness sanctified!'[151] Here we reach the theme that preoccupied Nietzsche, especially in the late phase of his thinking: theism is ultimately a form of nihilism; nihilism exists 'because the values we have had hitherto thus draw their final consequences';[152] it 'represents the ultimate logical conclusion of our great values and ideals'.[153] Christianity itself is a nihilistic religion. 'Nihilist and Christian [*Nihilist und Christ*]: they rhyme, and do not merely rhyme.'[154]

'What does nihilism mean? *That the highest values devaluate themselves. The aim is lacking; "why?" finds no answer.*'[155] Nihilism is the belief that 'there is no truth at all';[156] it includes 'disbelief in any metaphysical world'.[157] But Nietzsche distinguishes between 'the weary nihilism that no longer attacks', and the active nihilism that perceives previous goals to be inadequate and is strong enough 'to posit for oneself, productively, a goal, a why, a faith'.[158] 'An aim? a new aim? – *that* is what humanity needs.'[159]

Nietzsche clothes his own answer to the question of aim in various metaphors. The most important of these is his talk of the Superman in *Thus Spoke*

Zarathustra. The figure of the Superman makes its appearance when the death of God has become a reality. '*Dead are all gods: now we want the Superman to live.*'[160] But what is this Superman? For Nietzsche he is 'the meaning of the earth'[161] and the meaning of man.[162] For 'man is something that shall be overcome'; 'What is great in man is that he is a bridge and not an end: what can be loved in man is that he is an *overture* and a *going under*.'[163] Superman is the man who has overcome all the former alienations. He is therefore not an other-worldly man, but rather remains '*faithfull to the earth*' and does not believe in other-worldly hopes.[164] He also breaks in pieces the 'tables of values';[165] he is not one of 'the despisers of the body';[166] he rejects the old virtues and lives 'beyond good and evil'. He is the man who is at one with himself, who has overcome all tension and division between being and meaning; he is the man who has himself become God and replaced the vanished and slain God. Only in order to become God could man kill God.[167] '*If* there were gods, how could I endure not to be a god!'[168]

Nietzsche explains the way to Superman by means of another image: the metaphor of the three metamorphoses, or 'how the spirit becomes a camel; and the camel, a lion; and the lion, finally, a child'. The camel humbles itself; it submits to higher values. The lion seeks freedom; he is an image of the man who wants to win happiness and fulfillment for himself in and by his own freedom. But as for the child: 'The child is innocence and forgetting, a new beginning, a game, a self-propelled wheel, a first movement, a sacred "Yes".'[169] Yes-saying brings redemption from transitory time. The creative will says: 'But thus I will it.'[170] 'Was *that* life? . . . Well then! Once more!'[171]

In the third part of *Thus Spoke Zarathustra* Nietzsche logically extends the idea of Superman to an 'abysmal thought': the idea of eternal recurrence.[172] He means by this the presence of eternity in every instant: 'In every Now, being begins; round every Here rolls the sphere There. The center is everywhere. Bent is the path of eternity.'[173] Nietzsche gives expression to this insight in the image of the great Noon.[174] 'The world is deep, / Deeper than day had been aware. / Deep is its woe; / Joy – deeper yet than agony: / Woe implores: God! / But joy wants all eternity – / Wants deep, wants deep eternity.'[175] Instead of accepting the negation of life, Nietzsche wants to break through 'to a Dionysian affirmation of the world as it is, without subtraction, exception, or selection'.[176] He wants to understand the previously denied aspects of existence as not only necessary but desirable and to accept the eternal recurrence of all things. His formula for this is '*amor fati* [love of fate]'.[177]

This doctrine of the eternal recurrence of the same is undoubtedly meant to contradict the historical and eschatological world view of Christianity, and this dissolution of all contrarieties and oppositions, represents a rejection of the very foundations of Western metaphysics. It is possible to see in it a critical revival of mythical religiosity, which would show that even Nietzsche was not really finished with the God-question and that instead it returns in a new form in his writings. Nietzsche is not alone in thus having recourse to myth. Before him Görres, Schelling and Hölderlin had already called for a new mythology. In his poem *Die Götter Griechenlands* [The Gods of Greece] Schiller grieves over a world that has lost its soul, and summons back the ancient world in which 'everything was a footprint of God'.[178] Even more filled with a sense of urgency, if this be possible, are Hölderlin's elegies, his grief at the disappearance of the gods, and his call for and even expectations of their return. 'Close is the God and difficult to grasp. But where danger threatens, redemption is also at hand.'[179] Later on, Stephan George and Rilke (in the form of the angel in the *Duino Elegies*) point in a similar direction. In Thomas Mann and, though differently, in Günther Grass we again come upon the fascination with myth. No one, of course, has dared to gaze so deeply as Martin Heidegger into the abyss of nothingness that is the present world with its technological image of reality, while at the same time joining Hölderlin and Nietzsche in looking for a new revelation of being.[180]

Nietzsche himself asks: 'Is not just this godlike that there are gods but no God?'[181] Even in his late notes we find the question: 'How many new gods are still possible?' He answers: 'I should not doubt that there are many kinds of gods.'[182] Therefore: 'We believe in Olympus – and *not* in the "Crucified".'[183] This longing finds its clearest expression in the well-known 'Dionysus Dithyramb': 'Oh, come back, / My unknown god! My *pain*! My last – happiness!'[184] However these verses are to be interpreted, Nietzsche was preoccupied with the God-question until the very end, and he supplies the reason: 'I fear we are not getting rid of God because we still believe in grammar.'[185] We are caught in the snares of grammar, which is 'the metaphysics of the people';[186] due to it, nothing hitherto has as direct a power of persuasion as the error regarding being: 'Every word, every sentence we utter speaks in its favour.'[187] Is it even possible, then, to express Nietzsche's conception? Is it possible to think it?

Nietzsche does not simply confront us with the question of theism or atheism. Certainly he does not criticize only sentimental and moralistic caricatures of Christianity; it is therefore not possible to meet his criticisms by touching up our image of God a bit. He confronts us rather with the question of being or not being; his focus is on the foundations of our entire Western culture, both Greek and Christian. He unveils its nihilistic tendency and sees nihilism coming as a result. Due to his diagnosis of the present age, Nietzsche is an uncannily contemporary thinker, much more so than Marx, who still lived by the principles of meaning embodied in humanity and history. In Nietzsche faith in reason and thus in modernity is shattered. He reveals the lack of meaning and direction, the boredom of modern civilization. He knows the consequences of de-divinization, including the emptying out of the world which Platonism and Christianity together had built and which achieved its full practical results in modern science and technology. The statement that God is dead is as it were an abbreviated expression of this far-ranging process.

But, challenging though Nietzsche's diagnosis is, his answer may not be convincing. Is life – healthy, vital, robust life – and the will to life really the ultimate thing? May not life itself be only a perspective, an expression of the will to power, a despairing effort to survive the nihilism that threatens? Nietzsche's attempt to locate eternity in the present life and not in a world beyond, and thus to eternalize our present life, can only lead (as no one saw more clearly than Nietzsche himself) to an eternalizing of what is meaningless, to deadly boredom and a disgust with life. Another point: if man is to remain human, can he do away with the distinction between good and evil? Can he say Yes to evil, to lying, murder, violence? For the sake of a human kind of life must he not make distinctions here? And finally: Is recourse to myth enough? The distinction between Yes and No, true and false is at bottom identical with the discovery of thought, which it is impossible to reject without falling into absurdities. When the contradictions in the thinking of Nietzsche seem to be reconciled, they end up reappearing. For the principle of contradiction, according to which something cannot simultaneously be and not be in the same respect, is the basis of all thinking; even the attempt to deny the principle presupposes it. As a consequence, the passage from *mythos* to *logos* cannot be revoked. Of course, there is also the counter-question: if this is so, then are not also the consequences unavoidable that lead to a de-divinized, unsouled and objectified world in which as a final logical step God must be dead? Or is it possible to think *theos* and *logos* – theo-logy – in a new and non-nihilistic way? What positive role would mythological language have in this enterprise?

In his *Anti-Christ*, of all places, Nietzsche points to such a way out. For, despite his very cutting criticism of Christianity and the church, he retains a certain respect for Jesus, whose good news the church turned into a dysevangel. Nietzsche sees Jesus not as a genius or a hero, but as Dostoievsky did (to whom Nietzsche is so close in many ways and yet from whom he is so totally alien): as an idiot who lives 'love as the sole, as the *last* possibility of life'.[188] In this 'life lived in love, in love without deduction or exclusion, without distance' there is no question of a new faith but rather of a different way of acting; and '*evangelic practice alone* leads to God, it *is* God'.[189] For the kingdom of God is within us; it is not something one waits for: 'it is everywhere, it is nowhere'.[190] Thus in the life and life-project of Jesus Nietzsche thinks he finds what he proclaims: a life at one with itself, a claiming back for man of the attributes squandered on God. A life lived in love as the essence of the gift-giving virtue which Nietzsche praises:[191] would this be the new unalienated existential project, which though not entirely Christian is at least that of Jesus? Is it an atheistic following of Jesus, in which the biblical statement that God is love is affirmed only in its converse, namely, that love is God?

Recent theology has often sought to follow this path as a way out of the crisis. Undoubtedly the Nietzsche to whom appeal is made in this context is a carefully selected Nietzsche.[192] In addition, the questions of principle which Nietzsche raises are by no means answered in such short-cut adaptions. Nietzsche's remarks do, however, supply a stimulus which it will be worth accepting in a critical way. But if absolute love is to be the answer on which there is agreement in principle, then man can never be this absolute love; he can only allow it to be bestowed on him.

This brings us back once again to the basic question involved in the modern idea of autonomy: can the concept of a radical human autonomy in the sense of a pure self-mediation ever succeed? Or must not a successful human identity rather be only a freedom that is given to man from another? Being from man's own resources – or being that is received? Can autonomy find an other than theonomous foundation? And how can theonomy be so conceived that it does not signify heteronomy, but rather both grounds autonomy and brings it to fulfillment? The word 'love' already points to the answer given by theology. For love means a union which does not absorb the other but sets him free to be himself and thus brings him to fulfillment. The response which theology gives to a modern atheism that appeals to human autonomy is, then, the following: greater union with God means greater and more fulfilled freedom for humanity.

In order that it may give its answer to modern atheism in a reasoned way, theology is challenged to a basic self-definition and self-criticism. In closing this chapter, therefore, let me once again call to mind the fundamental question raised by modern atheism. The fundamental question is not the one that arises when the confession of faith 'God exists', is met by the contrary assertion:. 'God does not exist,' so that theology is forced to ask: 'Does God exist?' The confession of faith has never asserted the existence of God in an abstract way; it has always spoken instead of the one God shows himself as creator of heaven and earth and as Father of our Lord Jesus Christ. Neither has modern atheism in its reflective forms ever simply asserted the non-existence of God; it has, rather, denied a very particular God who acts as oppressor toward humanity, and life, and this in order that it might then ascribe the divine attributes to humanity.

The fundamental question that lies behind this historical process was already brought out into the open by Fichte during the atheism controversy (the *Atheismusstreit*). The question is whether and to what extent we can speak of God at all in terms of being and existence, or whether we can only assign predicates based on action.[193] Classical theology concluded from God's action to his being and said, for example, that because God shows himself good to me, God is good. It thus understood God as a substance to which certain predicates could be applied. Modern philosophy criticized this approach. Fichte[194] and later Feuerbach[195] were of the opinion that when such statements about being in the sense of substance are used of God, he is being thought of as a being who exists in space and time and is thus objectified and rendered finite. The answers given by modern philosophy itself are admittedly ambiguous, to say the least. The Fichte of the atheism controversy gives the impression that he applies the divine predicates to the moral order, somewhat as Spinoza applies them to nature and as myth does to the cosmos. Feuerbach for his part applies them to humanity, and Marx to society. The later Fichte and the later Schelling wanted to avoid these atheistic consequences by speaking of God not as a substance but as a subject (in the modern sense of the term); that is, by thinking of God within the horizon of freedom. They thought therefore that they could overcome modern atheism on the very ground where it had arisen: on the ground of the modern philosophy of subjectivity when this is thought through to the end.

The fundamental question raised by modern atheism is thus the question of the meaning or meaninglessness of sentences such as 'God exists' or 'God does not exist'. It is the question of the condition for the possibility of existential (*existential*) statements as made about God. This clarification is necessary because the word 'is' is profoundly ambiguous. At first glance it seems to assert an identity. If this is the case, then it is possible to convert the New Testament statement that God is love, exchange subject and predicate, and say: Love is God; that is, where love occurs, there God is and there something divine occurs. Now this statement may be quite legitimate from a Christian point of view, but it can also be interpreted atheistically unless an explanation is given of who the subject of this love is, or how human and divine subjects are related to one another in the loving. Thus, in the matter of the God-question modern philosophy ultimately confronts us with the problem of whether and how the question of being, or the question of the meaning of being, can be asked anew within the modern philosophy of subjectivity. It is the merit of Nietzsche and of Martin Heidegger's interpretation of Nietzsche to have posed the problem in this radical manner.

III

The Predicament of Theology in the Face of Atheism

1. The traditional apologetic position

Modern atheism has put theology in a difficult position. Of particular importance here is mass atheism, a phenomenon unparalleled in past history; it regards the practical, if not theoretical denial of God or at least indifference to belief in God as being by far the most plausible attitude to take. As a result, theology has been stripped of its power to speak to people and to communicate with them. There are now no generally accepted images, symbols, concepts and categories with which it can make itself understood. This crisis in the presuppositions for understanding talk about God is the real crisis of present-day theology. To put the matter in more Scholastic terms; the crisis of contemporary theology arises from the loss of the *praëambula fidei*, that is, of the presuppositions which faith needs if it is to be possible as faith and if it is to be able to make itself intelligible as faith. The quandary becomes clear when we consider the various ways in which theology comes to grips with modern atheism.

In dealing with modern atheism, the theology of the second half of the nineteenth century and the first half of the twentieth understandably had recourse to the forms in which the scripture, the Fathers, and the Scholastic theology of the Middle Ages and the modern era dealt with the forms of atheism of their day or with what was then designated as atheism. This type of treatment can be described as apologetic in two senses of this term. On the negative and critical side, the attempt was made to refute the arguments of the adversaries as being non-probative; on the positive side and in response to criticism, the attempt was made to show that faith in God is reasonable, and in this way to offer a defense (*apologia*) of the faith.[1]

This kind of approach is already germinally present in scripture.[2] Only fools say: 'There is no God' (Pss.14.1; 10.4; 36.2). In the view of the psalmist this kind of folly is wicked, since God's rule over creation and

48   *The God-Question Today*

history is only too obvious. From this experience the wisdom literature of
the Old Testament already derives an intellectual argument. According to
this literature, all who lack knowledge of God are foolish, 'for from the
greatness and beauty of created things comes a corresponding perception
of their Creator' (Wisdom 13.5). The New Testament adopts this argument
(Rom. 1.18–20; Acts 14.14–16; 17.26–29). Like the Old Testament, the
New Testament can see in godlessness only a wicked heart that refuses to
acknowledge the God it knows (Rom 1.20) and that therefore worships
earthly things as idols (Rom. 1.23; Gal. 4.8) and may move on from this
to the worst kind of moral corruption (Rom. 1.24ff.; I Thess. 4.5). The
Letter to the Ephesians speaks explicity of the *atheoi* who have no hope
(Eph. 2.12); the reference is evidently not to atheists in our present-day
sense of the word but to pagans who worship idols. Their thinking is futile,
their understanding darkened; their ignorance cuts them off from true life,
and the reason for it all is their hardness of heart. As a result, they give
themselves up to licentiousness; they are full of greed, and practise every
kind of uncleanness (Eph. 4.17–19). Moral wickedness is thus both the
source and consequence of godlessness; moral depravity is a sign of
godlessness. The New Testament thus shows its awareness of the practical
atheism of those who 'profess to know God, but . . . deny him by their
deeds' (Titus 1.16; cf. II Tim. 3.5).

According to the Old and New Testaments, atheism in the sense of
godlessness includes every attitude that fails to acknowledge the true God,
and therefore every form of idolatry; idolatry, meaning the absolutization
of finite realities, is in fact a possibility and a reality not only in times past
but in the present as well. Such an absolutization of honour (prestige),
power, possessions, sex, nation, race and so on does in fact by its nature
lead to morally reprehensible actions and to the alienation not only to
human beings from God but of human beings from one another and of the
individual from himself. Only one who acknowledges the true God has
true life. In other words: only one who believes is saved. This connection
between faith in God and human salvation is expressly stated in Heb. 11.6:
'Without faith it is impossible to please him [God]. For whoever would
draw near to God must believe that he exists and that he rewards those
who seek him.' The reference here is clearly not to a purely natural
knowledge of God that is achieved by reason but to faith in the true God
who has revealed himself as the God of history and as redeemer and judge.
Atheism, which springs from wickedness and leads to wickedness, is thus
an expression of man's loss of salvation.

The fathers of the church[3] further develop these suggestions given in
scripture. They often define atheism in a very broad way that includes not

only pagan polytheism but frequently Jewish and Islamic monotheism as well. Atheism conceived in such a comprehensive way by comparison with our modern usage presents the fathers with not only a theoretical but also, and even more, a moral problem. Since God is naturally knowable, they regard atheism as a refutable and even absurd position. Consequently a complete ignorance of God that is also inculpable seems to them an impossibility. They tend to regard atheism rather from a practical view-point, as a consequence and expression of moral failure and, in the final analysis, as a demonic attack on God.

Scholasticism provided some further explanations that are important especially for present-day discussion. In particular, in his *Proslogion* Anselm of Canterbury, the father of medieval Scholasticism, develops the thought of Augustine and explains that God cannot rationally be thought of as non-existent.[4] Anselm thus prepares the way for the Thomist theory according to which God is implicitly known in every act of knowing.[5] This means that there can be no such thing as absolute atheism and that the athiest who (for example) makes matter ultimate and therefore absolute does know of God in a manner which under some conditions may be hidden from him, although he gives an erroneous interpretation of this knowledge. Nonetheless, with Heb. 11.6 Thomas maintains as necessary for salvation a faith that is not simply implicit but explicit.[6] He gives two reasons for this view. On the one hand, even what we are able to know of God by our natural powers cannot be known easily and without admixture of error by all. On the other hand, human beings can by their natural powers know the existence of God, but knowledge of God as man's salvation is beyond the natural powers of man to obtain. Consequently an explicit faith in response to revelation is necessary if man is to be saved. Here Thomas presupposes, of course, that the message of God as man's salvation is known to all human beings. If then (says Thomas) there is a human being who lives in the primeval forest or among wild beasts and has not heard this message, God will certainly convey to him by an interior enlightenment the revelation of what is necessary for salvation, or else he will send the person an evangelist.[7] It is possible that at a later stage, in his theological *Summa*, Thomas moved beyond this emergency solution, which really requires a miracle. He says that every adult human being who is capable of the full use of reason must reflect on himself and on the meaning and goal of his life and, with the help of grace, has the power to turn to God as meaning and fulfillment or, in other words, as man's salvation.[8] It would follow from this that anyone is saved who in his conscience directs himself toward ultimate values, insofar as he is capable of recognizing these in his concrete situation.

It is against this theological background that we must interpret the statements of the *magisterium* on atheism. It was only at a very late point in history that atheism became the subject of doctrinal statements. The Syllabus of Pius IX (1864) only summarizes the older condemnations of pantheism, deism and indifferentism; atheism is not mentioned.[9] The first mention of it comes in Vatican I. In its preface to the Constitution *Dei Filius* 'on the Catholic faith' the Council harks back to the Council of Trent and sees the modern errors of rationalism, naturalism, pantheism, materialism and atheism as consequences of the Protestant principle that every Christian may exercise private judgment in matters of Christian doctrine. It regards atheism as a contradiction of reason and as destructive of the foundations of human society.[10] In keeping with this view, the Council defines the possibility of a natural knowledge of God[11] and condemns atheism, materialism and pantheism as opposed to Christian faith.[12] The line is thus set down which will be followed in future papal statements of doctrine: those of Leo XIII,[13] Pius XI (especially in his Encyclical *Divini Redemptoris* against atheistic communism),[14] and Pius XIII.[15] But all these statements give only summary indications. An extended commentary comes for the first time in John XXIII's Encyclical *Mater et Magistra* (1961), although in other respects this remains within the traditional framework:[16] Atheism contradicts reason and unsettles the foundations of every human and social order. There is no careful analysis of the phenomenon itself or of its often humanistic, even if misguided impulses to the establishment of a more just and human world. The Encyclical *Ecclesiam Suam* of Paul VI (1964) is the first to introduce new standards in that despite its rejection of atheism in principle it establishes a new attitude of dialogue.[17]

2. The new attitude of dialogue

The Second Vatican Council opens a new chapter in the church's relation to atheism. It counts atheism as 'one of the most serious problems of our times', but adds immediately that it 'deserves more thorough treatment'.[18] This change, especially in relation to Marxist atheism, has been summed up in the formula: 'From anathema to dialogue.'[19] The formula correctly captures the new pastoral emphasis of the Council, but it is also exaggerated, inasmuch as while the Council does set new emphases, these do not replace the old statements. On the contrary, for the Council says: 'The Church, as given over to the service of both God and man, cannot cease from reproving, with sorrow yet with the utmost firmness, as she has done in the past, those harmful teachings and ways of acting which are in conflict with reason and with common human experience, and which cast man down from the noble state to which he is born.'[20] On the other hand, there is something new here in that the Council is not simply issuing an abstract judgment but is accepting a concrete historical approach and shifting the discussion from the purely essentialist level to the existential.

This new approach to the problem manifests itself in three ways. First, there is the effort to offer a description that differentiates various forms of the phenomenon of atheism, as well as an attempt to do justice to its positive motives and impulses: the freedom of man, justice in society, and a protest against evil in the world. Second, the Council turns these arguments and impulses into a question directed at its own position.

For atheism, taken as a whole, is not present in the mind of man from the start. It springs from various causes, among which must be included a critical reaction against religion and, in some places, against the Christian religion in particular. Believers can thus have more than a little to do with the rise of atheism.

By a misleading presentation of Christian teaching and through deficiencies in their private and social life they may 'conceal rather than . . . reveal the true nature of God and of religion'.[21] Effective remedies against atheism include therefore not only its refutation but also an improved presentation of one's own doctrine and a creditable living of this teaching.[22]

Third, there are also new emphases in the arguments against atheism. To begin with, the knowledge of God gained by reason is supplemented by knowledge gained from human experience.[23] But the real argument is based on the dignity of man, who without God remains in his own eyes an unanswered question. The acknowledgment of God is therefore not opposed to human dignity but rather provides its foundation and fulfillment.[24] This anthropological argument is then further developed in christological terms, since only through the mystery of Jesus Christ is true clarity brought to the mystery of man himself; only thus is light thrown on the riddle of suffering and death.[25] No longer, then, does the Council base its arguments on the natural knowledge of God; rather, it takes as its point of departure the heart of the Christian faith itself. This anthropological and christological approach runs through almost all the utterances of Pope John Paul II.[26]

Admittedly, the conciliar text is cause for some dissatisfaction, inasmuch as the intellectual questions raised by atheism are not to be answered solely by a concrete, historical and existential approach. The historical aspect should therefore have been more clearly connected with the traditional teaching on the possibility of a natural knowledge of God. In the process, the fundamental objections raised by K. Barth and many Protestant theologians would also have to have been met. In addition, the Council passed over the doctrine of the *theologia negativa*, the doctrine of the hiddenness of God. This might have been of help in bringing out even more clearly the positive, purificatory function atheism has in relation to faith in God. Finally, we miss any reference to the moral presuppositions of faith in God; among these are not only *ratio pura* (unprejudiced reason) but also the *cor purum et purificatum* (the pure and purified heart). This aspect of the matter has deep roots in scripture and in the Augustinian tradition.[27] But despite these criticisms it must be said that chapters 19–22 of the Pastoral Constitution 'may be counted among the most important pronouncements of Vatican II',[28] and even that they 'are a milestone in the church history of our century'.[29]

Vatican II would obviously not have been possible without intensive theological preparation. So, too, after the Council Catholic theology has taken up and developed further the suggestions given there. A complete survey of the extensive discussion of the God-question is, not of course, possible here,[30] and I shall limit myself to some of the kinds of discussion of atheism that are to be found in post-conciliar Catholic theology.

K. Rahner's efforts to do theology as anthropology or to make anthropology the context for theology is of special importance in view of the humanistic thrust that characterizes modern atheism and of the corresponding anthropological arguments it uses. Following J. Maréchal, Rahner makes his own the transcendental starting point adopted in the modern era, but he endeavours to overcome Kant's agnosticism and to move beyond him to a new basis for metaphysics. The ascent from beings to Being and ultimately to an absolute mystery is for Rahner the condition for the possibility of finite knowledge. According to Rahner – and entirely in the spirit of Thomas Aquinas – in this pre-apprehension (*Vorgriff*) of being as the condition for the possibility of knowledge of beings the reality of God is always already affirmed.[31] The unthematic experience of God thus occurs with transcendental necessity in every spiritual act, even in the act of denying God. This thesis is of radical importance in coming to grips with atheism. There are four possibilities:[32]

(*a*) The person interprets his transcendental relatedness categorically as theism and accepts this by a free decision.

(*b*) The person interprets his transcendental relatedness categorically as theism, but denies God by a free decision. This represents the conventional idea of culpable practical and theoretical atheism.

(*c*) The person accepts his transcendental relatedness but interprets this with the aid of an erroneous concept of God, which he rejects, or else reaches no concept of God at all. This is inculpable atheism, which at bottom is an anonymous theism.

(*d*) The person violates his conscience and denies even the transcendental relatedness, and then goes on to reject both correct and erroneous concepts of God, or else he reaches no concept of God at all. This is culpable atheism; as long as the person remains in this attitude, he has no possibility of being saved.

Rahner's theory, which on the whole is entirely in the line of Scholastic tradition, represents a tremendous advance because it makes it possible for the first time to reflect on the inherent possibilities in the phenomenon of atheism and to do so in theological terms, instead of immediately rejecting it as alien and even absurd. This theory makes a dialogue possible for the first time, since dialogue by its nature presupposes a common basis. Nonetheless questions remain that have to do with Rahner's central idea of a necessary affirmation of God. If this idea is presupposed, is any real atheism still possible, that is, an atheism which is not a veiled anonymous theism? For, according to the theory, every individual, whether or not he realizes it, whether or not he wills it, must with transcendental necessity direct his life to an absolute. The only questions remaining are whether this absolute is God or an idol and, should the case arise, whether or not the decision against God and for an idol is culpable. In a sense, then, it can be said that Rahner's theory of atheism is the antitype of the atheistic theory of religion.³³ The latter theory interprets theism atheistically as a projection of man, while Rahner interprets atheism theistically as a false interpretation of man and his transcendence.

Rahner thus remains within the framework provided by classical metaphysics as well as within that provided by the modern point of departure. His merit is to have shown that there is no opposition between classical thinking in the line of Thomas Aquinas and modern transcendental thought. On the other hand, as the entire modern development has made clear, it is highly ambiguous to claim God as the interpretation of human transcendence, for there is the danger either of no longer being able to preserve fully the transcendence of God or – as is rather the danger in Rahner – of turning this transcendence into an ineffable mystery in which man exists but which he must rather be silent about than speak of. Today, at the end of modern times (R. Guardini), at the end of modernity (A. Gehlen) and at the end of modern consciousness (R. Spaemann), when we have become clear on the limits of these starting points, this position is no longer adequate as an answer to modern atheism.

M. Heidegger in particular has attempted to move beyond both traditional metaphysics and the modern philosophy of subjectivity. B. Welte and H. Urs von Balthasar have followed him in a critical and creative way, while reaching different conclusions. Heidegger's basic objections to both traditional meta-physics and the modern philsophy of subjectivity is their forgetfulness of being.[34] They think of being only in relation to what is and have forgotten the question of the meaning of being itself. This functional type of thinking has not only produced the modern scientific and technical picture of the world, with all its consequences that are today becoming increasingly clear;[35] it has also led to thinking of God solely as the ground of what is and thus to stripping him of his divinity. 'Man can neither pray nor sacrifice to this God. Before the *causa sui*, man can neither fall to his knees in awe nor can he play music and dance before this God. The god-less thinking which must abandon the god of philosophy, god as *causa sui*, is thus perhaps closer to the divine God.'[36] Nietzsche's saying that 'God is dead' is the summary result of metaphysical thinking as such.[37] In response, Heidegger wants to take seriously the ontolog-ical difference between being and what is. At the beginning of his thinking stands not admiration of the beauty of what is but astonishment that anything exists at all, rather than nothingness.[38]

After the collapse of metaphysics God can no longer be thought of as necessary ground. As a result, the hiddenness of God comes into view once more. According to B. Welte, the being to which all knowing points as the condition for its possibility is profoundly equivocal.[39] It can also be interpreted as nothingness. The question then is whether this nothingness is empty nothingness or whether on the contrary the nothingness is the hidden presence of the Absolute. The answer to this question cannot be reached by sheer logic; it calls for a decision which is ultimately a decision about the meaning or unmeaning of life. Welte thus realizes that nihilism has shattered the intellectual premises which the classical humanistic atheism of the modern age still took for granted.[40] On the other hand, unlike Nietzsche and in direct disagreement with him, Welte regards as itself absurd and impermissible the option for absurdity and therefore nothingness. For the distinction between good and evil may not be surrendered; love is meaningful, no less than the struggle for freedom and justice. Given the non-necessity of God, Welte finds it possible to preserve the hiddenness of the divine God as well as the freedom and ethical dimension of faith in God. In this regard his post-metaphysical thinking is substantially closer to biblical thinking than was traditional metaphysics. He is able to comprehend the inherent possibility of atheism and at the same time is better able than Rahner to let atheism be atheism and not turn it into an anonymous theism. But precisely at this point the limitation of this position also becomes clear. Atheism has almost become a possibility and danger of faith in God as such, and one of its virtualities. The post-metaphysical understanding of God comes very close to the mysticism of Eckhart: God is in danger of being swallowed up in 'modelessness', of vanishing into nothingness; the (rightly) non-objective understanding of God is in danger of losing its object.[41] The difference between atheism and theism becomes extremely thin. Texts expressive of atheism can therefore provide almost as much of a basis for a new God-talk as texts expressive of theism can.[42]Such a mystical understanding of God is in its own way once again very far removed from the personal God of the Old and New Testaments who speaks and acts in history.[43]

Like Heidegger, H. Urs von Balthasar starts from being as cause of radical astonishment.[44] However he sees the question of being as mediated, from the outset, through other persons. 'The self is awakened by its experience of the Thou: by the smile of the mother, from which the child experiences that it is accepted, affirmed and loved within an environment that is incomprehensibly self-sacrificing, already real, protective and nourishing.'[45] The light of being arises in the experience of the love shown by the Thou. Being and love are co-extensive. By its very non-necessity, love becomes the radically astonishing dimension of being, the meaning of being. It is the answer to the question of why there is a world instead of no-world.[46] The basis of this approach is already to be found in Plato, for whom the Idea of of the Good that is beyond Being is at the same time the light which illumines all beings. The Good can only be grasped 'suddenly' (*exaiphnēs*) in a kind of ecstasy.[47] But this philosophical mysticism is by its nature incapable of being brought to fulfillment. For the divine Absolute proves to have no content and to be inexpressible, and it turns into atheism unless it is thought of as Thou and personal love – but it alone can demonstrate or reveal itself to be such. The ontological difference that is experienced in the phenomenon of love and love's non-necessity must therefore be supplemented by a theological difference in which all that is must be grounded in an ungrounded and freely bestowed love. This absolute love is at one and the same time necessary for man and yet given to him not necessarily but freely and as an act of grace. It is more than necessary.[48] Therefore it can be conceived as reasonable, but at the same time it is seen to be beyond reason and therefore to be received only by a free act. The Christian answer to modern atheism is to prove not that God is necessary but that he is the ever-greater.[49] We do not need him in order to explain the profane world; he is beyond all worldly reality, beyond everything that serves a functional purpose in and for the world; he is Love and can only be grasped in love and therefore in freedom. Every argument offered in this area presupposed an option. Or, in the language of Thomas Aquinas: knowing and willing are profoundly interdependent. In thus moving from philosophy to theology Balthasar has preserved the positive possibilities for dialogue that Welte has opened up in relation to atheism, but at the same time he has unequivocally eliminated the ambiguities that necessarily persist in the realm of philosophy. He is able on the basis of hints to be found in Thomas Aquinas himself to break out of self-enclosed classical metaphysics into a metaphysics that is open: that remains incomplete in itself and only in theology is both preserved and transcended.

All the theological approaches to atheism that I have thus far discussed are challenged by political theology[50] and by the questions it raises in the form of the theology of liberation.[51] These two theologies promote a new kind of theology which is conceived of not primarily as a reflection on faith but as a reflection on the practice of faith. They regard even modern atheism as primarily a practical and political problem that can be resolved only through a new practice. Their concern is thus with a new acceptance and new definition of the theory-practice relationship, which past theology has neglected. This theology has undoubtedly performed a service by reacting against the tendencies to privatization that are found in transcendental and in dialogical theology and by calling attention to the practical and political dimension of theology in general and of modern atheism in particular. Political theology and the theology of liberation have thus intensified our awareness of certain problems. The insight that the modern privatization of religion has produced modern atheism leads these theologies to the programmatic statement of a post-bourgeois religion and theology that will not uncritically accept into theology the modern subject which is the result of the modern age and its process of privatization.[52] Put concretely, the antithesis is: theology of the people.[53] The people, or the base of the pyramid as the case may be, is here not only the goal and addressee of theology but its subject and the place where it is carried on. The struggle about God becomes a struggle for the right of all to be free subjects before God.[54] The new God-talk is thus possible only in the context of a liberating practice.

Political theology in fact calls our attention to aspects which are short-changed in the theologies of the modern age which take as their point of departure the subject or the I-Thou relationship. The only question is whether it in turn does not fall victim to possibly even more deleterious simplifications. I have already pointed out that society and therefore the political dimension is not the only dimension, and certainly not the most inclusive one, or the one in which alone the God-question can appropriately be raised.[55] And in fact, with the passage of time, political theology has substantially broadened its approach, by maintaining that religion must be at once political and mystical.[56] But atheism calls in question the very condition for the possibility of mysticism, insofar as mysticism is understood in the traditional theistic sense. This question can be tackled under the rubric of 'practice' only if practice is understood strictly in the sense given it by modern philosophy: the practice of freedom; in other words, only if one accepts the despised modern philosophy of freedom and then, within the horizon of freedom, raises anew the metaphysical question of the meaning of freedom within reality as a whole.

Since catch-word simplifications are repeatedly to be found in connection with political theology and in its wake, there are a few points that need further brief discussion, First, a preliminary question. If the catch-phrase 'post-bourgeois religion and theology' is not to conceal a reversion to a pre-bourgeois theology, then we must take with us into this post-bourgeois religion all the positive achievements of bourgeois modern subjectivity, and specifically the advance in knowledge and the winning of individual freedom. But this is possible – especially in view of the long rejection of modernity by Catholic theology – only if we look at the modern problematic in a concrete way instead of turning it into an all-inclusive abstraction and then spurning it. The *real question* then is whether this task can be appropriately tackled solely under the catch-word 'practice'.[57] Practice is a word with many meanings; it can mean both productive work (subject-object relation) and the activity of free communication (subject-subject relation). If the concept of practice is used as a slogan and magical incantation against a supposedly purely abstract theorizing, and understood as a call to concrete reality, then it becomes a form of abstract opposition to theory; it becomes an abstraction without conceptual content. In the fact of such a development we need to be reminded of the truism that the relation of theory and practice is itself first and foremost a theoretical problem. Especially worth noting in this context are T. W. Adorno's warnings against a conceptless practice which accepts no criterion but itself and therefore becomes irrational and totalitarian. 'The face of practice wears an expression of deadly seriousness . . . Theory represents all that is not narrow-minded. Despite all its lack of freedom it becomes the representative of freedom in the midst of unfreedom.'[58] Theory, properly understood, is itself a practice, just as responsible practice is rational and thus the result of theoretical reflection. Finally: a confession of faith in God is neither a theory nor a practice in the modern sense of the term; rather, it is a unique linguistic expression in which theoretical and practical elements intermingle. For this reason it cannot be adequately understood within the pre-established framework of a theory-practice dialectic which is interpreted in ultimately neo-Marxist terms. However great a use faith in God may make of human ways of understanding, in the final analysis it can only be understood on its own terms.[59] Any other approach leads to the reductions of faith that are typical of modern atheism.

The attempt to ground faith in God purely in itself and to take a radical position of faith as the starting point for a debate with modern atheism brings us to a final model of theological encounter with atheism; it is a model that may be described as dialectical. The dialogical model looks to the natural-theology tradition for a common basis of understanding that allows faith in God and atheism to comprehend and discuss each other and thus enter into a dialogue. The dialectical model, on the other hand, challenges the existence of this common basis. It acknowledges no positive connection between the two, but only a connection in the form of a contradiction. This is the direction in which a large part of contemporary Protestant theology has moved in its exchanges with modern atheism.

3. Dialectical relationship between Christianity and atheism

In the sixteenth century the question of natural theology was not a subject of controversy between the Catholic churches and the churches of the Reformation. The natural, that is, rational knowableness of of God was taught in Protestant orthodoxy of the seventeenth century just as it was in the Catholic theology of the time. Only in the nineteenth century, especially in liberal theology, did the radical break come, while in our own century the dialectical theology of Karl Barth[60] turned the question of natural theology into a new, hitherto unrecognized subject of controversy and in fact even turned it into *the* subject of controversy par excellence.[61]

The early Barth of *The Epistle to the Romans* (first German publication in 1918; second ed. in 1922) took as its starting point the contrast between God and the world. God is the wholly other, who judges and annuls the world. The saving message of God is 'not a religious message to inform mankind of their divinity or to tell them how they may become divine. The Gospel proclaims a God utterly distinct from men. Salvation comes to them from Him, because they are, as men, incapable of knowing Him, and because they have no right to claim anything from Him.'[62] Correspondingly, the *analogia entis* is for Barth (according to the well-known passage in the Foreword to the first volume of his *Church Dogmatics*) 'the invention of Antichrist' and the only serious reason for not becoming a Catholic.[63] The basis for this extremely harsh statement is clear: Barth sees the analogy of being and the natural theology based on it as cut from the same cloth as the modern theology of the Enlightenment and of liberalism, against which his own battle is being waged. In natural theology nature, reason, history and man's natural religiosity become the context for and criterion of faith, while Christianity becomes a particular instance of a phenomenon that is neutral in itself and found universally in human beings.[64] It is against this background that we must understand the famous chapter on 'The Revelation of God as the Abolition of Religion' in Volume I/2 of the *Church Dogmatics*. His central thesis here is: 'Religion is unbelief. It is a concern, indeed, we must say that it is the one great concern, of godless man.'[65] It is a self-willed human manufacture, an arrogant attempt by man to take control of God and in the process to form God after man's image and likeness. It is idolatry and self-righteousness.[66] Mysticism therefore turns into atheism; both are forms of religion. Feuerbach is right: 'Atheism is the blabbing out of the true secret of religion.'[67] Revelation does not link up with a human religion that is already present and practised. It contradicts it, just as religion previously contradicted revelation. It displaces it, just as religion previously displaced revelation.'[68] The contradiction is admittedly of a dialectical kind; it displaces or abolishes religion in the two senses of negating and exalting it. Therefore: 'The Christian religion is the true religion.'[69]

Materially, if not in formal statement, Barth subsequently modified in large measures his harsh judgment of natural theology as understood by Catholic theology as distinct from the theology of the Enlightenment, and he made more positive statements about the religions.[70] His earlier position, however, exercised an almost incalculable influence on the Protestant theology of our century; these effects can only be hinted at here. They have in common an attempt to establish a position beyond theism and atheism and thus, by rejecting theism, to make its own the legitimate aspirations of atheism. In this way, the statement that God is dead, which, as I pointed out earlier, goes back to an old Lutheran hymn, was to be taken back into theology and, to that extent theologically *aufgehoben* (i.e., negated, retained and lifted to a higher level).

This attempt is to be seen in its most authentic form in the notes which D. Bonhoeffer jotted down during his imprisonment by the Nazis.[71] We find in them an outline of a religionless Christianity. Even though Bonhoeffer's concept of religion is not that of Barth, the two are nonetheless in agreement that at least today and in the time to come the religious presupposition is lacking in our society which has become irreligious.[72] But the Christian need not bemoan this turn of events, since it brings us to 'a true recognition of our situation before God'. The God of Jesus Christ allows himself to be expelled from the world through the cross; he is helpless and weak in the world, and only under these conditions does he abide with us and help us. Therefore 'before God and with God we live without God'. The atheistic situation makes it possible to see the God of the Bible 'who wins power and space in the world by his weakness'.[73] 'The world that has come of age is more godless, and perhaps for that very reason nearer to God than the world before its coming of age.'[74]Bonhoeffer thus takes a renewed theology of the cross as the starting point for his answer to modern atheism.

It was not until the 1960s, when the situation had completely changed since his time, that Bonhoeffer began to exert an extensive, although unfortunately often quite superficial, influence. In German theology his influence showed itself first in the radical wing of the Bultmann school, where H. Braun extended Bultmann's program of demythologization to the understanding of God that is presupposed in the New Testament, and interpreted God in existential terms as 'the ground of my drifting', 'the ground of the security I find in my fellow man and of the obligation I have to him', 'a certain kind of human fellowship'.[75]

In like manner, D. Sölle looks for a way of believing atheistically in God.[76] 'God happens in what happens between human beings';[77] faith is 'a certain kind of living',[78] 'a certain way of being there',[79] an 'existential movement'.[80] By means of this Christian atheism Sölle attempts to reach a position beyond theism and atheism, although in the process she oversimplifies both by taking them to be objectivizing positions.[81] In the final analysis, her position, like that of Braun, leads to exactly what Feuerbach wanted, and is indistinguishable from a pure humanism.[82]

In non-German theology there was a direct connection between K. Barth, D. Bonhoeffer and, to some extent, Hegel, on the one hand, and, on the other, the 'death of God' theology[83] that caused so much shaking of heads within and especially outside theological circles. 'Death of God' actually had a variety of meanings: from the death of God in modern secularized culture (G. Vahanian), in language (P. van Buren), in the silence of God (W. Hamilton), all the way to the extreme kenosis-theologies according to which God in Jesus Christ died on the scene of world history (T. J. J. Altizer). These ideas were popularized in the book *Honest to God* by the Anglican bishop J. A. T. Robinson; this book, though it was an undigested mixture full of over-simplifications, nonetheless gave expression to what many people were vaguely feeling.[84] It soon became clear, of course, that this theological fad was self-contradictory. For if God is dead then so is theology – a fate that has since befallen at least the Death-of-God theology. This current of thought has not really grappled with modern atheism, but has simply capitulated to it and thus surrendered any chance of arguing on other than an atheistic basis. All that was left was a theological verbal facade with nothing theological behind it.

The first new serious attempt has come in J. Moltmann's *The Crucified God*. Following closely in the footsteps of Barth and Bonhoeffer, Moltmann takes as his starting point 'the cross of Christ as the foundation and criticism of Christian theology'.[85] This approach thus excludes natural theology which, in Moltmann's view, ignores the cross and attempts to argue back from experienced reality to its absolute ground in God, reaching in the process the theistic notion of a God who is incapable of suffering.[86] The rejection of this theistic God justifies our speaking of a 'Christian atheism'.[87] Moltmann's epistemological starting point is not analogy but dialectic.[88] That is, God is known here in terms of his opposite, and godlessness is in a sense the presupposition for knowing God. In other words, if we start with the death of God on the cross and really take this seriously, then atheism is integrated into the reality of God and, at the same time, is therein negated, preserved and transcended. On the cross God has anticipated atheism, made it his own, and blunted it. Atheism and theism alike have been negated and transcended by the cross. 'With a trinitarian theology of the cross faith escapes the dispute between and the alternative of theism and atheism.'[89] The conclusion, to be sure, that Moltmann draws from all this is that God is, in an almost Hegelian manner, entangled in the history of human sin, so that God's existence in and for himself (the immanent Trinity) can no longer be distinguished from the history of God's suffering in the world. At this point, a radical approach 'from above' in terms of the theology of revelation and of the cross is dialectically converted by Moltmann into a conception of God that no longer adequately distinguishes God from the world and is almost mythological and tragic in character. The dialectic with which Moltmann started turns into an identity. The extremes touch.

The question that has to be asked[90] of the dialectic theology which K. Barth inaugurated is whether the transcendence of God and his word can be preserved otherwise than by *not* making man and his positive or negative answer a phase in the word and action of God; for if man and his answer are given such a role, the next easy step is to make God a phase of man. It is necessary, in other words, to understand the human person as a partner who has been brought on the scene by God and established as free, that is, as a relatively independent partner whom God, in revealing himself, presupposes as one capable of hearing and understanding his word (*poeentia oboedientialis*, obediential potency). The correspondence at the level of faith (*analogia fidei*, analogy of faith) thus presupposes, on its own behalf, a correspondence at the level of creaturehood (*analogia entis*, analogy of being). This second correspondence does not function as a pregiven, independent framework for revelation, restricting the scope of the latter and turning it into a special application of a pre-given general principle; it is, rather a presupposition for revelation, and a presupposition which revelation itself requires if it is to be possible. It exists for the sake of revelation and formulates the pure potentiality of the creature for God, utterly beyond any active power of its own.[91]

Contemporary Protestant theology has by no means lost sight of the authentic concern of natural theology. In the context of the God-question this concern is very much alive in theologians who approach the question from the vantage point of Paul Tillich's correlation theology; for example, in the phenomenological analyses of L. Gilkey[92] and in the recent natural philosophy of the process theologians.[93] This concern emerges most emphatically in W. Pannenberg.[94] Pannenberg raises the objection to K. Barth and his radical stance of faith, that Barth does not get beyond an empty assertion of God and thus is himself an extreme example of modern subjectivity. 'Amongst the examples of an excessive adaption of theology to the intellectual fashions of the age was the belief of dialectical theology that it is possible to accept atheistic arguments and trump them by a radical belief in revelation . . . In terms of the intellectual effort a theologian has to extend, this represents the cheapest form of modernity'.[95] In the final analysis dialectical theology paradoxically makes atheism the natural presupposition for faith and thus turns it into a natural theology.[96] But if faith no longer finds any foothold in the questionableness of human existence, it becomes irrational and authoritarian.[97] Today, however, theology and the church must drop their authoritarian approach and come to grips with modern atheism at the level of argument.

Barth's position is not the only one that serves contemporary Protestant theology as a basis for coming to grips with atheism. The Lutheran position is also brought to bear on the discussion, especially in the writings of G. Ebeling[98] and E. Jüngel.[99] Luther agrees with Barth that true knowledge of God is to be had only through faith. 'For the two go together: faith and God! Anyone who tries to find God apart from faith finds only the devil. But it is faith that gives shape to both: God and idols.[100] When faith and God are connected in such a close way. Feuerbach's suspicion of a projection seems to make itself felt with special intensity. Luther's position is by its innermost nature exposed to the temptation of atheism.[101] Objectively, of course, it is worlds removed from atheism. For while Luther says: 'That to which you attach and surrender your heart is really your God,'[102] Feuerbach's principle is: 'His heart is his god.'[103]

The question, of course, is how this fundamental difference can be not only asserted but also made clear to the unbeliever or, in words, how what is believed can be made universally intelligible and thus its rationality be proved. At this point the Lutheran position differs from the Barthian in that the former claims a correlation not only between God and faith, but also between faith or word and situation.[104] In the word 'God' and in the word of God it is not only God who makes himself known; light is also shed on the situation of man. In fact, the word 'God' and the word of God look to the basic situation of man as a word situation; they lay hold of man in his linguisticality.[105] The word 'God' shows us 'that man in his linguisticality is not master of himself. He lives from the power of a word that is not his own, and at the same time he thirsts after the power of a word that likewise cannot be his own.'[106] God is thus the mystery of reality.[107] But because of his linguisticality man gains knowledge of this mystery only in and through the word; only in the word does the truth about God and man come to light. Only the word of God makes it known that man is always one who is already being approached by God. For this reason, before the word comes to him man cannot know God as the mystery of reality; on the other hand, the word 'God' and the word of God are verified in the being of man and the world – 'verified' in the sense of *verum facere*, 'make true' and bring to the truth.[108]

The contest with atheism is thus a contest for the world and man. But the contest is not waged – as it is in natural theology and to some extent also and especially when the relation between faith in God and modern atheism is conceived as dialogical – on the ground of a shared neutral base, namely a natural power of knowing God that precedes both faith and unbelief. Faith is not a particular case under an overarching universal category (on this point Luther's criticism is in agreement with Barth's).[109] The starting point is the reality of faith, which encounters the reality of unbelief as man's factual situation and seeks to convince man in this situation of his lostness and lack of truth. The starting point is God's promise, the *promissio* of the word of revelation, to which faith responds but which unbelief opposes. Luther's thinking moves not in the framework of natural and supernatural knowledge of God but in the framework of law and gospel.[110]

The thesis that true knowledge of God is to be had only through faith in the word of God has for a consequence that we can never speak of God while prescinding from man, but only of God for me and for us, or of God in his relation to man.[111] If we abstract from this relation and speak abstractly of God's being in itself, we are in danger of turning God into an object and thus stripping him of his divinity. One acts as an atheist by asserting the existence of God no·less than by denying it.[112] The old ontology of substance must therefore be replaced by relational thinking. The following principle is valid: 'The idea of God without the world is a pure limit notion which gives expression to the truth that when God and world are taken together the absolute primacy of God emerges.'[113] For the rest, it remains true that *Deus supra nos, nihil ad nos*, God is beyond us and no business of ours.[114] With this, the classical distinction between the being of God thought of as at rest and the same being thought of as active is eliminated. From the insight that we may not speak of God's being while prescinding from his activity it follows that 'God's being is in becoming'.[115]

At this point we are dangerously close to Hegel's highly ambiguous position that God cannot exist without the world.[116] The dialectical definition of the relation between faith and unbelief is thus in danger, even in Luther's version of it, of turning into an identification of the two, so that it is no longer possible to distinguish between the two in a rationally argued way, but instead the distinction must be arbitrarily asserted. Neither in the old ontology of substance nor in the relational theology developed out of Luther does the danger of atheism seem to be eliminated in principle.

It is interesting, to be sure, that Luther and Thomas are not only threatened by the same danger but also astonishingly close in their positive assertions. As everyone knows, according to Thomas we can know better what God is not than what he is. Less well known is the fact that for Thomas the same holds true of faith. Even through revelation we do not know what God is; we are united to him *quasi ignoto*, as to one unknown to us. Through revelation we gain knowledge only of more and greater works of his.[117] There is no denying that this thesis of Thomas is at odds with the many passages in which he makes statements about the being of God. Nonetheless, the passage to which I have referred shows that there is no mutual opposition between the metaphysically based theology of Thomas and a relational theology of Lutheran extraction. We are dealing rather with two complementary schemes and approaches which intend to say materially the same thing but which also have limits and dangers, so that each needs to be criticized and supplemented by the other. On this fundamental question, which is a matter of life or death for both, they can fulfill their common task only in conjunction with each other and not in opposition to each other.

As we look back and try to summarize, we can identify a profound aporia that is common to all the theological positions discussed as they face up to modern atheism. The aporia affects the apologetic and dialogical positions, both of which make use of natural theology, and the dialectical positions, which reject natural theology and precisely for that reason are in danger of themselves turning into a purely natural theology. We would probably not be mistaken if we were to claim that the aporia affects all the contemporary theology. We lack the language and the adequately developed categories that would enable us to speak unambiguously about God. Ever since philosophy has become atheistic, whether professedly or tacitly or even only methodically, all philosophical concepts – the concept of substance no less than the concept of relation – are open to misunderstanding along atheist lines. Faced with atheism, faith and theology as well have no choice but to raise anew and at a fundamental level the question of their own presuppositions and of the conditions for their own possibility. But this basic theological question has become further specified as compared with the question asked at the end of the previous chapter. That chapter ended with our saying that the basic metaphysical question, the question of being, could alone provide the adequate horizon within which to raise the question of God. Now, however, we must define this question more closely. This further definition is necessary both by reason of the intra-philosophical criticism directed at traditional ontotheology and by reason of the critical questions asked by dialectical theology. The question now is how the question of God and the question of being are specifically related to each other; that is, whether we must ask the question of God within the horizon of the question of being, or the question of being within the horizon of the question of God. This means that the question of the relation between faith and thought, theology and philosophy, natural theology and theology based on revelation is raised anew. This brings me to the foundations of my own answer to the challenge of modern atheism.

IV

Experience of God and Knowledge of God

1. The problem and concern of natural theology

For many people today the Christian message about God has become a foreign language they are unable to understand or grasp. In fact, in the context of modern experience the questions asked in this message and the answers given seem to have become meaningless. This loss of the basic presuppositions needed for understanding affects in our day not only peripheral and borderline truths but even the terms that are central to the Christian proclamation (God, sin, redemption, grace). The real issue today is no longer primarily this or that truth but the very ability to believe. We have to a large extent lost the dimension of faith, which is the dimension of mystery. Theologically, therefore, we are forced back to the rudiments of understanding; our capacity for experience has become in good measure limited to what can be grasped by the senses, to what can be counted and produced. As a result, in our secularized society dogmatic theology is compelled, more than in the past, to reflect on the presuppositions of understanding that are proper to it. This reflection on the presuppositions for the understanding of faith is known as natural theology.[1]

The present situation of natural theology is admittedly a quite paradoxical one. For in the measure that the call has been increasingly sounded in present-day theology for a discussion of the presuppositions of understanding, natural theology has falled into disrepute. Natural theology has become as it were the neuralgic point in contemporary theology (E. Jüngel).

The Bible does not as yet contain any reflection on the presuppositions for the understanding of faith. To that extent there is no natural theology in the Bible. On the other hand, the Bible practises natural theology to a surprising degree. For the life mirrored in the Bible goes on in a world that is religious to the core; the Bible can therefore, in a still utterly unreflective way, have recourse not only to religious ideas and experience but also to universal human, every-day experiences and from these derive images for use in religious statements. We see this process at work on the opening pages of the Bible, in the two accounts of creation. These take very ancient religious ideas of the human race (ideas which we today describe as mythical) and interpret them in a new and critical way in the light of the experience of faith. The creation psalms in particular show how the devout of the Old Testament derive from wordly reality a knowledge of the power and glory of God (cf. Pss. 8; 19; 29; 104; 148). Only the fool says in his heart: There is no God (Ps. 14.1). In the late period of the Old Testament this 'natural' knowledge of God is already being expressed in didactic form: 'All men who were ignorant of God were foolish by nature . . . For from the greatness and beauty of created things comes a corresponding perception of their Creator' (Wisdom 13.1–5).

In the New Testament, Jesus' practice of speaking in parables is highly significant. In the parables of Jesus the world as it presents itself to human beings in their everyday experience becomes an image of the reign of God. All the processes in nature and history are capable of serving in this context as images of eschatological salvation. Jesus takes the everyday experiences of human beings as his starting point and uses them as a mirror in which to make his message intelligible. Conversely, however, these same everyday experiences often have a new and unexpected light thrown on them by the parables of Jesus (contrast parables). Through the parables of God's reign the world at last acquires its definitive meaning. When Jesus speaks in parables he turns the world into a parable of the reign of God.

The New Testament shows parabolic language being used in varying measures. The link with wordly experience shows up with greatest immediacy in Luke's Acts of the Apostles. According to Acts Paul appeals in his missionary discourses not only to the Old Testament but also to the religious experiences of the pagans: to the testimony God has given to himself in nature and history (Acts 14.16f.; 17.22–28).

In the letters of Paul the reference to 'natural' experience and knowledge does not take this direct and positive form but rather a critical and dialectical form. Paul does indeed speak of God being known from created reality (Rom 1.19f.), and especially from conscience (Rom. 2.14f.). But he also says that while the pagans knew God they did not acknowledge him as God, but refused to honour him and transferred to creatures the homage due to him alone. In so doing, their hearts were hardened and their minds darkened. They have no excuse for their godlessness and corruption (Rom. 1.20). When Paul thus makes the pagans responsible for their unbelief, he indirectly recognizes the possibility and actuality of the pagans' knowledge of God. It is possible here to speak of contact amid contradiction. In other words: it is not legitimate to make Paul's theology of the cross simply a contradiction of the concern at work in natural theology. For although Paul emphasizes the foolishness of the cross (I Cor. 1–2), he would also rather speak five words with his mind than stammer ten thousand words in an ecstatic tongue (I Cor 14.19); in fact, he wants to take all thinking captive for Christ (II Cor 10.5).

The situation is again different to Johannine theology. John accepts the questions of human beings with regard to bread (John 6), light (John 8), and way, truth and life (John 14), in order then to proclaim Jesus Christ as the definitive answer to these questions. He starts therefore with the assumption that the lives of human beings are inspired by the quest for salvation and that in this way men and women have a preunderstanding of salvation. On the other hand, it is only through Jesus Christ that definitive clarity comes on what light, life and truth are. Just as an answer is intelligible only in the light of the question being asked, so conversely the answer throws a definitive light on the meaning of the question. John's proclamation of Jesus Christ as the incarnate Word proved to be especially momentous (John 1.1–14), for it meant the acceptance of a concept which Philo, a Jewish philosopher of religion, had already used as a way of mediating between Old Testament faith and Hellenistic thought. Behind John's application of Logos to Jesus stands the conviction that the Logos at work in creation is no other than the Logos who in the fullness of time became a human being in Jesus Christ. In similar fashion, the theology of later ages drew Stoic, Platonic and finally also Aristotelian concepts into the service of the faith. The purpose in so doing was to give expression to the fact that the Logos who holds sway in a seminal and traceable manner in all reality (*logos spermatikos*) has manifested himself fully in Jesus Christ.[2]

In summary we may say that while the Bible does not expressly reflect on the natural presuppositions of faith, it does in fact appeal to these presuppositions to a quite notable extent and in manifold ways. In the background of this unreflective yet extensively practised natural theology there is a convinction that is basic to both the Old and the New Testament: the conviction that the order of creation and the order of salvation fit together. The Bible understands the revelation given in the course of salvation history as being a prophetic interpretation of reality. Consequently, faith, as understood in the Bible, is not a blind venture, not an irrational feeling, not an uncalculated option and certainly not a *sacrificium intellectus* (sacrifice of the understanding). Rather, faith can and must give a rational account of itself. According to the New Testament, believers are

called upon to explain to all men the reasons for the hope which they have
(I Peter 3.15).

Early tradition provides a copious development of the testimony found in
scripture. The fathers speak of the possibility of a twofold natural knowledge
of God: according to them, God can be known both from visible things and
from the human soul. Irenaeus already speaks of the cosmological way to God:
'For creation points to the one creator, the work requires a master-builder,
and the order in the world reveals the one who ordered it.'[3] The psychological
way of knowing God finds expression above all in the doctrine of the idea of
God as innate in man.[4] Tertullian says that the knowledge of God is a dowry
of the soul (*animae dos*).[5]

A radical reflection on the relation between faith and natural knowledge
was forced upon the fathers especially by the conflict with the gnostic
movements of the ancient world. The origin of the gnostic idea has not yet
been fully explained. Gnosis is characterized by an absolute dualism between
God and world, spirit and matter. Redemption is conceivable only as a
redemption from the world, not as a redemption of the world. The conflict
with this dualistic world-view turned into a life-or-death struggle for early
Christianity; it was in the course of this struggle that the foundations of the
Christian idea were first clarified. In response to the gnostic separation of the
order of creation from the order of redemption the church drew up its canon
of scripture, deliberately adopting the Old Testament, which contains the story
of creation, and the New Testament as a single canon or norm of ecclesial
faith. The formation of the canon thus gives expression to what is probably
the most important of all hermeneutical principles for the interpretation of
scripture: the Old and New Testaments, the revelations regarding creation
and salvation, are to be interpreted according to their inherent unity and their
reciprocal correspondences (analogy). In our present context this means that
biblical revelation is to be interpreted in the light of reality and in view of it;
biblical revelation must demonstrate its internal intelligibility be continuing
to be a prophetic interpretation of reality.

The Scholastic tradition expresses this unity of creation and redemption
chiefly by means of the classical axiom: 'Grace presupposes nature' (*gratia
supponit naturam*) or 'Faith presupposes reason' (*fides supponit rationem*)[6] I
cannot here review the complicated history of this axiom and the questions of
interpretation that this history raises. In its original form the axiom does not
mean that faith presupposes a mind cultivated to the highest possible degree.
Natural prerequisites of that kind would mean that grace and faith were no
longer free gifts and would contradict the experience already attested in the
New Testament that faith 'is accepted' by the little ones and the simple folk.
The meaning of the axiom is rather that God's revelation presupposes a subject
capable of hearing, understanding, and making a free decision. For this
reason God can issue his call to faith only to human beings endowed with

understanding and free will and not, for example, to dead objects or to living things that do not possess a spiritual soul. The human person as such, and not the human person as possessing a particular cultural development, is what faith presupposes.

Not until the modern age do we find statements of the *magisterium* regarding these natural presuppositions of faith. This late appearance is not accidental. For it was not until the modern age that the presuppositions of faith were initially seen as doubtful and then even denied in principle. This new situation came about in two ways: through an over-estimation of reason (rationalism) which led to an unqualifiedly autonomistic view of man and the world, and then, in reaction against this over-estimation, through a devaluation of reason, which led to the claim that God is accessible only in faith (fideism) and by way of religious tradition (traditionalism).

The First Vatican Council (1869–1870) condemned both views. It harked back to relevant earlier papal decrees and explained that faith is an act of obedience consistent with reason (*obsequium rationi consentaneum*).[7] On this basis the Council maintained, in opposition to fideism and traditionalism, that by the natural light of reason man can know God with certainty from created reality.[8] We will correctly understand this definition of the possibility of a natural knowledge of God only if we realize that it is deliberately couched in general terms. It speaks of 'knowledge' in the broadest sense of the term and not of purely argumentative and deductive thinking. It is not defined, therefore, that one can prove God by the natural light of reason.[9] In addition, the definition speaks only of the possibility of knowing God (*certo cognosci posse*) and deliberately says nothing about whether such a natural knowledge of God actually exists. The issue, therefore, is simply the openness, in principle, of reason to God, and not whether in fact specific human beings have ever reached knowledge of God solely by their natural powers of knowing. The dogma of the First Vatican Council is thus making a theological statement of a transcendental kind; that is, it is concerned with the condition for the possibility of faith which faith itself presupposes. This transcendental theological statement is meant to bring out the accountability of man for his belief or unbelief, and thus the reasonableness and intellectual probity of faith.

The Second Vatican Council (1962–1965) accepted and repeated the fundamental assertions of the First Vatican Council.[10] At the same time, however, it integrated the abstract, transcendental theological approach of Vatican I into a concretely historical and salvation-historical perspective. On the one hand, the Council describes in detail the difficulties which contemporary man has with the natural knowledge of God, and the resultant forms of modern atheism. On the other hand, it brings out the fact that the answer to the question which man is for himself is given, in the final analysis, not through the natural knowledge of God but only through Jesus Christ.[11] The connection between the transcendental starting point and the historical or salvation-historical aspect is admittedly left more or less undetermined by the Council; the two aspects stand side by side in relative isolation in the conciliar texts. The integration of the two viewpoints is therefore an important task for a dogmatic foundational reflection.

This question has a practical as well as theoretical side to it. In its *Declaration on Religious Liberty* the Second Vatican Council takes up its own various earlier magisterial statements and says that it is the church's duty to proclaim and teach with authority the truth which is Christ and 'at the same time, to declare and confirm by her authority the principles of the moral order which spring from human nature itself'.[12] This doctrine of the church's task as teacher of the natural moral law is the basis for the church's instructions on individual and social ethics; above all, it is the basis of the church's social teaching and its more recent acceptance of universal human rights. The problems which this teaching raises are obvious. Nonetheless, anyone who does not wish to deny that the order of creation and the order of redemption fit together and who does not wish to turn Christianity into a purely theoretical matter, cannot reject this teaching in principle, quite independently of the fact that it has a basis in the Bible (cf. Rom. 2.15). The problem raised by this teaching must therefore be defined more precisely. The problem is comparable to that raised by the natural knowledge of God; it finds expression in the oft-repeated criticism that the moral directives of the church are based on a non-historical concept of nature. Here again, therefore, in the area of the church's moral directives, there is a need to connect the transcendental presuppositions of faith with the historical or salvation-historical situation of the human person.

The statements of scripture, tradition and the ecclesiastical magisterium can be validated by a more systematic reflection on the realities involved. In fact, an initial consideration of the matter already yields a first approach to the subject of natural theology. That is, a relatively simple kind of reflection shows that we never possess the Christian faith 'in itself', in as it were a 'chemically pure' state. We 'possess' the Christian faith only as a faith that is humanly heard, humanly understood, humanly affirmed and humanly appropriated. Faith is 'given' as it were only in the medium of human hearing and understanding. Whatever else, therefore, must be said about Christian faith as a free gift, it is a fully and wholly human act (*actus humanus*) and, as such, is subject to a human and therefore rational accountability. A faith for which no human and rational account can be given would be unworthy not only of man but of God.

We achieve a comparable result if we engage in a second reflection that starts not with the subject of the testimony of faith but with its addressees. The Christian faith claims to be the universal truth about salvation for all human beings. Consequently it cannot be the intention of the testimony of faith to express only private religious experiences. The Christian faith stands and falls by its universal communicability. Christians must therefore not only answer for their faith before the bar of their own consciences; they must render an account to all men of the hope that is theirs (I Peter 3.15). In the nature of things, then, it is impossible that the Christian faith should not refer to what all human beings have in common and what links them as human beings amid all their cultural differences: their reason or understanding. Especially in a situation like ours today, when everything depends on the Christian faith making the transition to new cultural horizons and a new epoch, there can be no question of the Christian retreating into the realm of private experience. Today, as hardly ever before in the history of Christianity, it is essential that the Christian faith emphasize its reasonableness which is accessible to all human beings.

The highlighting of the reasonableness of the Christian faith, as I mean it here, has nothing to do with a rationalistic reduction of faith. There is no question of comprehending faith from outside, as it were, with the aid of a supposedly neutral mind. As will be made clear, faith can be substantiated only by itself or, more accurately, by its proper object, which is the revelation of God in Jesus Christ. Natural theology cannot substitute for this substantiation or even attempt simply to supplement it. The task of natural theology is rather to show the internal reasonabless of a faith which has its substantiation in and from itself. This monstration of the reasonableness of the Christian faith likewise has nothing to do with an intellectualistic abridgement of faith. It is utterly beyond denial that faith is not simply an act of the mind but a personal act of the whole human being. In the language of the Bible: faith springs from the heart. In this sense faith is simple and also guileless. But this undividedness of faith does not exclude but includes the understanding. For this reason a 'childlike', that is, blind faith, which shuns the bright light of reason and, in a kind of pre-Pentecostal way, simply continues to believe behind closed doors, is not an especially intense faith but rather a very deficient form of faith, that expects not too much but too little of faith. Those who are really convinced of the truth of the faith also trust that their faith will enable them to come to grips with the intellectual challenges to it. The kind and extent of this intellectual grappling will depend, of course, on the kind and degree of the Christian's education in other areas, on his faith and on his mission and position in the church and the world. In principle, however, those who proclaim the Christian faith carry out their tasks in the proper way only when they do not communicate the faith through clever psychological manipulation or force it upon people in a dictatorial way but rather when the proclamation liberates people and renders them capable of a responsible decision to believe. Natural theology is meant to be of service in the execution of this task.

A deeper understanding of the business of natural theology requires a survey of the different forms it has taken in history. Three classical types of natural theology may be distinguished.

(a) Natural theology in the Greek philosophers

From the standpoint of cultural history it was the great achievement of the Greek mind that it was not satisfied with the imagery of myth but inquired into the logos that was hidden within it. The natural philosophers of the seventh to fifth centuries BC were already taking this approach. The Sophists fifth to fourth centuries BC showed at this early stage a critical and distrustful attitude toward the mythical tradition. This led them to distinguish between *physis*, that is, what gods and men are by their nature, and *thesis*, or what they are by reason of arbitrary human determination. The critical meaning of the concept of 'nature' is also evident in Plato. In Plato we find for the first time the concept of 'theology'. He is aware of the pernicious character of many of the mythical stories and wants types of theology to be distinguished, that is, critical norms for discourse about the gods.[13] In Aristotle theology, becomes identical with first philosophy, which discourses in a rational way about first principles or the first Principle[14] and is later distinguished as natural theology from mythical theology and from political theology, that is, the theology publicly acknowledged and celebrated in the polis. The Stoic Varro in the first century BC expressly reports this threefold division of theology into natural, mythical and political.[15] Augustine criticizes this threefold division on the grounds that it is really twofold because the mythical theology is in fact the theology of the polis and the theology of the polis is in fact the mythical one. But both ascribe to the gods a good deal that is absurd and unworthy. In any case, even the best natural theology, that of Plato, is in Augustine's view far inferior to the Christian truth.[16] Nonetheless early Christianity took over this natural theology to such an extent that Tertullian could speak of an *anima naturaliter christiana*.[17] In this tension-filled reception there found expression a new and specifically Christian understanding of natural theology which

incorporated and carried even further the critical side of the natural theology
of antiquity.

(b) The Christian form of natural theology

The Bible is not concerned with the nature of things, that is, with what things
are by reason of the origin peculiar to each of them (*natura* from *nasci*, 'to be
born') but only with what man and the world are by reason of their origin in
God. The Bible thus looks upon reality not as nature (*physis*) but as creature
(*ktisis*). Reality as created is, on the one hand, wholly dependent on God and,
on the other, infinitely different from him; moreover, insofar as it is entirely
distinct from him even while being dependent on him, it enjoys a relative
independence over against him. Because of this relative independence the Bible
has no hesitation about speaking of a nature that has been given to man by
God himself and that inspires him (cf. Rom. 1.26; 21.4; I Cor. 11.14). This
relative independence also makes it possible for human beings to turn against
God and in this way to corrupt their own natures (cf. Rom. 1.18ff.). Now they
are by nature children of wrath (cf. Eph. 2.3), but because they owe their entire
being to God, they remain, even as sinners, wholly related to God. Precisely as
sinners, they are, in their corrupt state, a question to themselves, a question
which they themselves cannot answer. The Bible thus expounds the being of
world and man in the form of an extremely tension-filled history of relations
between God and human beings. But despite all the vicissitudes that mark this
history, there is something that abides and retains its identity and that, even
though profoundly distorted by sin, cannot be radically negated or cancelled
out. At the same time, however, this abiding nature is henceforth drawn into
the dynamic movement of the historical dealings between God and man, a
history of which Greek philosophy could have had no knowledge. In the Bible,
therefore, nature is not the basis for an order of being which is independent of
grace; it is rather the term which expresses a relatively independent meaningful
structure within the order of grace.

  This integration of natural theology into the history of salvation is to be
found in all the great theologians of the classical tradition: Augustine, Anselm
of Canterbury, Bonaventure, Thomas Aquinas. The dynamiç movement of
salvation history into which the concept of nature has been incorporated finds
expression especially in the axiom mentioned earlier: 'Grace presupposes
nature and completes it.' The axiom makes it clear that nature exists entirely
for the sake of grace; it is the extrinsic presupposition of grace, just as,
conversely, grace is the intrinsic presupposition of nature, that for the sake of
which nature exists. Nature is therefore not an independent, self-enclosed and
self-completing or fulfilling realm. It is dynamically ordered beyond itself to a
fulfillment which it cannot bestow upon itself but rather achieves through
grace alone. Only through grace does nature attain to its own full determina-

tion. When it closes itself to grace through sin it becomes contradictory to itself and is deeply perverted.

A twofold order, one of nature and one of grace, is at most suggested as a possibility in the classical tradition; the idea has been developed only in the modern age. This momentous development was set in motion by the heresy of Baius, a theologian at Louvain in the sixteenth century. Baius taught that nature is not only ordered to grace but even has a right to grace. As a way of maintaining the gratuitousness of grace the theologians of the Baroque and Neo-scholastic periods constructed the idea of a pure nature (*natura pura*).[18] This was originally intended simply as an auxiliary construct, a conceptual hypothesis, enabling theologians to grasp the gratuitousness of grace. But it led in turn to the development of a twofold order of natural and supernatural theology. This elaboration of something initially proposed simply as a conceptual possibility is intelligible only in the light of the indirect influence exercised by a new understanding of natural theology that developed in the modern Enlightenment.

(c) Natural theology in the Enlightenment

For many reasons the modern age liberated itself from many of the historical presuppositions of Christianity. After the division of the church in the sixteenth century and after the religious wars that resulted from this division, Christianity could no longer be the force holding society together. Modern society had to find a new and religiously neutral basis, and for this purpose it turned to nature and reason as common to all human beings. The result was a new form of natural theology: a knowledge of God and a doctrine of God that were derived from the contemplation of the nature of man and the world as seen solely by the natural light of human understanding. This new and independent natural theology became the equal partner of theology based on revelation. In fact, the old relationship was soon reversed. Natural theology had previously been a presupposition for theology based on revelation; now it became the norm for this theology.[19] Revelational theology had to submit to being judged by whether it served the advancement of reason and happiness. Revelational theology became a historical presupposition and a vehicle for natural theology.

However much it criticized this rationalism, Catholic theology preserved a tone of moderation in its reaction. It objected not only to rationalism but also to the opposite extreme of fideism and traditionalism, both of which denied reason any capacity or competence in the area of faith. Catholic theology thus sought to travel a middle way between rationalism and fideism. In opposition to rationalism it made a distinction in principle between faith and understanding; against fideism it maintained the conformity between faith and reason. This led to the theory of a twofold order of knowledge, one natural, the other supernatural, no contradiction between the two being possible. But however justified the underlying concern for mediating between faith and reason, the intellectual form in which the concern found expression calls for criticism in the light of the older tradition. For this 'two-storey model' of natural and supernatural theology ends up simply in a relatively loose juxtaposition of the two or a superposition of the one on the other; it effects no real mediation. In fact, the model is even dependent on the spirit of the Enlightenment to the extent that it develops natural theology in an abstract and unhistorical manner and fails to grasp its proper integration into the history of salvation.

In its reaction to the modern age, the theology of the Reformation followed a different path than Catholic theology, and this difference developed in our own century into almost a new kind of disagreement dividing the church, a disagreement of which the sixteenth century knew nothing as yet in this form.[20] Luther's statements on the question of the natural knowledge of God are ambivalent. He knows that God has given all human beings a general knowledge of God; apart from revelation, however, human beings do not know who God is for them. As a result they turn God into an idol, a figure created by human desires. According to Luther, the word of God alone makes it possible to have a right knowledge not only of God but even of man. The object of theology is *cognitio Dei et hominis* (the knowledge of God and man); but the 'man' thus known is *homo reus et perditus* (man guilty and lost), and God is *Deus justificans et salvator* (God who justifies and saves).[21] For Luther, then, there is no universal natural knowledge of God and man within which the knowledge gained through revelation occurs as a special case. The generally conceived being of God and man can be specified only by the very concrete knowledge given through revelation and justification.

These tension-filled foundations served as the basis later on for various approaches to a solution. In early Protestant theology, or what is called the 'Protestant orthodoxy' of the seventeenth century, the subject of natural theology was known and accepted in a way that was fully in accordance with Catholic presentations of the same subject. Only in the Neo-Protestantism of the nineteenth century did natural theology become a subject for criticism. But the way in which this occurred seems to confirm rather than refute the proper concern of natural theology. In F. Schleiermacher the criticism of natural theology serves as a means of turning away from the Enlightenment. In contrast to the indeterminate and vague meaning of 'natural' as understood in the modern philosophy of subjectivity, Schleiermacher wants to give due attention to the reality of freedom and history. Accordingly his dogmatics begin with lemmata taken over from ethics. This means that Schleiermacher is simply criticizing a particular natural theology and replacing it with another. Something comparable is the case with A. Ritschl, the leader of the liberal theology school. His position against natural theology is for him part of his criticism of metaphysics. In his view, religion and revelation are concerned not with nature but with the spiritual. His rejection of natural theology is thus in keeping with the bourgeois consciousness of his age; philosophical parallels to his view are

Neo-Kantianism and the effort of the human sciences to escape from the grip of the natural sciences.

The strongest criticism of natural theology comes from the representatives of dialectical theology, and especially from K. Barth, who on this account parted company with his former comrade-in-arms, E. Brunner.[22] In Barth's eyes natural theology is evidence of the bourgeoisification of Christianity; in criticizing it he hopes to vanquish the liberal theology of culural Protestantism (*Kulturprotestantismus*).[23] But in this criticism of bourgeois cultural Protestantism he is in harmony, in a new way, with the changed consciousness of the age. For in the meantime, the criticism of religion that had been developed by Feuerbach, Marx and Nietzsche had destroyed the optimistic expectations of Enlightenment rationalism that man could know God by his own powers, and had endeavoured to unmask knowledge of God as a projection by man. In a manner that is structurally comparable Barth explains natural theology as a manufacture of idols; he sees in it man's mongrel effort to take control of God. Consequently, the theological criticism of religion represents for dialectical theology the possibility of getting in contact with the general consciousness of the age; paradoxically, atheism has here become a form of natural theology.[24]

It thus becomes clear that the old natural theology contains questions and themes that did not cease to be valid when the historical form they once took was dropped, but rather have come to the fore repeatedly in changed form, even in those who criticize it most severely. The criticism of natural theology sees to it, as it were, that the business most proper to natural theology is carried on: reflection on the intellectual presuppositions of the Christian faith. It is therefore not at all surprising that the concerns of natural theology are reappearing in contemporary Protestant theology. To a certain extent this was already true of the later K. Barth and is being continued today, although in different ways, by W. Pannenberg, G. Ebeling and E. Jüngel.

(d) Contemporary problematic

The historical survey has shown that the concept of natural theology is very ambiguous. The ambiguity of the concept 'natural theology' is connected with the ambiguity of the concept of 'nature'.[25] For the concept of nature changes its meaning depending on the relational framework in which it is used. The philosophical concept of nature relates (that is, opposes) nature to culture and history. Culture and history are what emerges from the free creative activity of man; nature, on the other hand, is what we men presuppose at each point in our activity, namely the reality of the world, of other human beings, and of ourselves as a natural pregiven reality. Nature is what we do not make and are incapable of making but rather must presuppose in all our making and doing. In this sense we speak of raw or untouched and unshaped nature.

The theological concept of nature must be distinguished from the philosophical concept just described. The theological concept relates nature not to freedom and history but to grace. Nature is now what grace presupposes: man as a being endowed with intellectual knowledge and with freedom, a being who as such is capable of encountering and receiving grace. The theological concept is thus broader and more comprehensive than the philosophical; it includes what the philosophical concept of nature excludes, and in fact it includes this especially, because it is precisely spirit and freedom that are the transcendental presuppositions for faith and for the grace that is given through faith.

In the light of this explanation of concepts we may arrive at this summary statement: natural theology originates in a transcendental reflection of faith on the conditions for its own possibility. Faith, however, presupposes a subject endowed with freedom. Natural theology is therefore connected not with what philosophers mean by nature, but with what, from a philosophical standpoint, is contrasted with nature, namely, freedom. The theological concept of nature has to do, then, with freedom and therefore history. This in turn means that natural theology may not be satisfied with an abstract transcendental reflection and must instead involve itself with the concrete historical conditions and presuppositions of faith. Natural theology must establish itself by coming to grips with concrete historical reality.

Such a concretization of abstract transcendental theological reflection emerges from the constellation of problems dealt with in contemporary philosophy as well as from the more sharply focused constellation of problems in recent Catholic and Protestant theology. Modern philosophy achieved a clarification of Enlightenment views with regard to itself; more particularly, it achieved a clarification of Enlightenment views about its own historical presuppositions. In the process, the abstract, unhistorical understanding of nature and reason found in the Enlightenment was transcended. It was recognized that human reason and what it accepts as natural and reasonable are subject to cultural and historical changes. Quite independently of whether these changes in the horizon of understanding, in the modes of thought, in the understanding of being, and so on, are interpreted idealistically in terms of a history of ideas or materialistically as an epiphenomenon of economic changes, the intrinsic historicity has, ever since Hegel and Schelling, Marx and Nietzsche and not least Heidegger, Gadamer, Habermas and others, become a generally accepted insight which moves the transcendental approach beyond the point to which Kant took it. Unlike Kant, thinkers today know that the *a priori* conditions of human understanding can vary in the course of history.[26] This means that new presuppositions of understanding have been established for the understanding of the integration of nature and reason into the history of salvation, and that a natural theology which abstracts from the historical presuppositions of faith has become definitively impossible. Paradoxically, this thesis derives its strongest confirmation from the significant fact that projected natural theologies which prescind at least methodically from the revelation of God in Jesus Christ and seek to establish a purely natural presupposition for faith in God, are indeed of some help to Christians who have become unsure of themselves, but usually seem to carry little conviction to non-Christians. The critical evaluation which W. Weischedel has given of these attempts is very instructive and worth heeding.[27] The proof of the reasonableness of faith thus presupposes faith and its horizon of understanding and cannot by itself make these available.

The same result is yielded by the constellation of problems in contemporary theology. From this point of view, the original meaning of natural theology in High Scholasticism and the new approaches of the Reformation to it are not so far apart as they might seem to be at first sight. In both approaches there is no question of a neutral pre-structure and sub-structure for revelational theology or for a general framework in which the special revelation in salvation history could be subsequently inserted. In the theology of the High Scholastic period the point is rather that there is a relatively independent reality which revelational faith presupposes and which achieves its own fulfillment only through faith. Natural theology does not substantiate the faith; rather the faith grounds natural theology, although only as a relatively independent entity. Natural theology is therefore concerned with the reasonableness and universality of faith. This proof of the reasonableness of faith has for its starting point the fact that in Jesus Christ the definitive truth about God, man and the world has made its appearance. This primordial confession of the Christian faith can be shown to be reasonable by showing how in the light of Jesus Christ the light which enlightens the world shines in a new, more complete and even definitive way.

The reasonableness of faith can be shown concretely in two ways. On the one hand, and in a more negative way, it can be shown by the fact that faith, being convinced of the fact that in principle created reality and the realities of salvation are not contradictory, builds on this to show that the arguments brought against it are not coherent and sound even from the standpoint of pure reason.[28] On the other hand, and in a more positive way, it can be shown by the fact that faith proves its value as a prophetic interpretation of reality, that is, that faith gives access to a meaningful experience of reality, a meaningful understanding of reality, a liberating practice, and so on. The conflict between faith and unbelief is thus not a conflict regarding some sort of higher or ulterior world but a conflict regarding our present reality. Faith claims knowledge of the ultimate ground and the ultimate meaning and goal of all reality and asserts that for this reason only its own light makes it possible for the light proper to creation to shine out fully. It seeks to prove itself by the fact that unlike the ideologies which always absolutize a single aspect or single area of reality, it does not do violence to phenomena but can 'save' them as ancient philosophy claimed to do.[29] Above all, faith does justice both to the greatness and to the wretchedness of man. Faith can therefore ask other interpretations of reality whether they are able to say anything greater and more comprehensive about the world and man or whether on the contrary it is true to say that he who believes sees more.

2. Experience of God

As far as the God-question is concerned, we are being forced back today to the rudiments of understanding. Consequently, when we speak of a natural knowledge of God, there can be no question simply of abstract proofs of God. Such proofs are meaningful and intelligible only if they have a basis in experience and represent an affort to penetrate more deeply into this experience and defend it against intellectual challenges. Like all knowledge, the knowledge of God requires a basis in experience. But what is experience? To what extent is it possible to speak at all of an experience of God?[30]

The theme of faith and experience is an extremely difficult and perplexing one. This is due not least to the fact that both the concept of experience and the concept of faith are many-levelled and ambiguous. Experience may mean: personal experience of life, and the methodically disciplined experience of the modern experimental sciences; everyday experience in the secularized world of our day, and devotional experience and the experience of faith all the way up to mystical experience; practical experience, especially that gained in political practice, and experience taken over and imported from the experimental sciences. It is clear that these distinct concepts of experience, to which others might be added, point in very different and to some extent contradictory directions. When someone appeals to experience, he has not yet said anything clear and unequivocal; he has called attention to a problem, but he has not answered any questions.

The concept of faith likewise has a number of meanings. In theological parlance faith may mean the act of faith (*fides qua creditur*, the [act of] faith by which one believes) but also the content of faith (*fides quae creditur*, the faith-contents which are believed). In the first case, to ask about the relation between faith and experience is to ask how the act of trust, self-surrender and obedience toward the impenetrable mystery which in religious language we call God can be reconciled with our sober, enlightened, rational experience of the world. In the second case, the relation between faith and experience has to do with the problem of how certain contents of faith can be reconciled with our modern world-picture and especially with the results of the modern experimental sciences. The two problems cannot be wholly separated, but they must nonetheless be carefully distinguished.

It is not only the concepts of experience and faith but also the relation between faith and experience that can be defined in very different ways. At the present time two opposed positions call for particular discussion. The first and traditional formulation of the relation says: faith comes from hearing (Rom. 10.17) and has for its criterion not our present experience of reality but the authoritatively proclaimed gospel message which is transmitted through the church. The second and basically modernistic definition of the relation says: faith is an expression of religious experience, and the traditional confessions of faith must be measured by their ability to express our changed modern experience or at least to make this experience possible. Both positions have something true to say, but both are also one-sided.

True though it is that the Christian faith has for its norm the faith delivered once and for all (Jude 3), it is also true to say that we encounter this faith in a quite limited historical experiential tradition and that this tradition is no longer directly ours but must be appropriated via our own experience. This fact points to the truth in the second position. The latter, however, overlooks the fact that experience never begins at point zero but is historically mediated. Above all, it overlooks the fact that not the word of God as such but the historical form in which it is transmitted to us (and it comes to us only in a historical form) needs to be criticized, tested and sounded more fully. Our always limited and historically changing experience cannot and may not be the criterion for what is to be accepted as the word of God; rather, the word of God is meant to, and must, make known to us what true experience is as compared with illusory appearances. The word of God proves itself to be true by opening up new experience to us, experience which proves its worth by other experiences.

Finally, the point must be made that faith is not only related to an experiential reality which antecedes it, but also has experience which is proper to it. This aspect finds expression particularly in the biblical understanding of knowledge (*Yādā*) which is never acquired with the mind alone but is mediated through the whole of existence and through the existential centre, the heart of man. This experience which is proper to faith has been known especially by the mystics, for to them mysticism is *cognito Dei experimentalis* (an experiential knowledge of God).[31]

It follows from all this that the relation between faith and experience can only be described as a relation of critical correlation. The resultant hermeneutical circle between the transmission of faith and the experience of faith cannot be eliminated. The decisive point, of course, is that within this circle primacy belongs to the message; this means that we may never absolutize our present experience and that our experience is rather always a historically open experience that is and must be open to new experience. The question, then, is this. Where is faith to find its correlative in present-day experience of reality?

Our present situation is characterized by a far-reaching loss of religious experience. If, then, we are to make such experience at all accessible again, we must take as our point of departure a general understanding of experience and then show how the dimension of religious experience opens up 'in, with and under' everyday human experience. This very attempt is still difficult enough, since, as I already said, the concept of experience is extremely complex and multi-leveled; it is one of the most difficult and obscure concepts in all philosophy.

In our everyday linguistic usage we speak of an experienced person, meaning that he is one who knows people and things not simply by hearsay or from books but repeated direct dealings with them; one, therefore, who combines knowledge and ability. The German word for 'to experience', *erfahren*, is derived from *fahren*, which means 'to journey'. An experienced man is thus a 'travelled' man, who does not know the world only by hearsay but has rather been out in the midst of it and has shared the life, sufferings and activities of other human beings. The Romance languages take a different approach to the idea. They speak of *experientia* (the Latin word behind the Romance words). The expert is the *peritus*, the man who through experimentation, trial and error, and confirmation has as it were piled up insights within his own person.

This everyday linguistic usage shows that experience may not be reduced to an objectivist understanding of experience, such as is often attributed to the so-called experimental sciences. Experience is not only what we can establish and test by experiment and then reduce to the simplest kind of factual descriptions. Such a narrowly empiricist understanding of experience has in fact now been rejected even by the experimental sciences. Down to the present, no science, not even the natural sciences, has succeeded in convincingly reducing all knowledge to purely empirical data. The very development of modern physics, especially quantum physics, has shown that we never know reality in itself but always and only through human images, models and concepts. We never experience reality in itself; we always experience it as something that has a specific meaning for us; objective experience and interpretation of experience can never be completely separated. In any case, an absolutization of what is experimentally ascertainable would be a contradictory claim, since the thesis that the empirically ascertainable is alone real is itself not an empirically ascertainable assertion. Anti-metaphysical positivism is, paradoxically, a metaphysics of the positive. Consequently it is not a valid objection against belief in God to observe that God is not empirically observable; for there is no conceivable empirical method that could show that God is. The God who is is not a given. But there is also no conceivable empirical method that could ever prove the non-existence of God.

The critique of a one-sidedly objectivist concept of experience should not, of course, lead to a reduction of religious experience to the opposite, that is, to subjective experience (*Erlebnis*) or even to subjective moods. Every experience doubtless takes place in the medium of human subjectivity, calling forth therein an echo and a reflex response. Religious experience affects the human person to the depths and in all the fibres of the being; it sets humming all the chords of existence. One cannot encounter God and remain a distant spectator, for God lays total claim to the person. In the language of the Bible: the experience of God takes place in the heart, that is, in the core or centre of the human person. But the primary element in the person's being subjectively touched is that he or she comes in contact with and is even overwhelmed by a reality not himself or herself. This holds even for religious experience. Significantly, it is precisely the great mystics who are most critical and reserved toward inward personal experiences. The hunger for religious experiences can be very unreligious and self-centred. If, then, the person wants to encounter God and not simply himself or herself he or she must not seek such experiences for their own sake. Were we to reduce the experience of God to personal life-experience, we would confine ourselves to the realm of the subjective, of non-commitment; the suspicion of projection would then immediately arise.

The twofold limitation on the concept of experience brings us to a positive definition of the essence of experience. Experience is not to be reduced to something purely objective or to something purely subjective. It includes both elements: objective contact and subjective feeling. Experience arises from the interplay of objective reality and subjective intercourse with the milieu and our times. Experience is inseparably a being affected by reality and an interpretation of this contact through words, images, symbols and concepts. It thus has a dialectical structure; that is, it is historical, for 'history' means the reciprocal interaction of the person and the world.

The historicity of experience has, in turn, several aspects. It means, to begin with, that experience never takes place at an isolated point of time through the here-and-now digestion of momentary perceptions. Experiential knowledge emerges, rather, from repeated and increasingly proficient intercourse with reality. It comes into existence by the fact that certain impressions and the interpretation made of them are repeatedly confirmed. Experience thus requires a familiarity and practice in dealing with things and persons, a mastering of patterns of action. This is why Aristotle connects experience with memory.[32] But the memory of which he speaks is not simply the individual memory of each person; it is also the collective memory that is recorded especially in the language of a community. Language is the precipitate of the experience of many generations. This means that experiences are always likewise the we-experience of a community, a people, a race or class. These various human communities are characterized by a common remembrance of basic experiences that are constantly revived through the retelling of myths, sagas, legends, anecdotes and other stories. In other words, experiences are communicated through narrative.

This last statement points to a second aspect of the historicity of our experience. Through the mediation of language not only do former experiences come alive again today; language and the experience 'stored up' in it also help to interpret our present experience and pass it on to a future generation. Experience thus exists, at any given time, in a tension between remembrance of past experience, the experience of the moment, and the transmission of this experience in the hope that the future will preserve and confirm it. In other words: experience is a constantly renewed and never finished learning process. It is 'experience of life' in the proper sense of the phrase. The experienced person is not one who has a definitive answer for everything but the person who realizes that experience can never be complete, is open to new experience on the basis of past experience, knows how to experience, and understands how to undergo new experiences and correlate them in a productive way with past experience.

This historical tension between past, present and future experience has a twofold critical significance. First, the remembrance of past experience has a critical significance. For there are not only memories that shed light on the past but also dangerous memories in which unfulfilled hopes or experience of profound suffering are revived and present their claims. As a result, the delusive coherence of a personal universe now taken for granted can be suddenly destroyed and a new world opened up. Consequently, nothing would be more foolish and uncritical than to absolutize present and possibly very impoverished experiences and make them the sole criterion for judging past experiences by applying the simplistic saying: 'That no longer says anything to us today.' On the contrary, the remembrance of great past experiences can provide an impulse toward the future and render us capable today of new and more profound experiences.

On the other hand, there can evidently be no question of simply integrating new experiences into old experiential patterns. We undergo truly fundamental experiences only when we experience the stubborn resistance of reality to the model of thought and action which we have cultivated up to now; when we experience something surprisingly new which alters our previous views, thwarts our plans, opens up new perspectives to us and forces us to advance in new directions. The capacity for experience is always linked to a readiness to change our minds and be converted. The experiences that are fruitful are not our everyday experiences but rather those contrasting experiences that challenge us to a decision. In other words: experiences are dis-illusioning, in the positive sense of the term; they dissolve previous illusions and delusive coherences and thus reveal the truth about our previous experience.

The understanding of experience as historical, as I have thus far presented it, leads to a final point. It is this: the historical dialectic between past, present and future experiences shows that we not only have immediate and direct experiences but also experiences of our experiences[33] or indirect experiences. These indirect experiences represent the beginning of reflection. The reflection is not yet of a conceptual kind but consists rather in the fact that 'in, with and under' our immediate experience a deeper experience takes place.

This experience of our experience is in the final analysis an experience of the finiteness and incompleteness of our experience; it is thus an experience of suffering. From Aeschylus onward Greek literature repeated the play on the words pathos and mathos: experiential learning (mathos) through suffering (pathos). Nietzsche provides a clear formulation of this idea: 'As deeply as a man sees into life, he also sees into suffering.'[34] 'It almost determines the order of rank how profoundly human beings can suffer.'[35] From this it follows that the widespread expulsion of suffering from public life by hiding it behind a mask of youthfulness, vitality and health leads to an alarming shallowness and impoverishment of our experience and a declining sensitivity to 'the sigh of the oppressed creature' (Karl Marx). No one has experienced humanity to the full unless he or she has experienced its finiteness and suffering. But then experience becomes a way leading into an open immensity, into a mystery that is ever greater and never to be completely plumbed.

I may sum up by saying that our experience of our experience is in the final analysis an experience of the finiteness and mysteriousness of our experience. At this point we have reached the religious dimension of experience. Religious experience is an indirect, not a direct type of experience; it is an experience which we have 'in, with and under' our other experiences. It is therefore not just one experience alongside other experiences, but rather the basic experience present in our other experiences; it is an experience that presides over and gives a pervasive tone to all other experience. For this reason, K. Rahner and J. B. Lotz speak of transcendental experience.[36] At first hearing, this description sounds like a contradiction. For the term 'transcendental' applies to a type of consideration that is concerned with the conditions that precede and make possible any and all experience. It is impossible, or so it seems, for an experience to be its own condition; experiential knowledge cannot grasp the conditions that *precede* any and all experience. But the paradoxical character of the concept simply reflects the paradoxical character of the reality. For on the one hand it is transcendentality that makes experience possible to begin with; on the other hand, this transcendentality is itself historically contingent as far as its concrete form is concerned, and to this extent it can be the content of a special experience at the level of horizontal disclosure. In religious experience there is revealed to us, *via* other experiences, the ultimate, all-inclusive, sheltering horizon of human experience, namely, the dimension of that mystery out of which all experience emerges and to which all experience points.

Having pointed out the dimension of religious experience, I must now turn to the reality of religious experience itself. Religious experience would be simply a general, vague mood, were there no individual experiences to which the religious dimension became 'manifest'. In Anglo-Saxon philosophy, 'disclosures situation' has become the accepted term for such experiences.[37] What is meant are individual experiences in which more than just this individual experience is revealed to us: 'suddenly' the whole of our experience is clarified; the overall coherence of our experience, and the mystery that holds sway in it, become the subject of experience 'in, with and under' a concrete experience.

Such disclosure situations can take many forms: a situation of joy, for example, in which we feel a blissful delight and in which the world, and our own life, seems infinitely rich, beautiful and lovable; or a situation of sorrow, in which the world no longer makes sense to us and the question of 'Why?' forces itself ineluctably upon us; or a situation of anxiety, in which firm ground suddenly vanishes from beneath our feet, the world reels, and the utter unfathomableness of it all is made clear to us; or a situation of consolation, in which we feel supported, embraced and protected; or a situation of love and fidelity coming to us from our fellows, when we are unconditionally accepted and affirmed, and are ourselves so taken by the lovableness and beauty of another that everything about us seems transformed and even under a spell; or a situation of appalling boredom in which everything becomes slack and indifferent and reality proves to be empty, a hollow facade; a situation of encounter with death, when a human being falls for ever silent and everything is taken from him and put beyond his control, and when we ourselves are for ever deprived of a familiar, intimate and beloved friend. In the face of death the definitive truth about the human person is made pitilessly clear: that in the final analysis a human being belongs neither to himself nor to others; that an unfathomable mystery envelops the human person; that he himself is a mystery which he can never master.

Such religious experiences are profoundly ambivalent. In his well-known book, *The Idea of the Holy*, R. Otto spoke of a 'harmony of contrast'.[38] He described a holy mystery as *mysterium tremendum et fascinosum*, a mystery that is distant and rejects us but is also, at the same time, close to us and attracts us. Insofar as this experienced mystery is an inaccessible horizon of all our experience it encounters us as the Wholly Other, a frightening abyss, a wilderness of nothingness. Insofar as it is close to us in everything, it appears to us as a protecting Ground, as grace and fulfillment. The encounter with this mystery can be terrifying or blissful; it can repel and attract, fill us with anxiety and fear or with gratitude, joy and consolation. Augustine knew long ago of this ambivalence. 'I tremble and I catch fire. I tremble because I am so unlike him; I catch fire, because I am so like him.'[39]

Because of this ambivalence and ambiguity it has been possible for this mystery to be given many names in the history of human culture and to be susceptible of many interpretations. It would therefore be very premature to present the experience of this mystery as unqualifiedly an experience of God. The experience can be interpreted in theistic terms; but it can also be interpreted in pantheistic, atheistic or nihilistic terms. Or finally – as is often the case in our contemporary civilization – it can also be left anonymous and unnamed. When this happens, of course, it nonetheless succeeds in finding distorted expression, whether in the form of modern ideologies or in the form of psychic disorders. In the long run it is not possible to dismiss this dimension of experience completely. For the mystery is the foundation of all experience. It is therefore something different in nature from the riddles or problems which can, at least in principle, be solved one after another. In our experience we will always experience ourselves as finite beings who are surrounded by an unfathomable mystery.

The experience of the mystery that holds sway over our lives and all of reality is accompanied by a question that is no less unavoidable and insoluble: the question of the universal meaning of all reality. Since on the one hand we constantly experience both meaning and meaninglessness within history and since, on the other, the mystery that makes itself known to us in all experience is profoundly ambivalent, we will never be able to answer this question in a definitive way on the basis of experience. As in the case of all other experience, so in the case of religious experience the real meaning is disclosed only in a religious language and the tradition behind it. We must therefore go further and ask: What is this mystery? What name can we give it? Can we name it at all, or does it not continually evade our grasp and withdraw into a nameless beyond? May we even call it God? Is such religious language meaningful to begin with?

3. God in human language

The path of experience leads us to the threshold of an ultimate mystery which we can experience not directly but only indirectly, 'in, with and under' our everyday experience. Moreover, as soon as we attempt to describe this mystery, our language proves useless. What reveals itself to us in our experience is something that ultimately lies beyond the boundaries of language. This difficulty has always been felt in the mystical tradition, but in our day modern linguistic philosophy has given the problem a new degree of acuteness.[40] Modern linguistic philosophy asks: Is it possible to speak at all of the religious dimension? Is God a meaningful word in our language? Or must we not in the final analysis be dumb and silent before the mystical dimension of our experience? The answer to these questions is a matter of life and death for the church's proclamation and confession of its faith; on the answer also depends the very possibility of theology as linguistically communicated rational discourse on the Christian faith.

The answers given by modern linguistic philosophy have undergone a dramatic development in the course of our century; I can only present them in a very schematic way here. At the beginning of the century came logical positivism or logical empiricism, usually known as neo-positivism. The authoritative figures were B. Russell and L. Wittgenstein, and the Vienna Circle around H. Schlick and R. Carnap, who had been influenced by Russell and Wittgenstein. Logical positivism took as its point of departure the ideal of an exact unified science, the propositions of which can be expressed in a symbolic language that reflects the world and follows a logical syntax. For this reason, only those propositions are to be regarded as scientific and meaningful which are demonstrable and repeatable and to this extent are susceptible of inter-subjective proof. In addition to the criterion of logic there was also an empirical criterion of meaning, according to which all propositions must be capable of empirical verification. Metaphysical and religious propositions cannot meet either of these criteria. Metaphysical and religious questions are therefore unanswerable; they represent pseudo-problems and meanlingless propositions.

The classical expression of this position is to be found in L. Wittgenstein's *Tractatus Logico-Philosophicus*. In the very Preface of the book the author sets down the statement: 'What can be said at all can be said clearly, and what we cannot talk about we must pass over in silence.'[41] Anything that falls outside these limits of language is meaningless. 'Most of the propositions and questions to be found in philosophical works are not false but nonsensical. Consequently we cannot give any answer to questions of this kind, but can only establish that they are nonsensical . . . And it is not surprising that the deepest problems are in fact *not* problems at all.'[42] At the end of the *Tractatus* Wittgenstein admittedly comes to the realization: 'We feel that even when *all possible* scientific questions have been answered, the problems of life remain completely untouched. Of course there are then no questions left, and this itself is the answer.'[43] Nonetheless he observes: 'There are, indeed, things that cannot be put into words. They *make themselves manifest*. They are what is mystical.'[44] On the other hand, he concludes that 'what we cannot speak about we must pass over in silence'.[45]

Where this position was adopted, theology was reduced to speechlessness. Once neo-positivist presuppositions were allowed dominance, 'God' seemed to be no longer a meaningful word. (A. J. Ayer, A. Flew). We may speak in this context of a semantic atheism or the death of God. But such descriptions are, if anything, too innocuous, since they are meaningless.

But logical positivism, which was wholly inspired by the paradigm of the modern natural sciences, soon proved to be untenable from the standpoint of natural science itself. Its presupposition was that our language is an image of reality, but this presupposition was rejected as a result of modern quantum physics and its interpretation by N. Bohr and W. Heisenberg of the Copenhagen school. According to the latter view we cannot describe microphysical natural processes in an exact way but only with the help of complementary images and concepts from our macrophysical world.[46] In addition, difficulties were met with in reflection on the theory of scientific knowledge. These had to do, on the one hand, with the impossibility of strict verification and, on the other, with the unavoidability of conventional language both in the establishment of a universally valid formal language and in the statement of the basic propositions of a theory. The result was to undermine the presuppositions of logical positivism, along with its ideal of scientific statement.

The first consequences of these new insights were drawn especially by K. Popper in his *The Language of Scientific Discovery*[47] and, following him, by H. Albert.[48] According to these men the basic principles of a science are drawn from convention; they are stipulations accepted by the scientific community. They cannot be verified, although they can certainly be falsified. In this view, science is an open-ended process that proceeds by way of hypotheses and must obey the method of trial and error. Truth is thus a regulative idea: we can strive for the truth in a process that is always open-ended, but we can never reach it. What finds expression here is a radical scepticism with regard to unconditional truth-claims and an opposition to every philosophy of being (metaphysics). This position was developed in critical fashion by T. S. Kuhn in his studies of scientific revolutions.[49] According to Kuhn, scientific development proceeds not in an evolutionary manner (the view still maintained by Popper) but in a revolutionary way through changes of paradigm. A paradigm is an accepted typical case or model for the solving of a problem. In the normal practice of science the cases that arise are forced into the framework of this paradigm until the paradigm proves incapable of resolving further problems and, as the result of a revolution, is replaced by a new paradigm. Examples of such scientific revolutions may be seen with special clarity in Copernicus, Newton and Einstein.

In this context I need not enter into the details of the several theories I have been presenting. I introduce them here only to show that the logical positivism which prevailed at the beginning of the century has for practical purposes been generally rejected today. But this change does not at all mean that theology has already been saved. For the thinking neither of K. Popper nor T. S. Kuhn allows the possibility of speaking of something that is unconditioned and possesses a definitive ultimacy. The question still remains, therefore: how is it possible to speak meaningfully of God?

In a second phase of the discussion the question of the possibility of religious speech was approached in a completely different way. L. Wittgenstein subsequently subjected his earlier starting point to a radical criticism. This turnabout in Wittgenstein's thinking finds expression in his *Philosophical Investigations*. The meaning of a word or proposition is now seen as residing not in its representation of an object but in its use. 'The meaning of a word is its use in the language.'[50] Uses are many, depending in each case on the vital situation, the context, the language game (which at the same time represents a way of living). A word or sentence can function as blame, challenge, explanation, instruction or communication. The meaning of a proposition can therefore be explained only in terms of the language game being used. Instead of artificial scientific language, ordinary everyday language became the focus of attention (ordinary language philosophy).

In the framework of linguistic usage as a starting point two theories were developed to explain religious statements: the non-cognitive theory and the cognitive theory. According to the non-cognitive theory (R. Braithwaite, R. M. Hare, P. M. van Buren and others) the word 'God' has no cognitive content but serves rather to express an ethical attitude, to explain a commitment, a life-style or a conviction, or to express a certain way of viewing reality. Thus the sentence 'God is love' is not meant as a statement of fact, but is rather a declaration of the person's intention of living a life governed by *agape*; it means that love is God, i.e. is the highest, ultimate and most definitive reality. Allowing for all the progress which this theory represents, we must nonetheless ask whether it does justice to the religious use of language. For beyond any doubt a believer (when he prays, for example) is not simply explicitating his moral approach and his view of the world; he is invoking and addressing God. The various non-cognitive theories are thus removed from the religious use of language; they reduce religious faith to ethics.

The foundations of the cognitive theory were laid by J. Wisdom, and the theory's chief representatives have been I. T. Ramsey[51] and, following him, W. A. de Pater.[52] Ramsey's theory of religious language is closely connected with his theory of disclosure situations. The situations meant are those in which suddenly a person 'sees the light', in which suddenly 'the penny drops', or, in other words, a broader and deeper coherence is revealed. In such situations there is both a reality to be observed and something that transcends observation. The insights gained in such situations are not themselves verifiable, but neither are they irrelevant; rather, they fit in with experiences and organize the latter into a meaningful whole (empirical fit). But the understanding of these insights depends on an interior involvement; it demands an interior commitment. In religious disclosure situations what is at issue is the total coherence of reality, our experience in their totality; in these situations the universe acquires depth and comes alive. Religious language is not descriptive but evocative; it aims at opening up a particular view of the world, a view which, for the person who accepts it, is authenticated by reality itself. Once again, though Ramsey's theories contain much that is useful, they are in the final analysis vague. In the final analysis, the exact nature of the connection between religious language and reality and of the reality intended in such language remains unclear. Ramsey has nonetheless managed to show that there is a specifically religious use of language which is not reducible either to an empirical content or to ethics.

A further step is taken in J. L. Austin's *How To Do Things with Words*;[53] his views have been further developed by J. R. Searle.[54] Austin's theory distinguished between a constative and a performative use of language. In the performative use of language, reality is not only observed, but is accomplished by the speech-act. In this sense we can say, for example, that someone is passed over in silence or something is verbally torn to pieces or someone puts something in its place or someone lays a problem on the table, and so on. These examples make it clear that language can have the character of a happening. Especially clear examples of such effective speaking are statements that assert a claim or establish a status: 'I christen this ship the Elizabeth'; 'I take you for my wedded wife'; 'The session is opened'. Such speech-acts do not simply record an objective reality and information communicated regarding it; rather, the speech effects what it says. This theory of speech-acts is very important for religious speech. For religious speech does not convey neutral information, but rather has the nature of a testimony; that is, in dealing with it it is impossible in the final analysis to separate word and reality, the person of the speaker and the object spoken of. In the word 'God', God is 'uttered' in a literal sense; he becomes present and active in the world and in human life. On the other hand, when we pass God over in silence, he becomes dead as far as we are concerned; that is, no life goes forth from him.

We may say in a general way that the recognition of the historicity of language and human knowledge was the result of the second phase of the debates carried on in linguistic philosophy. Our language is not a neutral, objective reflection of reality; it is a subjective 'achievement' of human beings who through language are introduced into a historical inter-subjective speech-community and its historical way of life. One of the functions of the pre-understanding that is communicated through language is to disclose reality. But this pre-understanding is very diverse and historically changeable when considered at the level of individuals, so that in each instance reality 'happens' historically in language. Language thus understood does not express reality as such, but the meaning which reality has for us in each case. Such a historical understanding of reality brings with it new points of departure for a positive understanding of religious language. In fact, theology had long since perceived the tasks and possibilities set before it, independently of the more recent discussion in linguistic philosophy. For the form-critical study of the various literary genres and the sociological context (*Sitz im Leben*) proper to each had to a large extent objectively anticipated the new approaches opened up by linguistic philosophy.

We must, however, also recognize the limits of this linguistic-philosophical approach. Religious language and the manner of life that corresponds to it are here seen as one language-game alongside others. The question remains. How do I enter into this language-game? Simply by blindly trusting myself to it and practising the corresponding way of life? In this context commentators have often spoken critically of the fideism of Wittgenstein's language-game theory. If religious language is not to be a specialized idiom but universally communicable, then it has to be understood in terms of a general theory of language. Only under these conditions can there be a universal response to talk about God.

A third stage in the discussion arose from the convergence of the two orientations thus far discussed. For all the positions converge in an understanding of language as a practice of communication. The dependence of scientific language on a consensus among researchers already pointed in this direction; the theory of language games and speech-acts likewise highlighted the inter-subjective conditions for the validity of language. This understanding of language as a practice of communication is represented in Germany by the Erlangen School (Lorenzen, Kambartel, Mittelstrass); it has been developed especially by J. Habermas and K. O. Apel in ways that are relevant to theology. K. O. Apel has developed the theory of the *a priori* that is represented by the communication-community.[55] According to him, the language of a communication-community is the transcendental presupposition of all knowledge. On a similar foundation, J. Habermas developed the consensus theory of truth.[56]

He contrasts this theory with the classical correspondence theory: the correspondence theory is concerned with the agreement between language and reality, while the consensus theory is concerned with the agreement among those who participate in the communication process. In our present circumstances of disrupted communication every act of communication is also a pre-apprehension of an ideal communication community, an anticipation of a life unmarked by alienation. But the ontological status of this pre-apprehension remains ultimately unexplained in Habermas' writings.

The understanding of language as a practice of communication is of direct importance to religious language. For the testimony of faith is given through word and deed. Religious speech is not primarily a theological and systematic teaching of the faith; it is a testimony to the truth and as such is in the nature of an action and has its place within the community gathered for worship and liturgy, within the practice of proclamation, liturgy and *diakonia* (service). Its primary purpose is not to instruct but to urge a conversion of life. H. Peukert therefore justifiably looks to the understanding of language as communicative practice for a new approach to talk about God.[57] He introduces an idea taken from W. Benjamin and argues as follows. If the hope and longing implied in every act of linguistic communication is not to end in nothingness, and if communication is to be, above all else, truly universal and to include solidarity with the dead, this is possible only if God exists and if he is the God who gives life to the dead. Every act of linguistic communication is therefore at the same time a question and a pre-apprehension of the living and life-giving God. Every speech-act draws its vitality from the hope of a beatifying universal communication and is therefore an act of hope that anticipates the coming reign of God. Religious language is therefore not a specialized idiom alongside other kinds of language; rather, it makes explicit the condition for the possibility of all other language.

The question that arises at this point is whether we can be satisfied with this undoubtedly impressive result. A first question to be put may be derived from linguistic philosophy itself. According to C. W. Morris we must distinguish three meanings in language: the syntactic or grammatical (intra-linguistic), the semantic (relative to reality), and the pragmatic (related to action).[58] The theories previously considered have essentially concentrated to explaining the syntactic and pragmatic dimensions but have left the semantic dimension untouched. We must therefore ask more specifically what the reality is of which the word 'God' speaks. The same question is also raised by a philosophical consideration. J. Simon has made the acute observation that an opposition between correspondence theory and consensus theory is untenable since the consensus theory is itself a covert correspondence theory.[59]

For the consensus consists in people having the same view of the 'same thing'. As a practice of communication, language is at the same time an interpretation of reality. But what is the reality that is meant by the word 'God'? If this ontological question is no longer raised, then the proposition that God is becomes a statement of what the word 'God' means to us. This kind of transformation of ontological statements into statements of meaning and function empty the word 'God' of its cognitive content. It becomes either the embodiment of universal communication or a code-word and impulse for a certain attitude of solidarity or some other ethical attitude, or a perspective on the meaning of reality. Under such circumstances, the word 'God' is used in a merely allegorical way, that is, it always stands for something else and therefore can in principle be exchanged and replaced. In short: the question of the truth of religious language and therefore the question of the reality of God is unavoidable.

In a fourth stage of our reflections the ontological significance of language may be best brought out with the aid of the later philosophy of M. Heidegger.[60] In Heidegger's eyes the human person is *das Da-sein* (literally: 'the "being-there"'); he does not exist solely by interacting with reality that is simply 'at hand', but is rather concerned always with the meaning of being as a whole. Being is concretely present in language, through which reality is at each moment disclosed to us in a historical way. Language is therefore 'the house of being'. Language (for example, the language of science and technology that aims at communicating information) can indeed obstruct the question of being; but language can also disclose being in new ways, especially the language of myth and creative literature. Language is a story in which the mystery of being either conceals itself or addresses us.

The difficult views and approaches of Heidegger have been fruitfully applied to theology in various ways, especially by H. Gadamer[61] and P. Ricoeur.[62] In order to explain the semantic function and ontological significance of religious language we may not profitably start with metaphorical language or the language of symbols and similes (or parables), as this has been explored by P. Ricoeur and E. Jüngel.[63]

As everyone knows, the language of simile is also the language used by Jesus. Metaphors and similes do not have for their function simply to depict a set of familiar facts; rather, they offer a new and creative description of reality. In so doing they employ a dialectic of the familiar and the strange. When, for example, it is said that 'Achilles is a lion', a familiar concept is being employed in an unusual and unfamiliar way in order to turn something familiar into something strange and thus to shed an entirely new light on it and illumine it. Metaphors are meant to open up a new vision of reality. Like scientific models and paradigms they are a heuristic tool and a speech strategy that serves to demolish a previous inadequate interpretation and pave the way for a new and more adequate one. Metaphor thus gives expression to a plus of reality, or, we may say, it makes reality speak to us in such a way that at the same time something more than the reality we encounter reaches expression. This is especially the case with the word 'God'. In the word 'God', reality expresses itself in such a way that at the same time the world becomes a place in which 'something' more than the world is seen. Talk about God makes the world a simile or parable of God; this takes place in such a way that the world shows itself capable of serving as a parable of God. The word 'God' is thus a simile which gives expression to the world as itself a simile. Consequently, metaphor, and especially talk about God, is always an effective word. It is not concerned with what the world has always been, with its abiding nature, but with its open-ended future. The word 'God' is thus an invitation to look upon the world as a simile and to enter into it as such, that is, to undergo a change of thinking and a conversion, to believe and hope. The semantic meaning of the word 'God' thus discloses at the same time the pragmatic meaning of the word. If the word 'God' is understood as a simile which discloses the simile-nature of the world, then it is not a projective extrapolation of reality (a projection) but an anticipation of a reality which invites us to a new practice that in turn proves itself to be authentic through experience and the doing of the truth. The word 'God' is a word that opens up a place of freedom and a future.

By way of summary I may say that both from the syntactico-grammatical standpoint and from the pragmatic and semantic standpoints language contains a movement to transcendence. Not only can it, but it intends always to say more than what the factual case is. Language draws its life from a pre-apprehension of the total meaning of reality and gives expression to this meaning in metaphors and similes. Thus language is at the same time a remembering of an unfulfilled hope of the human race and an anticipation of this hope. Even before language becomes explicitly religious language, it always already implies a religious dimension. Only in religious language does language reach its full stature. The fact is that the word 'God' is not a meaningless word; rather, where God is passed over in silence, speech itself is endangered. When God is no longer spoken of, there is danger of a Babel-like confusion of tongues.

If we try to adopt the results of the developments in linguistic philosophy and take seriously the creative power of language, which does not simply reflect the pre-given reality of our everyday or scientific experience but at every point embodies a preapprehension of a total meaning for reality and thus of the religious dimension, and which is consequently capable of a creative new description of reality in metaphor and of giving voice to something truly new, then we come face to face with the doctrine of analogy which is to be seen as the linguistic doctrine of faith.[64]

The dialectic of familiarity and strangeness which is characteristic of metaphorical speech is taken over in a new way in the doctrine of analogy. Analogous predications occupy a position between univocal and equivocal predictions.[65] A term is univocal when it is applied with one and the same meaning to various objects. For example, in the statements 'Peter is man' and 'Paul is man', the concept 'man' has the same meaning in both cases and is therefore predicated univocally. A term is equivocal when it has a different meaning as applied to different objects. Thus the word 'foot' is used with different meanings and therefore equivocally when it is applied to the appendage at the end of a human or animal leg, to a unit of measure, to a unit of verse meter, and to the lower edge of a sail. Analogous terms fall in between univocal and equivocal terms; they convey the idea of a similarity and comparability that includes both sameness and difference. More precisely, analogy means a similarity of relations. The idea was originally developed in mathematics (A:B = C:D), but is found in practically all the sciences; in biology, for example, it describes the similarities between various organisms, where the similarities are not the result of kinship (for example, the 'wings' of insects and birds, or even the parallel between the wings of birds, the fins of fish and the legs of higher vertebrates). Last but by no means least, metaphors can be translated into analogies. When, for example, we speak metaphorically of the evening of life, the meaning is that evening is related to day as old age is to life.

At first glance, analogous predication may seem to be a derivative and non-literal manner of speaking as compared with unambiguous, univocal predications. In reality, analogy is primary and not secondary in relation to unambiguous, univocal statements.[66] Unambiguous statements are possible only through differentiation from and correlation with other statements. Unambiguousness or univocity thus presupposes comparability, which includes both sameness and difference. Analogy is thus the presupposition and ground of possibility of univocal statements. Not without reason, then, do all the sciences, even the so-called exact sciences, depend on analogies.

Ancient philosophy prepared the way for the theological use of analogy as a linguistic form. On foundations laid by Parmenides and Heraclitus[67] Plato first introduced the concept of analogy into philosophy. He regards analogy as the most beautiful of all bonds,[68] as what binds reality together, mediates between all things, and creates unity and coherence. This centre assigns the extremes their place and links them together. Analogy here is thus a structural principle of the universe. For Aristotle, too, the *analogon* (the proportional) is a *meson*, an intermediate;[69] this is especially important to him philosophically when he comes to describe the unity (which embraces the various genera) of all reality insofar as it is being.[70] This unity cannot be strictly defined, because every definition presupposes a genus and a specific difference, whereas when there is question of being, there is no conceivable specific difference that is not itself somehow being. Being can therefore only be ascribed proportionately, that is, analogously, to the various spheres of being.[71] It is possible to speak of being only in relation to the one and in terms of the one.[72] Analogy, like metaphor, proves to be an indirect discourse that points beyond itself.

Wisdom 13.5 already makes it clear how fundamental a role analogy plays in speech about God, for we are told there that we can gain knowledge of God from the world by analogy (*analogōs*) because the order and beauty of the world point beyond the world. Of course, the ancient philosophers were already aware that the statements which we can make about God or the divine in this process are of a more negative character.[73] Properly speaking, we can say of God or the divine only what it is not: incorporeal, invisible, infinite, and so on. But these negative statements have a positive meaning. They point not to a nothing but to that which is beyond being and unity and cannot be grasped in concepts[74] and before which the mind that seeks conceptual knowledge can only stand silent and still.[75] The fathers of the church took over this *theologia negativa* and applied it even more radically. Dionysius the Pseudo-Areopagite (so called because he was wrongly identified with the disciple who attached himself to Paul on the Areopagus) already gives classical expression to the idea: 'In dealing with the divine, negations (*apophaseis*) are true, affirmations (*kataphaseis*) inadequate.'[76] The ultimate possibility for thought in this area is thus a realization that we do not know, a *docta ignorantia* (learned ignorance).[77] These insights ultimately found their way into the confession of faith of the Fourth Lateran Council (1215): 'For no similarity can be asserted between creature and creature unless an even greater dissimilarity is included.'[78] Here the self-enclosed philosophical doctrine of analogy, which sought to bring all oppositions into unity through a mean, was forced open in the direction of God, dynamically oriented beyond itself, and directed towards an Ever-Greater. The theological doctrine of anology when thus understood does not serve as the basis for a closed cosmological or ontological continuity, but on the contrary is a principle of ever greater openness. It directs us toward the ever greater mystery and as such does not supply the basis for a natural theology in the sense of a doctrine of God with a purely rational content, but is rather the grammar of faith.[79]

If we look more closely at the theological doctrine of analogy, we find that it contains three phases or three interconnected steps.[80] The *via affirmationis* (way of affirmation) takes as its starting point the positive connection between the finite and the infinite, as this emerges from creation; it knows God from his effects in the world. The *via negationis* (way of negation) denies the finite mode inherent in our statements and in the embodiment of all perfections in the finite realm. The *via eminentiae* (way of eminence), finally, says that these finite perfections belong to God in a higher degree, in a more sublime manner, and, in fact, in a simply all-surpassing way (*eminenter*). By following these steps we come to know more what God is not than what he is; we come to know that we cannot know him. Nonetheless we do know that we do not know. Ours is not an unqualified *ignorantia* but a *docta ignorantia*, an informed ignorance or conscious not-knowing. This does not mean, as Hegel thought, that our statements tail off into indeterminancy. Rather, we may say with Hegel that the *via negationis* presupposes the *via affirmationis*; the negation is not total but limited, denying only the finite mode of the positive perfection and not the perfection itself; the *via eminentiae* in turn negates the negation and to that extent posits something higher. It expresses the positive meaning of the negation. We are dealing therefore with a coherent process of mediation that in the end does not close in on itself but is entirely open.[81]

A more detailed examination reveals that in Scholastic theology there were various interpretations of the doctrine of analogy. Even the teaching of Thomas Aquinas, which is regarded as the classical statement of analogy, is not monolithic but shows some not unimportant changes at various stages of his literary production, and is therefore susceptible of divergent interpretations.[82] One important point is that Thomas speaks of an *analogia nominum* (analogy of names or terms) and thus an analogy of the names of God,[83] and not yet of an *analogia entis* (analogy of being), a concept which Cajetan introduces only in the sixteenth century and which acquired its status as a principle only in our own century through the work of E. Przywara. The Franciscan theologians, especially Bonaventure, show even greater reserve than Thomas does; in their view knowledge of God is possible only on the basis of revelation and of the analogy of faith which revelation establishes.[84] But, as G. Söhngen[85] and H. Urs von Balthasar[86] have shown, the analogy of faith presupposes an analogy of being, although as a pure possibility, that is, in the form of the human person's capacity for being addressed by God. Duns Scotus goes farthest in this direction. According to him, reason can attain only to a 'confused concept' of God as supreme being.[87] Reason cannot, however, know the nature of God. What God is can be known and expressed only in faith, in which God freely makes himself known.

In view of these intra-scholastic and thus intra-catholic differences the abrupt antitheses between *analogia entis* and *analogia fidei*, as formulated by K. Barth and, following him, a large number of Protestant theologians in their opposition to the doctrine of *analogia entis*, are very much relativized. Barth thought that the doctrine of *analogia entis* lumped God and the world together within an overarching ontological continuity and thus made God cease to be God. For this reason he regarded the analogy of being as an invention of Antichrist.[88] Later on, however, he developed his own *analogia relationis* and *operationis* (analogy of relation and operation) that is established by revelation but is also reflected in creation, which the covenant presupposes as an extrinsic basis.[89] This view of Barth's is structurally not very different from the Franciscan conception of analogy. There is, however, this difference, that the *analogia relationis* grounds only an external correspondence (*analogia proportionalitatis extrinsecae* – an analogy of extrinsic proportionality) and not an ontological correspondence (*analogia proportionalitatis intrinsecae* – an analogy of intrinsic proportionality) or, in other words, there is an analogy based on God's historical action and speaking (*analogia nominum!*) but not an analogy embodied in being itself.[90] This raises the deeper problem of the relation between being and history or a (salvation-)historical understanding of being. The question, then, is this: how can we transform the classical doctrine of analogy into a (salvation-)historical mode of thought?

A (salvation-)historical transformation of the doctrine of analogy is possible provided that we do not adopt the Greek metaphysics of the cosmos but follow modern philosophy in taking freedom as our point of departure.[91] For it can be shown that analogy represents an interpretation of the exercise of freedom. Freedom has its existence in the tension between infinite and finite, absolute and relative. It is possible for us in a free act to distance ourselves from the finite and conditioned experience of the moment and to conceive this as finite and conditioned, only because we reach beyond it to what is infinite and unconditioned. Only within the horizon of the infinite can we grasp the finite as finite; only in the light of the unconditioned and absolute can we grasp the conditioned as conditioned. Every finite concept presupposes a pre-apprehension of the infinite. Because of this structure of pre-apprehension that is proper to human freedom and understanding, there is always present in human freedom and understanding an implicit and latent knowledge of the unconditioned and infinite. We may even say: there is an analogical knowledge. For we cannot speak of the infinite and absolute in the same univocal way that we do of the finite and conditioned; otherwise we would render it finite and conditioned. But neither may we speak of the two as simply equivocal, for then the infinite could not serve as a horizon for the finite and shine out of the finite. Therefore, despite all the qualitative as well as quantitative distinctness there must be a correspondence between the two poles of our freedom, and to this relation of correspondence we give the name analogy.

Once analogy is no longer understood primarily as an interpretation of the cosmos but is conceived in light of the basic exercise of freedom, it takes on a historical shape; it then participates in the structure of freedom and even represents the very heart of freedom. It expresses the 'more' and the 'new' of freedom as compared with the pure facticity of the world. It leads us to see the world anew within the horizon of freedom and to understand the world as the place where freedom is exercised, or, in other words, to conceive the world as a historical world. The doctrine of analogy, when thus transformed, can therefore disclose to us the possibilities present in reality; this means, it can disclose reality's dimension of futurity. The pre-apprehension characteristic of freedom is thus an anticipation of a future that is more than an extrapolated past and present. A doctrine of analogy that is renewed in this way can be regarded as a speculative interpretation of the form of speech we call metaphor and of the gospel parables.

If we attempt to think of God within the horizon of freedom as perfect and absolute freedom to which our finite freedom reaches forward,[92] and if we then conceive of the world as the place for the exercise of freedom, there is no possibility of showing God to be a necessity posited by thought. As perfect freedom, God is more than necessary; because he is free, he can be recognized only in freedom, if and when he freely discloses himself to human beings. For this reason, when we attempt to think of God within the horizon of freedom, we are not indulging in abstract speculation about God but listening in concrete ways to the world, to determine whether and where traces of God's free revelation are to be found, and then, in the light of these traces, conceiving reality in a new way as the space of freedom and as history. The doctrine of analogy constrains us, then, to turn to the testimony of the Bible and to allow reality, in the light of that testimony, to disclose itself to us anew. At the same time, analogy equips us with a language that presupposes the self-disclosure of God and makes it possible for us in turn to give expression to this self-disclosure. In this sense the *analogia fidei* presupposes the *analogia entis* or *libertatis* and brings the latter to its fulfillment.

4. Knowledge of God

In our present-day world of science and technology the basic question of natural theology, which is the problem of responsible talk about God, will be answered, in the final analysis, not in terms of religious experience and religious language but in the light of reason. Without 'the exertion of the concept' experience and language become empty (Hegel). The question, then, is this: is faith in God intellectually honest and responsible or is faith in God possible only through the mind's abandonment of itself (*sacrificium intellectus*)? What is the relation between faith in God and human knowledge? Can we know or even prove God in a purely natural way?[93]

Let me get into the subject by asking first of all: what does it mean to know? Knowledge evidently includes far more than proof. Knowledge is a many-leveled vital process of the entire person; it is not a matter simply of conceptual abstraction but has a personal dimension and, above all, always presupposes experience. But knowledge differs from experience in that it is not only in contact with reality but also knows that it is in contact.[94] While direct experience involves only an absorption in its object and subjective interiorization of this object, knowledge is entirely present to the other but in that very act also entirely present to itself. It is reflective, that is, it turns back from the object to itself and becomes conscious of itself. Knowledge thus presupposes a relative independence from what is known; it is immediately linked to freedom. In knowledge we are one with things and human beings, but in such a way that at the same time we distance ourselves from them and distinguish them as objects from ourselves as subjects.

In agreement with Aristotle I may describe the difference between experience and knowledge in this way. Knowledge asks not only what is but also why it is; it also inquires into the grounds of this knowledge – including knowledge of and talk about God.[95] To that extent knowing also includes supplying arguments and proving. We must realize, of course, that proof is an analogous concept which derives its specific meaning from the object of the proof in each instance.[96] Common to all forms of proof is the fact that there is a process of substantiation that can be repeated by people generally. But proofs take different forms: the proof of a mathematician, the proof of a natural scientist who proceeds by experiment, the proof of a lawyer, a historian, a literary researcher, or the proof of a doctor when he diagnoses an illness. It is not surprising, therefore, that a proof of God's existence must be of a different kind from a proof in mathematics or the natural sciences. The 'proofs of God's existence' reach beyond the dimension of the physical and of the purely rational into the metaphysical world and the realm of the infinite, which by its very nature can no longer be conceived and comprehended in finite definitions. If we were to attempt to prove God as though he were just like any other being, and to reach him through calculation and establish his factuality after the manner of the scientist who objectifies and keeps his own distance, then, far from knowing him, we would profoundly fail to know him. Therefore we should not expect more from the proofs of God's existence than a well-founded invitation to faith. If freedom and knowledge are always interconnected, then it can be said of the knowledge of God that it is in a special way possible only in freedom. The proofs of God's existence are therefore a reasonable appeal to human freedom and an account rendered of the intellectual honesty of faith in God.

(a) The cosmological argument

The cosmological argument is probably the oldest of the proofs for God's existence. Its point of departure is the reality of the cosmos with its order and beauty, but also its mobility, frailty and contingency. Starting with experience of these aspects of the world, the argument inquires into the ultimate ground of the world; to this ground if finally gives the name 'God', which is derived from the language of religion.

The cosmological argument has been in use since practically the beginning of Western thought. The early Greek natural philosophers already argue back from the cosmos and its order to the ground of these. The fathers of the church take over this approach at a very early point in church history.[97] The argument is given its classical form in the East in the three ways of John Damascene[98] and in the West in the five ways of Thomas Aquinas.[99] Thomas takes as his starting point various aspects of the world of our experience (movement, causality, contingency, degrees of being, purposefulness). He then inquires into the cause of these phenomena. In this search for a cause it is not possible to engage in an infinite regress in its entirety as a series, no less than in its individual members since the series of causes is itself contingent and therefore requires an explanatory ground. There must therefore be a first cause that is not to be understood simply as the first member in a series of causes, but that grounds this series in its entirety and cannot itself have its ground in a higher cause. It must therefore be understood as self-subsistent, complete being, as that fullness of being which we call God. Even Kant, who subjected this proof to a searching critique, is of the opinion that it has an abiding importance. In Kant's view the arguments are not indeed compelling, but they do impose on the mind, so that even in the future attention will have to be paid to this proof. In particular, the so called teleological argument from purposefulness will always have to be mentioned with respect. It is 'the oldest, the clearest, and that most in conformity with the common reason of humanity'.[100]

As a matter of fact, even among present-day natural scientists arguments are to be found that resemble the cosmological argument, especially as this takes the form of the teleological proof. The natural scientist sees a marvellous order everywhere in nature. Admittedly, we know today that natural laws are laws formulated by man and that they have only a very high degree of probability; on the other hand, we also know that we can rely on these laws, for without such reliance technology, for example, would be impossible. There must therefore be something in the reality of nature itself that corresponds to the designs worked out by the human mind in the natural sciences; nature must be controlled by a rational order that cannot originate in man but only from a mind that embraces reality in its entirety. This consideration leads prominent natural scientists to a kind of new Platonism. They see in reality the embodiment of intellectual ideas which we creatively reconstruct in our natural laws. Thus nature, precisely as known by the natural sciences, makes it possible to accept the existence of God. This acceptance can, of course, take many forms. The argument just explained still leaves the way open for pantheism or panentheism (A. Einstein), for the acceptance of a personal God (W. Heisenberg) or for a Neoplatonic *theologia negativa* (C. F. v. Weizsäcker). But whatever the more specific interpretation of the relation between God and world, these various positions are in agreement that God alone can ground the scientific intelligibility of reality.

Nowadays it is philosophy rather than the natural sciences that challenges the proofs of God's existence. It was Kant that dealt them a first blow from which they have still not entirely recovered. Yet the more serious challenge to them comes today from nihilism rather than from Kant. For this reason, for us the starting point for the proofs of God's existence can no longer be simply an inquiry into the ground of the order in the world. For it is not only the 'what' but the 'that' of reality that calls for an explanation. The basic philosophical question is: why is there anything at all instead of nothing?[101] With this dimension of the question Thomas deals rather in his third way, the proof from contingency.[102] For the contingency of reality means its radical problematicalness. Everything that is was not at one time and will at some point cease to be; even more, everything that is could also not be. Everything that is is therefore suspended over the abyss of non-being; it is inclined toward nothingness and controlled through and through by nothingness. This nothing is not a minimally structured, perhaps ever so weak and shadowy reality; nothing is nothing. It is a pure concept of the understanding which we use in order to bring out the problematical character of being. It is with this radical problematical character that we must begin.

If we do start here, we notice something remarkable; it is precisely when we take the possibility of not-being as our horizon that we realize the positive character of being. Despite its vanity, being does not fall prey to nothingness; rather, the wonder of being reveals itself to us precisely in the face of nothingness. Precisely when confronted with the non-evidentiality of reality we experience its reliability, solidity and beauty. Thus being reveals a power within it that resists nothingness. This may be stated formally in the classical principle of contradiction: insofar as it is, what is cannot not be. Thomas says the same thing in a more substantive way: nothing is so contingent that it does not contain within itself some element of necessity. This element of the unconditioned in the conditioned is not first brought home to us by a complicated proof; it is grasped unthematically in every knowledge of the conditioned, since it is only in the light of the necessary that we know the conditioned as conditioned. When thus understood, the cosmological argument is in the final analysis simply reflecting this primordial knowledge; it is an explanation of the astonishment felt at the wonder of being.[103]

In its radical form, the proof from contingency, the cosmological argument, thus brings us into the presence of the marvellous fact that being is, even though (to use a paradox) non-being could exist. We are therefore confronted with a pure 'that', the 'what' of which we are unable to grasp.[104] We are dealing here with a limit-concept of the mind, for we grasp something of which we can say only that we do not grasp it. We know what it is not but not what it is. In this idea the mind that seeks to conceive and explain reaches beyond itself. We are confronted with a groundless ground that lies beyond our explanatory thinking. Precisely when we deal with the ultimate ground we must put aside our explanatory thinking and trust ourselves to the absolutely Groundless. And that which is an abyss for our thinking is also an abyss for our conduct and our striving for security. Man faced with groundlessness, with the abyss, is overcome by anxiety. There is nothing to which he can hold tight in the abyss of *Dasein*. He can only trust himself to the groundless Ground. When finite values that have been absolutized collapse, when the idols fall, only God, the Absolute, can give life stability and meaning. A conversion of mind and conduct is needed, and only through such a conversion is knowledge of God possible. Such a conversion does not disclose to us God's being in itself, but it does allow us to grasp reality in a new way as an image and likeness of the mystery of God and thus to understand it as meaningful. Even in its incomprehensibility, the knowledge of God is authenticated by the fact that it makes the world and its order intelligible and thus proves its authenticity by means of the phenomena of reality. This is due not least to the fact that the acknowledgment of God means a demythologization and de-ideologization of all the finite realities that have been turned into absolutes. Man thus becomes free over against the world; he need not become the slave of anything or anyone. The acknowledgment that God alone is God makes it possible to be human in a human way. At this point the cosmological argument leads into the anthropological argument.

(b) The anthropological argument

The anthropological argument takes as its point of departure not the external reality of the cosmos but the inner reality of the human spirit. Depending on whether one prefers here to start with intellectual knowledge or with moral willing (or freedom), one will speak of the noetic (ideological) proof or the moral proof.

The writers of antiquity already saw that in the spiritual nature of man there is a presentiment and tacit presupposition that something divine exists. These writers pointed especially to the phenomenon of conscience as a testimony to God. The fathers of the church took up this notion and spoke of an idea of God that is innate in the human person.[105] Tertullian even speaks of the witness given by the *anima naturaliter christiana* (the soul that is by its nature Christian).[106] Above all others, however, it was Augustine who pointed the way inward and taught men to look for God in the heart that is restless until it finds him.[107] In his own spirit man finds truth regarding which he can, in principle, have no doubt. For, long before Descartes, Augustine says: '*Si enim fallor sum*' (If I am deceived then I exist).[108] He finds it impossible to interpret this truth as being anything but an enlightenment from God. 'Therefore we cannot know God except by going beyond ourselves within ourselves.'[109] The same arguments are to be found in Thomas Aquinas. According to him, in every act of knowledge of a finite entity we apprehend infinite being, for it is only in the light of the infinite that we can know the finite as finite. Thus in every act of knowledge we implicitly know God.[110] In like manner our willing strives beyond all that is finite.

In this process there cannot be an infinite regress; there must therefore be a final goal. We are free in the face of finite goods only because we strive toward the absolute good. All of our striving is implicitly a striving toward God; he is loved along with everything else we love. In Scholasticism these arguments admittedly take second place to the cosmological argument; only in the modern age do they move into the foreground. In his third Meditation Descartes takes as his point of departure the idea of God that is given in human consciousness; he cannot find the ground for this in the finite human mind itself but only in the reality of God.[111] The idea of God is of fundamental importance to Descartes especially because he can ensure the certainty of our knowledge of the external world only through the idea of God who embraces both man and world. As Descartes needs God as guarantee of knowledge, so Kant needs him as a postulate of freedom. For freedom can find the blessedness it seeks only if there is a pre-established harmony between freedom and nature. But this in turn is possible only if both nature and freedom are embraced by the all-inclusive freedom of God.[112]

It was owing to the Belgian Jesuit J. Maréchal that the modern approach through subjectivity was accepted into Catholic theology.[113] Maréchal influenced K. Rahner, J. B. Lotz, M. Müller, B. Welte, J. Möller, E. Coreth, W. Kern and others. J. H. Newman had already independently pointed out the presence in the human conscience of a real apprehension of God.[114] In the following remarks I shall adopt the approach of the Maréchal school, but with H. Frings I shall take freedom as my starting point rather than consciousness.[115]

It is constitutive of human freedom that it is in tension between the finite and the infinite. Only because it is open to the infinite can it be free in relation to the finite. For this reason there is no intra-wordly encounter that can bring human freedom its proper fulfillment. The person can reach fulfillment only through encounter with a freedom that is unconditioned not only in its formal claims but also in its material possession of the good. Only in encounter with absolute freedom can the person reach inner peace and inner fulfillment. In every other exercise of freedom there is a hopeful but always unsatisfied pre-apprehension of the complete realization of freedom. This pre-apprehension of complete fulfillment makes possible, and supplies the light and strength for, every free act. The idea of an utterly fulfilled and all-fulfilling absolute freedom is thus a necessary idea; it is a transcendental condition for the possibility of freedom.

But is there a reality that corresponds to this idea? As in the case of the cosmological argument, so here we are confronted with a limit-definition. For the encounter with absolute freedom is outside the conditions of our present mode of existence. If possible at all, it is possible only in death. It would therefore be possible to speak of God only in a pre-apprehension of 'eternal life' and the 'vision of God'. In our present life we must be satisfied with fragmentary anticipations. Is it not, therefore, enough for us to settle for grasping the absolute in ever-new symbols that constantly elude us? According to a view that is widespread today it is better to be modest and renounce any absolute determination of meaning. But is human freedom adequately grounded by means of an indeterminately infinite horizon, or must it derive its ultimate grounding from a determinately infinite goal? Only this much can be said by way of answer: *if* there is to be an absolute fulfillment of meaning for man, this requires absolute freedom as a condition. The question then is: is there then to be an absolute fulfillment of meaning? It was Christianity that brought into the world such an absolute fulfillment of meaning. In the final analysis this fulfillment stands or falls in dependence on a decision in which freedom decides about itself and its own meaning. Only in freedom can the meaning of freedom be decided. This means, however, that God as perfect freedom which brings our freedom to fulfillment cannot be demonstrated to anyone from outside unless that person interiorly opens himself to this truth. The person must be ready to anticipate death and to surrender himself in order to gain himself. The anthropological argument can only explicitate the alternatives on which a decision must be made. It can, in addition, show that the choice of God is meaningful and even the more meaningful of the alternatives. When all is said and done the anthropological argument boils down to Pascal's 'wager': 'If you win you win everything, if you lose you lose nothing.'[116]

The anthropological argument has a decisive advantage over the cosmological argument: it points not to a necessary absolute being, a supreme Good, and so on, but to perfect freedom. Freedom is something the human person can recognize only if it discloses and reveals itself in history. For this reason, what we encounter in the anthropological argument is not an abstract God but the living God of history. Thus the anthropological argument leads us to the proof of God's existence from the philosophy of history.

(c) The argument from the philosophy of history

Down to the present time, relatively little attention has been paid in Catholic theology to the argument from the philosophy of history; this is still the case today. The lack is all the harder to understand since the argument from divine providence in connection with scripture already plays a role in the fathers of the church.[117]

It was Augustine who in his *The City of God* wrote the most brilliant of all theologies of history and one that was influential for many centuries. The thesis that history is a work and, at the same time, a sign of divine providence exerted an influence into the modern age, in Vico and Bossuet and finally Hegel.[118] Hegel looks upon his entire philosophy of history as a proof that providence rules the world; for this reason he interprets his philosophy of history as a theodicy that is being worked out in history and that he wishes to see replacing the metaphysical theodicy of Leibniz.[119]

More than any other, it was J. S. Drey, the father of the Catholic Tübingen school, who, in critical and creative dialogue with German idealism, developed the idea of God in the perspective of universal history.[120] In contemporary Protestant theology W. Pannenberg has expounded a theology in the light of universal history; in his work he harks back to Hegel but also depends on Dilthey, Heidegger and Gadamer.[121] In its Marxist or Neo-marxist form, Hegel's philosophy of history has exerted a wide influence on political theology and liberation theology.[122] For Hegel's idealist interpretation of history, according to which it is spirit that determines history, became problematical to the post-idealist thinkers (the later Schelling, Feuerbach, Marx, Kierkegaard, etc.). They acknowledged the facticity of reality as both incapable of being derived from spirit and as nonetheless a given that cannot be ignored. K. Marx believed that idealism should be turned upside down and that history should be derived from changing socio-economic conditions. According to Marx, mediation between humanity and world is through practice and more specifically through work, in which humanity shapes the world but at the same time is determined by the world,[123] until finally humanity is entirely reconciled to the world in the communist kingdom of freedom.[124]

The Scholastic tradition, to which I attach myself here, intends to move beyond the one sidedness of both idealism and materialism and sees itself as a realism or, in many cases, more specifically an ideal-realism.[125] It acknowledges subject and object, spirit and matter, intellectual knowledge and sense experience as each having a relative independence, and thus does not simply derive any one of them from the others. However, realism, being an ideal-realism, does see spirit as the more comprehensive reality. For in the act of intellectual knowledge and in free practice human beings appropriate reality for themselves. On the one hand, this appropriation is of such a kind that in this very act of becoming one with the world spirit sees itself as a relatively independent entity, while at the same time acknowledging the relative independence of material reality. On the other hand, this relative unity and relative penetration of matter by spirit presupposes that matter is not unqualifiedly spirit-less but rather has a structure that makes it analogous to spirit.[126] If matter did not 'somehow' have a spiritual character and if it were not ordered to spirit, we would be unable to discern laws of nature which are more than human projections. The very knowledge of nature, and especially the sciences of nature, presuppose that spirit embraces both subject and object, establishing each of them in relative independence. This interconnection is revealed and realized in the historical intercourse of man and world. Consequently, a historical vision of the world signifies that reality is not simply something objectively pregiven, but rather that the subject plays a part in the constitution of the world, just as the subject in its turn is mediated through the world. Thus reality is constituted in a dialectical interplay of world and humanity.[127]

This historical understanding of reality entails consequences for the God-question. For, given this basic approach, it follows that the basic human situation in the world is at first sight a paradoxical one.[128] On the one hand, the human intellect stands superior over all reality, for in principle it can make all reality its own by knowing it. In its freedom with respect to pregiven reality it can inquire into everything and overwhelm it with questions. As Aristotle and Thomas Aquinas used to say, the intellect is '*quodammodo omnia*' – it is 'in a manner, all things'.[129] But this very '*quodammodo*' (in a manner) points to a limitation that must not be overlooked and that signifies a boundary which may not be crossed (unlike what we find in rationalism and idealism). On the other hand, then, this 'in a manner' indicates that reality is also greater than man and his mind. Man can never completely know, still less completely control, reality as a whole; reality always proves larger, broader and deeper than man's reach, until in death man finally succumbs to reality. But even the details of reality man can likewise never completely penetrate; he can never completely comprehend them. In the final analysis, matter eludes man's grasp.

Is man's situation therefore meaningless and absurd? The suspicion of meaninglessness that was fostered by nihilism at the collapse of idealism is countered by our experience that partial fragmentary meaning is available; I refer to successfully acquired knowledge of reality, such as may be seen, for example, in technology, and above all to the experience of the happiness of love between human beings. In every successful knowing and every successful practice meaning is revealed that checks the acceptance of total meaninglessness and that keeps alive the question of the meaning of reality as a whole and even leads to a well-founded hope that the experience of partial meaning presupposes the meaningfulness and therefore the rationality of the whole.[130] Every experience of partial meaning proves to be a hope-inspired pre-apprehension of the unconditioned meaning of the whole. But, given the finiteness of human knowledge and action, it is not possible to establish and prove this unconditioned meaning of the whole, either theoretically or practically. All that is possible here is a founded hope, a *docta spes*. Above all, the meaningfulness of the whole cannot come from finite man but only from a meaning and a spirit that embraces both man and the world, from a spirit which is at the same time the all-determining reality and thus from what in the language of religion we call God.

This argument can be made a bit more concrete. The historical hope of man is ultimately a hope of justice, that is, a hope of being acknowledged as man. Hope thus understood is not a position taken or a plank in a party platform; it is a transcendental condition for the possibility of a common being-human. As human beings we simply cannot stop hoping that in the end the murderer will not triumph over his innocent victim.[131w10] If we were to abandon this hope, we would abandon ourselves. On the other hand, unjustified violence can be eliminated only by violence. Consequently we are caught up in a satanic cycle of guilt and revenge from which we can be redeemed only by a wholly new beginning that cannot be derived from the conditions of history. The pre-apprehension of the future thus implies a pre-apprehension of the new justice of God and his reign. But this justice must also be applied to the dead. Any hope of the future would be cynical that was built on the toil, suffering and renunciation of previous generations and that offered these as victims on the altar of the future. Consequently, unless we are willing to cut hope in half, as it were, and limit it to a future generation and to those who are in the vanguard of progress, our hope must imply the God of hope who gives life to the dead.[132] The future cannot therefore be simply a prolongation and intensification of the present (future as *futurum*); it must rather be the future of a self-sufficient power of the future (future as *adventus*).

The God of hope to which the historico-philosophical argument brings us is not the God who stands at the end: the God who makes his appearance at the term of an intellectual regression to the ground of reality and who as the unmoved Mover can only be an end and never a beginning. Rather, this God of hope is the living God who can be a beginning; he is the power of the future, the one who is coming. The God of hope cannot be thought of as other than absolute freedom. Therefore this proof of God's existence can only be a kind of hypothesis that only the advance of history can verify. It represents a justifiable decision in behalf of a particular way of viewing reality, a paradigm which has proved its validity according to the testimony of the biblical writers and of all true Christians down to our own day and which we in turn must verify in our own experience. The arguments from the philosophy of history make especially clear a point that has already emerged in connection with the other arguments: in the final analysis it is impossible to prove God's existence from some authority external to him; he must show himself. The idea of God can be established as a true one only if we take into account its specific implications. This is the way followed by the so-called ontological argument, to which all the other arguments boil down.

(d) The ontological argument

All the proofs of God's existence that have thus far been discussed have a common underlying structure: they start with cosmological, anthropological or historical experiences and ask what the ground and meaningful goal of these experiences must be. A third step in the argument then identifies absolute being with God: 'and this is what everyone calls "God".' Because of this identification of being or the ultimate ground of being with God it is possible to speak of the onto-theological constitution of classical metaphysics.[133] The classical tradition admittedly paid little attention to this identification; there was a tactic consensus that the ultimate, supreme and all-embracing reality is God. Modern atheism and especially nihilism has destroyed this consensus. Debate with these positions had made it clear that no obvious statements about this ultimate reality are possible. Only

God can make God plain. But this means that God cannot be proved in the strict sense of the word 'prove'; he must make himself known. Therefore our thinking must not move solely from the world to God; it must also move from God to the world, and the idea of God must be tested by the reality of man, world and history. This is the way followed in the proof of God's existence that was set forth by Anselm of Canterbury and that has since Kant been called the ontological argument.[134]

Anselm develops the ontological argument in his *Proslogion*, in which he seeks to concentrate into a single argument the many arguments offered in his previous work, the *Monologion*. He tells us that he had in despair decided to drop this plan, but finally the idea forced itself upon him and ended by filling him with joy.[135] The ontological argument thus represents an intellectual experience, an intellectual breakthrough, or, more accurately, the experience of truth breaking through into thought, a being overpowered by truth. Correspondingly, this argument, unlike the others, moves from above downward; it starts from above, from a grasp of, or a being grasped by, the idea of God, in order to demonstrate the reality of God. For this reason Anselm begins with a prayer: 'Teach me to seek You, and reveal Yourself to me as I seek; for unless You instruct me I cannot seek You, and unless You reveal Yourself I cannot find You.' Where and how does God reveal himself? By creating 'in me Your image so that I may remember, contemplate, and love You'.[136] Anselm's ontological argument is thus connected with his doctrine of the image of God in man. This connection is usually overlooked. If it is taken into consideration, his argument ceases to seem purely aprioristic and deductive and proves to be close to the teaching of the church fathers on the image of God or the idea of God innate in man.

Anselm now attempts to bring God's image in man into consciousness. Thought grasps God as that 'than which nothing greater can be thought' (*'aliquid quo maius nihil cogitari potest'*).[137] Thought experiences the reality of God not in an ordinary concept but in a limit-concept, which expresses the dynamic movement of thought beyond itself. Logically, therefore, Anselm defines God simply as that 'than which nothing greater can be thought', but also as 'something greater than can be thought'.[138] Consequently, it must be said of the mind that it 'rationally comprehends that [God] is incomprehensible'.[139] In the idea of God, then, which is innate in the human spirit as image of God, thinking is radically directed beyond itself. The ontological argument is simply a logical 'ex-plication' or unfolding of the ontological constitution of reason, (*ratio*). Anselm states the argument as follows: 'Surely that than which a greater cannot be thought cannot be only in the understanding. For if it were only in the understanding, it could be thought to exist also in reality – which is greater [than existing only in the understanding]. Therefore if that than which a greater cannot be thought existed only in the understanding, then that than which a greater *cannot* be thought would be that than which a greater *can* be thought! But surely this conclusion is impossible. Hence, without doubt, something than which a greater cannot be thought exists both in the understanding and in reality.'[140] In short, the idea of God cannot without contradiction be thought of as merely an idea.[141]

Anselm's thinking is caricatured when objection is raised to him that in the ontological argument he is deducing existence from the concept of existence or arguing from the idea of God to the existence of God. This objection to the ontological argument was already being voiced during the lifetime of Anselm. In a work entitled *Liber pro insipiente* (Book On Behalf of the Fool) the monk Gaunilo objected that Anselm was making a leap from the ideal order to the real; but from the idea of a perfect island its real existence does not follow.[142] Kant raised a similar objection later on, though he started with different presuppositions: a hundred dollars in the mind are not a hundred real dollars; you cannot derive existence from the concept of existence.[143] In the language of the schools the objection runs thus: the ontological argument is a sophism because it contains four terms. True enough, from the concept of God it follows that God exists, but the concept of existence is ambiguous, for it can mean either existence in the mind or real existence. From the idea that existence is necessary follows only a conceptual existence, not a real existence. These criticisms fail to grasp the structure of the ontological argument. The argument is concerned with the existence not of just any idea but of the supreme idea which is required for thinking and in which thinking transcends itself.

Anselm is entirely a Platonic thinker for whom thinking is inconceivable except as a participation in being and as an interpretation of being. Augustine had already characterized God as that 'than which there is nothing greater' ('*quo nihil superius*').[144] We can, to be sure, know God only in the light of the truth which is God himself and which is present to the soul.[145] Knowledge of God therefore presupposes illumination by the truth which is God. In the *Proslogion* Anselm relates this idea to the image of God in the interior of man where the reality of God directly manifests itself. The ontological argument is meant to give expression to this ontological connection. It is therefore typical that thinkers in the Augustinian tradition (Alexander of Hales, Bonaventure, Duns Scotus and others) should, in connection with the doctrine of illumination, give their adherence to Anselm. The idealist thinkers of the modern age – Descartes, Spinoza, Leibniz, Hegel and others – likewise accept his arguments, although they reinterpret it in their own manner. Especially for Hegel, the self-interpretation of the Absolute takes place in thinking; the proofs of God's existence are an exegesis of this necessary connection.[146]

These idealist presuppositions provide the basis for a second objection that carries the criticism an essential step further. It, too, is already to be found in Kant. Precisely because the concept of God is a necessary and supreme concept, it is a limit-concept which the mind cannot more fully define. It is 'an abyss on the verge of which human reason trembles in dismay'.[147] Kant concludes that we can use this concept only in a regulative and not in a constitutive way.[148] It is at this point that the later Schelling begins his critique of the ontological argument. According to him, in the idea of God thought constructs something 'in the presence of which thought falls silent and reason humbles itself', and in which reason 'is carried outside of itself in a state of unqualified ecstasy'. When it proposes this idea it is 'as it were rendered immobile, as it were rendered paralysed'.[149] Therefore Schelling characterizes this entire philosophy with its ascent through dialectic as a negative philosophy. Admittedly, thought cannot rest content with this negative outcome. Man longs for meaning and he can find this only in absolute freedom.[150] Schelling therefore drafts a second, positive philosophy. Its starting point is necessary being, interpreted as absolute freedom, and it seeks to show that this absolute freedom is the Lord of being, that is, God. It thus follows a course opposite to that of the ontological argument: It moves not from concept to existence but from existence to nature or concept.[151] Schelling's purpose, then, is to show the divinity of the absolute and to 'conceptualize the absolute in the form of God'.[152] Here, according to Schelling, is the difficulty encountered by the whole of metaphysics. Metaphysics has identified the concept of supreme existence with the concept of God; in so doing it became an ontotheology. Schelling's thesis in opposition to ontotheology is: 'The necessarily existent is not necessary, but is in actuality the necessary, necessarily existing essence of God.'[153] This non-necessary but factual connection cannot be shown *a priori*, but only *a posteriori*. This is done not by having thought ascend from experience to God but rather by having it descend to experienced reality in order to conceive reality in the light of what necessarily exists and thus to prove that what necessarily exists is Lord of being, or God.[154] Schelling himself, indeed, did not apply this brilliant insight in a consistent way. Had he remained consistent with himself, he would not have begun his positive philosophy with speculative considerations on the intra-divine powers; he could only have projected it as a reflection on the historical self-manifestation of God.

In contemporary philosophy, the ontological argument is once again being more and more widely accepted, although in a form that corresponds to a changed context of the problem.[155] It is no longer possible today, of course, to accept without qualification the Platonic idea of participation which forms the background of the argument, since this idea already presupposes the existence of God and simply shows the intrinsic necessity of the presupposition. We must start with the more restrictive post Hegelian context for the problem, in which thinking, which since Anselm's time has established itself as pure thought set free of all ties to theological justifications, finds itself in an aporia with regard to the God-question. It must necessarily think an ultimate, absolute and infinite, but it is no longer able to grasp this conceptually and to define its nature univocally. In the end thinking necessarily transcends itself, inasmuch as it thinks something which it is essentially incapable of thinking out any further, because the infinite cannot be captured in any finite concept. God, therefore, can be known only through God; he can be known only when he himself allows himself to be known. In the final analysis, that is also the meaning of the Augustinian doctrine of illumination, and Anselm's argument is in that tradition. It was along this line, too, that the theologians of the Tübingen School, especially J. E. Kuhn, tried to restore the ontological argument.[156]

According to Kuhn, the arguments which start from experience – the cosmological, anthropological and historico-philosophical proofs – have probative force only in the light of the idea of God that is innate in man. This idea is already part of us in a general and still indefinite form by reason of the image of God that is in us as creatures; the idea is renewed, deepened and defined by the revelation of God. Consequently the proofs of God do not introduce the idea of God for the first time; they do not produce the idea but rather explicitate and concretize it and prove its truth by way of a reflective meditation on the world. The idea of God is as it were the light that illumines these considerations. In contemporary theology it is W. Pannenberg who most fully represents Anselm's concern as modified in the modern age. According to him, the historically transmitted idea of God must be measured by its own implications. 'The idea of God as, by definition, the reality which determines everything must be substantiated by the experienced reality of man and the world.' Pannenberg says that this method 'is identical in form with the ontological proof of the existence of God, the self-proof of God'.[157]

As compared, then, with the aporia of pure thought in its movement from below to above, the ontological argument effects an intellectual turnabout and in its thinking moves from above, interpreting reality from the standpoint of the historically transmitted idea of God, which in pure thought sheds only a very general, indefinite and ambiguous light. This argument thus effects a definition of the idea of the absolute, which is itself indeterminate, and it intellectually substantiates this definition by means of the reality of world, man and history. The substantiation is accomplished in such a way that in the reflective contemplation of reality the idea of God shows itself capable of opening up reality, making connections visible, facilitating life and encouraging freedom. The conflict between faith and unbelief is therefore not a disagreement about some kind of other or higher world but about the understanding and existence of the reality of man and world. Faith in God thus makes a claim: the believer sees more. It aims to show, in the empirically ascertainable, something more than is empirically ascertainable. It opens up the sign and symbol dimension of reality. The parabolic and metaphorical language of faith shows reality itself to be a parable. This 'more' is not susceptible of proof in the sense of an incontrovertible demonstration. But in the light cast by an unconditional option for meaning a plurality of signs and pointers to meaning yield a certainty at the level of the whole person.

It was J. H. Newman especially who worked out this proof from probabilities.[158] Newman is particularly interested in knowledge of the concrete. Abstract conclusions are of no real help in this area; at both ends they are as it were suspended in the air: on the side of the first principles which they must in every instance presuppose, and on the side of the results achieved, which never reach down to concrete reality. When we deal with concrete knowledge, the only possible way to proceed is through a cumulus of probabilities which, taken together, lead to certainty. Such a procedure admittedly requires a certain intuition, an instinct, a discernment, a power of judgment; Newman himself speaks of an illative sense, which acts as a light illumining our concrete deductions. In this respect he is at one also with the Neoplatonic and Augustinian doctrine of knowledge, which speaks of an illumination. Pascal speaks in a comparable way of the knowledge of the heart: 'The heart has its reasons of which reason knows nothing.'[159] As examples of this kind of concrete reasoning process Newman cites the archeologist, who from individual finds reconstructs an entire world with its cultural life, or the lawyer who from clues reconstructs the course of a crime, or the doctor who from particular symptoms of illness forms a comprehensive diagnosis. In each case a degree of brilliance and originality is required. Put more generally and in the terms I have been using, this means: only in the light of pre-apprehension of unconditioned meaning can we grasp the connections of meaning in the reality of our experience.

The option for meaning that is made in faith in God proves itself adequate to our experience of reality by virtue of the fact that since it is a pre-apprehension of irreducible mystery, it cannot claim to be a complete explanation of reality and all its phenomena. On the contrary, the option for meaning that is present in faith is supremely critical of any total explanation of the world. This option brings with it a decided capacity for being critical of ideologies, because it points beyond all absolutizations of finite values – possessions, power, pleasure, honour, or nation, race or class to an ever greater freedom, and thus constantly makes us free and keeps history open-ended. It has not only an affirmative function but a critical one as well. The credibility of the faith is thus shown precisely in the fact that it has no need of suppressing any kind of experience of reality. It has no need of putting on ideological blinders and of reducing the many-leveled and ambiguous whole of reality to a single dimension, be this the dimension of the positivist or the spiritualist, the pessimist or the optimist. Faith can do justice to both the greatness and the wretchedness of man.

It is not possible apodictically to demonstrate the validity of this outlook to anyone; it is possible, however, to bear witness to it with good arguments. It becomes evident only to one who is ready to enter into it and change his views; one who, in Augustine's terms, purifies his heart and, in the language of the Bible, contemplates reality with the eyes of the heart. This means that in faith man finds the meaning of his existence, provided that he makes a personal commitment to faith. Faith itself rejects the philistine view that truth and goodness will 'prevail' 'by their own power' and without a commitment of the person. Faith is the noble and courageous decision to accept the risks life entails and in the process to risk life itself.

Faith in God is the foundational and primordial act of the spirit. Faith engages neither the mind alone nor the will alone, but the whole person. Knowing and willing are thus parts of a single act of faith; in faith the two meld into an inner unity. For this reason, faith in God is neither a purely intellectual belief-faith nor a purely volitional decision-faith nor a matter simply of feeling. It is an act of the whole person, an act in which alone the person reaches fully human stature.

With this recapitulatory thesis we have reached the goal of our reflections on the problem of natural theology. The question with which we began was the question of the human accountability of faith in God and in his revelation. The result of our reflections is this: man is the being who in the experiences, of his life, in his speaking and in his knowing, pre-apprehends the absolute mystery of an unconditioned, perfect freedom. It is this believing and hoping pre-apprehension that sets the mark of freedom on his knowing and acting in this world. Consequently he is in quest of signs in which the absolute mystery of an unconditioned freedom addresses him and communicates itself to him. He is the being who lives in the presence of the infinite mystery and who waits and hopes for the free self-revelation of this mystery. He goes in search of signs and words in which God reveals himself to him.

V

Knowledge of God in Faith

1. The revelation of God

The result of all that has been said so far can be summed up thus: the divine mystery is manifest in the midst of our world. We can encounter it in nature which, being God's creature, points to its creator; in the mystery which becomes visible within man himself; and in history which is vitalized by a hope that looks for more than history. The mystery of man, of his world and of history points beyond itself. To this first thesis we must, of course, add a second: in the mystery of man and his world God is also hidden. We can grasp the 'that' of this mystery, but its 'what' is concealed from us. As a result the mystery remains indeterminate for pure thought and is susceptible of varying interpretations. There are indeed arguments which explain this mystery as an existent, holy mystery that is distinct from the world. But a final clarity in this area is not possible to isolated thought. We cannot penetrate the nature of the mystery, because all the similarity that marks our statements about it is accompanied by an ever greater dissimiliarity. The inner nature of this divine mystery is therefore hidden from us, inaccessible, a closed book. As finite beings, all of our living, thinking and acting is always already being done in the light of a pre-apprehension of the infinite; but this 'infinite' is only a pre-apprehension and not a concept; it is a limit-concept which we are unable to turn into a concept. Our thinking is always struck dumb in its presence. If the infinite is to be accessible to us, it must disclose and make itself known to us; it must reveal itself. For this reason revelations are an essential part of all religions.[1]

At all times and in all religions human beings have looked for traces and signs that would help them grope after the mystery of God. The word 'revelation' serves as a categorical expression for those worldly experiences, areas of experience and aspects of experience in which man sees signals, signs and symbols in which the inexpressible divine mystery is disclosing itself to him. Revelation is therefore first of all an indirect experience, that is, an experience 'in, with and under' other experiences in which God or the divine makes its appearance (theophany) or makes his will known (divination). Among such experiences are astonishing – i.e., wonder-awakening – experiences in nature (storms, lightning, thunder, gales, sun, etc.), in inter-personal encounter (especially the fascination of man and woman for one another), in history (victories and defeats, the establishment of cities and states, etc.); also cultural events, dreams and the interpretations of dreams, the drawing of lots as oracles, the ordeal (understood as a 'judgment of God'), and so on. Ecstatic phenomena such as auditions and visions play a role no less than do tradition, reflection, meditation and contemplations.

These experiences are accessible to people generally and can nowadays be scientifically 'explained', at least in principle, by psychology, for example, or sociology. But for the religious man something more takes place in, with and under these worldly experiences; he sees them as signs and symbols of the divine mystery revealing itself. For religious man a new horizon and all-embracing coherence makes itself known in and under these worldly experiences which are available to everyone; for him a light is turned on, as it were, in which the whole of reality is seen in a new way. In the terminology of contemporary linguistic philosophy we may speak of disclosure situations in which a particular event opens up a total meaning and a total context.[2] We must therefore distinguish between the categorical concept of revelation (revelations) in the sense of individual revelatory events and the transcendental concept of revelation, that is, that supra-categorical occurrence in which the mystery that holds sway in and above all reality discloses itself.[3] In this second sense of the word, revelation is not a given but something that gives itself; not a fact, but an occurrence (a verbal noun). And since this occurrence is the basis of religious faith, it cannot in turn be justified. One 'has' it only insofar as one accepts to be involved in it and opens oneself to it, and therefore in an act of religious faith (these two words being understood here in a provisionally very broad and general way).

Faith in this broad sense is not a categorical belief in certain suprarational truths; rather it is the fundamental choice whereby the person opens himself to this dimension of divine mystery and, in terms of it, understands and encounters life, world, man and history. Religious faith does not have its existence, therefore, at the level of a regional and categorical act; it is neither an act of understanding alone nor willing alone nor feeling alone.

Religious faith exists at the level of a decision regarding life, a decision that embraces the whole person and all his acts. It is a kind of primordial choice, a fundamental option, a decision in behalf of a certain understanding of reality as a whole, together with a decision to adopt a specific practical attitude to this reality. As a responsible human act the decision is a response to revelation; the person knows himself to be invited, challenged and supported by this revelation. His decision is an act of primordial trust, understood as an act of self-giving.

Biblical revelation freely acknowledges the existence of such revelatory events outside the 'official' salvation history of the Old and New Testaments. The Bible tells us in various passages of 'saintly pagans' who are witnesses to the living God: Abel, Enoch, Melchizedek, Job, and others. After all, God 'desires all men to be saved and to come to the knowledge of the truth' (I Tim. 2.4). For this reason the Second Vatican Council teaches:

> Throughout history even to the present day, there is found among different peoples a certain awareness of a hidden power, which lies behind the course of nature and the events of human life. At times there is present even a recognition of a supreme being, or still more of a Father . . . The Catholic Church rejects nothing of what is true and holy in these religions. She has a high regard for the manner of life and conduct, the precepts and doctrines which, although differing in many ways from her own teaching, nevertheless often reflect a ray of that truth which enlightens all men.[4]

The meaning of this general history of God's revelation is first made known to us when we reach the history of special revelation, that is, the history of revelation as set down in the Old and New Testaments. For in the general history of revelation the picture of God remains ambiguous. Alongside noble insights is often to be seen the grimacing of the demonic. A further consideration is that God does not will to approach man solely as an individual, independently of his reciprocal ties with others, but also wills to reveal himself to man as a social and historical being. His will is to gather human beings into a people and to make this people the light of the nations (Isa. 42.6).[5]

The theological concept of revelation is admittedly a very obscure one and extremely hard to pin down.[6] The usual procedure is to start with individual revelations or truths of revelation; by 'truths of revelation' is meant individual truths which are not accessible to the unaided human mind and which God, through his messengers of revelation, authoritatively sets before human beings for their belief. This authoritarian understanding of revelation, which is modelled on the phenomena of information and instruction, by its nature comes into inevitable conflict with the responsible use of human reason and human freedom. It is therefore significant that more recent theology usually replaces this authoritarian understanding of revelation with another that is based on the model of communication. In this new context theologians speak not of revelations in the plural but of revelation in the singular, with revelation understood not as a revelation of objective facts but as a self-revelation of a person. What God reveals is first and foremost not something but himself and his saving will for humanity. In revealing himself and his mystery, he also reveals to humanity themselves and their own mystery. Revelation is thus the determination of the indeterminately open mystery of humanity and its world and history.

This newer understanding of revelation can appeal to scripture. Of course, when we ask what scripture understands by revelation, we must be aware that the Bible contains no concept of revelation in the strict sense of the term. The Bible is familiar rather with a great variety of phenomena which it interprets with the aid of concepts that are likewise quite varied. It speaks, for example, of unveiling, of granting knowledge, of coming to light, of making plain, of appearing. The best known of the phenomena which it interprets with the aid of these various concepts is the prophetic communication of revelation. In the prophets we constantly find such phrases as: 'Thus says the Lord'; 'Go, and say to this people' (Isa. 6.9); 'Go and proclaim in the hearing of Jerusalem, Thus says the Lord' (Jer. 2.2). The authoritarian understanding of revelation, which I mentioned a moment ago, can to a certain extent appeal to this language of the prophets. But the prophetic language in turn must not be isolated from the fact that in what they say the prophets remind the people of God's great acts in the past and announce a present and future action of God. The prophets are thus concerned with an authoritative interpretation of the history in which God is revealing himself to his people. Thus the prophetic type of revelation leads over into the narrative form of revelation as we find it especially in the historical books of the Old Testament, in the New Testament Gospels and in the Acts of the Apostles. In the telling of this history the historical events are interpreted as God's revelation. In this history God speaks to human beings and deals with them as with his friends.

Revelation takes still another form in the Torah. Here too it is linked to revelation in the history of salvation: 'I am the Lord, your God, who brought you out of the land of Egypt, out of the house of bondage' (Ex. 20.2; cf. Deut. 5.6). The acts by which God established his covenant with his people dictate the human conduct that is in keeping with the covenant. At this point the personal character of revelation emerges with particular clarity. Revelation is thus an invitation and challenge to covenant and communion with God. But only in the doing of the truth does the human person accede to the light of the truth (John 3.21). Different again is the form revelation takes in the wisdom literature: wisdom as revelation of reality and its laws, with the accompanying conviction that only in Israel and in the law has wisdom found its definitive dwelling (Sir. 24.8ff.). Revelation also occurs in the songs of the Old and New Testaments, in the prayers of complaint, praise and petition, and especially in the psalms, where the life and experiences of those praying become a revelatory history of God's dealings with men. In the apocalyptic literature, finally, revelation takes the form of bringing to light the eternal divine decree of salvation and in unveiling the mystery 'which was kept secret for long ages' (Rom. 16.25; cf. Eph. 1.9). The eschatological disclosure of the mystery of God takes place, according to the New Testament, in Jesus Christ as he is attested by the church.

Thus the entire history of revelation in the Old and New Testaments is one long illustration of what the New Testament sums up when it says: 'In many and various ways God spoke of old to our fathers by the prophets; but in these latter days he has spoken to us by a Son' (Heb. 1.1–2).

From the various types of revelation in the Bible it follows that as understood by the Bible revelation is not simply something that is manifestly present in the world or which through meditation and reflection human beings are able by their own power to read off from the world. It is rather a free self-disclosure of God, not deducible from anything else, by which alone man and the world are brought into the light of the truth. Consequently revelation does not occur always and everywhere but here and now. It is historical revelation, and always accompanied by an indispensable temporal reference.

More specifically, according to the Bible revelation takes place through words and deeds. 'Word' includes the prophetic word but also the word of the law (instructions) and the words of wisdom and of song (songs of praise, petition, and lament). Revelation through deeds occurs in creation (according to the wisdom literature), and above all in God's historical acts of salvation. Revelation through word and revelation through acts are intrinsically related to each other. The word-revelation interprets the act-revelation; it is related by way of remembrance, interpretation and promise to the act-revelation in creation and history. Conversely, the act-revelation reinforces the word; the word-revelation is thus demonstrated and confirmed by historical experience.[7]

In the human realm, word and act or deed are already the ways in which persons reveal and communicate themselves. Without such revealing words and actions another person is a closed book to us; by means of them he discloses himself and allows himself to be known. Thus the historical character of revelation is also the corporeal-symbolic aspect of an irreducible personal freedom which without this revelation would be hidden from us. Biblical revelation is thus not primarily a revelation of objects, not a revelation of truths, teachings, commandments, and 'supernatural' realities, but a personal self-revelation of God. What God primarily makes known to us in revelation is not various truths and realities but himself and his saving will for human beings.[8] This personal character of God's revelation finds varied expression in the Bible. In God's self-disclosure the pronoun 'I' is constantly being used in a very emphatic manner. This is true especially of the self-presentation formula: 'I am the Lord, your God' (Ex. 20.2; Deut. 5.6; cf. Ezek. 20.5; Hos. 12.10; etc.). In fact, revelation occurs precisely in order that we may know that he, the Lord, is our God (Ex. 6.7; Ezek. 20.26, 38, 42, 44). In Yahweh's self-revelation his personality is brought with special impressiveness in the metaphorical language of the Bible, according to which God reveals his face (Ex. 34.20; Deut. 10.8; 18.7; Ps. 86.9; etc.), his heart (Hos. 11.8; Jer. 31.20; etc.), and his name (Ex. 6.3; John 17.6; etc.). All this shows that in his revelation God is not an It but an I and a Thou.[9]

This self-disclosure of God occurs historically 'in, with and under' words and deeds. It thus makes use of many different forms of categorical revelation.[10] The one revelation occurs in many individual revelations. The climax and completion of this historical revelation is Jesus Christ.[11] In him, personal content and historical form become identical. For in Jesus Christ the form is the form of God's self-communicating and self-emptying love. This radically self-giving and self-emptying love is the utmost that is possible for God. It is therefore not an ultimately arbitrary decree of God that turns Jesus Christ into the completion of God's historical revelation; rather it is because of the intrinsic nature of this revelation that he is its fulfillment than which no greater historical fulfillment is possible. Jesus Christ is that 'than which a greater cannot be thought', and he is therefore in person the eschatological self-definition of God. Anyone who sees him sees the Father (John 14.9). For this reason, a Christian doctrine of God cannot be concerned with 'just any' God but only with the one God of Abraham, Isaac and Jacob, the God of Jesus Christ. As Love (I John 4.8, 16), he is the definitive determination of the mystery of God and man. In this eschatological self-revelation of God in Jesus Christ a Christian doctrine of God has both its ground and its content, and by this self-revelation it must be constantly judged anew.

The personal self-disclosure of God in his word is answered by faith as a personal self-giving of man to God.[12] Since faith is the answer to God's word which finds expression in word and deed and is summed up in Jesus Christ, it always has a concrete content. It finds God not in vague feeling but in concrete words, events, human beings. But faith is far more than an acceptance-as-true of revealed truths and facts. It looks beyond the concrete forms which revelation takes and in them seeks the God who is personally revealing himself. The basic form of faith is therefore not: 'I believe that . . . ' or 'I believe something', but rather: 'I believe you' and 'I believe in you'. As Augustine and Thomas Aquinas showed, faith contains three elements: *credere Deum*, to believe that God is; *credere Deo*, to give credence to God in the sense of trusting God; and *credere in Deum*, to move toward God, to rely on him and depend on him.[13] Faith is therefore not a simple act of understanding (an acceptance-as-true) or of the will (trust) or of feeling; it is rather a life-project that lays hold of all these powers and includes them, and a comprehensive mode of existing. Faith is at the same time an act (*fides qua creditur*) and a content (*fides quae creditur*). Faith is the comprehensive re-action of the human being to the prior action of God in revealing himself; it is a trusting in God and a building on God, a gaining of a foothold in God, a saying of 'Amen' to God, with all the consequences this entails. To have faith is to take God seriously as God, without reservations; it is to give him the honour and to glorify him as Lord; it is to acknowledge his lordship with praise and thanksgiving.

What is the ultimate ground and justification for such a comprehensive faith? This is one of the most difficult questions raised in fundamental theology, and I cannot go into it in detail in the present context.[14] Our various reflections up to this point have already made it clear that in the final analysis we cannot justify faith by rational proofs or historical documents. The ultimate cannot be justified by the penultimate, the all-embracing and infinite by the finite; since God is the one than whom a greater cannot be thought, it is impossible to find a greater and more comprehensive horizon in view of which and within which we can conceive him. Much less can freedom be proved; it can only be known and acknowledged in freedom. Reason and history provide indications which show faith to be reasonable; but these indications themselves become fully certain only in the light of faith or, more accurately, in the light of the self-revelation of the truth of God, which truth shines out in the act of faith itself. Scripture tells us that no one can come to faith in Jesus Christ unless the Father draws him (John 6.44). For this reason it is true that 'he who believes in the Son of God has the testimony in himself' (I John 5.10). For this reason the First Vatican Council defined that 'inspired and assisted by the grace of God, we believe, not because we have grasped the inner truth of things by the natural light of reason, but because of the authority of the revealing God himself, who can neither deceive nor be deceived'.[15] It is to be observed that this definition says, not that we believe on the authority of God who commands (*authoritate Dei imperantis*), but rather that we believe on the authority of God who reveals (*auctoritate Dei revelantis*). The ultimate ground of faith is thus the unveiled truth of God itself. It is the very truth of God that enlightens man in faith and convinces him.[16] This enlightenment does not take place 'vertically' from above, as it were; it takes the form, rather, of a coming of the light in and through the historical forms of revelation. In the final analysis the enlightenment comes through the self-evidence of God's love, which cannot be demonstrated from outside but can only convince by its innate power. For love alone is credible.[17]

Only where God is acknowledged as God in faith does his divinity make itself felt in the world; only where he is thus glorified as Lord is it possible for his glory to radiate out and for his lordship to take historical shape. Thus revelation does not occur in the form of something objectively ascertainable which is then subsequently known by faith. It occurs in human faith and in the mode of life that develops out of this faith. The truth of revelation is thus the truth of witnessing (*martyria*). This means, further, that God's revelation never exists in itself but only in a human, historical mediation. We encounter the self-revealing God only as the God who is hidden in his human and historical revelatory forms. The profession of faith in God on the basis of his revelation never does away with the mystery of the God who is hidden from man, but rather brings this mystery to bear on man. Revelation within history is therefore an image and likeness, a foretaste and anticipation of the eschatological revelation in which we will see God face to face (I Cor. 13.12) as he is (I John 3.2). In revelation there is an anticipatory appropriation of the eschatological meaning and eschatological fulfillment in which God will be all in all (I Cor. 15.28). For this reason every historical form of revelation points beyond itself to the mystery of God.

2. The hiddenness of God

'Self-revelation of God' means that the mystery which makes itself known to man is not simply a kind of code for the depth-dimension of man himself and the world. It is not a predicate to be applied to the world but rather a holy mystery that is independent of the world, a self-sufficient subject who can speak and act. The mystery is not a silent mystery concerning which man in turn can only only keep silence; it is a mystery that utters itself, one that addresses us and that we can address in turn. But such revelation is something other than an enlightenment in a superficial sense of the term.

In the act of revealing himself God does not do away with his own mystery; he does not unveil it in such a way that we are now well informed about God. Revelation consists, rather, in God making known his hidden mystery, that is, the mystery of his freedom and his person. Revelation is thus revelation of the hiddenness of God.[18]

This hiddenness and mysteriousness of revelation is abundantly brought out in the Bible. In the accounts of manifestations of God there is never talk of God taking a visible form. In every case all that is visible are the signs of God's presence: the burning bush (Ex. 3.2), the pillar of cloud at the exodus from Egypt (Ex. 13.21); clouds and tempest on Sinai (Ex. 19.9, 16; cf. Deut. 4.33–36). Moses is expressly told that he cannot see the face of God, 'for man shall not see me and live'; he may only see God's back (Ex. 33.20).

Especially significant is the Old Testament prohibition of images: 'You shall not make for yourself a graven image' (Ex. 20.4; Deut. 5.8). We would misunderstand the prohibition if we were to interpret it as indicating that the worship of God was marked by a high degree of spirituality and if we were to take it as meaning that the adoration of God is more a matter of the heart than the eye and that it is not possible to make a visible representation of the invisible God. Our starting point in understanding the prohibition must rather be the notion current in the ancient world, according to which the divinity is present in his image and the world in its totality makes the godhead transparent. The prohibition of images is meant to state precisely that this notion contradicts the very essence of the revelation of Yahweh. Neither through images nor by speaking the name of God can human beings gain power over God. God's freedom to reveal himself when, where and how he will must remain inviolable.

> This then means that the commandment forbidding images is bound up with the hidden way in which Jahweh's revelation came about in cult history . . . The relentless shattering of cherished concepts of God . . . stands in a theological relationship which is perhaps hidden, but which is, in actual fact, very close to the commandment forbidding images. Any interpretation which deals in isolation with the impossibility of representing Jahweh by an image, and which does not see the commandment as bound up with the totality of Jahweh's revelation, misses the crucial point.[19]

Thus the Old Testament prohibition of images transcends the alternatives of idolatry and iconoclasm. It is meant to safeguard the hiddenness that is part of God's revelation.

The dialectic of God's revelation and his hiddenness is still present at the climax of revelation in Jesus Christ. As the eternal Son of God Jesus Christ is the image, the icon of God the Father (II Cor. 4.4; Col. 1.15), the radiance of his glory and the perfect copy of his being (Heb. 1.3). In him is made vividly clear who God is: he is the God with a human face. Whoever sees him sees the Father (John 14.9). But this seeing is a seeing by faith. For in Jesus Christ 'being in the form of God' has shared in the emptying out 'in the form of a slave' and in the 'obedience unto death on a cross' (Phil. 2.6–8). But the language of the cross is a shocking scandal to the Jews and foolishness to the pagans; only for believers is the cross the power and wisdom of God (I Cor. 1.23f.). In God's self-revelation in Jesus Christ God is therefore – as Martin Luther puts it in his *theologia crucis* – hidden *sub contrario*, 'under his opposite'.[20] This hidden presence of God in Jesus Christ is in a manner continued in his presence in the brothers and sisters of Jesus Christ, especially the poor, the lowly, the sick, the persecuted, and the dying (Matt. 25.31–46). Theologically, therefore, the hiddenness of God does not refer to a *Deus absolutus* who is other-worldly and distant, but to the *Deus revelatus* who is present amid the alienations of the world. In the death and resurrection of Jesus the reign of God is present under the conditions of the present aeon: God ruling in human weakness, wealth in poverty, love in abandonment, fullness in emptiness, life in death.

In the apocalyptic literature the revelation of the mysteries or mystery of God becomes the express theme. The unveiling (*apokalypsis*) of divine mysteries is even the real theme of late Jewish apocalyptic.[21] The 'mysteries' here are hidden realities which have been prepared in heaven since the very beginning and are to be made known at the end of time, and into which the apocalyptic seer has been given insight even now through mysterious images, visions, and so on. The revelation of these eschatological mysteries is the revelation of the mystery of time and the historical eras. The focus of these mysteries is God's eschatological decree of salvation, a decree that has been effectively carried out since the very beginning but will emerge from its hiddenness only at the end of time and then openly shows its effectiveness. These apocalyptic writings intend to offer not confused speculations but concrete words of consolation and hope. At a difficult moment of history believers are told that the coming of God's reign is absolutely certain. The New Testament takes over this apocalyptic concept of mystery. Jesus speaks of the mystery of the reign or kingdom of God, and says that it is revealed to the disciples but hidden from others (Mark 4.11; cf. Matt. 13.11; Luke 8.10). What is new by comparison with Jewish apocalyptic is the fact that it is Jesus who reveals this mystery of God's kingdom and that he does so not only through his words and his actions but through his entire person. He is in his person the revelation and carrying out of the mystery of God.[22] The Pauline and even more the Deutero-pauline letters take up this theme. Jesus Christ is the accomplishment of the eternal and hitherto hidden mystery of God, that is, of the eternal decree of his will. The mystery that has thus manifested itself in Jesus Christ is made plain, communicated and proclaimed through the preaching of the apostles and the testimony of the church (cf. Rom 16.25; I Cor. 2.1–6; Eph. 1.9; 3.9; Col. 1.26f.; I Tim. 3.9, 16).

The most emphatic summation of this conviction of faith is to be found in Isaiah: 'Truly, thou art a God who hidest thyself' (45.15). The Bible regards it as obvious that in this sense God is invisible (Rom. 1.20; Col. 1.15) and incomprehensible (Ps. 139.6; Job 36.26); that his thoughts and decrees are unfathomable (Rom. 11.33f.); and that he dwells in unapproachable light (I Tim. 6.16).

The theological tradition was fully aware of the mysteriousness of God. From the beginning it taught that God is invisible (*invisibilis*), incomprehensible (*incomprehensibilis*) and ineffable (*ineffabilis*).[23] It was obliged to defend this teaching especially against the Eunomians, in the context of the disturbances caused by Arius. The Eunomians claimed the possibility of an exhaustive, adequate and comprehensive knowledge of God even in the present life. In opposition, the fathers – especially Basil, Gregory of Nazianzus, Gregory of Nyssa and Chrysostom – developed the doctrine of the incomprehensibility of God.[24] John Damascene sums up the teaching of the Greek fathers in a lapidary statement: 'The divine nature is ineffable and incomprehensible.'[25] All the great theologians of the West – Augustine, Anselm of Canterbury, Bonaventure, Thomas Aquinas, Duns Scotus and, not least, Nicholas of Cusa – bear unanimous witness that the supreme knowledge of God is to know that he is unknowable. A *docta ignorantia* (Nicholas of Cusa) is the most that is possible for us human beings.[26] These insights have also become part of the church's official teaching. An avowal of the *Deus invisibilis* occurs even in the early professions of faith; the confession of *Deus incomprehensibilis* is to be found above all in the Fourth Lateran Council (1215)[27] and the First Vatican Council (1869–70).[28]

It is admittedly striking that the theological tradition says almost nothing of the hiddenness of God and prefers to speak of his incomprehensibility. From the viewpoint simply of terminology there is a shift of accent here as compared with the Bible. The tradition usually meditated on the mystery of God not in terms of the history of salvation and revelation but in epistemological and metaphysical terms, seeing it as the mystery of the infinite being of God which is beyond the reach of finite human knowledge. Such an approach did not bring out the full depth of the biblical teaching on the hiddenness of God. In modern times, moreover, a concept of knowledge became prevalent in which knowing was understood as grasping or conceiving, thoroughly penetrating and even controlling. This rationalistic ideal of knowledge led to the disintegration of the theological category of mystery in Enlightenment theology. In their efforts to counter this trend, theologians developed a concept of mystery that focused negatively on the non-conceivable and supra-rational. Mystery was now an impassable boundary for knowledge, rather than the ultimate overflowing fulfillment of all knowing. This led to an understanding of mystery that was narrowly anti-rationalistic: a mystery in the strict sense (*mysterium stricte dictum*) is a truth which is absolutely inaccessible to human reason; if we are to know it, revelation must not only set the mind in motion (so that we might subsequently gain insight), but it, together with faith, remains the sole abiding basis of our knowledge.

In this understanding of mystery there is a twofold narrowing of vision. 1. The concept of mystery is defined in a purely negative way in relation to human reason. The fact is overlooked that the human mind as such is so constituted that it reaches beyond itself into an impenetrable mystery. There is also a failure to see that the revelation which makes this mystery known as mystery is for this very reason man's salvation. In this positive understanding of it, the mystery of God is not a mystery for the mind but a mystery of salvation. 2. The concept of mystery, because it is thus negatively defined by contrast with categorical knowledge, itself falls indirectly under the control of that ideal of knowledge. Theologians taking this approach no longer speak of the one mystery of God but of many mysteries (*mysteria*). No longer are the saving events and the reality of salvation in their totality a mystery, but only 'the higher and nobler part of it [Christianity]' (Trinity, incarnation, grace, transsubstantiation, etc.).[29] The incomprehensibility of God becomes one divine attribute alongside others and therefore no longer even an attribute that systematically determines and grounds the whole. In short: the mystery of God is itself conceived categorically as one of the mysteries.

It is thanks especially to Karl Rahner that we now have a more profound theology of mystery.[30] He has shown that while the tradition does maintain the incomprehensibility of God, it does not give this a determining role in the formation of a system. In the tradition the incomprehensibility of God is simply one divine attribute alongside others, but it does not become the dimension that determines, grounds and qualifies all other statements about God; it does not become the recapitulatory statement about God, in the sense that anyone who does not speak of God's hiddenness is not speaking of God at all but only of an idol. Rahner's own point of departure is the human being as a being of mystery. In every concept they have, human beings are directed beyond all concepts to a nameless reality that cannot be circumscribed or comprehended. Mystery is even the *a priori* condition for all categorical knowledge. Thus the knowledge of mystery is not a defective kind of knowledge, not something negative, not a boundary of knowledge, but the original type of knowledge that alone makes all other knowledge possible. Man's fulfillment consists not in penetrating the mystery of God but rather in having this mystery come definitively into his ken. The revelation of the mystery of God is the response to the mystery of humanity. Revelation does not, however, signify an 'enlightenment' (*Aufklärung*); it does not bring dissonances into harmony and do away with the mystery. Rather it is the revelation precisely of mystery and thus the definitive acceptance of the mystery of humanity. Knowledge of God's incomprehensibility is therefore the beatifying fulfillment of the human person.

The revelation of God as mystery means, in positive terms, that God is a Freedom which is reserved to itself and withdrawn from our grasp. The revelation of God is the revelation of him as a Freedom that discloses itself and offers itself to us, a freedom in love. The mystery of divine revelation is thus his free self-communication to us in love. This self-communication in love is the single mystery of revelation, the basic mystery which interprets itself and unfolds in the many mysteries of faith. Christians are convinced that the self-interpretation of the one mystery of God takes place definitively and comprehensively in Jesus Christ; he is God's self-communication in person, he is the mystery of God made manifest. This self-communication of God is made present to us in the Holy Spirit. For we can accept the mystery of God as mystery only if God himself gives us the power to accept it. God can be known and acknowledged only through the power of God. For this reason we need a new self-communication of God to us whereby we become sons and daughters of God in the image of the only Son of God, Jesus Christ. This gracious self-communication of God in the Holy Spirit is only a kind of deposit or pledge that will be completed in the eschatological vision face to face. All of revelation is thus concerned with the revelation of the single mystery of God the Father's love that communicates itself through Jesus Christ in the Holy Spirit. The trinitarian profession of faith is therefore not only the summation of the revelation of the mystery of God; it is also the concrete exposition of the hiddenness of God, which is the origin, goal and essential content of all revelation.

As a result of what has been said here three statements may be made about the mystery of God.

1. In the Bible, the proposition that God is mysterious and hidden has for its context not a theory about the scope and limits of human knowledge, but the self-revelation of God. It is a theological and not an epistemological proposition; it is the first word in the knowledge of faith which God gives to us, and not the last word in human self-knowledge. Consequently, when the Bible speaks of the mystery and hiddenness of God, it means something

different from when Plato and especially Plotinus talk about the idea of
the Good and the One being above all existence and essence, or when Kant
says that the rational idea of God is beyond our power and a real 'abyss
on the verge of which human reason trembles is dismay'. The mystery of
God is not the ultimate, still attainable but ever withdrawing horizon of
our knowledge; rather, it is the foundational content of God's revelation.
It is positive, not negative; it is not a word that condemns us to silence, but
a word that enables us to speak or, more accurately, to praise and honour
God, to adore and glorify him. This does not mean that we are fully
informed about God. Revelation as revelation of the mystery of God is not
an enlightenment in the sense that it removes the mystery from God; rather
it is the definitive establishment and confirmation of this mystery. The
believer is not better informed about God than the unbeliever, and
theologians are not God's 'privy councillors'. On the contrary, the unbeliever thinks he really knows all about God; the believer, on the other hand,
knows that he cannot provide himself with answers and that the answer
which God gives him is a message about an abiding mystery. If, then, we
speak of the revelation of God, we must stress both words: *revelation*, in
which God communicates himself to be known by human beings, and the
fact that it is the revelation *of God*, a revelation in which God is both
subject and object and in which he makes known his utter hiddenness and
his being utterly beyond our power to manipulate and dispose of him.

2. In the Bible, the proposition that God is mysterious and hidden refers
not to his being as withheld from man but to his being as offered to man
and to his eternal decrees of salvation and their execution in history. God's
hiddenness is not God's being-in-itself prior to, beyond and 'behind' the
history of salvation, but his being-for-us and being-with-us in history.
Therefore the revelation of the mystery of God does not lead us, as it does
in Neoplatonism, 'to the nihilistic heights of a purely negative concept
of God that lacks all content',[31] or to an unobjective, indeterminate
transcendence that can be expressed only in cipher form, but rather to the
God of human beings who descends into the determinations of space and
time, to the God who condescends. God's hiddenness is hiddenness within
revelation; more concrete, the hiddenness of his glory in the suffering and
death of Jesus Christ. The theology of God's hiddenness is in the final
analysis the theology of the cross (*theologia crucis*). The mystery of God
is therefore also not, as in nominalism and many statements of Luther and
Calvin, a hidden remnant and dark border, as it were, consisting of God's
unfathomable majesty that strikes anxiety and terror into human beings;
the mystery of God is rather his saving will, his turning to us, his total and
unreserved self-communication in grace or, in a word, his love. It is for

this reason that the New Testament can summarily define the mystery of God as love (I John 4.8, 16). It does not mean that God is *der liebe Gott* (the dear, kindly God) in the innocuous sense in which we tend to use the phrase. It means rather that the incomprehensible mystery to which man is introduced is not one of remote, judgmental distance but one of gracious, giving, protecting nearness, by means of which human beings are unconditionally and definitively accepted in Jesus Christ.

3. The revelation of the mystery and hiddenness of God is not a message concerned with theoretical speculation, but a 'practical' message of salvation. It is a message both of judgment and of grace. It is a message of judgment because it ultimately says that man has no power over the mystery of God either through knowledge or through action. To that extent the revelation of the mystery of God is a judgment on human hybris which wants to be like God (Gen. 3.5). The revelation of God is thus a judgment on all home-made idols, on our images of God, and on the things of which we make absolutes that enslave us instead of setting us free. But insofar as the revelation of the mystery of God reminds us of our limits and sets us straight, it also confers a benefit on us and conveys a message of grace. It abrogates the law of achievement, of the will to achievement and of the pressure to achieve, and tells us that we cannot and need not give fulfillment to our own lives. We are definitively accepted with our limitations; we must therefore not only know our limitations, but we can and may also accept them. As those who have been unqualifiedly accepted by God we must affirm both ourselves and all others. In the language of theology: the revelation of the mystery of God abrogates the law of self-justification through works and proclaims the gospel of grace as alone justifying. Thus the revelation of the mystery of God is the revelation of the mystery of our salvation; it is the fundamental and central saving truth of the Christian faith. Our profession of faith in the revelatory and saving action of God the Father through Jesus Christ in the Holy Spirit sets forth the implications of this one mystery of our salvation.

PART TWO

The Message about the God of Jesus Christ

I

God, the Father Almighty

1. The problem of an almighty Father-God

The Christian confession of faith begins with the sentence: 'I believe in God, the Father almighty.'[1] This statement sums up in a valid and binding way the essential message of Jesus: the coming of the reign of God and specifically of the God whom Jesus called 'my Father' and whom he taught us to invoke as 'our Father'. At the same time, the indeterminate and ambiguous concept 'God' is specified and interpreted by the concept 'Father'.

This interpretation, it must be admitted, hardly makes the God-question any simpler for us today. On the contrary, the statement, so central to the New Testament, that God is the Father of Jesus Christ and the Father of us all, has today become difficult for many to understand and assimilate. This observation is all the more momentous since 'father' is a primordial word in the history of cultures and religions. In the course of history down to the present, 'father' in this context has been understood as meaning far more than simply 'begetter'. The father is the creative source and at the same time the protector and nourisher of life. One's life depends on one's father, but at the same time the father makes this life something independent and accepts it as such. Thus the father represents the binding order of life. He represents power and authority as well as gift, goodness, solicitude and aid. After a long prior history this picture of the father has become uncertain to us today.[2] M. Horkheimer observes that there are no fathers any more, if by 'father' you understand what society has for centuries understood by it.[3] In continuity with S. Freud, A. Mitscherlich speaks of a society without fathers.[4] The question that arises here is an obvious one: if the experience of a human father is lacking or if the experience is even a primarily negative one, how is it possible to have a positive relationship to God as Father? How will we be able to proclaim and confess God as the Father almighty? The background of this 'collapse of the father' (H. Tellenbach) contains many and varied elements. From a sociological standpoint we might take as our starting point the termination of the patriarchal form of society by our modern industrial society that is based on exchange. When everything is based on an exchange of services of equal value, and when everything is geared to independence, promotion, progress, emancipation and self-fulfillment, there is no longer any place for authority and rank, certainly not for the authority of the ancient and the primitive. Like society at large, the structure and culture of the family, and with these the authority of the father, have been caught up in a process of revolutionary transformation and even of dissolution. The problem here is not only the protest against and rejection of the father, but the father's own renunciation of responsible fatherhood and of any binding and responsible authority.

S. Freud analysed the problem from the standpoint of depth psychology[5] and A. Mitscherlich has carried the analysis further while adding the viewpoint of social psychology. Freud explains the ambivalent attitude to the father as a father-complex and more specifically as an Oedipus complex. According to Freud, this is at the heart of all neuroses. For the rebellion against the father and the murder of the father led to a struggle of all against all, to a chaos that begot anxiety, and to a reign of terror. As a result, human beings embark on a search for the lost father, and endeavor to give new life to the ideal of fatherhood. According to Freud, it is Christian doctrine that most clearly bears witness to the primal guilty act. Christ sacrifices his own life and thus frees the multitude of his brothers and sisters from original sin. But in the very act by which he offers to the Father the greatest possible atonement, he also reaches the fulfillment of his own wishes against the Father. He himself becomes a god alongside and even in place of the Father. The religion of the Son eliminates the religion of the Father. These theses of Freud are more than questionable from the historical point of view. From a psychological point of view, however, they do make intelligible the difficulties many people have with God as Father. They explain the God-complex (Richter)[6] or, to put it more strongly, the way people suffer from God, as impressively described by, for example, T. Moser in his book 'Poisoning by God'.[7] Finally, these ideas make understandable the paradox involved in the death-of-God theology, which boils down to the slogan: God is dead, and Jesus Christ is his only Son. Here we have an extreme theology of the Son that has radically freed itself from the Father-God.

The broad connections thus established by sociology and depth psychology also provide the context for the modern women's liberation movement and its accompanying feminist theology.[8] The protest against the patriarchal form of society and against the setting of man above woman leads the movement and the theology to criticize the idea of a Father-God, since they see in this the sacralization of the patriarchal relationship and the ideological exaltation of male superiority and of the repression of both women and womanly values. This criticism need not lead, as it does in M. Daly,[9] to a post-Christian religion of the mother goddesses; it may instead lead, as it does in R. Ruether, to an emphasizing of the prophetic criticism that has for its point of departure the biblical understanding of God as Father.[10] This prophetic criticism is based on the idea that God is the Father of all human beings and that he alone is truly the Father (Matt. 23.9). If this is so, then there must be no oppression of one human being by another, since all of them are brothers and sisters. Of course, they are brothers and sisters only so long as they have God as their common Father. Viewed in this light, feminist theology is a challenge to reflect more profoundly and more critically on the idea of father and gain a new grasp of its meaning.

The sociological and psychological approaches already bring us to the threshold of the radically metaphysical dimension of the father problem. The problem must be understood, in the final analysis, against the background of the modern philosophy of emancipation, of which the emancipation of women is but one aspect, though an important and typical one.[11] Emancipation in the sense of liberation from all imposed dependencies is a watchword that applies to the whole modern age and its experience of reality; it is also a fundamental historico-philosophical category that helps characterize the modern processes of enlightenment and liberation.[12] For while emancipation in Roman law meant the graciously granted liberation of slaves or the release of the adult son from his father's authority, it has come to mean in the modern age the autonomous self-liberation of the human person or social groups (peasants, citizens, proletarians, Jews, Blacks, women, colonial territories, etc.) from intellectual, legal, social or political tutelage, from discrimination, or from a domination perceived as unjust. The extent to which at the end of the modern age emancipation has become an all-embracing ideological category may be seen from K. Marx's definition: '*Every* emancipation is a *restoration* of the human world and of human relationships to *man himself.*'[13]

We must not, of course, fail to realize that behind the philosophy of emancipation and its accompanying loss of the father there ultimately lies a new form of gnosis. By gnosis I mean here an attitude of mind that can develop in varied cultural contexts. It was an attitude that became particularly dangerous to Christianity during the cultural collapse of the

Hellenistic world in the second century after Christ. The world was no longer experienced as an ordered, harmonious cosmos, as it had been in the classical age of Greece, but rather as alien, sinister and menacing. Anxiety about life became widespread; the basic mood was a sense of being lost in the present world. The experience of alienation led to an attempt to break out of a cosmos and its structures that were felt to be a prison, and to an abandonment of the material world in order to rescue the truly divine in man. H. Jonas gives the following summary description of this Promethean rebellion on the part of man as he seeks to free himself from the traditional father-religions:

> That turning-point in the history of religions (or myths) was in truth a real revolt against the gods and a collapse of the gods, and the establishment (clear in terms of myth) of a new dominion; in allegorical symbols we experience on the scene of world-history the replacement of the old, powerful father-religions by religions of the son, the replacement of cosmic religion by acosmic religion: 'man' or the 'son of man' is exalted above the ancient gods and becomes the supreme god or the divine center of a religion of salvation . . . The great gods who are fathers of the world, and who themselves had come to the fore in historical time and were characteristic of a millennial stage of human culture, now everywhere abdicate their power.[14]

G. Bornkamm observes: 'Not the least reason why the Christian faith stood up against the drag of this religious movement and did not succumb to it is that due to the crucified Jesus who was Son it had a renewed faith in God as Father and therefore could not abandon the world which is God's creation.'[15]

We can hardly be mistaken if we claim that today again Christianity is undergoing a similar test. Modern science and technology and the industrial society which these have made possible have eroded the concept of a metaphysical order. They were a gigantic attempt on man's part to understand and control the world and man's material, physical, biological, sociological and economic dependencies. At the end of this development man is in the position of the sorcerer's apprentice who can no longer free himself from the spirits he has summoned up.[16] The world that he himself projected and constructed has become a barely intelligible system with its unavoidable constraints; it has become a kind of second-order destiny. Once again anxiety is spreading abroad, and the anxiety often turns into a cynical contempt for the world. Nietzsche foresaw the nihilistic consequences of the death of God, and said: 'There is no more up or down, we plunge in all directions and wander as through an infinite nothing.'[17]

In this situation in which all thinking based on a metaphysical order has collapsed Christianity must raise anew the question of the ground of all reality, the ground from which everything comes and which sustains everything and assigns everything its measure. Christianity must learn once again to affirm the world as coming from God's positive creative will and to defend it and man's natural ties to it against a radical denigration of them. Only in this way is it possible to resist the loss of all norms, direction and stability and to re-establish the security within which alone freedom is possible and meaningful. We must therefore reflect anew on the first article of the faith and ask ourselves what it means to confess God as the Father almighty.

2. The Christian message of God the Father

(a) God as Father in the history of religions

The idea of the Godhead as Father of the world and of human beings is extremely old.[18] The invocation of the divinity under the name of father is one of the primordial phenomena of the history of religions. It is found in simple and undeveloped religions and among culturally advanced peoples, among the inhabitants of the Mediterranean area as well as among the Assyrians and Babylonians. Everywhere the divinity is understood as Father of the universe, the one from whom everything comes and who controls everything. A central dogma of Greek religion was that Zeus is the father of gods and men. In the mystery religions, too, the invocation of God as 'father' was current. Both Platonic and Stoic philosophy, each in its own way, accepted this idea and the vocabulary attendant on it and integrated it into its philosophical speculation. The concept of father was especially helpful in understanding God as ultimate source and as the principle which establishes the unity and connectedness (relatedness) of all reality.

Behind this mythical and philosophical language of fatherhood there are essentially two influences. First, there is the idea of a begetter; this presupposes the existence of an overarching oneness of life that embraces God, the world, and human beings. There is nothing in myth of a divine transcendence in the biblical sense, still less of a purely natural or secular and immanentist idea of the world. The divine is the depth dimension of the world; it is as it were a predicate applied to a cosmos that is understood as numinous.[19] Second, behind the use of the name 'Father' for God in the history of religions there is an apotheosis and sacral legitimation of the position of the father of the family as master of the household and as domestic priest. In the ancient world, 'father' was not only a genealogical concept but also a sociological and juridical concept; particularly in the Latin and Roman world the *pater familias* ('father of the household') and the *patris potestas* (paternal authority) played a very prominent role.[20] 'Father' was a symbol and summation of what was ancient and venerable, of authority, of the power that not only bestowed but also sustained life. To that extent the concept of father combined the motifs of strictness and respect with those of kindness and solicitude. Consequently we have fallen victim to misunderstanding if we interpret and criticize the patriarchal order in the light of the Marxist ideology of domination and exploitation. The *auctoritas* or authority of the father is based on the fact that he is the source and augmenter of life (*auctoritas* is from the verb *augere*, to augment, increase).

The father is essentially the source on which the child indeed depends but to which it also owes its existence. He is the source that renders the child an independently existing entity and justifies that existence. The father-child relation is thus a symbol of the human condition as such; it gives expression to the fact that human freedom is a conditioned and finite freedom. The abolition of the father is made possible only by indulging in a hybrid utopianism that combines absolute freedom and an inhuman kind of human mastery. Since, however, the father-child relation is not only an inalienable aspect of being human but also cannot be replaced by other relation, 'father' is a primal word in the history of humanity and religion; it cannot be replaced by another concept and cannot be translated into another concept. It is against this background that the full extent of the present crisis becomes visible.

(b) God as Father in the Old Testament

The God of revelation is a God of human beings, and he speaks the language of human beings. The primal word 'father' is therefore also a basic word in biblical revelation.[21] On the other hand, the two motifs – the genealogical and mythological and the sociological and juridical – which underlie the use of the concept 'father' in the history of religions were no small obstacle to the acceptance of word into the Bible. For the God of the Bible is not simply the depth dimension of the world; he is the freely acting lord of history.[22]

The Old Testament gives central importance to the 'God of the fathers' (Ex. 3.13; etc.), the God of Abraham, Isaac and Jacob, and to the people of Israel as son of God, not on the basis of natural descent but on the basis of historical election and vocation (Ex. 4.22; Hos. 11.1; Jer. 31.9). The fatherhood of God and the sonship of Israel are therefore based not on myths but on the concrete experience of a saving divine historical act. The divine sonship thus established is still regarded by Paul as the greatest of Israel's privileges (Rom. 9.4).

Allusions to the mythological understanding of God's fatherhood are admittedly not entirely absent from the Old Testament (e.g. Deut. 32.8; Ps. 29.1; 89.7; etc.); they are, however, sublimated almost to the point of being unrecognizable. The mythologoumenon of the father of the gods is 'no more than a stylistic intermezzo, a poetic formulation' which 'abandons the mythological concept'.[23] If God is said on one occasion to have 'begotten' the king (Ps. 2.7), the relationship that is meant is not one of kinship but one established by an act of choice which we might best describe as an act of adoption.

Taking as its point of departure the idea of vocation and election, the Old Testament is able to make its own in a critical way the legitimate point of the myth. For the concept of covenant points back to the concept of creation. God's sovereign call and choice presupposes that he is the master of all reality, that is, that he is the Father who has created everything (Deut. 32.6; Mal. 2.10) and that he is therefore ground and lord of all reality (Isa. 45.9f.; 64.7). However, the father motif that is based on the idea of the covenant does not simply point back to creation; it also points forward. Only in the final age will people say to the children of Israel: 'You are "the sons of the living God"' (Hos. 2.1; cf. II Sam. 7.14; Ps. 89.27). In the Bible, therefore, the historical basis of the father motif is to be seen not only in the idea of origin and of the authority of what is ancient, venerable and primeval, but also in the idea of the future and of hope in the new. This primordially new reality consists ultimately in the forgiving and merciful paternal love of God (Hos. 11.9; Isa. 63.16; Jer. 31.20). 'As a father pities his children, so the Lord pities those who fear him' (Ps. 103.13). Israel can always call upon this merciful love of the Father with the repeated cry: 'Thou art our Father' (Isa. 63.15f.; 64.7f.). The devout Jew of the Old Testament is already able to call upon this Father-God as 'Father' with great reverence and confidence (Sir. 23.1; 51.10). God is in a special way 'Father of the fatherless' (Ps. 68.6). It can be said of him that even if 'my father and my mother have foresaken me . . . the Lord will take me up' (Ps. 27.10).

The aspects which I have just pointed out show that the covenantal idea of God as Father can be turned in a prophetic and critical way against the concrete fathers of this world. In all truth the dignity of father belongs to God alone. It is not any earthly father but God, from whom all fatherhood is derived (Eph. 3.15), who defines what true fatherhood is. According to the Bible, therefore, our talk of God as Father is not simply a sacral apotheosis of paternal authority; God's fatherhood, being the source, is also the norm of paternal authority and the critical standard by which it is judged. At the same time, any sexist misunderstanding of the religious concept of father is also excluded. This is clear, for example, from the fact that the Old Testament can also translate the Father's loving mercy into the language of womanliness and motherhood. (Isa. 66.13).

The new form which the Old Testament gives to the father motif as compared with the form it has in the history of religions brings out what is proper and specific to Old Testament faith in God: namely, God's freedom and sovereignty, and his transcendence which is a freedom in love and therefore manifests itself historically as a descent into immanence and as a being-with-us. As Father, God is not only the origin but also embraces present and future; he is a God of history. Judgmental distance and redemptive nearness, judgment and grace, omnipotence and merciful forgiveness: in the Old Testament father motif all these are integrated into a unity-in-tension. The tension point beyond the unity and presses for a final clarification.

(c) God as Father in the New Testament

In the New Testament the Old is brought to its superabundant fulfillment by the fact that the word 'Father' or 'the Father' becomes *the* name for God. There is a broad consensus among exegetes that this practice goes back to Jesus himself. The name 'Father' for God is found on his lips no less than 170 times in the Gospels. It is even possible to detect in the gospel tradition a growing tendency to include the description of God as Father in the sayings of Jesus. It would be wrong, however, to conclude from this to the operation of a later community theology. The tendency is due rather to the recollection of Jesus' characteristic way of speaking of God as 'my Father', 'your Father', and even 'the Father' or 'the heavenly Father'.

In Jesus himself the practice of speaking of God as Father is connected with the center and horizon of his entire preaching and ministry: the message of the coming of God's reign.[24]

The concept 'reign of God' is a relatively late abstract formation for the verbal statement that Jahweh is Lord or King (Ps. 47.6–9; 93.8; etc.). The idea of the reign of God does not therefore, have to do, primarily with a kingdom understood in spatial terms, but with the historical manifestation of God's lordship through events, with the revelation of his glory and with the proof of his divinity. In the final analysis the reign of God represents a radicalizing interpretation of the first commandment and its justification through God's control of history: 'I am the Lord your God . . . You shall have no other gods before me' (Ex. 20.2f.). For this reason, the message of the coming of God's reign is directly and inseparably connected in the preaching of Jesus with a call to conversion and faith (Mark 1.15).

Because the reign of God and its coming are the doing and concern of God alone, they cannot be merited, caused or coerced by either religious and ethical achievements or by political struggles. The reign of God is given (Matt. 21.43; Luke 12.32) and bestowed as an inheritance (Luke 22.29). This state of affairs finds its clearest expression in the parables: the coming of God's reign in God's own marvelous accomplishment and without relation to any human expectations, resistances, calculations or plans. We cannot 'bring it to pass' by conservative or progressive activity, by any evolutionary or revolutionary practice; all we can do is prepare for it by conversion and faith. Only in exterior and interior poverty, weakness and powerlessness can the human being be attuned to the godliness of God. He can only pray: 'Thy kingdom come' (Matt. 6.10; Luke 11.2). One who thus believes and prays may experience the omnipotence of God (Mark 9.23); therefore the principle holds that he who prays already receives (Luke 11.9f.; Matt. 7.7f.). Prayer made in faith is not only assured of a future hearing; it itself is already an anticipation of the reign of God because it makes room for God to be Lord and to act. It is not academic discourse about God but talking with God or prayer that is for Jesus the vital context (*Sitz im Leben*) of authentic theology.

The reign of God is thus characterized for Jesus by an absolute lack of world-immanent conditions and a pure graciousness. His concern for sinners and the godless is as it were only one side of his message; his talk of God as a loving and merciful Father is the other and the one that is objectively foundational. It makes it utterly clear that God's reign has its source in God alone, and that it is therefore pure grace, unalloyed mercy. That these two aspects belong together is strikingly shown in Jesus' parable of the lost or prodigal son, which might more accurately be called the parable of God's fatherly love (Luke 15.11–32). Man's salvation consists not in a departure that is meant as a protest and an assertion of emancipation, but in a return to the house of the Father – though admittedly a Father who does not humiliate the prodigal but restores him to his rights as son. God's reign does not suppress man's freedom; rather it raises it up from degradation and restores it to its rightful place.

Also characteristic of Jesus' ministry and preaching is the way in which he connects the coming of God's reign as the reign of love with his own coming.[25] He tells the parable of the lost son as a response to the grumbling of the Pharisees over his association with sinners (Luke 15.2). The point he wishes to make is this: as I behave toward sinners, so too does God. He dares to act as it were as God's substitute. If *he* drives out demons, then the reign of God has come (Matt. 12.28; Luke 11.20). Correspondingly it is he who first reveals God to us as a Father. In this connection the cry of jubilation in Matt. 11.27 is especially important: 'All things have been delivered to me by my Father; and no one knows the Son except the Father, and no one knows the Father except the Son and any one to whom the Son chooses to reveal him.' According to this saying, 'the Father' or 'my Father' is a revelatory term that expresses a revealed christology. Jesus himself and he alone it is who discloses God to us as Father and teaches and empowers us to pray: 'Our Father' (Matt. 6.9).

The truth about the Father is no naturally known general truth as it is in Stoicism, but a historical, revealed truth that is connected with the Son. Only through the Son does it become known that God is the Father of all human beings; he makes his sun to rise on the evil and the good, and sends rain on the just and the unjust (Matt. 5.45); he is solicitous for all, even for the birds of the air and the grass of the field (Matt. 6.26, 32) and for the sparrows in their flight (Matt. 10.29). Thus we find that in the preaching of Jesus the application of 'father' to God has the same basic structure as in the Old Testament: a truth revealed at one point in history but disclosing the universal meaning and ground of all reality. What is new in the New Testament is the concentration of revelation in the person of the eschatological revealer of the Father; through him Old Testament revelation is brought to its surpassing fulfillment.

Along with this christological concentration there is a further distinction: the unparalleled intimacy that attaches to Jesus' use of 'Father'. This becomes clear above all in the characteristic word Jesus uses in addressing God: *Abba*. It is quite certain that in this use of *Abba* we have the very word of Jesus himself. Otherwise there would be no explaining why we find the Aramaic word even in originally Greek texts of the New Testament (Gal. 4.6; Rom. 8.15). Evidently *Abba* was a word which the later church regarded as especially important and sacred, being characteristic of Jesus' relationship to God. *Abba* has its origin in the speech of children; it is originally a child's babble, comparable to 'papa' or 'dada'. But it was also applied to other esteemed persons with whom one had a confidential relationship ('Little father'). Consequently, when applied to God *Abba* expressed a great and even familiar intimacy and personal closeness which every Jew must have regarded as shocking. On the other hand, we must not read into the word a commonplace familiarity with God or even a degrading of God's divine stature. In Jesus' usage *Abba* has for its context the proclamation of the coming reign of God. The Father-God is at the same time the Lord God whose name must be hallowed, whose kingdom is coming, and whose will must be done (Matt. 6.9f.). God our Father is also the Father almighty, creator of heaven and earth, and the eschatological judge who will pass sentence on all injustice and sin (Matt. 7.21; 18.23–35).

In the final analysis Jesus' message about the Father sums up the whole of his message in a most personal way. It is the answer to man's hope, which can find its fulfillment only in the unconditional and definitive acceptance of love, and it is the answer to the question about the ground of all reality, a ground which is not at man's disposal and in which he can share only through faith – not because God is distant but precisely because he is close to us in love, and love can only be a gift.

The New Testament writings are a faithful echo of Jesus' message about the Father. In Paul, God (*theos*) and Father (*Patēr*) are indissolubly connected. In the greetings at the beginning and the blessings at the end of the Pauline letters the apostle always speaks of 'our God and Father' or 'the God and Father of our Lord Jesus Christ' (I Thess 1.1; Gal. 1.3; I Cor. 1.3; II Cor. 1.2; Rom. 1.7; Phil. 1.2; etc.). Paul's statements about the Father evidently have the liturgy and prayer for their *Sitz im Leben* (vital context or sociological context). These liturgically influenced greetings and blessings of the Pauline letters are already preparing the way for the forms used in later dogmas. Paul uses 'Father' almost as a proper name for God; but it never appears without an ensuing mention of him as 'Father of our Lord Jesus Christ'. In Paul's eyes Jesus is the Son who alone makes us to be sons and daughters (Rom. 8.15; Gal. 4.6). The Father is the origin, point of departure and goal of the redemptive work of Jesus Christ. From him come blessing, grace, love, mercy, consolation and joy. For this reason he must be the addressee of prayer, praise, thanksgiving and petition. But for Paul, to have God for Father does not mean an enslavement; on the contrary, to have God for Father means a being freed from slavery and anxiety and a being established as mature sons and daughters (Gal. 4.1ff.; Rom. 8.15ff.). Maturity to Paul does not mean, however, acting according to arbitrary and selfish whim; rather, it means a freedom that shows itself in love and service. According to Paul, then, the revelation of the lordship and glory of the Father means the coming of the reign of freedom in love.

In an even more decisive way John develops the linguistic usage of Jesus in the light of theological reflection. In many passages he speaks in an unqualified way of 'the Father' and 'my Father'. The message of Jesus regarding the Father is here broadened until it becomes an explanation of the whole idea of revelation. The Father is the origin and content of revelation, and the Son is the revealer. These ideas find expression as early as the Prologue. Because Jesus alone is eternally with the Father and, in fact, is himself God and rests on the Father's bosom, he is able to bring knowledge of the Father (1.18). He comes by order of the the Father (5.43); whoever sees him sees the Father (14.7–10). The purpose of his life's work is to reveal the name of the Father (17.6, 26). The arguments with the Jews, which become critical in the Gospel of John, have to do in the last analysis with the relationship between Jesus and the Father. Jesus is accused not only of violating the sabbath but of calling God his Father and thus making himself equal to God (5.18; cf. 8.54). The confession of God as the Father of Jesus Christ is thus in John's view the properly and specifically Christian element, which he puts into words by saying: 'God is love' (I John 4.8, 16).

It can be said by way of summary that when the New Testament speaks in a concrete and determinate way of God as *ho theos*, the Father is always meant, except for a few and disputed instances (e.g., Rom. 9.5f.).[26] In other words, the New Testament interprets the word God, which in itself is ambiguous, by the word Father. God is thus defined as the originating but himself unoriginated source of all reality. To that extent the New Testament accepts, in its own fashion, the basic question of ancient philosophy: the question of the ultimate ground that gives existence, unity and meaning to all reality and is at the same time the ultimate goal of human action. Of course, when the Bible speaks of God as the Father, its meaning goes beyond this abstract philosophical idea of God. By calling him 'Father', it is saying that he is a personal being who acts and speaks freely in history and enters into a covenant with humanity. As Father, God is a God with a personal face; he has a name and can be invoked by his name. The personal freedom of God is the reason why God is the liberating origin of all reality; why he therefore freely accepts what he makes; why he is freedom in love. As freedom in love God is not only the origin but also the future of history; he is a God of hope (Rom. 15.3). In fact, we might sum up the New Testament proclamation of God in this formula: God is the One who loves freely and remains free in his love.

(d) God as Father in the history of theology and dogma

Early Christian theology followed the Bible in speaking of God as Father and described him simply and without qualification as 'the Father'.[27] Justin, Irenaeus and Tertullian show the same usage. Whenever reference is made to 'God', it is always the Father who is meant.
Origen approaches the matter more critically and distinguishes between *ho theos* (with the article) and *theos* (without the article). *Ho theos designates the Father; he is autotheos*, very God, God in the proper sense.

The Son, on the other hand, is *theos*; he is of divine origin, an idea which in Origen reflects a subordinationist tendency that finds expression in his characterization of the Son as *deuteros theos* (a second or secondary God).[28]

The basic conviction that 'God' means first and directly the Father also finds expression in the church's early professions of faith. These early professions of faith are always directed to 'God, the Father almighty'.[29] Correspondingly the Father alone is regarded as the unoriginated origin (*archē*) of all reality, the *principium sine principio*.[30] Especially indicative is the language of prayer in the earliest liturgies. The oldest eucharistic prayer that has come down to us is addressed to the Father: 'We thank you, our Father, for the holy vine of David your servant, which you have given us to know through Jesus your servant; to you be honor for ever.'[31] The Council of Hippo (393) expressly orders that 'when the service is celebrated at the altar, prayer is always to be addressed to the Father'.[32] This is why the liturgical doxology takes this form: 'Glory to the Father through the Son in the Holy Spirit'.[33] Not only the Eastern Church but the Roman liturgy as well has retained this form of prayer down to the present time in the ending of the orations (presidential prayers) and in the great doxology at the end of the eucharistic canon: 'Through him, with him, in him, in the unity of the Holy Spirit, all glory and honor is yours, almighty Father, for ever and ever.'

Different emphases are indeed already to be heard in the Apologists of the second century (Justin, Tatian, Athenagoras, Theophilus of Antioch). These men are writing for the educated individuals of the pagan world and are therefore compelled to speak their language. The Apologists took advantage of the fact that the word Father had been used as early as Plato to characterize the supreme being in whom everything has its origin.[34] In Neoplatonism (and also in gnosticism) the Father is the supreme reality beyond being, whereas for the Stoics the description of God as Father is meant to express the unity of nature between God and the world and the kinship among all human beings.[35] Justin takes this as his point of contact when he describes God as 'Father of the universe' and 'Father of all human beings'.[36] This kind of language undoubtedly has a basis in the Old and New Testaments, but its use leaves out the christological mediation of the Fatherhood of God. The Fatherhood of God seems to be almost an idea accessible to reason, although Justin expressly insists that the fullness of the Logos has appeared only in Jesus Christ. The whole approach had in its favor the fact above all that the word 'Father' was particularly suited to be the focus of a synthesis between the philosophical question of the ultimate ground (*archē; principium*) of all reality and the biblical message concerning the origin and goal of creation and salvation history.[37] What the Bible says about the Father could be taken as an answer (for which philosophy itself paved the way) to the basic question asked in philosophy.

The attempt of the Apologists to present the Christian message in the garb of philosophy was a courageous and necessary step. It was not the result of a feeling of weakness but rather an expression of the vitality of early Christianity which thereby pressed forward with bold missionary zeal into a new cultural realm. Such attempts, of course, rarely succeed on the first attempt. The step taken by the Apologists led intially to a crisis, because these men did not distinguish clearly enough between two different questions: the relationship between the world and God as its source, and the relationship of Jesus as Son to the Father, or, to use another terminology, between the eternal and the temporal Fatherhood of God. The two questions were even frequently mixed in together. This was especially the case with Arius, who understood the Son as a kind of mediator in creation (a demiurge) and as the supreme creature. It took the two councils of Nicaea (325) and Constantinople (381) to bring clarification, as they defined the Son to be the same (or: one) in substance with the Father (*homoousios*).[38] It was thus determined that God is from eternity the Father of a Son who is of the same substance as himself.[39] Within God, then, the Father is origin (*archē*) and source (*pēgē*), as the Greeks expressed it,[40] or principle, as the Latins expressed it.[41] In relation to what is outside of God, on the other hand, creation and the history of salvation are the work of the entire Trinity.[42] The Greek Fathers in particular[43] set great store on the doctrine, for which Origen had already provided the foundations,[44] that the Father is the origin and source of the Godhead;[45] John Damascene summarizes it once again in his *De fide orthodoxa*, which became practically the textbook of the Eastern Church.[46] But Augustine, too, who became the founder of Western theology, writes that 'the Father is the source (*principium*) of the entire Godhead (*divinitas*) or, perhaps better, deity (*deitas*)'. The Councils of Toledo adopted the same language and described the Father as 'therefore the source and origin of the whole Godhead'.[48] Even in Thomas Aquinas there is an echo of this usage.[49] Of all the Scholastics, Bonaventure is the most emphatic in describing the Father as the *auctor* (author) and *fontalis plenitudo* (fontal fullness) of the Godhead, and in making *innascibilitas* (impossibility of being begotten or born) his essence.[50]

The clarifications made in the course of the history of theology and dogma also had negative effects. The emphasis on the true divinity of Christ led to the term 'God' being increasingly used not for the Father but for the one divine being possessed in common by Father, Son and Holy Spirit. The change could be seen even in the liturgical language of the church. Thus in Basil the liturgical doxology 'Glory be to the Father through the Son' was changed to read: 'Glory be to the Father with the Son and with the Holy Spirit',[51] until finally it became: 'Glory be to the Father and to the Son and to the Holy Spirit.' The effects became especially clear in Augustine's doctrine on the Trinity, which was to be so normative for the Latin West, and in particular in the prayers Augustine composed. It is clear, of course, that in the many prayers in his *Confessions* he *also* addresses God as Father; usually, however, he adopts the language of the Old Testament psalms and addresses him as 'God' or 'Lord'. But where he adopts a language of his own, he uses remarkably abstract and philosophical-sounding expressions: 'O eternal truth and true love and beloved eternity!'[52]

These changes in the language of prayer point to a danger: that the intra-trinitarian Fatherhood of the Father may become irrelevant to God's relationship with the world and human beings, so that the Trinity becomes a doctrine which is of interest to theologians but irrelevant to the world and history. Thus we find that in their treatises *De Deo uno* (on God as One) the Scholastics can speak of God, his nature, his attributes and thus also about his relation to the world without saying a word about the Father; of this they wait to speak until they come to the treatise *De Deo trino* (On God as Triune). This division of the one doctrine of God into two distinct treatises, *De Deo uno* and *De Deo trino*, is, however, highly problematical when seen from the standpoint of the scriptural witness and the early tradition, according to which the one God is always the Father.[52a] I shall therefore attempt to develop the material concerns of the treatise *De Deo uno* in the form of a doctrine on God the Father.

This development shows that even in the history of dogma and theology there are no gains without losses. The definitions that bring clarification also narrow the focus. We do not risk losing the gains they brought when we attempt to recover that which, as seen from the vantage point of our present knowledge of the history of theology, was either short-changed or simply lost. The attempt to articulate the Christian faith in the language of the day reflects not so much a problem peculiar to a past age as a perennial task of preaching and theology. The communication of a philosophical and theological doctrine of God is therefore not an outmoded speculative problem but an attempt to give an intellectually honest account of the Christian message about the Father. Given the contemporary challenge in principle to the very idea of God and in particular to any talk of a Father-God, the task has become a significantly more urgent one than it was in earlier centuries.

3. Theological definition of the essence of God

(a) The definition of God's essence in the horizon of Western metaphysics

While the philosophical inquiry into the ultimate ground (*archē*) of all reality is different in many respects from the biblical message about God as Father, that is, as the personal origin and source of all reality in the orders of creation and redemption, there is nonetheless an internal correspondence between them. This fact led at a very early date to a synthesis of the two approaches taken by faith and reason. In the course of this theological reflection on the testimony of scripture and tradition there arose a theological definition of God's essence which then served as a foundation for the entire theological tradition. The biblical name for God yielded a theological statement about the being of God. This synthesis locates us at the point where all the problems of the traditional doctrine on God intersect.

The starting point for this reflection was the Old Testament revelation of the name of God in connection with the burning bush in Ex. 3.14.[53] According to the Hebrew text, God reveals himself to Moses as 'I am there who am there.' The Hebrew verb *hayah*, used here, which we usually translate as 'to be,' means basically 'to effect, be effective'.[54] This passage of revelation, then, is not concerned with God's mere existence or with God as absolute Being. God's statement is a promise, a pledge that he is there, i.e., is with his people in an active, effective way. The second part of the statement adds that God is there as the one who is there, that is, he is present in a manner that cannot be calculated or defined. God's protecting and rescuing presence remains a mystery of his freedom. His being-there is absolutely certain, yet it is not at our disposal; God is always unconditionally true to his promise, yet always new in the way he carries it out. This historical self-definition of God is also given in other passages of scripture: God is the first and the last (Isa. 41.4; 44.6; 48.12; Rev. 1.17). He is the Alpha and the Omega (Rev. 1.4). But the Septuagint had already translated the promise of being-there into a statement about being: '*Egō eimi ho ōn*' (I am the One who is). The Vulgate follows suit: '*Ego sum qui sum*' (I am who am). English translations have traditionally followed the same line: 'I am who am' or 'I am who I am'. In these translations the historical promise becomes a metaphysical statement and a definition. But the transition can be seen already taking place within the Old Testament, when Wisdom 13.1 describes God as *ton onta*, 'him who exists'.

This transposition of the name of God into a definition of essence, after showing up in the Bible itself and in the translations of it, was taken as a foundation by the later tradition. We find the Jewish religious philosopher Philo of Alexandria already claiming on the basis of Exodus 3.14 that God's name is 'he who is' (*ho ōn*) or 'that which is' (*to on*).[55] Philo set a precedent with this thesis and it occurs repeatedly in the fathers of the church.[56] Augustine thought it possible to claim that on this particular point Philo and Moses were saying the same thing.[57] Athanasius, who led the fight at the Council of Nicaea, interprets in this light the conciliar assertion that the Son is from the being of the Father.[58] The medieval Scholastics accepted this synthesis and made it the basis of their systems.[59] It is obvious, of course, that the synthesis altered not only the interpretation of the Bible but philosophy as well. We must not assume that thinkers of the stature of Origen, Augustine and Thomas accepted traditional thought patterns in an unintelligent way; rather, all of them endeavoured to apply the formulas in a critical and creative way. This can be shown in all great theologians; I shall restrict myself in what follows to Thomas Aquinas.

Thomas Aquinas justifies the identification of the biblical name of God with the philosophical concept of being by this argument, among others, that being is the most universal of all concepts. The more comprehensive a concept, the more suited it is to being applied to God, since God embraces all being in himself. Thomas is here indirectly taking from Gregory of Nazianzus, by way of John Damascene, the idea of being as *pelagus substantiae infinitum et indeterminatum* (an infinite and unbounded ocean of being).[60] He links this idea with Neoplatonist images. In Neoplatonism Being (*ipsum esse*) stands at the apex of the pyramid of the Ideas; it is the first perfection after the One of Supra-Being. Thomas adopts this idea of *ipsum esse* as the supreme Idea, but he himself calls it *esse commune*, i.e., being in general, in which all existent things, but not God, participate.[61] For, as the origin of all being, God does not 'have' being but rather 'is' being. Unlike Neoplatonism, therefore, Thomas does not think of God as beyond being but rather as *ipsum esse subsistens*, subsistent being itself, in whose being all other existing things share.[62] For this reason God does not participate in *esse commune*; rather, *esse commune* participates in God;[63] it is the first and proper effect produced by God.[64] As subsistent being, God is then himself the origin and ground, or, in biblical language, the Father, of all reality.

This doctrine of God as subsistent being enables Thomas to save God's transcendence in relation to the world. For there is an infinite qualitative difference between the being-being of God and the having-being of creatures. When God is defined as *ipsum esse subsistens*, he is not being located within an ontological continuity that embraces both God and the world; on the contrary, Thomas expressly maintains that God is not in any genus nor even included in being.[65] He is infinitely exalted above all other reality. On the other hand, Thomas' definition of God, unlike that of Neoplatonism, also enables him to maintain the immanence of God in the world that goes with the idea of creation. For if God is the reality that embraces all being, it is not possible to think of his relation to the world and man as one purely of opposition; if God were simply opposed to the world, he would be limited by the world and would therefore be a finite being. But if God is thought of as Being in itself, then everything that exists participates in the reality of God; then God is in all things.[66] He is therefore not simply the distant and inaccessible one who is beyond being, rather, he is the God who is present in the world; he is omnipresent. Thus God is both transcendent and immanent.

From the definition of God as *ipsum esse subsistens* it follows that as the fullness of being God is not subject to any deficiency of being (= potentiality), but is unqualifiedly the absolutely perfect being and therefore pure actuality (*actus purus*). This identity of essence and existence in God is the reason both for his simplicity and his immutability. It means that God does not realize his essence in successive moments or acts but simply is his essence.[67] The eternity of God means, therefore, not simply that God is without beginning or end, but rather that he is simultaneously beginning and end. Since he does not need to realize his being through any succession, his eternity consists in the *tota simul et perfecta possessio* (instantaneously whole and perfect possession) of his being.[68]

The immutability and eternity that are entailed in the definition of God as *ipsum esse subsistens* do not mean that God is in every respect a fixed and motionless being. On the contrary, for from this definition it follows that he is pure knowing[69] and therefore has life in the highest possible degree.[70] Even, and in fact precisely, the God who is conceived with the help of the categories of classical metaphysics is not a dead God but in the highest possible measure a living God.

What Thomas expresses with the help of the concept of *ipsum esse subsistens*, later theologians, following the church fathers, tried to express with the help of the concept of aseity.[71] In so doing, they did not understand aseity only according to the immediate sense of the word, that is, as something negative. They meant to say not simply that God does not owe his existence to another, but rather that he exists exclusively by himself or that, without having become and in complete independence of any other reality, he is the absolutely unconditioned reality. Aseity is thus also understood in a positive sense; it says that God is the self-explanatory reality and that he is being by reason of his very essence. But asiety does immediately express only the negative side, whereas the concept *ipsum esse subsistens* expresses the positive ground, 'God is *ipsum esse subsistens*' must therefore be taken as the properly metaphysical definition of God's essence.

The now classical synthesis of Thomas Aquinas is an impressive work of genius. But is it tenable? The more deeply one goes into it, the more one has the impression of walking a lonely ridge between two abysses. The synthesis has been radically challenged in our century, especially by dialectial theology. E. Brunner regarded the translation of the name Yahweh into the concept of being as a 'tragic misunderstanding' and 'an error that bore disastrous fruit'.[72]

It must be responded, however, that Brunner himself has utterly misunderstood Thomas. In using the concept of *ipsum esse subsistens* Thomas is not trying to do what Brunner accuses him of doing, i.e. to locate God within a continuity of being that includes both God and world; on the contrary, he is seeking to maintain the transcendence of God. At the same time, however, there is a kernel of truth in Brunner's criticism. The differences between the biblical name for God and the traditional definition of God's essence are obvious. The Bible is talking not of God's being but of his being there, in the sense of being with us and for us. The classical definition of God's essence is incapable, at least at first sight, of expressing this living God of history and his intensely personal nature. God seems rather to become an abstraction, something neutral, even a faceless conceptual idol to whom we may ascribe everything else, but not the traits of personality. The philosophy of being seems incapable of doing full justice to the testimony of scripture.

The most penetrating criticism of the onto-theo-logical constitution of metaphysics and the theo-onto-logical constitution of theology comes from M. Heidegger. He summarizes as follows: 'Man can neither pray nor sacrifice to this God. Before the *causa sui*, man can neither fall to his knees in awe nor can he play music and dance before this God.' In fact, Heidegger even thinks that god-less thinking which feels obliged to abandon the God of philosophy, God as *causa sui*, is perhaps closer to the divine God. 'God-less thinking is more open to Him than onto-theo-logic would like to admit.'[73] Yet this criticism, too, is at least not fully just to the intellectual achievement of Thomas Aquinas. The definition of God as by essence *ipsum esse subsistens* has for its purpose precisely to differentiate God from *esse commune*. It is at least very open to question whether Thomas can be accused of a forgetfullness of being in the sense Heidegger gives to this phrase.[74]

J. E. Kuhn in particular has shown the great extent to which the Scholastic synthesis includes the idea of God's personality, which is so central to the Bible. Kuhn attempts a synthesis of the various Scholastic definitions of God's essence.[75] His point of departure is infinity, which is the Scotist definition of God's essence. Infinity distinguishes God from all finite creatures. But this negative approach would turn into a pantheism unless we were to go along with many Thomists and define God positively as absolute spirit (intellectuality), to whose essence it belongs to be infinite, not simply in intention (as in the case with the human spirit) but actually. But spirituality in turn implies reflectiveness and thus a conscious being-in-himself and for-himself; in an absolute spirit this means aseity. When the aseity of God is thus combined with his spirituality, his freedom is established. God can therefore be defined as absolute freedom and absolute person. In thus synthesizing the various Scholastic views Kuhn showed at the same time the extent to which the classical metaphysical definition of God's essence is thoroughly scriptural in what it says; it does not hide the personal face of the Father but endeavors to give the biblical message an intellectual form and to defend it before the bar of thought.

Kuhn's interpretation accomplished something further: it showed the connection that exists between the classical metaphysical definitions of God's essence and a definition formulated in the context of the modern philosophy of freedom. It made it clear that there can be no exclusive opposition between the two but rather that there are intrinsic continuities.

The man who ventured furthest in this question was the Würzburg dogmatic theologian H. Schell, who defined God as *causa sui*.[76] In doing so he was going back to Neoplatonism and to occasional formulas found in many of the church fathers; at the same time, he was making a link with the modern philosophy of self-positing freedom. According to Schell, no nature and no inherently inactive substantial being can procede absolute freedom, which in this respect differs from finite freedom. In Schell's view, therefore, God 'is not first a datum or being and only then active; he is primordial deed and therefore primordial datum'; he is 'the eternal actuation of infinite active power . . . the actuation of self-conscious truth and holiness'. Later on, Schell spoke somewhat more reservedly of the subsistent reality and subsistant act of God, rather than of self-causation and self-position. This definition of God as *causa sui* was rejected by most theologians because a being that causes itself must act before it exists; it must be before it is, and this violates the principle of contradiction. In addition, most theologians feared that the idea of self-realization would introduce becoming and therefore potentiality into God. These objections are irrefutable, given the presuppositions of classical metaphysics. But they do not come to grips with Schell's concern, which has validity despite his not fully successful formulations. His purpose is to overcome a reificatory and substantialist understanding of being and, on the basis of modern thought, to conceive God as being-in-action, as freedom and life. In so doing, Schell came far closer not only to the modern intellectual starting point but also to the biblical understanding of God than did his Scholastic adversaries, who managed to have his work put on the Index in 1898. To the detriment of the Christian faith they thus prevented his approach to the problem from bearing fruit in a new synthesis of faith and knowledge that would respond to the intellectual situations of the modern age. Should nineteenth- and twentieth-century theology have shown less courage for a critical and creative synthesis than the church fathers of the first centuries showed?

(d) The definition of God's essence in the horizon of the modern philosophy of freedom

While classical metaphysics moves in thought from being to freedom and understands freedom as the highest form of being, that is, as being that exists in itself and independently, modern philosophy starts with the subject and more particularly with freedom and proceeds then to think of being in the horizon of freedom. Kant speaks in this connection of a Copernican revolution,[77] which Fichte even more categorically defined as an option for freedom.[78] Not observable fact but free activity is the reality that alone brings the self-disclosure of the world. Being, therefore, is act, accomplishment, happening, event. Not self-contained being but existence, or freedom that goes out of itself and fulfills itself in action, is now the starting point and horizon of thought. It is clear that, given the horizon of this new starting point and this new mode of thought, God too must be thought anew.

At first glance there seems to be an inherent relation between biblical thought and modern thought. Efforts have therefore been made at times to represent modern thought as a secularized version of biblical thought and as the realization of the latter in the wordly sphere. But we must not overlook the dangers which the modern starting point represented for the Christian understanding of God. In the philosophy of freedom there was constant danger of God becoming a moment or element in the self-realization of the subject and his freedom; God was then the medium of moral freedom and the summation of the kingdom of freedom, but no longer a personal being over against man.[79] The danger showed itself in paradigmatic fashion in the 'atheism controversy' which Fichte set in motion in 1798 with his article 'Concerning the Foundation of Our Belief in the Divine Government of the World'. Since 'persons' exist only over against other persons of our world, Fichte concluded that personality implies limitation and finiteness and therefore cannot be predicated of God.[80] We find a similar objection being raised in our own century by K. Jaspers;[81] it also inspires trends in modern theology which for fear of objectifying God reject theism[82] or prefer to define God as suprapersonal rather than personal.[83] This problem is not a new one. It is to be found not only in the pantheistic and panentheistic currents of the modern age – in the world-centered piety of Goethe and the philosophy of G. Bruno and B. Spinoza – but also in the monistic understanding of reality that characterizes the Asiatic high religions, especially Buddhism, which is unwilling to ascribe either positive or negative attributes to God. The concept of person, especially in its application to God, is perhaps the most difficult point in the dialogue between Christianity and the Eastern religions.

A definition of God's essence in the horizon of freedom can already be justified, in a first reflection, in terms of the classical concept of person. For on the one hand the classical definition of the person includes individuality in the sense of an irreplaceable and inalienable uniqueness. Boethius' definition of person became normative for the entire tradition: '*naturae rationalis individua substantia* (an individual substance possessing a rational nature'.[84] This individual mode of existence of a spiritual nature seems to imply finiteness and therefore to exclude application of the concept of person to God. On the other hand, however, rationality and therefore infinity is part of the person. According to Thomas, who follows Aristotle, even the finite spirit is '*quodammodo omnia* (in a way all things)'; it is directed without limit to the whole of reality. Ex-istence – a being out of itself and beyond itself – therefore belongs to a spiritual nature. This aspect was brought out especially by Richard of St Victor in his definition of person: '*naturae intellectualis incommunicabilis existentia* (an intellectual nature existing incommunicably)'.[85] Each person, while being unique, is at the same time ordered to reality in its entirety. Even in the finite world, therefore, the person is characterized by a tension between an always concrete and irreplaceable individuality and an unlimited openness to the whole of reality. In other terms: in the person the whole of reality is present, but always in a unique way. The person is *Da sein* (being there), that is, the person is the 'there' of being.[86] The finite person is in an intentional manner the subsistence of being and to that extent is a *subsistens intentionale*. Because the whole of being is 'there' in an intentional way in the person, the person cannot be subordinated and sacrificed to any supposedly higher goal, value, coherence or whole; its personhood is instead the basis of its unconditional dignity, because of which it is never a means to an end, but always an end in itself.

With the classical concept of person as our starting point we can now in a second act of reflection reproduce the anthropological shift characteristic of the modern age. This need not lead the understanding of God into the aporias already mentioned. For, because of its dynamic ordering to the totality of being the person cannot find full satisfaction in anything finite, in any finite values whether material or spiritual, nor even in finite persons. This accounts for the restless and unquiet constant movement and self-transcending of man. The human person can reach definitive fulfillment only if it encounters a person who is infinite not only in its intentional claims on reality but in its real being; that is, only if it encounters an absolute person. Thus a more appropriate concept of person as the always unique 'there' of being leads necessarily to the concept of an absolute, a divine person.[87] If we understand the person as an always unique realization of being, then the category of person as applied to God does not mean an objectification of God. On the contrary, the concept of person is able to express in a new way the fact that in God being subsists in a unique way, that is, that God is *ipsum esse subsistens*.

The definition of God as a person both includes and goes beyond the classical definition of God's essence. It no longer looks at God in terms of substance and therefore does not define him as absolute substance, but thinks of him rather in the horizon of freedom and defines him as perfect freedom. This definition of God as essentially person has the advantage that it is more concrete and alive than the abstract metaphysical definition adopted by the tradition. It is also closer to the biblical picture of God as Father. This is especially so because personality necessarily says relationality. A person exists only in self-actualization in response to another person and as ordered to other persons. In the concrete a human person is not even able to live unless accepted and affirmed by other persons and unless he or she receives and at the same time gives love. We attain to fulfillment only by emptying ourselves out in love, so as to realize our own intentional infinity. Seen in the horizon of the person, the meaning of being is love. This thesis is of basic importance for a proper understanding of the personality of God. To call God a person is to say that God is the subsistent being which is freedom in love. Thus the definition of God's essence brings us back to the biblical statement: 'God is love' (I John 4.8, 16).

It is obvious, of course, that we can apply the category of person to God only by analogy. This does not mean that God is less a person than we are, but rather that he is a person in an incomparably higher way than we are. But the statement that God is person in an incomparably higher way than we are is to be distinguished from the thesis that God is supra-personal. When all is said and done, this thesis really says nothing, because 'person' is the highest category we have at our disposal. We can predicate the category in an analogous way, but to try to move beyond it into a higher, supra-personal dimension would mean leaving behind the realm of meaningful and responsible language. God's essence would then disappear into utter vagueness, indeterminacy and generality. This would be to misunderstand the biblical God, who has a concrete name. The category of person has three positive values:

1. The category of person holds fast to the truth that God is not an object or thing that can be observed and thus pinned down; he is, instead, a subject that exists, speaks and acts in a freedom which cannot be reduced to anything else. The category of person thus protects the unmanipulability and hiddenness that God displays in the revelation of his name. Since according to the Scholastic tradition *persona est ineffabilis* (the person is ineffable', the category of person keeps God from being assumed into some general concept or system. Thus the definition of God as a person stipulates, paradoxically, that in the final analysis God cannot be defined. As a person God is utterly and irreplaceably unique.

2. The category of person holds fast to the truth that God is not a predicate either of the world or of man; it emphasizes the fact that God is a sovereign subject. He is not the explanation and ideologization of the

world, or man, or any ideas, movements and interests. Therefore he may not be appropriated ideologically in behalf of any intra-worldly interest; we may not take his name in vain and misuse it, but must rather regard it as holy. God is therefore to be distinguished from idols, which are absolutizations of wordly values (power, money, sexuality, reputation, success, and so on). To put it in modern terms: faith in God as understood in the Bible has as one of its functions to exercise a critique of ideologies. Through a prophetic criticism of the idols and absolutizations of every kind that enslave human beings this faith can promote the freedom of man and protect the transcendence of the human person.[88] Acknowledgment of God's reign means freedom for man. But since God is, to an incomparably higher degree than the human person, an end in himself and never a means to an end, this concentration on the intra-worldly relevance of faith in God is subject to certain limits which may not be violated. The concept of person precludes any reduction of God to a function, whether the intention be conservative and affirmative or progressivist and critical. The primary thing is not the significance of God for us, but the acknowledgment of the Godness of God and the adoration and praise of him. 'We praise you for your glory.' The concept of person thus gives expression to the glory and holiness of God.

3. The category of person not only asserts the existence of God as a unique subject; it also says that God is the reality which determines everything. It takes seriously the fact that God is not simply an other-worldly being and not simply a person over against other persons, but rather is in all things, can be found in all things, and in particular can be encountered in all human beings. Yet even this does not say enough. When we define God, the reality that determines everything, as personal we are also defining being as a whole as personal. This entails a revolution in the understanding of being. The ultimate and highest reality is not substance but relation. For Aristotle, relation belongs among the accidents which are added to substance; he even regards it as the weakest of all entities. But when God reveals himself as the God of the Covenant and of dialogue, the God whose name means being-for-us and being-with-us, then relation takes priority over substance. For then the free turning of God to the world and to us grounds all intra-worldly substantiality. The meaning of being is therefore to be found not in substance that exists in itself, but in self-communicating love. The biblical idea of God thus has a positive significance as well as a negative. It says that the human person is accepted and loved without qualification as a person. Wherever, then, love 'occurs', there too the definitive meaning of all reality is realized in an anticipatory way and there too the reign of God has come, even if only in a fragmentary

and provisional manner. To believe in God the Father almighty means, then, to believe in the omnipotence of love and in love's eschatological victory over hatred, violence and egoism; it entails, too, the duty of living by this omnipotence and for this victory.

At this point a question arises which is utterly decisive for the further progress of our discourse about God. What does it mean to say that 'God is love'? After all that has been said thus far it certainly does not mean that that short statement can be inverted and that we can say 'Love is God'. To accept such an inversion is to fail to realize that God is a subject; it is to locate God once again under some more universal notion. But the ultimately decisive question is this: for whom is this love which is God himself? Is God in his love a pure outpouring of himself upon the world? Is it impossible, therefore, as Hegel claimed, for God to be without the world? If this is so, is he still God? Or must we rather say that God is love within himself? That he is communication and self-emptying within himself? Is God not only Father of the world and of human beings but first of all Father of his eternal consubstantial Son? Thus the definition of God's essence as perfect freedom in love turns us back, as does the biblical image of God as Father, to the christological ground for the way the Bible talks about God.

II

Jesus Christ, Son of God

1. The question of salvation as point of departure for the God-question

The church's profession of faith is not concerned with God in an unspecified sense of this word; its faith is in the God of Jesus Christ, the God who is the Father of our Lord Jesus Christ. For this reason, after confessing God as the Father almighty, the creed continued: . . . 'and in Jesus Christ his only Son'. The question of God is therefore inseparable from the question of Christ. But, once again, the creed does not speak of Jesus Christ as God's Son in an abstract way; it adds the meaning for us of this central point of the Christian faith: 'who for us men and for our salvation came down from heaven.' The question of Christ and therefore the question of God as well is placed within the framework of the question of salvation. The Christian's concern is not with God in himself but with God-for-us, the God of Jesus Christ, who is a God of human beings (Heb. 11.16). A preaching and teaching about God that spoke of God in himself without saying what he means for me and for us would be irrelevant and suspect of being an ideology. The concern is therefore always with the concrete God who is the salvation of human beings and whose glory is man alive.[1] In setting forth this thesis, the Christian profession of faith reverses the basic dogma of the modern critique of religion: God is not dead; he is the living God of human beings and is professed as being the hope and fulfillment of man.

In making the question of salvation the point of departure for the question of God and of Christ we are, of course, opening ourselves to very serious objections, especially in our day. The obvious question arises: if God is and if he is truly a God of human beings, what is the source of evil, of unmerited suffering in all its varied forms? Why and for what purpose is there exploitation and oppression, guilt, anxiety, sickness and death, persecution and rejection? Not least of all: why and for what purpose is the suffering of children who are not only personally innocent but are exposed to suffering without any possible protection? These experiences of unmerited and unjust suffering are existentially a much stronger argument against faith in God than are all the epistemological and scientific arguments, all the arguments used by critics of religion and ideology, all the other philosophical arguments of whatever kind. These experiences are in fact the rock on which atheism stands.[2] No one has formulated this argument more forcefully than Epicurus. Either God wants to get rid of evil but cannot – and then he is helpless and not God; or he can get rid of it but chooses not to – then he himself is wicked and at bottom is really the devil; or he does not want to and is not able – then both of the previous conclusions follow or he wants to and is able to – but then whence comes evil?[3] A. Camus gives the argument in this form: 'Either we are not free and God the all-powerful is responsible for evil. Or we are free and responsible but God is not.' All the Scholastic subtleties have not made this paradox any more telling nor, on the other hand, have they been able to take the edge from it.[4] After the dreadful horrors our century has seen, post-Auschwitz theology believes it now impossible to speak responsibly of a God who is both omnipotent and good.[5]

The objections raised here against the Christian message of redemption were raised against Christianity from the beginning by Jewish theologians. How is it possible to claim that the world has been redeemed when it is in such an obviously unredeemed state? Like Christianity, Jewish theology maintains, of course, that God is a God of human beings, a God who speaks and acts in history. But, in addition, it has 'always maintained a concept of redemption as an event which takes place publicly, on the stage of history and within the community. It is an occurrence which takes place in the visible world and which cannot be conceived apart from such a visible appearance.'[6] That kind of redemption is still an eschatological hope for Judaism.

We encounter this hope in a secularized form in the various modern utopian visions, among which the faith in evolutionary progress and the revolutionary utopianism of Marxism with its coming kingdom of freedom have been the most influential. Both of these assume that man must take his destiny into his own hands and be the author of his own happiness. When its radical implications are accepted, this modern idea of human autonomy excludes in principle any idea of a mediator and therefore any idea of a redemption that is not a self-redemption and self-liberation of man by himself.[7] In this perspective the hope of redemption and liberation by God seems to suppress human freedom, to devalue its efforts, even to condemn man to prove passivity and pure endurance, and thus to sanction the status quo.[8] It seems to take away man's responsibility for himself and conditions in the world; the idea of a substitute or representative redeemer seems a refusal to take such a responsibility seriously.

The passage of time has made it clear that the modern Enlightenment was based on an abstract picture of man. It failed to see that human freedom is a situated freedom and therefore is subject to physiological, biological, sociological, economic and psychological conditions, so that the person does not unqualifiedly 'possess' freedom and the ability to use it, provided only that he or she wants to. The freedom of the individual is interwoven with a universal situation of disaster. Every attempt to alter this situation is itself subject to the conditions created by the disaster. The result is an unending satanic cycle of guilt and revenge, violence and counter-violence. There is therefore no revolution that will not later be betrayed. In addition, there is the finiteness of man, which finds its starkest expression in death. Death is, above all else, a sign that all of man's attempts to deal with his disastrous situation must remain fragmentary and ultimately fail. At best man can limit evil; attempts to eliminate it always end in violence and totalitarianism, which are themselves evils.

These insights into the suffering that is inherent in human existence have changed the situation of theology. Whereas modern theology's partner in dialogue used to be the enlightened unbeliever, the partner in dialogue of any contemporary theology is suffering man who has concrete experience of the persisting situation of disaster and is therefore conscious of the weakness and finiteness of his human existence. This suffering can take many forms: exploitation and oppression, guilt, sickness, anxiety, persecution, rejection, and the many shapes of death.[9] And all these experiences of suffering are not peripheral and residual aspects of existence, not the shadow side of human life, as it were; rather; they characterize the human condition as such. Nietzsche rightly observes that the depth of suffering of which human beings are capable almost determines the order of their rank.[10] A theology that takes the human experience of suffering as its starting point starts, therefore, not with a borderline phenomenon but with the center and depths of human existence.

There is another reason why the question of God and the question of suffering belong together. We would not be able to suffer from our situation unless we had an at least implicit pre-apprehension of an undamaged, happy fulfilled kind of existence; unless we were at least implicitly looking for salvation and redemption. Only because we as human beings are meant for salvation do we suffer at our disastrous situation and rebel against it. If we had no 'longing for the wholly other' (M. Horkheimer), we would make the best of what is and accept what is not. Experiences of suffering are experiences of a contrast; it is precisely in our wretchedness that we also experience our greatness (B. Pascal). Therefore even the atheism for which this world is everything suffers shipwreck on the reef of suffering. 'For even the abolition of God does not explain suffering and does not assuage pain. The person who cries out in pain over suffering has his own dignity, which no atheism can rob him of.'[11]

If hope is to be all possible in the face of the universal situation of suffering and disaster, if in the face of injustice that cries out to heaven human beings are not to surrender their dignity, then a new beginning must be possible that cannot be derived from the conditions present in our situation, and there must be a final authority that is above all injustice and will have the last word to say at the end of history. Thomas Aquinas formulated this idea with unparalleled intellectual boldness, by reversing the thesis that evil is an argument against God and saying: *'quia malum est Deus est* (because evil exists, God exists).'[12] For hope in the face of despair is possible only in the light of redemption.[13] It would be futile to seek an absolute meaning without God.[14]

The question of God, then, and the question of suffering belong together. But the question of suffering also alters the question of God. The attempt to articulate the question of God in the perspective of the question of suffering has traditionally been called 'theodicy'.[15] This idea occurs as such for the first time in Leibniz,[16] but the thing itself is far older. The point has always been to justify God despite the existence of evil. Because of the presuppositions of the Christian faith two possible solutions were excluded in advance, since they would have attacked the Christian concept of God (and indeed any rational concept of God) at its very roots. I refer to the attribution of evil to God himself (monism) and the attribution of evil to a primordial evil principle which is independent of God (dualism). Plato had already realized that from God only good can come.[17] All the more then must Christian theology, which defines God as absolute freedom in love, exclude both dualism, which limits the absolute freedom of God, and monism, which jeopardizes his love. The traditional solution, therefore, was that God can only allow freedom for the sake of good, as a means to achieve the purposes of divine providence and bring order into the universe. Consequently, God allows evil either as a punishment for sin and a test and purification for man, or else as a way of bringing out the full riches and variety of the universe and the beauty of the good.[18] There has recently been a comparable attempt to explain evil as an unavoidable by-product of evolution.[19] Leibniz went furthest in this direction when he sought to prove that the present world is the best of all conceivable worlds, and in this way to justify God. But this optimistic version of theodicy is almost indistinguishable from a pessimistic, even tragic view of the world. Finiteness must be understood as a metaphysical evil and to that extent turned into a human evil, while evil understood as a service to the good is in the last analysis stripped of its evilness. But this way of mediatizing evil ultimately outmanoeuvers freedom and at bottom fails to take it seriously. What is left, in this explanation, of respect for the suffering of the individual, who is not simply a particular instance of something universal nor simply an element in a world-order, however magnificent? D. Sölle goes so far as to characterize these attempted solutions of the problem of theodicy as theological sadism.[20] In any case, Dostoievsky rightly objected that such harmony is secured at too great a cost: 'Therefore I hasten to return my ticket of admission'.[21]

Despite these legitimate criticisms, there is a valid insight in traditional theodicy: that for all its horror evil is only a secondary reality which can exist only be contradicting the good and can be experienced as evil only in the framework of the good. But this valid basic insight needs to be plumbed far more than it is in traditional theories. For the relativity of evil by comparison with the good allows no harmonization and adjustment and certainly no balancing of the one against the other. On the contrary, the relativity of evil brings out the contradictory character of evil. Because of this internal contradiction, evil is ultimately not nothing, but it is in itself an emptiness.[22] For this reason, scripture tells us, the sinner has forfeited his right to exist; he merits death. This amounts to saying that the real problem is not the justification of God but the justification of the sinner. The very fact that despite his sin the sinner continues to live shows that sin is always encompassed by an ever greater love which, precisely by accepting and justifying the sinner, exposes and overcomes the vanity of evil. An answer to the problem of evil and suffering becomes visible here in the mode of hope; precisely because it takes both sinful man and suffering man seriously, it redeems sin and suffering by an ever greater love. The hope is hope in the coming of absolute love that identifies itself with suffering and with the sufferer in the world. For sufferers the quest for God is a quest for a divine com-passion (in the proper sense of this word), an identification of God with the suffering and death of human beings.

The coherence of the question of God, the question of salvation, and the question of Christ has now become clear. The very nature of things makes it clear that for the Christian faith Jesus Christ or, more accurately, the cross of Christ is the place where the real decision is made on the question of God. The question of God, when given concrete form in the presence of evil and suffering, can therefore be answered only christologically and staurologically in the form of a *theologia crucis* (theology of the cross).

When Christian faith undertakes such an answer, it is not answering the question of the meaning of suffering by an appeal to an abstract cosmic order. The good to which God orders everything has, according to the Bible, a concrete name: Jesus Christ, for whom everything was created and in whom all things hold together (Col. 1.16f.). He is the concrete predestination of all reality (Eph. 1.4); God intends to unite all things in him at the end (Eph. 1.10) and so be 'all in all' (I Cor. 15.28).

2. The salvific proclamation of Jesus the Christ

(a) The messianic promise of salvation in the Old Testament

The Acts of the Apostles proclaims that Jesus is the Messiah or, as the Greeks would say, that he is the Christ (Acts 17.3; 18.5 etc.). It thus proclaims that Jesus of Nazareth is the fulfillment of the messianic expectation of the Old Testament and the eschatological bringer of salvation. This messianic consciousness impressed itself so deeply on Christanity that the original confession 'Jesus is the Christ' could later on turn into the proper name 'Jesus Christ'. Accordingly, the followers of Jesus of Nazareth were quite soon called 'Christians' (Acts 11.26), that is, Messiah-people. Because of this conviction regarding the messiahship of Jesus the christological interpretation of the Old Testament became fundamental for the New Testament and for the interpretation of scripture in the early and medieval church.

The opposition which Judaism raised against this christological use of the Old Testament has been taken up in a new way in modern biblical criticism. The majority of critics are of the opinion that the messianic hope plays only a secondary role and represents only a secondary current of thought in the Old Testament, and is by no means to be regarded as the center of the Old Testament or the key to its understanding. What is central to the Old Testament is rather the promise that God himself will be the salvation of his people; the focus of interest is in the coming of God and his kingdom and not in the coming of the Messiah. By and large, modern biblical criticism has also adopted a second presupposition, namely, that while Jesus understood himself wholly against the background of the Old Testament, he did not think of himself as the Messiah and did not proclaim himself to be the Messiah.[23] If these two principles of biblical criticism are valid, then the question becomes unavoidable of the continuity between the Old Testament and the New, and even between Jesus and Christianity, as the latter is already attested in the New Testament. Does Jesus even still belong to Judaism, as M. Buber and R. Bultmann both claim, though on the basis of very different presuppositions?[24] Moreover, what legitimacy has Christianity, if it cannot appeal either to the Old Testament or to Jesus himself?

This much is now clear: the messianic claim of Christianity obviously compels the question of the relation between the coming of Jesus and the coming of God. The messianic question can be answered if we raise the question of the relation between Jesus and God, and thus the God-question itself.

The messianic question cannot be answered if we take as our basis only isolated passages of the Old Testament. The reason is that certainly messianic prophecies are not very numerous. The situation changes when with H. Gese we take as our point of departure the entire combined witness of the Old and New Testaments.[25] The basic structure of biblical revelations assigns a fundamental importance to a mediator of revelation. For the personal encounter of God with human beings is part of biblical revelation, and in this encounter human beings are represented by individuals from among them, in accordance with the law of representation.

The history of revelation, which has the idea of representation as a distinguishing mark, entered a new phase with the institution of the Davidic monarchy. The early Israelite tradition had begun with the experience of the exodus, that is, with the liberation from slavery under the Egyptian monarchy; as a result, that tradition had been inherently anti-monarchical (cf. Judg. 9.8–12; I Sam. 8.1–22). Now, however, the Davidic monarchy had brought peace at home and abroad. As a result, the office of king could be thought of as an institution through which Yahweh acted to save, and even as 'an institutional guarantee of that history of his people's liberation which Yahweh himself had inaugurated'.[26] In the prophecies of Balaam (Num. 24) and Nathan (II Sam. 7), but especially in the royal psalms (Ps. 2; 45; 72; 89; 110), the monarchy was given theological legitimacy. This development took place as a result of contact with, or at least by analogy with, the ideology of kingship in the ancient Near East: the king was given the title of Son of God and enthroned, he was promised the whole earth as his realm, and finally he was assured of victory over all enemies. Such influences from the outside world around Israel were possible only if analogous approaches to problems had already taken shape in Israel's own tradition; these made such a takeover possible and then could, with the help of the outside influences, be further interpreted and formulated. In other words, there must have been an internal preparation for the external influence. H. Gese finds this point of contact in the Zion tradition. When the ark of God is transferred to Zion, God takes possession of a piece of ground; he enters into the space of the present world. God becomes earthly;

he condescends to dwell here. For this reason, the son of David who is enthroned on Zion is at the same time a Son of God. The Bible, of course, understands this divine sonship not in physical terms, as the surrounding world did, but in the context of the historical faith in election, and therefore in a demythologized sense, which we can best describe as adoptionist.[27]

At his enthronement and adoption as son of God each son of David was, of course, given a cloak to wear that was too big for him. Existing power relationships were in flagrant contrast with the elevated claims made for him. Every enthronement therefore raised the question: are you he that is to come, or must we wait for another? As a result, the Davidic monarchy pointed beyond itself; it was a promise of a future fulfillment and almost necessarily gave rise to messianic expectations. It could not but awaken hopes of a new son of David who would truly be God's Son and the definitive bringer of universal peace and salvation.[28]

Messianic hopes in the narrow and proper sense of the term came into existence only after the catastrophe of the destruction of Jerusalem and after the collapse of the historical monarchy due to the afflictions of the exilic period. That period brought a sweeping eschatologization of all ideas of salvation. The great saving acts of the past – the exodus, the covenant at Sinai, and the establishment of the Davidic monarchy – were projected into the future in an even more exalted form.[29] The situation in which the messianic idea originated shows that it is not a legitimation of existing power relationships, but rather a critical and utopian reverse image of the experiences Israel had of its historical kings and now of the political institutions of the various occupying powers.[30]

Individual messianic expectations took varying forms. The most important of these expectations is to be seen in the Emmanuel prophecy of Isaiah. The promise to King Ahaz that a virgin would conceive a child and bear a son (Isa. 7.14) was originally a promise that judgment would fall on the unbelieving House of David; later on it turned into a promise of salvation in the form of a new messianic king. 'For to us a child is born, to us a son is given; and the government will be upon his shoulder, and his name will be called "Wonderful Counselor, Mighty God, Everlasting Father, Prince of Peace". Of the increase of his government and of peace there will be no end, upon the throne of David, and over his kingdom, to establish it, and to uphold it with justice and with righteousness from this time forth and for evermore' (Isa. 9.5ff.). Isa. 11.2 adds the promise of the Spirit; to a vision of peace among the nations is added one of universal cosmic peace (Isa. 11.6–9). The prophet Zechariah makes his own this hope of a just and non-violent, humble and poor prince of peace: 'Rejoice greatly, O daughter of Zion! Shout aloud, O daughter of Jerusalem! Lo, your king comes to you; triumphant and victorious is he, humble and riding on an ass, on a colt the foal of an ass . . . . He shall command peace to the nations; his dominion shall be from sea to sea, and from the River to the ends of the earth' (Zech. 9.9f.; cf. Jer. 23.5; Micah 5.1f.). This spiritualizing tendency led to a twofold messianic expectation: alongside the Davidic anointed appeared a high-priestly Messiah (Zech. 4.1–4), hope of whom lived on subsequently at Qumran. In Ezekiel, the promise that Yahweh himself will be the eschatological shepherd of his people is connected with a promise to appoint a single shepherd, a servant David (34.23). Only in the Maccabean period, a time of persecution, does the messianic hope gradually take the form of an individual, personal figure. The Messiah is now seen as a warrior and even as a martyr (Zech. 13.7). There is also the Pharisaic Messiah, who is an observer of the Law.[31] Finally, in the apocalyptic literature, beginning in Daniel 7, the figure of the Messiah is fused with the figure of the apocalyptic Son of Man. He brings not only a new period but a new aeon, that is, a radically and qualitatively new beginning after the complete collapse of the old aeon, a new beginning that is not only national but universal and cosmic. According to the metaphorical discourses of the Book of Enoch, this son of man figure is endowed with the spirit of wisdom[32] (cf. already Sir. 24.10ff.).

Thus all the major lines of Old Testament tradition converge in the expectation of a Messiah: Davidism, prophetism, sapiential theology and apocalyptic. All these movements find their fulfillment in Jesus the Christ, the poor, non-violent, humble and suffering Messiah, the coming Son of Man, who as the Logos is Wisdom itself. In him God has definitively brought to fulfillment the promise regarding Zion; in him God has definitively entered into history in order to establish his rule as a kingdom of freedom in love. Jesus Christ sums up and at the same time goes beyond the Old Testament hope.[33] What, then, is new and specifically Christian in the New Testament?

(b) Ministry and preaching of Jesus of Nazareth

There is today a broad consensus among exegetes that New Testament christology[34] has its starting point and original basis in the disciples' faith that Jesus, who had been crucified, was raised from the dead. According to this view, there was no explicit christological profession of faith before Easter. All the biblical titles indicating Christ's high estate: Christ (Messiah), redeemer, servant of God, Son of God, and so on, are post-Easter confessional testimonies which Jesus did not expressly claim for himself. The one exception is the idea of 'Son of Man' which in the Gospels occurs, with one exception, only on the lips of Jesus, but which did not form part of a later confession of faith.

At the center of the preaching and ministry of Jesus is not the person of Jesus himself but the coming reign of God. Mark 1.15 given a valid summation of this central and all-inclusive content of the ministry and preaching of Jesus: 'The time is fulfilled, and the kingdom of God is at hand; repent, and believe in the gospel.' Attempts have often been made to remove the message of the kingdom of God from its central place in the preaching of Jesus. According to A. von Harnack Jesus' real concern is with the fatherhood of God and the infinite value of the human soul.[35] According to H. Conzelmann the preaching of Jesus, the doctrine of God, eschatology and ethics are juxtaposed in a relatively unconnected way.[36] But it can be shown that all these themes have an intrinsic connection with Jesus' message about the kingdom of God and that the latter is the center, and provides the framework, of his entire preaching.[37]

In the Old Testament 'kingdom of God' is a relatively late abstraction based on the statement: 'Yahweh is (has become) king' (cf. Ps. 93.1; 96.10; 97.1; 99.1).[38] It follows from this that in the reign of God the Old Testament is asserting not primarily a kingdom in the sense of a space ruled by God, but rather God's exercise of lordship here and now in history, or the revelation of the Godness of God. In the Old Testament this exercise of lordship is already connected with the reign of justice, peace and life. The concept of the reign or kingdom of God therefore sums up the entire Old Testament history of promise and hope. Jesus deliberately makes all this his own: 'The blind receive their sight and the lame walk, lepers are cleansed and the deaf hear, and the dead are raised up, and the poor have good news preached to them' (Matt. 11.5). But Jesus also connects his message about the kingdom of God with the apocalyptic idea of a new aeon. The linking of the two ideas is made clear by the fact that Jesus also describes the kingdom of God as a realm of salvation which human beings can inherit (Matt. 25.34) and enter (Mark. 9.46). The incorporation of this apocalyptic idea has two results. On the one hand, it becomes clear that the reign of God is entirely God's very own doing, which we can neither plan for nor bring to pass; it is not a better world but a new world. It is therefore also not a supreme good, not the kingdom of the spirit and of freedom, as liberal theology maintained, and not a social and political utopia, as political theology, old and new, often would like it to be. On the other hand, the message of the reign of God, precisely when understood in the apocalyptic framework, subsumes not only the quest and hope of Israel but also the human quest of peace, freedom justice, and life. It is the irreducible new beginning which God alone can provide; but this new brings the old to a superabundant fulfillment. The revelation that God is indeed God means at the same time the realization of the humanity of human beings, the salvation of the world. Therefore, in the context of his preaching of God's kingdom, and especially in his parables, Jesus is able to rediscover the world as God's creation and proclaim God as lord of all reality. The miracles of Jesus, the historical nucleus of which is indisputable, are signs and anticipations of this new and reconciled world that has been made whole.

The fact that God's reign comes wholly from God and thus brings the world to its salvation does not mean that God's action eliminates human action; rather, the coming of God's reign categorically demands human action, while also making this action possible and setting it free. This is not to say that we can plan, effect and build the reign of God. No, that reign is God's doing. But as God's saving act for the sake of human beings it does not ignore the latter. The concrete coming of the reign of God is therefore bound up with conversion and faith. The response of man is a constitutive element in the coming of God's reign. This reign would not make its way into our history if it did not make its way into hearts and therefore into the freedom of faith. God's reign is therefore entirely God's doing and entirely man's doing. But it is not an act of violence; it comes by man allowing it to be bestowed on him and by his giving it in turn to others. The reign of God consists in the coming of God's non-violent love into the world.

Here we have reached the new element in Jesus' preaching of the kingdom of God. Jesus proclaims the reign of God not under the sign of judgment, as John the Baptist still does, but under the sign of grace, forgiveness, mercy and love. He proclaims God as a Father who loves human beings, forgives sin, and makes sinners his children once more (Luke 15). This merciful and forgiving love of God is unconditional. Jesus does in fact think of himself as sent only to Israel; but the unconditionality of the salvation he proclaims is the material basis and point of departure which could lead after Easter to the missionary proclamation that disassociated salvation from membership in Israel and thus from the Jewish Law. Consequently, even though Paul did not know Jesus personally, he understood him best when he transposed Jesus' message of the *basileia* into a proclamation of justice from God through faith alone. John also understood correctly, though differently, the meaning of Jesus' preaching when he summed everything up in the statement: 'God is love' (I John 4.8, 16).

What is new about the message of Jesus is not only its content but also the fact that he linked his 'cause', namely, the kingdom of God, indissolubly with his own person. We hear over and over of 'now', 'today' (cf. Luke 4.21; 10.23f.; Matt. 11.5). The connection between the decision one makes regarding his person and message and the eschatological decision of the Son of Man when he comes for judgment is clearest in Mark 8.38: 'For whoever is ashamed of me and my words in this adulterous and sinful generation, of him will the Son of man be ashamed, when he comes in the glory of his Father with the holy angels.' In the decision of faith or unbelief the eschatological judgment is already being made. In the ministry, preaching and whole person of Jesus God's 'cause' is already present and at work; in Jesus the condescending movement of God, which can already be seen in the entire Old Testament, reaches its climax. In Jesus, God has definitively entered the time and space of this world. For this reason the Davidic expectations of an eschatological kingship as well as the expectations of the prophets, have been fulfilled in Jesus.

Even though Jesus does not explicitly claim christological titles, and even though in particular he does not speak of himself as the Son of God, the claim does find indirect and implicit expression of a very emphatic kind. This indirect christology of Jesus himself can be shown in various ways.

A first way starts from the preaching of Jesus. At first glance Jesus comes on the scene like a rabbi, a prophet or teacher of wisdom. But closer examination discovers some characteristic differences between him and the three groups named. The contemporaries of Jesus were obviously aware of the difference, for they asked one another in astonishment: 'What is this? A new teaching! With authority . . . ' (Mark 1.22, 27; etc.). When Jesus contrasts the words of the Old Testament with his own 'But I say to you. . . ' (Matt. 5.22, 28; etc.), he is not only giving a binding interpretation of the Old Testament Law but at the same time going beyond it. His formula 'But I say to you . . . ' sets his words alongside and even above what 'was said to the men of old', that is, what God himself had said under the former covenant. In his 'But I say to you . . . ' Jesus is thus claiming to speak the definitive word of God. And in uttering this definitive words he speaks differently from the prophets. He never says, like the prophets; 'Thus says the Lord', 'Oracle of Yahweh'. Unlike the prophets, Jesus does not distinguish his own words from the word of God. He says simply: 'Amen, amen, I say to you.' He evidently understands himself to be the mouth of God, the voice of God. This is a claim without parallel in Judaism.

A second way of bringing out the implicit christology of Jesus himself takes for its starting point the ministry and conduct of Jesus. One of the best attested traits of Jesus' ministry is that he used to eat at table with sinners and tax collectors; in other words, that he associated with those who at that times were labeled as godless. He was therefore abused as the companion of sinners and tax collectors (Matt. 11.19). This conduct on the part of Jesus had only an indirect connection with his criticism of society or with social changes. In the East a sharing of the table meant a sharing of life; in Judaism, it meant in particular a communion in the sight of God. Every meal was ultimately a prefiguration of the eschatological meal and of eschatological communion with God. The meals Jesus takes with sinners and tax collectors are therefore eschatological meals, anticipatory celebrations of the banquet of salvation in the final age. When therefore

Jesus accepts sinners to share his table with him, he is indirectly accepting them into communion with God. Once again, then, this behavior of Jesus toward sinners implies an unparalleled christological claim. Jesus himself voices it indirectly: when he is attacked for his behavior toward sinners (Luke 15.2), he narrates the parable of the lost son, which is really a parable of the Father's forgiving love (Luke 15.11–32). Jesus thus identifies his own activity with the action of God toward sinners. Jesus acts as one who stands in God's place. In him and through him God's love and mercy become real here and now. It is not a long step from this to what Jesus says in John: 'He who has seen me has seen the Father' (John 14.9).

There is still a third way of bringing out the implicit christology of the earthly Jesus. It can hardly be denied that as a historical fact Jesus gathered a band of disciples and, in particular, that the choice of the Twelve goes back to him. At first glance, Jesus is here acting simply like a Jewish rabbi who gathers a group of disciples. But there are significant differences between discipleship under the rabbis and discipleship under Jesus. The difference is already clear from the fact that one could not ask Jesus to be accepted as a disciple; Jesus chose with sovereign freedom 'those whom he desired' (Mark 3.13). Furthermore, there is no question, as there was with the rabbis, of a temporary master-disciple relationship that would last until the one-time disciple became a teacher in his turn. There is but one teacher (Matt. 10.24f.; 23.8). Therefore the ties binding the disciples of Jesus to their master are more extensive than with the rabbis: they share his journeying, his homelessness, and his dangerous destiny. There is an individed community of life, a sharing of destiny for better or for worse. The decision to follow Jesus means a breaking of all other ties; it means 'leaving everything' (Mark 10.28); ultimately one risks one's life and even the gallows (Mark 8.34). Such a radical and wholehearted following amounts to a confession of Jesus and thus implies a christology. The christology implied in following also shows that not only is there a material continuity of confession in the pre-Easter and post-Easter periods but also that there is a sociological continuity between the pre-Easter and post-Easter groups of disciples.

Finally, there is a fourth way. The most important pointer to an indirect christology in Jesus himself is the way he addresses God. It can hardly be denied that Jesus called God *Abba* and that the manner in which he did so was characteristic of him. Also significant is the fact that he always distinguishes between 'my Father' (Mark 14.36 par.; Matt. 11.25 par.) and 'your Father' (Luke 6.36; 12.30, 32) or 'your heavenly Father' (Mark 11.25 par.; Matt. 23.9). He never includes himself with his disciples by saying 'our Father'. The Lord's Prayer is not evidence to the contrary, because he begins it by saying: 'When you pray, say . . .' (Luke 11.2; Matt. 6.9). This differentiated usage is maintained throughout all the strata of the New Testament down to the classical formulation in the gospel of John: 'My Father and your Father' (John 20.17). There are good reasons for asserting that the substance of this differentiation goes back to Jesus himself. This exclusive 'my Father' points to an incommunicable and unique relationship between Jesus and God. The linguistic usage renders perceptible his special consciousness of being Son. Whether or not he explicitly claimed the title 'Son' for himself, the way in which he speaks implicitly says that although all are the children of God (Matt. 5.9, 45), he is God's Son in a special and unique way. He is *the* Son, who alone makes of us the sons and daughters of God.

This indirect approach to the Son-christology is not simply a new argument and justification for the traditional dogmatic christology, which is also the christology contained in the post-Easter testimony of the New Testament. Rather we have here, even materially, a new christological starting point. This is so in two respects. First, we no longer start, like the two-nature christology of Chalcedon, with the question of the relation between the human and divine natures in Jesus Christ; rather, we see the two-nature doctrine as indirectly and in its substance grounded in the relationship of Jesus to his Father.[39] In his being as Son Jesus has his radical origin in God and radically belongs to God. The turning of Jesus to the Father implies the prior turning of the Father to Jesus. The relation of Jesus to the Father implies the prior relation of the Father to him, the self-communication of God to him. The subsequent Son-christology is therefore simply the interpretation and translation of what is secretly present in Jesus' obedience as Son and his self-surrender as Son. What Jesus lived out ontically before Easter is interpreted ontologically after Easter. But there is more. The new approach provided by an indirect christology makes it possible, secondly, to link christology and soteriology right from the start. Jesus is the mode in which the self-communicating, self-outpouring love of God exists on the human scene; he is this for us. The being of Jesus is thus inseparable from his mission and his service; conversely, his service presupposes his being. Being and mission, ontological christology and functional christology cannot be played off against each other; they cannot even be separated from each other, for they condition each other. The function of Jesus, his being-there (*Dasein*) for God and for others, is at the same time his very being.

The indirect christology of the earthly Jesus is thus a personal summation of his message about the coming reign of God as the reign of love. He is this reign of God in his very person. Henceforth there can be no more talk of God that ignores Jesus; in Jesus God defines himself in an eschatological and definitive way as the Father of Jesus Christ; Jesus therefore belongs to the eternal being of God. In his person he is the definitive interpretation of the will and being of God. In him God has entered history once and for all.

Finally, I must mention a third and perhaps decisive novelty about the ministry and preaching of Jesus. The revolutionary novelty and even scandal of the cross for Jews and Gentiles alike (I Cor. 1.23) becomes clear to us if we consider the popular Jewish messianic expectation and the abhorrence felt by Romans at execution by crucifixion.[40] Many exegetes today are admittedly of the opinion that Jesus himself did not understand his death as a saving event.[41] On the other hand, we may point to the fact that his violent death was a consequence of his ministry and preaching. Jesus probably glimpsed the possibility of a violent end, for the hostility of his adversaries and their intention to trap him were only too clear. He had before his eyes the fate of the prophets and especially the fate of the Baptist. He knew the Old Testament songs about the Servant of God in Second Isaiah and the late Jewish ideas about the death of the just man. (Wisdom 2.20) and the expiatory significance attached to it (II Macc. 7.18, 37f.; II Macc. 6.28f.; 17.22). Since he understood his entire existence as one of obedience to the Father and service to human beings, it is certainly natural to think that he made use of these pregiven ways of interpreting his own destiny. How else are we to explain that the primitive community at a very early stage preached the cross as an act of redemption? This was done especially in the tradition about the Last Supper (Mark 10.22–25 par.; I Cor. 11.23–25) and in the saying about ransom in Mark 10.45. In their basic content these pericopes most likely go back to Jesus himself.[42]

The *basileia* message of Jesus and a soteriological understanding of his death are in no way exclusive of one another. On the contrary, the violent death of Jesus is as it were the concrete form taken by the breakdown of the old aeon. Here God's omnipotence is completely absorbed into outward weakness; here God takes the human condition, the human destiny, upon himself, with all its consequences. He enters into abandonment by God. There is no longer any human situation that is in principle cut off from God and salvation. To that extent the death of Jesus on the cross is not only the extreme consequence of his courageous ministry but a recapitulation and summary of his message. The death of Jesus on the cross is the final elucidation of what had been his sole concern: the coming of the eschatological reign of God. This death is the form in which the reign of God becomes a reality under the conditions of the present aeon; it is the form in which the reign of God comes to pass in human weakness, riches in poverty, love in abandonment, fullness in emptiness, life in death.

(c) The Son-christology of the New Testament

Soon after the death of Jesus the New Testament was proclaiming that after his ignominious death on the cross Jesus was established as Son of God through his resurrection and exaltation (Rom. 1.3f.) and that he who is in the form of God (Phil. 2.6) is the Son whom God had sent into the world (Gal. 4.4; Rom. 8.3). For Paul the message about the Son of God is the central content of his gospel; he describes the latter simply as 'the gospel concerning his [i.e., God's] Son' (Rom. 1.3). Finally, in the Prologue of his Gospel John sums up the New Testament profession of faith by proclaiming Jesus Christ as the Word of God that in the very beginning is with God and in fact is God (John 1.1) and that in the fullness of time became flesh (1.14). At the end of his Gospel there is this comprehensive confession: 'My Lord and my God' (John 20.28).

The question at this point is: 'how could such a development take place? Liberal theology, represented by, for example, A. von Harnack, saw the development as a suppression of the historical Christ by the pre-existent Christ of speculative and dogmatic theology. 'The living Christ seems to have been transformed into a confession of faith, and devotion to Christ into Christology.'[43] Harnack therefore called for a return to the simple gospel of Jesus. According to the history of religion school, whose theses R. Bultmann recapitulated in an impressive way,[44] the adoption of motifs from Hellenistic piety and philosophy brought about a Hellenization of the gospel, a process that has begun even in the New Testament itself.[45] Scholars pointed variously to parallels from Greek mythology or philosophy or from the mystery religions, to ideas of 'divine men' (*theioi andres*), or, above all, to the gnostic myth of redemption. All these theses have since proved to be pseudo-scientific myths inspired by fantasy. Our sources for the mystery religions and gnosticism come only from the second and third centuries AD; there is no justification for projecting these witnesses back into the first century and postulating an influence on early Christianity; there is better reason to ask whether on the contrary the sources in question were not influenced by Christianity.

The situation is different with regard to influences from the world of the Old Testament and Judaism. The title 'Son of God' has a firm basis in the royal messianism of the Old Testament.[46] For this reason it is not an accident that the two royal psalms, Ps. 2 and 110, could become the most important supports for the early church's christological proof from scripture. Ps. 2.7 says: 'You are my son. Today have I begotten you' (cf. Ps. 110.3). In the New Testament, too, the Davidic sonship of the Messiah and the divine sonship of Jesus are seen as closely connected (Rom. 1.3f.; Luke 1.32–35). Jesus' characterization of himself as Son of Man inevitably called attention as well to the statements in the apocalyptic literature about exaltation and pre-existence, as these are to be found in the metaphorical discourses of the Book of Enoch and IV

Esdras.[47] Most important, of course, is the idea of wisdom as a pre-existent hypostasis that is already present at the creation (Prov. 8.22ff.) and that looks everywhere for a place to dwell but finds it only in Israel on Zion (Sir. 24.8–12). The parallels to the idea of the Logos in the Prologue of John's Gospel are obvious.[48] The writings of the Jewish religious philosopher, Philo of Alexandria, show how easy it was to connect these Jewish speculations on wisdom with Greek philosophical ideas. As a result all the essential components of New Testament christology were prepared in the Judaism of the inter-testamental period.

But the New Testament christology is not simply reducible to such Jewish ideas. It is completely original and represents an unparalleled innovation.[49] The message of the exaltation and pre-existence of the crucified Jesus was an intolerable scandal to both Jews and Greeks. The material basis of New Testament christology can therefore be looked for only in the preaching and ministry of the earthly Jesus himself as well as in the experience of Easter that overcomes the scandal of the cross and in the message thereof. According to the conviction of almost all exegetes the message of the resurrection and exaltation of the crucified Jesus must be considered the point of departure for the development of christology in the New Testament.

Given this point of departure the Son-christology of the New Testament was inevitable. The categories supplied by the history of religions served a secondary purpose: to help give expression to an originally Christian matter. The idea of pre-existence, in particular, proved to be not only helpful but even necessary in the effort to hold fast to the unique filial relationship of Jesus to God as expressed in his use of 'Abba' in addressing God. Only the idea of pre-existence could guarantee that in the earthly life and in the cross and resurrection of Jesus God himself was involved and that in Jesus Christ God was revealing himself definitively and eschatologically. The eschatological character of the person and work of Jesus made it necessary, in the very nature of things, to say that Jesus belongs to the eternal being of God. Otherwise Jesus could not have 'defined' God in an eschatological and definitive way. Furthermore, only thus could the universal significance of Jesus Christ as the fulfillment not only of the Old Testament but of all reality have been adequately expressed. This makes it clear that in the Son of God statements of the New Testament we are dealing not with speculations inspired by theory but with soteriologically motivated assertions in which the issue is the definitiveness and unsurpassableness as well as the universality of salvation. It must be maintained that Jesus Christ is the only Son of God, who makes us in turn the children of God (Rom. 8.14–17; Gal. 3.26; 4.5); in him God has predestined us 'to share in the being and image of his Son' (Rom. 8.29).

These theses can easily be substantiated with the help of the most important passages embodying the Son-christology of the New Testament. At the same time and by the same means it can be shown that this Son-christology is not simply a late product of New Testament development but is already present in the earliest, pre-Pauline strata of the New Testament. According to the general judgment of exegetical scholarship Rom. 1.3f. is such a pre-Pauline confession of faith: 'his Son, who was descended from David according to the flesh and designated or: constituted Son of God in power according to the Spirit of holiness by his resurrection from the dead'.[50] This ancient 'two-stage christology' contrasts, on the one hand, the messianic dignity of Jesus which has to do with the earthly history of salvation and is based on Davidic descent, and, on the other hand, his divine glory and to that extent his divine sonship which are based on his resurrection from the dead. Expressed here is the idea that because he is Son of God Jesus fulfills the messianic hope of the Old Testament in a qualitatively new way that is mediated by cross and resurrection. As the Messiah on the cross he is also the Messiah in the Spirit. The striking thing is that this ancient confession as yet says nothing explicitly about pre-existence. Paul, who already presupposes the idea of pre-existence, interprets the ancient confessional formula by using 'Son' as title of the subject even of the first part of the confession. He is clearly saying that Jesus does not first become Son by reason of the resurrection but is already the Son even during his earthly life. But this assertion of pre-existence is not an invention of Paul the Apostle; he has taken it from the tradition. This is shown by the so-called mission formulas in Rom. 8.3 and Gal. 4.4 (cf. also John 3.17; I John 4.9f., 14). Talk of the Son being sent by the Father clearly presupposes the pre-existence of the Son.

The most important pre-Pauline testimony is the hymn to Christ in Phil. 2.6–11. 'Who, though he was in the form of God, did not count equality with God a thing to be grasped, but emptied himself, taking the form of a servant [or: slave], being born in the likeness of men. And being found in human form he humbled himself and became obedient unto death, even death on a cross.'[51] There can be no question here of my going into all the complicated exegetical problems which this passage raises. There is a broad consensus among exegetes that this hymn to Christ is pre-Pauline. Generally speaking, the exegetes are also in agreement that the self-emptying is of the pre-existent Christ and not of the earthly Jesus. The incarnation of the pre-existence Christ thus begins a journey of self-emptying that reached its completion on the cross; the incarnation is understood in the light of the cross and as directed to the cross. The decisive question, then, is what is meant by the self-emptying (*kenōsis*). In the literal sense the very *ekenōthen* means 'he made himself empty'; a person described in the New Testament as *kenos* is one who is empty-handed because he has been deprived of something he previously possessed. A person who makes himself empty gives up his wealth and becomes poor. The hymn to Christ is therefore in agreement with II Cor. 8.9, where it is said of Jesus Christ that 'though he was rich, yet for your sake he became poor, so that by his poverty you might become rich'. The riches of Jesus Christ are described by the term *morphē theou*, and his poverty by *morphē doulou*. The term *morphē* may mean either the outward phenomenal form or visible figure, or else the being itself. A third interpretation, often offered at the present time, which explains *morphē* as meaning status, position, attitude, and so on, is inferred from biblical thought patterns, real or supposed, rather than documented lexicographically. Since it is not possible to speak of God having an outward form and since in the New Testament the verb *metamorphousthai* always refers to a transformation in the order of being, it is hard to avoid concluding that the present passage is speaking of 'essential form'.

This important text, then, is speaking of Jesus Christ who from eternity existed in the essential form of God, but then emptied himself to the extent of suffering death on the cross and was finally exalted to be *Kyrios* i.e., world-ruler possessed of divine rank. The christology of pre-existence and the christology of cross or kenosis and exaltation are united in a vast drama that embraces heaven and earth. Christology here emerges within the framework of soteriology. That is, because the pre-existent Christ, God's equal, in free obedience takes upon himself the lot of a slave, *anankē* (necessity) or inevitable domination by the cosmic powers is replaced by freedom under the new Lord of the world. There is thus a change of reigns, but a change accomplished not by violence but through the obedience and weakness of the cross.

Pauline assertions about pre-existence are thus located within a firm prior tradition. An important fact about these assertions is that Paul is not interested in formal and abstract pre-existence as such. Rather he fills the statements about pre-existence with a specific content; in every case the statements are soteriological statements. This is shown by the consecutive clause that is at times added to the mission formula and clarifies the soteriological significance of the statement about pre-existence; these clauses assert liberation from the power of sin and the establishment of a relation of filiation between human beings and God. The fact that the mission is in the flesh and under the law shows that early christology was not solely a christology of the incarnation but also and above all a christology of the cross. The handing-over formulas, which are analogous to the mission formulas, also make this point clear (Rom. 8.32; Gal. 2.20; cf. John 10.11; 15.13; I John 3.16).[52] They show that the point to be made when pre-existence is asserted is that in Jesus Christ God's eternal self-giving love has entered once and for all into history in order that this self-disclosure of God's freedom in love may ground the freedom of the children of God. In the incarnation of the Son of God an exchange therefore took place: 'He was rich, yet for your sake he became poor, so that by his poverty you might become rich' (II Cor. 8.9; cf. Gal. 4.5; 2.19; 3.13; II Cor. 5.21; Rom. 7.4; 8.3f.). The soteriological and universal cosmic significance of the assertion of Jesus as Son of God is again taken up and developed in the hymn to Christ in Col. 1.15–17. Jesus Christ is here said to be 'the image of the invisible God, the first-born of all creation'; 'All things were created through him and for him. He is before all things, and in him all things hold together.'[53] Behind this statement about Christ as mediator of creation there is once again a soteriological concern; the aim is to prove the universality of the salvation given through Christ and at the same time to assert that all other 'principalities and powers' have been deposed and that we are bound to no other Lord save Jesus Christ and are to live in the world with a Christian freedom.

The most important statements of a Son-christology and the ones most momentous for subsequent development are in the writings of John. The Prologue[54] of the Fourth Gospel already makes three basic assertions: Verse 1a begins: 'In the beginning was the Word.' Here it is said that the Word which became flesh in Jesus Christ (1.14) already was in the beginning, that is, that it exists in an absolutely timeless and eternal way. This is why Jesus Christ can say of himself in the Fourth Gospel: 'Before Abraham was, I am' (John 8.58). Verse 1b continues in greater detail: 'And the Word was with God.' This being with God is described in 1.18 as a personal communion, a communion in glory (17.5), love (17.24) and life (5.26), so that in the Fourth Gospel Jesus can say of himself: 'I and the Father are one' (10.30). A climax is reached in verse 1c: 'And the Word was God.' 'God' without an article is a predicate here and not the subject; it is therefore not identical with *ho theos*, of which we spoke earlier. What is being said is that the Word is divine in nature. Despite all the distinction between God and Word and two are united by the one divine nature. But this statement about essence is ordered to a soteriological statement. For, as the eternal divine Word, Christ is truly light and life (1.4). In him is revealed therefore the origin and goal of all reality.

What the Prologue presents in a kind of programmatic fashion is often the subject of discourse in the gospel that follows. At the climax of the dispute between Jesus Christ and the 'Jews' the statement is made that 'I and the Father are one' (10.30). And at the end everything is once again summed up in Thomas' profession of faith: 'My Lord and my God' (20.28). Finally, in 20.31 we are told that the purpose of the entire Gospel is 'that you may believe that Jesus is the Christ, the Son of God, and that believing you may have life in his name'. In like manner the First Letter of John ends with the statement: 'This is the true God and eternal life' (5.20).

It is neither possible nor necessary to present in detail all the New Testament statements having to do with a Son-christology: that Jesus Christ is the image of God (Rom. 8.29; II Cor. 4.4; Col. 1.15), the radiant light of God's glory and the perfect copy of his nature (Heb. 1.3), the epiphany of God (I Tim. 3.16; II Tim. 1.9f.; Titus 3.4). There is one and the same theme in all these statements: Jesus Christ is the word and image of the Father, and in him the hidden God is revealed to us. But the revelation is a revelation on the cross, a revelation in hiddenness; God reveals his power in weakness, his omnipotence is at the same time an omnipatience or omni-suffering; his eternity is not a rigid immutability but movement, life and love that communicates itself to that which is distinct from it. The Son-christology thus implies both a new interpretation of God and a change in our reality. The revelation, *krisis* and even revolution in the picture of God leads to the *krisis*, transformation and redemption of the world. It is only too easy to understand that this new picture of God, as it has emerged in Jesus Christ, could not but lead to violent opposition and that its implications could be brought to light only through lengthy debate.

(d) The explanation of the divine sonship of Jesus Christ in the history of dogma and theology

It is not possible to provide here a complete picture of the development of christological teaching in the early church. I must be satisfied with highlighting a few decisive phases and a few Leitmotifs of this development.[55] In the earliest phase the development of christology was naturally shaped by two types of discussion: the discussion with Judaism and the discussion with Hellenism.

The encounter with Judaism and its strict monotheism led to the danger of diminishing the true divinity of Jesus Christ. The Jewish Christian group that sought to rank Christ with the prophets, the specially graced and chosen ones of God, or the angels, have come to be known as the Ebionites. We find the same approach being taken again in the adoptionist christology of Theodotus the Tanner and his disciple Theodotus the Money-Changer. This christology is fully developed in Paul of Samosata, who presents the man Jesus Christ as endowed with an impersonally conceived power (*dynamis*).

The other extreme is found in Hellenistic circles, where there is a diminishment of the true humanity of Jesus Christ. The Docetists, as they are called, sought to resolve the difficulty created by the incarnation, which was unworthy of a God, and by the scandalous suffering of the Son of God. They did so by adopting a dualistic and spiritualistic approach, and ascribing to Christ only the semblance of a body or at least only the semblance of suffering. The later New Testament writings, in particular the First and Second Letters of John and probably the Letter to the Colossians and the Pastoral Letters, had already had to resist preliminary forms of this docetist error. The confession of Jesus Christ as having truly come in the flesh is regarded in these writings as the line of demarcation between Christianity and non-Christianity or even anti-Christianity (I John 4.2f.; cf. 4.15; 5.5f.; II John 7). Ignatius of Antioch then launches himself unreservedly into the battle. His line of argument is wholly soteriological: every denial of the reality of the humanity of Jesus means a denial of the reality of our redemption, for if Jesus only seemed to have a body, then he only seemed to redeem us (*Smyrn.* 2); then the eucharist too is only an illusion (*Smryn.* 7); then, finally, it is senseless for us to suffer in body for Jesus and to endure persecution for him (*Smyrn.* 4.1). The whole of Christianity then evaporates into a mere semblance of reality. Thus Ignatius already achieves a christological vision in which the unity of Christ's two modes of being (flesh – spirit; having become – not having become; from Mary – from God; etc.) is explicitly highlighted (*Eph.* 7.2).

The great divergence of views regarding the proper understanding of Jesus Christ came in the second and third centuries in the struggle with gnosticism.[56] In this struggle Christianity was compelled for the first time to set forth its teaching on God, redemption, man and the world in a systematic way; only now did this teaching take a firm didactic and institutional form. There is, of course, a good deal of disagreement among scholars on the origin and nature of gnosticism. We know today that gnosticism already existed in pre-Christian times as a syncretistic religious movement and that, as the Qumran texts show, it had gained entrance into Judaism. The widespread and speedy success of the gnostic current of thought was based on a new experience of God, world and man that had no previous parallel in antiquity. The human being of late antiquity no longer felt at home in the universe; he experienced the world rather as alien and impenetrable, as a prison and a rigid system from which he sought liberation. At the center of the extreme dualism that characterized gnostic thinking stood the enigmatic figure of the god 'Man' who had fallen into the sphere of matter and who liberates his self, which has been thrown into the world and almost buried there, through knowledge (gnosis) of the right path. In this context, therefore, redemption is conceived in physical terms as redemption from matter and the body, and not, as in Christianity, in spiritual terms as redemption from sin that is conceived as disobedience to God. Over against Christian dualism which is historical and based on freedom, gnosticism set a metaphysical dualism in which God is the totally other, alien and new, unknown and unworldly God, while redemption consists in an emancipation from the pre-given order of things. Irenaeus of Lyons, Clement of Alexandria, Tertullian and Hippolytus took up the cudgels against this teaching which threatened the very foundations of Christianity. They were obliged to defend the reality of creation, no less than the reality of God and redemption, against the calumnies leveled against them.

Once the church's theologians had defended the reality of the God of history who speaks, acts and is present corporeally in Jesus Christ, the christological problem in the narrow sense inevitably made its appearance: how can God be and remain God and yet be truly present in history? Celsus, an opponent of Christianity, and a shrewd one, had already noted this problem: 'Either God really changes himself, as they claim, into a mortal body . . . or he does not change, but makes onlookers think he has so changed, and thus leads them into errors and tells lies.'[57] The debate over this question was the major theme in the fourth-century conflict with Arius and Arianism. It was in this context that the Council of Nicaea (325) issued its decision which was to be normative for the whole subsequent tradition.

The conflict had long been in the making, at least since the Apologists of the second century had taken over the Logos concept of Greek philosophy (but by that time for practical purposes an idea that had invaded every part of life) in order to clarify conceptually the relation between the Father and the Son. The way had been paved for this step by the wisdom literature of the Bible and by John's hymn to the Logos in the Prologue of the Fourth Gospel. The acceptance of the Stoic Logos doctrine now turned the wisdom teaching and the Logos idea of John into a comprehensive doctrine that explained everything: God, world and history. The Logos was conceived as the rational principle at work in the cosmos and in history. He is present in fragmentary form in every reality (logos spermatikos), but only in Jesus Christ has he appeared in his full form.[58] As far as the relation of the Logos to God is concerned, Justin thinks of it in subordinationist terms. The Logos is God's first production;[59] only in view of the creation of the world does he become independent in relation to what is outside God,[60] that is, he becomes a divine person but one subordinate to the Father.[61] In developing this teaching the Apologists were able to call upon the anthropological distinction between the immanent Logos (logos endiathetos) and the expressed Logos (logos prophorikos) and apply it to God.[62]

The Apologists with their first attempts were soon outstripped by two men of genius who determined the course of the entire subsequent development: Tertullian in the Latin West and Origen in the Greek East. With a sure touch and with juridical preciseness Tertullian had by about 200 already coined the decisive concepts used in later trinitarian theology.[63] By so doing he spared the

West a good deal of the protracted and wearisome debate that the East was to endure. But in Tertullian there is still a subordinationist tendency. The Logos indeed exists prior to the creation of the world, but it is only through creation that he achieves his 'complete birth' (*nativitas perfecta*).[64] The Son proceeds from the Father as the fruit from the root, the river from the source, the ray of sunlight from the sun.[65] The Father alone possesses the entire fullness of divinity, the Son has only a part of it.[66]

The theology of Origen († 253–54) is doubtless superior to that of Tertullian in speculative power. We are confronted in him by one of the greatest and boldest of all theological projects. Origen unhesitatingly asserts the eternity of the Son.[67] The Son is the brightness of the Light.[68] He is a hypostasis that is substantially distinct from the Father[69] and is not a part of the Father.[70] On the other hand, he is not unqualifiedly good as the Father is;[71] he is not 'very God' (*autotheos*) but a 'second God' (*deuteros theos*).[72] The transcendental attributes of the Father take form and figure in the Son.[73] The Son is therefore mediator of redemption.[74] Even though Origen's intention is first and foremost to do biblical theology within the framework of the church's tradition, his theology nonetheless represents the birthday of speculative theology, and one in which the influence of Platonic thinking is unmistakable.[75]

This encounter with contemporary philosophy was neither a calamity nor a mere accident, as objectors to the Hellenization of Christianity believe; it was hermeneutically necessary and was in the final analysis the form which aggiornamento or 'updating' took at that time. On the other hand, the steps then taken did ultimately lead to the crisis that is associated with the name of Arius. The crisis was at bottom nothing else than the outbreak of fever in a process that in its germinal stage was marked by a hidden virulence of which the Apologists had little conception. For the Logos of the Stoics was essentially monistic and made sense only in relation to the world. In later Middle Platonism, on the other hand, there was an excessive emphasis on the absolute transcendence, invisibility and unknowableness of God; in this context the Logos served as a principle of mediation. The result was the danger of subordinationism, that is, of making the Son less than the Father. The Logos is begotten by the Father with a view to creation; the procession of the Logos from the Father is thus made dependent on creation. The Bible's soteriological teaching on salvation was in danger of turning into cosmological speculation, and this danger became acute in Arius, a 'leftist' disciple of Origen.[76] Arius ventured to remedy in a one-sided way the imperfections in theological subordinationism. For him God is ineffable, unbegotten, free of becoming, without origin and immutable, as he is in Middle Platonism. The basic problem then became how to mediate between the indivisible being which is incapable of becoming, and the world of becoming and multiplicity. Here was the usefulness of the Logos, a second God (*deuteros theos*), whom Arius understood as being the first and most excellent creature and at the same time mediator in creation. Consequently, the Logos was created out of nothing, in time, as mutable and fallible; only because of his ethical behavior has he been adopted as Son. In Arius' thinking the God of the philosophers has evidently supplanted the living God of history. His theology represents an extreme Hellenization of Christianity.

The Council of Nicaea[77] was convoked in order to reach a decision in the debates caused by Arius' teaching and to restore unity to the church and the empire; it did not enter into the speculative questions raised by Arian teaching. Its sole aim was to defend the teaching of scripture and tradition. To this end it had recourse to the baptismal creed – whether of the church of Caesarea or of the church of Jerusalem – and to the essential biblical formulations contained in this confession of faith it made interpretative additions which were intended to exclude Arius. The decisive statement in the creed of Nicaea is as follows: 'We believe . . . in one Lord Jesus Christ, the Son of God, the only-begotten generated from the Father, that is, from the being (*ousia*) of the Father, God from God, Light from Light, true God from true God, begotten, not made, one in being (*homoousios*) with the Father, through whom all things were made, those in heaven and those on earth. For us men and for our salvation He came down, and became flesh, was made man.'[78]

The Nicene profession of faith is important in several respects:

1. It responds to the tension between tradition and interpretation. It does not try to present abstract speculation but is a liturgical confession originating in biblical and ecclesial tradition. The new dogma is thus meant to serve faith and be an interpretation of the tradition. The church bases its faith not on private speculation but on common and public tradition that is articulated above all in the church's liturgy. But it understands this tradition not as an inflexible letter but as a living tradition that develops under the pressure of new questions. The use made of Hellenistic concepts does not, therefore, represent a diminution or weakening of Christianity; at issue was the self-assertion and not the self-surrender of Christianity. In the final analysis, the Nicene creed was the *aggiornamento* or updating of that age, the hermeneutically necessary effort to express the permanently valid Christian message in the language of the day and in response to new questions. The supposed 'Hellenization' was in fact a sign of incarnational power and spiritual presence.

2. The 'new' statements about the nature of God represent not a Hellenization but a de-Hellenization of Christianity. Arianism was an illegitimate Hellenization that dissolved Christianity into a cosmology and a morality. The Council's intention, on the contrary, was to hold fast to what the New Testament says about the Son and to reaffirm that in Jesus

Christ God himself has made his appearance. For this reason, the Council has to say that Jesus Christ belongs on the side not of creatures but of God, and that he has not been created but begotten and is of the same being (*homoousios*) as the Father. The idea expressed in *homoousios*[79] does indeed come from the teaching of the Valentinian gnostics on emanation and was therefore highly suspect to many of the Fathers at Nicaea and especially to many bishops and theologians after Nicaea. But in using the term the Council had no intention of 'Hellenizing' the concept of God that is found in revelation and in the church's kerygma and superimposing on it a philosophical concept of being. Its concern was rather with the truth that the Son is by his nature divine and stands on the same level of being as the Father, so that whoever encounters him encounters the Father himself. For this reason it was also not the Council's intention to explain more precisely how this oneness of being in God the Father and God the Son is related to the distinction between the two. Like most conciliar decisions, that of Nicaea was an *ad hoc* solution. The clarification of such a statement as Nicaea's is the task of subsequent theological reception and interpretation.

3. The concern in the conciliar statement of Nicaea is not a speculative one but first and foremost a soteriological one. Athanasius, the champion of the church in the struggle with Arius, insisted over and over again: if Jesus Christ is not the true Son of God, then we have not been redeemed by him, that is, he has not made of us the sons and daughters of God. Athanasius is even able to say: 'He did not, because he was a man, subsequently become God, but because he was God, he subsequently became man in order to make Gods of us.'[80] The teaching on the true divinity of Jesus Christ must therefore be understood in the framework of the entire soteriology of the early church with its idea of redemption as the divinization of the human person. This teaching on divinization is much criticized nowadays, as though it called for a magical natural transformation. On the basis of a mistaken appeal to Ignatius of Antioch[81] interpreters speak disparagingly of a pharmacological process. They overlook the fact that in Athanasius 'divinization' means simply that through the action of him who is Son of God by nature we become the children of God through grace and divine acceptance,[82] because we receive the Holy Spirit who cries out in us: 'Abba, Father!'[83] The whole idea is thus a thoroughly biblical one; in contrast to similar sounding Hellenistic notions there is here not the slightest blurring of the distinction between God and man, and the thought is concerned not with natures but with persons.

4. Nicaea's concern, then, is to maintain the teaching of the Bible against a philosophical falsification of it. On the other hand, the Council is able

to ward off the attack only by taking up the same weapons and speaking the language of philosophy as it adopts the non-biblical concept of *homoousios*. To this extent the dogma of Nicaea means the entrance of metaphysical thinking about substance into the preaching of the church and into theology. Thereafter the eschatological and historico-salvational thinking of the scriptures was often overlaid by speculation and to some extent even supplanted by it. This is the kernel of truth in the thesis about the de-eschatologization of Christianity being both a presupposition and a consequence of its Hellenization.[84] The immediate consequence of the shift – but a consequence contrary to the intentions of Nicaea – was that the traditional picture of God had imposed upon it the Greek idea of the immutability, impassibility and dispassionateness (*apatheia*) of God. It was no longer possible to give full value to the kenosis statements of scripture, which are very closely connected with the biblical assertions about the incarnation. The incarnation of God – which was Athanasius' central theme – and especially the suffering and death of God became a problem precisely after Nicaea. We are becoming fully conscious of this same problem only today when we have reached the end of metaphysics in its classical form. For us the question is whether a God incapable of suffering can help us in our suffering. Is such a God still a God of human beings and of history? Is he even the God revealed to us through the incarnation and cross of Jesus Christ?

In solving one problem while remaining faithful to scripture and trad-ition, Nicaea created another for which we today must find a new solution on the basis of Nicaea. The dogma stated by the first ecumenical council thus makes it already clear that dogmatic formulations are never simply the concluding clarification of a dispute but are at the same time always the beginning of new questions and problems. Precisely because dogmas are true they are in constant need of new interpretation.

3. Theological interpretation of the divine Sonship of Jesus Christ

(a) Logos-christology

Theology is 'faith in search of understanding'; its intention is not simply to ascertain the self-revelation of God in an extrinsic and positivist way but also to understand it from within. This kind of understanding is gained by trying to grasp the many truths of revelation in their internal connection with one another and thus as forms of the one mystery of God, and by trying to relate the one mystery of God to the mystery of man so that an analogous conceptualization of the divine mystery may become possible.

This second attempt in particular was important for christology. The very statement that Jesus Christ is Son of God already represents an analogy from the human realm that expresses both the oneness of being and the distinction of God the Father and Jesus Christ. But in order to keep the relation of Jesus Christ to his Father free from all-too-anthropomorphic ideas of natural generation, and in order to be able to say that Jesus and his Father have not only the same being but a single being, there was need in addition of an analogy from the spiritual realm. There was need, as it were, to conceptualize the image of the Son, and this was accomplished with the aid of the concept of 'word'. Thus the decisive step in christology was the interpretation of the biblical image of Jesus Christ as the Son of God by means of the concept 'Word of God'.

This step from image to concept had already been prepared for in Old Testament wisdom literature and was expressly taken in the Prologue of John.[85] The thesis that the Johannine concept of Logos was of gnostic origin was popular for a long time, but today scholars are laying much greater emphasis on its Old Testament and primitive Christian roots. John harks back to the biblical understanding of 'word' and to Jesus' own implicit claim of being the final and definitive Word of God. The absolute use of the term 'the Word' is not, of course, to be derived solely from the Old Testament and Jewish tradition. In this matter John is located rather in the intellectual and spiritual world of Jewish Hellenism, represented by the Jewish religious philosopher Philo, who linked Old Testament speculation on wisdom with Greek philosophical speculation on the Logos. On the other hand, the differences between Philo and the Prologue of John must not be overlooked. Philo has nothing of a personal conception of the Logos and even less of the idea of an incarnation; for Philo, unlike John, the Logos is a power intermediate between God and the world. The synthesis offered in the Prologue of John must therefore be regarded as an independent achievement which operated in the framework of biblical and early Christian thinking but served to disclose to Hellenistic Jews the being and meaning of Jesus.

The Logos christology of the Gospel of John proved to be immensely influential for the course of history, for it was taken over by the entire Christian tradition. We find the same approach already being taken by Ignatius of Antioch, by Justin and the other Apologists, by Irenaeus of Lyons and even more by the later fathers.[86] And yet, despite its solid biblical basis, it soon led, as I have shown, to a serious crisis; it was from this crisis that classical christology emerged in the fourth century. The crisis resulted from the different understandings of the Logos in Greek philosophy and in the Bible. The concept of Logos had served Greek philosophers since

Heraclitus as a way of expressing the intrinsic rationality and coherent meaning of all reality.[87] The Logos is the reason that governs and unifies all reality. But this coherent meaning and rationality that marks all reality first reveals itself in the rational mind of man. Only through human reason and the human word – both of them being defined as Logos – is the knowableness of reality actually brought to light.[88] The Logos concept is therefore concerned with the revealedness of being in thought and thus with the unity of thinking and being. As a result, there is a formal correspondence between the biblical understanding of 'word' and the Greek understanding of Logos, but at the same time a radical difference in content. Despite the difference in content both are interested in the revelation of reality. But what for the Bible is an irreducible historical event is conceived in Greek thought as being the inner substance of reality. Consequently, the overall understanding of God, world and man that is contained in the Greek concept of Logos is marked by a monistic tendency which could not be taken over by Christian theology. The situation changed in late antiquity when the experience of a harmoniously ordered universe was undermined. The divine was no longer understood as the deepest ground of reality; God was now conceived rather as an absolutely transcendent and unknowable and even an alien God. In this new situation the Logos served as mediator between this transcendent God and the world. But this dualistic conception of things again left no place for the biblical faith in creation as well as faith in the God of history and human beings. Given this complicated situation and set of problems it is understandable that an authentic Christian Logos-christology became possible only after a lengthy process of purification and critical discernment.

In this process a reflection on the relation between the interior word and the exterior word proved useful. Greek philosophy had long since done the preliminary work on this question. In his dialogue *Cratylus* Plato discusses the position of the Sophists according to whom the external word is only an ultimately arbitrary sign based on convention. According to Plato this view of the Sophists is intrinsically untenable because any convention can be established only in and through language, so that language is already presupposed. Plato therefore asserts a correspondence between external word and internal word, that is, between internal understanding and the outward form this understanding takes in words. He understands the external word to be an image and sign of things.[89] But for Plato the knowledge of things is not due primarily to sensible experience of things and therefore not to the external word, but to internal insight into reality itself.[90] For this reason knowledge, according to Plato, is in the final analysis, a wordless dialogue of the soul with itself.[91]

Plato's reflections led, especially in Augustine, to a clarified Logos-christology. Augustine understands the outward word as a sign 'of the word that shines forth within . . . All words, whatever the language in which they achieve the status of sound, are also thought in silence.'[92] The decisive thing for Augustine, then, is the interior word, which has the greater right to be called 'word'. This interior word arises through a creative act which is comparable to an act of generation and in which something distinct from the begetter and yet consubstantial with it emerges. 'When we speak what we know, a word is inevitably born from the knowledge contained in our memory; this word is fully of the same kind as the knowledge from which it is born. The idea which is formed of the known object is the word which we speak in our heart.'[93] 'The spirit retains, hidden away in the treasury of the memory, everything which it has appropriated and knows by its own power or through the bodily senses or through the testimony of others. Out of this the true word is begotten when we express what we know: I mean the word that precedes every spoken sound and even every thought of spoken sound.'[94] Even though Augustine is fully aware of the difference between divine knowledge and human knowledge,[95] he is nonetheless convinced that he has found an analogy for understanding the relation of Father to Son, the distinction between them and also their sameness and unicity of being. 'The word of God the Father is the only-begotten Son, who is like and identical with the Father in everything: God from God, light from light, wisdom from wisdom, essence from essence . . . Therefore the Father begot his Word, which is identical with himself in all respects, by expressing himself as it were.'[96]

Thomas Aquinas accepted and developed this conception of Augustine. But he states more clearly than Augustine that the word is a process (*processio*), an event and an accomplishment; showing very great courage in the light of the history of philosophy, he also describes this word as an intellectual emanation. The thing that is peculiar to this word-occurrence is that there is no going from one subject to another and that the emergence of the word takes place rather in the knowing subject himself,[97] so that it is possible to speak of this word as a *perfectio operantis* (a perfection of the agent).[98] For the higher a being is, the more independent it is and the more fully it is concentrated within itself and reflected back upon itself. The highest form of such interiority belongs to the spirit, which reflects on itself and is thus able to understand itself. But whereas the human spirit's self-consciousness yields but an image of its being, in God being and consciousness coincide; in knowing himself God does not simply have an intellectual image of himself, but his being is identical with this image or word. The act of divine self-knowledge is thus an act of intellectual generation, an emanation of the spirit. There is of course a difference here as compared with the Neoplatonic doctrine of emanation, inasmuch as that which is begotten is not a lesser being but possesses the same ontological reality as the being of God.[99] Were one to deny this generation of the Word, one would be forced to deny that God is life and spirit and to maintain that he is dead and without spirit.[100] The living God can therefore be thought of only as Father and Son, while a non-trinitarian, purely monotheistic God would in fact have to be declared dead.

The explanation of the divine sonship of Jesus Christ by means of the concept of word not only helps Thomas to explain this individual, though admittedly central, dogma of the faith; the explanation also enables him to grasp in faith the whole of reality. Because in a single act God understands both himself and everything else, the eternal Word is an expression and representation not only of the Father but of creatures as well. To state this more accurately: in his Son, the eternal Word, the Father knows not only himself but also created reality.[101] Thomas is thus able, with the help of the concept of word, to make it intelligible that all things have been created in Jesus Christ and for him (Col. 1.16f.) and that from eternity we have been known and chosen in him (Eph. 1.4f.).

It is impossible to deny the spaciousness, depth and coherence of this classical Word-theology. It has a very satisfactory basis in scripture and tradition, and is a help that cannot be overvalued for a deeper understanding of revelation and of the latter's internal coherence and its correspondence to human knowledge. Logos-christology can help us understand that in Jesus Christ God's innermost being as well as the ultimate ground and meaning of all reality are made known to us. It explains how Jesus Christ is the head of the whole creation and how in him as the single Word of the Father all of reality finds expression and its deepest meaning. Only one who knows Jesus Christ has an ultimate understanding of man and the world.

Nonetheless, questions remain. Does not this theology of the word have its ultimate center of gravity in philosophy rather than in theology? And even when viewed simply from the standpoint of philosophy does the significance of the word and of language find its proper expression? Does the interior soliloquy of the soul yield an adequate understanding of the word, or must we not rather start with dialogue and therefore with the external word, with the word as a self-emptying? These questions lead in turn to the properly theological question. Does the classical Logos-christology adequately express the intentions of the biblical theology of the Word, as these are shown to us in the Prologue of John? Can it explain why the culmination of the Prologue of John is the statement: 'The Word became flesh'? 'Flesh' designates the human person in its frailty and subjection to death. The incarnation thus already suggests a christology of the cross and of kenosis, according to which in Jesus Christ God empties himself and, as it were, reveals himself in his opposite, so that God's revelation of himself is at the same time a revelation of his hiddenness. This element of self-emptying is neglected in the classical Logos-christology. This fact constrains us not indeed to renounce the classical solution but rather to take it a step further and deeper in light of the idea of self-emptying.

(b) Kenosis-christology

If we take the testimony of the New Testament consistently as our starting point and if we make this testimony the basis for the speculative development of our faith in Christ, then we must take seriously the fact that the Gospels are 'passion narratives with extended introductions' (M. Kähler). The cross is then not simply the consequence of the earthly ministry of Jesus but the very goal of the incarnation; it is not something adventitious but the meaning and purpose of the Christ-event, so that everything else is ordered to it as to a goal. God would not have become truly a human being had he not entered fully into the abyss and night of death. But this means that we must approach the question of the nature of Jesus' divine sonship not from the vantage-point of his eternal and temporal birth but from that of his death on the cross. The starting point of christological reflection must be the giving of the Son by the Father and the self-giving of the Son to the Father and for the many, rather than the generation of the Son by the Father as conceived according to the analogy of the production of the intellectual word.[102]

Basic to such a christological approach is the hymn to Christ in Phil. 2.6–11, which speaks of the kenosis or emptying (Greek: *kenōsis*) of him who was in the form of God and accepted the form of a slave.[103] In interpreting this important text we must take careful note of the fact that it is not speaking of a transformation of nature, still less of a de-divinization of God. Such an interpretation would contradict not only II Cor. 5.19: 'God was in Christ', but also what is said here in Philippians, for according to this text the kenosis consists in the taking of the form of a slave and not in the surrender of the form of God. Augustine is fully correct in his interpretation: 'It was thus that he emptied himself: by taking the form of a slave, not by losing the form of God; the form of a slave was added, the form of God did not disappear.'[104] On the other hand, it is only with this interpretation that the real problem becomes clear. We must negotiate the narrow path of making him who is God's equal the subject of the emptying and of taking this emptying seriously while yet not depriving him of his divinity. How is it possible, then, that the immutable God should at the same time be mutable? How can the history of God in Jesus Christ be so thought that it really affects God and is God's very own history, while at the same time God remains God? How can the impassible God suffer?

The Bible makes unavoidable the question of the suffering of God. The Bible tells us over and over that God is affected by the action and suffering of human beings or, as the case may be, allows himself to be affected through compassion, anger and pity (Gen. 6.6; Ps. 78.41; Isa. 63.10; Hos. 11.8f.; Jer. 31.20; etc.).[105] Consistently with this, rabbinical theology often speaks of the pain in God.[106] The New Testament continues this line of thought by telling of the anger of Jesus (Mark 3.5), his compassion (Mark 6.34), and his weeping over Jerusalem (Luke 19.41). Fundamental in this context are the words of Jesus about being abandoned by God (Mark 15.34; Matt. 27.46) and the statement of principle in the Letter to the Hebrews: 'We have not a high priest who is unable to sympathize with our weaknesses, but one who in every respect has been tempted as we are, yet without sinning' (4.15). 'He can deal gently with the ignorant and wayward, since he himself is beset with weakness . . . Although he was a Son, he learned obedience through what he suffered' (5.2, 8; cf. 2.18; 4.15). It is impossible to dismiss all this as simple anthropomorphism, or to ascribe it solely to the human nature of Jesus, while leaving his divinity untouched by it. For the kenosis is that of the pre-existent Son of God (Phil. 2.7), and it is the humanness of God that has made its appearance (Titus 3.4). In his humanness, then, and in his living and dying Jesus Christ is the self-interpretation of God.

The fathers were compelled to differentiate this God of history as understood in the Bible from mythological conceptions of gods who undergo becoming and who suffer and change, and of their mythologically interpreted incarnations. In effecting the differentiation the fathers were to appeal to motifs of Greek philosophy and its axiom of God's impassibility (*apatheia*: the apathia-axiom).[107] In the process they doubtless often defended God's impassibility in a way that betrays the influence more of Greek philosophy than of the testimony of the Bible.[108] It is not the case, however, as is often claimed, that the fathers simply took over the apathia-axiom and thus abridged the Bible's testimony regarding the living God of history.[109]

The early fathers simply let the paradox stand. According to Ignatius of Antioch, 'The timeless and invisible one became visible for our sake; the incomprehensible and impassible one became capable of suffering for our sake.'[110] Irenaeus[111] and Melito[112] use similar language. Tertullian, known for his paradoxes, says: 'God's Son was crucified, and precisely because it was ignominious I am not ashamed of it. God's Son also died, and this is credible precisely because it was in such bad taste. He died and rose again, and this is certain because it is impossible.'[113] In other passages he speaks of the *Deus mortuus* (dead God)[114] and the *Deus crucifixus* (crucified God).[115] He thus anticipates the formula of the Scythian monks in the theopaschite controversy of the sixth century: 'One of the holy Trinity suffered in the flesh.'[116]

A mode of expression that was less bizarre and that showed a balance achieved through reflection was very difficult for the fathers because they regarded *pathos* (suffering) as a non-free external passive experience[117] and even as an expression of the human fallenness brought about by sin.[118] Given such presuppositions, such *pathē* (sufferings) could be ascribed to God only insofar as he freely accepted them, with the result that in him they would not be the expression of finiteness, lack of freedom, and sinfulness but, on the contrary, an expression of his power and freedom. This is the line taken in the response of Gregory Thaumaturgus[119] and Hilary[120] and even of Augustine: 'If he was also weak, this was due to his own fullness of power.'[121] Gregory of Nyssa is very emphatic: 'But his descent into lowliness represents a certain excess of power, so that even what is as it were contrary to his nature is not a hindrance to him.'[122] From here it is but a relatively short step to the most important patristic discussion of the apathia-axiom, that of Origen.[123] Origen moves beyond the idea of free acceptance to that of love. If the Son had not from eternity felt compassion for our wretchedness, he would not have become man and would not have allowed himself to be crucified: 'First he suffered, then he came down. What was the suffering he accepted for us? The suffering of love.' Not only the Son but the Father as well is not simply 'impassible': he too 'suffers something of the suffering of love'.[124] Here a solution is insinuated which has its basis in the innermost being of God himself, in his freedom in love.

Unfortunately, the Scholastic tradition took hardly any advantage of these rudiments of a solution in the theology of the fathers.[125] A shift from the one-sidedly metaphysical theology of Scholasticism came only with Luther's theology of the cross.[126] Luther was attempting a consistent exposition not of the cross in the light of a philosophical concept of God, but of God in the light of the cross. In his teaching on the *communicatio idiomatum* (communion of properties; reciprocal predication of properties) he tries to transfer to the human nature all the sublime statements proper to the divine nature; in particular, the humanity of Christ is made to share in the omnipresence of the divinity. Conversely, the divinity shares in the abjectness of the humanity and in its suffering and death.[127] In this he was opposed especially by the Calvinists with their *Extra Calvinisticum*, by which they sought to maintain the transcendence of the Logos in relation to Jesus Christ.[128]

The still unsettled problem led to the kenoticism controversy of the sixteenth and seventeenth centuries, first between Chemnitz and Brentz and later between the schools of Giessen and Tübingen. According to both schools the human nature of Christ participates in the omnipresence, omniscience and omnipotence of the divine majesty. According to the Giessen school, however, the incarnate Word renounces the use of these attributes (*kenōsis chrēseōs*, a kenosis of use); the Tübingen school, on the contrary, maintained that he simply hid these attributes and did not reveal them externally (*kenōsis krypseōs*, a kenosis of concealment). No matter which of the two approaches is taken, it is clear that Luther's doctrine on the communication of idioms leads to aporias that are hardly soluble. It ends up opposing the picture of Jesus that is given to us in the scriptures. For if the humanity of Jesus participates in the attributes proper to the divine majesty, how is it still possible to maintain that Jesus is authentically human? If, on the other hand, the divinity itself suffers, how are we to understand the abandonment of Jesus on the cross by God?[129]

German idealism made a new attempt to give intellectual form to the kenosis teaching of scripture. For Hegel the absolute is not a substance but a subject; this subject exists, however, only in emptying itself out to what is other. It is of the essence of the absolute Spirit that it reveal and manifest itself, that is, that it show itself in and for what is other and so become objective to itself.[130] It is thus of the essence of the absolute Spirit that it establishes within itself the distinction from itself; that it be identical with itself in distinction from itself. In Hegel's mind this theory is a philosophical exegesis of the biblical saying that God is love. For it belongs to love to find itself in the other, in self-emptying. 'Love is a differentiation of two who nonetheless are not unqualifiedly distinct.'[131] In this self-emptying, death is the highest point of finiteness, the supreme negation, and therefore the best way of seeing the love of God. In this way Hegel manages to conceptualize the death of God. As I noted earlier, he cites the Lutheran hymn: 'O great affliction, God himself is dead,' and he speaks of this event as 'a monstrous, fearful idea that confronts the mind with the deepest abyss of estrangement'.[132] But love means that in the midst of division there is at the same time reconciliation and union. Thus the death of God means at the same time the removal of alienation, the death of death, the negation of negation, the reality of reconciliation. The message of God's death means therefore that God is a living God; that he is able to take negation into himself and at the same time cancel it in himself. The basic problem of Hegelian philosophy is its irremediable ambiguity. If God must necessarily externalize himself, then he cannot be God apart from the world.[133] But in that case the distinction between God and world is cancelled out in a dialectical process.

This leads to the question whether Hegel has not turned the scandal of the cross into a speculative Good Friday. For if the cross can be speculatively understood, it is dialectically cancelled out and reconciled. But then it is no longer an irreducible historical event, but simply an expression of a principle of love, a necessary destiny of God. If, however, the death of God is conceived as necessary, is it still being taken seriously? Is not the full depth of human suffering simply by-passed? At this point the words of Goethe would apply: 'There the cross stands, thickly wreathed in roses, / Who put the roses on the cross?'[134] In summary: on the one hand, the modern philosophy of subjectivity offers new intellectual possibilities of mastering the problem of the suffering of God, for which a solution is hardly possible in the metaphysically oriented theological tradition; on the other hand, this philosophy in turn contains undeniable dangers, since it is exposed to the temptation of emptying the cross of Christ (I Cor. 1.17).

The possibilities and dangers of thinking that takes its direction from Hegel become clear in the kenotic theory of the nineteenth and twentieth centuries. The intention of this theology is to preserve the christological tradition of the early church and at the same time to develop it. We find the new approach to christology in the kenoticists of the nineteenth century: G. Thomasius, F. H. R. Frank, W. F. Gess. Their teaching has been described as 'the complete kenosis of the mind'; K. Barth's view of that 'there is even worse than that to be said of it'. For in fact the kenoticists were compelled to surrender the divinity of Jesus Christ, a move which, however, brought them only scorn and mockery from the liberals. The Anglican kenoticists at the end of the last and the beginning of the present century were likewise influenced by Hegel, but they made an independent attempt to reconcile patristic theology with the realistic picture of the man Jesus of Nazareth that had emerged from the study of the Gospels. The emphasis in the writings of these men was therefore more on the empirical side of the self-consciousness of Jesus. To be mentioned here are C. Gore, F. Weston, C. E. Rolt, W. Temple, R. Brasnett, and others. Hegel's ideas, combined to some extent with those of Boehme and Schelling, also exercised an influence on some Russian Orthodox theologians and thinkers, especially on Soloviev, Tarajev, Bulgakov, and Berdyaev. Close to them in many respects is the Spanish philosopher Miguel de Unamuno, who in turn influenced Reinhold Schneider.

The same problem, mediated through the post-idealist critique of Hegel, has been taken up again today, although with changed premises, by many contemporary Catholic and Protestant theologians: K. Rahner, H. Urs von Balthasar, H. Mühlen, J. Galot, H. Küng, W. Kasper, J. Moltmann, E. Jüngel, G. Koch, and others.[135] On the basis of entirely different presuppositions the same problem is taken up in process theology (C. Hartshorne, J. B. Cobb, S. Ogden, and others), which makes use of A. N. Whitehead's distinction between primordial nature and consequent nature of God.[136] It is not always clear in these theologians how the legitimate concern expressed in the immutability axiom can be respected. K. Kitamori's *Theology of the Pain of God* [137] shows how relevant a theology of the passion and of suffering is for Asiatic thinking. The last offshoots of this kenoticist tendency are to be found in the death-of-God theology which, being a momentary fad, a may-fly, is itself already dead. [138]

This survey shows that the biblical and ecclesial confession of Jesus as the Son of God is something that theology has still not completely assimilated. The theology of the nineteenth and twentieth centuries is the attempt on a grand scale to effect a new interpretation of the concept of God and his immutability in the light of that confession or, more accurately, in the light of the cross of Jesus Christ, and so to give new relevance to the biblical understanding of the God of history. It has become clear in the process that there are valid points of contact in patristic theology. But the attempt to understand God and Jesus Christ in terms of the kenosis idea must be antecedently aware that such an understanding must not turn into a wisdom of this world but must hold fast to the folly of the message of the cross, which is the wisdom of God (cf. I Cor. 1.18–31). The point of departure for such an attempt can therefore only be the testimony of the Bible and not some philosophy or other, whether classical metaphysics with its apathia-axiom, or idealism with its conception of the necessary self-renunciation of the absolute, or modern process philosophy. We must therefore resist all the attempts, anticipated long ago in gnosticism, to turn the cross of Christ into a world principle, a world law or a world formula or to explain it as a symbol of the universal principle of 'dying and living again' (*Stirb und Werde*). [139]

The decisive argument can be set forth in two steps:

1. On the cross the incarnation of God reaches its true meaning and purpose. The entire Christ-event must therefore be understood in terms of the cross. On the cross God's self-renouncing love is embodied with ultimate radicalness. The cross is the utmost that is possible to God in his self-surrendering love; it is 'that than which a greater cannot be thought'; it is the unsurpassable self-definition of God. This self-renunciation or emptying is therefore not a self-abandonment and not a self-de-divinization of God. The love of God that is revealed on the cross is rather the expression of God's unconditional fidelity to his promise. It must be said of the living God of history that precisely as the God of history he remains true to himself and cannot deny himself (II Tim. 2.13). The cross is therefore not a de-divinization of God but the revelation of the divine God. It is by the very unfathomableness of his forgiving love that he proves he is God and not a man (Hos. 11.9). For the Bible, then, the revelation of God's omnipotence and the revelation of God's love are not contraries. God need

not strip himself of his omnipotence in order to reveal his love. On the contrary, it requires omnipotence to be able to surrender oneself and give oneself away; and it requires omnipotence to be able to take oneself back in the giving and to preserve the independence and freedom of the recipient. Only an almighty love can give itself wholly to the other and be a helpless love.

> God's omnipotence is therefore his goodness. For goodness is to give oneself away completely, but in such a way that by omnipotently taking oneself back one makes the recipient independent ... It is incomprehensible that omnipotence is not only able to create the most impressive of all things – the whole visible world – but is able to create the most fragile of all things – a being independent of that very omnipotence.[140]

Here we have reached the key point: God's self-emptying, his weakness and his suffering are not the expression of a lack, as they are in finite beings; nor are they the expression of a fated necessity. If God suffers, then he suffers in a divine manner, that is, his suffering is an expression of his freedom; suffering does not befall God, rather he freely allows it to touch him. He does not suffer, as creatures do, from a lack of being; he suffers out of love and by reason of his love, which is the overflow of his being. To predicate becoming, suffering and movement of God does not, therefore, mean that he is turned into a developing God who reaches the fullness of his being only through becoming; such a passage from potency to act is excluded in God. To predicate becoming, suffering and movement of God is to understand God as the fullness of being, as pure actuality, as overflow of life and love. Because God is the omnipotence of love, he can as it were indulge in the weakness of love; he can enter into suffering and death without perishing therein. Only thus can he redeem our death through his own death. In that sense Augustine's statement is valid: 'Slain by death, he slew death.'[141] 'He destroyed our death by dying and restored our life by rising' (Hymn to the Cross). Thus God on the cross shows himself as the one who is free in love and as freedom in love.[142]

2. If God shows himself as the one who loves in freedom and who is free in loving and if the cross is the eschatological self-revelation of God, then God must in himself be freedom in love and love in freedom. Only if God is in himself love can he reveal himself as such in an eschatological and definitive way. From eternity, therefore, God must be self-communicating love. This in turn means that God possesses his identity only in a distinction within himself between lover and beloved who are both one in love. Here we have a starting point for the understanding of the Trinity, and one that

proceeds not from knowledge in the word but from self-communicating love. This starting point helps us to do greater justice to the phenomenon of self-emptying, which is essential to love, than is possible when, with the tradition, we take the word as the starting point. On the other hand, since love presupposes and includes knowledge of the beloved, this approach is broad enough to integrate and make fruitful the profound insights of Logos-christology. In addition, there is the fact that contemporary linguistic philosophy starts with the external, spoken word and not with the interior word as Plato and Augustine did, and that it understands the spoken word as a self-surrender on the part of the speaker and as a turning to other human beings. This is a further point of view which allows Logos-christology to be taken into a kenosis-christology, that is, a christology of self-emptying and self-surrender, and thereby to be developed and deepened.

There is a basis in the tradition for thus taking love as the point of departure. As early as Origen we find the teaching that the Son proceeds from the will, that is, from the love of the Father.[143] It is Augustine, above all, who recognizes that the Trinity discloses itself in light of the concept of love. 'See, there are three things: lover, beloved and love. What is love but a kind of life that unites or endeavors to unite two with one another, namely, lover and beloved?'[144] Augustine did not, however, pursue this insight further. Or, more accurately, he begins with love but then introduces the element of knowledge by arguing: 'The spirit cannot love itself if it does not know itself.' 'Thus the spirit, its love and its knowledge form a kind of trinity.'[145] Within the approach by way of love there is thus the basis for the theology of the word, but the latter was subsequently developed, for the most part, in isolation. The only real exception is the approach of Richard of St Victor (twelfth century) who thinks consistently in terms of love.[146] I shall be discussing him in greater detail later on.

Love entails a unity that does not absorb the other person but rather accepts and affirms the other precisely in his otherness and only thus establishes him in his true freedom. Love, which gives to the other not some thing but its very self, involves, in this very self-communication, a self-differentiation and self-limitation. The lover must take himself back because his concern is not with himself but with the other. More than this, the lover allows the other to affect him; he becomes vulnerable precisely in his love. Thus love and suffering go together. The suffering of love is not, however, a passive being-affected, but an active allowing others to affect one. Because, then, God is love he can suffer and by that very fact reveal his divinity. The self-emptying of the cross is therefore not a de-divinization of God but his eschatological glorification. The eternal intra-divine distinction of Father and Son is the transcendental theological condition for the possibility of God's self-emptying in the incarnation and on the cross. This statement is not simply a more or less interesting piece of speculation; it signifies that from eternity there is place in God for man, place also for a genuine sym-pathy with the suffering of human beings. The Christian God, that is, the God who is thought of in terms of Jesus Christ, is therefore not a God of a-pathia, but in the real sense of the term a God of sym-pathy, a God who suffers with man.

This 'sym-pathetic' God as he reveals himself in Jesus Christ is the definitive answer to the question of theodicy, the question on which theism and atheism alike founder. If God himself suffers, then suffering is no longer an objection against God. On the other hand, if God suffers, this does not mean that he divinizes suffering. God does not divinize suffering, he redeems it. For the suffering of God, which springs from the voluntariness of love, conquers the fateful character of suffering, which attacks us from without as something alien and unintelligible. Thus the omnipotence of God's love removes the weakness of suffering. Suffering is not thereby removed, but it is interiorly transformed – transformed into hope. Kenosis and suffering now no longer have the last word; the last word belongs to exaltation and transfiguration. Once again, then, kenosis-christology points beyond itself to a christology of Easter exaltation and transfiguration, and is very closely connected with pneumatology. For according to scripture the eschatological transformation and transfiguration of the world is the work of the Spirit of God. Because according to the theological tradition the Spirit unites lover and beloved, Father and Son, in their very distinction, he is also the power that brings the world to its eschatological transfiguration and reconciliation.

III

The Holy Spirit, Lord and Giver of Life

1. Problem and urgency of a theology of the Holy Spirit today

'I believe in the Holy Spirit, the Lord and giver of life': thus begins the third section of the Christian confession of faith. Only with this final statement does the confession reach its end and completion. For the life that has its origin in the Father, and is given to us in the Son, is made our interior, personal possession by the Holy Spirit, operating through the ministry of the church. That which has its origin in the Father and its center in the Son reaches its completion in the Holy Spirit.

The statement about the Holy Spirit is, of course, also full of intellectual difficulties. As a matter of fact, the Holy Spirit does not play an outstanding part in the average ecclesial and theological consciousness. The Holy Spirit is the most mysterious of the three divine persons, for while the Son has shown himself to us in human form and we can form at least an image of the Father, we have no concrete grasp of the Spirit. Not without reason has he frequently been called 'the unknown God'. Forgetfullness of the Spirit is a charge often leveled against the Western tradition in particular, and it is true that the triad, Father – Christ – Spirit is replaced, in the minds of many by the triad God – Christ – church.[1] I will have occasion to discuss in greater detail the reasons and consequences of this forgetfullness of the Spirit.

The real intellectual difficulties in pneumatology are to be seen as springing not primarily from the ecclesial and theological tradition but rather from the intellectual situation of the age and its lack of 'spirit'. The loss of the dimension and reality which Western thinking has described by the term 'spirit' is perhaps the most profound crisis of the present time.[2] The discovery of the world of the spirit was the great accomplishment of Greek thought, and Christian theology was able to make use of it in a manner both critical and creative. In Western philosophy spirit used to be not simply one reality among others, but the truest of realities. In the philosophy of the modern age, spirit even became the dominant basic concept; spirit was for it the totality that gave meaning and unity and grounded everything else amid the multiplicity of phenomena. The spirit which permeated all reality made it possible to recognize what was one's own in what was alien and to be at home in it. After the passing of Goethe, Hegel and Schleiermacher this philosophy of spirit suddenly collapsed. Since that time the idealist interpretation of spirit has largely yielded the field to a materialistic and evolutionary interpretation. Reality is no longer viewed as a manifestation of spirit, but rather spirit is understood as an epiphenomenon of reality, being conceived as a superstructure built on the economic and social process or as a surrogate and sublimation of man who is defined as a being made up of needs. Finally, a positivist and supposedly 'exact' understanding of science demanded the renunciation of the concept of 'spirit' because of its multiplicity of meanings and the impossibility of providing an exact definition of it; it demanded that we remain silent regarding that which we cannot define with precision. It is obvious that this kind of materialist and positivist thinking could not but give way to nihilism and turn into a devaluation and revaluation of all previous ideas, values and ideals, which now become suspect of being mere ideological cloaks for individual and collective interests.

What I have been saying represents, of course, only one half of our situation. For that which past European history understood by 'spirit' is present anew today in the mode of absence and in a way that is truly terrifying. Our experience is of the spiritless condition of a reality which has lost its soul and turned into a facade, a reality in which every organization of things can only be felt as a form of coercion and in which the isolated subject finds himself confronted by impenetrable processes that generate anxiety and a sense of oppression. The experience is accompanied by a search for what used to be meant by spirit, but in the form now of various utopian visions of a better, more human, and reconciled world. Two such visions in particular call for mention: the utopian vision of evolution or progress, and that of revolution. The two have in common that they want to turn a reality alien to man into a human world in which will be brought to pass something of 'that which manifested itself to everyone in childhood and wherein as yet no one dwelt: home' (E. Bloch). Yet both of these utopian visions must today be regarded as shattered. The collapse of the vision of progress is evident on a wide scale in view of external economic conditions and of the dangers lurking in technological development. In the interim it has also become clear that any revolution is subject to the conditions of injustice and violence which it is resisting, so that the injustice and violence of which the revolution itself makes use bring into the desired new order of things the seeds of new injustice and new violence. Therefore no revolution is possible that will not later be betrayed as the formerly oppressed become oppressors in their turn. The flight to the interior and the flight to ecstasy, whether religious ecstasy or one of its surrogates, are evidently not solutions. Moreover, even in these kinds of flight the cry for the spirit cannot be missed.

The only real replacement for human fulfillment and for the utopian ideal of a reality that is unrent, undivided, and successful is art. According to classical philosophy the beautiful is the sensible manifestation of the idea; it is freedom made manifest or, in the language of today's thinkers, the anticipation of definitive reconciliation.[3] In a work of art, then, there is, at least according to the classical understanding of art, a foretaste of that which Christian faith looks to with hope as to be accomplished by the Holy Spirit; the transfiguration of reality. On the other hand, contemporary artists think it possible to carry out the task of art only in the form of criticism, protest and negation, given the spiritless condition of the present age. Where all idea of the spiritually supra-sensible has been abandoned and the beautiful has been separated from the true and the good, as in nihilism,[4] the beautiful can only be understood as taking the form of a life-enhancing ecstasy, an affirmation of the sensuous, a will to appearances, or pure form. In contemporary art, therefore, the question is largely left unanswered how a transformation of the world and man, a real reconciliation of the world and man, are possible. The question is raised of that which used to be expressed in the term 'spirit', but no answer is in sight. The Christian message of the Holy Spirit raises this question and intends to provide a super-abundant answer to it. It is the answer to the distress of our times and the crisis of our age.

2. The Christian message of God's life-giving Holy Spirit

(a) The Spirit of God in creation

The basic meaning of the Hebrew and Greek words for 'spirit', namely *ruach* and *pneuma*, is 'wind, breathing, breath'; the second meaning – since breathing is the sign of life – is 'life, soul'; the final, transferred meaning is 'spirit'.[5] The spirit or spirits played an extensive role in the many myths and popular religions of the ancient world. Especially widespread in divination and poetry was the idea of the life-giving and life-engendering power of the spirit as well as its power to sweep along, throw into ecstasy, inspire and, in the literal sense, 'enthuse'. The spirit was thus a dynamic and creative reality that gave life to everything, raised or snatched human beings out of the everyday, fixed order of things, and brought about the extraordinary and the new.

In the time of the pre-Socratics the concept of spirit had already become part of philosophy. According to Anaximenes, air is the origin of all things; it holds everything together and surrounds the whole universe.[6] According to Aristotle the pneuma is the breath of life that animates all living things.[7] Finally, Stocism made the pneuma the basis of a universal speculative theory, looking upon it as the power and life that orders the universe and all individual beings, including God.[8] But even in this speculative use the original basic meaning of the word 'spirit' is preserved. By this I mean that pneuma was never something purely spiritual; rather it was always linked to a corporeal substratum, and was even itself only a sublimated form of the material. It was an intra-worldly, impersonal, vital natural power that dwelt in the organism of the cosmos and in all its parts. In Greek thought pneuma therefore remained something neutral and never became a person.

The description just given already indicates both the connection with and the difference from the biblical understanding of spirit. In the Bible, too, the spirit is the vital principle of the human being, the seat of its sensations, intellectual operations, and attitudes of will. On the other hand, spirit is not a principle immanent in man's nature, but rather designates life as given and authorized by God. 'When thou hidest thy face, they are dismayed; when thou takest away their breath, they die and return to their dust. When thou sendest forth thy Spirit [or: breath], they are created; and thou renewest the face of the ground' (Ps. 104.29f.; cf. Job 34.14f.). Yahweh's Spirit is thus the creative power of life in all things. His Spirit moves over the primeval waters at the beginning of creation (Gen. 1.2). 'By the word of the Lord the heavens were made, and all their host by the breath of his mouth' (Ps. 33.6; cf. Job 33.4). The Spirit of God gives man his artistic sense and his shrewdness, and bestows insight and wisdom on him.

The Bible thus has something in common with the religious outlook and the philosophy of antiquity. According to both, everything that exists exists only through sharing in the divine fullness of being. But, in contrast to the religions, the Spirit of Yahweh is not an impersonal principle that is immanent in the world. On the contrary, his Spirit is characterized by its difference from the weakness and frailty of man and from human power and wisdom (Isa. 31.3); it is beyond man's ability to penetrate and explain (Isa. 40.13). The biblical conception of the Spirit is thus marked by the same transcendence that characterizes the whole biblical conception of

God. Only in this sense is the Spirit of God the creative life-giving power of God, the power that produces, sustains, rules and directs all things. The Spirit is the *Spiritus creator* that is at work throughout the whole of created reality. 'The Spirit of the Lord has filled the world, and that which holds all things together knows what is said' (Wisdom 1.7; cf. 7.22–8.1).

The teaching on the Holy Spirit must therefore be located within a universal perspective. This teaching is concerned with life as such and with the meaning of all life, with the origin and goal of life, with the power that gives life. Pneumatology is concerned not with some special esoteric knowledge but with a completely exoteric reality. Pneumatology is therefore possible only through looking for and listening to the traces, expectation and futilities of life, through attention to the 'signs of the time' which are to be found everywhere that life breaks forth and comes into being, everywhere that new life as it were seethes and bubbles, and even, in the form of hope, everywhere that life is violently devastated, throttled, gagged and slain. Wherever true life exists, there the Spirit of God is at work. 'He is the gravitational pull of love, the attraction upward, that resists the gravitational pull downward and brings all things to their completion in God.'[9]

(b) The Holy Spirit in the history of salvation

The church's creed says of the Holy Spirit: 'He has spoken through the prophets.' Evidently, then, as far as the church's confession of faith is concerned, the Spirit is not simply God's creative power but also his power over history; through the Spirit he intervenes by word and action in history in order through him to bring history to its eschatological goal: God all in all. (I Cor. 15.28).

In the Old Testament we find prophetic inspiration coming from the Spirit as far back as Moses (Num. 11.25) and Joshua (Num. 27.17) and Balaam the seer (Num. 24.2); we find it frequently in the Book of Judges, in the cases of Othniel, Gideon, Jephthah and Samson (Judg. 3.10; 6.34; 11.29; 13.25; 14.6, 19; etc.) and in Saul, last of the judges and first of the kings (I Sam. 10.6; 19.24). From David onward, the coming of God's Spirit no longer takes the form solely of an unexpected, sudden event, a striking ecstatic and charismatic phenomenon, a kind of 'happening'. Rather, the Spirit remains upon David and rests on him (I Sam. 16.13; cf. the prophecy of Nathan, II Sam. 7). Finally, the inspiration of the writing prophets by the Spirit is attested by Third Isaiah (Isa. 61.1), Ezekiel (2.2; 3.24) and Zechariah (7.12; on prophetic inspiration cf. I Peter 1.11; II Peter 1.21).

The salvation-historical and eschatological goal of this activity of the

Spirit finds expression in the great writing prophets, especially Isaiah and Ezekiel. The coming Messiah (Isa. 11.2) or Servant of God (Isa. 42.1) is promised as one filled with the Spirit. The Spirit of God will change the wilderness into a paradise and make it a place of justice and righteousness (Isa. 32.16f.). He will raise the expiring people to new life (Ezek. 37.1–14) and create a new heart in them (Ezek. 11.9; 18.31; 36.27; cf. Ps. 51.12). Finally, in the last time there will be a universal outpouring of the Spirit 'on all flesh' (Joel 3.1f.). In all these texts the Spirit is conceived of as the power that produces a new creation. The entire creation that now impatiently waits amid groans will be led by the Spirit to its goal, which is the kingdom of the free children of God (Rom. 8.19f.). This does not mean that the Spirit will act only in the future and not in the present. 'My Spirit abides among you; fear not' (Hag. 2.5). But the present action of the Spirit has for its purpose the eschatological transformation and fulfillment. 'Not by might, nor by power, but by my Spirit, says the Lord of hosts' (Zech. 4.6). As God's power over history the Spirit will effect the transformation and transfiguration of the world in a non-violent way, because the change will first take place in the human heart.

The New Testament proclaims that this kingdom of freedom has begun in Jesus Christ. All four evangelists place at the beginning of their Gospels the account of the baptism of Jesus by John and the descent of the Spirit on Jesus (Mark 1.9–11 par.).[10] According to the predominant view among exegetes the baptism of Jesus is one of the surest facts of his life. The evangelists however, do not, report it as a call-vision and a datum in Jesus' biography; they understand it theologically and as an interpretative vision which explains the entire messianic activity of Jesus in a summary way and in terms of its source. According to Mark the baptism of Jesus is 'the beginning of the gospel of Jesus Christ, the Son of God' (Mark 1.1). For the apocalyptic motifs – the opening of the heavens, the sound of God's voice, and the coming of the Spirit who has been promised for the last times – are intended to make just one point: with the coming of Jesus Christ the eschatological time of salvation has begun; he is the messianic bearer of the Spirit of God; he is the Servant of God, who does not cry out or lift up his voice, does not break the bruised reed or quench the dimly burning wick, and truly brings justice (Isa. 42.2f.). In his 'inaugural sermon' at Nazareth Jesus is therefore able to claim that Isa. 61.1 is fulfilled in him: 'The Spirit of the Lord is upon me, because he has anointed me to preach good news to the poor. He has sent me to proclaim release to the captives and recovering of sight to the blind, to set at liberty those who are oppressed, to proclaim the acceptable year of the Lord' (Luke 4.18f.).

According to the view of all four evangelists, in the time before Easter

Jesus was the exclusive bearer of the Spirit. In his own preaching and activity, statements about the activity of the Spirit play no part. This becomes especially clear in the much-debated saying about blasphemy against the Holy Spirit (Matt. 12.31f.; Luke 12.10). Here a contrast is established between the time when the Son of man is active on earth and exercises authority and the time when the Spirit will be at work. John 7.39 says explicitly: 'As yet the Spirit had not been given, because Jesus was not yet glorified.' Yet Matthew is already concerned to look back and connect statements about the Spirit with the activity of Jesus. According to the older version of a saying of Jesus in Luke 11.20, Jesus expels demons 'by the finger of God', but Matthew's version of the saying reads: 'if it is by the Spirit of God that I cast out demons . . . ' The earthly activity of Jesus is then consistently interpreted in pneumatological terms in Luke (4.14, 18; 10.21). In keeping with this, the two infancy narratives of Luke and Matthew see Jesus as being from the moment of his conception not only the bearer of the Spirit but the creation of the Spirit (Luke 1.35; Matt. 1.18, 20).

The older New Testament tradition connects the activity of the Spirit with the resurrection and exaltation of Christ. Typical of this view is the ancient piece of tradition in Rom. 1.3f. which confesses of Christ that he was 'constituted Son of God in power according to the Spirit of holiness by his resurrection from the dead'. Finally, the Letter to the Hebrews says that it was by the power of the Spirit that Christ offered himself to God in sacrifice on the cross (9.14).

The New Testament itself makes no effort to harmonize these various strands of tradition. Their common denominator is, of course, quite clear; in the entire ministry and activity, life death and resurrection of Jesus Christ, in his person as well as in his work, the Spirit is bringing about the eschatological fulfillment. Consequently, the pericope on the baptism of Jesus makes it clear that what takes place in Jesus the exemplar at the baptism takes place ever anew in the baptism of Christians as images of Jesus: the Spirit of God lays hold of the baptized person and gives him a share in the eschatological divine sonship.

In describing the post-Easter activity of the Spirit the New Testament again shows several theological traditions:

According to Luke's Acts of the Apostles the presence and action of the Spirit characterizes the age of the church, which lasts from the ascension of Jesus to his return. The Spirit is given to the church at Pentecost (2.1–13). In the Pentecost pericope there are clear echoes of the Sinai event, for Pentecost has to do with the new law and the covenant which embraces not only Israel but the pagan nations as well. From what had been the pagan peoples (*ethnē*) emerges the people (*laos*) of God (15.14). But echoes, too, of the confusion of languages at Babel (Gen. 11.1–9) are to be heard in the account of the miracle of speaking (or hearing) on Pentecost. The divided and estranged peoples can once again understand one another by the power of the one Spirit. Thus is fulfilled the prophecy of Joel that in the final time God will pour out his Spirit on all flesh (2.16–21). It is also the Spirit that leads the young church on its missionary way and guides it as it goes. According to Luke the Spirit acts in a somewhat disconnected way; that is, there are, as it were, a series of repetitions of the Pentecostal miracle in Jerusalem (2; 4.25–41), Samaria (8.14–17), Caesarea (10.44–48; 11.15–17), and Ephesus (19.1–6). Here the Spirit manifests himself in striking miracles and extraordinary charisms such as glossolaly and prophecy. But Luke is also aware of the connection between baptism and the communication of the Spirit (1.5; 2.38; 9.18; 10.47; etc.) and between the laying on of hands by the apostles and the bestowal of the Spirit (8.14–17). Above all, despite the great emphasis on the freedom of the Spirit, Luke is also concerned to show the continuity of the Spirit's activity. Even though the Spirit keeps on opening up new mission fields and new tasks, there is a continuous history that begins in Jerusalem and has Rome for its goal. For this reason, the collection taken up in the Gentile Christian communities for the poor of Jerusalem as a sign of abiding union with the mother community of Jerusalem is also, in Luke's mind, an inspiration of the Holy Spirit (11.27–30; 24.17; Gal. 2.10; Rom. 15.26–28; I Cor. 16.1–4; II Cor. 8.4, 6–15). In his idealized and exemplaristic description of the primitive community of Jerusalem Luke is thus able to tell us how the Spirit acts in the church: by effecting a communion (*koinonia*) in apostolic faith, celebration of liturgy, and service that reaches the point of sharing earthly goods (2.42–47).

According to the writings of Paul, the Spirit has a fundamental part to play in Christian life and in the church. According to Paul, Christians are even defined by the fact that they possess the Spirit of God and allow him to guide them (Rom. 8.9, 14). 'To be in Christ' and 'to be in the Spirit' are interchangeable expressions for Paul. On the other hand, the pneumatology of Paul the Apostle is clearly distinguishable from that of Luke. Paul does, of course, know of extraordinary gifts of the Spirit; he claims to have them himself. But the important thing for Paul is that the Spirit works not only externally but also internally, not only in striking, extraordinary phenomena but in ordinary Christian life. He is not simply the power that makes the extraordinary possible, but the power that enables us do the ordinary in an extraordinary way. In dealing, therefore, with the enthusiastic tendencies especially of the Corinthian community, Paul emphasizes two criteria in particular for the 'discernment of spirits':

1. The confession of Jesus Christ as Lord: 'No one can say "Jesus is Lord" except by the Holy Spirit' (I Cor. 12.3). In Paul's view, the Spirit is the Spirit of Christ (Rom. 8.9; Phil. 1.19), the Spirit of the Lord (II Cor. 3.17), and the Spirit of the Son (Gal. 4.6). The famous formula: 'The Lord is the Spirit' (II Cor. 3.17) means that the Spirit is the effective mode of presence and the present effectiveness of the exalted Lord in the church and in the World.

2. Paul connects the efficacious action of the Spirit with the building up of the community and with service in the church. The Spirit is given for the advantage of all; the various gifts of the Spirit are therefore meant for mutual service (I Cor. 12.4–30). There can be no question, therefore, of invoking the supposed charismatic structure of the Pauline communities against an institutionally structured church. Quite the contrary, for Paul lays decided emphasis on the fact that God is a God not of confusion but of peace (I Cor. 14.33). The Spirit works, therefore, not through opposition of his gifts to each other, but through their combination and mutual support. He is inseparably linked to baptism (I Cor. 12.13) and the preaching of the gospel (I Thess. 1.5f.; I Cor. 2.4f., 13,; etc.) Above all, however, the charisms are not to be understood as external activities in the church but as varied expressions of the one grace of God (Rom. 12.6; cf. the identification of charism and eternal life in Rom. 6.23). The various gifts of grace, thus understood, bring with them a diversity of functions. The greatest of these gifts of the Spirit is love (I Cor. 13.13). In love, the Spirit becomes the norm and the source of power for Christian life.

According to Paul, Christian existence in the Spirit consists in our allowing ourselves to be led not by the flesh but by the Spirit; in our doing the works not of the flesh but of the Spirit; in setting our hearts not on what is passing but on what is abiding (Gal. 5.17–25; 6.8; Rom. 8.2–15). In positive terms, life in the Spirit means openness to God and neighbor. Openness to God finds expression above all in the prayer 'Abba, Father!' (Rom. 8.15, 26f.; Gal. 4.6). Because of the Spirit we possess the freedom of the children of God; we have access to God and know that in every situation we are under his protection. Galatians 5.13–25, finally, makes it clear that to walk in the Spirit means to serve one another with love. Love of God and of neighbor is true Christian freedom in the Spirit (Gal. 5.13). For the free person is not the one who does whatever he wants; one who acts in that manner is very much unfree because he is the slave of himself, his moods, and his changing circumstances. The free person is rather one who is free from himself and thus able to be there for God and for others.

The selflessness of love is true Christian freedom, and it is this that provides the context for the fruits of the Spirit: love, joy, peace, patience, kindness, goodness, faithfulness, gentleness and self-control. (Gal. 5.22f.). Through all these fruits the Spirit is bringing into existence the kingdom of the freedom of God's children (Rom. 8.8–10). Our present experience of the Spirit and his freedom is really only a first installment (Rom. 8.23; II Cor. 1.22; 5.5; Eph. 1.14). As a result, the Christian who lives in the Spirit is caught in a tension between the 'already' and the 'not yet'. To live by the Spirit means above all, therefore, to live our lives in the power of hope and to await the definitive transformation of the world and our own bodies.

In John[11] the eschatological character of the Spirit finds an expression peculiar to the Fourth Gospel. God himself is Spirit and wishes to be worshipped eschatologically in Spirit and in truth (John 4.24). Unless, therefore, a man is born again of water and Spirit, he cannot enter the kingdom of God (John 3.6). As John expressly points out, the Spirit rests permanently on Jesus (John 1.32). Jesus is the eschatological revealer because he gives the Spirit without limit (John 3.34; cf. 7.39). His words are spirit and life (John 6.63). But like the Synoptic writers John is also aware of the difference between the earthly life of Jesus and the time of his glorification. Only after he has been glorified can the Spirit be given (John 7.39; 16.7). At his death Jesus surrenders his spirit (John 19.30) and gives it to the church, which is represented beneath the cross by John and Mary. After his resurrection Jesus expressly communicates his Spirit to the disciples: 'Receive the Holy Spirit' (20.22).

The Spirit who is present after the resurrection and exaltation of Jesus is also called by John the 'Paraclete', that is, the helper and supporter (not: consoler). This Paraclete is identified with the Spirit of truth (John 14.17; 15.26; 16.13) and, as a 'second' or 'another' supporter, is paralleled with Jesus. As Jesus has been sent by the Father and proceeds from the Father, so the Spirit too proceeds from the Father (John 15.26), but he is given because of the prayer of Jesus (John 14.16) and in the name of Jesus (14.26). His function is to teach the disciples everything and to remind them of everything that Jesus had told them (John 14.26); he will bear witness to Jesus (15.26) and will lead the disciples to the complete truth, not saying anything on his own authority but glorifying Jesus and proclaiming his word (John 16.13f.). The Spirit acts, moreover, not only in the preaching of the community of disciples but also in its sacraments; he is associated especially with baptism (John 1.33; 3.5) and the eucharist (John 6.63; I John 5.6–8). This activity of the Spirit can be carried out only amid confrontation with the world that does not believe and therefore cannot receive the Spirit (John 14.17). In relation to the world it is the

Spirit's task to convict the world and make known what sin, justice and judgment are (John 16.8). The faithful, however, who are recognized by the Spirit, by their confession of Jesus Christ, and by their love (I John 4.6, 13), have already reached eschatological fulfillment. They no longer need to be taught by anyone (I John 2.27); they no longer need to inquire, and their joy is complete (John 16.20–23). Thus in the coming of the Spirit the second coming of Jesus is already taking place; the Spirit is the reality of eschatological fulfillment; he is the way in which God, who is Spirit, is present in the world.

The experience of the early church is reflected in the first Letter of Clement: 'All were granted a profound and blessed peace and an unquenchable desire to do good; and the fullness of the Holy Spirit was poured out on them.'[12] All the early Christian writers tell first and foremost of the gifts of the Spirit in the communities.[13]

The struggle with the movements of enthusiasts that have continually appeared on the scene in the course of the church's history led unintentionally to a repression of the charismatic element and a certain institutionalization of the Spirit. Montanism in the second half of the second century already marks an important turning-point.[14] As the danger grew of the church becoming 'bourgeois', Montanism sought to revivify the original enthusiasm. The call to conversion in face of the imminent end of the world, together with an ethical rigorism and ecstatic forms of communal life, awoke a powerful echo in hearts. Tertullian set up an opposition of principle between the *ecclesia spiritus* (church of the Spirit) and *ecclesia numerus episcoporum* (the church which consists of a number of bishops).[15] Irenaeus takes a different approach: he sees the Spirit of God as active in the church, which is made up of followers of the apostles. The church is the vessel in which the Spirit 'rejuvenates and keeps rejuvenating' faith; 'Where the church is, there the Spirit of God is; where the Spirit of God is, there the church is and all grace.'[16] According to the *Apostolic Tradition* of Hippolytus of Rome it is the Spirit who guarantees the preservation of the tradition;[17] therefore 'let him [the believer] hasten to the church where the Spirit flourishes.'[18]

Because of the polemic against the Montanists and later against enthusiasts generally, the striking charisms gradually faded away. But the charismatic dimension of the church lived on in the martyrs, as it did in monasticism, from which many bishops came, and later in the saints.[19] But even though there have been repeated severe struggles between charismatic movements marked by uncontrolled enthusiasm and often by a rigoristic understanding of the church's holiness, and the institutional great church, the church's theologians have never allowed themselves to be forced into setting up an opposition of principle between Spirit and institution; they have rather seen the church as the place and even the sacrament of the Spirit, and the Spirit as the vital principle or soul of the church.[20] On the other hand, a certain absorption of the Spirit by the church is unmistakable in this approach.

Beginning in the twelfth and thirteenth century the discussion of the reality and effective action of the Spirit in history took on a new dimension. Joachim of Flora, a Calabrian abbot,[21] prophecied a coming new age of the church, an age of the Spirit which would replace the age of the Father (the Old Testament) and the age of the Son (the clerical church) with an age of monks, contemplatives, and *viri spirituales* (men of the Spirit). In this outlook the hope of the eschatological transformation by the Holy Spirit became the expectation of a renewal within history. In being thus historicized, the Spirit became a principle of historical progress. While this renewal and progress was originally thought of by the Fraticelli as a renewal of the church, Joachim's ideas were soon given a secularized form. In that form these ideas became the source of the modern idea of progress and the various modern utopias. We find Joachim's ideas reappearing, transformed, in Lessing, Kant, Hegel, Schelling and Marx, and even in the dreadful dream of a Third Empire. In the present as in the past, Joachim's ideas or fragments of them have been at work in many theological trends and movements of renewal within the church.

The church's theologians have taken a critical attitude toward Joachim's ideas. Bonaventure was able, indeed, to find one positive element in Joachim's thinking, inasmuch as Francis of Assisi was for Joachim an eschatological sign.[22] But on the key issue Bonaventure and Thomas Aquinas took the same stand: there is no salvation-historical advance beyond Jesus Christ; the Holy Spirit must therefore be understood as the Spirit of Jesus Christ. Thomas himself was extremely harsh in his judgment of Joachim; he would have nothing to do with any theological interpretation of individual historical events.[23] In his view the new covenant consists in 'the grace of the Holy Spirit, which is given through faith in Christ' ('*gratia spiritus sancti, quae datur per fidem Christi*'). The 'new law' (*lex nova*) or 'evangelical law' (*lex evangelica*) is therefore primarily an 'inward implanted law' (*lex indita*) and only secondarily connected with anything external; externals serve only in preparation and implementation. Therefore the law of the new covenant is a law of freedom and not of the letter that kills; it is not law but gospel.[24] Every historicization of the activity of the Spirit must therefore fall short of the gospel and turn into a new legalism.

The church's pneumatology was therefore inspired chiefly by the intention of safeguarding the unity of the history of salvation and of understanding the Holy Spirit as the Spirit of Jesus Christ, the Spirit who is inseparably connected with the person and work of Jesus and whose task it is to make the person and work of Jesus present in the church and the individual Christian and thus bring them to their completion. The new thing which the Spirit brings is that he constantly makes Jesus Christ present anew in his eschatological newness. The Spirit's work is renewal in the newness of

Jesus Christ. This means that we are continually linked to the humanity of Jesus and that the tension between letter and spirit cannot be overcome through historical progress. Rather, the transition from letter to spirit must be repeated over and over, without the tension ever being removed within history. These concerns on the part of ecclesial tradition are undoubtedly faithful to the testimony of scripture. At the same time, however, the struggle with the various movements of enthusiasm led to certain narrowings of vision in the tradition: on the one hand, to an identification of the Spirit with the church or, more accurately, with office in the church, and, on the other, to a restrictive spiritualization. The freedom and universality of the Spirit no longer received their full due. Finally, talk of the Holy Spirit was largely restricted to the doctrine of the Trinity, where indeed it had its proper place but also where it could bear little fruit. Thus it was not only the struggles with the enthusiasts but also the very teaching of the church on the Holy Spirit as a divine person that led to a certain forgetfulness of the Spirit. Of this I shall now speak in greater detail.

(c) The Holy Spirit as a person

According to the creed, the Holy Spirit is not a mere impersonal gift, nor is he simply God in his creative, life-giving and saving presence in the world and in the church; he is also a personal giver of these gifts, he is the third Person of the Trinity. In the New Testament the confession of the Trinity appears only in rudimentary form; this is true in particular of the personal aspect of the Holy Spirit. Nonetheless there are clear indications that the Bible, too, understands the Spirit as being not simply an impersonal gift but a personal giver.

The wisdom literature of the Old Testament already contains the idea of hypostases which enjoy a relative independence over against God. Among these belong especially wisdom, and the pneuma which is largely identical with wisdom (Wisdom 1.6f.; 7.7, 22, 25). In post-biblical Judaism categories proper to the person are applied to the Spirit, who is said to speak, cry out, admonish, grieve, weep, rejoice and console; he is even represented as speaking to God. He appears as a witness against human beings, or is presented as their advocate.[25] The New Testament uses similar language. It speaks of the Spirit groaning and praying in us; the Spirit pleads for us with God (Rom. 8.26). The Spirit bears witness to our spirit (Rom. 8.16). He distributes gifts as he chooses (I Cor. 12.11). He speaks in the scriptures of the old covenant (Heb. 3.7; I Peter 1.11f.; II Peter 1.21) and in the church (I Tim. 4.1). He instructs the community (Rev. 2.7). All these statements indicate a person or at least a personification. In the Gospel of John, the Spirit is the church's helper and supporter (John 15.26). He is in particular the 'other' helper along with Jesus (John 14.16) and must therefore be understood as personal by analogy with Jesus Christ. He is sent by the Father in the name of Jesus, but also possesses an independence over against the Father (I John 2.1); he is not only the returning Christ, but also bears witness to Jesus (John 15.26). It is worth noting, too, that though 'Spirit' is a neuter noun in Greek, he is described in John 14.26 by a masculine and therefore personal demonstrative: 'that one' (*ekeinos*). In all this we can see clear indications of a relative independence of the Spirit and of a personal understanding of his being. In keeping with this, the New Testament already has trinitarian formulas (Matt. 28.19; II Cor. 13.13; etc.), which I shall be discussing in detail later on.[26]

More important than individual passages is the objective context into which they fit. The question is: what is it that materially necessitates such statements as indicate the relative independence of the Spirit and his character as a person? In order to answer this question we shall take as our point of departure the function of the Holy Spirit. According to the New Testament it is the task of the Spirit to give a universal presence to the person and work of Jesus Christ and to make these real in the individual human being. The task is carried out, however, not mechanically but in the freedom of the Spirit. For 'where the Spirit of the Lord is, there is freedom' (II Cor. 3.17). The Spirit does not teach a doctrine of his own, independent of that of Jesus Christ, but he does teach in the prophetic mode by leading men to the complete truth and making known what is to come (John 16.13). This freedom of the Spirit is incompatible with the Spirit being simply an impersonal principle, a medium or dimension; rather, the freedom of the Spirit presupposes the relative independence of the Spirit. The explicit acknowledgment of the independent personality of the Spirit is therefore anything but speculative indulgence; at issue in it is the reality of Christian salvation: the Christian freedom that is based on the freedom of God's gift and grace. The development of the full doctrine on the Holy Spirit thus has for its vital context (its *Sitz im Leben*) an experience, namely, the experience of the irreducible freedom that characterizes the activity of the Spirit. This is the objective fact which allows the New Testament to take over certain ideas from post-biblical Judaism, use them for its own purposes, and at the same time develop them, on the basis of its own experience, into a confession of the Trinity.

Despite these New Testament beginnings, explicit clarification took a long time.[27] In a famous address Gregory of Nazianzus traces the slow advance of the revelation of the mystery of God. As he puts it, in the Old Testament the mystery of the Father was revealed, while the Son remained in the shadows; the New Testament reveals the Son and insinuates the divinity of the Holy Spirit. Only at the present time, however, is the Spirit revealing himself more clearly.[28] As a matter of fact, early Christian writers show some obscurity with regard to the Holy Spirit. He is frequently confused with the Son.[29] At bottom, the thinking of the Apologists was binitarian rather than trinitarian. Yet clarification came relatively soon in connection with the baptismal confession of faith. Like Matt. 28.19, the *Didache*[30] and Justin[31] are already familiar with a trinitarian baptismal confession. In Irenaeus of Lyons[32] and Tertullian[33] the baptismal confession in its trinitarian form is perfectly clear. The rules of faith proposed by Irenaeus[34] and Tertullian[35] bear witness to the same faith. In connection with the baptismal confession we find Irenaeus already explaining that there are three key points of faith[36] and that all heresies are based on a denial of one or other of these three points.[37]

In Jewish Christianity the theological clarification seems to have been effected initially with the help of apocalyptic images.[38] The first more speculative essays to come with Tertullian in the Latin West[39] and Origen in the East;[40] in both men the explanations show a subordinationist tendency. The question of subordinationism did not become acute, however, until the fourth century when, as I indicated earlier, Arius, an Origenist, denied the true divinity of Jesus Christ. In the final phase of the Arian controversy the same problem arose in an acute form with regard to the Holy Spirit. The Macedonians or, as the case might be, the Pneumatomachians (lit., 'battlers against the Spirit') were at bottom biblicists who refused to accept metaphysical claim as part of their faith. They understood the Spirit as a serving Spirit, as an interpreter of God or as a king of angelic being; for them he was either a creature or a being intermediate between God and creatures. These views were opposed especially by the three great Cappadocians: Basil the Great (*On the Holy Spirit*), Gregory of Nazianzus (*Fifth Theological Oration*), and Gregory of Nyssa (*Great Catechetical Oration*, cf. 2). The dispute came out into the open in 374 when Basil replaced the traditional liturgical doxology 'Glory be to the Father through the Son in the Holy Spirit' with a new and unfamiliar one: 'Glory be to the Father with the Son and the Holy Spirit'. This doxology placed the Spirit on the same plane as the Father and the Son. In his book *On the Holy Spirit* Basil defends this new formula with, among other arguments, an appeal to the baptismal confession of faith. Athanasius also entered the controversy (*Four Letters to Serapion*). He argued soteriologically as he had in the dispute about the true divinity of Jesus Christ: The Holy Spirit can give us a share in the divine nature and divinize us only if he himself is God.[41] In the view of the Fathers, therefore, the issue was not a speculative problem but a fundamental question of salvation.

The Council of Constantinople (381)[42] – which historically was a synod of the Eastern Church and became an ecumenical council only because it was received, especially by the Council of Chalcedon (451) – dealt with this dispute about the Spirit. The Council composed a didactic document (*Tomos*) which has been lost; we know its content, however, from a letter which the Synod of 482 sent to Pope Damasus and the Western Synod which he was chairing in Rome (382). This document speaks of the single divinity, power and substance (*ousia*) of the Father, Son and Holy Spirit, to whom belong equal honor and dignity and eternal dominion and who exist in three perfect hypostases or persons.[43] Accordingly, the Pneumatomachians are anathematized in canon 1, along with the Arians and other heretics.[44] The Western Synod of 382 under Damasus taught objectively the same doctrine.[45] Along with the *Tomos*, which used technical theological language, the Council of Constantinople also proposed a confession of faith or, more exactly, made its own the confession which Epiphanius gives us in his *Ancoratus*.[46] In this confession the doctrine on the Holy Spirit in the Nicene confession of faith is expanded: 'We believe . . . in the Holy Spirit, the Lord and giver of life, who proceeds from the Father, who with the Father and the Son is worshipped and glorified, who has spoken through the prophets.'[47] This teaching of the Nicene-Constantinopolitan creed, the church's great confession of faith, is binding on all churches of the East and West down to the present time.

It is striking that the article of faith on the Holy Spirit does not use the term *homoousios* that is used in the article on Jesus Christ. But churchmen had learned a lesson from the confusion that followed on Nicaea; it is likely, therefore, that they deliberately avoided this disputed term, which was open to misunderstanding and was not attested in scripture. Nonetheless, the teaching on the divinity of the Holy Spirit was made fully clear (as can also be seen from the *Tomos*). The Spirit was described as *Kyrios* and thus given the title which was the Septuagint translation of *Adonai*, the Hebrew name for God. It was recognized, of course, that the title 'the Lord' (*ho Kyrios*) was reserved to Jesus Christ, and therefore the Spirit was called *to Kyrion*. The Holy Spirit is thus one who belongs to the category of Lord and is God. The term 'Giver of life' expressed the same idea in terms of action and function. For the point of this term was to say that the Spirit is not only the gift of life but also the giver of the gift, the originator of spiritual life – something that can come only from God. The term also makes clear the soteriological and existential character of the confession of faith in the Holy Spirit. The Fathers consistently argued that if the Holy Spirit is not truly God, then we are not truly divinized by him.

The further expression, 'who proceeds from the Father', is based on John 15.26 and is meant to explain the relation of Father and Spirit within the Trinity. The Spirit must not be allowed to be thought a creature of the Father; at the same he must not be said to be begotten by the Father as the Son is; he stands in a unique relation to the Father as his origin. In the West the Spirit's relation to the Son was defined only later on by the addition of the *filioque* ('and from the Son'), in a way, admittedly, that led to a still unresolved conflict with the East.[48] In the next clause: 'who with the Father and the Son is worshipped and glorified', the doxological motif finds expression which had already played a key role for Basil at the beginning of the controversy. Emphasis is placed on the idea that the same worship and glorification belongs to the Spirit as to the Father and the Son, and even that he is to be worshipped simultaneously with the Father and the Son. Finally, in the anti-gnostic formula, 'who has spoken through the prophets', the role of the Holy Spirit in the history of salvation is brought out. The Old and New Testaments are linked by the one Spirit; they are related as promise and fulfillment.

Through its reception by the Council of Chalcedon (451), the 'Nicene-Constantinopolian Creed,' as it is called, became the common possession of all the churches of East and West. It is one of the strongest ecumenial bonds and can stand as a basic expression of the Christian faith. This is true as well of its teaching on the Holy Spirit. All subsequent pneumatological statements are at bottom only interpretative extensions of this confession; this is true not least of the well-known addition in the Western form of this confession, an addition not found in the Eastern form, according to which the Holy Spirit proceeds from the Father and the Son (*filioque*). In its original form the confession left a question open at this point. It explained the divinity of the Holy Spirit as a presupposition of his function in the history of salvation; it also explained the relation of the Spirit to the Father, but left open the relation of the Spirit to the Son. This relation is not simply a speculative question; the issue in it is rather the precise determination of the relation of the Spirit to the salvific work of the Son and – as part of this work – to the church. The common confession left room here for various theological interpretations which later led to serious conflicts and became an occasion for the division between the Eastern and Western church. We must now turn to a consideration of these divergent theologies of the Holy Spirit.

3. Theology of the Holy Spirit

(a) Different theologies in East and West

A theology of the Holy Spirit labors under special difficulties. It is not possible for us human beings to speak of the mystery of God except by using human images and likenesses. Even the scriptures use a variety of images to describe the action of the Holy Spirit: breath, air, wind, water of life, fire or tongues of fire, ointment and anointing, seal, peace, gift, love. Each of these images attempts to describe the one action and being of the one Spirit of God from a different angle. The various images can therefore ground diverse approaches to theological understanding.

This is precisely what happened in the diverse theological approaches of East and West.[49] There was a common ground of faith as attested in scripture and tradition, but the result was diverse theologies of the Holy Spirit. The differences have to do with both images and concepts and ultimately with the overall conception of pneumatology. Unfortunately, however, the development did not stop a point when there was still a legitimate and desirable unity pervading a plurality of speculative theologies. Instead, the theological differences made their way into the confession of faith of the Western church, and specifically in the much debated addition to the Nicene-Constantinopolitan creed: 'who proceeds from the Father and the Son (*filioque*)'. The *filioque* is not present in the original text or in the creed of the Orthodox Church down to the present time. Its introduction into the Latin confession of faith turned a theological difference into a dogmatic belief, which was subsequently interpreted as a difference separating the churches and is still an unresolved point of controversy between East and West. The controversy is intelligible and resolvable only against the background of different theologies of the Holy Spirit.

The different conceptions are based, to begin with, on the different images used in order to gain a deeper faith-understanding of the doctrine of the Holy Spirit. The dominant model of Latin theology takes for its point of departure the soul's two faculties of knowing and willing. The Father, who knows and expresses himself in his Son as in his Word, also wills or is moved by love to unite himself to this image of himself; in like manner, the Son gives himself wholly to the Father in love. This loving grasp and embrace is not a generative process comparable to the production of the Word by knowledge, in which something substantially the same yet different emerges; rather, there is a movement of the will, which seeks the union of what is distinct. Since the beloved exists in the will of the lover as a power that moves and impels, the beloved can be described as 'spirit' in the sense of a power that impels from within. M. Scheeben has an even better explanation of how a reciprocal love between Father and Son can be described as 'Spirit': 'When we wish to express the intimacy of union between two persons, we say that they are of one spirit, or even that they are one spirit'.[50]

This interpretation of the Holy Spirit as mutual and reciprocal love between

Father and Son is an essential of Latin pneumatology, which was established especially by Augustine. 'The Holy Spirit is in a sense the ineffable communion of Father and Son.'[51] 'This ineffable embrace of the Father and his Image is not unaccompanied by pleasure, love and joy. This love, this joy, this blessedness, this happiness, or however this reality is to be described in a way worthy of God has been called "use"' by Hilary. 'In the Trinity this "use" is the Holy Spirit, who is not begotten but is the sweet blessedness of the Begetter and the Begotten.'[52] This is how Anselm of Canterbury[53] and Thomas Aquinas,[54] in particular, understood the Holy Spirit in continuity with Augustine. Latin theology thus uses a symmetrical representational model, according to which the movement of trinitarian life is rounded off in the Holy Spirit in a kind of circular movement. But Latin theology was not able consistently to follow through on this model. For Augustine and the rest of the Western tradition also wished to regard the Father as sole origin. Therefore, despite his firmly asserted thesis that the Holy Spirit proceeds from both Father and Son,[55] Augustine also insists that he proceeds originally (*principaliter*) from the Father.[56] Thomas Aquinas accepts this formula and describes the Father as the *principium* or *fons totius trinitatis* (source or fountainhead of the entire Trinity).[57] It follows from this that the Son derives from the Father his power to produce the Spirit; Thomas is therefore also able to say that the Holy Spirit proceeds from the Father through the Son. Only in Anselm of Canterbury is no room made for this point of view. Unfortunately, it was Anselm who influenced the later theological tradition at this point!

Alongside this model a second is to be found in Latin theology; its point of departure is an analysis of love. According to Augustine, love has three elements: the lover, the beloved, and the love itself.[58] Later on it was Richard of St Victor in particular who developed this approach; Alexander of Hales, Bonaventure and the Franciscan School took it over from him.[59] According to Richard St Victor, perfect love, which is God, is wholly ec-static. It therefore exists as Father, that is, as pure giver (*gratuitus*). As gift wholly given away it also exists as Son, that is, as gift wholly received from another (*debitus*) and wholly given away in turn (*gratuitus*). Finally, it exists in the Holy Spirit as gift wholly received (*debitus*); the Spirit is the common beloved (*condilectus*) of Father and Son. He is gift in an unqualified sense.[60] This second model has the advantage that, unlike the first, it does not understand the Holy Spirit as the mutual love of Father and Son, but more clearly and consistently brings out the status of the Father as the source which gives love to the Son, a love which the Son, who possesses it as given to him by the Father, together with the Father who possesses it as ungiven, then bestows on the Spirit.

The Greeks, too, use human images and analogies for understanding the Son and the Spirit of God. But, unlike the Latins, the Greeks take as their starting point not the interior word but the external, spoken word. For us human beings this external word is associated with breath as a movement of the air. 'When we speak a word, this movement of the air produces the voice, which alone makes the meaning of the word accessible to others.' In an analogous manner, in God, too, there is a breath, namely, the Spirit 'which accompanies the word and reveals its efficacy'.[61]

Latins and Greeks thus start with different representational models. From the divergent images used come different theological conceptions. According to the Latins the Spirit proceeds from the reciprocal love of Father and Son; the Greeks, on the other, speak only of a procession of the Spirit from the Father. This does not mean that for the Greeks the Spirit is not also the Spirit of the Son.[62] For 'he proceeds from the Father and rests in the Word and reveals him'.[63] In this sense the Spirit 'proceeds from the Father, is communicated through the Son, and is received by every creature. He creates by his own power, makes all things be, sanctifies and holds together.'[64] The advantage of this conception is that it maintains the position of the Father as sole source within the Godhead and that the relation of the Spirit to activity in the world is brought out more clearly than in the Latin conceptions, which are in danger of turning the life of God in the Holy Spirit into something self-enclosed and not turning outward to the world and history.

The different analogies used are matched by different concepts. The common basis for the formation of concepts is John 15.26, where the Spirit is described as one 'who proceeds from the Father' (*ho para tou patros ekporeuetai*). All the traditions have in common that in the Nicene-Constantinopolitan creed they replace *para* with *ek* and replace *ekporeuetai* in the present tense with the participle *ekporeuomenon*, in order to bring out not only the temporal procession but the abiding eternal procession.[65] The difference between Greeks and Latins began when the Vulgate translated *ekporeuetai* as *procedit*, for *processio* in Latin theology has a much more general meaning than *ekporeusis* in Greek theology. *Ekporeuesthai* means 'emerge from, go forth from, stream forth from'. In this sense the concept is applicable only to the Father, the first, unoriginated origin; the co-operation of the Son in the procession of the Holy Spirit, on the other hand, must be described by the verb *proïenai*. Latin does not make this fine distinction. According to Latin theology *processio* is a general concept that can be applied to all of the inter-trinitarian processes, that is, not only to the coming forth of the Spirit from the Father, but also to the generation of the Son and to the breathing of the Spirit through the Son. As a result, Latin theology is faced with a problem that does not have a parallel in Greek theology. For Latin theology too must hold fast to the distinction between the *processio* of the Son from the Father and the *processio* of the Spirit from the Father. If the Spirit proceeded from the Father in the same manner as the Son, there would be two Sons and no longer any distinction between Son and the Spirit. Given the presuppositions of Latin theology, the distinction between Son and Spirit can be preserved only by giving the Son a role in the procession of the Spirit from the Father, whereas he does not have an active role in his own procession from the Father. Admittedly, he plays a part not *principaliter*, that is, as an origin, but only in virtue of the being he has received from the Father. For this reason, Latin theology has always insisted that in the procession of the Holy Spirit Father and Son form a single principle.[66] In fact, Latin theology can even say with Thomas Aquinas that the Spirit proceeds from the Father through the Son. The disadvantage, of course, is that the *filioque* does not express in credal form the differentiation of roles which is accepted in Latin theology.

The Greek theology of the Spirit likewise has its weaknesses. It is able to express the special role of the Father in the procession of the Spirit, but in its dogmatic credal formulas it is completely silent about the relation of the Spirit to the Son. Simply to leave open the relation of Son and Spirit is, not of course, a solution. For according to the scripture, in terms of the economy of salvation the Holy Spirit proceeds from the Father (John 15.26), but he is also communicated by the Son (John 14.16, 26). But if the economy of salvation and the theology of the inner life of the Trinity should not diverge but rather correspond, and if the Son has a share in the sending of the Spirit in the history of salvation, then he cannot fail to have a share in to the intra-trinitarian procession of the Spirit. According to the scriptures, after all, the Spirit is the Spirit of the Son (Gal. 4.6) or the Spirit of Jesus Christ (Rom. 8.9; Phil. 1.19). According to Rev. 22.1 the water of life 'flows (*ekporeuomenon*) from the throne of God and of the Lamb'.

These data from the Bible are probably the reason why the Greek fathers of the first centuries did not object to early formulations of the *filioque* or its equivalents in Ambrose, Augustine and Leo the Great. More than this, formulations are to be found in some Greek fathers, especially Athanasius, Cyril of Alexandria and even Basil, that sound like the Western *filioque*.[67] The Greek fathers do, of course, speak mostly of a procession of the Spirit from the Father through the Son,[68] a formula which is not wholly foreign to the Latins; this is true especially of Tertullian,[69] who, even before Augustine, had laid the foundation of Latin teaching on the Trinity. An interesting formula, which combines the concerns of both West and East, is to be found in Epiphanius of Salamis, who speaks of the Spirit 'who proceeds from the Father and receives from the Son'.[70] While Epiphanius seeks to mediate between the two traditions from the side of Latin theology, Maximus the Confessor in the seventh century starts with Greek presuppositions in his efforts to mediate;[71] in the later patristic period, as the latter is drawing to its close, he is an important witness to ecumenical unity between East and West.

The points of contact just indicated cannot and should not blur the differences between the two traditions; they were to show, however, that in the early centuries these differences were never taken as a challenge to the common faith and that, on the contrary, because of the common biblical basis and a common tradition there were bridges of many kinds between East and West. Both theologies were trying to say objectively the same thing. They bore witness to one and the same faith but in different conceptual forms. In other words, they were complementary theologies, each internally consistent and coherent but each also irreducible to the other. The difference in terminology presented no problem at all in the first eight centuries; it was never an occasion for controversy, much less for a rupture of ecclesial communion.

The *filioque* first became a problem when the Latins turned their theological formula into a dogmatic confessional formula and thus unilaterally changed the originally common text of the creed. The change took place initially in various provincial Synods of Toledo in the fifth to the seventh centuries.[72] The background of this development has still not been fully clarified. It is probable that in the *filioque* these provincial synods were reacting against an offshoot of Arianism, namely, Priscillianism. The intention of the *filioque*, in this case, was to assert the consubstantiality of the Son with the Father and to emphasize the point that the Spirit is the Spirit not only of the Father but also of the Son. These are concerns that were shared by the East as well. It is clear, therefore, that the *filioque* was in no way originally directed at the East but represented a development peculiar to the West at a time when contacts with the East had already been greatly weakened, so that eventually mutual understanding ceased. To this extent, then, the *filioque* is the Western form in which the Nicene-Constantinopolitan creed was received.

The controversy over the Latin tradition and reception broke out only when Charlemagne at the Council of Frankfurt (794) objected to the Second Council of Nicaea (787) and its confession of the procession of the Holy Spirit 'from the Father through the Son' and proclaimed instead the *filioque* which had meanwhile been received in the West. The Council of Aachen (809) officially added the *filioque* to the creed. For our present purposes we may ignore the political background of all this, although it did determine the emotional climate. Rome was very reserved and even opposed to the development. Pope Leo III defended Nicaea and thus the tradition and set himself against the Carolingian council. He maintained his position when Frankish monks in the monastery of St. Sabbas in Jerusalem introduced the *filioque* into the creed of the Mass and gave occasion for considerable controversy. The pope defended the teaching contained in the *filioque* but he refused its incorporation into the crowd. Pope Benedict VIII took a different attitude when Emperor Henry II demanded that the *filioque* be incorporated into the creed of the Mass at his coronation in 1014. With the agreement of the pope a new confessional tradition was begun in the West.[73]

The Fourth Lateran Council (1215) and in particular the Second Council of Lyons (1274) defined the Western doctrine of the procession of the Holy Spirit from the Father and the Son.[74] Lyons rejected the Eastern misunderstanding (which has lasted in part down to our own day) of the *filioque*: that there are two principles or origins in the Trinity. According to the teaching of the Lateran Council, Father and Son form a single principle in the procession of the Holy

Spirit. In a certain sense it can even be said that the West emphasizes the unity of the Trinity even more than the East does, since in the *filioque* it insists on the equality and even singleness of substance of the Spirit with the Father and the Son and, with regard to the distinction of persons, shows that the intra-trinitarian movement of life and love between Father and Son ends in the Holy Spirit as the bond of unity.

The introduction of the *filioque* created a canonical as well as a dogmatic problem for the East. From the canonical standpoint the East objected to the introduction of the *filioque* as illicit according to the canons. It saw in the action a violation of the seventh canon of the Council of Ephesus (431), which had forbidden the formation of a different confession of faith (*hetera pistis*).[75] The Latins, however, saw in the *filioque* not a different faith but an explication of one and the same faith as had been professed by Nicaea and Constantinople. It was above all Patriarch Photius in the ninth century who took up the objective dogmatic question.[76] He opposed the Latin *filioque* and set in its place the formula *ek monou tou patros* (from the Father alone). This formula has a legitimate meaning when *ekporeusis* is given its strict Greek meaning and taken in the Augustinian sense of *principaliter procedere*. But with the polemical meaning given it by Photius this formula is itself a novelty. In this Monopatrism the texts of the Greek tradition that had asserted a procession from the Father through the Son, or something comparable, were brushed aside, and any agreement with the West was rendered impossible. The Greek church canonized Photius' views, although without shelving the older fathers, as Photius had. The Greek tradition is broader and richer than it seems to be when viewed through Photius' polemical spectacles.

Gregory Palamas in the fourteenth century took a further and much more decisive step in the theological dispute.[77] According to him there is no real indwelling of the Holy Spirit in the faithful; what is poured out upon the faithful is not the substance of God but only the uncreated action, radiance and glory (*energeia*); only his uncreated gift and not the giver himself. For this reason it is not possible to argue back from the economic Trinity to the immanent Trinity. The question then arises whether this radical *theologia negativa* does not make the immanent Trinity irrelevant to the history of salvation and deprive it of any role therein. The Neopalamite theologians of our century (especially V. Lossky,[78] have renewed this rejection in principle of the *filioque*; they see in Latin filioquism the root of all Latin heresies including even the dogma of papal primacy. According to Lossky the *filioque* connects the Holy Spirit in a onesided way to the Son; this kind of chritomonism no longer assures the freedom of the Spirit in the church. On the other hand, since V. Bolotov, church historian at St Petersburg, published his 'Theses on the Filioque'.[79] a more historical judgment has to some extent prevailed even in the Orthodox churches; these now regard the *filioque* as canonically irregular, but not as a dogmatic error.

In the West the view can be found at an early date that non-acceptance of the *filioque* is heretical. But the positions of the great theologians of the high Middle Ages on this matter are far more nuanced than is usually assumed.[80] In consequence, there was good reason to expect reunion with the Greeks at the Council of Florence (1439–45).[81] The Council was aware of the Greek distinction according to which the Son is indeed *causa* of the procession of the Spirit but not, like the Father, its *principium*. To that extent, the Council acknowledges the formula 'through the Son', although it interprets this as equivalent to the Western *filioque* which, it says, was rightly and reasonably added to the creed.[82] Because of this Western attitude it is understandable that, even apart from political and emotional reasons, the East was not satisfied with the reunion offered and did not receive it. For the present-day Roman Catholic Church the decisions of Pope Benedict XIV (1742 and 1755) are normative: the Uniate Eastern Churches are allowed the use of the unaltered creed of 381. This is to acknowledge that the formulas used in the two churches are complementary.

The churches of the Reformation took over the confession of faith in its Western form and therefore with the addition of the *filioque*. In the present century K. Barth in particular has expressly defended the *filioque*.[83]

Only with the contemporary ecumenical discussion has the question entered a new phase.[84] The discussion has led to the feeling that the West should restore the original text by striking the *filioque* from the creed, and thus create the conditions for a new dialogue on the Holy Spirit. But this suggestion would produce fruit only if the East were at the same time to acknowledge that in what it intends to say the *filioque* is not heretical but theologically legitimate. In other words, East and West must reciprocally acknowledge the legitimacy of their divergent theological traditions. Of course, if this acknowledgement were to be given, there appears to be no reason why the West should renounce its confessional tradition. Conversely, the West need not impose its tradition on the East. Such a unity in multiplicity is, in my view, a far more appropriate ecumencial goal than a monolithic confessional unity would be. In order to reach this goal, it is necessary, of course, that the conversation between East and West on the theological motives behind the *filioque* or its rejection be carried to a significantly deeper level. For in the final analysis, as the Neopalamite controversy has shown, the issue here is not a remote and abstract theological problem but the relation between the economic Trinity and the immanent Trinity or, to put it more concretely, the way in which the Holy Spirit works in the faithful and in the church.

In light of what has been said, any further ecumenical dialogue on the *filioque* faces a twofold task. On the one hand, it must achieve a recognition that East and West have two different traditions, based on a common faith, which are both legitimate and which can therefore acknowledge and complement each other, without either being reducible to the other. There are present here complementary theologies and complementary formulas.

The essential concern of the *filioque* is twofold: to preserve the consubstantiality (*homoousios*) of the Father and the Son, and to emphasize the fact that according to the scripture the Holy Spirit is always the Spirit of Jesus Christ, the Spirit of the Son. Conversely, the East is more concerned than the West to maintain the monarchy of the Father and the freedom of action of the Holy Spirit. These concerns are not contradictory, although no one has as yet succeeded in reducing them to components and thus cancelling while also preserving them in a higher, single theology of the Holy Spirit.

On the other hand, as the fact just noted shows, the dialogue between East and West must make it clear that the two traditions are dealing with different problems. The East in its confession of faith leaves open the relation of the Spirit to the Son; the West for its part has difficulty in conceptually distinguishing the relation of the Spirit to the Son from the relation of the Spirit to the Father. The ultimate question that waits in the background is that of the relation between the activity of the Holy Spirit in the economy of salvation as the Spirit of Jesus Christ, and the being of the Spirit within the Trinity. A dialogue on the different formulas of the past must be conducted with an openness to the future, in order to bring clarification to the still unresolved problems on both sides.

Only the future can show whether such a dialogue can lead to a new common formula that accepts both traditions and at the same time opens a way forward. One possible formula would be: '*qui ex Patre per Filium procedit*' (who proceeds from the Father through the Son). But more important than such a commonly accepted formula is unity in the objective truth. I have no doubt that such unity exists today despite all the differences in images, concepts and accents, and that the differences of the theologies in this area does not amount to a difference that should divide the churches. Likewise more important than a new commonly accepted formula is that the misunderstandings of the past should stimulate us to be sensitive to the concerns of the other tradition and thereby to clarify and enrich our own tradition, thus deepening the existing unity in truth and making both parties more clearly conscious of it. The issue here is not a useless quarrel about words but a deeper understanding of our salvation, that is, the question of how the salvation effected by Jesus Christ is communicated through the Holy Spirit. Is the Holy Spirit himself the gift of salvation, or is salvation an uncreated or created gift that is distinct from the giver? In what manner are we incorporated into the life of the triune God? These are questions truly worth discussing. A hasty elimination of the *filioque* could easily tempt us to leave problems untouched instead of seeking an answer to them.

(b) Suggestions for a theology of the Holy Spirit

A more profound theology of the Holy Spirit[85] is confronted with the difficulty that, unlike the Father and the Son, the Spirit is faceless as it were. He is like the wind that blows where it will: 'You hear the sound of it, but you do not know whence it comes or whither it goes' (John 3.8). Thomas Aquinas long ago acknowledged the linguistic problem in speaking of the Holy Spirit.[86] The Holy Spirit is often described as 'the unknown God'.[87] H. Urs von Balthasar calls him the Unknown One beyond the Word.[88] In a special way the Holy Spirit expresses the mystery of God whose depths no one knows but he (I Cor. 2.11). It is possible within limits to see the differences between the Latin and Greek conceptions of the Holy Spirit, which found critical expression in the Latin addition of the *filioque* to the creed, as originating ultimately in the fact that the Greek emphasize especially the incomprehensibility of God and the mysteriousness of the Spirit, while the Latin doctrine of the Trinity with its analogies from the life of the human soul strike the Greeks as rational or even rationalistic. The Greeks regard the theological deductions which lead to the *filioque* as an intolerable injection of rational thinking into the realm of the mystery of God. This is not to deny, of course, that in its own way Latin theology likewise intends to preserve the mysteriousness and non-manipulable freedom of the love and grace of God, which the Holy Spirit is in person.

In view of the mysteriousness of the Holy Spirit a theology of this divine Person is possible only if we take as our point of departure what the word of God reveals to us about him and what we know of the activity and effects of the Spirit in the history of salvation. The starting point must not be speculation, Neoplatonic or idealistic, but the experience of the Spirit in history: such experience as is attested and authentically interpreted in scripture and in the traditions that explain scripture. The basis of a theology of the Holy Spirit is not to be found in analogies from the life of the human spirit. The Latin tradition in particular has been accustomed to such analogies ever since Augustine; in them the Son is correlated with knowledge through the interior word and the Spirit with the will and the loving union of Father and Son. Such analogies can indeed shed some light as supplementary aids to understanding; the starting point and foundation, however, even in Augustine, is the testimony of faith to the action of the Spirit in the history of salvation. Only in Scholasticism, and especially in Anselm of Canterbury and (with less genius, but with more hair-splitting to make up for the lack) in the decadent controversies of the thirteenth and fourteenth century schools, did such speculative deductions gain pride of place, whereas Thomas Aquinas is still resolute is starting from the faith of the church and the experience of the Spirit as gift.

Of the many images which scripture uses in describing the action and effects of the Holy Spirit (breath, air, wind, water of life, fire or tongues of fire, ointment and anointing, seal, peace), the most influential in the history of theology has been the characterization of the Holy Spirit as gift and, in connection with this, as love. According to scripture the Spirit is God's eschatological gift; as such he completes the works of God. The scriptures regard the Spirit as *the* gift without qualification (Acts 2.38; 8.20; 10.45; 11.17; Heb. 6.4; cf. John 4.10). New Testament statements about the Spirit are therefore frequently accompanied by the verbs 'give' and 'receive'. Through the gift of the Holy Spirit the love of God is poured out in our hearts (Rom. 5.5). This means that the Spirit is even now given to us as a first installment of eschatological fulfillment (II Cor. 1.22; Eph. 1.14). With sighs he is already bringing about the eschatological fulfillment of creation in the kingdom of the freedom of God's children (Rom. 8.18ff.). The same language recurs in the fathers of the church. Following Hilary,[89] Augustine in particular developed a pneumatology of the Spirit as gift[90] which Peter Lombard[91] and Thomas Aquinas[92] took up and carried further. In addition, the Greek fathers emphasized the point that as eschatological gift the Spirit is the sanctification, fulfillment, completion and goal of all reality; he effects the divinization of man and reality so that God may be all in all (I Cor. 15.28).[93]

It is the task of theology to develop these data of scripture and tradition into a theology of the Holy Spirit. This does not mean drawing conclusions from the data of scripture and tradition as though they were premises, and thus passing from the realm of binding faith into the realm of non-binding private speculation. The point is, rather, to penetrate more deeply into the inner spirit and meaning of what is believed, in order to reach an understanding of that which is believed (*intellectus fidei*). This is done by seeking to grasp the internal connection between the various experiences and interpretations of faith (*nexus mysteriorum*), as well as their mutual correspondences (*analogia fidei*), and thus come to understand the one mystery that is manifested in the various mysteries of faith. The point, therefore, is not to do away with the mystery of rationalizing it but to gain a deeper understanding of the mystery as mystery.

This penetration and understanding of the depths of the divinity is not possible to the human spirit by its own power, but is the doing solely of the Spirit of God (I Cor. 2.11). Theology itself is therefore a spirit-ual process, something done in the Holy Spirit. For if we could grasp the mystery of God with our finite intellectual powers, we would degrade his divinity; in knowing him we would misunderstand him; in trying to conceive him we would be laying violent hands on him. If God is to remain God in our knowing of him and not turn into an idol which we knock together or tailor to our own measure, then God must not only reveal himself to us 'objectively' but must also grant us the 'subjective' power to know him; he must give us the Holy Spirit as the Spirit of faith (II Cor. 4.13) who enlightens the eyes of our heart (Eph. 1.18). He is the Spirit of wisdom and understanding (Isa. 11.2). Only through the Holy Spirit is it possible for us to address God as Father (Rom. 8.15; Gal. 4.6). The Spirit gives us the ability and power to recognize as such the love of God that is given to us in Jesus Christ and to take delight in it. In the Holy Spirit who is God in us we are able to acknowledge God over us, God the Father, as the one who in his Son is God among us. The Spirit enables us to recognize God's grace as grace; through him we are able to grasp God's gift as a gift, his love as his love; the Spirit is the subjective possibility of revelation.[94]

Since the Spirit, in an eschatological and definitive way, reveals God's eschatological giftness and eschatological love in us and for us, he must also be in himself God's graciousness. For if he were not God's love and giftness in himself 'first of all' but were this only for us, he could not reveal to us the Godness of God, which, as we saw earlier, consists in the freedom of his self-communicating love. The Spirit would then not reveal God as he is but only God as and insofar as he shows himself in history. In order that the Holy Spirit may be the subjective possibility of the eschatological and definitive revelation of the love and thus the Godness of God, he must himself be this freedom in love; that is, he must be God's love in person. He must be not only God's gift but also the giver of this gift; he must embody in a manner personal to himself that which God is by his nature. This thesis is not an arbitrary inference from the Spirit's action in the history of salvation to his personal divine being. That kind of inference must inevitably be powerless in the face of the mysteriousness of the Spirit. We can say nothing about the inner divine being of the Spirit that is not revealed to us by the Spirit himself and attested in scripture. The only thing in our power is to be led and enlightened by the Spirit so as to know the internal connection and internal correspondence between what revelation says about the action of the Spirit in the history of salvation and what it says about his divine being.

These reflections are confirmed and carried further by Augustine's comments on the subject. Augustine asks himself the question: how is it possible to call the Spirit the gift and love of God when love and giftness are the very nature of God and therefore common to all the divine persons? In his answer he distinguishes between love in the substantial sense and love in the personal sense. In the substantial sense love is the very being of God and common to all the divine persons; in the personal sense it is said in a special way of the Holy Spirit.[95] According to Augustine, then, the Holy Spirit expresses in a personal manner the giftness and love of the Father and the Son; he is in his very person the reciprocal love of the Father and the Son.[96] Unlike the Son he proceeds from the Father *quomodo datus* (as given) and not *quomodo natus* (as born).[97] The Spirit thus shows that the giftness and love of God do not first become a reality in the form of a gift made in the course of history, but are instead a reality from all eternity; in other words that God is from eternity 'givable' (*donabile*).[98] The Spirit is thus 'God in such a way' 'that he can at the same time be called the gift of God'.[99] Here we have the deepest reason why the Holy Spirit as gift is at the same time giver of the gift.

We may sum up and say that the Holy Spirit reveals, and is, the giftness of God as gift, love as love. The Spirit thus expresses the innermost nature of God – God as self-communicating love – in such a way that this innermost reality proves at the same time to be the outermost, that is, the possibility and reality of God's being outside of himself. The Spirit is as it were the ecstasy of God; he is God as pure abundance, God as the overflow of love and grace.[100] On the one hand, then, the immanent love of God reaches its goal in the Spirit. But at the same time, because in the Holy Spirit the Father and the Son as it were understand and realize themselves as love, the love of God in the Spirit also moves beyond God himself. This loving streaming-out-beyond occurs not in the form of a necessary streaming-out but in the personal manner of voluntary sharing and free, gracious self-communication. In the Spirit God has as it were the possibility of being himself by emptying or divesting himself. In the Holy Spirit God is eternally givable. With this in mind the fathers often compared the Spirit to the wafted perfume of an ointment[101] or thought of him as the radiating beauty of God, the traces of which can be seen in created beauty, in the wealth of created gifts, and in the abundance that marks creation.[102] As completion within God the Spirit is, then, also the eschatological completion of the world.

This theology of the Holy Spirit affords correctives to numerous tendencies in Eastern theology as well as to the Neo-scholastic type of Western theology. Unlike the Palamite theologians, I understand grace not as uncreated energy but as the real self-communication of God in and through the indwelling of the hypostasis of the Holy Spirit. Through the indwelling of the Holy Spirit, who has been given to us, we participate in the divine nature (II Peter 1.4). But, differently from what took place in the self-communication of the Son of God, we do not, through the Spirit, become children of God by reason of a generation, that is, substantially; rather we become sons and daughters of God through gift and grace or, in other words, we become children of God by adoption. (Rom. 8.15, 23; Gal. 4.5).

In thus taking seriously what the New Testament says about the indwelling of the Holy Spirit and in speaking not only of an indwelling of God that is simply appropriated to the Holy Spirit but rather of a personal (hypostatic) indwelling, I also differ from Neo-scholasticism in its understanding of grace as a created reality distinct from God.[103] Grace is rather first of all uncreated grace, God's self-communication in the Holy Spirit. To say this is not to exclude created grace. For uncreated grace changes the human person within; it has created effects, and it requires an acceptance by man that is possible only through grace. Therefore uncreated grace, or the indwelling of the Holy Spirit, requires created grace to prepare the way for it, just as it also has created grace for a consequence. It is impossible, therefore, to conceive of the self-communication of God in the Holy Spirit apart from the manifold gifts of the Holy Spirit that are distinct from God and therefore created.

All this makes it clear that a theology of the Holy Spirit as both giver and gift, and thus a theology of the Holy Spirit as self-gift, is the ultimate ground or, in other language, the transcendental theological condition for the possibility of the reality and effective realization of the salvation that is bestowed on us through Jesus Christ. It is also clear, then, that the theology of the Holy Spirit does not take us out of the realm of faith but on the contrary leads us more deeply into to. This theology proves its value by giving us a deeper understanding of what salvation really is. Thomas Aquinas, in particular, has given a magnificent explanation of how the action and effects of the Holy Spirit are to be understood in the light of the Holy Spirit as divine love in person.[104]

Since the Spirit is divine love in person, he is, first of all, the source of creation, for creation is the outflow of God's love and a participation in God's being. The Holy Spirit is the internal (in God) presupposition of this communicability of God outside of himself. But the Spirit is also the source of movement and life in the created world. Wherever something new arises, whenever life is awakened and reality reaches ecstatically beyond itself, in all seeking and striving, in every ferment and birth, and even more in the beauty of creation, something of the activity and being of God's Spirit is manifested. The Second Vatican Council sees this universal activity of the Spirit not only in the religions of mankind but also in human culture and human progress.[105] We may even say that because the Spirit is the inner condition for the possibility of creation, the latter is already always more than pure nature.[106] Through the presence and action of the Holy Spirit creation already always has a supernatural finality and character.

Secondly, the Holy Spirit is in a special way a source in the order of grace. He is at work everywhere that human beings seek and find friendship with God. A loving union with God is possible for us only through the Holy Spirit.[107] Through the Spirit we are in God and God is in us. Through him we are God's friends, sons and daughters, who, because we are impelled from within, serve God not as slaves but as free beings and who are filled with joy and consolation by this friendship with God. The grace of the Holy Spirit, which is given through faith in Jesus Christ, is thus, as Thomas Aquinas has shown, the law of the new covenant. This law is a law written in the heart, as interior law that moves us from within, and therefore a law of freedom.[108] Joy in God is the real freedom of the children of God. This freedom manifests itself in the many charisms (I Cor. 12.4–11) and fruits (Gal. 5.22f.) of the Holy Spirit. The supreme gift and fruit of the Spirit is love (I Cor. 13), for he is truly free who is not tied to himself but can surrender himself in the service of love (Gal. 5.13). This freedom that is given by the Spirit shows itself most fully in a love that renounces self even in the situation of persecution and suffering. In perseverance under persecution and in the patient endurance of suffering, the interior independence of the powers and principalities that press on us from without reaches its most complete form. Not without reason is the Spirit often described both in scripture (John 15f.) and in tradition as strength (*robur*) for resistance. He is at the same time the Spirit of truth (John 15.26; 16.13) who brings true reality to light despite efforts to distort and suppress it by violence and lies, and thus allows the splendor of God's glory to radiate upon the world once again. This healing and transforming power of the Spirit finds its most beautiful expression in the well known hymns to the Holy Spirit *Veni Creator Spiritus* ('Creator Spirit, come'; ninth century) and *Veni Sancte Spiritus* ('Come, Holy Spirit'; twelfth century). In these hymns the Spirit is described as the life-giving creative Spirit who, as the Holy Spirit, also fills the heart with the breath of the grace-life of love. He expels the powers of evil, cleanses what is soiled, fructifies what is arid, gives warmth to what is cold and heals what is ill. In the sanctifying action of the Holy Spirit the eschatological transformation and fulfillment of man and world dawns in us.

Thirdly, what has been said of the Spirit has consequences for the understanding of the church. If the Spirit is the authentic presence and realization of the salvation given through Jesus Christ, then whatever is external in the church – scripture and sacraments, offices and certainly the discipline of the church – has for its sole task to prepare men for receiving the gift of the Spirit, to serve in the transmission of this gift, and to enable it to work effectively.[109] This means that the reign of Christ extends beyond and embraces more than the visible church. Wherever there is love, the Spirit of God is at work, and the reign of Christ becomes a reality even without institutional forms and formulas.[110] It also means that the Holy Spirit is the internal life-principle or soul of the visible church.[111] The church must live by the power of the Spirit and constantly renew itself by that power. The constant presence and operation of the Spirit keeps the church always young. The action of the Spirit in the church takes the form of making Jesus Christ present ever anew in his newness.[112] Precisely as the Spirit of Jesus Christ the Spirit is the Spirit of freedom from the letter that kills. The Spirit preserves the church in its fidelity to tradition by leading it in a prophetic way into the entire truth and making known to it what is coming (John 16.13). He is not a kind of ideological guarantee of the church's *status quo*, but rather the Spirit of continual renewal. Above all, he makes known to the church ever new missionary opportunities, and points out ever new ways for it to go. He urges the church to heed his action in the 'signs of the times', to interpret these, and in their light to gain a deeper understanding of the Christian message.

In all these ways, the Spirit, who searches and knows the depths of the godhead (I Cor. 2.11), enables us to gain an ever deeper knowledge and ever greater love of God. Therefore it is he who also leads us into the depths of God by enabling us to know who God is as Father, Son and Spirit. He discloses to us the triune being of God and makes possible that knowledge of the Trinity in which the deepest mystery of the God of Jesus Christ finds its abiding and binding expression.

PART THREE

The Trinitarian Mystery of God

I

Establishment of the Doctrine of the Trinity

1. Preparation in religious history and in philosophy

The confession of one God in three persons is rightly regarded as proper and specific to Christian faith in God.[1] This trinitarian confession is not, however, a specific difference that is added as a Christian characteristic, or perhaps oddity, to a general religious conception of God of one kind or another, rather, it is the Christian form of speaking about God, that at the same time claims to express the eschatologically definitive and universal truth about God from which alone all other talk about God can derive its full truthfulness. It is the objective and even objectively necessary and binding formulation of the eschatological revelation God has given of himself in Jesus Christ through the working of the Holy Spirit. The trinitarian confession is therefore the recapitulation and summary of the entire Christian mystery of salvation, and with it the entire reality of Christian salvation stands or falls. It is no accident that this confession has for its vital context (*Sitz im Leben*) not the unworldy speculations of monks and theologians but the act of becoming a Christian, that is, baptism, which is administered in all churches 'in the name of the Father and of the Son and of the Holy Spirit'. Becoming a Christian, like being a Christian, is unconditionally linked to the trinitarian confession.

But it is precisely at this point, which holds the entire edifice together like the keystone of a Gothic arch, that difficulties of understanding become particularly numerous. And in saying this I am far from thinking chiefly of logical difficulties or of the certainly far from simple problems raised by biblical theology and by the history of religions and of dogma. Far more important is the question of the practical relevance to Christian life. It is a fact that many Christians correctly repeat the trinitarian profession of faith, for example, when they recite the creed during the celebration of the eucharist; it is also a fact that these same people can make very little use of it in their Christian lives. Karl Rahner's observation that most Christians are in practice strict monotheists is probably correct.[2] The widespread custom, which occasionally makes its way even into official documents, of speaking of a personal God instead of a tripersonal God, as the trinitarian confession requires, fully confirms Rahner's thesis. Before discussing the strictly theological problems of the trinitarian confession, we must therefore concern ourselves first with approaches to the understanding of the Trinity, in order thus to advance to the theological dimension proper, within which alone this confession can become relevant for us. In these preliminary considerations I am not yet concerned to justify the trinitarian faith, but only to offer some preparatory and introductory reflections that will bring to light the question to which the confession claims to provide the answer.

The church's doctrine of the Trinity has obviously never made the completely absurd claim that is constantly attributed to it, namely that 1 = 3. The attribution would be correct only if the doctrine claimed that 1 person = 3 persons, or that 1 divine substance = 3 divine substances; that is, if it claimed that God is both unity and trinity in one and the same respect. Such a claim would violate the principle of contradiction, according to which one and the same reality cannot in one and the same respect be simultaneously one and three. But what the doctrine of the Trinity asserts is that in God there is a unity of substance and a trinity of persons or a unity of substance in a trinity of persons. The one and the three refer, therefore, to entirely different aspects, and therefore there is no inherent contradiction. This negative statement can be supplemented by a positive statement. In the trinitarian confession of faith the problem is not an arithmetical and logical one, that is, one that is relatively superficial from the existential standpoint. Rather, in the numbering of one and three as well as in the reciprocal relation between them, what is being articulated are age-old problems associated with man's understanding of reality and himself. The issue is the ultimate ground and meaning of all reality.

It is quite easy to show that the question of unity is a basic problem of humanity.[3] Unity is necessarily presupposed if a being is identical with itself and therefore identifiable. Everything that exists is given only in the mode of unity. 'Unity' here means that the being is undivided in itself and differentiated from others. Unity is therefore an all-inclusive (transcendental) primordial and foundational determination of being.[4] Unity as a transcendental determination of being is not equivalent to a number; on the contrary, unity is the presupposition of numerability and the measure of numbers.[5] The unity that is quantitative and can be counted is the most inferior form of unity; it is derived and presupposes the higher forms of unity. Thus a plurality of beings is thinkable only because of the overarching unity of the species and genus. It makes sense to talk of 'three or four men' only if these three or four share the same human nature, or, in other words, only on the supposition of a specific unity and of the universal concept 'man' that is based on this specific unity. Numerical unity thus presupposes the unity of species and genus. The question that arises at this point is whether beyond the distinct genera of reality there is a unity that embraces all of reality.[6] Only at this level does the question of unity become existentially urgent. For without such an all-embracing unity amid the multiplicity of the realms of reality the world would be nothing but a dust-heap piled up at random and lacking in any order and meaning.[7] The question of the unity of reality amid the multiplicity of the realms of reality is therefore the same as the question of the intelligibility and meaning of reality. Only within the horizon of this question can the meaning of the monotheistic faith in God be fully grasped.

The question of unity amid the multiplicity of reality had already been raised by myths in their own fashion.[8] The multiplicity of gods in polytheism is at bottom an expression of the multi-levelled, broken and unsynthesizable character of reality. The genealogies of the gods, on the other hand, are already an attempt to introduce order and unity into this multiplicity. Most religions, too, are not simply polytheistic; rather they acknowledge a supreme God or an inclusive divine reality that manifests itself in the many gods. Thus as early as 1350 BC there was in Egypt an enlightened attempt under Ikhnaton to establish a monotheism of the sun-god Aton. In particular, Buddhism and Hindu Brahmanism are religions which maintain that all reality is a single entity.

From its very beginnings in Heraclitus and Parmenides, Western thought has concerned itself with the problems of unity. As early as the sixth century BC a radical critique of religion brought Xenophanes to this insight: 'There is one god, among gods and men the greatest, not at all like mortals in body or in mind.'[9] Such insights as this are still at work in Aristotle, who ends the eleventh (theological) book of his *Metaphysics* with the well-known verse from Homer's *Iliad*: 'It is unprofitable to have many rulers. Let one be sovereign.'[10] This doctrine of monarchy, that is, of a single ruler and a single origin, served Aristotle as both a political and a metaphysical program; more accurately, in his view the political order had a metaphysical and theological basis. This political and metaphysical theology of unity was further developed by the Stoics. According to them it is the one, divine world-reason that holds everything together and orders it; this world-reason is reflected above all in human reason who is charged to live in accordance with the order of nature.[11] The philosophy of unity attained its supreme form in Neoplatonism. Aristotle has already seen that the supra-categorical, transcendental one which is beyond all the genera cannot be conceptualized and that our thinking must begin with the One and lead back to it.[12] Plotinus went a step further. Since all existence presupposes unity, the One must be beyond existence; it is beyond being and is therefore ineffable; only through an ecstasis of reason can contact be made with One.[13]

A properly understood conception of unity does not, therefore, lead to a closed system in which everything can be derived from a single principle. The question of unity leads rather to an open system insofar as the principle of this unity eludes purely rational thought. With the philosophy of Aristotle and Thomas one must say that unity as a transcendental predicate of being applies analogously and not univocally to the various spheres of being. The question of the unity of all reality – a unity without which meaningful speech, thought and action and, in the final analysis, meaningful human existence are impossible – leads ultimately to a mystery. Thus the Neoplatonic philosophy of unity was not simply abstract speculation but the foundation of an entire spirituality and mysticism. Its purpose was that the soul should be increasingly purified of the multiple and manifold in order to ascend to the One and come in contact with it in a mystical ecstasy. This mysticism also had a lasting effect on the Christian tradition. Augustine writes in his *Confessions*:

> Lo, my life is scattered. And your right hand laid hold of me . . . so that . . . I might be gathered together in striving for the One . . . . But now my years pass amid groans, and you, Lord, my Father and consolation, are eternal; but I am fragmented into successive times whose order I do not know, and in the tumult and vicissitudes of things my thoughts and the innermost vitals of my soul are torn apart, until at last, purged and wholly melted down in the fire of your love, I flow together in unity in you.[14]

The question of Trinity or threeness, as much as the question of unity, is a primordial question of man and mankind. Schemata involving three (triads, ternaries) make their appearance wherever reality resists the innate need of the human spirit for unity. Threeness thus represents the multiplicity and manifoldness of reality. Now, since a triad has a beginning, middle and end, it is not just any kind of plurality. Three is the simplest and the same time the most perfect form of plurality: it is an organized plurality and therefore unity in multiplicity. For this reason Aristotle calls it the number of completeness.[15]

Myths and religions are full of triads. In Greek mythology the regions of the world are divided among the three sons of Chronos: Zeus, Poseidon and Hades. We often find three-headed or three-bodied divine personages. In cultic rituals and in music and architecture rhythms based on three have a privileged place. Everyone is familiar with the threefold repetition of oaths; elsewhere, too, trigemination or triplication in language and literature is an important stylistic device. Finally, division into threes is a favorite scheme for thinkers (e.g., antiquity, Middle Ages, modern times). Neoplatonic philosophy in particular is full of ternaries. Plotinus summed up the universe in three concepts: the One, spirit, soul. In Iamblichus, Proclus and Dionysius the Areopagite all of reality is comprehended with the aid of the law of division into three.[16] Especially important in antiquity were speculations regarding the triangle, which the Pythagoreans were already looking upon as not only a geometrical and arithmetical principle but a cosmic principle as well.[17] Plato developed this idea and interpreted the various types of triangular surfaces as the basic building blocks of the world.[18] A Christian use of the triangle as a symbol was, however, rendered impossible for a long time because the triangle was originally also a sexual symbol, and as such contained a reference to the primordial, maternal ground of all being. Only since the fifteenth century has the triangle served as a symbol of the Trinity.

Such ternaries and triads are also richly attested in the Old and New Testaments.[19] Nonetheless, the Christian doctrine of the Trinity is not to be derived from such symbols and speculations.[20] For nowhere do we find the specifically Christian idea of a single divinity in three persons, that is, of the unity of three divine persons in a single being. In contrast to the non-Christian ideas and speculations which I have been mentioning, unity in trinity according to Christianity is not a cosmological problem that embraces both God and the world, but a strictly theological and even intradivine problem. For this reason the Bible nowhere justifies the Christian doctrine of the Trinity with the aid of such cosmological speculations. The doctrine has its basis solely in the history of God's dealings with human beings and in the historical self-revelation of the Father through Jesus Christ in the Holy Spirit. On the other hand, it is not unimportant that in summing up the unity and comprehensiveness of its message and of reality itself Christianity, in a manner analogous to that of mythology and philosophy, holds fast to the unity and trinity of the ultimate primordial ground. In its own special way, then, the trinitarian confession proper to Christianity is an answer to the primordial question of man and mankind. In a way that distinguishes Christianity and is peculiar to it alone, the confession of one God in three persons answers the primordial question of the human person: the question of unity in multiplicity, of unity that does not absorb multiplicity but turns it into a unified whole, a unity that is notimpoverishment but fullness and completion. The distinguishing element in Christianity is ultimately this: that the ultimate ground of the unity and wholeness of reality is not a scheme, a structure, a triadic law or abstract principle; according to the Christian faith the ultimate ground and meaning of all reality is personal: one God in three persons.

2. Foundations in revealed theology

(a) The unity of God

The Christian confession of faith begins with the statement: '*Credo in unum Deum* – I believe in the one God.' In these words the creed legitimately sums up the faith of the Old and New Testaments. We read in the Old Testament: 'Hear, O Israel: The Lord our God is one Lord; and you shall love the Lord your God with all your heart, and with all your soul, and with all your might' (Deut. 6.4–5; cf. II Macc. 7.37).[21] This basic statement later became part of the *Shema*, the prayer which every Jew was obliged to recite twice daily. The New Testament takes over the Old Testament faith in the singleness of God (Mark 12.29, 32), and in its missionary preaching contrasts it anew with the polytheism of the Gentiles (Acts 14.15; 17.23; I Cor. 8.4; Rom. 3.29f.; Eph. 4.6; I Tim. 1.17; 2.5). In the perspective of the history of religions, Christianity is therefore reckoned, with Judaism and Islam, among the monotheistic religions.

The biblical faith in one God has a long history which is not without its importance for a theological understanding of the doctrine. In the beginning the Old Testament accepts, with a relative lack of embarrassment, the existence of alien gods (cf. Gen. 35.2, 4; Josh. 24.2, 14). The oneness of the biblical God shows itself initially only in the fact that Yahweh is superior to the other gods; he makes an exclusive claim and shows himself a jealous God who will suffer no other gods besides himself (Ex. 20.3ff.; 34.14; Deut. 5.7). In the beginning, this intolerance extends only to the worship of other gods, because such worship indicates a lack of trust in Yahweh. One who adores other gods does not love Yahweh with his whole heart and soul and strength. Initially, then, the monotheism was of the practical order. The question of the existence or non-existence of other gods was not yet raised; it is likely even that their existence was accepted as a fact (cf. Judg. 11.24; I Sam. 26.19; II Kings 3.27). But beginning with Elijah, the prophets engaged in a resolute battle against all syncretistic deviations; Yahweh was now regarded as the one and only God. The 'other deities' were explained as being nonentities (Isa. 2.8, 18; 10.10; 19.3; Jer. 2.5, 10, 15; 16.19) and non-gods (Jer. 2.11; 5.7). Finally, we read in Second Isaiah: 'There is no other god besides me' (Isa. 45.21; cf. 41.28f.; 43.10). Yahweh is now the God of all peoples (cf. Isa. 7.18; 40.15ff.).

This history makes two points clear:

1. In the Bible, monotheism is not a philosophical question but the fruit of religious experience and an expression of practice based on faith. At issue is a practical monotheism. Faith in the one God is therefore not primarily a matter of intellectual verification. The issue in this profession of faith is, rather, a radical decision in behalf of the one thing necessary, of that which alone suffices because at bottom it is everything. For this reason it can lay total claim to human beings. In confessing the one God, the ultimate issue is a radical decision between faith and unbelief, a radical answer to the question of where alone and in all situations unconditional trustworthiness is to be found. The issue is conversion from the non-existent gods to the one true God (Acts 14.15). The problem or issue here is not one that is outmoded and belongs to the past. False gods take many forms. One's false god can be mammon (Matt. 6.24) or one's belly (Phil. 3.19); it can be one's honor (John 5.44) or the Baal of unrestrained pleasure and uncontrolled sensuality. In the final analysis, one's false god can be anything in this world that is absolutized. But the truth is that you cannot serve two masters (Matt. 6.24). God alone is God; on him alone can one build unconditionally, in him alone can one trust without reserve. One who in addition to believing in the one God also serves false gods does not really believe and trust in God. The confession of faith in the one God is therefore a radical decision that obliges the person to a continual conversion. At issue is the one thing on which everything else depends and which determines whether our way leads to life or to death (Mark 10.21; Luke 10.42).

2. The oneness of God involves far more than a quantitiative and numerical unity. The creed does not mean simply that there is only one God and not three or four gods. The singleness and uniqueness of God is qualitative. God is not only one (*unus*) but also unique (*unicus*); he is as it were unqualified uniqueness. For by his very nature God is such that there can only be one of him. From the nature of God as the reality that determines and includes everything his uniqueness follows with intrinsic necessity. 'If God is not one, then there is no God.'[22] Only one God can be infinite and all-inclusive; two Gods would limit one another even if they somehow interpenetrated. Conversely: as the one God, God is also the only God. The singleness of God is therefore not just one of the attributes of God; rather his singleness is given directly with his very essence.

Therefore, too, the oneness and uniqueness of the biblical God is anything but evidence of narrow-mindedness. On the contrary, for precisely as the one and only God he is the Lord of all peoples and of all history. He is the First and the Last (Isa. 41.4; 43.10f.; 44.6; 48.12; Rev. 1.4, 8, 17), the ruler of the universe (Rev. 4.8; 11.17; 15.3f.; 19.6). The oneness of God is at the same time his universality which binds all human beings.

In their message of the one God, the Old and New Testaments are responding to a primordial question of the human race: the question of the unity to be found in all the multiplicity and fragmentation of reality. Polytheism gives expression to the manifoldness and fragmentation of reality and to the impossibility man feels of reducing it to unity. But as I indicated earlier, thinking men, human beings looking for meaning, could not be satisfied with this state of affairs. For this reason monotheistic tendencies are to be found in the religions and philosophies of antiquity; they provide parallels to the Old Testament.

Early Christianity was able to make use of these tendencies.[23] The early Christian Apologists constantly appealed to the idea of the *monarchia* (oneness) of God.[24] Evidently, the doctrine of the *monarchia* of God had its set place in the instruction that accompanied Christian baptism.[25] In a letter to his namesake, Bishop Dionysius of Alexandria, Pope Dionysius says that the divine oneness is a most august part of the church's teaching.[26] This conviction of scripture and tradition found binding expression in the church's profession of faith in one God who is creator of heaven and earth.[27]

This monotheistic confession links Christianity to Judaism and Islam. On the other hand, Christianity is distinguished from these others by its concrete understanding of unity as unity in trinity. The question which Judaism and Islam then address to Christianity is this: has not Christianity by its confession of the Trinity proved unfaithful to its confession of the one God?

The answer to this question emerges if we trace the speculative considerations which the church fathers offered from a very early date as they made use of Greek philosophical thought on the nature of God's oneness. We find such considerations as early as Irenaeus, Tertullian and Origen,[28] and at a later time in Thomas Aquinas, among others.[29] In these reflections an effort is made, first of all, to ground the oneness and singleness of God in the very concept of God. The absoluteness and infinity of God leave no room for a second God. If there were several gods, they would limit one another and God would no longer be God but a finite being. Secondly, absolute oneness entails absolute non-division and therefore absolute simplicity. God's unity thus excludes materiality, since this is by its nature quantitative and therefore characterized by multiplicity. If the unity of God is thought out in a radical manner, it entails God being a pure spirit who in his absolute simplicity must be thought of as being absolutely transcendent in relation to all that is finite and especially to all that is material. In other words, if the idea of God's unity is thought through completely, it necessarily leads to the idea of the infinite qualitative difference between God and the world. The absolute unity of God means, thirdly, that the unity of God and the unity of created reality may no longer be confused as they are in ancient philosophy. If God is thought of as transcendent, then he can no longer be the immediate principle of unity amid the multiplicity of the world. The problem of the one and the many must be given a different answer than in ancient thought, once the idea of God's unity is radically thought through and once the transcendence of God, which is immediately connected with his unity, is taken into account.

The problem of the one and the many must now be seen as a problem of the unity of the world as well as a problem of the unity of God. In relation to God the question is this: is the radically conceived unity of God thinkable at all without at the same time thinking of a differentiation within God himself that does not cancel out the unity and simplicity of God, but on the contrary is required to make these meaningful? Without such a multiplicity in unity would God not be an utterly isolated being which would need the world for a counterpart and thereby lose its divine status? Such considerations lead to the conclusion that the assertion of God's unity does not exclude the question of the Trinity, but rather includes it. Against this background it is understandable that in the eyes of the church fathers the confession of the Trinity can become the concrete form taken by Christian monotheism.[30] We must now turn to a detailed discussion of how this can be so.

(b) The living God (Old Testament preparation)

It is the irrevocable conviction of the Old Testament that Yahweh is one and unique (Deut. 6.4). He is a jealous God who suffers no other gods alongside himself (Ex. 20.5; Deut. 5.7). Where such language as this is used, there seems to be no room, in principle as much as in fact, for a trinitarian revelation of God. Such a revelation seems antecedently excluded. So, at least, it seems to Judaism and Islam. They are correct insofar as nothing is said in the Old Testament about the trinitarian structure of God. On the other hand, there are significant bases in the Old Testament for the later trinitarian faith. These are to be found, above all, in the many statements, so fundamental to the Old Testament, about God as a living God (Ps. 42.3; 84.3; Jer. 10.10; 23.26; Dan. 6.27; etc.). For the Old Testament, God in his oneness and uniqueness is at the same time the fullness of life.[31] In this observation we have the justification, to some extent, for the trinitarian exegesis of various Old Testament passages by the fathers of the church.

There are a number of passages in the Old Testament in which God is depicted as speaking of himself in the plural; in these especially the fathers of the church saw intimations that there is more than one person in God. They appealed, for example, to the statement: 'Let us make man in our image, after our likeness' (Gen. 1.26; cf. 3.22; 11.7; Isa. 6.8). Contemporary exegetes cannot accept this explanation. Also improbable is the explanation often given in the past, that we have here a 'plural of majesty': God speaks of himself as 'we' just as kings and popes used to speak of themselves as 'we'. It is likely, in fact, that the plural is the stylistic device know as the 'plural of deliberation': the plural used when a person is taking counsel with himself and engaging in soliloquy.[32] The we-formulas do at least suggest, however, that the God of the Old Testament is not lifeless but a living God, characterized by a superabundant fullness of vitality and compassion.

For the church fathers and the medieval theologians a further important element in the biblical basis for the confession of the triune God was the manifestation of God in the form of three men or angels to Abraham under the oaks of Mamre (Gen. 18). This scene is extremely rich in meaning not only for theology but also for the history of piety and art. We find it in many iconographic representations and in particular in Rublev's famous fifteenth-century icon.[33] But once again it is less easy for us to accept this interpretation of the passage. On the other hand, the passage does suggest a mysterious interaction within the one God who speaks and acts and manifests himself in three figures. Finally, the church fathers cited the two angels near the throne of God in Isa. 6, and the triple 'Holy!' offered to God. This interpretation, too, seems impossible to us today. Once again, however, it has great symbolic importance, for in its own way it shows that in the time of the church fathers the trinitarian confession did not originate in pure theory and abstract speculation but rather had its vital context (*Sitz im Leben*) in the doxology, that is, in the liturgical glorification of God.[34]

More important than the texts thus far mentioned is the figure of the 'angel of Yahweh' (*malakh Jahwe*) in the Old Testament. He accompanies Israel on its journey in the wilderness (Ex. 14.19), helps those in need (Gen. 16.7; I Kings 19.5; I Kings 1.3), and protects the devout (Ps. 34.8). He makes known God's power (Zech. 12.8) and knowledge (II Sam. 14.20). While in these passages the angel of Yahweh is a revelatory figure distinct from God, at other times he is identical with Yahweh (Gen. 31.11, 13; Ex. 3.2,

4f.). The 'angel of the Lord' thus represents an effort to bridge the gap between the being of God, which to man is incomprehensible and hidden, and God's active and substantial presence in history.[35] The angel of Yahweh thus prefigures the whole later problem of the identity and difference between God in himself and the form he takes in revelation. It also brings out in a most expressive manner the fact that the Old Testament God is a living God of history.

In the later writings of the Old Testament the conviction that God is superabundant life finds expression in passages that talk of various hypostases. The most important of these is divine wisdom, which is spoken of as a kind of hypostasis distinct from God (cf. especially Prov. 8). Also noteworthy are the personifications of the divine Word (Ps. 119.89; 147.15ff.; Wisdom 16.12) and the divine Spirit (Hag. 2.5; Neh. 9.30; Isa. 63.10; Wisdom 1.7). 'These personifications bear witness to the wealth of life in Yahweh and, from the viewpoint of the history of revelation, are a first hesitant anticipation of the disclosure in the New Testament that the one divine substance is marked by a pluripersonal fullness of being.'[36] These personifications provided the New Testament with a point of departure.

Behind these various hints and indications there is a common objective question. By its very nature the Old Testament understanding of God as personal inevitably led to the question: who is God's appropriate *vis-à-vis*? An I without a Thou is unthinkable. But is man, the human race, or the people the appropriate or proper *vis-à-vis* for God? If man were God's sole *vis-à-vis*, then man would be a necessary partner of God. Man would then no longer be the one who is loved with an abyssal free and gracious love, and God's love for man would no longer be God's gracious act but rather a need of God and a completion of God. But such a conclusion would be utterly contradictory to the Old Testament. The Old Testament therefore raises a question to which it gives no answer. The Old Testament picture of the living God is not finished and complete but open to the definitive revelation of God. It is only 'a shadow of the good things to come' (Heb. 10.1).

(c) The basic trinitarian structure of the revelation of God (establishment of the doctrine in the New Testament)

The New Testament[37] gives an unequivocal answer to the question, left open in the Old Testament, of God's *vis-à-vis*. It tells us that Jesus Christ, the Son of God, is the eternal Thou of the Father, and that in the Holy Spirit we human beings are accepted into the communion of love that exists between Father and Son. Consequently the New Testament is already able to sum up the eschatologically definitive self-revelation of God in the sentence: God is love (I John 4.8, 16). The trinitarian confessions of faith that are attested in the New Testament are a spelling out of this sentence which interprets the revelational event that has taken place in Jesus Christ.

Given this thesis, which I shall justify below, it is not enough simply to set forth the individual trinitarian confessional statements of the New Testament. It is necessary rather to understand these *statements* of revelation as the interpretation, supplied by revelation itself, of the revelational *event*, and this trinitarian interpretation must in turn be seen as an explication of the New Testament's essential definition of God as love. I shall therefore proceed in three stages: 1. the trinitarian structure of the revelational event; 2. the trinitarian explanation of this event in the New Testament; and 3. the connection between this explanation and the essential definition of God that is given in the New Testament. Only if this three-stage demonstration is successful can we avoid a naive biblicist fundamentalism that relies on isolated *dicta probantia* (proof texts), and at the same time make it clear that the confession of the Trinity is far from being a later, purely speculative addition to the original faith in Christ, an addition that is more or less superfluous and certainly unimportant in identifying the Christian faith. It can be shown, on the contrary, that the trinitarian confession provides the basic structure and ground plan of the New Testament witness, and that with it the belief in the God of Jesus Christ stands or falls.

The basic form taken by the New Testament revelational event consists in this, that Jesus reveals God as Father not only by his words and actions but also by his whole life and person. In the process Jesus reveals God as his own Father in an utterly unique and non-transferable way, while it is only through Jesus that we in turn become the sons and daughters of this Father.[38] In the unique and non-transferable Abba relation which Jesus has to God, God is revealed as being eschatologically and definitively 'Father'. The eschatological character of this revelation indirectly makes it clear as well that from eternity God is the God and Father of Jesus Christ and therefore that as Son of God Jesus belongs to the eternal being of God. Thus the New Testament statements about Jesus as Son are the legitimate and necessary explication of the Abba relation of Jesus to God. In this Abba relation our own filial relation to God is at the same time disclosed and rendered possible. To those who believe, that is, who in union with Jesus and in his name rely wholly on God, everything is possible (Mark 9.23); they share in the omnipotence of God, for to God everything is possible (Mark 10.27). In the Synoptic Gospels this participation in the power (*dynamis*) of God has as yet no fixed name. Only after Easter are the acceptance of believers into the relation of Jesus to the Father, and their participation in the power of the Father, ascribed to the action of the Pneuma. From this point on it is said that we are God's sons and daughters in the Pneuma. This pneumatological interpretation, like the christological, is grounded in the revelatory event itself.

The trinitarian explanation of the event of revelation is found in all the important strands of New Testament tradition. It is already in the Synoptic tradition and, significantly, at the beginning of the Synoptic Gospels, in the accounts of the baptism of Jesus. Mark places the baptism of Jesus[39] as a programmatic statement at the beginning of his Gospel; it is meant as a summation of the entire gospel (Mark 1.9–11; cf. Matt. 3.13–17; Luke 3.21f.). The passage on the baptism has a clear trinitarian structure: the voice from heaven reveals Jesus as the beloved Son, while the Spirit descends upon him in the form of a dove (Mark 1.10f. par). In the Lukan version of the cry of jubilation, Jesus, at the high point of his ministry, 'rejoiced in the Holy Spirit' and praised God as 'Father, Lord of heaven and earth' whom no one knows 'except the Son and any one to whom the Son chooses to reveal him' (Luke 10.21f.; cf. Matt. 11.25–27). According to Acts, the preaching of the apostles likewise begins in trinitarian form: God has raised Jesus to life and exalted him; after Jesus himself had received from the Father the promised Holy Spirit, he poured it out upon them (Acts 2.32f.). Finally, Stephen, the first martyr, is filled with the Holy Spirit and, looking up to heaven, sees the glory of God and Jesus standing at the right hand of God (Acts. 7.55f.).

The most important witness to the Trinity in the Synoptic tradition and even in the New Testament as a whole is undoubtedly the baptismal command in Matt. 29.19: 'Go therefore and make disciples of all nations, baptizing them in the name of the Father and of the Son and of the Holy Spirit.'[40] Even if the text does not represent a trinitarian reflection in the later sense of this phrase, that is, if it does not as yet reflect on unity and trinity in God, it nonetheless proves a clear basis for such relection, because it sets Father, Son and Spirit side by side as full 'equals'. The baptismal command is generally regarded today not as a saying of the historical Jesus himself but as a summary of the early church's development and practice which had been guided by the Spirit of Jesus Christ and to that extent were authorized by Jesus himself. What I have said thus far also shows that the baptismal text is not a novelty but simply gives concise expression to the basic trinitarian structure of the Synoptic tradition and even of the entire New Testament. At the same time, the summary makes it clear that the trinitarian confession is not the result of theoretical reflection and speculation. Rather, it summarizes the entire saving event which we appropriate in baptism. Consequently, it is baptism, that is, the act in which Christian existence is grounded, which is the vital and sociological context (the *Sitz im Leben*) of the trinitarian confession. The trinitarian confession thus expresses the reality from which the church and the individual Christian draw their life and for which they must live. The trinitarian confession is therefore *the* short formula of the Christian faith. The baptismal command, consequently, is rightly regarded as the most important basis for the dogmatic and theological development of the church's doctrine of the Trinity.

Later trinitarian doctrine is not based solely on the Synoptic tradition. The letters of Paul are likewise filled with trinitarian formulas. An allusion to the trinitarian structure can even be found in the old two-stage christology of Rom. 1.3f., according to which Jesus Christ is established as Son of God in power by the Father through the Spirit of holiness. Gal. 4.4–6 contains a complete summary of the Christian message of salvation: 'But when the time had fully come, God sent forth his Son . . . so that we might receive adoption as sons. And because you are sons, God has sent the spirit of his Son into our hearts, crying, "Abba, Father!"' (cf. Rom. 8.3f., 14–16). But a trinitarian structure characterizes not only the non-recurring action of God in the history of salvation but also his ongoing action in the church. In explaining the unity and multiplicity of charisms in the church Paul writes: 'Now there are varieties of gifts, but the same Spirit; and there are varieties of service, but the same Lord; and there are varieties of working, but it is the same God who inspires them all in every one' (I Cor. 12.4–6). It is not surprising, therefore, that when Paul sums up the whole reality of salvation in a doxology, he again uses trinitarian formulas. The most important of these is the liturgical conclusion of the Second Letter to the Corinthians: 'The grace of the Lord Jesus Christ and the love of God and the fellowship of the Holy Spirit be with you all' (II Cor. 13.33). Thus whenever Paul wishes to express the entire fullness of the saving event and of the reality of salvation, he has recourse to trinitarian formulas.

The Deutero-Pauline letters take over this trinitarian structure from the letter of Paul. In the prologue of the Letter to the Ephesians this structure is expanded into a hymnic exposition of God's plan of salvation. It speaks of the work of the Father who has predestined everything (1.3–11), the work of the Son in whom the fullness of time has come (1.5–13), and the work of the Holy Spirit who has been given to us as the seal and pledge of eschatological salvation (1.13f.; cf. I Peter 1.2; Heb. 9.14). This trinitarian structure is also applied to the church. In Eph. 4.4–6 the unity of the church is based on the Trinity: 'There is one body and one Spirit . . .; one Lord, one faith, one baptism; one God and Father of us all.' The church is thus 'a people brought into unity from the unity of the Father, the Son and the Holy Spirit' (Cyprian). In the Johannine tradition of the New Testament we even find the beginnings of trinitarian reflection. The first half of the gospel of John (1–12) has basically a single theme: the relation of the Son to the Father. On the other hand, the Johannine farewell discourses of the second half (14–17) are concerned with the sending of another Paraclete (14.16), his procession from the Father (15.26), his sending by Jesus Christ (16.7), and his task of recalling and making present the work of Christ (14.26; 15.26; 16.13f.). In John 14.26 the trinitarian unity of the two themes emerges clearly: 'But the Counselor, the Holy Spirit, whom the Father will send in my name, he will teach you all things, and bring to your remembrance all that I have said to you' (cf. 15.26). The high point of this reflection is provided by what is known as the priestly prayer of Jesus.[41]

The Leitmotiv or dominant theme is stated in the very first verse: the glory of the Father and the Son. This glory includes salvation or, to use John's term, life. In turn, life consists in knowing the only true God and Jesus Christ whom he has sent, (17.3). In John, 'to know' is more than a simple act of the intellect; true knowledge includes acknowledgment of the lordship (in being and action) of God; it includes the glorification of God. Those who know God as God and acknowledge and glorify him, are in the light; they have discovered the meaning of their life and the light that shines in all reality (John 1.4). Doxology is thus at the same time soteriology.

The theme is then developed in detail. The Son glorifies the Father by bringing to completion the work the Father has given him (17.4) and specifically by revealing the Father's name to men (17.6), leading them to faith (17.8) and sanctifying them in truth (17.17, 19). Parallel with the glorification of the Father through sanctification in truth is the communication of life. The Father has this life in himself; he has also granted the Son to have life in himself (5.26) and to bestow it on men (17.2). This life consists in knowing that Jesus Christ is life, because he is life from life, God from God, light from light (17.7). Life consists therefore in knowing the glory which Jesus has with the Father, even before the world existed (17.5). 'I desire that they . . . behold my glory which thou hast given me in thy love for me before the foundation of the world' (17.24). Those who acknowledge this fact share in this same eternal love (17.23, 26) and in the glory of the Father and the Son (17.22). The knowledge and confession of the eternal divine sonship of Jesus brings communion with him and through him with God (17.21–24).

The glorification of the Father by the Son thus has for its goal the participation of the disciples in this glorification and in eternal life. Thus Jesus' prayer of praise to the Father leads in the second part to a prayer of petition; doxology leads to epiclesis. The object of the petition is that the disciples may be preserved in truth (17.11) and may abide in unity with one another, with Jesus and, through Jesus, with God (17.21–24). This prayer of Jesus for his disciples is, in the final analysis, a prayer for the sending of the other Paraclete, the Spirit (14.16). This Spirit is the Spirit of truth (14.17), who will guide the disciples into the whole truth (16.13). He does this by glorifying Jesus (16.14) and bearing witness to him. He does not speak on his own authority but only of what Jesus is and of what is from the Father (16.14f.; cf. 14.26). Through the action of the Spirit, then, the union of Father and Son becomes the union of the disciples among themselves. The Spirit draws the faithful into the unity which is the mark of the divine being (cf. 10.38; 14.10f., 20, 23; 15.4f.; 17.21–26).

The unity of Father and Son thus becomes the ground that makes possible and vitalizes the unity of the faithful, and the unity of the latter is in turn to be a sign to the world (17.21). The revelation of eternal love leads to the gathering of the scattered flock under a single shepherd (10.16). The unity, peace and life of the world thus come about through the revelation of the glory of the Father, Son and Holy Spirit. The trinitarian doxology is the soteriology of the world.

In the First Letter of John we find various trinitarian groupings (4.2; 5.6–8). These include the so-called Johannine *Comma* [section of a sentence]: 'There are three who give testimony in heaven: the Father, the Word, and the Holy Spirit; and these three are one' (I John 5.7f.). This trinitarian formula is generally regarded today however, as a later insertion.[42] Extremely important is the summarizing statement that God is love (I John 4.8, 16). This means, to begin with, that in the revelational event which is Jesus Christ God has shown himself to be love. But this revelational event consists precisely in making known the eternal communion of love, life and reciprocal glorification between Father, Son and Spirit, in order that through this revelation the disciples and, with their help, mankind may be drawn into this same communion of love and life. The revelational statement 'God is love' is therefore at the same time a statement about the being of God and, as such, a statement about salvation. Only because God is love can he reveal and communicate himself to us as love. The unity of church and world, the peace and reconciliation of mankind have their ultimate ground and ultimate possibility, as seen by Christians, in the acknowledgment of the glory of God in the love of Father, Son and Spirit. This summary of the entire New Testament message already lays the foundation for the later speculative development of the doctrine of the Trinity, a development which has for its sole aim to understand the trinitarian confession of scripture in terms of its deepest roots and in the overall context of the whole reality of salvation.

The New Testament message thus proves to be trinitarian not only in the details of what it says but also in its basic structure. In saying this, I oppose the thesis of O. Cullmann that the basic structure of the New Testament profession of faith is purely christological, so that 'when all is said and done the development of christological formulas ultimately distorted the interpretation of the essence of Christianity'[43] This thesis is antecedently improbable in view of the fact that the revelation in the New Testament presupposes Old Testament revelation and brings it to its transcendent fulfillment. Therefore, contrary to what O. Cullmann believes, the New Testament does not concern itself solely with the journey of Jesus Christ to the Father; rather, faith in Jesus Christ is based in turn on the testimony of the Father (Matt. 3.17; 17.5; John 5.37f.). People believe in Jesus because the Father has raised him from the dead and established him as Lord. Moreover, the saving act of Jesus Christ includes the sending of the Holy Spirit. Only in the Holy Spirit is it possible to confess Jesus as Lord (I Cor. 12.5f.), and only in the Spirit do we have a share in the reality of Jesus. Consequently, a christological confession is possible only in the form of a trinitarian confession. Faith in Christ and existence as a Christian depend on the confession of the Trinity.

(d) The trinitarian confession as rule of faith

The early post apostolic church was fully aware of the trinitarian structure of Christian salvation.[44] This is clear both from the writings of Ignatius of Antioch[45] and from the First Letter of Clement.[46] Athenagoras, one of the Apologists, writes around 175 that the very desire Christians have is already enough to make them understand 'what the union of the Son with the Father is, what communion the Father has with the Son, what the Spirit is, what the union of these three is and what the distinction among the united, namely, the Spirit, the Son and the Father'.[47] This short passage basically anticipates all the questions taken up in the later doctrine of the Trinity. So too the decisive term and concept, *trias* or *trinitas*, are already to be found in Theophilus of Antioch and Tertullian.[48] It would obviously be a complete misinterpretation to see in this a degeneration following immediately upon the New Testament age and stemming from the swift invasion of Hellenistic speculation. The context from which the trinitarian confession drew its life was not pleasure in theoretical speculation but the life and practice of the church, especially baptism and the eucharist.

The most important vital context (*Sitz im Leben*) for the trinitarian confession of faith was baptism. Both the *Didache*[49] and Justin[50] bear witness to a trinitarian confession at baptism. The basic structure of the later creed had already developed out of this confession as early as the last third of the second century.[51] Irenaeus, who is also familiar with the trinitarian baptismal confession,[52] already speaks of the three main doctrines of the faith: God the Father, creator of the universe – the Word of God, God's Son, who brings communion and peace with God – the Holy Spirit, who re-creates human beings for God.[53] In Hippolytus of Rome we then find the later tri-membered creed in the form of the three questions at baptism.[54] In continuity with Paul, Tertullian sees the church as founded upon the trinitarian confession: 'For where the three are, that is, the Father, the Son and the Spirit, there too is the church which is the body of the three.'[55] Cyprian says the same thing a hundred years later,[56] and the Second Vatican Council accepts his trinitarian definition of the church as 'a people brought into unity from the unity of the Father, the Son and the Holy Spirit'.[57] Finally, Hilary of Poitiers[58] and Augustine[59] understand the mystery of the Trinity to be fully expressed in the baptismal command.

Along with baptism, the eucharist in particular provided the vital context for the trinitarian confession. This was true especially of the East, where the baptismal confession did not play the same role that it did in the West. While the eucharistic prayer in the *Didache* does not yet explicitly mention the Holy Spirit,[60] the prayer recorded by Justin does already have a trinitarian structure.[61] The same is true of the eucharistic prayer in the Apostolic Tradition of Hippolytus. This prayer says, in part: 'We thank you, God, through your Son Jesus Christ whom you sent to us at the end of days as Savior and liberator . . . And your Son was revealed by the Holy Spirit . . .' The prayer ends with a doxology addressed to the Father in the Holy Spirit 'through your Son Jesus Christ'[62] The same trinitarian structure can be seen in the epicleses, the conclusions of orations, and the doxologies. These are addressed to the Father, through his Son Jesus Christ, in the Holy Spirit.[63] Only later on, when the Arians sought to deduce from this type of prayer the subordination of the Son, and the Pneumatomacheans argued from it to the subordination of the Holy Spirit, did paratactical formulas come into use: 'Glory be to the Father and to the Son and to the Holy Spirit.'[64] Basil's work *On the Holy Spirit* is an extended reflection on the liturgical doxology and on the meaning of the prepositions 'through', 'in', 'from', and 'with' that are used in it. In its early stages, therefore, the doctrine of the Trinity was regarded not as indulgence in private speculation but as a reflection of the liturgy and the doxology.

On this basis of faith that was lived and prayed, Irenaeus and Tertullian developed the rule of faith or of truth (*kanōn tēs pisteōs* or *tēs alētheias; regula fidei* or *veritatis*). The rule of faith is not identical with the baptismal symbol, but represents, rather, a symbol or creed aimed at countering the gnostics. Furthermore, it is not a rule for faith, but rather the rule which consists of the faith preached in the church. It is the norm provided by the faith of the church or, if you will, by the truth of faith; it expresses the normative character of the truth as attested in the preaching of the church. Consequently, the rule of faith is not a set of individual formulas such as are contained in creeds and dogmas, but rather a concise normative summary of the entire faith which the church has received from the apostles. It is all the more significant, then, that these summaries are thoroughly trinitarian in character.[65] They provided not only the early Christian thinkers already mentioned but also such later 'speculative' theologians as Origen[66] and Augustine[67] with the basis for their teaching on the Trinity. This fact tells us that in their teaching on the Trinity the early theologians of the church were expounding not their private reflections and speculations but the common, public faith of the church that was binding on all. They were defending this faith against denials and misinterpretations and, not least, making it more accessible in the interests of a deeper understanding of the faith and the growth in love. The trinitarian doctrine of the early church is thus 'the' rule of faith and, as such, the normative exposition of the truth of Christianity. It is the church's normative explanation of the scriptures. It is the summation of the Christian faith.

3. History of theological and dogmatic development

A doctrine of the Trinity, as distinct from a trinitarian confession, appears when there is not only the confession of the same shared divine dignity of Father, Son and Spirit, but also reflection on the relation between faith in one God and this trinity of persons and on the relation of Father, Son and Spirit among themselves. The confession states in the form of an assertion what is attested in narrative form in the documents of revelation; the doctrine of the Trinity, on the other hand, takes a speculative form. It establishes a kind of 'mirror' (*speculum*) relation between the individual statements of the confession; to the extent that each is reflected in the others, it becomes clear that there is a reciprocal correspondence and intrinsic connection among them (the *nexus mysteriorum*) and that they form a structure and an organized whole (*hierarchia veritatum*). The doctrine of the Trinity seeks, therefore, to reconcile the trinitarian statements of scripture and tradition, to bring to light their internal harmony and logic, and thus to make them plausible in the eyes of faith.

The first hesitant attempts at a theological reflection on the trinitarian confession of the church are to be found in Jewish Christianity. Admittedly, we have only fragmentary knowledge in this area, since the relevant traditions were not subsequently developed further but on the contrary were even deliberately suppressed.[68] It is clear that in the teaching of Jewish Christianity on the Trinity a fundamental role was assigned to apocalyptic and rabbinic ideas of two angelic figures that stand as witnesses or paracletes at the right and left sides of the throne of God. The stimulus to these ideas came from the story of the three men or angels who visit Abraham (Gen. 18) and, above all, from the vision of the seraphim in Isa. 6.1–3.[69] It soon became clear, however, that a trinitarian doctrine involving angels could not express the divine rank of Jesus and the Spirit, but was leading instead to a subordinationist conception of them such as actually developed in heretical Jewish Christianity, among the Ebionites.[70] In light of this development the speculation on the Logos that arose in early Hellenistic Christianity can be understood as an attempt to de-apocalypticize the idea of the Trinity.[71] It has to be said, however, that the Apologists, the first to follow this path, were still unable to avoid the danger of subordinationism. The Logos was regarded very much as a second or secondary God (*deuteros theos*), and the Spirit even as a servant (*hyperatēs*) of the Logos. A Judaizing curtailment of the doctrine was thus followed by a Hellenizing reduction in which the Father, the Son and the Spirit were located in a kind of hierarchically descending pattern.[72]

The valid theological explanation of the doctrine of the Trinity[73] was achieved in the Hellenistic world in two phases: in the conflict with gnosticism in the third century and in the conflict with Hellenistic philosophy, which radicalized the direction taken by the Apologists and in the fourth century made its way into the church through Arius. This division of phases is, of course, to some extent a schematization, since there are numerous connections between the two conflicts, as is clear especially in the person of Origen, the greatest theologian of the early church.

The first phase in the development of the doctrine of the Trinity occurred in the conflict with gnosticism. Gnosticism,[74] a generic concept that sums up a many-leveled and multiform mentality, whose origin and nature has not yet been fully explained, arose out of the collapse of the cosmos-oriented thinking of antiquity. The men and women of late antiquity no longer experienced the world as a cosmos or ordered universe, but rather felt themselves to be estranged from the world even while they lived in it. The divine, as a result, became the totally other, an inconceivable and ineffable Absolute.[75] The resultant problem of communication between God and the world was solved by the gnostics with the aid of the concept of emanation (*aporrhoia; probolē*), which they regarded as fundamental. By it they meant that from the primal source, by reason of a necessity internal to God, reality flows forth in a series of descending steps, each more tenuous in character than the one before.[76] With the help of such speculations as these the gnostics believed they could attain to a superior grasp of Christianity. But the gnostic dualism of God and world was no less unacceptable to the Christian faith in God as creator than was the bridging of the abyss between God and the world by all kinds of intermediate entities which then blurred the original distinction between the two. For early Christianity, therefore, the very foundations and essence of what is Christian were at stake in the dispute with gnosticism, and this in regard both to its picture of God and to its understanding of the world. The issue in this struggle was the continued existence or disappearance of the Christian faith.

The decisive figure in this struggle was Iranaeus of Lyons. For Irenaeus, 'true gnosis is the teaching of the apostles and the ancient doctrinal structure of the church that is meant for the entire world'.[77] Therefore over against gnosis he sets the rule of faith: the apostolic faith, attested in the church, regarding the one God, who is the almighty Father and the creator of heaven and earth, the one Jesus Christ, who is God's Son, and the one Holy Spirit.[78] According to Irenaeus, no one has any knowledge of the supposed emanation; after all, one cannot call it ineffable and then try to talk about it and, as he remarks sarcastically, speak of it as though one had been present as midwife at the birth of the Son.[79] Irenaeus does not, of course, stop at this negative answer. He begins an intellectual analysis by showing the internal contradiction in the gnostic doctrine of emanation: that which comes forth from the source cannot be utterly alien to it. If in human generation mind is continued in the begotten person, then this will certainly be true in God who is totally mind.[80] Here the way is opened to an understanding of 'emanation' in which there is no attenuation of being and no gradation, but rather a relation of originated to origin at the same level. The key to this correction is that Irenaeus replaces the materialistic understanding of God by the gnostics with a concept of God as pure spirit. The gnostic doctrine of emanations presupposes some kind of divisibility of the divine and thus a quantitative, material understanding of God. By understanding God to be pure spirit Irenaeus preserves the unity and simplicity of God that excludes any divisibility.

The action of Irenaeus in laying the foundations of an emanation at one and the same level of being and thus of later trinitarian doctrine is connected with his thinking in terms of salvation history. As Irenaeus sees it, the unity of God excludes any dualistic separation of creation from redemption and grounds the unity of the divine plan of salvation and, in particular, the unity of creation and redemption; this unity is summed up and 'given a head' (*anakephalaiosis*) in the unity of manhood and Godhead in Jesus Christ.[81] Irenaeus' basic thesis is: it is one and the same God who acts in the order of creation and in the order of redemption.[82] Irenaeus thus defends not only the dignity of creation against the gnostic defamation of it but also the meaning of redemption: 'The Word of God became man and the Son of God became the Son of man in order that man might receive the Word into himself and, being adopted, might become the son of God.'[83] The soteriological meaning of the incarnation requires in turn the eternal existence of the Son and the Spirit.[84] The latter are as it were the two hands of God in the carrying out of his plan of salvation.[85] The unity of God thus grounds the unity of the order of salvation, while the order of salvation in turn presupposes the consubstantiality of the Son with the Father. In this brilliant vision of Irenaeus the economic Trinity and the immanent Trinity are one.

Irenaeus' grandiose vision had subsequently to be spelled out in greater conceptual detail. Two theologians in particular devoted themselves to this task at the beginning of the third century; Tertullian in the West and Origen in the East established a specific Christian doctrine of the Trinity. It is clear that such pioneering efforts could not escape uncertainties in expression and ambiguities in content. Nonetheless each made a beginning on which later generations could build.

Tertullian thought of himself as a churchman, for whom, as for Irenaenus, the *regula fidei*, or faith handed down in the church from the beginning, was the foundation and norm of his thinking.[86] Here was the decisive difference from gnosticism. On the sure foundation of the church's confession of faith, Tertullian was able to make critical use of the idea of emanation by excluding any and every separation of the emergent from its source[87] and linking the idea of emanation with the idea, originally completely alien to it, of *unitas substantiae* (oneness of substance).[88] The consequence of this line of thought was that the Trinity could no longer have the cosmological function it had for the gnostics and that the way was thus opened for the doctrine of an immanent Trinity, a doctrine that for Tertullian as for Irenaeus was soteriologically motivated. For only if God himself has become man can the humanity of Christ be the *sacramentum humanae salutis* (sacrament of *human salvation*).[89] Tertullian's doctrine of the Trinity thus preserved both the *monarchia* of the Father, from whom everything proceeds, and the *oikonomia*,[90] that is, the concrete ordering of this *monarchia*, by reason of which the Father gives the Son a participation in his dominion and exercises this dominion through him.[91] Tertullian is thus able to preserve unity in God and yet expound the distinction as well. In this he differed from the Modalists, from whom Tertullian differentiates himself especially in his discussion with Praxeas. The Modalists see in the Son and the Spirit only different manifestations of the Father; they forget that the Father is a Father only in relation to the Son and conversely.[92] It must therefore be said with regard to the *unitas in trinitatem* that the Three differ *non statu sed gradu, nec substantia sed forma, non potestate sed specie* ('not in condition but in degree; not in substance but in form; not in power but in kind').[93] Contrary to what the gnostics say, there is no separation; but contrary to the modalists there is a distinction of persons, not of substances.[94] Tertullian's formula is unrivalled in its accuracy: *Tres unum sunt non unus* (the three are one substance, not one person).[95] Thus, despite the persistence of some expressions that sound subordinationist,[96] Tertullian created a new theological language and thus laid the foundations of the specifically Christian doctrine of the Trinity.

Tertullian's clarifications exercised a normative influence especially on the Western doctrine of the Trinity, which thus acquired firm basic traits at a relatively early stage. His influence can be felt especially in the clash of the two Dionysiuses. In a letter which Dionysius, Bishop of Rome, wrote in 262 to his namesake, Bishop Dionysius of Alexandria,[97] Dionysius of Rome objected both to the (supposed) tritheism of his fellow bishop in Alexandria and to the modalism of Sabellius. The divine unity may not be dissolved into three fully separate divinities (tritheism), nor may Father and Son be identified (modalism). If we ask, however, how these two truths are to be thought of as compatible, we will find no answer as yet in Dionysius. It is of interest, on the other hand, that like Tertullian, Dionysius sees the *monarchia* as resident not in a single divine substance but in the Father, to whom the Son is united and in whom the Spirit abides and dwells. Here the bond of unity in the Trinity is the Father, and not the Spirit, as Augustine will later maintain.[98] A century later in the Latin West Hilary will still be proposing a view similar to that of Dionysius.[99] Thus there was established in the Latin West a conception of the Trinity which went a long way towards meeting the Eastern concern to preserve the *monarchia* of the Father. Yet even here there was conflict between East and West. The reason is that Dionysius of Alexandria was a disciple of Origen and to that extent representative of Eastern thinking. In what does the difference consist?

The normative theologian of the East was Origen. Like Irenaeus and Tertullian he thought of himself primarily not as a philosopher but as a biblical theologian for whom Jesus Christ is the truth; more specifically, he thought of himself as an ecclesial theologian for whom the *ecclesiastica praedicatio* (preaching of the church) is the norm according to which scripture is to be interpreted.[100] Thus the boundaries were clearly drawn in relation not only to gnosticism but also to purely philosophical speculation in the form of Platonism. Nonetheless Origen goes more deeply than Irenaeus or Tertullian into gnostic and philosophical speculations, in order that in response to them he may for the first time project a comprehensive Christian view of reality. Origen's basic difference from gnosticism consists in his agreement with Platonic philosophy that God is a purely spiritual being.[101] Origen is therefore compelled to reject the concept of emanation because of its materialistic assertion of the divisibility of the divine.[102] He must look for some other way of deriving all reality from God who, in a thoroughly Platonic fashion, exists beyond spirit and essence[103] as Unity (*monas*) and Oneness (*henas*).[104]

In formal terms Origen follows the same path as the gnostics: the multiplicity of reality is due to a graduated decline from that transcendent unity to which in the end it will return.[105] Whether and to what extent Origen also accepted the idea of successive cycles of worlds[106] is a question we may leave untouched here. The more important thing is that while he takes over the formal gnostic scheme, he introduces radical material corrections. First of all, he understands reality to be God's free creation.[107] which remains always subject to divine providence; secondly, he sees the entire development as originating in a free decision of the will and thus makes freedom the vehicle of the world process;[108] finally, he sees everything as subject to God's judgment at the end.[109] As a result, Origen's entire system has a voluntaristic or, as we would say today, historical character which is profoundly opposed to the naturalism inherent in the gnostic idea of emanation[110]

In origen this comprehensive vision of reality, in which everything proceeds from God and returns to him, has in its turn trinitarian presuppositions. For both the coming forth and the return take place through Jesus Christ in the Holy Spirit. To begin with, God creates and rules the world through his Son.[111] The latter proceeds eternally from God; not, however, 'materialistically' through generation as with the gnostics, but spiritually in a procession that is due to the will and, more specifically, to love.[112] Also important for Origen, as it had already been for Tertullian, is the comparison of the relation between Father and Son with the relation between a light and its brightness.[113] Despite many formulas that suggest subordinationism Origen's intention at every point is to maintain the consubstantiality of the Son with the Father.[114] Since the Son springs from freedom in love and at such is a draft and prototype of the world,[115] God rules the world through him in a non-violent and non-coercive way, since the world is antecedently ordered, rather, to freedom.[116] The Logos is for us the image of God[117] and the way to knowledge of the Father.[118] We can understand the Son, of course, only through the Holy Spirit.[119] Just as God acts through Christ in the Spirit, so we return to the Father through Christ in the Spirit. Consequently, Origen too, despite numerous ambiguous statements, has a soteriological reason for not allowing an ontological subordination of Son and Spirit to the Father. Those who want to be reborn to salvation need the Father, the Son and the Spirit, and are unable to receive salvation if the Trinity be not complete.[120] This soteriological vision and the spirituality and mysticism based on it carries Origen beyond Irenaeus inasmuch as they become the basis for a comprehensive vision of reality. This explains why this brilliant synthesis has so many levels and facets.

Origen was in antiquity and still is today a sign of contradiction. Epiphanius, Jerome and Theophilus was already bringing severe indictments against him. A hundred years later Emperor Justinian condemned some theses regarded as Origenist.[121] The relation between Origen himself and the Origenism (especially of Evagrius Ponticus) that was condemned is still difficult to determine, and scholars disagree about it.[122] What seems certain is that the 'Left Origenist' tendency led *via* Lucian of Antioch to the heresy of Arius which brought the church into new and difficult conflicts just when it had surmounted the conflicts with gnosticism and the persecutions against Christians. On the other hand, it was only amid these new confusions and through the clarifications ultimately achieved that Origen's brilliant insights could become fruitful for the church.

Let me sum up. Despite all the lacunae and obscurities that still remained, the work of Irenaeus, Tertullian and Origen enabled the church to come to grips with the speculations of the gnostics and develop a trinitarian doctrine of its own in which the economic Trinity and the immanent Trinity are inseparably conjoined. The subordinationist tendencies discernible in both Tertullian and Origen were due at bottom to an excessive linking of the two approaches and a lack of adequate distinction between them. The inner logic of development as well as external challenges made a clear distinction between time and eternity, God and world, the task of the next phase of development.

This second phase of the development is distinguished chiefly by the name of Arius and by the direction taken in Arianism. Under the influence of Middle Platonic philosophy Arius radicalized the subordinationist tendencies present in the tradition up to this point. He worked out a system in which God and the world were radically separated and therefore had to be linked by the Logos understood as an intermediate being.[123] In so doing, Arius really did not take seriously the radical distinction between God and world with which he had begun; he overlooked the fact that there can be no mean between God and creatures, but only an either-or. As in the debate with gnosticism, so too in the debate with Arius the issue was not a matter of detail and certainly not a peripheral matter, but the entire Christian vision of God and the world. In fact, as Athanasius in particular made clear,[124] the Christian understanding of salvation itself was at stake. For in the hands of Arius the Christian doctrine of salvation was in danger of turning into a piece of speculation about the cosmos, a philosophical wisdom regarding the world.

The outcome of the Arian conflict (in which the outcome of the gnostic conflict played a part) and subsequent developments was the definition by the Council of Nicaea (325) of the oneness in being (*homoousios*) of the Son with the Father,[125] and the definition by the Council of Constantinople (381) of the Spirit as having the same dignity as the Father and the Son.[126] The confession of Nicaea culminates in the statement that the Son is one in being (*homoousios*) with the Father. But the term *homoousios* soon proved to be 'the sensitive point of the Nicene symbol, the arrow stuck in the side of Arianism, and the sign of contradiction that was to be debated for over half a century'.[127]

The concept did have several disadvantages: it was not biblical but gnostic in origin; in addition, it had been condemned in a different but not fully explained sense at a Council of Antioch which had been convoked in 269 against Paul of Samosata; finally, even its content was not completely unambiguous. The intention of the concept was to express the truth that the Son is not created but begotten and that he belongs on the side not of creatures but of God. The question that arose, however, was this: does *homoousios* mean the same being with the Father or of one being with the Father? The first interpretation could be misunderstood as tritheistic, the second as modalist. The answer to the question emerges from the context rather than from the term and concept itself. After all, the confession of Nicaea begins with a confession of the one God, the Father, who by his nature can only be one and unique. The Son, who is no less divine than the Father, is of the being and hypostasis of the Father (being and hypostasis still had the same meaning at Nicaea). It follows that the Son likewise possesses the essentially unique and indivisible divine being that is proper to the Father. The unity of being and not merely the sameness of being in Father and Son is thus clear only as a conclusion from the whole tenor of the confession.[128]

This interpretation of *homoousios* has certain implications for the doctrine of the Trinity that underlies and is implicit in the Nicene creed:

1. The Council does not proceed monotheistically from the one being of God and then speak in trinitarian language of the Father, Son and Holy Spirit as the three ways in which this one being concretely exists. The creed starts rather with the Father and understands him as the 'summit of unity' in which the Son and the Spirit are comprehended. We thus have a genetic conception of the divinity, in which the divinity originates in the Father and streams forth in the Son and the Holy Spirit.[129]

2. The Council obviously lacks the conceptual tools for expressing in an adequate way the unity of being and distinction of persons. At this point Nicaea presses beyond itself. The clear distinctions which Tertullian had already made could win adherence only after a long and difficult process of clarification.

The needed clarification was won in the half-century between Nicaea (325) and Constantinople (381). The Semi-Arians were of the opinion that the *homoousios* meant a modalistic blurring of the distinction between Father and Son, and they sought to rescue the distinction by adding a single letter to the word and speaking instead of *homoiousios* (i.e., like the Father but not identical with him). This compromise was untenable because it did not do justice to the profound concern expressed in the *homoousios*. A solution began to emerge when Athanasius, the great champion of the Nicene orientation, effected a rapprochement at the Council of Alexandria in 362 by accepting a distinction between three hypostases and one being. This meant that two concepts used as identical at Nicaea were now differentiated.[130]

The more precise conceptual clarification of this distinction was the work of the three Cappadocian Fathers (Basil of Caesarea, Gregory of Nazaianzus, and Gregory of Nyssa). Basil followed the Stoics in looking upon the being (*ousia*) as something general and not limited to a particular entity. Thus the generic concept 'man' is the common predicate of any individual human beings. The hypostases (*hypostaseis*), on the contrary, are the concrete individual embodiments of this common being. Hypostases come into being as complexes of *idiomata*, i.e., individualizing characteristics. These *idiomata* are here understood not as accidents but as constitutive elements of the concrete existent.[131] Peculiar to the Father is the fact that he owes his being to no other cause; peculiar to the Son is his generation from the Father; peculiar to the Holy Spirit is that he is known after and with the Son and that he has his substance from the Father.[132]

Westerners had trouble with this distinction, because *hypostasis* was often translated into Latin by the word *substantia*.[133] It would seem to Westerners, therefore, that three hypostases meant three divine substances, thus leading to tritheism or a doctrine of three Gods. Conversely, Tertullian's distinction between *natura* and *persona* was difficult for the East, because *persona* was translated as *prosōpon*; *prosōpon*, however, meant a mask, that is, a mere appearance, and thus suggested modalism. For this reason Basil issued a warning that, as understood in the confession of faith, the persons (*prosōpa*) in God exist as hypostases.[134] Once this equivalence was generally accepted, all the major church provinces were saying materially the same thing despite the different concepts used: Caesarea (Basil), Alexandria (Athanasius), Gaul (Hilary), Italy and especially Rome (Damasus). Thus after one of the most turbulent periods in the history of the church all the presuppositions for a solution were at hand.

The resolution came with the Council of Constantinople (381) and its reception by the Roman synod under Pope Damasus (382). In its doctrinal letter Constantinople gave expression to the distinction between the one substance (*ousia; substantia*) and the three perfect hypostases (*hypostaseis; subsistentiae*).[135] This meant that the Nicene formula, according to which the Son is from the being (*ousia*) of the Father was now dropped.[136] But the Roman synod, like Pope Damasus in his doctrinal letter of 374,[137] spoke of one *substantia* and three *personae*.[138] The difference was not merely one of terminology. While the creeds of Nicaea and Constantinople start with the Father and then confess the Son and the Spirit to be one in being or substance with the Father, the West replaces this dynamic conception with a more static approach that starts with the one substance and then says that it subsists in three persons. But these differences were not regarded at that time as dividing the church. The two formulas bring out the possible plurality and wealth of theologies that are based on a single common faith. A synthesis of the two differenct vocabularies and approaches came only at the fifth ecumenical council, the Second Council of Constantinople (553), which combined them in one and the same formula. Meanwhile Boethius and Leontius of Byzantium had clarified the concept of person, which the East had originally found so difficult.[139] As a result the Council could take hypostasis and person as synonyms, and state: 'If anyone does not confess that Father, Son and Holy Spirit are one nature (*physis; natura*) or essence (*ousia; substantia*), one might and power, a Trinity one in being (*homoousios*), one Godhead to be worshipped in three hypostases (*hypostaseis; subsistentiae*) or persons (*prosōpa; personae*), anathema sit.'[140] The Council then adds to this static and extremely abstract technical theological definition a statement that is more dynamic in character and based on the history of salvation: 'For one is the God and Father from whom all things are, one is the Lord Jesus Christ through whom all things are and one the Holy spirit in whom all things are.'[141]

A comparison of the two formulas shows the long and difficult road travelled in the doctrinal development leading from the Bible to the 'fully developed' dogmatic confessional formula. These passionate debates were not involved in useless hair-splitting and conceptual quibbles. The aim was the greatest possible fidelity and exactitude in the interpretation of the biblical datum. This last was so new and unparalleled that it turned all traditional conceptual thinking upside down. It was therefore by no means enough simply to apply concepts from Greek philosophy to the traditional confession of faith. All such attempts ended in heresy. The need was to reflect on the data of scripture and tradition and to break away from the one-sidedly essentialist thinking of Greek philosophy and into a personalist thinking that did justice to the scriptures, thus laying the foundation of a new type of thought. From the theological standpoint, this shift made it possible to bring out the specifically Christian form of monotheism as distinct from that of either Judaism or paganism. To that extent, the wearisome and difficult debates with gnosticism and with the heresies of right and left retain a permanent basic significance for the church and its identity. No wonder, then, that in the later period the formulas we have been examining were constantly repeated.[142] The best known example is the *Quicumque*, also know as the (Pseudo-) Athanasian Creed.[143] Of course, the price to be paid for this conceptual clarity also became clear in the course of time. This consisted in the increasing danger that the abstract conceptual formulas would become independent and lose their character as interpretations of the historical action of God through Christ in the Holy Spirit. The vital historical faith of scripture and tradition threatened to rigidify into abstract formulas which are materially correct but which, isolated from the history of salvation, become unintelligible and function-less for an existential faith.

The Nicene-Constantinopolitan confession was thus, on the one hand, the result of long and passionate debate; as such it has remained down to our own day the common foundation for all churches of both East and West. On the other hand, that confession was also the point of departure for further theological reflection. After Nicaea and Constantinople this reflection led to a momentous change of perspecitve. Tertullian and Origen were still taking as their starting point the divinity of the Father and then, in the interests of the economy of salvation, asserting the equality of Son and Spirit with the Father.[144] Origen even distinguished within this one economy specific areas of operation for Father, Son and Spirit.[145] Basil, however, rejected this view,[146] and on the basis of the one nature theologians now concluded that the three divine persons act together in all operations *ad extra*. This thesis was common to the fathers of both East and West,[147] although the Eastern fathers brought out more clearly the fact that this common action still expresses the internal trinitarian structure of God; that is, that the Father acts through the Son in the Holy Spirit.[148] The shift in outlook shows most clearly in the liturgical doxologies, thus indicating once again that these were the *Sitz im Leben* of the trinitarian confession of faith. In the original liturgical doxology glory is given to the Father through the Son in the Holy Spirit. But Basil already makes a change which is then taken over at Constantinople: the Spirit is glorified together with the Father and the Son. Thus a doxology based on the one nature or substance of God takes its place alongside the doxology that reflects the history of salvation: 'Glory be to the Father and to the Son and to the Holy Spirit.'[149]

This development took place in both East and West, although in different circumstances. In both cases the need was to eliminate the last traces of Arianism. In the East these traces took the form chiefly of Eunomianism, which reduced Arian thinking to a formal, dialectical, almost rationalistic system.[150] In order to counter it, the Greek Fathers were compelled to emphasize the mysteriousness of God and the eternal processions in God.[151] As a result, they no longer started with the order found in the economy in order then to make their way back to the order within God. Trinitarian theology and the economy were henceforth separated. The emphasis on the Father having shown his face to us concretely in Jesus Christ was replaced by a radically negative theology of a Neoplatonic cast, in which greater stress was put on the incomprehensibility of God than on the truth that the Incomprehensible had, in an incomprehensible way, made itself comprehensible in Jesus Christ.[152] God's trinitarian being was regarded as unknowable in itself; only its rays, or energies, are knowable.[153] Hints in this direction that are to be found in the Cappadocian Fathers were developed in the fourteenth century, especially by Gregory Palamas. The Trinity thus ceased to have any function in the economy of salvation.[154]

It is obvious that the West, too, regarded the incomprehensibility of the Trinity as beyond question.[155] But there, especially in Augustine, analogies between the human spirit as image of God and the Trinity played a key role. In the West, the conflict with Arianism led to such an emphasis on the *homoousios* that the one nature or substance of God became the basis on which the entire doctrine of the Trinity was explained. Over and over we find in Augustine such statements as: the Trinity is the one true God,[156] or: God is the Trinity.[157] The distinction of the three persons was made within the one nature and, in the final analysis, remained a problem for Augustine.[158] This Augustinian tendency was accentuated in Anselm of Canterbury.[159] The term of this development in the Latin West was the formula of the Fourth Lateran Council, according to which in their action *ad extra* the three divine persons are a single principle of operation.[160] This applied not only to the act of creating but also to the history of salvation. Thomas Aquinas even held the thesis that in the abstract any one of the divine persons could have become man.[161] Even in the early Middle Ages, however, and certainly in Thomas himself there were contrary tendencies in the direction of a Trinity that reflects the economy of salvation; of these I will be speaking further on.[162] But in late mediaval Nominalism a complete separation was made between God's being in itself and God's action in the history of salvation, and the *potentia ordinata* or 'ordered power' of God that is revealed in the history of salvation threatened to give place to a divine freedom that is completely arbitrary in its exercise [163] and no longer bears the stamp of the intra-divine trinitarian structure.

The Reformers took over the trinitarian confession,[164] but it was no more fruitful in their case than it had been in Scholasticism. With some attenuations the trinitarian confession has also become part of the basic unifying formula of the World Council of Churches.[165] In practice, however, many churches and even many Catholic communities and Catholic Christians seem to regard this confession as no more than a relic of venerable antiquity. The difficulty is that the churches have all too long emphasized and defended the internal triuneness of God without saying what this should mean for us. The doctrine of the immanent Trinity, which was originally meant to be the basis and guarantee of the doctrine of the economic Trinity, has in practice become an independent entity. No wonder, then, that at the time of the Enlightenment people asked what practical value it had. Since the answer was 'None', and the doctrine of the Trinity was either jettisoned[166] or, at best, preserved, from a sense of duty, as a kind of appendix. Characteristic of this second approach is F. Schleiermacher's thesis in his *The Christian Faith*: 'Our faith in Christ and our living fellowship with Him would be the same although we had no knowledge of any such transcendent fact [as the Trinity], or although the fact itself were different.'[167] And in fact many, if not the majority of Christians today are in practice pure monotheists, i.e., believers in a monopersonal God.

This situation, in which living and experiential faith is in danger of losing the basic structure proper to it as Christian, poses a powerful challenge to theologians. They will not succeed in once again making the trinitarian confession a vital part of experiential faith unless they are able to bring home to Christians the importance of this confession for their salvation. This in turn means that they must pay greater attention to the connection between the economic Trinity and the immanent Trinity. The soteriological motives which in Irenaeus and Tertullian and especially in Athanasius lead to the development of the *homoousios* doctrine, must once again be emphasized so that the Trinity may recover its importance for man and his salvation. There is need, in addition, to highlight once again the brilliant insights of Origen as clarified and purified with the aid of Nicaea and Constantinople and, in response to the neo-gnostic currents of our time, to develop a comprehensive and specifically Christian vision of reality on the basis of the trinitarian confession. There is need, in other words, to hold fast to the Nicene-Constantinopolitan confession of the independent reality of the immanent Trinity, while at the same time saying what this doctrine means for us within the economy of salvation. Here we have the basic task of a contemporary doctrine of the Trinity.

II

Exposition of the Doctrine of the Trinity

1. The point of departure

(a) The Trinity as mystery of faith

The history of modern thought is not only a history of the destruction of the trinitarian confession; it is also a history of the many attempts made to reconstruct the doctrine of the Trinity.[1] Admittedly, the credit for having kept alive the idea of the Trinity belongs less to theology than to philosophy. For while the theologians were either transmitting the doctrine of the Trinity in a Scholastically correct but uncreative way or else, as in the theology of the Enlightenment, were dismissing it with the aid of a great deal of exegetical and historical erudition, thinkers like Spinoza, Lessing, Fichte, Schelling[2] and Hegel were trying to revitalize what the theologians were treating, in one way or other, as a dead object. But the philosophers were doing this in a manner which the theologians and the churches rightly regarded as highly suspect and even downright unacceptable. Gnostic and Neoplatonic ideas which the churches all thought had been eliminated came alive again in a new form by way of Eckhart and Boehme. If the church did not wish to surrender the identity and continuity of its tradition, along with the insights gained therein, it could only react negatively. Unfortunately it did not have available an Origen or a Basil or an Augustine who might have handled this necessary clash in a creative way and drawn strength from the very strength of the opponent for a deeper understanding of his own tradition, so as to achieve a new synthesis and thus a renewal of the tradition itself.

It was Hegel who attempted the most important and momentous of these new approaches. In his philosophy of religion (to which I limit myself here) Hegel starts from the modern alienation and separation between religion and life, between weekday and Sunday.[3] As a result of this separation, the weekday becomes the world of the finite, lacking in any true depth, while religion for its part is emptied of all concrete content; religion turns cold and dead, wearisome and burdensome. 'Religion shrivels and becomes a matter of mere feeling, an empty elevation of the spirit to something eternal, and so on.'[4] For this reason theology has been reduced to a minimum of dogmas. 'Its content has become extremely attenuated despite all the talk and erudition and argumentation.'[5] But the exegesis and history serve in fact only to do away with the basic doctrines of Christianity. The symbol, the *regula fidei*, is no longer regarded as binding.[6] 'As a result, people have only a general knowledge that God is, and they regard him simply as a supreme being that is empty and dead in itself and cannot be grasped as a concrete content, as spirit. . . If God as 'spirit' is not to be simply an empty word for us, then he must be conceived as a triune God.'[7] In this respect, according to Hegel, there is a great deal more dogmatic theology in philosophy than in dogmatic theology itself.[8]

Hegel's intention, therefore, is to recover the living God and for him this means the triune God. But he wants to do this in his own fashion. He wants to reduce the naive representation of Father, Son and Spirit to concepts; he wants to understand God as a spirit whose essence it is to make himself an object for himself in order then to remove this distinction through love.[9] His intention, therefore, is to go beyond the abstract concept of God as supreme being and to think God as a spirit who becomes objective to himself in the Son and then recovers himself in love.[10] Hegel is here expressly harking back to gnostic and Neoplatonic thinking.[11] In the final analysis the divine Trinity is the interpretation of the statement that God is love. For 'love is a distinguishing of two who nonetheless are not simply distinct in relation to one another'.[12] This in turn means that the divine Trinity is a mystery for the imagination and for abstract thought but not for speculative thinking. 'The nature of God is not a mystery in the usual sense of the word, least of all in the Christian religion. Here God has given himself to be known as he is; here he is made plain.'[13] It was this reduction of religion to the level of the imagination and the speculative sublimation of religion in an absolute concept that first and foremost elicited the opposition of the theologians and the churches. They saw in Hegel's approach a failure to preserve the mystery and hiddenness of God.[14]

It would be wrong, however, to dismiss Hegel's speculation about the Trinity as simply a new form of gnosticism. For from one point of view it is directly opposed to the gnostic systems. The gnostic systems organize their thinking in a scheme of descent and decline, whereas Hegel's thinking must be regarded as a scheme of ascent and progress. At the beginning stands something abstract and general, namely, the Father, who then first defines himself in another self, namely, the Son, and finally, in a third, the Spirit, becomes a concrete idea. Admittedly, this process does not produce anything new. 'The third is also the first'; 'What is produced already exists from the beginning.' 'The process, then, is simply a game of self-preservation, of self-confirmation.'[15] It is a fact, however, that truth can be identified only with the whole, and that the whole exists only at the end.[16] In a sense Hegel has thus rediscovered the eschatological dimension of the Trinity, which the theological tradition had largely forgotten and according to which God will be 'all in all' (I Cor. 15.28) only at the end when the Son hands the kingdom over to the Father. But despite this point of contact, Hegel's thinking on the whole runs counter to the traditional view. For according to the biblical and traditional conception, what stands at the beginning is not emptiness but the fullness of being, namely, the Father as origin and source. Consequently, while it is possible to argue about whether Vatican I understood Hegel correctly, it did in fact make an important point when it condemned the proposition that 'God is the universal or indefinite begin which, by self-determination, constitutes the universality of beings differentiated into genera, species and individuals.'[17]

This condemnation at the same time alludes to a third area of problems in the debate with Hegel, and in fact to the basic problem: Hegel's determination of the relation between God and world. He does not indeed simply identify the procession of the Son with the act of creation; nor does he understand the world-process and the historical process as simply a theogonic process in which God becomes and finds himself. He keeps the levels clearly distinct. But how does he do so? For Hegel the Son is the abstract determination of otherness, while the world is the concrete realization of otherness, so that 'in themselves' the two are the same.[18] For Hegel it is valid to say: 'Apart from the world God is not God.'[19] 'God is creator of the world; it belongs to his being, to his nature, to be a creator.'[20] Consequently for Hegel the distinction between the economic Trinity and the immanent Trinity is in the last analysis an abstract one; considered concretely and in themselves, the two coincide. 'Spirit is the divine history, the process of self-distinction, separation, and return.' This process takes three forms: one in the realm of thought, apart from the world; another in the realm of representation, in the world and its history; and the other in the community,[21] in and for whose consciousness Jesus Christ is the manifestation of God, and in which therefore the eternal movement which is God reaches consciousness[22] and God as Spirit is present.[23] 'This Spirit insofar as it exists and reaches self-realization is the community.'[24] God and world; the history of salvation, the history of the world, and the history of the church: all these are here dialectically *aufgehoben* (reduced to components, annulled, preserved, and elevated to a higher level) in one another, but in such a way that the decisive point of the Christian faith is in danger of being lost: God as freedom that exists in and for itself and that communicates itself in the freedom of love. But God thus understood presupposes the real and not simply abstract distinction between the immanent and economic Trinities. At this point, which is the main point, Hegel's thinking remains profoundly ambivalent and irremediably ambiguous.

Given the ambiguity of Hegel's thinking it is not surprising that his system should have been received in various ways. Some, e.g., Ph. K. Marheineke, approached it from the ecclesial and orthodox standpoint; others, e.g., L. Feuerbach and K. Marx, were expressly interested in a critique of religion. For Feuerbach the mystery of theology is anthropology, while the mystery of the Trinity is the mystery of communal, societal life; it is the mystery of the necessity of the Thou for the I; it is the truth that '*no being whatsoever*, be it man or God or be it called "spirit" or "I", can be *true*, *perfect* and *absolute being in isolation*; that the *truth* and *perfection* are only the *union* and *unity* of beings that are similar in essence'.[25] The Trinity is therefore a projection and, so to speak, an encoded representation of human intersubjectivity and love. The human soul, which in the past supplied images and analogies of the Trinity, now becomes the prototype and the reality. For Feuerbach this amounts to saying that faith is to be replaced by love. For it is faith that sets God apart and turns him into a particular being; it thus separates believers from unbelievers and is the contrary of love, which embraces everything. Love makes God a universal being and converts the statement that God is love into the statement that love is God.[26] On the other hand, Feuerbach is far from sharing the naïveté of many theologians of our own day who think they can give Christianity a new opportunity in the time ahead by 'sublimating' a dogmatically defined faith in the practice of love. Feuerbach is aware that in setting faith aside for the sake of love he is striking a decisive blow at Christianity: 'Christianity owes its perpetuation to the dogmatic formulas of the Church.'[27] He does not reflect, however, that to maintain the Godness of God is also to defend the humanness of man. For the preservation of the difference between lovers that remains even in love also preserves the unconditional dignity and unconditional worth of the individual person within the human genus into which Feuerbach and, even more resolutely, Marx wish to absorb the individual.[28] The transcendence of God proves to be the sign and safeguard of the transcendence of the human person.[29]

Although theologians have a good deal to learn from modern philosophy and in particular from Hegel, at the decisive point they must say a resolute No. Reason cannot prove the necessity of the Trinity either from the concept of absolute spirit or from the concept of love. The Trinity is a mystery in the strict sense of the term.[30] What is said in the scriptures applies here: 'No one knows the Son except the Father, and no one knows the Father except the Son and any one to whom the Son chooses to reveal him' (Matt. 11.27; cf. John 1.18). No one knows God except the Spirit of God (I Cor. 2.11). The thesis regarding the Trinity as a strict mystery is directed primarily against rationalism who seeks to prove the doctrine of the Trinity by reason, whether it does this by way of the history of religions from the so-called extra-biblical parallels, or speculatively from the essence of divinity or the essence of human consciousness. The thesis is also directed against semi-rationalism, as it is called, which admits that prior to the revelation of them we cannot deduce the mysteries of faith, but then goes on to assert that once they have been revealed we are able to understand them.[31] It is a fact, of course, that the theological tradition offers rational arguments for faith in the Trinity. But the analogies from the life of the human spirit which Augustine in particular introduced into the discussion serve only to illustrate and never to demonstrate the truth of the Trinity.[32] Admittedly, some medieval Scholastics (especially Richard of St Victor and Anselm of Canterbury) did try to produce *rationes necessariae* (demonstrative reasons) for faith in the Trinity.[33] The question is, however, whether their cogent rational arguments were not in fact simply arguments of suitability and did not in fact presuppose the trinitarian faith and argue in the light of it. It was only with Albert the Great and Thomas Aquinas that a clear distinction was made between faith and knowledge; not until the modern age were the two separated. Therefore in the medieval theologians I have been discussing there may have been an exaggerated intellectual optimism, but we can hardly speak of them as rationalists in the modern sense of the word.

The positive reason for the basic incomprehensibility of the Trinity even after it has been revealed is that even in the economy of salvation God is revealed to us only in the medium of history and in the medium of human words and deeds, or, in other words, in finite forms. What Paul says holds at this point too: we see in a mirror and not face to face (I Cor. 13.12). Or, to use the language of Thomas Aquinas: even in the economy of salvation we know God only indirectly through his effects. These effects are clearer and less ambiguous in the history of salvation than they are in creation; nonetheless, they enable us to know only that God is and that he is triune, but do not permit us to understand his essence (*quid est*) from within. We are therefore united to God as to one unknown (*quasi ignoto*).[34] Nowadays we would say rather that we know the triune God only through his words and actions in history; these are the real symbols of his love that freely communicates itself to us. God's freedom-in-love in the form of a gratuitous self-communication would in fact be annulled if it could be shown to be rationally necessary. The revelation given in the history of salvation does not therefore explain the mystery of God to us but rather leads us deeper into this mystery; in this history the mystery of God is revealed to us as mystery.

There are three points in particular that remain incomprehensible and impenetrable to our minds: 1. the absolute unity of God despite the distinction of persons; 2. the absolute equality of the persons despite the dependence of the second on the first and of the third on the first and second; 3. the eternity of God as Father, Son and Spirit despite the fact that they are established as such by the activities of generation and spiration. But then, do we even grasp the absolute simplicity of God despite the multiplicity and differentiation of his attributes, or his absolute immutability and eternity despite the multiplicity of his activities and of his involvements in history? No, God is unknowable in every aspect of his being and not just in his internal personal relations. Neither the That of the triune God nor his What (his inner nature) nor his How are accessible to our finite knowledge.[35]

Up to this point, in dealing with the mysteriousness of the Trinity I have been taking 'mystery' in its Scholastic sense: a mystery is a truth which in principle transcends the powers of the human mind, is certified only by a divine communication, and, even after its communication, cannot be positively understood.[36] In this Scholastic approach mystery is understood, first of all, as a property of a proposition. It speaks of mysteries in the plural; it is asserted that there are many mysteries of faith, but there is no explicit reflection on whether these many mysteries are simply aspects of a single mystery. Secondly, mystery is understood in terms of reason, without the question being asked whether this reference is not too narrow and superficial and whether the standpoint adopted should not rather be that of the human person as a whole and the mystery of its existence. Thirdly, the revelation of mystery is understood as a transmission of true propositions (revelation as supernatural information and instruction) rather than being conceived as a personal communication. Fourthly, mystery is defined in a purely negative way as the unknowable and incomprehensible. Fifthly, and consistently with such a definition, mystery is thought of as something provisional; it will someday be eliminated, when we see God 'face to face' in the beatific vision. No account is taken of the fact that mystery is essentially connected with the self-transcendence of the human spirit and with the Godness of God and that it is to this extent something positive.

    This Scholastic concept makes it possible to distinguish a mystery from a riddle and a problem, both of which in principle can be gradually solved, whereas in principle mystery cannot be thus removed. But such a concept of mystery is not clearly distinguished from the everyday use of this word and from the unpleasant associations of secrecy connected with it. Such terms as secret diplomacy, secret police, military secrets and secretiveness suggest a distressing lack of openness and so on; they suggest the painful need of locks and keys. Especially in its religious application, the word mystery, thus understood, becomes suspect. It seems to abet a flight from the bright light of the intellect into the half-darkness of feeling and to provide religious justification for mental fatigue and even intellectual dishonesty. Against this background it is understandable that the attack of the Enlightenment on Christianity should have found expression especially in hostility to the concept of mystery. The very title of *Christianity Not Mysterious* (1696) by John Toland, an English deist, is typical. And in fact the concept of mystery can become 'the refuge of tendencies' 'which distort Christian talk about God and blur the distinction between belief and superstition'.[37]

A positive and more complete concept of mystery can be elaborated along two lines. To begin with, it can be shown from philosophy and anthropology that because of the self-transcendence proper to their spirit, human beings are beings of ineradicable mystery. The mystery in this case is not something that merely accompanies the other, rationally explicable traits of his existence; it is the all-inclusive totality of their existence, that which alone makes possible, comprehends and permeates everything else.[38] This many-faceted mystery of man determines revelation inasmuch as it is an image and likeness of the mystery of God and his freedom. Theologically, therefore, there are not many mysteries of all kinds, but only one mystery: God and his saving will as carried out through Jesus Christ and in the Holy Spirit. The entire Christian economy of salvation is thus a single mystery that can be summed up in one sentence: through Jesus Christ and in the Holy Spirit God is the salvation of man.[39] This triune mystery can be broken down into three mysteries: the triune being of God, the incarnation of God in Jesus Christ, and man's salvation in the Holy Spirit, a salvation which finds is eschatological completion in the vision of God face to face. In these three mysteries the one mystery of the self-communicating love of God is seen from various angles: in itself – in Jesus Christ – in all the redeemed.[40] The mystery of the triune God as it exists in God himself is here both the presupposition or intrinsic ground as well as the deepest reality of the mysteries of the incarnation and grace. The Trinity is the mystery present in all mysteries; it is, without qualification, *the* mystery of the Christian faith.

If mystery is understood in this positive sense and if the correspondence between the mystery which is man and the mystery of God is seen, then the Christian mystery cannot be simply non-rational or, worse still, contrary to reason. This positive understanding excludes not only the one-dimensional leveling down of faith and knowledge but also the dualistic definition of the two as antithetical in irrationalism and fideism. Fideism constantly appeals to the well-known saying of Tertullian (although it is the sense and not the words as such that are to be found in this writer): *Credo quia absurdum est* (I believe because it is absurd).[41] In the Middle Ages this critical attitude toward reason is to be seen in, for example, Peter Damian and Bernard of Clairvaux; it occurs then in late medieval Nominalism, in the supernaturalism of the Reformers, in the debate between P. Bayle and Leibniz, in Kierkegaard and in early dialectical theology.

In response to this attitude it must be said:

Reason that claims to lack any intrinsic connection with revelation and to be separated from and opposed to it by an unbridgeable chasm is no less dangerous than reason that asserts itself as equal in rank with revelation. . . In the final analysis, the claim that we cannot simultaneously hold fast in faith to the truth of revelation and have confidence in the knowledge of it which the mind can acquire turns out to be identical with the claim that we do not need both together and that speculative reason attains to full knowledge of the same content which the believer accepts on entirely external authority. In other words, once the human spirit becomes a thinking spirit it necessarily ceases to be a believing spirit; conversely, it can only believe when it ceases to think. This statement holds true in both approaches, so closely allied are the two extremes.[42]

'The light of divine truth does not need this kind of artificial eclipse in order to reveal its brilliance.'[43] Revelation is 'supra-rational, not irrational or anti-rational. It represents an enrichment of reason, not a spurning or constriction of it.'[44]

The correspondence between the mystery of man and the mystery of God means, to begin with, that reason can show that what the mystery of the Trinity asserts is not contradictory or nonsensical. It does not amount to the absurd claim that one equals three, or similar nonsense.[45] On the positive side, there are three ways of attaining to a deeper understanding of the mystery of the Trinity as accepted in faith: 1. by examination of analogies from the natural world; Augustine in particular travelled this path in his teaching on the Trinity; 2. by showing the *nexus mysteriorum* (the connection of the mysteries with one another) or the *hierarchia veritatum* (the hierarchy of truths):[46] all the mysteries of faith together form a structured whole, and by reason of the internal harmony and coherence of this structure the individual truths of faith become credible and intelligible. As far as the doctrine of the Trinity is concerned, this connection between the truths of faith means showing that the economic Trinity and the immanent Trinity are inseparable and, furthermore, that the trinitarian confession provides the basic structure for all the other truths of faith as well as their overarching context. 3. The third way is by showing the connection between the trinitarian faith and man's meaning and goal, namely, eternal communion with God, which is given through Christ in the Holy Spirit.[47] We may combine these three ways and say that the mystery of the Trinity can be understood as a mystery if it can be shown that it proves its worth as an interpretation of reality, that is, of the order of creation and the order of redemption.

(b) Images and likenesses for the trinitarian mystery

The First Vatican Council stated that with the help of grace reason can gain a certain understanding of the mysteries of God 'from the analogy with the objects of its natural knowledge'.[48] Theologians reflecting on the doctrine of the Trinity adopted this principle at a very early stage and looked to the natural world for images, parables and analogies that would enable them to penetrate more deeply into the mystery of the Trinity. As early as the second century we find the classical comparison with fire, which is not diminished by the fact that another fire is lit from it.[49] Another ancient comparison, between the source of light, the light and the radiance of the light[50] played an important role later on, especially in Athanasius.[51] In fact, this image even made its way into the church's confession of faith: 'Light from Light, true God from true God'.[52] Tertullian introduced a series of other comparisons: root and fruit, source and stream, sun and ray of the sun.[53]

Augustine was the most prolific of these theologians in discovering traces (*vestigia*) of the Trinity in creation. The whole eleventh book of his *De Trinitate* is devoted to this subject. In addition to the images already mentioned,[54] Augustine points out that according to Wisdom 11.20, God has arranged all things 'by measure and number and weight'. In this triad he sees an image of the divine Trinity.[55] But for him the true image of God is man (Gen. 1.28)[56] and, more specifically, the human soul.[57] This idea of man as image of God is the starting point for Augustine's psychological speculation on the Trinity, which in turn determined the course of all later reflection on the mystery of the Trinity in Latin theology. Here again Augustine can refer back to earlier beginnings and especially to the comparison with the interior word and with the will, these being analogies customary ever since the Apologists and Origen.[58] Within Latin theology, Augustine could build especially on preliminary work done by Tertullian, Hilary and Ambrose.[59] In the final analysis, however, Augustine proceeds in a fully independent manner; his psychological doctrine of the Trinity is the product of his own genius.[60] With great speculative power and depth Augustine detects in the human spirit ever new ternaries: *mens – notitia – amor* (mind – knowledge – love), *memoria – intelligentia – voluntas* (memory – intelligence – will), and others. I shall speak of these in detail further on.

There is, of course, a question that needs to be answered: what do these analogies really achieve? They are doubtless not meant as proofs in the strict sense of the term; they are not a demonstration but a subsequent illustration that presupposes the confession of the Trinity. They represent an attempt to put the mystery of the Trinity in the language of our present world. Admittedly, then, they move within a hermeneutical circle. They not only interpret the Trinity in terms of the world and more particularly of man but, conversely, they also interpret the world and man in the light of the mystery of the Trinity; on the basis of the doctrine of the Trinity they postulate a particular model for human knowing and loving. This reciprocal clarification has its basis in the correspondence (analogy) between God and world, the order of creation and the order of redemption.

It is understandable, then, that because of his divergent conception of analogy[61] Karl Barth should sharply criticize the doctrine of the *vestigia trinitatis*. He is afraid that this ambivalent undertaking may lead to a high-handed justification of the doctrine of the Trinity on the basis of man's understanding of the world and himself and thus to a defection from revelation. He therefore regards the attempt to find traces of the Trinity as frivolous and as distracting us from the real task, which is not to illustrate revelation but to interpret it, that is, to make it intelligibile in its own terms.[62] Catholic theology, which persists in maintaining the analogy between God and world, cannot accept this radical criticism. Riskiness is not a theological argument for abandoning a task seen as necessary; it is rather a challenge to do the task well, accurately and conscientiously.

One point in Barth's criticism is indeed valid: that theological under-standing must come primarily not from without, that is, from analogies with the world, but from faith itself or, more accurately, from the *nexus mysteriorum* or internal unity of the various assertions of faith.[63] The real *vestigium trinitatis* is therefore not man but the God-man Jesus Christ. A real understanding of the doctrine of the Trinity from within is gained only in the light of the economy of salvation. This brings us to the approach to the doctrine of the Trinity that is predominant today: namely, the unity of the immanent Trinity and the economic Trinity.

(c) The unity of immanent Trinity and economic Trinity

Since the Trinity is without qualification *the* mystery of faith, faith alone must provide the approach to the doctrine of the Trinity. Therefore we cannot start from modern philosophy or from any analogies drawn from the created realm; philosophy and analogies can only have subsequent auxiliary role in attaining a deeper understanding. The real starting point for understanding must be found in the economy of salvation. It is in this sense that K. Rahner has laid it down as the basic principle that 'the Trinity of the economy of salvation *is* the immanent Trinity and vice versa'.[64] K. Barth had already written a comparable statement: 'The reality of God in

His revelation is not to be bracketed with an "only", as though somewhere behind His revelation there stood another reality of God, but the reality of God which meets us in revelation is His reality in all the depths of eternity.'[65] Even an important Orthodox representative of Neopalamite theology, J. Meyendorff, proposes comparable theses. He says that God's being for us belongs to his being in himself.[66] It can be said, then, that what K. Rahner sets down as a basic principle, reflects a broad consensus among the theologians of the various churches. At the same time, the axiom sums up, in a critical and purified form, the results of an exchange of views with Hegel and Schleiermacher. Schleiermacher observed that 'we have no formula for the being of God in himself as distinct from the being of God in the world'.[67] This thesis retains its validity even though Schleiermacher himself drew false conclusions from it. In a way less open to misunderstanding than Schleiermacher's F.A. Staudenmaier, a representative of the Tübingen School, had already, in debate with Hegel, anticipated Rahner's basic axiom in his thesis regarding the 'vanity of the distinction between Trinity of being and Trinity of revelation'.[68]

With Karl Rahner we may adduce three arguments in justification of the basic principle or axiom:

1. Man's salvation is and can be nothing less than God himself; it cannot be simply a created gift distinct from God (*gratia creata*, 'created grace'). God's action through Jesus Christ in the Holy Spirit is therefore truly God's saving action only if in it we are dealing with God himself and if God himself is there for us as he is in himself. The economic Trinity would thus be deprived of all meaning if it were not at the same time the immanent Trinity. In addition, the eschatological character of the revelation in Christ makes it a necessity that in Jesus Christ God should communicate himself unreservedly and in a manner which cannot be surpassed. In the Christ-event there cannot be some unilluminated fringe and residue of a *Deus absconditus* left lurking 'behind' the *Deus revelatus*. Rather, the *Deus absconditus* is the *Deus revelatus*; the irremovable mystery of God is the mystery of our salvation. For this reason the so-called Athanasian Creed, which contains the most comprehensive doctrine of the Trinity to be found in any creed, begins by saying: '*Quicumque vult salvus esse, ante omnia opus est, ut teneat* . . . (whoever wishes to be saved must, first of all, hold . . .).'[69]

2. There is at least one case in which this identity of economic and immanent Trinity is a defined truth of faith: the incarnation of the Logos, or hypostatic union. Independently of the unproved and in fact false Scholastic opinion that in the abstract any one of the three divine persons could have become man, it is a fact that in Jesus Christ not God in general

but second divine person, the Logos, became man and this in the sense that he does not simply dwell in the man Jesus but is the subject (hypostasis) in which the humanity of Jesus subsists, so that the humanity of Jesus is not simply an external garment but a real symbol of the Logos.[70] In the man Jesus Christ it is God's very Son who speaks and acts. In the case of the incarnation, then, the temporal sending of the Logos into the world and his eternal procession from the Father cannot be completely distinguished; here immanent Trinity and economic Trinity form a unity.

3. The salvation brought to us by the Son of God consists in our becoming sons and daughters of God in the Holy Spirit; that is, the self-communication of God, which belongs by nature to the eternal Son of God, is given to us through grace in the Holy Spirit. Admittedly, with few exceptions the Scholastic theologians have asserted that, despite what scripture suggests, we may not speak of a personal indwelling of the Holy Spirit in Christians; according to most Scholastics scripture justifies only an indwelling that belongs to God as such and therefore to all three persons and that is only imputed (appropriated) to the Holy Spirit. But there are speculative objections, as well as solid biblical objections, to this thesis.[71] In this context, therefore, we may take as our starting point the assertion that grace is the free self-communication of God in the Holy Spirit; even in the tradition established by the Augustinian doctrine of the Trinity the Holy Spirit is precisely the eschatological gift in which God communicates himself. We may therefore say, too, that in the outpouring of the Spirit which brings the economy of salvation to its conclusion economic Trinity and immanent Trinity form a unity.

In K. Rahner, the original purpose of the axiom which is justified in the three ways just described originally was to overcome the non-functionality of the doctrine of the Trinity and to link the doctrine once again with the history of salvation, thus making it intelligible once again to the believer. In this perspective the axiom is correct, legitimate and even necessary.

The identification of the immanent and economic Trinities as established in this axiom is, of course, susceptible of several meanings and open to various misinterpretations. It would certainly be a misinterpretation if as a result of this identification the economic Trinity were stripped of its proper historical reality and were understood simply as a temporal manifestation of the eternal immanent Trinity; if, for example, we were not to take seriously the truth that through the incarnation the second divine person exists in history in a new way; and if, therefore, the eternal generation from the Father and the eternal mission to the world were no longer to be distinguished as well as internally connected. Today, of course, the opposite misinterpretation is more likely: the identification is taken to mean that the immanent Trinity is dissolved in the economic Trinity, as though the eternal Trinity first came into existence in and through history. In eternity the distinctions between the three persons would then at best be modal, and would become real only in history.[72] Finally, the axiom is being completely misunderstood when it is turned into a pretext for pushing the immanent Trinity more or less out of the picture and limiting oneself more or less to consideration of the Trinity in the economy of salvation.[73] Such a course only deprives the economic Trinity of all meaning and significance. For it has meaning and significance only if God is present in the history of salvation as the one who he is from eternity; more accurately, if God does not simply show himself to us as Father, Son and Spirit in the history of salvation, but is in fact Father, Son and Spirit from all eternity.

If, then, the axiom which states the identity of the immanent and economic Trinities is not to lead to the dissolution of the immanent Trinity instead of to its substantiation, this identity must not be understood along the lines of the tautological formula $A = A$. The 'is' in this axiom must be understood as meaning not an identification but rather a non-deducible, free, gracious, historical presence of the immanent Trinity in the economic Trinity. We may therefore rephrase Rahner's basic axiom as follows: in the economic self-communication the intra-trinitarian self-communication is present in the world in a new way, namely, under the veil of historical words, signs and actions, and ultimately in the figure of the man Jesus of Nazareth. The need is to maintain not only the kenotic character of the economic Trinity but also its character of graciousness and freedom in relation to the immanent Trinity and thus to do justice to the immanent mystery of God in (not: behind!) his self-revelation.[74]

To highlight the gracious freedom and the kenotic aspect of the economic Trinity is at the same time to emphasize the apophatic character of the immanent Trinity, that is, the fact that it eludes all language and thought. The immanent Trinity is and remains a *mysterium stricte dictum* in (not: behind!) the economic Trinity. This means that we cannot deduce the immanent Trinity by a kind of extrapolation from the economic Trinity. This was certainly not the path the early church followed in developing the doctrine of the Trinity in the form of confession and dogma. As we have seen, the early church's starting point was rather the baptismal confession of faith, which in turn was derived from the risen Lord's commission regarding baptism.[75] Knowledge of the trinitarian mystery was thus due directly to verbalized divine revelation and not to a process of deduction. This revelation in word is for its part the interpretation of the saving event that takes place in baptism, through which the saving event accomplished by Jesus Christ is made present by the power of the Spirit.

We come, therefore, to the conclusion that like all revelation, the revelation of the trinitarian mystery of God is given not in words alone nor in saving acts alone but in word and act, which are inter-related. The trinitarian baptismal confession and the eucharistic doxology are intended to interpret the trinitarian reality of salvation which is made present in baptism and the eucharist and in which God is our salvation through Christ in the Spirit; conversely, this saving reality turns revelation into a word that is living and has power over history.[76] Once it is understood in terms of the history of revelation, the axiom regarding the unity of the immanent and economic Trinity shows itself to be one from which it is not possible to deduce the immanent Trinity and which cannot be used in order to reduce the immanent Trinity to the economic Trinity. Rather, this axiom presupposes knowledge of the immanent Trinity and is meant to interpret and concretize the immanent Trinity in an appropriate way.

2. Basic concepts of the doctrine of the Trinity

(a) The classical basic concepts

The doctrine of the Trinity, as found in the manuals of dogmatic theology, begins with the doctrine of the immanent Trinity and specifically with the eternal processions of the Son from the Father and of the Holy Spirit from the Father and the Son; only at the end of the treatise do the manuals deal with the mission (sending) of the Son and the Spirit into the world in the history of salvation. Thus the dogmatic theology of the manuals follows the order of being, in which the eternal processions are antecedent to the missions and provide the basis for them. However, if we follow the order of knowledge, then we must begin with the missions as these occur in the history of salvation and with the revelation of these in words, and then come to know the eternal processions via the missions as their ground and presupposition. In the following discussion I shall follow this second path because it seems more in keeping with the nature of our human knowledge, which always starts from experience, and because it also seems more appropriate in view of the biblical witness.[77]The starting point and basic category of a doctrine of the Trinity that is based on the history of salvation must be the concept which in the traditional presentation of the Trinity comes only at the end: the concept of mission or sending. The scriptures tell us of the Son being sent by the Father (Gal. 4.4; John 3.17; 5.23; 6.57; 17.18) and of the Spirit being sent by the Father (Gal. 4.6; John 14.16, 26) and the Son (Luke 24.49; John 15.26; 16.7). While the mission of the Son in the incarnation takes visible form, the mission of the Spirit in the indwelling of the Spirit in the hearts of those who have been justified (I Cor. 3.16; 6.19; Rom. 5.5; 8.11) is invisible but does not utterly elude experience. The documents of the *magisterium* also use the concept of mission or sending.[78]

The concept of mission includes two aspects or factors.[79] In keeping with my approach from the history of salvation I shall deal with these in an order which reverses that followed in traditional theology. 1. The mission has for its goal the presence of the Son or the Spirit in the world and in history. As compared with the omnipresence of God that is entailed by God's very nature, this is a new, free and personal kind of presence. 2. The mission presupposes and has for its origin the eternal dependence of the Son on the Father and of the Spirit on the Father and the Son. The Son is eternally from the Father; the Spirit is eternally from the Father and the Son. The mission in time thus presupposes the eternal procession and adds to it a new, historical mode of presence in the created world.[80] The mission can therefore be regarded as a reproduction and diffusion, and even a prolongation of the eternal procession.[81]

The concept of mission thus leads to the concept of the intra-divine procession of the Son from the Father and of the Spirit from the Father and the Son (or originally [*principaliter*] from the Father and, in a mode bestowed on the Son by the Father, from the Son as well).[82] The scriptures only allude to these processions. For when they speak of the Son coming forth or proceeding (Vg.: *ex Deo processi*) from the Father (John 8.42) and of the Spirit proceeding (Vg.: *qui a Patre procedit*) from the Father (John 15.26), they are referring directly to the coming forth in time, or to the missions. Only indirectly is the eternal procession also expressed, in the form as it were of a transcendentally and theologically necessary condition for the possibility of the temporal procession. The eternal procession signifies an eternal relation of origin.

For an accurate grasp of the concept of procession we must distinguish between a procession to the outside, in which that which (or he who) proceeds emerges from his origin and passes beyond it (*processio ad extra* or *processio transiens*), and a procession in which that which (or he who) proceeds remains within his origin (*processio ad intra* or *processio immanens*).[83] It is in the first manner that creatures come forth from God; it is in the second that the Son proceeds from the Father, and the Spirit from the Father and the Son. For given the unity, simplicity and indivisibility of the divine being, only a *processio immanens* is possible in God. For the same reason the immanent processions in God cannot be understood as spatial or temporal movements, but are rather 'the foundation of the order of life and existence in God'. They are the immanent vital processes and vital movements in God. They are not a kind of graduated development of God out of the abyss and darkness of his mysterious being into the light of clear self-knowledge. There is no temporal succession in God, but only an eternal active reality (*actus purus*) of immense power, inexhaustible fullness of life, and yet profound interiority and repose.[84]

On the basis of the scriptures, tradition has endeavored to give more precise expression to the two processions in God.[85] The procession of the Son is described as generation, that of the Spirit (on the basis of John 15.26) as a procession in a narrower sense. In view of the original meaning of the word 'spirit' (namely wind, breathing, breath), traditional theology describes the procession of the Spirit as a 'breathing' or spiration (*spiratio*). But while the concept of generation is immediately intelligible, we experience some embarrassment in our attempts to characterize the procession of the Spirit. This conceptual poverty is only apparently lacking in Eastern theology. Because Eastern theology has no general concept to cover the intra-trinitarian 'comings forth', it is able to reserve the concept of 'procession' to the Spirit.[86] Yet we look in vain to this theology for some more precise explanation of the concept. As far as I know, the only attempt at such an explanation that is to be found in the tradition comes in Albert the Great,[87] to whom M. J. Scheeben refers.[88] According to Albert *processio* signifies an ecstatic going-beyond-oneself and self-transcending, a being-out-of-oneself such as is proper to love. As we compare the internal procession of the Son that is, his generation, with the procession of the interior word in the act of knowledge, so we compare procession of the Spirit, that is, his spiration, with the being-out-of-oneself or ec-stasy of love. Thus the Son is the Word and Wisdom of the Father, while the Spirit is the love of the Father and Son and the bond of love between them.[89]

The processions in God in turn are the basis of relations in God. Relation means reference to another.[90] The concept of relation therefore has three elements: a subject (*terminus a quo*), a term (*terminus ad quem*) and a foundation. There is a relative opposition between the subject and term of the relation. The two processions in God yield four such relations:

1. The relation of the Father to the Son: active generation (*generare*) or Fatherhood;

2. The relation of the Son to the Father: passive generation (*generari*) or sonship;

3. The relation of the Father and the Son to the Holy Spirit: active spiration (*spirare*);

4. The relation of the Holy Spirit to the Father and the Son: passive spiration (*spirari*).

Three of these relations are really distinct from each other: fatherhood, sonship and passive spiration. Active spiration, on the other hand, is identified with fatherhood and sonship and belongs to Father and Son in common, whereas passive spiration is really distinct from fatherhood and sonship. This means that the two processions in God ground three really distinct relative oppositions. The latter are the prototypes and primal ground of the dialogical and relational interaction and co-presence of Father, Son and Spirit in the history of salvation.

It was the brilliant insight of the fourth- and fifth-century fathers – an insight with a basis in Athanasius,[91] and developed in the East especially by Gregory of Nazianzus,[92] and in the West even more clearly by Augustine[93] – that fatherhood, sonship and passive spiration are relational realities, so that the distinctions in God affect not the one divine substance or one divine being but only the relations in God. This insight was later incorporated into official church teaching.[94] It led to the basic trinitarian principle: '*In Deo omnia sunt unum, ubi non obviat relationis oppositio* (In God everything is one where there is no opposition of relationship).'[95]

The statement that the distinctions in God are in the form of relations is of fundamental importance because it represents a break-away from a one-sidedly substantialist type of thought. The final word belongs not to the static substance, the divine self-containment, but to being-from-another and being-for-another. In the created world relations presuppose substance. Relations are essential only to the full self-realization of the being; they do not exhaust the reality of the being. A human being is and remains a human being even if he selfishly closes himself against relations with others; in fact he may not be regarded exclusively as a relational being that has meaning and value only to the extent that it exists for others and for the whole, since the human person has value and dignity in himself. In God, however, such distinctions between substance and relation are rendered impossible by the simplicity and perfection of the divine being. In God substance and relation are really identical; God is relation and exists only in the intra-divine relations; he is wholly love that surrenders and bestows itself. This relational reality of God, which is identical with his being or substance, presupposes real, mutually distinct relational realities. To that extent the distinction between the one substance of God and the relations is not a purely mental one (*distinctio rationis*) but one that has a foundation in reality (*distinctio virtualis*), in that the relation is directed to a term which is really distinct from the substance.[96] Thus the distinctions based on the relations once again bring out the ecstatic character of God's love.

The three mutually opposed relations in God – fatherhood, sonship and passive spiration – are abstract expressions for the three divine persons. Person (hypostasis),[97] as used in the early church and by the Scholastics, means the ultimate subject of all being and action (*principium quod*). The nature, for its part, is that by which the person or hypostasis is and acts (*principium quo*). The person or hypostasis is both irreducible to anything else and incommunicable to others; to that extent it is a unity distinct from every other such unity: the one here, the other there. For this reason the classical definition of person is: '*Persona est naturae rationalis individual substantia* (a person is an individual substance of a rational nature).'[98] The weakness of this definition, which comes from Boethius, is that it seems to understand personality and individuality as identical. Individuality, however, defines a what and not a who; it describes the person's nature, not the person as such. Nonetheless the content of Boethius' 'individuality' is incommunicability, an immediacy based on an ultimate indivisibility and unity.[99] This aspect finds expression especially in the definition of person that is given by Richard of St Victor: '*naturae rationalis incommunicabilis existentia* (an incommunicable existence of a rational nature).'[100] At bottom, Thomas Aquinas has the same thought in mind when he replaces the concept of substance (which is related to the concept of nature) with that of subsistence: that which is the subject that 'stands under' the nature or substance.[101] This conceptual refinement has importance not least for the doctrine of the Trinity. For talk of three substances is easily interpreted as meaning three Gods. Whereas if we speak of three subsistences, we are saying that the numerically one divine nature or substance is 'possessed' by three subjects or that it exists in three relatively distinct modes of subsistence.

In what does the ultimate, indivisible unity and therefore the ground of distinction in God consist? According to what has been said thus far it consists of the relations. This explains Thomas' definition of the divine persons: the divine persons are subsistent relations.[102] In fact, if not in terminology, this doctrine was also adopted by the Reformers; in our day it has been put forward among others by K. Barth.[103]

This definition of the divine persons as subsistent relations can be understood in two ways. First, the relation may be understood as the foundation of the subsistence, as in Anselm of Canterbury.[104] In this view an abstract approach with the nature as its point of departure predominates over the concrete approach based on the history of salvation. Then, of course, it is easy to lapse into modalism, since the persons seem to be simply modes of subsistence of the one nature. Second, the persons may be understood as grounding the relations. This is not to be interpreted as meaning that the persons are temporally prior to the relations; that is impossible since the persons are identical with the relations. The sense is rather that the persons are logically prior to the relations. This is the explanation given by Thomas Aquinas.[105] On this point he is materially close to the Eastern understanding of the Trinity, which starts not with the one nature but with the hypostases and is therefore closer to the concrete and salvation-historical language and thought of the Bible.

The persons are distinguished from one another by their characteristic properties (*idiōmata hypostatika*, 'personal properties').[106] Materially identical with the properties are the notions (*gnōrismata*), the attributes of the divine persons by which they are known and distinguished. Such personal properties (i.e., properties distinguishing the persons) are: father-hood, sonship, and passive spiration. The difference between the Eastern and Western doctrines of the Trinity can be seen in the divergent responses to the question of the role played by innascibility (*agennēsia*) as property of the Father.[107] Since the Eastern theologians start with the Father as unoriginated origin and as source of the Trinity, they see innascibility as the decisive property of the Father. The mainstream of the Western Latin tradition, however, sees innascibility as a property of the person of the Father but not as a property constitutive of the person. This view is connected with the fact that Western theologians usually see the persons as constituted and distinguished by the relations. Innascibility, however, is as such a denial of a relational dependence and cannot, therefore, be a property constitutive of a person. The East, on the other hand, regards this property as the starting point for the entire doctrine of the Trinity; this is because the Eastern theologians take innascibility as expressing the fact that God in his love is pure origin, receiving nothing from anyone, or that he is pure giving and unqualified bestowing.

The properties are to be distinguished from the appropriations, that is, the attribution of properties or activities which belong in common to all three persons because of their common nature but which are assigned to a particular person because they show a certain kinship with the property of that person.[108] Thus power can be appropriated to the Father, wisdom to the Son, and love to the Spirit. The appropriations are meant to illustrate the properties and distinction of persons in God.

At this point a serious logical difficulty arises. How can the absolute unity and simplicity of God permit of any numbering, any counting? Numbers, after all, have meaning only in the realm of the quantitative; there can be no counting in the sphere of pure spirit, which is the sphere of God. As Basil says, God is 'wholly beyond number'.[109] Or, as Augustine says, because God is not quantitative, he is not tripartite; the three persons cannot be counted up; God is not greater than each individual person.[110] In this sense we must join the Eleventh Council of Toledo in saying of the Trinity that it 'is not without number; yet it is not comprised by number (*nec recedit a numero nec capitur numero*)'.[111] The question, then, is whether and to what extent talk of 'three' persons is logically meaningful.

The point which prompts the question already makes it clear that in the realm of the spirit and above all in the realm of God number can only be predicated analogously, if at all. The application becomes meaningful only if we reflect on the ground and meaning of the possibility of numbers and counting, namely, unity as a transcendental property of being and one that adds nothing to being except a negation of division. This kind of unity belongs to every existent reality, although differently depending on its existential rank. Such unity belongs in the highest degree to the person, which is an 'individual' in the sense of possessing an ultimate undividedness and therefore incommunicability. When we talk of three persons in God, we are saying materially that the Father, the Son, and the Spirit are each that kind of undivided and indivisible ultimate unity.[112]

Since the number three is here used only analogously, it follows that the concept of person is not applied to the three persons as a generic concept.[113] The meaning of person here cannot be derived from any presupposed generic concept of person. We must rather heed what Hilary says and not determine the meaning of the reality from the words used but rather understand the words used in the light of the reality.[114] This point can also be made clear by looking at the reality, for in God it is not only the unity but also the distinction that is always greater than in the created world. In other words: not despite the fact that God is absolutely undivided unity but precisely because of this fact, he can and must also be infinite differentiation, and therefore he permits of personal distinctions which in each case are realized with an infinite differentiation by the mode of subsistence in which the one divine nature exists.

All the trinitarian concepts thus far examined lead to a final, all-inclusive basic concept: the being-in-one-another and mutual penetration of the divine persons, or the trinitarian perichoresis.[115] This concept has a scriptural basis in John 10.30: 'I and the Father are one' (cf. 14.9ff.; 17.21). This being-in-one-another and mutual penetration are attested in the tradition at a very early stage.[116] Hilary has a classical formulation of the relationship of Father and Son: 'One from the Other, and both are One; not One made up of Two, but One in the Other, because in the Both there is no otherness.'[117] 'God in God, because he is God from God.'[118] Augustine observes: In the Trinity 'there is no mixture or confusion. Each person is in himself, and yet three are each wholly in the others; each of them in the other two or the other two in each of them, and thus all are in all.'[119]

Following Fulgentius of Ruspe,[120] the Council of Florence describes as follows this reciprocal coinherence: 'On account of this unity the Father is wholly in the Son and wholly in the Holy Spirit; the Son wholly in the Father and wholly in the Holy Spirit; the Holy Spirit wholly in the Father and wholly in the Son.'[121]

The concept of perichoresis occurs first in Gregory of Nazanzius, although it is there applied to the relation between the two natures in Christ.[122] It is John Damascene who first applies the concept to the relation between the persons in the Trinity.[123] The Greek word *perichōrēsis* was initially translated as *circumsessio* (e.g., in Bonaventure), but from the thirteenth century on *circuminsessio* is also found (e.g., Thomas Aquinas). The former term denoted a more dynamic reciprocal penetration, while the latter signified a more static coinherence in repose. This translation with its variants once again points to differences between the Greek and Latin orientations, but also to different orientations even within the Latin doctrine of the Trinity. The Greeks start with the hypostases and understand the perichoresis as an active reciprocal penetration; the perichoresis is as it were the bond uniting the persons. The Latin theologians, on the contrary, usually start with the unity of the divine nature and understand the perichoresis more as a reciprocal coinherence on the basis of the one nature. In the Latins the perichoresis represents not so much movement in God as repose in God. Here, too, Thomas Aquinas seeks a synthesis; he bases the perichoresis both on the one nature and on the relations of origin.[124]

Pastorally as well as speculatively the doctrine of the perichoresis is of greatest importance, because it obviates both tritheism and modalism. The three persons are (in the language of christology) 'without confusion and without separation'.[125] From the speculative standpoint, the perichoretic unity in the Trinity provides a model for the union between Jesus Christ and human beings (John 14.20; 17.23), among human beings (John 17.21), and between God and man. We might take it as axiomatic that in the unity established by Jesus Christ unity and independence increase in direct and not in inverse proportion. Ever greater unity means ever greater independence, and conversely true independence is to be achieved only through and in unity in love. The unity with God that is established by Jesus Christ neither absorbs nor dissolves the human person; it means, rather, an abiding distinction and thus is the basic for authentic independence and freedom. In Christianity the mysticism of unity between God and man and between man and Christ is a mysticism of encounter, friendship and communion with God; it is realized in and through human encounter, friendship and communion, and in turn radiates outward into human friendship and communion and attains its full stature in these. Here once again it becomes clear that the trinitarian mystery is the deepest ground and ultimate meaning of the mystery of the human person and of the latter's fulfillment in love.

(c) The language of 'three persons'

Once the foundations had been laid in the fourth century for the church's doctrine of the Trinity and the concepts used in it, this doctrine and these concepts remained for a millennium (apart from a few disputes in the twelfth century) the undisputed joint possession not only of the churches of the East and the West but also of the churches of the Reformation and the Catholic Church. Anti-trinitarian trends came into existence only in the modern period: the Socinians and Arminians of the seventeenth century began the movement, and the high point was reached in eighteenth-century rationalism, which left its clear mark both on the theology of the Enlightenment and on liberal theology. The objections raised were of many kinds. But if we leave aside the historical arguments (exegetical and those from the history of religions and of dogma) and look at the arguments based directly on the content of the teaching, then one objection stands out as more important than the others: modern subjectivity and the modern concept of person which it has produced. In the modern period, person is no longer understood in ontological terms but is defined as a self-conscious free center of action and as individual personality.[126]

This modern ideal of person was quite compatible with the idea of a personal God. But once this new concept of person was accepted, the idea of three persons in one nature became impossible, not only logically but psychologically as well. For the modern self-conscious person could see in other persons only competitors. The combining of oneness and threeness became an insoluble problem. But even the idea of a unipersonal God – which was not a Christian but an Enlightenment notion; in the final analysis it was the heresy of Christian theism – soon proved to be an untenable post-Christian fossil. Modern critics of religion, and L. Feuerbach in particular, had an easy time of it when they set out to show that this idea is a projection of human self-consciousness and when K. Marx analysed it as an ideological construct of the bourgeois subject.

The possibility or impossibility of absorbing the modern concept of the person into the doctrine of the Trinity has been and still is a disputed matter in which there is far more at issue than a clever game among professional theologians and more, even, than a pastoral strategy for semantic adapt-ation to a changed situation. At issue in this question is, rather, the correct

286 *The Trinitarian Mystery of God*

conception of the center and basic structure of the Christian message in
the context of modern thought. The issue is the Christian answer to the
situation of atheism that has been brought about by Christian theism.
Above all, the issue is how, in continuity with and yet also in opposition
to the spirit of the modern age, the human person can be properly
understood as the image of the trinitarian God.

The traditional concept of person is undoubtedly an ancient and
venerable one. Admittedly, it is not found in scripture, but the same is true
of many important dogmatic concepts; this is certainly not a sufficient
reason for excluding it from use in dogmatic discourse. 'Not biblical' is far
from the same as 'unbiblical' or 'antibiblical'. The decisive question is not
whether a concept as such occurs in scripture, but whether it represents an
objectively valid interpretation of the biblical testimony. The tradition
undoubtedly regarded the concept of person as that kind of valid interpretation, and as such the concept formed part of the church's official
language beginning with the Second Ecumenical Council, the Council of
Constantinople (381).[127] The language of 'one God in three persons' thus
has the authority of tradition behind it.[128] Tradition as such is not, of
course, a decisive argument. But it becomes one when it gives an objective
interpretation and more precise statement of an original statement of
revelation itself. According to the Catholic view the church can unequivocally raise this kind of interpretation of scripture to the rank of a proposition
of faith. If the church does this and commits itself definitively to it, then
such a proposition is a dogma and no longer merely a theological statement
which in principle can always be revised. The status of dogma does not, of
course, mean that the content conveyed by a particular word cannot be
expressed better, more unmistakably and more profoundly by other
words.[129]

It is with the last-named kind of development that we are concerned
here. For the same tradition that transmits the concept of person also
shows an awareness of the problematic character of the concept of person.
Jerome in his day was already of the opinion that the language of
three hypostases was like honey in which poison was concealed.[130] Even
Augustine was conscious of being in a predicament. He is aware of a
linguistic inadequacy and a poverty of concepts, and he asks: three what?
His answer: 'Three persons – not because I want to say this but because I
may not remain silent.'[131] Anselm of Canterbury even speaks of 'three
something-or-other (*tres nescio quid*)'.[132] Thomas Aquinas, too, realizes
that the adoption of the concept of person, which is not in scripture, was
due to the need of debating with heretics.[133] Finally, Calvin, who takes his

stand on the doctrine of the Trinity as found in the early church, speaks sarcastically of the three mannikins in the Trinity.[134]

The problem was rendered even more acute in the modern age because the concept of person changed in relation to that which was current in the early church and in the Middle Ages. Ever since Locke, 'person' has been looked upon as characterized by self-consciousness: a person is a thinking, rational being endowed with understanding and reflection and capable of knowing itself as itself and as the same thinking being through different times and in different places; this continuity is possible only by reason of self-consciousness, which is inseparable from and essential to thinking.[135] The ontological definition of person was thus transformed into a psychological definition. Kant added a definition geared to morality: 'A *person* is a subject who is capable of having his actions imputed to him.'[136] The definition of person which had been current in the early church and in the Middle Ages and which the doctrine of the Trinity presupposes, thus became open to misunderstanding and even became unintelligible. For the one divine nature evidently excludes three consciousnesses. Now, since the church is not master of the history of concepts and since it must speak within a concrete pre-given linguistic situation and make itself understood therein, the question arises of whether the church in such a situation cannot best ensure the objective continuity of its confession by varying the linguistic expression of it; whether, therefore, in the doctrine of the Trinity it should renounce a concept of person that has become unintelligible and open to misunderstanding and replace it with a better one.

Two suggestions have been made. They come from a well-known Protestant theologian and well-known Catholic theologian. On the Protestant side, and for the reasons already indicated, K. Barth suggests that we 'do not say "person" but "mode of being", with the intention of expressing by this concept the same thing as should be expressed by "Person", not absolutely but relatively better, more simply and more clearly.'[137] K. Rahner rightly judges that such a change is in danger of being misunderstood along modalist lines. He therefore prefers to speak instead of 'three distinct manners of subsisting'.[138] Like Barth, his intention is not to eliminate use of the concept of person; he simply wants to use his own terminology as well, in order to make it clear that the concept of person as used in the doctrine of the Trinity is not perfectly clear and obvious. In addition, Rahner makes unequivocally clear the difference between his suggested language and that of modalism. Moreover, he can appeal in behalf of his suggestion to comparable formulas in Bonaventure and Thomas Aquinas.[139] All in all, we must agree that his suggestion is at least a possible and permissible contribution to discussion in the framework of a Catholic dogmatics.

In a technical theological context Rahner's suggestion can certainly provide the service he claims for it. It is another question, however, whether it is also kerygmatically meaningful – and that, after all, is Rahner's primary concern. It must in fact be said that if the concept of person is open to misunderstanding, the concept of 'distinct manner of subsistence' is unintelligible. Even more than the concept of person it is part of a special code language of theology. Independently of its philosophical use and its 'technical' definition the term 'person' immediately conveys some sort of meaning to every human being, whereas 'distinct manner of subsistence' is an exclusively metalinguistic concept which as such is antecedently unsuited for use in preaching. Furthermore, it is not enough that the trinitarian confession should be marked by logical clarity; this confession is also to be fit for doxological use. But no one can invoke, adore and glorify a distinct manner of subsisting. Finally, for anyone not trained in Scholastic theology, even the concept 'distinct manner of subsisting' can easily be misunderstood as modalist. And nowadays is not modalism or a weak theism a far greater danger than the tritheism which Barth and Rahner conjure up? If, then, we are not to conjure up new misunderstandings and if we are not to turn the trinitarian confession completely into a book with seven seals for the 'ordinary' Christian, we have no choice but to retain the traditional language of the church and interpret it to the faithful. As a matter of fact, Karl Rahner's reflections can be helpful in this area, even though his suggestion for a terminology is unsatisfactory.

All that has been said thus far is at best a preparation for the solution of the problem. For the critical acceptance of the modern concept of person is more a problem of content than of terminology. From this standpoint Barth and Rahner have only apparently rebuffed the modern concept of person as unusable; in reality they have in large measure accepted it. Precisely because they no longer think of God as absolute substance (as the early church and the Middle Ages did) but think of him rather as absolute subject, they have no place for three subjects but only for three modes of being or distinct manners of subsisting. To put it more clearly: because Barth and Rahner accept the modern concept of subject or person, they come to more or less negative conclusions regarding the three persons.[140] But the conclusion is neither cogent from the standpoint of the traditional doctrine of the Trinity nor necessary from the standpoint of the modern concept of person.

From the standpoint of the traditional doctrine of the Trinity it is clear that the unity of being in God entails unity of consciousness. It is impossible to accept three consciousnesses in God. But given this presupposition, which strictly speaking is self-evident in the context of the church's doctrine of the Trinity, Rahner too quickly concludes: therefore no three centers of consciousness and action. In thus rejecting the modern concept of person, Rahner is entirely dependent on Neo-scholasticism.[141] B. Lonergan, who otherwise is also within this tradition, has gone into this question more fully in the framework of the traditional terminology and has been able to show that in this question, as in others, the original Scholasticism was substantially more open than Neo-scholasticism, with its constricted apologetical outlook.[142] For, according to the traditional terminology, we must say that the one divine consciousness subsists in a triple mode. This means that a triple *principium* or subject of the one consciousness must be accepted and, at the same time, that the three subjects cannot be simply unconscious but are conscious of themselves by means of the one consciousness (*principium quo*). This assertion follows, on the one hand, from the fact that the divine persons are really identical with the one being and consciousness and, on the other hand, from the fact that they proceed from spiritual acts of knowledge and love, so that between them there exists a spiritual relationship which by its very nature cannot but be conscious. We have no choice, then, but to say that in the Trinity we are dealing with three subjects who are reciprocally conscious of each other by reason of one and the same consciousness which the three subjects 'possess', each in his own proper way.[143]

With the modern concept of person as his starting point, H. Mühlen in particular has taken an important step forward in applying personalist categories to the doctrine of the Trinity.[144] For what Rahner describes is in fact not at all the full modern understanding of person but rather an extreme individualism in which each person is a center of action who possesses himself, disposes of himself and is set off over against others. But Fichte and Hegel had already moved beyond such a point of view.[145] Ever since the time of Feuerbach modern personalism, as represented by M. Buber, F. Ebner, F. Rosenzweig and others, has made it entirely clear that person exists only in relation; that in the concrete, personality exists only as interpersonality, subjectivity only as intersubjectivity. The human person exists only in relations of the I-Thou-We kind.[146] Within the horizon of this modern understanding of person, an isolated unipersonal God is inconceivable. Thus it is precisely the modern concept of person that offers a point of contact for the doctrine of the Trinity.

It is clear that personalist categories can be applied only analogically to the Trinity. This means that every similarity is accompanied by an even greater dissimiliarity. Since in God not only the unity but also the differentiation and therefore the opposition is always greater than in human interpersonal relationships, the divine persons are not less dialogical but infinitely more dialogical than human persons are. The divine persons are not only in dialogue, they *are* dialogue. The Father is a pure self-enunciation and address to the Son as his Word; the Son is a pure hearing and heeding of the Father and therefore pure fulfillment of his mission; the Holy Spirit is pure reception, pure gift. These personal relations are reciprocal but they are not interchangeable.[147] The Father alone speaks, the Son responds in obedience; the Father, through the Son and with the Son, is the giver, the Holy Spirit is pure recipient. In his answer, therefore, the Son is not thought of as also speaking; the Spirit is not thought of as also giving. It does not follow from this, however, that there is no reciprocal Thou. Responding in obedience and owing one's being to another are also forms of Thou-saying, but a Thou-saying that takes seriously the uniqueness both of one's own and of the other's person. In other words: in God and among the divine persons, and because of, not despite, their infinitely greater unity, there is also an infinitely greater inter-relationality and interpersonality than in human inter-personal relations.

J. Ratzinger in particular has made his own these insights. According to him, the concept of person 'by reason of its origin expresses the idea of dialogue and of God as a dialogical being. It points to God as the being who lives in the Word and subsists in the Word as I and Thou and We'.[148] Ratzinger is aware of the revolution which this concept of person as relation represents.[149] Neither the substance of the ancients nor the person of the moderns is ultimate, but rather relation as the primordial category of reality. The statement that persons are relations is, of course, first of all simply a statement about the trinity of God, but important conclusions follow from it with regard to man as image and likeness of God. Man is neither a self-sufficient in-himself (substance) nor an autonomous individual for-himself (subject) but a being from God and to God, from other human beings and to other human beings; he lives humanly only in I-Thou-We relations. Love proves to be the meaning of his being.

3. Systematic understanding of the doctrine of the Trinity

(a) Unity in trinity

From the very beginning, the God-question, as we have seen, has been bound up with the question of the unity of all reality.[150] This generalization holds for the religions as well as for philosophy. The question of unity is not a purely academic one; in the final analysis it is *the* question of salvation.

Only where unity exists can there be meaning and order; disruption, alienation and chaos, on the other hand, are the signs of disaster. From the philosophical standpoint unity is the presupposition of truth, goodness and beauty; for all these transcendental properties of being signify in their different ways an order and coordination which presuppose unity in the sense of self-identity and are the ground for unity in the sense of wholeness and integrity. To say this much is already to suggest a second point: that unity is unthinkable without multiplicity, at least in the finite world. As Blaise Pascal puts it: 'Multiplicity which is not reduced to unity is confusion. Unity which does not depend on multiplicity is tyranny'.[151] The question of unity is therefore the question of how multiplicity and variety can be so brought into unity that the unity does not swallow up the multiplicity in a totalitarian way and, on the other hand, that the unity is not located beyond all the multiplicity and radically separated from the world, as it is in Neoplatonism. In other words, what solution is possible that is not either pantheistic or dualistic?

God's oneness and uniqueness is a part of the basic Old Testament message that is fully accepted in the New Testament.[152] In proclaiming this message the Bible is in its own way responding to a primordial question of the human race. For in the Bible the one God is the ground of the unity of salvation history in the orders of creation and salvation, and this under both the old and the new covenants. Salvation history has for its goal eschatological *shalom*: the salvation and wholeness of the human person as part of one human race in one world in which God is 'all in all' (I Cor. 15.28). Faith in the one God who effects salvation through the one Lord Jesus Christ and communicates this salvation in the one Spirit with his many gifts is therefore the salvation of humanity; in this one God, human beings find their identity and wholeness, for they are taken into the unity of Father, Son and Spirit. According to John 17.21, the unity of Father and Son is the ground of the unity of their disciples; and the unity of the latter is in turn directed to the unity of the world.[153] In other words: the Christian doctrine of the Trinity is the Christian form of monotheism that can and must prove its worth as the Christian answer to the world's quest of salvation.

In the history of theology and dogma this problem was debated and settled under the rubric of 'monarchianism'. That debate gave expression as it were to the primordial philosophical concern to trace everything back to a single supreme principle, as in the prophetic message regarding Yahweh as the sole God. The monarchy of God was therefore an essential part of early Christian catechesis.[154] It is all the more surprising, therefore, that the concept of monarchy, originally so basic and venerable, should soon have lost its importance as applied to God. The reason for this development is that at an early date heresies made their appearance which adopted as their slogan: '*Monarchiam tenemus* (We hold fast to the monarchy).'[155] Tertullian called such people 'Monarchians'.[156] These errors appeared in the second and third centuries in two forms.[157] The subordinationist Monarchians (a simpler form in Theodotus the Tanner and Theodotus the Money-Changer; a clearer form in Paul of Samosata) endeavored to preserve the monarchy of God by subordinating the Son and the Spirit to the one God. The modalist Monarchians (initially Noetus and Praxeas; a more developed form in Sabellius) sought to do the same by understanding Father, Son and Spirit to be three modes (*modi*) or three faces or masks (*prosōpon*, which later = person) of the one divinity. Both interpretations conflicted with the New Testament language of the one God, the one Son of God and the one Holy Spirit.

But there was more. Aristotle had already seen that underlying monotheism there is an entire political and metaphysical program.[158] This analysis was borne out in the debates over Christian monotheism. Arianism, the fully developed form of subordinationist Monarchianism, stated with a radical separation of God and the world and was therefore compelled to join the two by means of the Logos as an intermediary being. On the other hand, for modalistic Monarchianism, as for Stoicism, God and the world were pantheistically identified, so that the divine showed itself over and over again in the history of the world in constantly new forms.[159] The two conceptions got tangled up in positions contradictory to the Monarchian concern that inspired them. The first of the two ended up in a polytheism in which the one divinity expressed itself in the world in and through all sorts of subordinate divine beings. The second position ultimately amounted to atheism,[160] for if everything is God, then nothing is God; God adds nothing to the existence of the world. Pantheism is thus simply a more refined form of atheism. This makes it clear that these two errors, subordinationist and modalist Monarchianism, are not solely of historical interest but have an abiding relevance. They represent two possible – or impossible – ways of thinking about the relationship between God and the world; they crop up ever anew in theology, and in response to them the Christian understanding of God and the resultant Christian relation between God and world must likewise be expounded ever anew.[161]

Basil clearly recognized the importance of the issue. He saw in subordinationist monarchianism a relapse into polytheistic paganism[162] and in modalist monarchianism a 'Judaism in Christian clothing'.[163] He found himself caught up in a battle on two fronts.[164] Thus it is that in the effort to preserve and defend the biblical trinity-in-unity of God against pagan polytheism and Jewish monotheism the real issue is the proper and specific character of Christian monotheism.

The Christian response to heretical Monarchianism, along with the development of a Christian monotheism, was no easy matter, and it took time. A first, still provisional and inadequate answer is found in Tertullian and, in a different form, in Origen. Tertullian had recourse to the political concept of monarchy, which did not at all exclude the idea of the monarch giving his son a share in his rule or even exercising his rule through his son.[165] This conception has the advantage of making possible a salvation-historical vision of the Trinity. But the subordinationism it implies leads indirectly to a pagan polytheism in which the one invisible divine being encounters us in many subordinate intermediate forms. The only way of making valid progress at this point was to reflect on the metaphysical implications of the divine oneness.

Irenaeus, Tertullian and Origen were already moving in this direction when in their opposition to gnosticism they explained the unity of God along the lines of simplicity and spirituality.[166] A graduated participation in the divine being of God was thus excluded. Athanasius made this idea of the simplicity and indivisibility of God a cardinal point in his refutation of Arius.[167] Precisely because God is indivisibly one, the Son and the Spirit cannot be a kind of partial God and certainly not a second and third divinity. The subordinationism of the Arians was thus excluded from the nature of God. The three great Cappadocian fathers argued along the same lines: Basil at the head, his friend Gregory of Nazianzus, and his brother Gregory of Nyssa. Basil distinguished between one according to number (the numerically one) and one according to nature or substance (the essentially one). The numerically one presupposes quantity, and there can be no question of it in connection with God;[168] the essentially one entails the simplicity of the purely spiritual, by reason of which God is wholly beyond number and is therefore one not according to number but by nature.[169] The nature of God and its oneness thus excluded not only a threeness with various levels (subordinationism) but also a threeness at the same level (tritheism).

The question of how any trinity at all is thinkable within this essential unity becomes thematic in Gregory of Nazianzus. He makes reference to Plotinus, according to whom the many cannot be conceived without the one, but neither can the one be thought of without the many. Plotinus concludes from this that the one overflows into the many. Gregory emphatically rejects this necessary overflow, because it is incompatible with the concept of the divinity.[170] The intrinsic basis for this rejection is clear: if God necessarily overflows out upon the world, or in other words, if God needs the world in order to be able to be the one God, then he is not really God at all. The transcendence and freedom of God are preserved only if the world is not necessary for God to be himself. If, then, both the *unity* of God and the unity of *God* are to be conceivable, the reconciliation of unity and plurality must take place within God himself. We can put this point more precisely: if the unity of God is to be conceivable, then it can be conceived, on the one hand, only in relation to multiplicity and, on the other, only as qualitatively distinct from multiplicity and therefore only as absolutely transcendent. Both of these conditions are met in the confession of the trinity that is immanent in the unity of God. Later on, John Damascene developed this idea with full clarity: if we look at God from below, we encounter a single being; but if we express what this being comprises or what it is in itself, we must speak of the trinity of persons.[171] In this sense the Christian confession preserves the monarchy of God, but it concretizes and states in detail what this monarchy is in its inner nature. To that extent the trinitarian confession is monotheism in concrete form.[172] 'The doctrine of the three-in-oneness of God . . . means . . . not a removal or even a mere querying, but rather the final and decisive confirmation, of the insight that God is One.'[173] The trinitarian doctrine is concerned with the self-communication of God.[174] It says that the one God is not a solitary God.[175]

The church's confession of faith incorporated these clarifications. In fact, in the matter of the unity of God the creed is remarkably unambiguous. Ever since Nicaea and Constantinople I and II it has not simply confessed the one being and the one substance of God;[176] it has also rejected not only tritheism[177] but also a collectivist and symbolical understanding of a unity modelled on a community of persons, as proposed by Joachim of Flora.[178] The official language of the magisterium is extremely precise and differentiated in this area. The Eleventh Provincial Council of Toledo (675) remarks with regard to the concept of *trinitas*: 'not threefold but Trinity'.[179] The *Roman Catechism* expressly observes that we were baptized not in the names but in the name of the Father and of the Son and of the Holy Spirit.[180] Finally, in the Bull *Auctorem fidei* (1794) Pius VI states that we can talk of God as 'in three distinct persons (*in tribus personis distinctis*)', but not as 'divided into three persons (*in tribus personis distinctus*)'.[181]

The modern age has to a great extent abondoned this concrete Christian monotheism in favor of the abstract theism of a unipersonal God who stands over against man as the perfect Thou or over man as imperial ruler and judge.[182] In the final analysis this conception is the popular form of a Christianity half under the influence of the Enlightenment, or else the religious remnant of Christianity in a secularized society. From the theological standpoint we must speak more accurately of the heresy of theism. This theism with its unipersonal God is untenable for a variety of reasons. For one thing, if we imagine God as the other-worldly counterpart of man, then despite all the personal categories we use we will ultimately think of him in objectivist terms as a being who is superior to other beings. When this happens, God is being conceived as a finite entity who comes in conflict with finite reality and the modern understanding of it. Then we must either conceive God at the expense of man and the world, or conceive the world at the expense of God, thus limiting God in deistic fashion and finally eliminating him entirely with the atheists. This conversion of theism into a-theism also takes place for another reason: theism almost necessarily falls under the suspicion voiced by the critics of religion, that the theistic God is a projection of the human ego and a hypostatized idol, or that theism is ultimately a form of idolatry.

This legitimate criticism of a feeble theism must not, of course, be replaced by an ambiguous and wavering conception of a Christian a-theism.[183] Nor should the search for a position beyond theism and atheism be expanded into a rejection of monotheism. A trinitarian God that is not at the same time the monotheistic God must necessarily lead to a kind of tritheism.[184] In response to atheism, the need is rather to show the trinitarian confession to be the Christian form of monotheism, and to make it clear once again that the Trinity is the condition for a consistent monotheism. Against all the incorrectly posed questions it must be made clear that in the doctrine of the Trinity there is no question of denying either the revelation of the Trinity or the divine unity both as revealed and as known to reason. The church does not hold on to the unity of God despite the doctrine of the Trinity. Rather, in the doctrine of the Trinity it is precisely holding fast to Christian monotheism. It even maintains that the doctrine of the Trinity is the only possible and consistent form of monotheism[185] and the only tenable answer to modern atheism.

The considerations thus far proposed on trinity in unity are still very formal and abstract. They seem far removed from the concrete language the Bible uses in speaking of God the Father who reveals his love and communicates himself to us through Jesus Christ in the Holy Spirit. In fact, however, my intention in these considerations has been to express and safeguard this gracious freedom of God in his self-communicating love. Their point has been, against all emanationist systems, whether gnostic or Neoplatonic, that there is no necessary overflow of the divine One out upon the many of the world; that God rather reconciles unity and multiplicity within himself; that within his very being he is overflowing love and that only because he is love within himself can the overflow of his love upon the world be conceived as not necessary but free and gratuitous. Only because God is love within himself can he be love for us. Consequently, the abstract and formal considerations I have set forth are a way of saying: God is love. Love is that which reconciles unity and multiplicity; it is the uniting unity in the threeness.

Such is the common conviction of both the Eastern and the Latin Western traditions. However, the East and the West have developed different theological systems on this common basis.[186] The two systems may be described somewhat schematically as follows. In their theology of the Trinity the Greeks start with the three hypostases or persons; more precisely, they start with the Father as origin and source within the Godhead. Their concern is to protect the monarchy of the Father, who as sole origin ensures unity in the Trinity. According to the Greek understanding it is the one God the Father who bestows his divine nature on the Son, so that the Son possesses the one identical divine nature with the Father. The same holds for the Holy Spirit, who proceeds from the Father and receives the one divine nature from the Father (through the Son). The Greek conception thus starts with the persons and advances from one person to another. Unity is assured by the Father as origin and source of the divinity and as principle of its unity; the one nature is thus envisaged only indirectly.

The Latin approach is different and has largely been determined by the genius of Augustine. The Latins begin directly with the one divine nature or the one divine substance and one divine being. The three persons come into view only mediately as three personal, i.e., distinct manners in which the one substance subsists. The one divine being does not exclude the three persons (that would be Sabellianism), but rather exists only in these three personal manners of subsisting. Nonetheless, the one divine being is the basis on which everything is built in the effort to understand the three persons in God. For knowing and willing are the essential activities of the spiritual nature. In knowing himself, God begets his eternal Word; he is therefore Father and Son. The Holy Spirit then proceeds as the third person from the mutual love of both Father and Son. In this conception of the Trinity, unity in trinity is made psychologically intelligible; for this reason historians speak of a psychological doctrine of the Trinity in Augustine. The difference between the Greeks and the Latins can be formulated thus: The Greeks say 'One God in three persons', the Latins say 'Three persons in God.'

The difference between the two approaches can also be brought out with the help of images. The line is a suitable image for the Greek conception: the Father begets the Son, and through the Son the Holy Spirit proceeds from him. In the procession of the Spirit the life process in the Trinity reaches its completion, while at the same time in the Spirit it also presses out beyond itself. A triangle or a circle is a more suitable image for the Latin conception: the Father begets the Son; the circle of trinitarian life is then closed in the Spirit as the reciprocal love between Father and Son. The Greek conception is thus more open to the world, while the Latin is more self-enclosed. This difference can also be seen in artistic representations of the Trinity. The classical artistic representation of the Trinity in the Orthodox Church is of the three men or angels visiting Abraham (Gen. 18) – three figures who, however, in Rublev's famous ikon are depicted as forming an incomparably beautiful unity. The most important ecclesiastical representation of the Trinity in the Western church is the 'Throne of Grace', in which the three persons form a single united figure: the Father sits on the throne and holds the cross with the Son on it, while between the two the Spirit hovers in the form of a dove.

Each of the two conceptions is magnificent in its own way, but each also has its dangers. It is clear that the Greek conception is more concrete and more biblical and reflects the history of salvation. But it formally asserts the inner unity of the three persons rather than makes this unity intelligible from within. The Latin conception is by comparison the fruit of greater reflection and speculative thought, but it is also more abstract. It is in danger of being unable to bring out fully the distinction of the three persons and, ultimately, in danger of letting the three persons evaporate as it were into mere *modi*, modes of being of the one divine nature. This danger is especially present in the form which Anselm of Canterbury gave to the Latin doctrine of the Trinity. As a result, the Western conception has often been subjected to rather sharp attacks from Orthodox theologians, who even accuse it of being a radical revision of the trinitarian dogma.[187] Even among Catholics a latent preference for the Eastern conception is ascertainable today.

The clash of the two approaches comes to a head especially in the dispute about the *filioque*.[188] The Greeks accuse the Latin formula of eliminating the monarchy of the Father and dissolving the unity in God because it accepts two processions in God; they object, in addition, that it identifies the Spirit with the nature common to the Father and the Son and therefore unable to ensure the hypostatic independence of the Spirit. The Latins dismiss these objections as misunderstandings of their conception of the Trinity. They, too, say that it is from the Father that the Son has his 'power' to spirate the Spirit; consequently the Spirit proceeds *principaliter* from the Father, so that the latter's monarchy is preserved in the Latin conception no less than in the Greek. Finally, even in the Latin conception the Spirit does not proceed from the one divine nature but from the two persons (*duo spirantes*) who as persons form a single principle in the procession of the Spirit[189]

More important than such disputes, which are basically fruitless because they are based on mutual ignorance or misunderstandings, is the realization that the contrast between the two conceptions makes a valid point but also that these schematic generalizations do not do justice to a historical reality which shows far more diversity.[190] Thus in the East alongside the conception of the Cappadocians there is also that of the Alexandrians, and especially of Athanasius, which corresponds more to the Latin conception. Even John

Damascene, who sums up the patristic tradition in a way that has become normative for Orthodoxy, starts with the one God and only then passes on to a presentation of the three hypostases.[191] Elsewhere, too, among the Greek fathers we come upon formulas that have a very essentialist ring; for example, God from God, Light from Light, Essence from Essence, Wisdom from Wisdom, and so on.[192] Conversely, in addition to the essentialist tradition which was established by Augustine and was intensified to the extreme by Anselm of Canterbury[193] and which is represented today by K. Barth and K. Rahner,[194] there is also a more 'personalist' tradition. It was adopted in antiquity by Hilary of Poitiers and in the Middle Ages by William of St Thierry,[195] the friend of Bernard of Clairvaux and the adversary of Abelard, a modalist. Its most important representative is Richard of St. Victor, who wrote the most important treatise on the Trinity between Augustine and Thomas Aquinas. He was followed by Alexander of Hales and Bonaventure.[196] In their own way all of these theologians make their own the concern which the Greeks sum up in the 'monarchy of the Father' and which Augustine too respects, since he – like Bonaventure and Thomas Aquinas later on – teaches that the Spirit proceeds *principaliter* from the Father. A doctrine of the Trinity that is decidedly based on the history of salvation is to be found in the Middle Ages in Rupert of Deutz, Gerhoh of Reichersberg, Anselm of Havelberg, and others.[197]

In this as in many other questions Thomas Aquinas sought for a synthesis that would strike a balance between the various conceptions; he ended with one that is really not very far removed from that of John Damascene, whose writings Thomas knew well and esteemed highly.[198] Thomas Aquinas is thus proof that we must not exaggerate the differences between East and West. The differences exist, but they do not reach up to heaven, and the walls that have often been artificially erected are transparent and permeable in both directions. As Thomas Aquinas in particular shows, the Western tradition is in a position to make its own all the concerns of the East and to elevate these to a higher level of reflection.

The defect in the main strand of Western tradition is that it interprets the adjustment of trinity to unity as a matter of knowing and willing and therefore of essential actions of God. This brings with it the danger that the persons may be misunderstood as ideal phases in the self-fulfillment of the absolute spirit. This tendency, which ultimately leads to modalism, can be avoided only if we keep in mind that the spirit, and especially the absolute spirit, subsists concretely only as a person and that as far as man is concerned everything depends precisely on this understanding of God as person. For human beings, as persons, can find their salvation only in the absolute person of God. But according to the scriptures and the early Christian tradition the person God whom we seek is the Father. Therefore the doctrine of the Trinity must start with the Father and understand him as origin, source and inner ground of unity in the Trinity. We must start with the Father as the groundless Ground of a self-communicating love which brings the Son and the Spirit into being and at the same time unites itself with them in one love. If we thus take God's sovereign freedom in love as the starting point and focus of unity in the Trinity, we are moving, unlike the predominant Latin tradition, not from the nature of God but from the Father who originally possesses the being of God that consists in love. For love cannot be thought of except as personal and inter-personal.[199] The person, therefore, cannot exist except in self-communication to others and in acknowledgment by others. For this reason, once God is thought of from the start as personal, the oneness and unicity of God cannot possibly be conceived as meaning a solitary God. Here we have the deepest reason why the theistic notion of a unipersonal God cannot be maintained. Such a view will be compelled to look for a counterpart for God, find it in the world and man, and, by setting up a necessary relation between God and the world, be unable any longer to preserve the transcendence of God and his freedom in love. If we want to maintain, in an intellectually consistent way, the biblical message about God as absolute person and perfect freedom in love, the trinitarian confession of faith becomes plausible to the believing mind.

The objection against this thesis, that it infringes upon the mysteriousness of the Trinity, is not a real objection. The difference (which is not open to inspection by the human mind) between love among human beings and love in God consists in this, that a human being *has* love while God *is* love. Because a human being has love and this love does not constitute his entire being, he or she is united to other persons through love without thereby becoming one being with them; among human beings, love grounds a close and profound communion of persons but not an identity of being. God, on the contrary, *is* love, and this nature of his is absolutely simple and unique; therefore all three persons possess a single being; their unity is a unity of essence and not simply a communion of persons. The trinity in the unity of the one essence is the unfathomable mystery of the trinity; we can never plumb it by reason but can only make it accessible to the believing mind in rudimentary ways.

(b) Trinity in unity

Since the trinity of persons in the unity of the one divine nature is an unfathomable mystery for the human mind, the starting point for a systematic understanding of the trinity of divine persons can only be revelation. In order to understand this mystery of trinity in unity as a mystery we must therefore start not with the one divine nature and its immanent essential actions (knowing and willing) but with the revelation of the Father through the Son in the Holy Spirit. It is in the perspective of this one mystery of the Christian reality of salvation that we must seek to understand the mystery of the three divine persons. Along these lines we have at the present time two approaches in particular that seek, each in its own way, to understand the salvation-historical or economic Trinity by way of the immanent Trinity, and this in terms either of the root of the Trinity itself (K. Barth)[200] or of a systematic conception (K. Rahner).[201] The two theologians proceed in quite different ways that are characteristic of the theological thinking of each. Both have in common, however, that they do not start with the formula *una substantia – tres personae* (one substance, three persons) and that they think of God not as substance but as subject, whether as subject of a self-revelation (K. Barth) or as subject of a self-communication (K. Rahner).

K. Barth starts with the concept of revelation because he is convinced that this contains within itself the problem of the Trinity.[202] In his view, the root of the doctrine of the Trinity is the statement: 'God reveals Himself as the Lord.'[203] This sentence means that God is 'the same in unimpaired unity, yet also the same in unimpaired variety thrice in a different way', namely, as revealer, revelation and revealedness.[204] Revelation is 'the self-unveiling, imparted to men, of the God who according to His nature cannot be unveiled to men'. Because he is so sovereignly free, God 'can become so unlike Himself that He is God in such a way as not to be bound to His secret eternity and eternal secrecy, but also can and will and really does assume temporal form'.[205] But in this process he himself remains the Revealer. Precisely as *Deus revelatus* he is still the *Deus absconditus*.[206] He is the sovereign subject of his own revelation. Finally, revelation also means revealedness, for revelation also includes the self-unveiling that is granted to men. It is a historical event through which the existence of certain human beings is so affected that while they cannot indeed grasp God, they are able to follow him and respond to him.[207] Barth's doctrine of the Trinity thus brings out the unchangeable subjectivity of God[208] and is thereby a variant on the modern theme of subjectivity and its autonomy.[209] The three modes of being in which the Trinity manifests itself belong to the self-constitution of the absolute subject. This is a distinctly modern or, more accurately, a distinctly idealist pattern of thought, which links Barth to Hegel despite all the material differences between them.[210]

We find a similar thought structure in K. Rahner. In keeping with his anthropological approach to theology his starting point is of course the subjectivity not of God but of man. This means that he aims to understand the mystery of the Trinity as a mystery of salvation. Salvation occurs when man's indigent relatedness to an absolute mystery is filled by the irreducibly free and gracious self-communication of this mystery. In this sense Rahner can say: 'Man is the event of a free, unmerited and forgiving, and absolute self-communication of God.'[211] The concept of self-communication includes 'the absolute nearness of God as the incomprehensible mystery which remains forever such', 'the absolute freedom . . . of this self-communication', and 'that the inner possibility of the self-communication as such . . . can never be perceived'.[212] The doctrine of the Trinity emerges from this concept of self-communication by way of a kind of transcendental reflection on the conditions of its possibility.[213] The Trinity is thus the condition for the possibility of human subjectivity.

Rahner's starting point for a systematic understanding of the Trinity is thus the basic concept of his theology of grace: the concept of divine self-communication. According to Rahner, there are in fact two different but interrelated and mutually conditioning modes of free, unmerited self-communication on God's part: in Jesus Christ and in the Spirit. The two can be understood as moments in the one self-communication.[214] For self-communication signifies both origin and future (event of the radically new), history and transcendence, offer and acceptance, and, finally, truth as revelation personal being and love as the freely offered and freely accepted self-communication of the person.[215] But this self-communication in the history of salvation would not truly be God's self-communication unless it also belonged to God in himself, that is, unless the economic Trinity were also the immanent Trinity.[216] In the final analysis, by means of this transcendental theological deduction Rahner has renewed the essentials of Augustine's trinitarian speculation, although in doing so he has proceeded not by way of the *analogia entis* but by way of a synoptic presentation of the history of salvation itself. According to Rahner, too, there are two moments, knowledge and love, which yield two distinct manners of subsisting of the self-communicating God or, more specifically, of the Father.[217] Rahner can therefore summarize as follows the meaning of the doctrine of the Trinity: 'God himself as the abiding holy mystery, as the incomprehensible ground of man's transcendent existence is not only the God of infinite distance, but also wants to be the God of absolute closeness in a true self-communication, and he is present in this way in the spiritual depths of our existence as well as in the concreteness of our corporeal history.'[218]

We cannot but admire the coherent way in which with the economic Trinity as his starting point Rahner attempts a theology of the Trinity from within; how at the same time he theologizes on the Trinity in the context of the modern philosophy of subjectivity; and how, last but not least, he succeeds in doing justice to the meaning of the formulas of the classical tradition. The result is undoubtedly a bold and successful design that can only be classed with other great productions of Christian theology and that can best be compared with Anselm's deduction of the doctrine of the Trinity from *rationes necessariae*.

This new approach of Karl Rahner has, of course, some major consequences. This is already clear from the fact that in Rahner's *Foundations of Christian Faith* the doctrine of the Trinity no longer provides the supporting framework, as it did in the creed of the early church and in the theology which interpreted that creed. In fact, the doctrine of the Trinity does not even form a special part, but only a sub-section of about four pages, two of which are spent on a critical discussion of the traditional doctrine of the Trinity, so that the positive presentation is compressed into about two pages. This external allocation of space already makes it clear that the doctrine of the Trinity has handed over its structuring role to theological anthropology and is now studied only as a condition for the possibility of the doctrine of grace. This change of function, secondly, has important effects on the inner meaning of the doctrine of the Trinity. For when it is developed, as it is in Rahner, entirely under the sign of soteriology, it loses its character of doxology. While the subjectivity of man is in danger of being lost in Barth's thematizing of God as absolute subject in his theology of the Trinity, it is the Thou of God that is in danger of being lost in Rahner's thematizing of the subjectivity of man in his theology of the Trinity. Rahner does succeed in taking seriously the modern idea of man's subjectivity (although this is conceived in narrowly individualistic terms), but he does not succeed in thinking the Trinity in the mode of subjectivity. This accounts for his radical rejection of the modern concept of person as utilizable in the doctrine of the Trinity.[219] As I said earlier, we cannot invoke, adore and glorify 'distinct manners of subsisting'. We can only fall silent before Rahner's ultimately nameless mystery of God. It is not without reason that a well-known, beautiful, attractive and profound little book of Rahner on prayer bears the title 'Words into Silence'.[220]

Thirdly, when place and meaningful form are thus changed, alterations in internal structure are unavoidable. Since in Rahner's theology of the Trinity everything focuses on the relation and unity of God and man, there is really no room left for the relations and unity of the trinitarian persons themselves. They are moments in the economic self-communication of God to man, but not subjects of an immanent self-communication. Rahner does succeed in showing more clearly than Scholasticism has done the inalienable function of each of the three divine 'persons' in the history of salvation. He repeatedly attacks the view that in the abstract each of the three persons could have become man. But he does not succeed in arguing back from this to the immanent properties of the persons. His trinitarian speculation thus stops short of the goal; it is unable to show clearly in what the special character and difference of each hypostasis consists and what comprehensible meaning each has. Nor may one say that from an existential and soteriological standpoint such questions are simply an unimportant theological parlor game. For if the immanent Trinity is the economic Trinity, then deficiencies in the doctrine of the immanent Trinity must necessarily influence the understanding of the Trinity in the history of salvation. If the divine hypostases in God are not subjects, then they cannot speak and act as subjects in the history of salvation. This consequence shows up clearly in Rahner's statements about the hypostatic union. To the question: 'Which I speaks in Jesus Christ?' he rightly answers that we must attribute to Jesus a genuine human and creaturely self-consciousness if we are not to fall into a new form of monophysitism.[221] But it is not so clear in Rahner that this human I subsists in the hypostasis of the Logos, so that in Jesus Christ the Logos himself speaks and acts; it is not so clear that in the man Jesus Christ God is not only present in a unique and unsurpassable way but that in addition Jesus Christ *is* the Son of God.[222] In fact, Rahner sees the hypostatic union more as a unique and unsurpassable mode of a self-communication that is in principle promised to all human beings; he sees it as an intrinsic moment and a condition for the universal bestowal of grace on spiritual creatures.[223] Given his approach, this is a consistent position, but also one that shows the inherent limitations of the approach itself.

We can develop our own systematic approach to the doctrine of the Trinity if, while bearing in mind all the questions and answers of the tradition, we listen once again to the testimony of scripture, which is the primordial document of the faith. I shall once again start with the final prayer of Jesus, the so-called high-priestly prayer in John 17, which, as we saw earlier, provides the clearest New Testament basis for a doctrine of the Trinity.[224] This prayer was uttered at the moment when Jesus saw his hour coming, since the eschaton was at hand (17.1, 5, 7). As a result, this prayer, spoken at the moment of departure, contains as it were the testament of Jesus. At the moment of completion it once again summarizes the overall meaning of the saving work of Jesus Christ, and it does this in trinitarian form. The high-priestly prayer contains the entire doctrine of the Trinity in basic form and in a nutshell.

1. *The meaning of the doctrine of the Trinity.* The high-priestly prayer begins with the words: 'Father, the hour has come; glorify thy Son that the Son may glorify thee' (17.1). The reference is to the eschatological hour, the hour when the entire work of salvation is completed in a comprehensive and surpassing manner. This completion takes place in the cross and exaltation of Jesus as the eschatological revelation of God. When the Father glorifies the Son by exalting him, the Father himself is in turn glorified by the Son; in the glorification of the Son the Father's own glorification is made manifest. The Son's glory is that which he has from eternity with the Father (v. 5). The eschatological revelation, then, is a revelation of the eternal being of God, a revelation of the Godness of God. It is said that from eternity God possesses the glory of his Godness because the Father glorifies the Son and the Son in turn glorifies the Father.

Now the faithful are incorporated into this eternal doxology. They have accepted and acknowledged the revelation of the Father's glory by the Son and of the Son's glory by the Father. The Son is therefore glorified in them (v. 10). This glorification takes place through the action of the 'other Paraclete', the Spirit of truth. He guides the faithful into the whole truth; but because he says nothing on his own authority but only says what Jesus is and what Jesus has from the Father, he too acknowledges the glory of the Son and of the Father (16.13–15). The Spirit is, and effects, the concrete presence of the eternal doxology of Father and Son in the church and in the world. He is the eschatological accomplishment of the glory of God; he is its presence within the confines of history. This is possible only because he himself proceeds from the Father (15.26) and because as Spirit of truth he is the revealedness and radiance (*doxa*) of the eternal glory of God.

The intention of the trinitarian confession is thus not really a teaching about God but the doxology or eschatological glorification of God. The doctrine of the Trinity is as it were simply the grammar of the doxology. The trinitarian confession is concerned with the 'Glory be to the Father through the Son in the Holy Spirit'. In this liturgical hymn of praise the eternal glory of God the Father, Son and Holy Spirit is revealed in an eschatological and definitive way. The eschatological glorification of God is at the same time the salvation and life of the world. 'This is eternal life, that they know thee the only true God, and Jesus Christ whom thou hast sent' (v. 3). In the intention of scripture this confession is not abstract speculation but participation and communion of life. The issue in the trinitarian confession is therefore communion with God. The doctrine of the Trinity acquires its meaning from the unity-in-tension of doxology and soteriology. There is no need to choose between the approaches of Karl Barth and Karl Rahner.

The unity-in-tension of doxology and soteriology means that the acknowledgment of God's glory does not represent a humiliation for humanity. The acknowledgment of God's absolute subjectivity does not mean a suppression of our subjectivity; on the contrary, this acknowledgment redeems, liberates and fulfills humanity. Thus the trinitarian confession is the final concrete determination of our undetermined openness and of the idea of God that gleams indeterminately therein and lights the way for all thinking and action.[225] It is the surpassing answer to the question which we do not simply *have* but *are*. The meaning of humanity and the world, and the life and truth of humanity and the world, consist in the glorification of the triune God, and through this glorification we are incorporated into the intra-trinitarian glorification and we have communion with God. In the trinitarian confession, then, the meaning of Jesus' message about the coming of God's reign is fulfilled in an anticipatory manner. For that message too is concerned precisely with the revelation of the lordship and glory of God as life of the world and fulfillment of human hope.[226] In its deepest meaning the doctrine of the Trinity is the normative explanation of Jesus' message about the kingdom. It sums up the core of Jesus' message and is the summation of the Christian faith.

2. *The content of the doctrine of the Trinity.* According to the high-priestly prayer, the glorification of God and the life of the world consists in knowing and acknowledging the God of Jesus Christ as 'the only true God' (v. 3). Unity and uniqueness are essential predicates of God. Once again, then, there is question of the knowledge of the nature of God, of God's Godness. This knowledge of the oneness of God is distinguished both from philosophical monotheism and from the monotheism of the Old Testament by the fact that it includes knowledge of him whom the Father has sent (v. 3) and who is one with the Father (v. 21f.). The world has not known the oneness of God; he alone who from eternity is one with the Father has brought knowledge of this oneness and has revealed the name of the Father (v. 25f.; cf. 1.18). Knowledge of the unity and oneness of God is possible only through knowledge of the unity between Father and Son. Into this oneness, too, the faithful are to be incorporated. They are to 'be one even as we are one' (v. 22), and they are to be made perfect in this oneness (v. 23). This unity of the faithful among themselves as well as with the Father and the Son is the work of the Spirit, according to John as well as the rest of the New Testament. This connection is clearly brought out in John 14.15–24. The coming and remaining of the Spirit is at the same time the return of Jesus and his dwelling in the faithful, so that he is in them as he is in the Father.

The revelation of the Trinity is thus the revelation of the deepest and utterly hidden nature of the unity and oneness of God, which in turn grounds the unity of the church and, via the church, the unity of the world. In its content, then, the doctrine of the Trinity is the Christian form of monotheism. More accurately: the doctrine of the Trinity concretizes the initially abstract assertion of the unity and oneness of God by determining in what this oneness consists. The oneness of God is defined as a communion of Father and Son, but indirectly and implicitly also as a communion of Father, Son and Spirit; it is defined as unity in love.

The precise meaning of unity in love becomes known by contrasting it with other forms of unity.[227] In the material world we encounter quantitative unity and therefore units that can be counted. Each of these units is composed of various linked entities; science has not succeeded, at least thus far, in throwing light on the ultimate and smallest units. The delimitation and numerical pooling of such quantitative units presupposes universal concepts of species and genus. These generic and specific unities are the work of the human powers of abstraction. They presuppose the unity of the person. The person is a unity that exists in and for itself and is therefore capable of bringing into focus and reflecting on its own multiple dimensions in self-consciousness. But even though the person is a unity that cannot be communicated to a higher unity, its existence is nonetheless possible only in co-existence with other persons. The human person is possible only in the plural; it can exist only in reciprocal acknowledgment, and it finds its fulfillment only in the communion of love. Persons thus exist only in mutual giving and receiving.

In this final observation we have developed a preapprehension that enables us to understand the unity in love which according to the Gospel of John exists in God and is the very being of God. It is, of course, only a preapprehension that can be applied only analogically to God. For in the human realm the co-existence of persons is an expression of their finiteness and neediness. Human persons are dependent on each other in a great variety of ways. No single person is wholly identical with himself; none exhausts the nature of humanity and all of its possibilities. Among human beings, therefore, communion in love is always erotic as well; that is, the love is a love that seeks fulfillment. All this is excluded from God by his very nature. God does not possess being; he *is* Being in absolute perfection that has no slightest trace of neediness. He is therefore absolute oneness, perfect self-identity and complete self-possession, personal unity in the most perfect sense.

And yet if God is not to be understood as a solitary narcissistic being who (to put it paradoxically) would be highly imperfect by reason of his very perfection and would inevitably suffer from his own completeness, then God can only be conceived as co-existent. On the other hand, if God is to remain God and not become dependent on the world or man, then he must be co-existent within himself. Within the unity and simplicity of his being he must be a communion in love, and this love cannnot be a love marked by need but only a love that gives out of the overflowing fulness of his being. This is why in his farewell prayer Jesus speaks repeatedly of giving (vv. 2, 6, 22). Because God in his perfection and simplicity is everything and does not possess anything, he can give only himself. He can only be a pure giving and bestowing of himself. God's oneness must be thought of as love that exists only in the giving of itself. In God, therefore, the communion of love is not a communion of separate beings, as it is among men, but a communion within a single nature. The principle is valid here: 'All I have is yours and all you have is mine' (17.10 JB). Augustine has formulated this truth with the utmost accuracy: the Trinity is the one and only God, and the one and only God is the Trinity.[228] The doctrine of the Trinity is therefore concrete monotheism.

The understanding of God as communion-unity has far-reaching implications for our understanding of reality. Monotheism has always been a political program as well as a religious: one God, one realm, one emperor.[229] This connection is clear in John 17 from the fact that the unity in God is the model and ground of the unity of the church and that the unity of the church in turn is the sacrament, that is, the sign and instrument, of the unity of the world (v. 23). But what kind of unity is meant? Evidently not a rigid, monolithic, uniformist and tyrannical unity, which excludes, absorbs or suppresses every kind of otherness. A unity of that kind would be an impoverishment. God's unity is fullness and even overflowing fullness of selfless giving and bestowing, of loving self-outpouring; it is a unity that does not exclude but includes; it is a living, loving being with and for one another. This trinitarian understanding of unity as communion has implications for the political sphere in the broadest sense of this term and therefore for the formulation of the goals of unity in the church, in society and in the human race; in other words, for the peace of the world. E. Peterson has proposed the thesis that the doctrine of the Trinity puts an end to political theology.[230] It would be more accurate to say that it puts an end to a particular political theology that serves as an ideology to justify relations of domination in which an individual or a group tries to impose its ideas of unity and order and its interests to the exclusion of others. The doctrine of the Trinity inspires an order in which unity arises because all pool what they have and make it part of the common store. Such a vision is as far removed from a collectivist communism as it is from an individualistic liberalism. For communion does not eliminate the individual being and rights of the person but rather brings these to fulfillment through the giving away of what is the person's own and the reception of what belongs to others. Communion is thus a union of persons and at the some time maintains the primacy of the always unique person. This primacy, however, finds its fulfillment not in an individualistic having but in giving and thus granting participation in what is one's own.

K. Hemmerle has expounded the consequence for Christian spirituality of such a trinitarian understanding of unity as communion-unity.[231] The resultant spirituality is contemplative, but in all things it pays heed to the traces of love that it finds in all things and most of all in the cross of Jesus Christ. The self-giving of God in Jesus Christ is not only the ground but also the abiding measure upon which this spirituality repeatedly focuses its gaze in order to make it its own measure. While contemplative, this spirituality is also active and involved in the world. It attunes itself to God's self-giving for men. It thus becomes a service in the world and for the world. Finally, in its contemplation and its action it is community-orientated and ecclesial. It draws its vitality from union with others. It is not dependent on the pleasure and disposition of the individual, but recognizes 'binding obligations' in the full sense of the phrase.

3. *The abiding problem of the doctrine of the Trinity* or, better: *The mystery of the Trinity*. I said above that that the trinitarian communion-unity is radically different from communion-unity among human beings in that it is a unity in one and the same being and not simply a communion of separate beings. The analogy here involves an always greater dissimilarity despite all the similarity. The concrete mode of trinitarian unity amid the distinction of persons is therefore for us a mystery that cannot be eliminated. Recent discussion of an appropriate understanding of person as applied to the Trinity only shows once again the difficulties and aporias that face all theological thinking at this point. But even in this most difficult of all questions in the theology of the Trinity the high-priestly prayer offers us points of contact and guides for further and deeper reflection. The answer is once again suggested by the movement of giving and receiving, the movement of love, which God is. For if we pay careful attention to the text we see that in this movement there are three distinct relations.

The Father is purely a giver and sender. He is thus the unoriginated origin of divine love, a pure source, a pure outflowing. The Son receives life, glory and power from the Father; but he does not receive it in order to keep it for himself, to possess it, and to take full enjoyment of it for himself; rather, he receives it in order to empty himself of it (Phil. 2.6f.) and to pass it on. Love that terminated in the two-in-oneness of the lovers, and did not selflessly press out beyond itself, would be only another form of egoism. The Son is therefore the mediator; he is even pure mediation, a pure passing-on. Finally, in the Spirit the faithful receive the gift of the Father through the Son, so that they may share in this gift. The Spirit is nothing by himself; he is a pure receiving, pure donation and gift; as such he is pure fulfillment, eternal joy and blessedness, pure endless completion. Since he is the expression of the ecstasy of love in God, God is, in and through him, an eternal movement of pure exuberance reaching beyond himself. As gift within God, the Spirit is God's eschatological gift to the world; he is the world's definitive sanctification and completion.

Perfect and complete communion within the one being of God thus also includes distinctions in the way this one being is possessed. In the Father, love exists as pure source that pours itself out; in the Son it exists as a pure passing-on, as pure mediation; in the Spirit it exists as the joy of pure receiving. These three modes in which the one being of God, the one love, subsists, are in some sense necessary because love cannot be otherwise conceived; to that extent the trinitarian confession has an intrinsic plausibility for the believer. The Trinity nonetheless remains a mystery because there is a question here of a necessity in love and therefore in freedom, a necessity which cannot be deduced in advance of its self-revelation and of which there can be no rational grasp after it has been revealed. The logic of love has its own internal coherence and its own power to convince in, and not despite, its irreducible and unfathomable freedom.

Each of the three modes in which the one love of God subsists is conceivable only in relation to the other two. The Father as pure self-giving cannot exist without the Son who receives. But since the Son does not receive something but everything, he exists only in and through the giving and receiving. On the other hand, he would not have truly received the self-giving of the Father were he to keep it for himself and not give it back. He exists therefore insofar as he receives himself wholly from the Father and gives himself wholly back to the Father, or, as it is put in the farewell prayer of Jesus, glorifies the Father in his turn. As an existence that is wholly owed to another, the Son is therefore pure gratitude, eternal eucharist, pure obedient response to the word and will of the Father. But this reciprocal love also presses beyond itself; it is pure giving only if it empties itself of, and gives away, even this two-in-oneness and, in pure gratuitousness, incorporates a third in whom love exists as pure receiving, a third who therefore exists only insofar as he receives his being from the mutual love between Father and Son. The three persons of the Trinity are thus pure relationality; they are relations in which the one nature of God exists in three distinct and non-interchangeable ways. They are subsistent relations.[232]

These considerations bring us back by a new path to the Augustinian and Thomist concept of trinitarian person as subsistent relation. I have rendered this concept concrete with the help of the reflections offered by Richard of St Victor. At the same time, I have found a systematic conception of the doctrine of the Trinity in which the concerns of the Greek and Latin doctrines of the Trinity can be *aufgehoben* (set aside, preserved and elevated to a higher level) in a higher unity. In principle, this view of the Trinity begins, as does the Greek, with the Father, the unoriginated origin; but insofar as it conceives the Father as pure love, as pure self-giving, it is able to understand the processions of the Son and of the Spirit according to their inner 'logic', after the manner of Latin theology, and to conceive these processions, in faith, as forms of the one impenetrable and incomprehensible love of God and as expressions of the one mystery of salvation.

The question remains, of course: what is the value of such a systematic exposition of the doctrine of the Trinity? What does it have to do with the doxological and soteriological meaning of the confession of the Trinity? I have already given a first answer to this question: our concern is with the *intellectus fidei*, an understanding of the faith from within. What is meant is not a rationalistic understanding, an understanding according to the criterion and in the framework of the human reason, which would then, by comparison with faith, be the greater and more comprehensive power that could serve as measure and standard. The 'understanding of faith' is rather a conceptualizing on the basis of faith and an understanding in faith; it is an understanding that does not lead away from faith to a supposedly higher knowledge. The aim is a deeper initiation into the faith itself, a faith-filled understanding of the mystery as mystery, and specifically as the mystery of an unfathomable and for that very reason convincing love.

In these remarks I have already anticipated a second answer. Because the mystery of love is the supreme criterion and one established by revelation itself, it yields further criteria for understanding the reality in a new and more profound way. By way of analogy the trinitarian communion-unity shows itself to be the model for a Christian understanding of reality. The development of the doctrine of the Trinity means a breaking out of an understanding of reality that is characterized by the primacy of subject and nature, and into an understanding of reality in which person and relation have priority. Here the ultimate reality is here not the independent substance but the person, who is fully conceivable only in the relationality of giving and receiving. We might even say: the meaning of being is the selflessness of love. Such a 'trinitarian ontology',[233] like any other ontology, cannot of course be convincingly established by induction. Self-assertion, blind facticity, abstract historicity or the irreducible obscurity of reality constantly make their presence felt and seek to contradict such an interpretation. The interpretation is nonetheless plausible because it does justice in a greater degree to the human experience of reality while bracketing none of that experience. In addition, it is capable of incorporating and 'letting stand' those experiences of reality that will not fit into any system: guilt, loneliness, the grief caused by finiteness, failure. In the final analysis, it is an interpretation in the key of hope, an anticipation of the eschatological doxology under the veil of history.

Finally, the trinitarian confession yields a model for a Christian spirituality of hope and of the selfless service that hope inspires. For the trinitarian persons are characterized by their selflessness. They are, each in his own way, pure surrender, self-emptying. Their eternal kenotic existence is the condition for the possibility of the temporal kenosis of the Son, and thus a type of Christian humility and selfless service.[234] Consequently it is the very nature and content of the trinitarian confession that causes it to be pronounced in the act of baptism, which grounds Christian existence. This confession is the very heart not only of the Christian faith but also of the following of Jesus, which is based on this faith, and of the Christian's being incorporated into the death and resurrection of the Lord.

4. The systematic place of the doctrine of the Trinity follows from the point just made. This doctrine is in a sense the summation of the entire Christian mystery of salvation and, at the same time, its grammar. It is its grammar because it is the intrinsic condition for the possibility of the history of salvation. Only because God is perfect freedom in love within himself can he also be freedom in love in dealing with what is outside of himself. Because in his very being he is one with himself through being with and in another, he is able to empty himself out in history and in this very emptying reveal his glory. Because in himself God is pure gift, he is able to give himself in the Holy Spirit; as the innermost being of God, the Spirit is at the same time the outermost, the condition for the possibility of creation and redemption. Consequently the trinitarian confession is at the same time the summary of the entire Christian mystery of salvation. For the fact that God the Father is the salvation of the world through Jesus Christ his Son in the Holy Spirit – this fact is the one mystery of faith which is contained in the many mysteries of faith. The Father as unoriginated origin in God is also the ground and goal of the history of salvation; from his all comes forth and to him all returns. The Son as pure communication in God is the mediator whom the Father sends and who in turn gives us the Holy Spirit. The Spirit, finally, as completion in God is the eschatological completion of the world and man. Just as he is God's way to what is outside himself so also he effects the return of all created reality to God. Through the Spirit soteriology ends in doxology; at the end of time all of reality will be incorporated into this doxology when God is 'all in all' (I Cor. 15.28).

Finally, the thesis that the doctrine of the Trinity is the grammar and summation of the entire Christian mystery of salvation provides us with the answer to the much-discussed question of the place of the doctrine of the Trinity within dogmatic theology.[235] Given the importance of the doctrine of the Trinity, the question and its answer are not simply a matter of scientific organization but much more one of theological content that has serious implications and determines the overall theological approach to a dogmatic theology.

Three classical solutions call for discussion. The first solution, which received its classical formulation in Thomas Aquinas, puts the doctrine of the Trinity at the beginning of dogmatic theology, in keeping with a dogmatic epistemology. In practice the treatise *De Deo uno* precedes the treatise *De Deo trino*. This arrangement implies a twofold preliminary theological decision: it presupposes the priority of *theologia* (the study of God in himself) over *oeconomia* (the study of God's action in creation and history); and it takes seriously the fact that in the history of salvation and in the *theologia* which interprets it the most important thing is God's deeds and words and therefore that everything in theology must be studied *sub ratione Dei* (in the light of God). The positioning of the treatise *De Deo uno* before the treatise *De Deo trino* implies, in addition, a choice of the Western theology of the Trinity as established chiefly by Augustine, a theology that starts with the one essence of God, deals with the three persons in terms of this one essence or nature, and thus leads in practice to stripping the Trinity to a large extent of any function in the economy of salvation. Despite its being placed before the other dogmatic treatises the doctrine of the Trinity is, in this approach, largely without influence on the further presentation of dogmatic theology.

The second solution is represented by the renewed Protestant theology of our century, which has received its classical formulation in Karl Barth. In this theology the *solus Christus* (Christ alone) is not simply a basic material theological principle which says that all salvation comes to us through Christ alone. Rather it is also a fundamental formal theological principle that says we can speak of God only through Jesus Christ and his mediation. Given the critical assessment of natural theology to which this *solus Christus* principle leads, it follows that even the prolegomena to dogmatic theology – or, as post Barthian theologians like to say, theological hermeneutic – must already speak of christology and the doctrine of the Trinity. The prolegomena are now no longer simply a preamble to dogmatic theology but rather that which has to be said first and foremost in dogmatic theology itself, an instruction on the correct way to speak of God. It follows from this basic approach that the distinction between the treatises *De Deo uno* and *De Deo trino* is abandoned and the doctrine of the Trinity is shifted into the dogmatic prolegomena or, if you will, dogmatic hermeneutic, thus becoming the grammar for all other dogmatic statements. The result of such an a-theistic theology which is so radically grounded in christology is that the difference between it and real atheism is emphatically asserted in faith but hardly demonstrated in an intellectually satisfactory way.

At this point a third solution suggests itself. This is an approach consistently taken by F. Schleiermacher, the father of Neoprotestantism and one that is being attempted today even in Catholic theology, as, for example, in the 'Dutch Catechism'.[236] In this approach the Trinity is regarded as the crowning conclusion and to that extent the summation of all dogmatic theology. It is sufficiently clear from Schleiermacher that in this approach the doctrine of the Trinity can also become in practice a mere appendix. The intrinsic reason for this is easy to understand: if the doctrine of the Trinity is treated simply as a summation, then it is difficult to show how it can also serve as the grammar for all other dogmatic statements. The doctrine of the Trinity necessarily ceases to be the basic proposition of theology and becomes instead a postscript to theology.

From the idea, just mentioned, of the doctrine of the Trinity as the grammar of theology in its entirety it follows that an introductory treatise *De Deo trino* is indispensable at the beginning of dogmatic theology. 'But this initial treatise should not be an attempt to cover a theme which can be then marked as read, but a preliminary orientation with regard to a theme which is still to be dealt with.'[237] It might perhaps be said more accurately: this treatise would have to deal with a theme that subsequently keeps surfacing in different variations as in a fugue. For dogmatic theology does not form a system in the sense that everything can be logically deduced from a principle. It is a structured whole in which each partial statement reflects the whole in a different way. For if the Trinity is the one mystery in the many mysteries, then in the nature of things there is a 'perichoresis' of the individual dogmatic treatises, each of which deals with the whole from a particular point of view. In the theology of the Trinity the one theme that is present in the many themes of dogmatic theology becomes itself thematic. But in this reflection on the oneness and wholeness of dogmatic theology the theology of the Trinity presupposes not so much the other dogmatic treatises as the church's confession of faith, which it reflects upon in its entirety in the perspective of its ultimate ground and ultimate goal. The material object of the doctrine of the Trinity is thus the entire confession of faith with all three of its parts: 'I believe in one God, the Father almighty . . . And in one Lord, Jesus Christ . . . I believe in the Holy Spirit.' The formal object or point of view from which the doctrine of the Trinity deals with the whole of the Christian faith is God as ground and goal of all these confessional statements. The material dogmatic statements made in the other treatises are intelligible as theological statements only when their formal object is first named; that is, when it has been made clear what we as Christians mean when we speak of God, namely, the God of Jesus Christ to whom we have access in the Holy Spirit. In view of all these considerations we must maintain the priority of the treatise on the Trinity over the other treatises.

If, however, we are to avoid the negative consequences which this approach has had both in classical Catholic and in modern Protestant theology, we must reflect anew on the inner structure of the doctrine of God or, concretely, on the relation between the treatise *De Deo uno* and the treatise *De Deo trino*. We must therefore take seriously the fact that when we speak of God and to God we always mean – according to the Bible and the early church – the Father who is known to us through the Son in the Holy Spirit. The one God, as Augustine repeatedly insists, is therefore the triune God. This means that we cannot first speak in a general way about the being of God and only then of the three divine persons. On the contrary, after the fashion of the Eastern doctrine of the Trinity, we must start with the Father as the origin and source of the Trinity and show that the Father possesses the one divine substance in such a way that he gives it to the Son and to the Spirit. In other words, the abstract doctrine of the being of God must once again be incorporated into the doctrine of the concrete revelation of God's being and thus into the doctrine of the Trinity. It is to the credit of the dogmatic theology presented by M. Schmaus that it made a significant advance in this direction.[238] This new approach, which we owe to the tradition of the Eastern church, need not lead to an abandonment of the achievements of Augustinian trinitarian theology. For if we start with the Father as the origin and source of the Trinity we are led to conceive of the one divine nature as love. Then it becomes possible, more than in Eastern theology, to understand the Trinity entirely in terms of its innermost root, as is done, for example, by Richard of St Victor; that is, as the mystery of perfect love that communicates and empties itself and, to that extent, as the grammar and summary of the entire Christian mystery of salvation.

This approach from the economy of salvation likewise need not lead to the dismissal of natural theology and, with it, of the legitimate concern at work in the old treatise *De Deo uno*. For the economy of salvation presupposes the natural or, better, the creaturely quest of man for God and responds to it in a surpassing manner.[239] The trinitarian self-revelation of God is thus the surpassing answer to the question and quest which man not only has but is: the question and quest of God. The trinitarian revelation and the trinitarian confession of faith are the ultimate, eschatological and definitive determination of the indeterminate openness of man. The doctrine of the Trinity is concrete monotheism. This thesis closes the circle of our reflections, which began with the contemporary atheistic situation. It has been shown that the trinitarian confession is the Christian answer to the challenge of modern atheism. This thesis brings me to a concluding summary reflection.

(c) Conclusion: the trinitarian confession as the answer to modern atheism

The journey from the situation that is given its character by modern atheism to the trinitarian confession of faith has been a long one; for many, perhaps too long. It seems to them that the real question calling for an answer today is the question of God's existence and not that of his inner mystery. In addition, they regard the theology of the Trinity as often nothing but an impertinent prying into the mystery of God. They are therefore more or less content with a theistic confession of faith. But this kind of theological contentment has, I think, been shown in the chapters of this book to be based on an inherently untenable position. A theistic faith today is a Christian faith which has already been undermined by the Enlightenment and atheism, and in the nature of things it repeatedly turns into the atheism which it is intended to prevent, but whose arguments it cannot defend itself against. In the face of the radical challenge to the Christian faith, help will come not from a feeble, general and vague theism but only from a decisive witness to the living God of history who has disclosed himself in a concrete way through Jesus Christ in the Holy Spirit.

The way beyond theism and atheism, as travelled today by many influential representatives of Protestant theology, is safe from the dangers which threaten theism only if it does not throw the baby out with the bath water; that is, if it does not answer the questions of atheists by avoiding the problems of natural theology and making a direct leap into a supposedly radical faith and if it does not hastily extend its criticism of theism to a criticism of monotheism. For monotheism is the answer to the question raised at the natural level about the unity and meaning of all reality. It is precisely this ambiguous and open question that is specified in a concrete way by the trinitarian self-revelation of God, so that the trinitarian confession is concrete monotheism and as such the Christian answer to the God-question of the human person. The God of Jesus Christ – that is, the God who gives himself to be known through Jesus Christ in the Holy Spirit – is the ultimate, eschatological and definitive determination of the indeterminate openness of man; he is therefore also the Christian answer to the situation created by modern atheism. As a result, the proclamation of the triune God is of the greatest pastoral importance in the present-day situation.

It is obvious that the complicated exegetical, historical and speculative questions with which the theology of the Trinity must grapple are not the direct object of the proclamation of the trinitarian mystery of God. The discussion of such questions is necessary in order to defend the confession against challenges, to make it at least possible to discuss the doctrine with its 'cultured despisers', and, more important still, to open up the doctrine to those who venerate it in faith. Such discussions are therefore of fundamental importance for the proclamation of the doctrine, even if only indirectly.

The direct object of the proclamation, as the church's confession of faith, is the economic Trinity and the God of Jesus Christ who in the Spirit gives us life and freedom, reconciliation and peace. Of course, the proclamation cannot stop there. For according to the Lord's farewell prayer true life consists precisely in knowing and glorifying God. For its own sake therefore soteriology must pass over into doxology. For amid all the vicissitudes and instability of history man's salvation consists in having communion with the God who through all eternity *is* love. It is precisely an anthropologically oriented theology that must also be a theological theology which takes into account that the *ad maiorem hominis salutem* (to the greater salvation of man) is possible only by way of the *ad maiorem Dei gloriam* (to the greater glory of God). It is therefore possible for theology to develop the anthropological relevance of what it says only if it remains theology and does not turn into anthropology. It is the acknowledgment of the Godness of God that leads to the humanization of man.

It is undoubtedly pleonastic to speak, as I did at the beginning of this book, of theological theology as a program; the formula 'theological theology' makes sense only as a polemical formula which serves to remind theology of its own proper theme. The challenge raised by atheism and, even more, by the crisis in atheism must cause theologians to attend once again to the theological dimension which is denied by atheism and has been suppressed or simply forgotten, and to revive an awareness of it as the one supremely important thing for man. This is all the more necessary because the proclamation of the death of God has meanwhile led to the public proclamation of the death of man. If this answer is not to stop half-way and is to allow the God of Jesus Christ to have his full impact, then the answer must take the form of the confession of the Trinity. Precisely because this confession takes seriously the Godness of God, his freedom in love, it is able to rescue the freedom in love and for love that has been given us by God through Jesus Christ in the Holy Spirit, and thus to rescue the humanity of man at a time when it is most threatened.

Abbreviations

AnBib	Analecta biblica, Rome
BEvT	Beiträge zur evangelischen Theologie, Munich 1935ff.
BGPTM	Beiträge zur Geschichte der Philosophie und Theologie des Mittelalters, Münster 1891ff.
BSLK	*Die Bekenntnisschriften der evangelisch-luterischen Kirche*, ed. the Deutscher Evangelische Kirchenausschuss, Göttingen ³1956
CA	*Confessio Augustana*, in *BSLK*
Cath	*Catholica. Jahrbuch für Kontroverstheologie*, (Paderborn) Münster 1932ff.
CCL	Corpus Christianorum, Series Latina, Turnholt 1953ff.
COD	*Conciliorum oecumenicorum decreta*, ed. J. Alberigo *et al.* Bologna ³1973
CSEL	*Corpus scriptorum ecclesiasticorum latinorum*, Vienna 1866ff.
DBSup	*Dictionnaire de la Bible: Supplément*, Paris 1928ff.
DS	H. Denziger and A. Schönmetzer (eds.), *Enchiridion symbolorum, definitionum et declarationum de rebus fidei et morum*, Freiburg ³³1965
DTC	*Dictionnaire de théologie catholique*, Paris 1930ff.
ECQ	*Eastern Churches Quarterly*, Ramsgate 1936ff.
EKKNT	Evangelisch-katholischer Kommentar zum Neuen Testament
EKL	*Evangelisches Kirchenlexikon*, ed. H. Brunotte and O. Weber, Göttingen 1965ff.
EvT	*Evangelische Theologie*, Munich 1934ff.
Flannery	A. Flannery (ed.), *Vatican Council II: The Conciliar and Post-Conciliar Documents*, Collegeville 1975
FS	*Festschrift*
FZTP	*Freiburger zeitschrift für Theologie und Philosophie* (before 1914, *Jahrbuch für Philosophie und spekulative Theologie*; 1914–54, *Divus Thomas*), Fribourg
GCS	Die griechischen christlichen Schriftsteller der ersten drei Jahrhunderte, Leipzig 1897ff.
Ges. Schriften	Gesammelte Schriften
Greg	*Gregorianum*, Rome 1920ff.
HDG	Handbuch der Dogmengeschichte, Freiburg 1951ff.
HPG	*Handbuch philosophischer Grundbegriffe*

HTG	*Handbuch theologischer Grundbegriffe*, ed. H. Fries, 2 vols., Munich 1962–63
HTKNT	Herders theologischer Kommentar zum Neuen Testament, Freiburg
HWP	*Historisches Wörterbuch der Philosophie*, Basle 1971ff.
JTS	*Journal of Theological Studies*, London 1899ff.
KD	*Lexikon für Theologie und Kirche*, ed. J. Höfer and K. Rahner, Freiburg ²1957ff.
MTZ	*Münchener theologische Zeitschrift*, Munich 1950ff.
Mysal	*Mysterium salutis, Grundriss heilsgeschichtlicher Dogmatik*, ed. J. Feiner and M. Löhrer, Einsiedeln – Zürich – Cologne 1965ff.
ND	J. Neuner and J. Dupuis (eds.), *The Christian Faith in the Doctrinal Documents of the Catholic Church*, Staten Island, NY 1982
NZST	*Neue Zeitschrift für systematische Theologie*, Berlin 1959ff.
PhJ	*Philosophisches Jahrbuch der Görresgesellschaft*, Fulda 1888ff.
PhRu	*Philosophische Rundschau*
QD	Quaestiones disputatae, Freiburg
PG	Patrologia Graeca, ed. J.-P. Migne, Paris 1857–66
PL	Patrologia Latina, ed. J.-P. Migne, Paris 1878–90
RAC	*Reallexikon für Antike und Christentum*, ed. T. Klauser, Stuttgart 1941ff.
RevSR	*Revue des sciences religieuses*, Strasbourg 1921ff.
RGG	*Die Religion in Geschichte und Gegenwart*, Tübingen ³1956ff.
SacMundi	*Sacramentum mundi*
SANT	Studien zum Alten und Neuen Testament
SC	Sources chrétiennes, Paris 1941ff.
Schol	*Scholastik*, Freiburg 1926ff.
ST	Thomas Aquinas, *Summa theologiae*
StudGen	*Studium Generale*, Berlin – Göttingen – Heidelberg 1948ff.
Theol. Phil.	*Theologie und Philosophie*, Freiburg 1966ff.
TDNT	*Theological Dictionary of the New Testament*, ed. G. Kittel, Grand Rapids 1964ff.
TLZ	*Theologische Literaturzeitung*, Leipzig 1878ff.
TPS	*The Pope Speaks*, Washington DC 1954–75, Huntington Ind. 1975ff.
TQ	*Theologische Quartalschrift*, Tübingen 1818ff.
TRE	*Theologische Realenzyklopädie*, Berlin 1974ff.
TRu	*Theologische Rundschau*, Tübingen 1897ff.
TTZ	*Trierer theologische Zeitschrift* (until 1944: *Pastor Bonus*), Trier 1888ff.
TU	*Texte und Untersuchungen zur Geschichte der altchristlichen Literatur*, Leipzig-Berlin 1882ff.
VCaro	*Verbum caro*
VF	*Verkündigung und Forschung*

WA	Martin Luther, *Werke*, Kritische Gesamtausgabe ('Weimarer Ausgabe') Weimar 1883ff.
WW	Gesammelte Werke
WWeis	*Wissenschaft und Weisheit*
ZKG	*Zeitschrift für Kirchengeschichte*, (Gotha) Stuttgart 1887ff.
ZKT	*Zeitschrift für katholische Theologie*, Innsbruck and Vienna 1876ff.
ZNW	*Zeitschrift für die neutestamentliche Wissenschaft und die Kunde der älteren Kirche*, Berlin 1900ff.
ZST	*Zeitschrift für systematische Theologie*, (Gütersloh) Berlin 1923ff.
ZTK	*Zeitschrift für Theologie und Kirche*, Tübingen 1891ff.

NOTES

PART ONE

Chapter I God as a Problem

1. DS 150; ND 12.

2. What Vatican II says of scripture in particular is true of faith generally: its object is 'the truth which God' has revealed 'for the sake of our salvation' (*Dei Verbum* 11). In saying this the Council does not intend to delimit the material object of the statements of faith or scripture, but rather to define the formal object in the light of which all the statements of faith and scripture are to be understood.

3. Cf. Thomas Aquinas, *ST* I, 1, 7: 'In sacred doctrine all subjects are treated in terms of God, either because they are God himself or because they are related to him as their origin and end. It follows from this that God is indeed the object of this science.'

4. Cf. Augustine, *De civitate Dei* VIII, 1 (CCL 47, 217), who defines theology as 'thought or speech about the divinity' (*de divinitate ratio sive sermo*).

5. M. Buber, *Meetings*, La Salle Ill. 1973, 50–1.

6. Thomas Aquinas, *ST* I, 2, 3.

7. Anselm of Canterbury, *Proslogion* 2.

8. Ibid., 15.

9. *BSLK* 560.

10. P. Tillich, *Systematic Theology* 1, Chicago 1951, 12, etc., especially 211ff.

11. R. Bultmann, 'What Does It Mean to Speak of God?', in *Faith and Understanding* 1, ET L. P. Smith, London and New York 1969, 53.

12. G. Ebeling, *Dogmatik des christlichen Glaubens* 1, Tübingen 1979, 187.

13. K. Rahner, *Foundations of Christian Faith: An Introduction to the Idea of Christianity*, ET W. V. Dych, London and New York 1978, 65–6.

14. This is the justifiable starting point of W. Weischedel, *Der Gott der Philosophen. Grundlegung einer philosophischen Theologie im Zeitalter des Nihilismus*, 2 vols., Munich ³1975.

15. There is a synthesis, including an application to the God-question, in E. Fromm, *Psychoanalysis and Religion*, New Haven 1950, 21ff.

16. Thus G. Ebeling, op. cit., 168–9.

17. Thomas Aquinas, *ST* 1, 2, 3, arg. 1 and 2.

18. Anselm, *Proslogion*, Prooemium 1.

19. It is not possible here to go into all the theoretical problems of theology as a science. Cf. W. Kasper, *The Methods of Dogmatic Theology*, ET J. Drury, New York 1969; id., 'Dogmatik als Wissenschaft. Versuch einer Neubegründung', *TQ* 157, 1977, 189–203; id. 'Wissenschaftliche Freiheit und lehramtliche Bindung der

katholischen Theologie', *Essener Gespräche zum Thema Staat und Kirche* 16, Münster 1982, 12–44, especially 26ff. (bibliography in all three works).

20. Cf. M. Eliade, *Cosmos and History. The Myth of the Eternal Return*, ET W. R. Trask, New York 1954, 3–4

21. M. Heidegger, *Erläulterungen zu Hölderlins Dichtung*, Frankfurt 1951, 27.

22. M. Buber, *The Eclipse of God*, ET M. Friedman *et al.*, New York 1953.

23. D. Bonhoeffer, *Letters and Papers from Prison*, ET Frank Clark *et al.*, The Enlarged Edition, London and New York 1971.

24. A. Delp, *Im Angesicht des Todes. Geschrieben zwischen Verhaftung und Hinrichtung 1944–45*, Frankfurt, ⁸1963.

25. Vatican II, *Gaudium et spes*, 19.

26. On secularization: K. Löwith, *Meaning in History: The Theological Implications of the Philosophy of History*, Chicago 1949; T. Rendtorff, *Church and Theology: The Systematic Function of the Church Concept in Modern Theology*, ET R. H. Fuller, Philadelphia 1971; id., *Theorie des Christentums. Historisch-theologische Studien zu seiner neuzeitlichen Verfassung*, Gütersloh 1972; F. Gogarten, *Despair and Hope for Our Time*, ET T. Weiser, Philadelphia 1970; J. B. Metz, *Theology of the World*, ET W. Glen-Doepel, New York 1969; id., *Faith in History and Society: Toward a Practical Fundamental Theology*, ET D. Smith, New York 1980; P. L. Berger, *The Sacred Canopy: Elements of a Sociological Theory of Religion*, Garden City NY 1967; H. Lübbe, *Säkularisierung. Geschichte eines ideenpolitischen Begriffs*, Freiburg, and Munich ²1975; H. Blumenberg, *Die Legitimität der Neuzeit*, Frankfurt 1966; id., *Säkularistierung und Selbstbehauptung*, Frankfurt 1974; cf. W. Pannenberg, *Basic Questions in Theology* III (American title *The Idea of God and Human Freedom*), ET R. A. Wilson, London and Philadelphia 1973, 178–91; W. Kasper, 'Autonomie und Theonomie. Zur Ortsbestimmung des Christentums in der modernen Welt', in *Anspruch der Wirklichkeit und christlicher Glaube. Probleme und Wege theologischer Ethik heute (FS A. Auer)*, ed. H. Weber and D. Mieth, Düsseldorf 1980, 17–41; K. Lehmann, 'Prolegomena zur theologischen Bewältigung der Säkularisierungsproblematik', in his *Gegenwart des Glaubens*, Mainz 1974, 94–108; U. Ruh, 'Säkularisierung', *Christlicher Glaube in moderner Gesellschaft* 18, Freiburg – Basle – Vienna 1982, 59–100 (bibliog.).

27. Thus E. Troeltsch, *Das Wesen des modernen Geistes*, Gesammelte Schriften 4, Tübingen 1925 = Aalen 1966, 334.

28. *Hegel's Philosophy of Right*, ET T. M. Knox, Oxford 1942, 51, 84, 124.

29. This aspect has been brought out especially by W. Dilthey, *Weltanschauung und Analyse des Menschen seit Renaissance und Reformation* WW 2; Stuttgart and Göttingen ⁵1957, 254ff., etc.

30. K. Holl, 'Die Geschichte des Worts Beruf', in his *Gesammelte Aufsätze zur Kirchengeschichte* 2. *Der Westen*, Tübingen 1928, 189–219; M. Weber, *The Protestant Ethic and the Spirit of Capitalism*, ET T. Parsons, New York 1958.

31. On the basis of research done by J. Habermas, R. Koselleck, M. Riedel, B. Groethuysen, D. Schellong, L. Goldman and others, the category of 'bourgeois society' has been taken as the basis, especially in the new political theology of J. B. Metz, for a hermeneutic of Christianity in the context of the contemporary historical and social situation. Cf. J. B. Metz, *Faith in History and Society* (n. 26); id., *The Emergent Church: The Future of Christianity in a Postbourgois World*, ET P. Mann, New York 1981. There is a good and balanced summary in W. Müller,

'Bürgertum und Christentum', *Christlicher Glaube in moderner Gesellschaft* 18, Freiburg – Basle – Vienna 1982, 5–58 (bibliog.). The approach is a stimulating one and opens up avenues. But we also see its limitations. For the bourgeoisie which has existed from the twelfth century down into the nineteenth and twentieth underwent important changes during this long period of time, and who knows what capacity for change it may not display in the future as well? 'Bourgeois' is therefore a generic historical concept that stands at a high level of abstraction and is not suited, as such, for describing the concrete situation of our own day. Unless one states precisely the meaning attached to the term, it can only be a defamatory one nowadays; its emotional overtones prevent rational discussion. In addition, it overlooks the great accomplishments of bourgeois civilization in favor of a one-dimensional, more or less Marxist criticism: the value of individual freedom, the universal rights of the human person as a free being, the idea of tolerance, and so on. Instead of prematurely proclaiming a post-bourgeois religion, we ought to be seeing to it that these ideas, which are Christian in their inspiration, are put into practice and respected in the religions and churches. This is not to deny the limits or the critical state of bourgeois civilization. But these cannot be overcome by an abstract denial of what is bourgeois, but only by a transformational insertion of the bourgeois legacy into the larger context. As will be shown in a moment, this larger context does not consist only in the political dimension of religion as contrasted with the privatization of religion in a bourgeois culture. For on closer examination, bourgeois religion proves not to have been so unpolitical; in fact, it was overly political. It did not so to speak sleep through the new social problems because it was unpolitical; rather, it was unwilling to acknowledge these social problems because it was the prisoner of existing social structures and provided these with legitimacy. Consequently, the loss of the political dimension cannot be the reason for the failure of bourgeois religion. For this reason a more comprehensive point of departure is needed than the one we find in political theology.

32. H. Grotius, *De iure belli ac pacis*, Prolegomena 11 (ed. P. C. Molhuysen; Leiden 1919, 7).

33. Cf. below, 20ff.

34. Hegel, *Faith and Knowledge, or the Reflective Philosophy of Subjectivity in the Complete Range of Its Forms as Kantian, Jacobian and Fichtean Philosophy*, ET W. Cerf and H. S. Harris, Albany 1977, 57.

35. Ibid., 190; id., *The Phenomenology of Mind*, ET J. Baillie, rev. 2nd ed. London 1949, 752–3; id., *Vorlesungen über die Philosophie der Religion*, 3. Teil, *Die absolute Religion* (ed. G. Lasson, 157f.). [There is an English translation of this last work, by E. B. Spiers and J. B. Sanderson: *Lectures on the Philosophy of Religion* (3 vols.; London 1895; reprinted New York 1962), but I have decided not to use it in the present book but to translate directly from the text provided by W. Kasper. Tr.].

36. Nietzsche, *The Gay Science*, no. 125, ET W. Kaufmann, New York 1974, Vintage Book ed., 181.

37. L. Kolakowski, 'Die Sorge um Gott in unserem scheinbar gottlosen Zeitalter', in his *Der nahe und der ferne Gott. Nichttheologische Texte zur Gottesfrage im 20. Jahrhundert. Ein Lesebuch*, Berlin 1981, 10.

38. M. Buber, *Meetings* (n. 5), 51.

39. For more detailed justification of this statement cf. below, 77f., 87f.

40. Aristotle, *Metaphysica* II, 994a-b. For the concept of problem in Aristotle cf. his *Topica* 104b.

41. For the concept of mystery cf. below, 124ff.

42. Vatican II, *Gaudium et spes*, 25.

43. Cf. Aristotle, *Metaphysica* III, 1003a. I cannot here go into the history of the concept of metaphysics and into the changes that have taken place in the understanding of metaphysics and correspondingly in the meaning of the claim that the era of metaphysics is over. Nor is it possible here to define in a more detailed way the relationship between theology and philosophy. Cf. below, 65ff. 94ff.

44. H. U. von Balthasar, *Herrlichkeit. Eine theologische Ästhetick*, III/1: *Im Raum der Metaphysik*, Einsiedeln 1965, 974.

45. Vatican II, *Gaudium et spes*, 76.

46. Kolakowski, op. cit. (n. 37), 21.

Chapter II The Denial of God in Modern Atheism

1. On the concept of atheism and on the history of the concept, cf. W. Kern, *Atheismus – Marxismus – Christentum. Beiträge zur Diskussion*, Innsbruck 1976, 15ff. Basic works on atheism: H. Ley, *Geschichte der Aufklärung und des Atheismus*, 3 vols., Berlin 1966–72; F. Mauthner, *Der Atheismus und seine Geschichte im Abendland*, 4 vols., Stuttgart and Berlin 1920–23, reprinted Hildesheim, 1963; C. Fabro, *God in Exile: Modern Atheism*, ET ed. A. Gibson, Westminster Md. 1968; W. Schütte, 'Atheismus', *HWP* 1, 595–9.

2. Cf. Kern, op. cit., 17ff.

3. Justin, *Apologia* I, 6 (*Corpus Apol.*, ed. v. Otto, 20–22). Cf. A. Harnack, *Der Vorwurf des Atheismus in den drei ersten Jahrhunderten*, TU 28, Leipzig 1905; N. Brox, 'Zum Vorwurf des Atheismus gegen die alte Kirche', *TTZ* 75, 1966, 274–82.

4. Cf. G. Ebeling, 'Rudimentary Reflexions on Speaking Responsibly of God', in *Word and Faith*, ET J. W. Leitch, London and Philadelphia 1963, 374ff.

5. Cf. W. Kasper, 'Theonomie und Autonomie. Zur Ortsbestimmung des Christentums in der modernen Welt', in H. Weber and D. Mieth (eds.), *Anspruch der Wirklichkeit und christlicher Glaube. Probleme und Wege theologischer Ethik heute (FS Alfons Auer)*, Düsseldorf 1980, 17–41.

6. R. Descartes, *Meditations on First Philosophy* II, 25(20), ET L. J. Lafleur, Indianapolis 1978, 24.

7. *A Discourse on Method* IV, 1f., in *A Discourse on Method and Selected Writings*, ET J. Veitch, New York 1957, 28.

8. *Meditations on First Philosophy* II, 28(22) (Lafleur, 27): *The Principles of Philosophy* I, 7 (Veitch, 186).

9. I. Kant, *Critique of Pure Reason*, Preface to 2nd ed., 1787, ET J. M. D. Meiklejohn, in *Kant*, Great Books of the Western World 42, Chicago 1952, 7.

10. On this interpretation cf. W. Schulz, *Der Gott der neuzeitlichen Metaphysik*, Pfullingen 1957, 22ff., 31ff. Augustine is already familiar with this kind of thinking: *Confessions* X, 6, 9ff.; 8, 12ff.; 25, 36ff. (CCL 27, 159ff., 161f., 174f.). Augustine even has the formula: '*Si enim fallor sum*' ('If I am deceived, I exist', *De civitate Dei* XI, 26; CCL 48, 345f.). But Augustine's thinking is located wholly in the theological order.

11. Cf. R. Pohlmann, 'Autonomie', *HWP* 1, 701–19; M. Welker, *Der Vorgang Autonomie. Philosophische Beiträge zur Einsicht in theologische Rezeption und*

Kritik, Neukirchen-Vluyn 1975; W. Kasper, 'Autonomie und Theonomie' (n. 5); K. Hilpert, *Ethik und Rationalität. Untersuchungen zur Autonomieproblem und zu seiner Bedeutung für die theologische Ethik*, Moraltheologische Studien, Systematische Abteilung 6, Freiburg 1978; E. Amelung, 'Autonomie', *TRE* 5, 4–17.

12. Cf. below.

13. Cf. E. Troeltsch, *Das Wesen des modernen Geistes*, Ges. Schriften IV; Tübingen 1925 = Aalen 1966, 324; W. Dilthey, *Weltanschauung und Analyse des Menschen seit Renaissance und Reformation*, WW II, Stuttgart and Göttingen 1969, 90ff., and frequently.

14. Kant, *Fundamental Principles of the Metaphysic of Morals*, ET T. A. Abbott, in *Kant* (n. 9), 271.

15. Ibid., 279.

16. Ibid., 260

17. Hegel, *Faith and Knowledge*, ET W. Cerf and H. S. Harris, Albany 1977, 189–91.

18. There is an important differentiation and classification in *Gaudium et spes*, 19f.

19. Cf. below.

20. Cf. K. Lehmann and A. Böhm, 'Die Kirche und die Herrschaft der Ideologien', *Handbuch der Pastoraltheologie* II/2, Freiburg – Basle – Vienna 1966. 109–202.

21. K. Rahner, 'Science as a "Confession"', in his *Theological Investigations* 3, ET K.-H. and B. Kruger, London and Baltimore 1967, 390; cf. id., 'The Acceptance in Faith of the Truth of God', *Theological Investigations* 16, ET D. Morland, London and New York 1979, 169–70; 'Religious Feeling Inside and Outside the Church', *Theological Investigations* 3, 390; 'Atheism', *SacMundi* 1, 117–22.

22. F. Nietzsche, *Thus Spoke Zarathustra*, ET W. Kaufmann, New York, 1954, Zarathustra's Prologue 5 (Kaufmann, 17–18).

23. This is true especially of behaviorism. Cf. B. F. Skinner, *Beyond Freedom and Dignity*, New York 1971.

24. For a history of the problems tackled in the natural sciences and a history of the relation between theology and the natural sciences cf. A. C. Crombie, *Augustine to Galileo: The History of Science AD 400–1650*, London 1952; F. Wagner, *Die Wissenschaft und die gefährdete Welt*, Munich 1964; N. Schiffers, *Fragen der Physik an die Theologie. Die Säkularisierung der Wissenschaft und das Heilsverlangen nach Freiheit*, Düsseldorf 1968; W. Heisenberg, *Physik und Philosophie*, Stuttgart ²1972; C. F. v. Weizsäcker, *Die Tragweite der Wissenschaft* 1, Stuttgart ⁵1972; N. M. Wildiers, *The Theologian and His Universe: Theology and Cosmology from the Middle Ages to the Present*, ET P. Dunphy, New York 1977. Important for the Scholastic prehistory are the works of A. Meier, especially *An der Grenze von Scholastik und Naturwissenschaft. Studien zur Naturphilosophie des 14. Jahrhunderts*, Essen 1943.

25. On the 'Galileo Case' : F. Dessauer, *Der Fall Galilei und wir. Abendländische Tragödie*, Frankfurt ³1951; A. C. Crombie, 'Galileo's Conception of Scientific Truth', in *Literature and Science. Proceedings of the Sixth Triennial Congress*, *Oxford 1954*, Oxford 1955, 132–38; E. Schumacher, *Der Fall Galilei. Das Drama der Wissenschaft*, Darmstadt 1964; G. de Santillana, 'Galileo e la sua sorte', in *Fortuna di Galileo*, Biblioteca di cultura moderna 586, Bari 1964, 3–23; P. Paschini, *Vita e opere di Galileo Galilei*, Rome ²1965; H. Blumenberg, 'Das

Fernrohr und die Ohnmacht der Wahrheit', in *Sidereus Nuncius u.a.*, ed. H. Blumenberg, Frankfurt 1965, 7–75; O. Loretz, *Galilei und das Irrtum der Inquisition. Naturwissenschaft – Wahrheit der Bibel – Kirche*, Kevelaer 1966.

26. This failure is cautiously acknowledged by Vatican II in *Gaudium et spes*, 26, where the Council also speaks of the legitimate autonomy of the sciences.

27. C. F. v. Weizsäcker, *Der Garten des Menschlichen. Beiträge zur geschichtlichen Anthropologie*, Munich and Vienna 1977, 22, 93, 460, etc.

28. H. Blumenberg, *Die kopernikanische Wende*, Frankfurt 1965. Cf. especially M. Heidegger, 'The Age of the World Picture', in *The Question concerning Technology, and Other Essays*, ET W. Lovitt, New York 1977, 115–54

29. W. Heisenberg, *The Physicist's Conception of the Universe*, ET A. J. Pomerans, London 1958, 7ff., 59ff., 78ff.

30. Cf. the survey in S. Pfürtner, 'Pantheismus', *LTK* 8, 25–29. For modern pantheism cf. W. Dilthey, op. cit. (n. 13), 283ff., 326ff., 391ff.

31. Cf. the survey in F. Überweg, *Grundriss der Geschichte der Philosophie* 3, Darmstadt 1957, 30f., 48f., 632f.

32. B. Spinoza, *Die Ethik nach geometrischer Methode dargestellt*, ed. O. Baensch, Hamburg 1955, 187, 194.

33. Ibid., 32.

34. Cf. E. Spranger, *Weltfrömmigkeit. Ein Vortrag*, Ges. Schriften IX, ed. H. W. Bähr, O. F. Bollnow *et al.*, Tübingen 1974, 224–50.

35. A. Einstein, Letter to Max Born, 4 December 1936, in Albert Einstein, Hedwig and Max Born, *Briefwechsel 1919–1955*, Munich 1969, 129f.; cf. 118f., 224.

36. F. H. Jacobi, 'Uber die Lehre des Spinoza', in *Briefen an Herrn Moses Mendelsohn*, WW IV/1, ed. F. Roth and F. Köppen, Leipzig, 1819 = Darmstadt 1976, 216.

37. L. Feuerbach, 'Preliminary Theses on the Reform of Philosophy' (1842), in Z. Hanfi (ed.), *The Fiery Brook: Selected Writings of Ludwig Feuerbach*, Garden City 1972, 153–4.

38. Hegel, *Enzyklopädie der philosophischen Wissenschaften im Grundrisse* (1830), §50, ed. F. Nicolin and O. Pöggeler, Hamburg 1959, 76.

39. Cf. the following surveys: J. T. Engert, 'Deismus', *LTK* 3, 195–9; E. Troeltsch, *Der Deismus*, Ges. Schriften IV, Tübingen 1925 = Aalen 1961, 429–87; W. Dilthey, op. cit. (n. 13), 90ff., 246ff.; J. T. Engert, 'Zur Geschichte und Kritik des Deismus', *Bonner Zeitschrift für Theologie und Seelsorge* 7, 1930, 214–24; W. Philipp, *Das Werden der Aufklärung in theologiegeschichtlicher Sicht*, Göttingen, 1957.

40. Cf. Hegel, *Vorlesungen über den Begriff der Religion* II (ed. Lasson, 11).

41. Cf. W. Heisenberg, *The Physicist's Conception of Nature* (n. 29), 78ff., 86ff.

42. Cited in W. Kern, op. cit. (n. 1), 27.

43. Cited ibid.

44. For the history of materialism: F. A. Lange, *Geschichte des Materialismus und Kritik seiner Bedeutung in der Gegenwart*, 2 vols., Leipzig 1921; E. Bloch, *Das Materialismusproblem, seine Geschichte und Substanz*, Frankfurt 1972; N. Lobkowicz and H. Ottmann, 'Materialismus, Idealismus und christliches Weltverständnis', in *Christlicher Glaube in moderner Gesellschaft* 19, Freiburg – Basle – Vienna 1981, 65–141.

45. On this point cf. G. Altner, *Schöpfungsglaube und Entwicklungsgedanke in*

der protestantischen Theologie zwischen Ernst Haeckel und Teilhard de Chardin, Zürich 1965; id., Charles Darwin und Ernst Haeckel. Ein Vergleich nach theologischen Aspekten, Zürich 1966.

46. W. Heisenberg, Der Teil und das Ganze. Gespräche im Umkreis der Atomphysik, Munich 1969, 116–30, 279–95; id., 'Naturwissenschaft und religiöse Wahrheit', in Schritte über die Grenze. Gesammelte Reden und Aufsätze, Munich ³1973, 335–51, esp. 347; P. Jordan, Der Naturwissenschaftler vor der religiösen Frage. Abbruch einer Mauer, Oldenburg-Hamburg ²1948; W. Weidlich, 'Zum Begriff Gottes im Felde zwischen Theologie, Philosophie und Naturwissenschaft', ZTK 68, 1971, 381–94; C. F. v. Weizsäcker, Die Einheit der Natur. Studien, Munich ²1971; id., Der Garten des Menschlichen (n. 27), 441ff.; id., 'Gottesfrage und Naturwissenschaften', in M. Hengel and R. Reinhardt (eds.), Heute von Gott reden, Munich and Mainz 1977, 162–80; M. Schramm, 'Theologie und Naturwissenschafte – gestern und heute', TQ 157, 1977, 208–13.

47. Cf. below, 88f.

48. Cf. Kant, Critique of Practical Reason, ET T. A. Abbott, in Kant (n. 9), 344ff.

49. F. W. J. Schelling, Philosophische Briefe über Dogmatismus und Kritizismus (1795), WW I, ed. M. Schröter, 214. On this point cf. W. Kasper, Das Absolute in der Geschichte. Philosophie und Theologie der Geschichte in der Spätphilosophie Schellings, Mainz 1965, 188.

50. J. G. Fichte, Über den Grund unseres Glaubens an eine göttliche Weltregierung, WW III, ed. F. Medicus, 129f.

51. Ibid. 131; cf. 400.

52. Cf. Kasper, op. cit. (n. 49), esp. 181ff.

53. Hegel, Faith and Knowledge (n. 17), 190; id., The Phenomenology of Mind, ET J. Baillie, rev. 2nd ed., London 1949, 752–3, 782; id., Vorlesungen über die Philosophie der Religion II/2, ed. G. Lasson, 155ff.

54. Cf. K. Löwith, From Hegel to Nietzsche. The Revolution in Nineteenth-Century Thought, ET D. E. Green, New York 1964; Anchor Books ed. 1967, 339–47.

55. Ibid., 345.

56. Cf. H. Küng, Menschwerdung Gottes. Eine Einführung in Hegels theologisches Denken als Prolegomena zu einer künftigen Christologie, Ökumenische Forschungen 1, Freiburg – Basle – Vienna 1970, 503–22. In literature the radical change is most clearly marked in H. Heine; cf. E. Peters and E. Kirsch, Religionskritik bei Heinrich Heine, Erfurter Theologische Studien 13, Leipzig 1977.

57. On Feuerbach's criticism of religion: G. Nüdling, Ludwig Feuerbachs Religionsphilosophie. Die Auflösung der Theologie in Anthropologie, Paderborn ²1961; M. von Gagern, Ludwig Feuerbach. Philosophie und Religionskritik. Die 'Neue' Philosophie, Munich and Salzburg 1970; M. Xhaufflaire, Feuerbach et la théologie de la sécularisation, Paris 1970; H. J. Braun, Die Religionsphilosophie Feuerbachs. Kritik und Annahme des Religiösen, Stuttgart 1972; E. Schneider, Die Theologie und Feuerbachs Religionskritik. Die Reaktion des Theologie des 19. Jahrhunderts auf Ludwig Feuerbachs Religionskritik, Göttingen 1972; H. Lübbe and H. M. Soss (eds.), Atheismus in der Diskussion. Kontroversen um L. Feuerbach, Munich and Mainz 1975; H. Fries, 'L. Feuerbachs Herausforderung an die Theologie', in Glaube und Kirche als Angebot, Graz – Vienna – Cologne 1976,

62–90. On the acceptance of Feuerbach in Protestant theology cf. E. Thies (ed.), *Ludwig Feuerbach*, Darmstadt 1976.

58. Cf. A. Schmidt, *Emanzipatorische Sinnlichkeit. Ludwig Feuerbachs anthropologischer Materialismus*, Munich 1973.

59. Cf. K. Marx, 'Contribution to the Critique of Hegel's Philosophy of Right', in T. B. Bottomore (ed.), *Karl Marx: Early Writings*, New York 1964, 43.

60. Marx, 'Luther as Arbiter between Strauss and Feuerbach', in L. D. Easton and K. H. Guddat (eds.), *Writings of the Young Marx on Philosophy and Society*, Garden City 1967, 95.

61. L. Feuerbach, *The Essence of Christianity*, ET G. Eliot (1854), New York 1967, Torchbook ed., 2.

62. Ibid., 2.

63. Ibid., 5.

64. Ibid., 12–13

65. Ibid., 63

66. Ibid, 29–30

67. *Lectures on the Essence of Religion*, ET R. Manheim, New York 1967, 234.

68. *The Essence of Christianity*, 26, 27.

69. Ibid., 33.

70. Ibid, 184.

71 Ibid., 271.

72 Ibid., 276, 278.

73. Ibid., 32.

74. Cf. M. Buber, 'Zur Geschichte des dialogischen Prinzips', in WW I, Munich 1962, 293f.

75. Feuerbach, 'Principles of the Philosophy of the Future', in Hanfi (ed.), op. cit. (n. 37), 244.

76. Ibid.

77. 'The Necessity of a Reform of Philosophy', in Hanfi, 148–9.

78. 'Notwendigkeit einer Veränderung', in K. Löwith (ed.), *Kleine Schriften*, Frankfurt 1966, 231 n. 1 [not in the English version].

79. K. Barth, *Protestant Theology in the Nineteenth Century: Its Background and History*, London ²1972, 536–7.

80. J.-P. Sartre, 'Existentialism Is a Humanism', in W. Kaufmann (ed.), *Existentialism from Dostoievsky to Sartre*, New York 1956, 287–311, esp. 288–9, 294–6, 310–11. Cf. G. Hasenhüttl, *Gott ohne Gott. Ein Dialog mit J. P. Sartre*, Graz and Vienna 1972.

81. On Freud's criticism of religion: A. Plé, *Freud et la religion*, Paris 1968; K. Birk, *S. Freud und die Religion*, Münsterschwarzach 1970; J. Scharfenberg, *Sigmund Freud und seine Religionskritik als Herausforerung für den christlichen Glauben*, Göttingen ³1971; id., *Religion zwischen Wahn und Wirklichkeit. Gesammelte Beiträge zur Korrelation von Theologie und Psychoanalyse*, Hamburg 1972; H. Zahrnt (ed.), *Jesus und Freud. Ein Symposion von Psychoanalytikern und Theologen*, Munich 1972; E. Nase and J. Scharfenberg (eds.), *Psychoanalyse und Religion*, Darmstadt 1977. On the interpretation of Freud's work generally: E. Jones, *The Life and Work of Sigmund Freud*, 3 vols. London and New York 1953–7; P. Ricoeur, *Freud and Philosophy: An Essay on Interpretation*, ET D. Savage, New Haven 1970; W. Loch, *Zur Theorie, Technik und Therapie der Psychoanalyse*, Frankfurt 1972; A. Mitscherlich, *Der Kampf um die Erinnerung*.

Psychoanalyse für fortgeschrittenen Anfänger, Munich 1975. In this context the debate over the books of J. Pohier, *Au nom du Père. Recherches théologiques et psychoanalytiques*, Paris 1972, and *Quand je dis Dieu*, Paris 1977, is of some importance. The Declaration (3 April 1979) by the Congregation for the Doctrine of the Faith on Pohier's second book may be found in *TPS* 24, 1979, 227–8.

82. Freud, *The Future of an Illusion*, ET W. D. Robson-Scott, rev. J. Strachey, London 1961; New York 1964, Anchor Books ed., 30.

83. Ibid., 47.

84. Ibid., 71.

85. Ibid., 81–82.

86. On Marx's criticism of religion: M. Reding, *Thomas von Aquin und Karl Marx*, Graz 1953; R. Garaudy, *Gott ist tot*, Frankfurt 1969; V. Gardavsky, *God Is Not Yet Dead*, ET V. Menkes, London and Baltimore 1973; G. M. M. Cottier, *L'athéisme du jeune Marx. Ses origines hégéliennes*, Paris 1969; W. Post, *Kritik der Religion bei Karl Marx*, Munich 1969; J. Kadenbach, *Das Religionsverständnis von Karl Marx*, Munich – Paderborn – Vienna 1970; R. Garaudy, *From Anathema to Dialogue: The Challenge of Marxist-Christian Cooperation*, ET L. O'Neill, with Replies by K. Rahner and J. B. Metz, ET E. Quinn, London 1967; H. Rolfes (ed.), *Marxismus und Christentum*, Mainz 1974; V. Spülbeck, *Neomarxismus und Theologie*, Freiburg 1977. On Marxism in general: J. M. Bochenski, *Der sowjetrussische dialektische Materialismus*, Munich – Salzburg – Cologne 1958; G. A. Wetter, *Dialectical Materialism*, ET P. Heath, New York 1958, J. Habermas, 'Zur philosphischen Diskussion um Marx und Marxismus', in *Theorie und Praxis*, Neuwied-Berlin, ³1969, 261–335 [not included in the abridged *Theory and Practice*, ET J. Viertel, Boston, 1973]; I. Fetscher, *Karl Marx und der Marxismus. Von der Philosophie des Proletariats zur proletarischen Weltanschauung*, Munich 1967; K. Hartmann, *Die Marxsche Theorie*, Berlin 1970; L. Kolakowski, *Main Currents of Marxism: Its Origins, Growth and Dissolution*, ET P. S. Falla, 3 vols., New York 1978 (1981).

87. Marx, 'Contribution to the Critique of Hegel's Philosophy of Right', in Bottomore, op. cit. (n. 59), 43.

88. Ibid., 44.

89. 'Theses on Feuerbach', no. 6, in Easton and Guddat, op. cit. (n. 60), 402.

90. 'Contribution to the Critique. . .', in Bottomore, 43.

91. 'Notes to the Doctoral Dissertation', in Easton and Guddat, 52; cf. 'The Leading Article in No. 179 of the *Kölnische Zeitung*: Religion, Free Press, and Philosophy', in Easton and Guddat, 109–30; 'Contribution to the Critique. . .', in Bottomore, 51.

92. 'Theses on Feuerbach', no. 11, in Easton and Guddat, 402.

93. Ibid., no. 1f. (402–3).

94. 'On the Jewish Question', in Bottomore, 30–31; 'Contribution to the Crique. . .', in ibid., 52.

95. *Zur Kritik der Nationalökonomie – Ökonomisch – philosophische Manuskripte*, in *Werke – Schriften – Briefe* I, ed., J. H. Lieber and P. Furth, Darmstadt 1962, 488.

96. 'On the Jewish Question', in Bottomore, 31; 'Contribution to the Critique. . .' in ibid., 57–8.

97. Contribution to the Critique. . .', in ibid., 52.

98. Ibid., 43–44.

99. *Capital*, ET S. Moore and E. Aveling, reprinted New York 1967, I, 71.

100. Ibid., I. 72.

101. *Zur Kritik der Nationalökonomie* (n. 95), 595.

102. On this point cf. Fetscher, op. cit. (n. 86), 215.

103. Marx, *The German Ideology*, in Easton and Guddat, 414.

104. Ibid., 438

105. *Capital* I, 79.

106. 'Contribution to the Critique. . .', in Bottomore, 44.

107. Ibid.

108. Some surveys in this area: W. Kern, 'Gesellschaftstheorie und Menschenbild in Marxismus und Christentum', in id., *Atheismus, Marxismus, Christentum, Beiträge zur Diskussion*, Innsbruck 1976, 97–118; id., 'Die marxistische Religionskritik gegenkritisch betrachtet', in ibid. 119–33, esp. 127f.; id., 'Die Religionskritik des Marxismus', in H. Rolfes (ed.), *Marxismus – Christentum*, Mainz 1974, 13–33, esp. 27–30; H. Vorgrimler, 'Zur Geschichte und Problematik des Dialogs', in ibid., 245–61; M. Prucha, 'Wandlungen im Charackter des marxistisch-christlichen Dialogs', in ibid., 262–75.

109. Cf. Apostolic Letter *Octogesima adveniens*, no. 33f.

110. Cf. Marx, Letter of 25 September 1869 to F. Engels, in Karl Marx and Friedrich Engels, *Selected Correspondence: 1846–1895*, ET D. Torr, New York 1942, 263: 'This tour in Belgium, stay in Aix-La-Chapelle and voyage up the Rhein have convinced me that priests, especially in the Catholic districts, must be energetically attacked. I shall work on these lines through the International. The curs (e.g., Bishop Ketteler in Mainz, the parsons at the Düsseldorf Congress, etc.) are flirting, where they find it suitable, with the labour question.' Cf. Marx and Engels, *The Communist Manifesto*.

111. E. Bloch, *Das Prinzip Hoffnung*, Frankfurt 1959, 1413.

112. Id., *Atheism in Christianity: The Religion of the Exodus and the Kingdom*, ET J. T. Swann, New York 1972, 9.

113. K. Rahner, 'Marxist Utopia and the Christian Future of Man', in *Theological Investigations* 6, ET K.-H. and B. Kruger, London and Baltimore 1967, 57–68.

114. The interpretation of Marxism as secularized messianism is already to be found in S. N. Bulgakov, *Sozialismus im Christentum?* (1909–10) Göttingen 1977. This interpretation exercised a strong influence especially on K. Löwith, *Meaning in History: The Theological Implications of the Philosophy of History*, Chicago 1949, 33–53.

115. Marx, *Zur Kritik der Nationalökonomie* (n. 95), 605f.; cf. 645.

116. 'On the Jewish Question', in Bottomore, 11.

117. 'Contribution to the Critique. . .', in ibid., 52.

118. V. Gardavsky, *God Is Not Yet Dead* (n. 86), 154.

119. 'Synodenbeschluss: Kirche und Arbeiterschaft', 1, in *Gemeinsame Synode der Bistümer in der Bundersrepublik Deutschlands. Offizielle Gesamtausgabe*, Freiburg – Basle – Vienna 1976, 327.

120. M. Weber, *The Protestant Ethic and the Spirit of Capitalism*, ET T. Parsons, New York 1930.

121. Vatican II, *Gaudium et spes*, 12.

122. Ibid., 25.

123. Ibid., 76.

124. Ibid., 21.

125. This point of view derives from W. Benjamin, 'Theses on the Philosophy of History', in his *Illuminations*, ET H. Zohn, New York 1968, 255–66. It has been taken over into a theological framework and further developed there especially by H. Peukert, *Wissenschaftstheorie – Handlungstheorie – Fundamentale Theologie. Analysen zur Ansatz und Status theologischer Theoriebildung*, Düsseldorf 1976, 283ff.

126. On Nietzsche: K. Löwith, *Nietzsches Philosophie der ewigen Wiederkunft des Gleichen*, Berlin 1935; H. de Lubac, *The Drama of Atheist Humanism*, ET E. M. Riley, New York 1950; K. Jaspers, *Nietzsche und das Christentum*, Munich 1952; id., *Nietzsche. Einführung in das Verständnis seines Philosphierens*, Berlin ³1950; J. B. Lotz, *Zwischen Seligkeit und Verdammnis. Ein Beitrag zu dem Thema: Nietzsche und das Christentum*, Freiburg 1953; E. Benz, *Nietzsches Ideen zur Geshichte des Christentums und der Kirche*, Leiden 1956; G. G. Grau, *Christlicher Glaube und intellektuelle Redlichkeit. Eine religionsgeschichtliche Studie über Nietzsche*, Frankfurt 1958; B. Welte, *Nietzsches Atheismus und das Christentum*, Freiburg 1953; M. Heidegger, 'The Word of Nietzsche: "God Is Dead" ', in his *The Question concerning Technology, and Other Essays*, ET W. Lovitt, New York 1977, 115–54; id., *Nietzsche*, 2 vols. Prullingen, 1961; E. Biser, *'Gott ist tot.' Nietzsches Destruktion des christlichen Bewusstseins*, Munich 1962; id., 'Nietzsches Kritik des christlichen Gottesbegriffs und ihre theologischen Konsequenzen', *PhJ* 78, 1971, 34–64, 295–304; W. Müller-Lauter, *Nietzsche, Seine Philosophie der Gengensätze und die Gegensätze seiner Philosophie*, Berlin 1971; E. Fink, *Nietzsches Philosophie*, Stuttgart ³1973.

127. Nietzsche, *Human All-Too-Human*, no. 1, ET H. Zimmern in O. Levy (ed.), *Complete Works of Nietzsche*, reprinted New York 1964, 631. Cf. *The Gay Science*, Preface to the second edition, no. 3, ET W. Kaufmann, New York 1974, Vintage Books ed., 36.

128. *Beyond Good and Evil*, Part I, 'On the Prejudices of Philosophers', ET W. Kaufmann, New York 1966, Vintage Books ed., 9–31.

129. *The Will to Power*, no. 493, ET W. Kaufmann and R. J. Hollingdale, New York 1967, 272.

130. *On the Genealogy of Morals*, Part III, no. 12, ET W. Kaufmann, New York 1967, Vintage Books ed. 1969, 119; *The Will to Power*, no. 259 (Kaufmann-Hollingdale, 149).

131. *Beyond Good and Evil*, Preface (Kaufmann, 3).

132. *Human All-Too-Human*, no. 1 (Zimmern, 2).

133. *Thus Spoke Zarathustra*, Part II, no. 12: 'On Self-Overcoming' (Kaufmann, 115); *Beyond Good and Evil*, nos. 13 and 258 (Kaufmann, 21, 202), etc.

134. Nietzsche very often speaks of the Dionysian versus the Apollonian: *The Birth of Tragedy*, ET W. Kaufmann, New York 1967, Vintage Books ed., passim; *The Gay Science*, no. 270 (Kaufmann, 327–31); *Twilight of the Idols*, 'Expeditions of an Untimely Man', no. 20, ET R. J. Hollingdale, Baltimore 1968, 72; *Nietzsche contra Wagner*, 'We Antipodes', in W. Kaufmann (ed.), *The Portable Nietzsche*, New York 1954, 669–71; *The Will to Power*, nos. 417, 1050 (Kaufmann and Hollingdale 224, 539).

135. *Beyond Good and Evil*, Preface (Kaufmann, 3).

136. *The Gay Science*, no. 344 (Kaufmann, 280–82).

137. Ibid. (Kaufmann, 283).

138. Ibid., Appendix of Songs (Kaufmann, 351).

139. *Ecce Homo*, Part IV, 'Why I Am a Destiny', no. 8, ET W. Kaufmann, New York 1967, Vintage Books ed. 1969, 334.

140. *The Anti-Christ*, no. 40, ET R. J. Hollingdale, Baltimore 1968, 153.

141. M. Heidegger, 'The Word of Nietzsche: "God Is Dead" ' (n. 86).

142. Nietzsche, *The Anti-Christ*, no. 18 (Hollingdale, 128).

143. *The Will to Power*, no. 1052 (Kaufmann and Hollingdale, 543).

144. *Ecce Homo*, Part IV, 'Why I Am a Destiny', no. 9 (Kaufmann, 335); cf. *The Will to Power*, nos. 401 and 1052 (Kaufmann and Hollingdale, 217 and 543).

145. *The Gay Science*, no. 125 (Kaufmann, 181).

146. Ibid., no. 343 (Kaufmann, 279).

147. Ibid., no. 108 (Kaufmann, 167).

148. Ibid., no. 343 (Kaufmann, 280).

149. Ibid., (Kaufmann, 279).

150. Ibid., no. 125 (Kaufmann, 181).

151. *The Anti-Christ*, no. 18 (Hollingdale, 128).

152. *The Will to Power*, Preface, no. 4 (Kaufmann and Hollingdale, 4).

153. Ibid.

154. *The Anti-Christ*, no. 58 (Hollingdale, 182).

155. *The Will to Power*, no. 2 (Kaufmann and Hollingdale, 9)

156. Ibid., no. 598 (Kaufmann and Hollingdale, 325).

157. Ibid., no. 12A (Kaufmann and Hollingdale, 13).

158. Ibid., no. 23 (Kaufmann and Hollingdale, 18).

159. Ibid., no. 866 (Kaufmann and Hollingdale, 464).

160. *Thus Spoke Zarathustra*, Part I, no. 22: 'On the Gift-Giving Virtue' (Kaufmann, 79).

161. Ibid., Zarathustra's Prologue, no. 3 (Kaufmann, 13).

162. Ibid., no. 7 (Kaufmann, 20).

163. Ibid., nos. 3 and 4 (Kaufmann, 12 and 15).

164. Ibid., no. 3 (Kaufmann, 13).

165. Ibid., no. 9 (Kaufmann, 23).

166. Ibid., Part I, no. 4: 'On the Despisers of the Body' (Kaufmann, 34–5).

167. *The Gay Science*, no. 125 (Kaufmann, 181).

168. *Thus Spoke Zarathustra*, Part II, no. 2: 'Upon the Blessed Isles' (Kaufmann, 86).

169. Ibid., Part I, no. 1: 'On the Three Metamorphoses' (Kaufmann, 25–7).

170. Ibid., Part II, no. 20: 'On Redemption' (Kaufmann, 141); cf. Part III, no. 12: 'On Old and New Tablets' (Kaufmann, 208–9).

171. Ibid., Part IV, no. 19: 'The Drunken Song' (Kaufmann, 318).

172. Ibid., Part III, no. 2: 'On the Vision and the Riddle' (Kaufmann, 155–60).

173. Ibid., Part III, no. 13: 'The Convalescent' (Kaufmann, 217–18).

174. Ibid., Part IV, no. 10: 'At Noon' (Kaufmann, 275–8).

175. Ibid., Part IV, no. 20: 'The Sign' (Kaufmann, 324).

176. *The Will to Power*, no. 1041 (Kaufmann and Hollingdale, 536).

177. *Ecce Homo*, Part II, 'Why I Am So Clever', no. 10 (Kaufmann, 258); cf. *The Will to Power*, no. 1041 (Kaufmann and Hollingdale, 536); etc.

178. F. Schiller, *Die Götter Griechenlands*, Sämtliche Werke I, ed. G. Fricke and H. G. Göpfert, Munich ²1960, 169–73.

179. F. Hölderlin, *Patmos*, Sämtliche Werke II, ed. F. Beissner, Stuttgart 1953, 173.

180. M. Heidegger, *Erläuterungen zu Hölderlins Dichtung*, Frankfurt 1951, 38f., 61f., 73, etc.

181. Nietzsche, *Thus Spoke Zarathustra*, Part III, no. 8: 'On Apostates' (Kaufmann, 182); repeated in Part III, no. 12: 'On Old and New Tablets' (Kaufmann, 203).

182. *The Will to Power*, no. 1038 (Kaufmann and Hollingdale, 534).

183. Ibid., no. 1034 (Kaufmann and Hollingdale, 533).

184. *Thus Spoke Zarathustra*, Part IV, no. 5: 'The Magician' (Kaufmann, 255).

185. *Twilight of the Idols*, Section ' "Reason" in Philosophy', no. 5 (Hollingdale, 38).

186. *The Gay Science*, no. 354 (Kaufmann, 300); cf. *Beyond Good and Evil*, Nietzsche's Preface and nos. 20, 34, 54 (Kaufmann, 2, 27–8, 47, 67).

187. *Twilight of the Idols*, Section ' "Reason" in Philosophy', no. 5 (Hollingdale, 38).

188. *The Anti-Christ*, no. 30 (Hollingdale, 142).

189. Ibid., nos. 29 and 33 (Hollingdale, 141, 146).

190. Ibid., no. 34 (Hollingdale, 147).

191. Cf. Nietzsche's criticism of Jesus in *Thus Spoke Zarathustra*, Part I, no. 21: 'On Free Death' (Kaufmann, 73): 'He died too early: he himself would have recanted his teaching, had he reached my age. Noble enough was he to recant.'

192. *Thus Spoke Zarathustra*, Part I, no. 22: 'On the Gift-Giving Virtue' (Kaufmann, 74–9).

193. J. C. Fichte, *Rückerunnerungen, Antworten, Fragen* (1799), WW III, ed. F. Medicus, 235.

194. Fichte, *Appellation an das Publikum*, WW III, 176.

195. L. Feuerbach, 'Preliminary Theses on the Reform of Philosophy' (1842), in Hanfi, op. cit. (n. 37).

Chapter III   The Predicament of Theology in the Face of Atheism

1. There is a classical formulation of both approaches in Thomas Aquinas, *ST* I, 1, 8.

2. Cf. J. M. Gonzáles-Ruiz, 'L'ateismo nella Bibbia', in *L'ateismo contemporaneo* 4, Turin 1969, 5–20.

3. Cf. A. M. Javierre, 'L'ateismo nei Padri della chiesa', in ibid., 4, 21–42.

4. Anselm of Canterbury, *Proslogion* 3f.

5. Thomas Aquinas, *De ver*. 22, 2 ad 1; *In I Sent*., d. 3, q. 1, a. 2.

6. Id., *ST* II-II, 2, 3 ad 5; *De ver*. 14, 11.

7. Id., *De ver*. 14, 11 ad 7.

8. Id., *ST* I-II, 89, 6; cf. M. Seckler, *Instinkt und Glaubenswille nach Thomas von Aquin*, Mainz 1961, 237–58.

9. DS 2901f.; ND 411/1–2.

10. *COD*, 804f.

11. DS 3004, 3006; ND 113, 216.

12. DS 3021–23; ND 414–16.

13. Cf. A. Rohrbasser (ed.), *Heilslehre der Kirche*, Freiburg/Switz. 1953, no. 184, 1093–5.

14. Cf. ibid., no. 992–6.

15. Cf. ibid., no. 736, 751, 936, 1589. In addition, in his Encyclical *Humani*

generis (1950) Pius XII again emphasizes the possibility of natural knowledge of the personal (!) God, although he does discuss in detail the difficulties against this position. Cf. DS 3875, 3992; ND 144, 2135.

16. John XXIII, Encyclical *Mater et Magistra* (1963), 207–15.

17. Paul VI, Encyclical *Ecclesiam Suam* (1964), 96–8.

18. Vatican II, *Gaudium et spes*, 19. Cf. P. 'Ladrière, L'athéisme au Concile Vatican II', *Archives de sociologie des religions* 16, 1971, no. 32, 53–85; C. Moeller, 'History of the Constitution', in H. Vorgrimler (ed.), *Commentary on the Documents of Vatican II 5*, ET W. J. O'Hara, New York 1969, 1–76; J. Ratzinger, 'Commentary on Part I, Chapter I, Articles 19–22', in ibid., 143–63; J. Figl, *Atheismus als theologisches Problem. Modelle der Auseinandersetzung in der Theologie der Gegenwart*, Tübinger Theol. Stud. 9, Mainz 1977, 31–81.

19. R. Garaudy, *From Anathema to Dialogue: The Challenge of Marxist-Christian Cooperation*, ET L. O'Neill, with Replies by K. Rahner and J. B. Metz, ET E. Quinn, London 1967.

20. Vatican II, *Gaudium et spes*, 21. It is important that the documents use the word *reprobat* instead of *damnat*. It is also significant that despite numerous petitions to the contrary the Council avoids specifically naming and condemning communism. Cf. Ratzinger, art. cit., 151–2, 149–50.

21. Vatican II, *Gaudium et spes*, 19.

22. Ibid., 21.

23. Ibid.

24. Ibid.

25. Ibid., 22.

26. Cf. especially the Encyclical *Redemptor hominis* (1979).

27. Cf. Ratzinger, art. cit., 154f.

28. Ibid., 145.

29. Ibid., 150.

30. Contemporary discussion of the God-question (exclusive of writers to be discussed subsequently in the text): J. Lacroix, *The Meaning of Modern Atheism*, ET G. Barden, New York 1965; H. Gollwitzer, *Die Existenz Gottes im Bekenntnis des Glaubens*, Munich 1963; J. C. Murray, *The Problem of God: Yesterday and Today*, New Haven 1964; H. Zahrnt, *The Question of God: Protestant Theology in the Twentieth Century*, ET R. A. Wilson, London 1969; id. (ed.), *Gespräch über Gott. Die protestantische Theologie im 20. Jahrhundert. Ein Textbuch*, Munich 1968; id., *What Kind of God? A Question of Faith*, ET R. A. Wilson, London 1971; C. H. Ratschow, *Gott existiert. Eine dogmatische Studie*, Berlin 1966; N. Kutschki (ed.), *Gott heute. Fünfzehn Beiträge zur Gottesfrage*, Mainz and Munich 1967; H. J. Schultz (ed.), *Wer ist das eigentlich – Gott?*, Munich 1969; E. Castelli (ed.), *L'analyse du langage théologique. Le nom de Dieu*, Paris 1969; W. Kasper, *Glaube und Geschichte*, Mainz 1970, esp. 101–43; E. Coreth and J. B. Lotz, *Atheismus kritisch betrachtet*, Munich and Freiburg 1971; E. Biser, *Theologie und Atheismus, Anstösse zu einer theologischen Aporetik*, Munich 1972; J. Blank *et al.*, *Gott-Frage und moderner Atheismus*, Regensburg 1972; J. Ratzinger (ed.), *Die Frage nach Gott*, QD 56, Freiburg – Basle – Vienna 1972; H. Fries (ed.), *Gott, die Frage unserer Zeit*, Munich 1972; id., *Abschied von Gott? Eine Herausforderung – Versuch einer Antwort*, Freiburg – Basle – Vienna ³1974; K. Rahner (ed.), *Ist Gott noch gefragt? Zur Funktionslosigkeit des Gottesglaubens*, Düsseldorf 1973; B. Casper, *Wesen und Grenzen der Religionskritik. Feuerbach – Marx – Freud*,

Würzburg 1974; R. Schaeffler, *Die Religionskritik sucht ihren Partner. Thesen zur einer erneuerten Apologetik*, Freiburg – Basle – Vienna 1974; J. Möller, *Die Chance des Menschen – Gott genannt. Was Vernunft und Erfahrung von Gott sagen können*, Zürich – Einsiedeln – Cologne 1975; W. Kern, *Atheismus, Marxismus, Christentum*, Innsbruck 1976; H. Döring, *Abwesenheit Gottes. Fragen und Antworten heutiger Theologie*, Paderborn 1977; H. Küng, *Does God Exist? An Answer for Today*, ET E. Quinn, Garden City and London 1980; W. Brugger, *Summe einer philosophischen Gotteslehre*, Munich 1979; H. R. Schlette (ed.), *Der modern Agnostizismus*, Düsseldorf 1979; K. H. Weger (ed.), *Religionskritik von der Aufklärung bis zur Gegenwart. Autoren-Lexikon von Adorno bis Wittgenstein*, Freiburg – Basle – Vienna 1975; id., *Der Mensch vor dem Anspruch Gottes. Glaubensbegründung in einer agnostischen Welt*, Graz – Vienna – Cologne 1981.

31. On K. Rahner's theological approach: B. van der Heijden, *Karl Rahner. Darlegung und Kritik seiner Grundposition*, Einsiedeln 1973; K. Fischer, *Der Mensch als Geheimnis. Die Anthropologie Karl Rahners*, Ökumenische Forschungen II/5, Freiburg – Basle – Vienna 1974; K. Lehmann, 'Karl Rahner', in H. Vorgrimler and R. van der Gucht (eds.), *Bilanz der Theologie im 20. Jahrhundert. Bahnbrechende Theologen*, Freiburg – Basle – Vienna 1970, 143–81; P. Eicher, *Offenbarung, Prinzip neuzeitlicher Theologie*, Munich 1977; K. H. Weger, *Karl Rahner. An Introduction to His Theology*, ET D. Smith, New York 1980; W. Kasper, 'Karl Rahner – Theologe in einer Zeit des Umbruche', *TQ* 159, 1979, 263–71. Karl Rahner laid the foundations for this theory in his early work, *Spirit in the World* (1939), ET W. V. Dych New York 1967; he developed it along religio-philosophical lines in his *Hearers of the Word*, ET M. Richards, New York 1969; it is summarized in *Foundations of Christian Faith: An Introduction to the Idea of Christianity*, ET W. V. Dych, New York and London 1978.

32. K. Rahner, 'Atheism and Implicit Christianity', in his *Theological Investigations* 9, ET G. Harrison, London and New York 1972, 145–64; 'Theological Considerations on Secularization and Atheism', in ibid., 11, ET D. Bourke, New York 1974, 166–84; 'Atheism', *SacMundi* 1, 117–22.

33. Cf. J. Figl, op. cit. (n. 18), 175f.

34. This thesis is already present in Heidegger's *Being and Time*, ET J. Macquarrie and E. Robinson, London and New York 1962, 19, 43, 487, etc.; cf. id., 'What Is Metaphysics?', ET R. F. C. Hull and A. Crick in Martin Heidegger, *Existence and Being*, Chicago 1949, 355ff.; id., *Holzwege*, Frankfurt 1957, 195f., 238–47, etc.

35. 'The Age of the World Picture', in his *The Question concerning Technology, and Other Essays*, ET W. Lovitt New York 1977, 115–54; id., 'The Question concerning Technology', in ibid., 3–35.

36. *Identity and Difference*, ET J. Stambaugh, New York 1969, 72.

37. 'The Word of Nietzsche: God Is Dead', in *The Question concerning Technology*, 104–6.

38. 'What is Metaphysics?', 378.

39. For what follows cf. especially B. Welte, 'Die philosophische Gotteserkenntnis und die Möglichkeit des Atheismus', in his *Zeit und Geheimnis. Philosophische Abhandlungen zur Sache Gottes in der Zeit der Welt*, Freiburg – Basle – Vienna 1975, 109–23; id., 'Versuch zur Frage nach Gott', ibid., 124–38; id., *Religions-philosophie*, Freiburg – Basle – Vienna, 1978, 150–65.

40. This post-nihilist position is also to be found in H. Küng, *Does God Exist?* (n. 30).

41. For Welte's interpretation of Eckhart, cf. 'Meister Eckhart als Aristoteliker', in his *Auf der Spur des Ewigen*. *Philosophische Abhandlungen über verschiedene Gegenstände der Religion und der Theologie*, Freiburg – Basle – Vienna, 1965, 197–210; id., *Meister Eckhart. Gedanken zu seinen Gedanken*, Freiburg – Basle – Vienna 1979.

42. Cf. Welte, 'Nietzsches Atheismus und das Christentum', in his *Auf der Spur des Ewigen*, 228–61.

43. Cf. Figl, op. cit., 205f.

44. For what follows cf. H. Urs von Balthasar, *Herrlichkeit. Eine theologische Ästhetick* III/1, Einsiedeln, 1965, 943–83; id., 'Der Zugang zur Wirklichkeit Gottes', *Mysal* I, 15–45.

45. *Herrlichkeit* III/1, 945.

46. 'Der Zugang. . .', 18.

47. Plato, *Republic* VI, 505a–509c; *Ep*. VII, 341c. Other philosophical testimonies in Balthasar, 'Der Zugang. . .', 22f.; Balthasar also refers to Thomas Aquinas, *De ver*., 22, 2, ad 2.

48. This is the formula of E. Jüngel, *Unterwegs zur Sache. Theologische Bemerkungen*, BEvT 61, Munich 1972, v, and often.

49. Cf. H. Urs von Balthasar, *The God-Question and Modern Man*, ET H. Graef (original title *Science, Religion and Christianity*, Westminster, Md. 1958), 111–19. On this basic theme in Balthasar's thinking, cf. H. P. Heinz, *Der Gott des Je-mehr. Der christologische Ansatz Hans Urs von Balthasars*, Disputationes Theologicae 3, Frankfurt 1975.

50. I limit myself here to the political theology represented by J. B. Metz. Metz's most important statements on the subject are: *Theology of the World*, ET W. Glen-Doepel, New York and London 1969, 89–97, 107–24; 'Apologetics 1. Apologetics in General', *SacMundi* 1, 66–70; id., *Faith in History and Society: Toward a Practical Fundamental Theology*, ET D. Smith, New York 1980; id., *The Emergent Church: The Future of Christianity in a Postbourgois World*, ET P. Mann, New York 1981. For discussion: H. Peukert (ed.), *Diskussion zur 'politischen Theologie'*, Mainz and Munich 1969; H. Maier, *Kritik der politischen Theologie*, Einsiedeln 1970; G. Bauer, *Christliche Hoffnung und menschlicher Fortschritt. Die politische Theologie von J. B. Metz als christliche Begründung gesellschaftlicher Verantwortung des Christen*, Mainz 1975; S. Wiedenhofer, *Politische Theologie*, Stuttgart 1976, with bibliography. Cf. also the bibliography in Metz, *Faith in History and Society*, 77 nn. 1–2.

51. I shall mention here only a few works from a very extensive literature: G. Gutiérrez, *A Theology of Liberation*, ET Sr. C. Inda and J. Eagleson, Maryknoll, NY and London 1973; H. Assmann, *Theology for a Nomad church*, ET P. Burns, London and Maryknoll, NY 1975; L. Segundo, *The Liberation of Theology*, ET J. Drury, Maryknoll, NY and London 1976; J. M. Bonino, *Doing Theology in a Revolutionary Situation*, Philadelphia and London 1975; P. Hünermann and G. D. Fischer (eds.), *Gott im Aufbruch. Die Provokation der lateinamerikanischen Theologie*, Freiburg – Basle – Vienna 1974; K. Rahner *et al*. (eds.), *Befreiende Theologie. Der Beitrag Lateinamerikas zur Theologie der Gegenwart*, Stuttgart 1977.

52. Metz, *Faith in History and Society*, 46.

53. Ibid., 136–53; cf. id., *The Emergent Church*, 82–94; L. Boff, *Die*

Neuentdeckung der Kirche. Basisgemeinden in Lateinamerika, Mainz 1980, A. Exeler and N. Mette (eds.), *Theologie des Volkes*, Mainz 1978.

54. Metz, *Faith in History and Society*, 60, 67ff.

55. Cf. above, 14f.

56. Cf. especially J. B. Metz, *Followers of Christ: The Religious Life and the Church*, ET T. Linton, New York 1978.

57. On the concept of practice and on its history and problems cf. M. Theunissen, 'Die Verwirklichung der Vernunft. Zur Theorie-Praxis-Diskussion im Anschluss an Hegel', *PhRu*, 1970, Beiheft 6; P. Engelhardt (ed.), *Zur Theorie der Praxis. Interpretationen und Aspekte*, Walberberger Studien der Albertus-Magnus-Akademie, Philosophische Reihe 2, Mainz 1970; L. Bertsch, *Theologie zwischen Theorie und Praxis. Beiträge zur Grundlegung der praktischen Theologie*, Frankfurt 1975; K. Lehmann, 'Das Theorie-Praxis-Problem und die Begründung der Praktischen Theologie', in F. Klostermann and R. Zerfass (eds.), *Praktische Theologie Heute*, Munich and Mainz 1974, 81–102; R. Bubner, *Theorie und Praxis – eine nachhegelsche Abstraktion*, Frankfurt 1971.

58. T. W. Adorno, 'Marginalien zur Theorie und Praxis', in his *Stichworte. Kritische Modelle I*, Frankfurt 1969, 173.

59. Metz has tried to do justice to this viewpoint in his thesis on *memoria*. For the most recent statement of this thesis cf. *Faith in History and Society*, 184–204. But he discusses this basic category only in the framework of past and present philosophical concepts of *memoria* and pays hardly any attention to the biblical and sacramental-liturgical meaning of anamnesis-*memoria*.

60. The literature on Barth has grown beyond all bounds since he wrote. I limit myself to the presentation by Hans Urs von Balthasar, *The Theology of Karl Barth*, ET J. Drury, New York 1971, which is still authoritative for the Catholic view of Barth and for the criticism of Barth generally. There is an excellent survey of the entire discussion of Barth in E. Jüngel, 'Karl Barth', *TRE 5*, 251–68.

61. Cf. below, 74ff.

62. K. Barth, *The Epistle to the Romans*, ET E. C. Hoskyns, London 1933, 28.

63. *Church Dogmatics* I/1, ET G. T. Thomson, Edinburgh 1936, x.

64. Ibid., 44, 385f., etc.

65. *Church Dogmatics* I/2, ET G. T. Thomson and H. Knight, Edinburgh 1956, 280.

66. Ibid., 302f., 314.

67. Ibid., 320.

68. Ibid., 303.

69. Ibid., 326.

70. Cf. the statements in *Church Dogmatics* III/2, ET G. W. Bromiley and T. F. Torrance, Edinburgh 1961–62, 220f., 323f., on the *analogia relationis* (analogy of relation), which is different from the *analogia entis* (analogy of being) and yet in its content approximates very closely to what Catholics mean by the latter. Barth goes still further in *Church Dogmatics* IV/3.

71. On D. Bonhoeffer, cf. E. Bethge, *Dietrich Bonhoeffer. Man of Vision – Man of Courage*, ET E. Mosbacher *et al.* London and New York 1970; E. Feil, *Die Theologie Bonhoeffers. Hermeneutik – Christologie – Weltverständis*, Gesellschaft und Theologie: Systematische Beiträge 6, Munich and Mainz 1971.

72. D. Bonhoeffer, *Letters and Papers from Prison*, ET Frank Clarke *et al.*, The Enlarged Edition, London and New York 1971.

73. Ibid., 360–1.

74. Ibid., 362.

75. H. Braun, 'Die Problematik einer Theologie des Neuen Testaments', in his *Gesammelte Studien zum Neuen Testament und seiner Umwelt*, Tübingen 1962, 341.

76. D. Sölle, *Atheistisch an Gott glauben. Beiträge zur Theologie*, Olten – Freiburg 1968.

77. Id., *Das Recht ein anderer zu werden. Theologische Texte*, Theologie und Politik 1, Neuwied-Berlin 1972, 86.

78. *Atheistisch an Gott glauben*, 79.

79. Ibid., 82.

80. Ibid., 81, 86.

81. Id., *Christ the Representative: An Essay in Theology after the 'Death of God'*, ET D. Lewis, London and Philadelphia 1967, 11–12.

82. For discussion: H. Gollwitzer, *Von der Stellvertretung Gottes: Christlicher Glaube in der Erfahrung der Verborgenheit Gottes. Zum Gespräch mit Dorothee Sölle*, Munich ²1968 id., *Die Existenz Gottes im Bekenntnis des Glaubens*, BEvT 3, Munich, ⁵1968; W. Kern, *Atheismus – Marxismus – Christentum. Beiträge zur Diskussion*, Innsbruck – Vienna – Munich 1971, 134–51, especially 137f.; H. W. Bartsch (ed.), *Post Bultmann locutum. Zur Mainzer Diskussion der Professoren D. Helmut Gollwitzer und D. Herbert Braun*, Vol. 2, Theologische Forschung 37, Hamburg-Bergstedt, ²1966; Figl, op. cit., 225–8.

83. Cf. J. Bishop, *Die 'Gott-ist-tot-Theologie'*, Düsseldorf 1968; S. M. Daecke, *Der Mythos vom Tode Gottes. Ein kritischer Überblick* Hamburg 1969; L. Scheffczyk, *Gottloser Gottesglaube*, Regensburg 1974.

84. J. A. T. Robinson, *Honest to God*, London and Philadelphia 1963. For discussion: H. W. Augustin (ed.), *Diskussion zu Bischof Robinsons Gott ist anders*, Munich 1964; E. Schillebeeckx, *Personale Begegnung mit Gott. Eine Antwort an John A. T. Robinson*, Mainz 1964; id., *Neues Glaubensverständnis, Honest to Robinson*, Mainz 1964.

85. J. Moltmann, *The Crucified God: The Cross of Christ as the Foundation and Criticism of Christian Theology*, ET R. A. Wilson and John Bowden, London and New York 1974.

86. Ibid., 207–19.

87. Ibid., 251.

88. Ibid., 25–8.

89. Ibid., 252.

90. Cf. H. Urs von Balthasar, *The Theology of Karl Barth*.

91. Cf. E. Przywara, *Analogia entis. Metaphysik*, Schriften 3, Einsiedeln 1962, 206f.

92. L. Gilkey, *Naming the Whirlwind. The Renewal of God-Language*, Indianapolis and New York 1969.

93. A. N. Whitehead, *Process and Reality. An Essay in Cosmology*, New York 1929; C. Hartshorne, *The Divine Relativity. A Social Conception of God*, New Haven ²1964; J. B. Cobb, *A Christian Natural Theology. Based on the Thought of Alfred North Whitehead*, Philadelphia and London, 1960; S. M. Ogden, *The Reality of God*, New York and London 1967.

94. W. Pannenberg, 'Types of Atheism and Their Theological Significance', in his *Basic Questions in Theology*, ET G. H. Kehm, 2 vols., London and Philadelphia

1970–71, 1, 184–200; id., 'The Question of God', ibid., 1, 201–33; id., *Basic Questions in Theology* III (American title *The Idea of God and Human Freedom*), ET R. A. Wilson, London and Philadelphia 1973.
95. *Basic Questions III/The Idea of God*, 87–8.
96. Ibid., 100.
97. Ibid., 141–2.
98. G. Ebeling, *Wort und Glaube* 3 vols., Tübingen 1960–75 (Vol. 1 of *Word and Faith* has been translated by J. W. Leitch, London and Philadelphia 1963); id., *Lutherstudien* 1, Tübingen 1971, 221–72; id., *Dogmatik des christlichen Glaubens* 1, Tübingen 1979.
99. E. Jüngel, *God as the Mystery of the World*, ET D. L. Guder, Grand Rapids 1982, id., *Entsprechungen: Gott – Wahrheit – Mensch. Theologische Erörterungen*, BEvT 88, Munich, 1980.
100. M. Luther, *Der grosse Katechismus*, in *BSLK*, 560.
101. Ebeling, *Dogmatik des christlichen Glaubens* 1, 216; cf. 212ff.
102. Luther, ibid.
103. L. Feuerbach, *The Essence of Christianity*, ET G. Eliot (1854), New York 1967, Torchbook ed., 12.
104. Cf. especially G. Ebeling, *God and Word*, ET J. W. Leitch, Philadelphia 1967; id., *Dogmatik des christlichen Glaubens* 1, 60ff., 189ff.
105. *God and Word*, 28; same idea in E. Jüngel, *God as the Mystery of the World*, 203ff., 307ff.
106. Ebeling, ibid., 29.
107. Ibid., 31; cf. the title of Jüngel's principal work: 'God as the Mystery of the World'.
108. Ibid., 44.
109. Ebeling, *Dogmatik des christlichen Glaubens* 1, 209, 218f.; id., *Lutherstudien* 1, 216f.; Jüngel, *Entsprechungen*, 169.
110. Ebeling, *Dogmatik des christlichen Glaubens* 1, 234.
111. Ibid., 219ff., 230ff.
112. Ibid., 212.
113. Ibid., 224
114. Jüngel, *Entsprechungen*, 202–51.
115. Ebeling, *Dogmatik des christlichen Gaubens* 1, 230ff., who refers to E. Jüngel, *The Doctrine of the Trinity: God's Being Is in Becoming*, Grand Rapids and Edinburgh 1976.
116. Cf. L. Oeing-Hanhoff, 'Die Krise des Gottesbegriffs', *TQ* 159, 1979, especially 291–4, although what for Jüngel is a problem becomes here the object of unhesitating criticism.
117. Thomas Aquinas, *ST* I, 12, 13 ad 1. I am indebted to my colleague M. Seckler for the reference to this passage and its importance.

Chapter IV Experience of God and Knowledge of God

1. On the problem and concerns of natural theology: G. Söhngen, 'Natürliche Theologie', *LTK* 7; 811–16; H. Urs von Balthasar, *The Theology of Karl Barth*, ET J. Drury, New York 1971; K. Riesenhuber, *Existenzerfahrung und Religion*, Mainz 1968; id., 'Natural Theology', *SacMundi* 4, 167–71; B. Welte, *Heilsverständnis. Philosophische Voraussetzungen zum Verständnis des Christentums*,

Freiburg–Basle–Vienna, 1966; K. Rahner, *Hearers of the Word*, ET M. Richards, New York 1969. From the vantage-point of Protestant theology: H. J. Birkner, 'Natürliche Theologie und Offenbarungstheologie. Ein theologiegeschichtlicher Überblick', *NZST* 3, 1961, 279–95; C. Gestrich, 'Die unbewältigte natürliche Theologie', *ZTK* 68, 1971, 82–120; E. Jüngel, 'Das Dilemma der natürlichen Theologie und die Wahrheit ihres Problems. Überlegungen für ein Gespräch mit Wolfhart Pannenberg', in his *Entsprechungen: Gott – Wahrheit – Mensch. Theologische Erörterungen*, BEvT 88, Munich 1980, 158–77; id., 'Gelegentliche Themen zum Problem der natürlichen Theologie', ibid., 198–201; id., 'Gott – um seiner selbst willen interessant. Plädoyer für eine natürlichere Theologie', ibid., 193–7.

2. Justin, *Apol. I*, 46 (*Corpus Apol.* I, ed. Otto, 128–30); *Apol.* II, 8; 10; 13 (ibid., 220–3, 224–9, 236–9).

3. Irenaeus, *Adv. Haer.* II, 9. 1 (SC 294, 82–5).

4. Justin, *Apol.* II, 6 (*Corpus Apol.* I, 212–17); John Damascene, *De fide orth.* I, 1 (*Die Schriften des Johannes von Damaskus*, ed. B. Kotter, II, Berlin and New York 1973, 7).

5. Tertullian, *Adv. Marc* I, 10 (CCL 1, 451).

6. Thomas Aquinas, *ST* I, 2, 2 ad 1.

7. DS 3009; ND 119. Cf. H. J. Pottmeyer, *Der Glaube vor dem Anspruch der Wissenschaft. Die Konstitution über den katholischen Glauben 'Dei Filius' des I. Vatikanischen Konzils und die unveröffentlichten Voten der vorbereitenden Kommission*, Freiburger Theol. Studien 87, Freiburg – Basle – Vienna 1968.

8. DS 3004, 3026; ND 113, 115.

9. The idea that it can be proved occurs first in the anti-modernist Oath: DS 3538; ND 143/1.

10. Vatican II, *Dei Verbum*, 6.

11. Vatican II, *Gaudium et spes*, 19–22.

12. Vatican II, *Dignitatis humanae*, 14.

13. Plato, *Republic* II, 379a.

14. Aristotle, *Metaphysica* VI, 1026a.

15. Augustine, *De civitate Dei* VI, 5 (CCL 47, 170–2).

16. Ibid., VI, 6 (CCL 47, 176–8).

17. Tertullian, *Apol.* 17, 6 (CCL 1, 117–18).

18. On this development cf. G. Söhngen, 'Natürliche Theologie', *LTK* 7, 811–16.

19. Cf. M. Seckler, 'Aufklärung und Offenbarung', in *Christlicher Glaube in moderner Gesellschaft* 21, Freiburg – Basle – Vienna 1980, 5–78.

20. Cf. H. J. Birkner, 'Natürliche Theologie und Offenbarungstheologie' (n. 1), 279ff.

21. M. Luther, *Enarratio Psalmi LI* (1532), WA 40/2, 327f.

22. K. Barth, *Natural Theology*, ET London 1946.

23. Cf. Barth, *Church Dogmatics* I/1.

24. Cf. Birkner, art. cit., 293ff.

25. On the concept of nature cf. Balthasar, *The Theology of Karl Barth* (n. 1), 217ff.

26. Cf. R. Schaeffler, *Fähigkeit zur Erfahrung. Zur transzendentalen Hermeneutik des Sprechens von Gott*, QD 94, Freiburg – Basle – Vienna 1982.

27. Cf. W. Weischedel, *Der Gott der Philosophen. Grundlegung einer philosophischen Theologie im Zeitalter des Nihilismus*, 2 vols., Darmstadt 1971–72.

28. Thomas Aquinas, *ST* I, 1, 8.

29. There is already a suggestion of this in Aristotle, *Metaphysica* XI, 8, 1074a.

30. On the problem of experience of God: H. G. Gadamer, *Truth and Method*, ET G. Barden and J. Cumming, London and New York 1975, 378–87; K. Lehmann, 'Experience', *SacMundi* 2, 307–9; P. L. Berger, *A Rumour of Angels: Modern Society and the Rediscovery of the Supernatural*, Garden City, N.Y. and London 1969; id., *The Sacred Canopy: Elements of a Sociological Theory of Religion*, Garden City, N.Y. and London 1967; W. Kasper, *Glaube und Geschichte*, Mainz, 1970, 120–43; K. Rahner, 'The Experience of God Today', in *Theological Investigations* 11, ET D. Bourke London and New York 1974, 149–65; M. Müller, *Erfahrung und Geschichte. Grundzüge einer Philosophie der Freiheit als transzendentale Erfahrung*, Freiburg and Munich 1971; E. Schillebeeckx, *The Understanding of Faith: Interpretation and Criticism*, ET N. D. Smith, London and New York 1974; id., *Jesus: An Experiment in Christology*, ET H. Hoskins, London and New York 1979, 636–68; id., *Christ: The Experience of Jesus as Lord*, ET John Bowden, London and New York 1980; id., *Interim Report on the Books Jesus and Christ*, ET John Bowden, London and New York 1981; id., 'Erfahrung und Glaube', in *Christlicher Glaube in moderner Gesellschaft* 25, Freiburg – Basle – Vienna 1980, 73–116; A. Kessler, A. Schöpf and C. Wild, 'Erfahrung', *HPG* 1, 373–86; J. Splett, *Gotteserfahrung im Denken*, Frankfurt 1973; G. Ebeling, 'Die Klage über das Erfahrungsdefizit in der Theologie als Frage nach ihrer Sache', in *Wort und Glaube* 3, Tübingen 1975, 3–28; D. Tracy, *Blessed Rage for Order: The New Pluralism in Theology*, New York 1975; J. Track, 'Erfahrung Gottes. Versuch einer Annäherung', *KD* 22, 1976, 1–21; D. Mieth, 'What Is Experience?', in E. Schillebeeckx and B. van Iersel (eds.), *Revelation and Experience*, Concilium 113, New York 1979, 40–53; B. Casper, 'Alltagserfahrung und Frömmigkeit ', in *Christlicher Glaube in moderner Gesellschaft* 25, Freiburg – Basle – Vienna 1980, 39–72; R. Schaeffler, *Fähigkeit zur Erfahrung. Zur transzendentalen Hermeneutik des Sprechens von Gott*, QD 94, Freiburg – Basle – Vienna 1982.

31. Cf. A. M. Haas, 'Die Problematik von Sprache und Erfahrung in der deutschen Mystik', in W. Beierwaltes, H. Urs von Balthasar and A. M. Haas, *Grundfragen der Mystik*, Einsiedeln 1974, 75 n. 1.

32. Aristotle, *Metaphysica* I, 980a-b.

33. G. Ebeling, art cit. (n. 30), 22; E. Jüngel, *Unterwegs zur Sache. Theologische Bemerkungen*, BEvT 61, Munich 1972, 8.

34. F. Nietzsche, *Thus Spoke Zarathustra*, Part III, no. 2: 'On the Vision and the Riddle' (Kaufmann, 157).

35. Nietzsche, *Beyond Good and Evil*, no. 270 (Kaufmann, 220).

36. J. Lotz, *Transzendentale Erfahrung*, Freiburg – Basle – Vienna 1978; K. Rahner, 'The Experience of God Today' (n. 30), 160ff.; id., *Foundations of Christian Faith*, ET W. V. Dych, New York and London 1978, 66–8.

37. The theory of disclosure-situations was developed chiefly by I. T. Ramsey, especially in his *Religious Language: An Empirical Placing of Theological Phrases*, London ²1969. It was further developed by A. de Pater, *Theologische Sprachlogik*, Munich 1971.

38. R. Otto, *The Idea of the Holy*, ET J. W. Harvey, New York 1923, ²1950.

39. Augustine, *Confessions* I, 9, 11 (CCL 27, 199–200).

40. On the problem of religious language: F. P. Ferré, *Language, Logic and God*,

London and New York 1961, G. Ebeling, *Introduction to a Theological Theory of Language*, ET R. A. Wilson, London and Philadelphia 1973; H. Fischer, *Glaubensaussage und Sprachstruktur*, Hamburg 1972; D. M. High, *Language, Persons and Belief*, New York 1967; A. Grabner-Haider, *Semiotik und Theologie, Religiöse Reden zwischen analytischer und hermeneutischer Philosophie*, Munich 1973; id., *Glaubenssprache. Ihre Struktur und Anwendbarkeit in Verkündigung und Theologie*, Freiburg – Basle – Vienna 1975, J. Splett, *Reden aus Glauben. Zum christlichen Sprechen von Gott*, Frankfurt 1973; J. Macquarrie, *God-Talk: An Examination of the Language and Logic of Theology*, London and New York 1967; B. Casper, *Sprache und Theologie. Eine philosophische Hinführung*, Freiburg – Basle – Vienna 1975; W. D. Just, *Religiöse Sprache und analytische Philosophie. Sinn und Unsinn religiöser Aussagen*, Stuttgart 1975; H. Peukert, *Wissenschaftstheorie – Handlungstheorie – Fundamentale Theologie. Analysen zu Ansatz und Status theologischer Theoriebildung*, Düsseldorf 1976; J. Track, *Sprachkritische Untersuchungen zum christlichen Reden von Gott*, Forschungen zur systematischen und ökumenischen Theologie 37, Göttingen 1977; J. Meier zu Schlochtern, *Glaube – Sprache – Erfahrung. Zur Begründungsfähigkeit der religiösen Überzeugung*, Regensburger Studien zur Theologie 15, Frankfurt 1978; T. W. Tilley, *Talking of God: An Introduction to Philosophical Analysis of Religious Language*, New York 1978; E. Biser, *Religöse Sprachbarrieren. Aufbau einer Logaporetik*, Munich 1980; I. U. Dalferth, *Religiöse Rede von Gott*, BEvT 87, Munich 1981; R. Schaeffler, *Fähigkeit zur Erfahrung* (n. 26)

41. L. Wittgenstein, *Tractatus Logico-Philosophicus*, ET D. F. Pears and B. F. McGuinness, Oxford and New York 1961, 3.

42. Ibid., 4.003 (37).

43. Ibid., 6.52 (149).

44. Ibid., 6.522 (150).

45. Ibid., 7 (151).

46. Cf. W. Heisenberg, *The Physicist's Conception of the Universe*, ET A. J. Pomerans, London 1958, 17f., 21, 28f.

47. K. R. Popper, *The Logic of Scientific Discovery*, London and New York 1959.

48. H. Albert, *Traktat über kritische Vernunft*, Die Einheit der Gesellschaftswissenschaften. Studien in den Grenzbereichen der Wirtschafts-und Sozialwissenschaften 9, Tübingen ²1969; id., *Plädoyer für kritischen Rationalismus*, Munich ³1973. On H. Albert: K. H. Weger, *Vom Elend des kritischen Rationalismus. Kritische Auseinandersetzung über die Frage der Erkennbarkeit Gottes bei Hans Albert*, Regensburg 1981.

49. T. S. Kuhn, *The Structure of Scientific Revolutions*, Chicago 1962.

50. L. Wittgenstein, *Philosophical Investigations*, ET G. E. M. Anscombe, Oxford 1953, no. 43, p. 20.

51. Especially: I. T. Ramsey, *Religious Language: An Empirical Placing of Religious Phrases*, London ²1969.

52. W. A. de Pater, *Theologische Sprachlogik*, Munich 1971.

53. J. L. Austin, *How To Do Things With Words*, Oxford 1962; id., *Philosophical Papers*, Oxford 1961.

54. J. R. Searle, *Speech-Acts: An Essay in the Philosophy of Language*, London 1969; id., *Philosophy of Language*, London 1971.

55. K. O. Apel, 'Der transzendentalhermeneutische Begriff der Sprache', in his

342   *Notes to pages 91–96*

Transformation der Philosophie II. *Das Apriori der Kommunikationsgemeinschaft*, Frankfurt 1973, 330–57; id., 'Das Apriori der Kommunikationsgemeinschaft und die Grundlagen der Ethik. Zum Problem einer rationalen Begründung der Ethik im Zeitalter der Wissenschaft', ibid., 358–435.

56. J. Habermas, 'Wahrheitstheorien', in *Wirklichkeit und Reflexion (FS Walter Schulz)*, ed., H. Fahrenbach, Pfullingen 1973, 211–65; id., 'Vorbereitende Bemerkungen zu einer Theorie der kommunikativen Kompetenz', in J. Habermas and N. Luhmann, *Theorie der Gesellschaft oder Sozialtechnologie – Was leistet die Systemforschung?*, Frankfurt 1975, 101–41, esp. 123ff.

57. H. Peukert, op. cit. (n. 40), 209ff., 230ff.

58. C. W. Morris, *Foundations of the Theory of Signs*, Chicago 1938, 1964, 6.

59. L. B. Puntel, 'Wahrheit', *HPG* 3, 1649–68; J. Simon, *Wahrheit als Freiheit. Zur Entwicklung der Wahrheitsfrage in der neueren Philosophie*, Berlin and New York 1978, 1ff., 11ff., 27ff.

60. M. Heidegger, *Unterwegs zur Sprache*, Pfullingen, ³1965.

61. H. Gadamer, *Truth and Method* (n. 30).

62. P. Ricoeur, *The Conflict of Interpretations: Essays in Hermeneutics*, ET D. Ihde, Evanston 1974, id., *Metapher. Zur Hermeneutik religiöser Sprache*, Sonderhaft *Evangelischer Theologie*, Munich 1974, 24–45; id., 'Stellung und Funktion der biblischen Sprache', ibid., 45–70.

63. E. Jüngel, 'Metaphorische Wahrheit. Erwägungen zur theologischen Relevanz der Metapher als Beitrag zur Hermeneutik einer narrativen Theologie', in *Entsprechungen* (n. 1), 103–57.

64. On the doctrine of analogy: G. Kittel, 'analogia', *TDNT* 1, 347–48; E. Przywara, *Analogia entis. Metaphysik – Ur – struktur und All-rhythmus*, Schriften 3, Einsiedeln 1962 (contains *Analogie entis. Metaphysik*, 1932); id., *Deus Semper Maior. Theologie der Exerzitien*, 3 vols., Freiburg 1938–40 (reprint, with the addition of 'Theologoumenon und Philosophoumenon der Gessellschaft Jesu', Vienna and Munich 1964); id., 'Die Reichweite der Analogie als katholischer Grundform', *Schol.* 15, 1940, 339–62, 508–32; E. Coreth, 'Dialektik und Analogie des Seins. Zum Seinsproblem bei Hegel und in der Scholastik', *Schol* 26, 1951, 57–86; id., 'Analogia entis I', *LTK* 1, 468–70; L. B. Puntel, *Analogie und Geschichtlichkeit* I. *Philosophiegeschichtlich-kritischer Versuch über das Grundproblem der Metaphysik*, Philosophie in Einzeldarstellungen 4, with a Preface by Max Müller, Freiburg – Basle – Vienna, 1969, W. Pannenberg, 'Analogie', *RGG* 1, 350–3; id., 'Analogie', *EKL* 1, 13f.; W. Kluxen, 'Analogie I', *HWP* 1, 214–27; J. Track, 'Analogie', *TRE* 2, 625–30 (with abundant bibliography).

65. Cf. Thomas Aquinas, *ST* I, 13, 5 and 10.

66. Ibid., a. 5 ad 1: 'All univocal predications depend on a single predicate which is not univocal but analogical, namely, being.'

67. E. Jüngel, 'Zum Ursprung der Analogie bei Parmenides und Heraclit', in *Entsprechungen* (n. 1), 52–102.

68. Plato, *Timaeus* 31a; cf. 53c, 56c, 69b.

69. Aristotle, *Ethica Nicomachea* II, 5, 1106a.

70. Aristotle, *Metaphysica* V, 6, 1016b–1017a.

71. Ibid., IV, 2, 1003a.

72. *Ethica Nicomachea* I, 4, 1096b.

73. For the history of negative theology cf. J. Hochstaffl, *Negative Theologie. Ein Versuch zur Vermittlung des patristischen Begriffs*, Munich 1976; W. Kasper,

'Atheismus und Gottes Verborgenheit', in *Christlicher Glaube in moderner Gesellschaft* 22, Freiburg – Basle – Vienna 1982.

74. This idea is already in Plato, *Republic* VI, 508b, and fully in Plotinus, *Enneads* V, 4; VI, 9.

75. Plotinus *Enneads* VI, 9.

76. Dionysius the Pseudo-Areopagite, *De coelesti hierarchia* II, 3 (SC 58, 77–80).

77. The formula has a basis in Socrates (*Apol.* 23b) and Augustine (*Ep.* 130, 15, 28 = PL 33, 505f.; 197 = PL 33, 899ff.), and occurs as such in Bonaventure, *Breviloquium* V, 6, 7; *II Sent.*, d. 23, 2.2, q. 3, and especially in Nicholas of Cusa, *De docta ignorantia*, Opera I, ed. P. Wilpert, Berlin 1967.

78. DS 806; ND 320.

79. This is true also and not least for E. Przywara, who in his *Analogia entis* (n. 64), 206, has this to say about the analogy of being: 'The *analogie entis* is thus only the expression of the fact that at the very starting point of thinking as thinking the most remainderless potentiality of the creaturely is actuated (down to the very *potentia oboedientialis* itself). It is not a principle by which the creaturely is grasped and can therefore be manipulated but in which the creaturely soars unhindered with all of its potentiality.' On Przywara cf. B. Gertz, *Glaubenswelt als Analogie. Die theologische Analogie-Lehre Erich Przywaras und ihr Ort in der Auseinandersetzung um die analogia fidei*, Düsseldorf 1969.

80. Thomas Aquinas, *ST* I, 13, 2f.

81. E. Heintel, 'Transzendenz und Analogie. Ein Beitrag zur Frage der bestimmten Negation bei Thomas von Aquin', in H. Fahrenbach (ed.), *Wirklichkeit und Reflexion (FS Walter Schulz)*, Pfullingen 1973, 267–90.

82. Cf. Kluxen, art. cit. (n. 64), 221ff.

83. Thomas Aquinas, *ST* I, 13; *De nominibus divinis*, esp. aa. 8–11.

84. Cf. G. Söhngen, 'Bonaventura als Klassiker der *analogia fidei*', *WWeis* 2, 1935, 97–11; L. Berg, 'Die Analogielehre des heiligen Bonaventura', *StudGen* 8, 1955, 662–70; J. Ratzinger, '*Gratia praesupponit naturam.* Erwägungen über Sinn und Grenzen eines scholastischen Axioma', in J. Ratzinger and H. Fries (eds.), *Einsicht und Glaube (FS Gottlieb Söhngen)*, Freiburg – Basle – Vienna 1962, 135–49.

85. G. Söhngen, 'Analogia fidei: I. Gottähnlichkeit allein aus Glauben?', *Cath* 3, 1934, 113–36; id., 'Analogia fidei: II. Die Einheit in der Glaubenswissenschaft', ibid., 176–208; id., 'Analogia entis oder analogia fidei?' *WWeis* 9, 1942, 91–100; id., 'Analogia entis in analogia fidei', in *Antwort (FS Karl Barth)*, Zollikon-Zürich 1956, 266–71; id., *Analogia und Metapher. Kleine Philosophie und Theologie der Sprache*, Freiburg and Munich 1962.

86. H. Urs von Balthasar, *The Theology of Karl Barth* (n. 1), 217–46.

87. J. Duns Scotus, *I Sent.*, pol., q. 1 schol. Cf. E. Wölfel, *Seinsstruktur und Trinitätsproblem. Untersuchungen zur Grundlegung der natürlichen Theologie bei Johannes Duns Scotus*, BGPTM 11/5, Münster 1956; M. Schmaus, *Zur Diskussion über das Problem der Univozität im Umkreis des Johannes Duns Skotus*, Bayerische Akademie der Wissenschaften, Philosophisch-historische Klasse 1957, Heft 4, Munich 1957.

88. K. Barth, *Church Dogmatics* I/1, X. Cf. H. Diem, 'Analogia fidei gegen analogia entis. Ein Beitrag zur Kontroversetheologie', *EvT* 3, 1936, 157–80; W. Pannenberg, 'Zur Bedeutung des Analogiegedankens bei Karl Barth. Eine Auseinandersetzung mit Urs von Balthasar', *TLZ* 78, 1953, 17–24; E. Jüngel, 'Die

Möglichkeit theologischer Anthropologie auf dem Grunde der Analogie. Eine Untersuchung zum Analogieverständnis Karl Barths', *EvT* 22, 1962, 535–57; H. G. Pöhlmann, *Analogia entis oder Analogia fidei? Die Frage der Analogie bei Karl Barth*, Göttingen 1965; K. Hammer, 'Analogia relationis gegen analogia entis', in *Parrhesia (FS Karl Barth)*, Zürich 1966, 288–304; E. Mechels, *Analogie bei Erich Przywara und Karl Barth. Das Verhältnis von Offenbarungstheologie und Metaphysik*, Neukirchen-Vluyn 1974. Cf. also the writings of G. Söhngen and H. Urs von Balthasar listed in nn. 85 and 86.

89. K. Barth, *Church Dogmatics*, III/2, 220f., 323f.

90. Similarly W. Pannenberg, 'Möglichkeiten und Grenzen der Anwendung des Analogieprinzips in der evangelischen Theologie', *TLZ* 85, 1960, 225–28; id., 'Analogy and Doxology', in *Basic Questions in Theology*, ET G. H. Kehm, 2 vols. London and Philadelphia 1970–71, 2, 212–38

91. J. Möller, *Von Bewusstsein zu Sein. Grundlegung einer Metaphysik*, Mainz 1962, 179ff.

92. Cf. below, 105f.

93. On the question of the knowledge of God and the proofs of God's existence: H. Ogiermann, *Hegels Gottesbeweise*, Rome 1948; id., *Sein zu Gott. Die philosophische Gottesfrage*, Munich 1974; F. van Steenberghen, *Hidden God. How Do We Know That God Exists?*, ET T. Crowley, St Louis 1966; W. Cramer, *Gottesbeweise und ihre Kritik. Prüfung ihrer Beweiskraft*, Frankfurt 1967; J. Schmucker, *Die primären Quellen des Gottesglaubens*, QD 34, Freiburg – Basle – Vienna 1967; id., *Das Problem der Kontingenz der Welt*, QD 43, Freiburg – Basle – Vienna 1969; Q. Huonder, *Die Gottesbeweise. Geschichte und Schicksal*, Stuttgart and Mainz 1968; C. Bruaire, *Die Aufgabe, Gott zu denken. Religionskritik, ontologischer Gottesbeweis, die Freiheit des Menschen*, Freiburg – Basle – Vienna 1973; J. Splett, *Gotteserfahrung im Denken. Zur philosophischen Rechtfertigung des Redens von Gott*, Freiburg and Munich 1973; E. Hirsch, *Das Ende aller Gottesbeweise? Naturwissenschaftler antworten auf die religiöse Frage*, Hamburg 1975; J. Fellermeier, *Die Philosophie auf dem Weg zu Gott*, Munich – Paderborn – Vienna 1975; W. Kern, 'Der Gottesbeweis Mensch. Ein konstruktiver Versuch', in *Atheismus, Marxismus, Christentum. Beiträge zur Diskussion*, Innsbruck 1976, 152–82; B. Welte, *Religionsphilosophie*, Freiburg – Basle – Vienna 1978; W. Brugger, *Summe einer philosophischen Gotteslehre*, Munich 1979; K. H. Weger, *Der Mensch vor dem Anspruch Gottes. Glaubensbegründung in einer agnostischen Welt*, Graz – Vienna – Cologne 1981.

94. Cf. Thomas Aquinas, *De ver.* 1, 9c.a: 'Truth is known by the intellect inasmuch as the intellect reflects on its own act and not only knows its own act but also knows the proportion of its act to the object.'

95. Aristotle, *Metaphysica* I, 981a-b.

96. Cf. Kern, art. cit. (n. 93), 154f.

97. Cf. W. Pannenberg, 'The Appropriation of the Philosophical Concept of God as a Dogmatic Problem of Early Christian Theology', *Basic Questions in Theology* (n. 90), 2, 119–83.

98. John Damascene, *De fide orthodoxa* I, 3, *Schriften*, ed. Kotter (n. 4), 2, 10ff.

99. Thomas Aquinas, *ST* I, 2, 3; *CG* I, 13; 15; 16, 44.

100. Kant, *Critique of Pure Reason*, ET J. M. D. Meiklejohn, in *Kant*, Great Books of the Western World 42, Chicago 1952, 188.

101 M. Heidegger, 'What Is Metaphysics?', ET R. F. C. Hull and A. Crick, in Heidegger, *Existence and Being*, Chicago 1949, 380.

102. J. Schmucker, *Das Problem der Kontingenz der Welt* (n. 93).

103. On wonder as the origin of philosophizing: Plato, *Theatetus* 155d; Aristotle, *Metaphysica* I, 982b: 'It was because men were curious that they began to reflect and still do.' Cf. H. J. Verweyen, *Ontologische Voraussetzungen des Glaubensaktes. Zur transzendentalen Frage nach der Möglichkeit von Offenbarung*, Düsseldorf 1968, esp. 159ff.; H. Urs von Balthasar, *Herrlichkeit. Eine theologische Ästhetik*, III/1: *Im Raum der Metaphysik*, Einsiedeln 1965.

104. F. W. J. Schelling, *Philosophie der Offenbarung*, WW, Erg. Bd. 6, ed. M. Schröter, 57f., 155ff.

105. Justin, *Apologia* II, 6, *Corpus Apol.* I, ed. v. Otto, 213–17; Origen, *Contra Celsum* I, 4 (SC 132, 84–87); Augustine, *De spiritu et littera* 12 (PL 44, 211ff.); *De civitate Dei* VIII, 6 (CCL 47, 222ff.).

106. Tertullian, *Apolog.* 17, 6 (CCL 1, 117f.); *De testimonio animae* (CCL 1; 173–83); *Adv. Marcionem* I, 10, 3 (CCL 1, 451): 'The soul precedes prophecy. For the knowledge the soul has from the beginning is a dowry from God; it is the same and no different in Egyptians and Syrians and people from Pontus.'

107. Augustine, *Confessiones* I, 1, 1 (CCL 27, 1); cf. III, 6, 11 (CCL 27, 32f.); X, 25, 36 (CCL 27, 174); 26, 37 (CCL 27, 174f.); 27, 38 (CCL 27, 175).

108. Augustine, *De civitate Dei* XI, 26 (CCL 48, 345f.).

109. Augustine, *Confessiones* X, 26, 37 (CCL 27, 174f.).

110. Thomas Aquinas, *De ver.* 22, 2 ad 1.

111. Descartes, *Meditations on the First Philosophy* III, ET L. J. Lafleur, Indianapolis 1978, 33–50.

112. Kant, *Critique of Practical Reason*, in *Kant* (n. 100), 344ff.

113. J. Maréchal, *Le point de départ de la metaphysique*, esp. Cahier V: *Le Thomisme devant la philosophie critique*, Museum Lessianum, Sect. phil. 7, Brussels and Paris ²1949. Further philosophical development especially in E. Coreth, *Metaphysik. Eine methodisch-systematische Grundlegung*, Innsbruck – Vienna – Munich ²1964.

114. J. H. Newman, *An Essay in Aid of a Grammar of Assent* (1870), New York 1906.

115. H. Krings, 'Freiheit. Ein Versuch, Gott zu denken', *PhJ* 77, 1970, 225–37; id., with E. Simons 'Gott', *HPG* 2, 614–41.

116. B. Pascal, *Pensées*, fr. 418 (Br. 233), ET A. J. Krailsheimer, *Pascal's Pensées*, Baltimore 1966, 151.

117. While pagan writers (Polybius, for example) saw the power of fate at work in history, the church fathers spoke of the providence of God as directing everything, and even of a divine plan for educating man: Irenaeus, *Adv. haer.* II, 28, 3 (SC 294, 274–9); IV, 20, 1ff. (SC 100, 625ff.); 38, 3 (SC 100, 952–7); Clement of Alexandria, *Stromata* VII, 7 (PG 9, 449b–472a); Origen, *Contra Celsum* IV, 99 (SC 136, 430–5); Augustine, *De vera religione* XXV, 46 (CCL 32, 216); *De civitate Dei* V, 18; 21–26 (CCL 47, 151–4, 157–63); VII, 30–2 (CCL 47, 211ff.).

118. K. Löwith, *Meaning in History: The Theological Implications of the Philosophy of History*, Chicago 1949.

119. Hegel, *Die Vernunft in der Geschichte* (ed. J. Hoffmeister), 28ff., 28, 77, etc.

120. J. S. Drey, *Die Apologetik als wissenschaftliche Nachweisung der Göttlichkeit des Christentums in seiner Erscheinung* II, Mainz ²1847.

121. W. Pannenberg, 'Redemptive Event and History', *Basic Questions in Theology* (n. 90), 1, 15–80; 'Hermeneutic and Universal History', ibid., 1, 96–136; 'On Historical and Theological Hermeneutic', ibid., 1, 137–81.

122. Cf. above, 35f., 55f.

123. Cf. above, 33f.

124. Cf. above, ibid.

125. J. de Vries, 'Realismus', *Philosophisches Wörterbuch*, ed. W. Brugger, Freiburg – Basle – Vienna ¹⁴1976, 316–18. For the history: H. Krings, 'Realismus', *LTK* 7, 1027f.; id., 'Die Wandlung des Realismus in der Philosophie der Gegenwart', *PhJ* 70, 1962, 1–16.

126. Cf. Thomas Aquinas, *De ver.* 1, 1–4.

127. Cf. W. Schulz, *Philosophie in der veränderten Welt*, Pfullingen 1972, 10, 143f., 470ff., 602ff., 841ff.

128. On what follows cf. R. Spaemann, 'Gesichtspunkte der Philosophie', in H. J. Schultz (ed.), *Wer ist das eigentlich-Gott?* Munich 1969, 56–65; id., 'Die Frage nach der Bedeutung des Wortes "Gott" ', *Internationale Katholische Zeitschrift* 1, 1972, 54–72.

129. Aristotle, *De anima* III, 8, 431b; Thomas Aquinas, *De ver.* 1, 1; *ST* I, 14, 1; etc.

130. This aspect of anticipation of the whole in the detail has been developed especially by W. Pannenberg. Critical distinctions are made in E. Schillebeeckx, 'Erfahrung und Glaube', in *Christlicher Glaube in moderner Gesellschaft* 25, Freiburg – Basle – Vienna 1980, 103ff.

131. M. Horkheimer, *Die Sehnsucht nach dem ganz Anderen. Ein Interview mit Kommentar von Hellmut Gumnior*, Hamburg 1970, 62.

132. H. Peukert, *Wissenschaftstheorie – Handlungstheorie – Fundamentale Theologie* (n. 40), 293ff.; J. B. Metz, *Faith in History and Society: Toward a Practical Fundamental Theology*, ET D. Smith, New York, 1980. 109ff.

133. M. Heidegger, *Identity and Difference*, ET J. Stambaugh, New York 1969, 42. The concept of ontotheology is already to be found in Kant, *Critique of Pure Reason* (n. 100), 190.

134. On the ontological argument: K. Kopper, *Reflexion und Raisonnement im ontologischen Gottesbeweis*, Cologne 1962, C. H. Hartshorne, *Anselm's Discovery: A Re-examination of the Ontological Proof for God's Existence*, La Salle, Ill. 1965, D. Henrich, *Der ontologische Gottesbeweis. Sein Problem und seine Geschichte in der Neuzeit*, Tübingen ²1967; H. K. Kohlenberger, *Similitudo und ratio. Überlegungen zur Methode bei Anselm von Canterbury*, Münchener philosphische Forschungen 4, Bonn 1972; J. Brechtken, 'Das Unum Argumentum des Anselm von Canterbury. Seine Idee und Geschichte und seine Bedeutung für die Gottesfrage von heute', *FZTP* 22, 1975, 171–203; K. Barth, *Anselm: Fides quaerens intellectum. Anselm's Proof of the Existence of God in the Context of His Theological Scheme*, ET I. W. Robertson, London and Richmond, Va. 1960.

135. Anselm, *Proslogion*, Preface.

136. Ibid., ch. 1, ET J. Hopkins and H. Richardson in *Anselm of Canterbury* 1, London and New York 1974, 93.

137. Ch. 2 (ibid.).

138. Ch. 15 (104).

139. Anselm, *Monologion*, ch. 64 (73).

140. Anselm, *Proslogion*, ch. 2 (94).

141. Ch. 3.

142. Thomas Aquinas raises this objection, *ST* I, 2, 1 ad 2.

143. Kant, *Critique of Pure Reason*, in *Kant* (n. 100), 181.

144. Augustine, *De libero arbitrio* II, 6, 14 (CCL 29, 246f.).

145. Ibid., II, 12, 34; 15, 39 (CCL 29, 260f., 263f.).

146. Hegel, *Vorlesungen über die Philosophie der Religion* I/1 (ed. Lasson), 207–25.

147. Kant, *Critique of Pure Reason*, in *Kant*, 185.

148. Ibid., 187.

149. F. W. J. Schelling, *Philosophie der Offenbarung* (n. 104), 161, 163, 165.

150. Ibid., 45f., 91ff., 125ff., 203ff.

151. Ibid., 168.

152. Ibid., 170.

153. Ibid., 169.

154. Ibid., 57ff., 111ff., 130f.

155. The process began with Karl Barth's interpretation of Anselm (cf. n. 134). Barth takes Anselm's argument to be a strictly theological implementation of his program of *fides quaerens intellectum*; that is, Barth takes the argument as showing the internal coherence and reasonableness of faith. In taking this approach Barth does not, of course, do full justice to the ontological profoundity of the argument.

156. J. E. Kuhn, *Katholische Dogmatik* I/2: *Die dogmatische Lehre von der Erkenntnis, den Eigenschaften und der Einheit Gotts*, Tübingen ²1862, 648–68.

157. W. Pannenberg, *Theology and the Philosophy of Science*, ET F. McDonagh, London and Philadelphia 1976, 300.

158. Newman, *Grammar of Assent* (n. 114), chapters 8–9.

159. Pascal, *Pensées*, fr. 423 (Br. 277), in Krailsheimer (n. 116), 54.

Chapter V   Knowledge of God in Faith

1. On the concept of revelation: R. Garrigou-Lagrange, *De revelatione per ecclesiam catholicam proposita*, Rome 1931; R. Guardini, *Die Offenbarung*, Würzburg 1940; P. Althaus, 'Die Inflation des Begriffs Offenbarung in der gegenwärtigen Theologie', *ZST* 18, 1941, 131–49; H. Schulte, *Der Begriff Offenbarung im Neuen Testament*, Munich 1949; K. Barth, *Church Dogmatics*, I/1 and 2; W. Pannenberg *et al.*, *Revelation as History*, ET D. Granskou, London and New York 1968; H. Fries, 'Offenbarung. III. Systematisch', *LTK* 7, 1109–15; D. Lührmann, *Das Offenbarungsverständnis bei Paulus und in paulinischen Gemeinden*, Neukirchen - Vluyn 1965; R. Latourelle, *Theology of Revelation*, Staten Island, NY 1966; A. Dulles, *Revelation Theology: A History*, New York 1969; F. Konrad, *Das Offenbarungsverständnis in der evangelischen Theologie*, Munich 1971; M. Seybold, H. Waldenfels *et al.*, *Offenbarung*, HDG I/1 and 2, Freiburg – Basle – Vienna 1971, 1977; P. Eicher, *Offenbarung. Prinzip neuzeitlicher Theologie*, Munich 1977; P. Ricoeur *et al.*, *La révélation*, Brussels 1977; M. Seckler, '*Dei verbum religiose audiens*: Wandlungen im christlichen Offenbarungsverständnis', in J. J. Petuchowski and W. Strolz (eds.), *Offenbarung im jüdischen und christlichen Glaubensverständnis*, QD 92, Freiburg–Basle–Vienna 1981, 214–36.

2. Cf. above, 85, 90.

3. P. Eicher, op. cit. (n. 1).

4. Vatican II, *Nostra aetate*, 2 (Flannery, 738–39).

5. Vatican II, *Lumen gentium*, 9.

6. It is obviously impossible for me to present here a complete doctrine of revelation. To do so would amount to setting down the entire treatise on revelation that is part of fundamental theology, and this is evidently not feasible. My discussion of the subject will be limited to what is relevant to a doctrine of God.

7. Vatican II, *Dei verbum*, 2.

8. This point is already made in Vatican I: DS 3004; ND 113. It is made even more clearly in Vatican II, *Dei verbum*, 2.

9. Cf. A. Deissler, *Die Grundbotschaft des Alten Testaments. Ein theologischer Durchblick*, Freiburg – Basle – Vienna ⁵1972, 43ff.

10. This aspect has been brought out especially by H. Urs von Balthasar. In what follows I am essentially adopting his standpoint. Cf. especially his *The Glory of the Lord: A Theological Aesthetics* 1, *Seeing the Form*, ET Erasmo Leiva-Merikakis, ed. Joseph Fessio and John Riches, San Francisco and Edinburgh 1982, esp. Part 3; 'The Objective Evidence'.

11. On this cf. below, 166ff.

12. Vatican II, *Dei verbum*, 5.

13. Augustine, *In Johannis Evangelium tractatus* 26, 6 (CCL 36, 286f.); *Enarrationes in Psalmos* LXXVII, 8 (CCL 39, 1072f.); Thomas Aquinas, *ST* II-II, 2, 3. Cf. J. B. Metz, 'Credere Deum, Deo, in Deum', *LTK* 3, 86–8.

14. On the problem of the justification of faith: S. Harent, 'Foi', *DTC* 6, 1920, 55–514, esp. 109–15; H. Lang, *Die Lehre des Hl. Thomas von Aquin von der Gewissheit des übernatürlichen Glaubens*, Augsburg 1929; R. Aubert, *Le problème de l'acte de foi*, Louvain ²1950; A. Brunner, *Glaube und Erkenntnis. Philosophisch-theologische Darlegung*, Munich 1951; J. Trütsch, 'Glaube und Erkenntnis', in J. Feiner *et al.*, *Fragen der Theologie heute*, Einsiedeln – Zürich – Cologne 1957, 45–68; F. Malmberg, 'Analysis fidei', *LTK* 1, 477–83; J. Beumer, 'Glaubensgewissheit', *LTK* 4 941–42; M. Seckler, *Instinkt und Glaubenswille nach Thomas von Aquin*, Mainz 1961; J. Alfaro, 'Faith' and 'Motive of Faith', *SacMundi* 2, 313–22, 322–24.

15. DS 3008; ND 188.

16. Thomas Aquinas, *ST* II-II, 1, 1c: 'If then we consider the object of faith under its formal aspect [i.e., that by reason of which we assent] this is nothing else than the first Truth itself.'

17. H. Urs von Balthasar, *Love Alone*, ET A. Dru, New York 1969. [The German title of this book is *Glaubhaft ist nur die Liebe* – Love Alone Is Credible. Tr.]

18. On God's mysteriousness and hiddenness: R. Garrigou-Lagrange, *Le sens du mystère*, Paris 1934; P. Siller, *Die Incomprehensibilitas Dei bei Thomas von Aquin*, Innsbruck 1963; id., 'Unbegreiflichkeit', *LTK* 10, 470–2; P. Wess, *Wie von Gott sprechen? Eine Auseinandersetzung mit Karl Rahner*, Graz 1970; K. Rahner, 'The Hiddenness of God', in *Theological Investigations* 16, ET D. Morland, London and New York 1979, 227–43; 'An Investigation of the Incomprehensibility of God in St Thomas Aquinas', ibid., 244–54; C. Schütz, *Verborgenheit Gottes. Martins Bubers Werk – Eine Gesamtdarstellung*, Zürich – Einsiedeln – Cologne 1975; W. Kasper, 'Atheismus und Gottes Verborgenheit in theologischer Sicht', in *Glaube in moderner Gesellschaft* 22, Freiburg – Basle – Vienna 1982, 32–52. Cf. Part I, chapter 4, n. 73, and, further on in this chapter, nn. 29–31.

19. G. von Rad, *Old Testament Theology*, ET D. M. G. Stalker, 2 vols., Edinburgh and New York 1962–65, 1, 218.

20. M. Luther, *Heidelberger Disputation* (1518), WA 1, 134, 362. Cf. W. von Loewenich, *Luther's Theology of the Cross*, ET H. J. A. Bouman, Minneapolis 1976; E. Jüngel, *Zur Freiheit eines Christenmenschen*, Munich 1978, 28–53.

21. G. Bornkamm, 'Mysterion', *TDNT* 4, 802–28.

22. Cf. below, 166ff.

23. DS 16, 293f., 501, 525, 683, 800, 853, 3001; ND 4, 611f., 627/1, 308, 19, 24, 327.

24. J. Hichstaffl, *Negative Theologie. Ein Versuch zur Vermittlung des patristischen Begriffs*, Munich 1976, 99–119; E. Mühlenberg, *Die Unendlichkeit Gottes bei Gregor von Nyssa*, Göttingen 1966.

25. John Damascene, *De fide orthodoxa* I, 12 (*Schriften* II, ed. B. Kötter, 35f.).

26. Nicholas of Cusa, *Of Learned Ignorance*, ET G. Heron, London 1954.

27. DS 800; ND 19.

28. DS 3001; ND 327.

29. M. J. Scheeben, *The Mysteries of Christianity*, ET C. Vollert, St Louis 1946, 15. Scheeben is here objecting to the still worthwhile article of W. Mattes (of the Tübingen School), 'Mysterien', *Kirchenlexikon* 7, 1851, 428–37; in the spirit of the church fathers Mattes is here pointing out that the whole of Christianity is a single mystery.

30. K. Rahner, 'The Concept of Mystery in Catholic Theology', in *Theological Investigations* 4, ET K. Smyth, London and Baltimore 1966, 36–73. On the Protestant side cf. G. Ebeling, 'Profanität und Geheimnis', in *Wort und Glaube* 2, Tübingen 1969, 184–208.

31. K. Barth, *Church Dogmatics* II/1, ET T. H. L. Parker *et al.*, Edinburgh 1957, 179ff. [but I have not been able to find the quoted words in the ET. Tr.].

PART TWO

Chapter I   God, the Father Almighty

1. DS 30; ND 5.

2. H. Tellenbach (ed.), *Das Vaterbild in Mythos und Geschichte*, Stuttgart 1972; id. (ed.), *Das Vaterbild im Abendland*, 2 vols., Stuttgart 1978; id. (ed.), *Vaterbilder in den Kulturen Asiens, Afrikas und Ozeaniens*, Stuttgart 1979. Cf. G. Marcel, 'The Creative Vow as Essence of Fatherhood', in *Homo Viator*, ET E. Craufurd, Chicago 1951, 98–124.

3. M. Horkheimer, *Kritische Theorie*, 2 vols., Frankfurt 1968; in the present context cf. 1, 277ff.; id., *Die Sehnsucht nach dem ganz Anderen. Ein Interview mit Kommentar von H. Gumnior*, Hamburg 1970.

4. A. Mitscherlich, *Auf dem Weg zur vaterlosen Gesellschaft. Ideen zur Sozialpsychologie*, Munich 1963.

5. Especially important are Freud's *Totem and Taboo*, ET A. A. Brill, London and New York 1938; *The Future of an Illusion*, ET W. D. Robson-Scott, rev. J. Strachey, London and New York, 1961; *Civilization and Its Discontents*, ET J. Strachey, London and New York, 1961; *Moses and Monotheism*, ET K. Jones, London and New York 1939.

6. H. E. Richter, *Der Gotteskomplex. Die Geburt und die Krise des Glaubens an die Allmacht des Menschen*, Hamburg 1979.

7. T. Moser, *Gottesvergiftung*, Frankfurt 1976.

8. Cf. the survey in J. B. Metz and E. Schillebeeckx (eds.), *God as Father?*, Concilium 143, New York 1981.

9. M. Daly, *Beyond God the Father*, Boston 1973.

10. R. R. Ruether, *New Woman/New Earth: Sexist Ideologies and Human Liberation*, New York 1975.

11. Cf. M. Greifenhagen, 'Emanzipation', *HWP* 2, 448f.; G. Rohrmoser, *Emanzipation und Freiheit*, Munich 1970; R. Spaemann, 'Autonomie, Mündigkeit, Emanzipation', in *Kontexte* 7, Stuttgart – Berlin 1971, 94–102.

12. J. B. Metz, 'Erlösung und Emanzipation', in L. Scheffczyk (ed.), *Erlösung und Emanzipation*, QD 61, Freiburg – Basle – Vienna 1973, (120–40) 121.

13. K. Marx, 'On the Jewish Question', in Karl Marx, *Early Writings*, ET ed. T. B. Bottomore, New York 1964, 31.

14. H. Jonas, *Gnosis und spätantiker Geist*, 1. *Die mythologische Gnosis*, Göttingen ³1964, 219.

15. G. Bornkamm, 'Das Vaterbild im Neuen Testament', in H. Tellenbach (ed.), *Das Vaterbild in Mythos und Geschichte* (n. 2), (136–54) 153.

16. J. W. Goethe, *Der Zauberlehrling*, WW 1, Zürich ²1961, 149ff.

17. F. Nietzsche, *The Gay Science*, no. 125, ET W. Kaufmann, London and New York 1974, Vintage Books ed., 181.2.

18. In addition to the literature already cited cf. especially G. Schrenk and G. Quell, 'Pater', *TDNT* 5, 946–1016 (in this context, 948–59).

19. Cf. above, 16f., 116ff.

20. Cf. Schrenk and Quell, art. cit., 950–1; A. Wlosok, 'Vater und Vatervorstellungen in der römischen Kultur', in H. Tellenbach (ed.), *Das Vaterbild im Abendland* (n. 2), 1, 18–54.

21. Cf. Schrenk and Quell, art. cit., 981–1016; W. Marchel, *Abba, Père! La prière du Christ et des chrétiens*, AnBib 19a, Rome 1971; J. Jeremias, *Abba. Studien zur neutestamentlichen Theologie und Zeitgeschichte*, Göttingen 1966 (partial ET by John Bowden, *The Prayers of Jesus*, London 1967); L. Perlitt, 'Der Vater im Alten Testament', in H. Tellenbach (ed.), *Das Vaterbild in Mythos und Geschichte* (n. 2), 50–101; G. Bornkamm, 'Das Vaterbild im Neuen Testament', ibid., 136–54.

22. Cf. above, 16f., 116ff.

23. Schrenk and Quell, art. cit., 966.

24. From the boundless literature cf. H. Kleinknecht, G. von Rad, K. G. Kuhn and K. L. Schmidt, 'Basileus', *TDNT* 1, 564–93; N. Perrin, *The Kingdom of God in the Teaching of Jesus*, London 1963; R. Schnackenburg, *God's Rule and Kingdom*, ET J. Murray, London and New York 1963; H. Schürmann, 'Das hermeneutische Hauptproblem der Verkündigung Jesu', in H. Vorgrimler (ed.), *Gott in Welt (FS Karl Rahner)*, 2 vols., Freiburg – Basle – Vienna 1964, 1, 579–607; H. Merklein, *Die Gottesherrschaft als Handlungsprinzip. Untersuchung zur Ethik Jesu*, Forschung zur Bibel 34, Würzburg 1978.

25. Cf. below, 168ff.

26. This has been brought out especially by K. Rahner, 'Theos in the New Testament', in *Theological Investigations* 1, ET C. Ernst, London and Baltimore 1961, 79–148.

27. Cf. *Didache* 1, 5 (SC 248, 144ff.); Justin, *Dialogus cum Tryphone* 74, 1; 76,

3; 83, 2; etc. (*Corpus Apol.* II, ed. von Otto, 264ff.); Clement of Alexandria, *Protrepticus* X, 94, 3 (SC 2, 162).

28. Origen, *Contra Celsum* V, 39 (SC 147, 117–21); *In Joan.* VI, 39 and 202 (SC 157, 158f., 280f.).

29. Cf. DS 1–5; only DS 6 differs.

30. Cf. DS 60, 75, 441, 485, 490, 525, 527, 569, 572, 683, 800, 1330f.; ND 16, 308, 310, 19, 325f.

31. *Didache* 9, 2 (SC 248, 174ff.).

32. A Schindler, 'Gott als Vater in Theologie und Liturgie der christlichen Antike', in H. Tellenbach (ed.), *Das Vaterbild im Abendland* (n. 2), 1 (55–69) 66.

33. On the entire problem cf. J. A. Jungmann, *The Place of Christ in Liturgical Prayer*, ET A. Peeler, Staten Island, NY 1965.

34. Plato, *Timaeus* 28c.

35. Schindler, art. cit., 57f.

36. Justin, *Dialogus* 56, 15; 60, 3; 61, 3; 63, 3 (*Corpus Apol.* II, 186f., 210f., 212f.; 222f.).

37. W. Pannenberg, 'The Appropriation of the Philosophical Concept of God as a Dogmatic Problem of Early Christian Theology', in *Basic Questions in Theology*, ET G. H. Kehm, 2 vols., Philadelphia 1970–71, 2, 119–83.

38. Cf. below, 182ff., 257f.

39. DS 125f., 150; ND 7f., 12.

40. Cf. John Damascene, *De fide orthodoxa* I, 8 (*Schriften*, ed. Kotter, 2, 18–31).

41. Cf. Augustine, *De Trinitate* IV, 20 (CCL 50, 195–202); Thomas Aquinas, *ST* I, 33, 1.

42. DS 800, 1331; ND 19, 326.

43. Gregory of Nazianzus, *Oratio* II, 38 (SC 247, 138–41).

44. Cf. Y. Congar, *I Believe in the Holy Spirit* 3. *The River of Life Flows in the East and in the West*, ET David Smith, London and New York 1983, 133–37.

45. Origen, *In Joan.* II, 20 (SC 120, 220).

46. John Damascene, *De fide orthodoxa* I, 8; 12 (*Schriften*, ed. Kotter, 2, 18–31, 35f.).

47. Augustine, *De Trinitate* IV, 20 (CCL 50, 195–202).

48. DS 525, 568; ND 308.

49. Thomas Aquinas, *In I Sent.*, d. 28, q. 1, a. 1; *In III Sent.*, d. 25, q. 1, a. 2; *ST* I, 33, 1; 39, 5 ad 6.

50. Bonaventure, *In I Sent.*, d. 27, p. 1, q. 2 ad 3; d. 28, q. 1–3; d. 29, dub. 1; *Breviloquium* p. 1, c. 3.

51. Basil, *De spiritu sancto* 6f. (SC 17, 126ff.).

52. Augustine, *Confessiones* VII, 10, 16 (CCL 27, 103f.).

52a. K. Rahner, 'Remarks on the Dogmatic Treatise "De Trinitate"', in *Theological Investigations* 4, ET K. Smyth London and Baltimore 1966, 77–102.

53. For the interpretation cf., in addition to the relevant commentaries, M. Buber, *Moses*, Oxford 1946, 39–55; T. C. Vriezen, ''Ehje 'ašer 'ehje', in W. Baumgartner et al., *Festschrift für A. Bertholet*, Tübingen 1950, 498–512; A. Deissler, *Die Grundbotschaft des Alten Testaments. Ein theologischer Durchblick*, Freiburg – Basle – Vienna, ⁵1972, 48ff.

54. T. Boman, *Hebrew Thought compared with Greek*, ET J. L. Moreau, London and Philadelphia 1960, 38ff.

55. Philo, *Quod Deus sit immutabilis* 14 (*Philonis Alex. opera*, ed. P. Wendland, 2, Berlin 1897, 72); *De vita Mosis* 14 (ibid., 4, 136f.); *De Abraham* 24 (ibid., 28).

56. Athanasius, *De synodis* 35 (PG 26, 753f.); Gregory of Nazianzus, *Oratio* II, 45, 3 (SC 247, 148); Gregory of Nyssa, *Contra Eunomium* I, 8 (PG 45, 255ff.); Hilary, *De Trinitate* I, 5 (CCL 62, 4f.).

57. Augustine, *De civitate Dei* VIII, 11 (CCL 47, 227f.); *De Trinitate* V, 10 (CCL 50, 217f.).

58. Athanasius, *De decretis nicaenae synodi* (PG 25, 449); cf. Cyril of Alexandria, *De Trinitate dialogi* I (PG 75, 672BD).

59. Thomas Aquinas, *ST* I, 13, 11.

60. Ibid.

61. Cf. K. Kremer, *Die neuplatonische Seinsphilosophie und ihre Wirkung auf Thomas von Aquin*, Leiden 1966.

62. *ST* I, 3, 4; 7, 1; etc.

63. *Summa contra Gentiles* I, 26.

64. *ST* I-II, 66, 5 ad 4.

65. *ST* I, 3, 5.

66. *ST* I, 8, 1.

67. *ST* I, 9, 1f.

68. *ST* I, 10, 1.

69. *ST* I, 14, 5; 19, 1.

70. *ST* I, 18, 3.

71. Cf. F. Lakner, 'Aseität', *LTK* 1, 921f.

72. E. Brunner, *Dogmatics* 1. *The Christian Doctrine of God*, ET O. Wyon, London and Philadelphia 1950, 120.

73. M. Heidegger, *Identity and Difference*, ET J. Stambaugh, New York 1969, 72.

74. Cf. G. Siewerth, *Das Schicksal der Metaphysik von Thomas zu Heidegger*, Einsiedeln 1959.

75. J. E. Kuhn, *Katholische Dogmatik* I/2. *Die dogmatische Lehre von der Erkenntnis, den Eigenschaften und der Einheit Gottes*, Tübingen 1862, 758ff.

76. H. Schnell, *Katholische Dogmatik* I, Münster 1888, 238ff.

77. Kant, *Critique of Pure Reason*, ET J. M. D. Meiklejohn, in *Kant*, Great Books of the Western World 42, Chicago 1952, 7.

78. J. G. Fichte, 'Über den Grund unseres Glaubens eine göttliche Weltregierung', *WW* III, ed. Medicus, 119–33.

79. Cf. above, 26f.

80. Fichte, op. cit.

81. K. Jaspers, *Philosophical Faith and Revelation*, ET E. B. Ashton, New York 1967, 141ff.

82. On the death-of-God theology cf. J. Bishop, *Die Gott-ist-tot Theologie*, Düsseldorf 1968; D. Sölle, *Christ the Representative: An Essay in Theology after the 'Death of God'*, ET D. Lewis, London and Philadelphia 1967; id., *Atheistisch an Gott glauben. Beiträge zur Theologie*, Olten-Freiburg 1968.

83. H. Küng, *Does God Exist? An Answer for Today*, ET E. Quinn, New York and London 1980, 631–5.

84. A. M. S. Boethius, *Liber de persona et duabus naturis* 3 (PL 64, 1343).

85. Richard of St Victor, *De Trinitate* IV, 22, 24 (ed. Ribaillier, 187f., 189f.).

86. Cf. M. Müller and W. Vossenkuhl, 'Person', *HPG* 2, 1059–70.

87. H. Krings, 'Freiheit, Ein Versuch, Gott zu denken', *PhJ* 77, 1970, 225–37; id., 'Freiheit', *HPG* 1, 493–510; H. Krings and E. Simon, 'Gott', *HPG* 2, 614–41.

88. Vatican II, *Gaudium et spes*, 76.

Chapter II Jesus Christ, Son of God

1. Irenaeus, *Adv. haer.* III, 20, 2 (SC 211, 388–93).

2. G. Büchner, *Dantons Tod*, Act 3, cited in J. Moltmann, *The Trinity and the Kingdom of God*, ET M. Kohl, London and New York 1981, 48. On the whole problem cf. W. Kasper, 'Das Böse als theologisches Problem', in *Christlicher Glaube in moderner Gesellschaft* 9, Freiburg – Basle – Vienna 1981, 176–80.

3. Cited in Lactantius, *De ira Dei* 13 (PL 7, 121).

4. A. Camus, *The Myth of Sisyphus and Other Essays*, ET J. O'Brien, London and New York 1955, 42.

5. Cf. R. L. Rubenstein, *After Auschwitz: Radical Theology and Contemporary Judaism*, Indianapolis 1966.

6. G. Scholem, 'Toward an Understanding of the Messianic Idea in Judaism', in *The Messianic Idea in Judaism and Other Essays on Jewish Spirituality*, ET M. A. Meyer and H. Halkin, New York 1971, 1.

7. Cf. K. Marx, 'On the Jewish Question', in Karl Marx, *Early Writings*, ET ed. T. B. Bottomore, New York 1964, 11.

8. E. Bloch in particular has endeavored to make a place in the Marxist system for the positive, utopian, world-transforming impulses unleashed by the idea of redemption, although in the process he imposes a strictly atheistic interpretation of them. Cf. *Das Prinzip Hoffnung*, Frankfurt 1959; *Atheism in Christianity: The Religion of the Exodus and the Kingdom*, ET J. T. Swann, New York 1972.

9. On this subject cf. E. Schillebeeckx, *Christ: The Experience of Jesus as Lord*, ET John Bowden, London and New York 1980, 670ff.

10. F. Nietzsche, *Beyond Good and Evil*, no. 270, ET W. Kaufmann, New York 1966, Vintage Books ed., 220; *Nietzsche contra Wagner*, 'The Psychologist Speaks Up', no. 2, ET W. Kaufmann in *The Portable Nietzsche*, New York 1954, 678–9.

11. Moltmann, op. cit., 48.

12. Thomas Aquinas, *Summa contra Gentiles* III, 71.

13. T. W. Adorno, *Minima Moralia. Reflections from a Damaged Life*, ET E. F. N. Jephcott, New York 1978, 247.

14. M. Horkheimer, *Die Sehnsucht nach dem ganz Anderen. Ein Interview mit Kommentar von H. Gumnior*, Hamburg 1970, 69.

15. Cf. A. D. Sertillanges, *Le problème du mal*, 2 vols., Paris 1948–51; F. Billicsich, *Das Problem des Übels in der Philosophie des Abendlandes*, 3 vols., Vienna and Cologne 1952–59; T. Haecker, *Schöpfer und Schöpfung*, Munich ²1949; B. Welte, *Über das Böse*, QD 6, Freiburg–Basle–Vienna 1959; P. Ricoeur, *Fallible Man*, ET C. Kelbley, Chicago 1965; id., *The Symbolism of Evil*, ET E. Buchanan, New York 1967; K. Lüthi, *Gott und das Böse*, Zürich 1961; Y. Congar, 'Schicksal oder Schuld? Das Problem des Übels und des Bösen', in J. Hüttenbügel (ed.), *Gott – Mensch – Universum. Der Christ vor den Fragen der Zeit*, Graz – Vienna – Cologne 1974, 653–75; J. Maritain, *God and the Permission of Evil*, ET J. W. Evans, Milwaukee 1966; W. Brugger, *Theologia Naturalis*, Pullach 1954, 369–90; O. Marquardt, 'Idealismus und Theodizee', in *Schwierigkeiten mit der Geschichtsphilosophie*, Frankfurt 1973, 52–65; W. Kern and J. Splett, 'Theodicy', *SacMundi* 6, 213–18; L. Oeing-Hanhoff and W. Kasper, 'Negativität und Böses',

in *Christlicher Glaube in moderner Gesellschaft* 9, Freiburg – Basle – Vienna 1981, 147–201.

16. G. W. Leibniz, *Theodicy: Essays on the Goodness of God, the Freedom of Man, and the Origin of Evil*, ET E. M. Huggard, New Haven 1952.

17. Plato, *Republic* 379.

18. Augustine, *De ordine* I, 7; II 7 (CCL 29, 97–9, 117–20); *Enchiridion* 11 (CCL 46, 69–70); Thomas Aquinas, *ST* I, 22, 2; 42, 2; *Summa contra Gentiles* III, 71.

19. Cf. especially P. Teilhard de Chardin, *The Phenomenon of Man*, ET B. Wall, London and New York 1959, 309–11.

20. D. Sölle, *Suffering*, ET E. R. Kalin, Philadelphia 1975, 22ff.

21. F. M. Dostoievsky, *The Brothers Karamazov*, Book 5, ch. 4, ET D. Magarshack, Harmondsworth and Baltimore 1958, 1, 297.

22. Cf. Kasper, art cit. (n. 15), 193ff.

23. E. Zenger, 'Jesus von Nazaret und die messianischen Hoffnungen des alttestamentlichen Israels', in W. Kasper (ed.), *Christologische Schwerpunkte*, Düsseldorf 1980, 37–78.

24. M. Buber, *Two Types of Faith*, ET N. Goldhawk, London 1951; R. Bultmann, *Theology of the New Testament*, ET K. Grobel, 2 vols., New York and London 1951–55, 1, 1f.

25. H. Gese, 'Der Messias', in his *Zur biblischen Theologie. Alttestamentliche Vorträge*, Munich 1977, 128–51.

26. Zenger, art. cit., 43.

27. H. Gese, 'Natus ex virgine', in *Vom Sinai zum Zion. Alttestamentliche Beiträge zur biblischen Theologie*, Munich 1974, 136.

28. G. von Rad, *Old Testament Theology*, ET D. M. G. Stalker, 2 vols., Edinburgh and New York 1962–65, 1, 320ff.

29. Ibid., 2, 116f.

30. Zenger, art. cit., 50.

31. H. L. Strack and P. Billerbeck, *Kommentar zum Neuen Testament aus Talmud und Midrasch* 1, Munich 1922, 6ff.

32. *Enoch* 45–50, in R. H. Charles (ed.), *The Apocrypha and Pseudepigrapha of the Old Testament*, Oxford 1913, 2, 213–18.

33. Gese, 'Der Messias' (n. 25), 150f.

34 V. Taylor, *The Names of Jesus*, London 1954; W. Marxsen, *The Beginnings of Christology: A Study in Its Problems*, Philadelphia 1969, H. Ristow and K. Matthiae (eds.), *Der historische Jesus und der kerygmatische Christus. Beiträge zum Christusverständnis in Forschung und Verkündigung*, Berlin 1960; R. Bultmann, 'The Primitive Christian Kerygma and the Historical Jesus', in C. E. Braaten and R. A. Harrisville (eds.) *The Historical Jesus and the Kerygmatic Christ*, Nashville 1964, 15–43; id., *Jesus and the Word*, ET L. P. Smith and E. H. Lantero, New York 1934; F. Hahn, *The Titles of Jesus in Christology: Their History in Early Christianity*, ET H. Knight and G. Ogg, London and New York 1969; id., 'Methodenprobleme einer Christologie des Neuen Testaments', VF 2, 1970, 3–41; L. Cerfaux, *Christ in the Theology of St Paul*, ET G. Webb and A. Walker, New York 1959; R. H. Fuller, *The Foundations of New Testament Christology*, Philadelphia and London 1965; M. Hengel, *The Son of God: The Origin of Christology and the History of Jewish-Hellenistic Religion*, ET John Bowden, London and Philadelphia 1976; W. G. Kümmel, 'Jesusforschung seit 1950', *TRu*,

NF 31, 1965–66, 15–46, 289–315; O. Cullmann, *The Christology of the New Testament*, ET S. C. Guthrie and C. A. M. Hall, Philadelphia and London ²1963; X. Léon-Dufour, *The Gospels and the Jesus of History*, ET J. McHugh, New York 1967; W. Trilling, *Fragen zur Geschichtlichkeit Jesu*, Düsseldorf 1966; id., *Christusverkündigung in den synoptischen Evangelien. Beispiele gattungsgemässer Auslegung*, Munich 1969; H. R. Balz, *Methodische Probleme der neutestamentlichen Christologie*, Neukirchen-Vluyn 1967; E. Schweizer, *Jesus*, ET D. F. Green, Richmond 1971; G. Bornkamm, *Jesus of Nazareth*, ET I. and F. McLuskey with J. M. Robinson, London and New York 1960; H. Braun, *Jesus of Nazareth. The Man and His Time*, ET E. R. Kalin, Philadelphia 1961; J. Gnilka, *Jesus Christus nach den frühen Zeugnissen des Glaubens*, Munich 1970; J. Jeremias, *New Testament Theology 1. The Proclamation of Jesus*, ET John Bowden, London and New York 1971; G. Schneider, *Die Frage nach Jesus. Christus-Aussagen des Neuen Testaments*, Essen 1971; H. Schürmann, *Das Geheimnis Jesu. Versuche zur Jesusfrage*, Leipzig 1972; K. Rahner and W. Thüsing, *A New Christology*, ET D. Smith and V. Green New York and London 1980; H. Küng, *On Being a Christian*, ET E. Quinn, New York and London 1976; C. H. Dodd, *The Founder of Christianity*, London and New York 1970; W. Pannenberg, *Jesus, God and Man*, ET L. Wilkins and D. A. Priebe, Philadelphia and London ²1972; E. Schillebeeckx, *Jesus: An Experiment in Christology*, ET H. Hoskins, London and New York 1979; W. Kasper, *Jesus the Christ*, ET V. Green, London and New York 1976; W. Thüsing, *Die neutestamentlichen Theologen und Jesus Christus 1*, Düsseldorf 1981.

35. A. von Harnack, *What Is Christianity?*, ET T. B. Saunders, London and New York ²1901, 63.

36. H. Conzelmann, 'Jesus Christus', *RGG* 3, 633f.

37. H. Merklein, *Die Gottesherrschaft als Handlungsprinzip. Untersuchung zur Ethik Jesu*, Forschung zur Bibel 34, Würburg 1978, 31ff.

38. G. von Rad, 'Basileus', *TDNT* 1, 570.

39. W. Kasper, *Jesus the Christ* (n. 34), 233.

40. M. Tullius Cicero, *Oratio pro C. Rabirio perduellionis reo*, cap. 5.

41. R. Bultmann, 'The Primitive Christian Kerygma and the Historical Jesus' (n. 34), 23–4.

42. R. Pesch, *Wie Jesus das Abendmahl hielt. Der Grund der Eucharistie*, Freiburg – Basle – Vienna ²1978.

43. A. von Harnack, *Lehrbuch der dogmengeschichte 1*, Tübingen ⁵1931, 121 [I have not been able to find the passage in the ET: *History of Dogma 1*, ET N. Buchanan, New York 1958, reprint. Tr.]

44. R. Bultmann, *Primitive Christianity and Its Contemporary Setting*, ET R. H. Fuller, London and New York 1956; id., *Theology of the New Testament* (n. 24); id., 'The Christology of the New Testament', in *Faith and Understanding* 1, ET L. P. Smith, New York 1969, 262–85.

45. Cf. M. Hengel, *The Son of God* (n. 34).

46. H. Gese, 'Der Messias' (n. 25), 129ff.

47. *Enoch* 37–41, in R. H. Charles, op. cit. (n. 32), 2, 208–13.

48. R. Schnackenburg, *The Gospel of John 1*, ET K. Smyth, London and New York 1968, 481–93; H. Gese, 'Der Johannesprolog', in *Zur biblischen Theologie* (n. 25), 152–201; E. Schweizer, *Neotestamentica. Deutsche und Englische Aufsätze, 1951–1963*, Zürich and Stuttgart 1963, 110–21.

356   *Notes to pages 174–181*

49. Hengel, op. cit. (n. 34), 59.

50. Cf. E. Käsemann, *Commentary on Romans*, ET G. Bromiley, Grand Rapids and London 1980, 10ff.; H. Schlier, *Der Römerbrief*, HTKNT 6, Freiburg – Basle – Vienna 1977, 24ff.; U. Wilckens, *Der Brief an die Römer* 1, EKKNT 6/1, Neukirchen – Vluyn – Zürich 1978, 64ff.; Hengel, op. cit., 59ff.

51. Cf. E. Lohmeyer, *Kyrios Jesus. Eine Untersuchung zu Phil 2, 5–11*, Sitzungsberichte der Heidelberger Akad. der Wissen., Phil-hist. Kl., 1927–28, 4. Abhandlung, Heidelberg ²1961; E. Käsemann, 'Kritische Analyse von Phil 2, 5–11', in *Exegetische Versuche und Besinnungen* 1, Göttingen 1970, 51–59; G. Bornkamm, 'Zum Verständnis des Christus-Hymnus Phil 2, 6–11', in *Studien zu Antike und Urchristentum. Gesammalte Aufsätze 2*, Munich 1959, 177–87; J. Gnilka, *Der Philipperbrief*, HTKNT 10/3, Freiburg – Basle – Vienna 1968; C. Hofius, *Der Christushymnus Philipper 2, 6–11. Untersuchung zu Gestalt und Aussage eines urchristlichen Psalms*, Tübingen 1976.

52. Cf. W. Popkes, *Christus traditus. Eine Untersuchung zum Begriff der Dahingabe im Neuen Testament*, Zürich 1967.

53. J. Gnilka, *Der Kolosserbrief*, HTKNT 10/1, Freiburg – Basle – Vienna 1980, 51ff.; E. Schweizer, *Der Brief an die Kolosser*, EKKNT, Neukirchen – Vluyn – Zürich 1976, 50ff.

54. R. Bultmann, *The Gospel of John: A Commentary*, ET G. R. Beasley-Murray, R. W. N. Hoare and J. K. Riches, Oxford and Philadelphia 1971, 13ff.; R. Schnackenburg, *The Gospel of John* 1 (n. 48), 232ff.; F. M. Braun, *Jean le théologien. Les grandes traditions d'Israël d'accord des écritures d'après le quatrième évangile*, Paris 1964; R. E. Brown, *The Gospel according to John*, AB 29A, Garden City 1970.

55. Cf. A. Grillmeier, *Christ in Christian Tradition* 1, ET John Bowden, Oxford and Atlanta 1975; A. Gilg, *Weg und Bedeutung der altkirchlichen Christologie*, Munich 1955; G. L. Prestige, *God in Patristic Thought*, London ²1952; I. Ortiz de Urbina, *Nicée et Constantinople*, Histoire des conciles oecuméniques, ed. G. Dumeige, 1, Paris 1963; J. Liébaert, *Christologie. Von der Apostolischen Zeit bis zum Konzil von Chalkedon (451)*, mit einer biblisch-christologischen Einleitung von P. Lamarche, HDG III/1a, Freiburg – Basle – Vienna 1965; P. Smulders, 'Dogmengeschichtliche und lehramtliche Entfaltung der Christologie', *Mysal* III/1, 389–475.

56. A. Orbe, *Cristología gnóstica*, 2 vols., Madrid 1976; H. Jonas, *Gnosis und spätantiker Geist*, Göttingen ³1965.

57. Origen, *Contra Celsum* IV, 18 (SC 136, 224–29).

58. Justin, *Apologia* I, 46; II, 8; 10; 13 (*Corpus Apol.* I, ed. von Otto, 128ff., 220ff., 224–8, 236ff.).

59. Justin, *Apologia* I, 21 (ibid., 64–8).

60. Justin, *Apologia* II, 6 (ibid., 212–16); *Dialogus cum Tryphone* 61 (ibid., II, 212–16); Athenagoras, *Supplicatio pro Christianis* (TU 4/2, 8–10).   ⋅

61. Justin, *Apologia* I, 13 (ibid., 40ff.); cf. *Dialogus cum Tryphone* 56; 128 (ibid., 186–96, 451–4).

62. Theophilus of Antioch, *Ad Autolycum* 2, 10; 2, 22 (SC 20, 122–4, 154).

63. Tertullian, *Adv. Praxean* 2; 8, 25 (CCL 2, 1160f., 1167f., 1195f.); *De pudicitia* 21, 16 (CCL 2, 1328).

64. Tertullian, *Adv. Praxean* 7 (CCL 2, 1165ff.); *Adv. Hermogenem* 2 (CCL 1, 397f.).

65. Tertullian, *Adv. Praxean* 8 (CCL 2, 1167f.); cf. 13 (CCL 2, 1173–6).

66. Ibid. 9(CCL 2, 1168f.).

67. Origen, *De principiis* I, 2, 2 and 9 (SC 252, 112ff., 128ff.); IV, 4, 1 (SC 268, 400–5).

68. *De principiis* I, 2, 5 (SC 252, 118–21); IV, 4, 1 (SC 268, 400–5).

69. Ibid., I, 2, 7 (SC 252, 124f.).

70. Ibid., I, 2, 2 (SC 252, 112–15); *De oratione* 15, 1 (GCS Orig. 2, 333f.).

71. *De principiis* IV, 4, 1 (SC 268, 400–5).

72. Ibid., I, 2, 13 (SC 252, 140–43); *In Joan.* II, 6 (SC 120, 210–13).

73. *Contra Celsum* V, 39 (SC 147, 116–31).

74. *De principiis* I, 2, 8 (SC 252, 126–9).

75. Ibid., II, 6, 1 (SC 252, 308–11); *Contra Celsum* III, 35 (SC 136, 82f.).

76. Grillmeier, op. cit., (n. 55), 1, 219–48.

77. Ortiz de Urbina, op. cit. (n. 55); J. N. D. Kelly, *Early Christian Creeds*, London and New York [2]1960, 205–30; Grillmeier, op. cit., 1, 249–73 (with bibliography).

78. DS 125; ET in ND 7.

79. H. Kraft, 'Homoousios', *ZKG* 66, 1954–55, 1–24; A. Grillmeier, 'Homoousios', *LTK* 5, 467f.; F. Ricken, 'Das Homoousios von Nikaia als Krisis des altchristlichen Platonismus', in B. Welte (ed.), *Zur Frühgeschichte der Christologie*, QD 51, Freiburg – Basle – Vienna 1970, 74–99.

80. Athanasius, *Adv. Arianos* I, 39 (PG 26, 91–4); II, 47, 59, 69f. (PG 26, 245–48, 271–4, 293–6).

81. Ignatius of Antioch, *Ad Ephesios* 20, 2 (*Patres Apostolici*, ed. Funk-Diekamp, 2, 204).

82. Athanasius, *Adv. Arianos* I, 38; III, 19 (PG 26, 89–92, 361–4).

84. Ibid., II, 59 (PG 26, 271–4).

84. Cf. M. Werner, *The Formation of Christian Dogma: An Historical Study of Its Problem*, ET S. G. F. Brandon, New York 1957.

85. Cf. above, n. 48.

86. Ignatius of Antioch, *Ad Magnesios* 8, 2; *Ad Ephesios* 3, 2; 17, 2 (*Patres Apostolici*, ed. Funk-Diekamp, 2, 86, 184, 200)); Justin, *Dialogus cum Tryphone* 61 (*Corpus Apol.* II ed. von Otto, 212–16); Athenagoras, *Supplicatio pro Christianis* 10 (TU 4/2 , 10f.); Irenaeus, *Demonstratio* (TU 31/1, 29 22).

87. Cf. H. Kleinknecht, '*Lego*, 3: The Logos in the Greek and Hellenistic World', *TDNT* 4, 80ff.

88. H. Krings, 'Wort', *HTG* 2, 835–45.

89. Plato, *Cratylus* 434b.

90. Ibid., 438a–439b.

91. Plato, *Sophist* 363c, 364a.

92. Augustine, *De Trinitate* XV, 11 (CCL 50A, 486–90).

93. Ibid., XV, 10 (CCL 50A, 483–6).

94. Ibid., XV, 12 (CCL 50A, 490–4).

95. Ibid., XV, 13 (CCL 50A, 494f.).

96. Ibid., XV, 14 (CCL 50A, 496f.); cf. *In Joannis Evangelium tractatus* I, 8–10 (CCL 36, 4–6).

97. Thomas Aquinas, *ST* I, 27, 1; 34, 1.

98. Thomas Aquinas, *De pot.* 10, 1.

99. Thomas Aquinas, *Summa contra Gentiles* IV, 11.

100. Thomas Aquinas, *De pot.* 10, 1.

101. Thomas Aquinas, *ST* I, 34, 3; *De ver.* 4, 5.

102. On what follows cf. H. Urs von Balthasar, 'Mysterium Paschale', in *Mysal* III/2, 133–326.

103. For the interpretation cf., in addition to the literature listed in n. 51, P. Henry, 'Kénose', *DBS* 5, 7–161; L. Oeing-Hanfoff, 'Der in Gottesgestalt war. . .', *TQ* 161, 1981, 288–304. For the history of the exegesis of this passage: J. Gewiess, 'Zum altkirchlichen Veständnis der Kenosisstelle', *TQ* 128, 1948, 463–87.

104. Augustine, *Serm.* 4, 5 (CCL 41, 21f.).

105. J. Scharbert, *Der Schmerz im Alten Testament*, Bonn 1955, 215ff.

106. P. Kuhn, *Gottes Selbsterniedrigung in der Theologie der Rabbinen*, Munich 1968; id., *Gottes Trauer und Klage in der rabbinischen Überlieferung*, Leiden 1978.

107. Cf. W. Maas, *Die Unveränderlichkeit Gottes. Zum Verhältnis von griechisch-philosophischer und christlicher Gotteslehre*, Paderborner theologische Studien 1, Münster – Paderborn – Vienna 1974, 34ff.

108. This is true, for example, of Clement of Alexandria; cf. Maas, ibid., 125ff.

109. This can be seen from the very fact that the fathers of the church, following scripture, often attribute to God such emotions as anger, love and pity.

110. Ignatius of Antioch, *Ad Polycarpum* 3, 2 (*Patres Apostolici*, ed. Funk-Diekamp, 2, 188ff.).

111. Irenaeus, *Adv. Haer.* IV, 20, 4 (SC 100/2, 634–7).

112. Melito of Sardis, *In Pascha* 3 (SC 123, 60–2).

113. Tertullian, *De carne Christi* 5, 4 (CCL 2, 881).

114. Tertullian, *Adv. Marcionem* II, 16, 3 (CCL, 493).

115. Ibid., II, 27, 7 (CCL 1, 507).

116. Cf. R. Lachenschmid, 'Theopaschismus', *LTK* 10, 83.

117. Cf. Augustine, *De civitate Dei* VIII, 17 (CCL 47, 234f.).

118. Cf. Athanasius, *Adv. Arianos* III, 32–34 (PG 26, 389–98); Gregory of Nyssa, *Contra Eunomium* VI (PG 45, 721B–725B).

119. Cf. H. Crouzel, 'La Passion de l'Impassible', in *L'homme devant Dieu (FS H. de Lubac)*, Théologie 56, Paris 1963, 1, 269–79.

120. Hilary, *De Trinitate* VIII, 45; X, 10, 24 (CCL 62A, 357f., 466f., 478f.).

121. Augustine, *De civitate Dei* XIV, 9 (CCL 48, 425–30).

122. Gregory of Nyssa, *Oratio catechetica magna* 24, 1 (PG 45, 64f.).

123. Origen, *De principiis* II, 4, 4 (SC 252, 288f.).

124. Origen, *Homiliae in Ezechielem* 6, 6 (GCS Orig. 8, 383ff.); cf. *Commentarium in Epistulam ad Romanos* VII, 9 (PG 16, 1127C–1130A).

125. Cf. Thomas Aquinas, *ST* I, 13, 7; *De pot.* 7, 8–11.

126. Luther, *Disputatio Heidelbergae habita*, Theses 19f. (WA 1, 254); cf. W. von Loewenich, *Luther's Theology of the Cross*, ET H. J. A. Bouman, Minneapolis 1976.

127. Cf. P. Althaus, *The Theology of Martin Luther*, ET R. C. Schultz, Philadelphia 1966, 193–99; T. Beer, *Der fröhliche Wechsel und Streit. Grundzüge der Theologie Luthers*, Einsiedeln ²1980, esp. 323–453.

128. J. Calvin, *Institutio christianae religionis* (1559) II, 13, 4 (*Opera selecta* III, ed. B. Barth and W. Niese, Munich 1928, 456–8), ET *Calvin's Institutes*, LCC , London and Philadelphia 1960, 480f. Cf. K. Barth, *Church Dogmatics* I/2, 159–71.

129. Cf. M. Lienhard, *Luther, Witness to Jesus Christ: Stages and Themes of*

the *Reformer's Christology*, ET E. H. Robertson, Minneapolis 1982; Y. Congar, 'Regards et réflexions sur la christologie de Luther', in A. Grillmeier and H. Bacht (eds.), *Das Konzil von Chalkedon. Geschichte und Gegenwart III*, Würzburg ⁴1973, 457–86.

130. G. W. F. Hegel, *Vorlesungen über die Philosophie der Religion* II/2 (ed. Lasson), 53f.

131. Ibid., 75.

132. Ibid., 158; cf. id., *Faith and Knowledge, or the Reflective Philosophy of Subjectivity in the Complete Range of Its Forms as Kantian, Jacobian and Fichtean Philosophy*, ET W. Cerf and H. S. Harris Albany 1977, 190; id., *The Phenomenology of Mind*, ET J. Baillie, rev. 2nd ed., London 1949, 753, 780.

133. Id., *Vorlesungen über die Philosophie der Religion* I/1, 148.

134. Cited by J. Moltmann, *The Crucified God: The Cross of Christ as the Foundation and Criticism of Christian Theology*, ET R. A. Wilson and John Bowden, London and New York 1974, 35.

135. Cf. the survey in H. Küng, *Menschwerdung Gottes. Eine Einführung in Hegels theologisches Denken als Prolegomena zu einer künftigen Christologie*, Ökumenische Forschungen 1, Freiburg – Basle – Vienna, 1970, 637–70; J. Galot, *Vers une nouvelle christologie*, Paris 1971, 67–94; id., *Dieu souffre-t-il?*, Paris 1976.

136. A. N. Whitehead, *Process and Reality: An Essay in Cosmology*, New York 1960, 524.

137. K. Kitamori, *Theology of the Pain of God*, Richmond, Va and London 1965.

138. J. Bishop, *Die Gott-ist-tot-Theologie*, Düsseldorf 1968; S. M. Daecke, *Der Mythos vom Tode Gottes. Ein kritischer Überblick*, Hamburg 1969; H. M. Barth, 'Der christologische Ansatz der nordamerikanischen Tod-Gottes-Theologie', *KD* 17, 1971, 258.

139. Cf. H. Urs von Balthasar, 'Mysterium Paschale', in *Mysal* III/2, 164ff.

140. S. Kierkegaard, *Journals and Papers*, ET H. V. Hong and E. H. Hong, 2, Bloomington 1970, 62 (no. 1251).

141. Augustine, *In Joannis Evangelium tractatus* XII, 10f. (CCL 36, 126f.).

142. K. Barth, *Church Dogmatics* II/1, §28: 'The Being of God as the One Who Lives in Freedom' (257ff.).

143. Origen, *De principiis* I, 2, 5 (SC 252, 118–21); IV, 4, 1 (SC 268, 400–5).

144. Augustine, *De Trinitate* VIII, 10 (CCL 50, 290f.); cf. IV, 2 and 4 (CCL 50, 294f., 297–300).

145. Ibid., IX, 3 and 4 (CCL 50, 295–300).

146. Richard of St Victor, *De Trinitate* (ed. J. Ribaillier); on Richard cf. below, 216.

Chapter III   The Holy Spirit, Lord and Giver of Life

1. Cf. Y. Congar, *I Believe in the Holy Spirit* 3. *The River of Life Flows in the East and in the West*, ET David Smith, London and New York 1983, 165f.

2. L. Oeing-Hanhoff, 'Geist', *HWP* 3, 154–212.

3. Plato, *Phaedo* 251d; *Symposium* 209a–212; Augustine, *De vera religione* 41, 77 (CCL 32, 237f.); G. W. F. Hegel, *Vorlesungen über die Ästhetik* I (WW XII, ed. H. Glockner), 153ff.

4. F. Nietzsche, *The Will to Power*, no. 822, ET W. Kaufmann and R. J. Hollingdale, New York 1967, 435.

5. Literature on biblical pneumatology: F.Büchsel, *Der Geist Gottes im Neuen Testament*, Gütersloh 1926; H. Kleinknecht *et al.*, 'Pneuma', *TDNT* 6, 332–455; C. K. Barrett, *The Holy Spirit and the Gospel Tradition*, London and Philadelphia ²1966; I. Hermann, *Kyrios und Pneuma. Studien zur Christologie der paulinischen Hauptbriefe*, SANT 2, Munich 1961; E. Schweizer, *Neotestamentica. Deutsche und Englische Aufsätze, 1951–1967*, Zürich and Stuttgart, 1963, 153–79; K. H. Schelkle, *Theology of the New Testament 2*, ET W. A. Jurgens, Collegeville 1976, 231–35; Y. Congar, *I Believe in the Holy Spirit*, 1, *The Experience of the Spirit*. London and New York 1983, 3ff.

6. Anaximenes, *Fragm.* 2, in H. Diels and W. Kranz (eds.), *Die Fragmente der Vorsokratiker* 1, Berlin, ⁶1951, 95.

7. Aristotle, *De motu animalium* 10, 703a.

8. H. Kleinknecht, 'Pneuma', *TDNT* 6, 354–5.

9. Augustine, *Confessiones* XIII, 7, 8 (CCL 27, 245).

10. Cf. F. Lentzen-Deis, *Die Taufe Jesu nach den Synoptikern. Literarkritische und gattungsgeschichtliche Untersuchungen*, Frankfurter theologische Studien 4, Frankfurt 1970.

11. H. Schlier, 'Zum Begriff des Geistes nach den Johannesevangelium', in his *Besinnung auf das Neue Testament*, Exegetische Aufsätze und Vorträge 2, Freiburg – Basle – Vienna 1964, 264–71 [not included in the ET: *The Relevance of the New Testament*, ET W. J. O'Hara, New York 1969. Tr.].

12. *I Clem* 2, 2 (*Die apostolischen Väter*, ed. J. A. Fischer, Darmstadt 1956, 26).

13. *I Clem* 38, 1 (ibid., 72); 46, 6 (ibid., 82); *Didache* 11, 8 and 12; 13 (SC 248, 184ff., 186ff., 190); Justin, *Dialogus cum Tryphone* 39, 2–5; 82; etc. (*Corpus Apol.* II, ed. von Otto, 296–9, etc.).

14. Eusebius, *Historia Ecclesiastica* V, 3–4, 14–19 (GCS 9/1, 432f., 458–81).

15. Tertullian, *De pud.* 21, 17 (CCL 2, 328).

16. Irenaeus, *Adv. haer.* III, 24, 1 (SC 211, 471–5).

17. Hippolytus, *Traditio Apostolica*, Prol., in G. Dix (ed.), *The Treatise on the Apostolic Tradition of St. Hippolytus of Rome*, London 1937, 1f.

18. Ibid., 31; 35 (Dix, 57f., 61f.).

19. Y. Congar, op. cit., 1, 68ff.

20. Augustine, *Serm.* 267, 4 (PL 38, 1231); cf. below, n. 111.

21. On Joachim of Flora cf. E. Benz, *Ecclesia spiritualis. Kirchenidee und Geschichtstheologie der franziskanischen Reformation*, Stuttgart 1934; K. Löwith, *Meaning in History: The Theological Implications of the Philosophy of History*, Chicago 1949, 145–59; Congar, op. cit., 1, 126ff.; H. de Lubac, *La postérité spirituelle de Joachim de Fiore*, Paris and Namur 1979.

22. Cf. J. Ratzinger, *The Theology of History in St. Bonaventure*, ET Z. Hayes, Chicago 1971.

23. Thomas Aquinas, *ST* I, 39, 5; I-II, 106, 4; cf. M. Seckler, *Das Heil in der Geschichte. Geschichtstheologisches Denken bei Thomas von Aquin*, Munich 1964.

24. Thomas Aquinas, *ST* I-II, 106 and 108.

25. H. L. Strack and P. Billerbeck, *Kommentar zum Neuen Testament aus Talmud und Midrasch* 2, Munich 1924, 134–8.

26. Cf. below, German 243ff.

27. On the history of pneumatology: H. B. Swete, *The Holy Spirit in the Ancient Church*, London 1912; T. Ruesch, *Die Entstehung der Lehre vom Heiligen Geist bei Ignatius von Antiochia. Theophilus von Antiochia und Irenäus von Lyon*, Studien zu Dogmengeschichte und systematischen Theologie 2, Zürich 1952; G. Kretschmar, *Studien zur frühchristlichen Trinitätstheologie*, Beiträge zur historischen Theologie 21, Tübingen 1956; id., 'Le développement de la doctrine du Saint-Esprit du Nouveau Testament à Nicée', VCaro 88, 1962, 5–55; id., 'Der Heilige Geist in der Geschichte. Grundzüge frühchristlicher Pneumatologie', in W. Kasper (ed.), *Gegenwart des Geistes. Aspekte der Pneumatologie*, QD 85, Freiburg – Basle – Vienna 1970, 92–130; H. Opitz, *Ürsprünge frühchristlicher Pneumatologie. Ein Beitrag zur Entstehung der Lehre vom Heiligen Geist in der römischen Gemeinde unter Zurgrundelegung des I. Clemens-Briefes und des 'Hirten' des Hermas*, Theologische Arbeiten 15, Berlin 1960; A. Orbe, 'La teología del Espíritu Santo', in his *Estudios Valentinianos* 4, Rome 1960; W. D. Hauschild, *Gottes Geist und der Mensch. Studien zur früchristlichen Pneumatologie*, BEvT 63, Munich 1972; H. J. Jaschke, *Der Heilige Geist im Bekenntnis der Kirche. Eine Studie zur Pneumatologie des Irenäus von Lyon im Ausgang vom altchristlichen Glaubensbekenntnis*, Münsterische Beiträge zur Theologie 20, Münster 1976; Congar, op. cit., 1: 173ff.

28. Gregory of Nazianzus, *Oratio* 31, 26 (SC 250, 326–9).

29. *Shepherd of Hermas* 41; 58; 59 (SC 53, 188–91, 24–37, 238–41); Justin, *Apologia I*, 39 (*Corpus Apol.* I, ed. von Otto, 110–13).

30. *Didache* 7, 1 (SC 248, 232).

31. Justin, *Apologia* I, 61 (op. cit., 162–9).

32. Irenaeus, *Adv. haer.* III, 17, 1 (SC 211, 328–31); *Demonstratio* 3; 6f. (SC 62, 32, 39f.).

33. Tertullian, *De baptismo* (CCL 1, 288f.).

34. Irenaeus, *Adv. haer.* I, 10, 1 (SC 264, 154–9).

35. Tertullian, *De praescript. haer.* 12 (CCL 1, 197f); *Adv. Praxean* 2 (CCL 2, 1160f.); *De virg. vel.* 1 (CCL 2, 1209f.).

36. Irenaeus, *Demonstratio* 5 (SC 62, 39f.).

37. Ibid., 99 (SC 62, 168f.).

38. Echoes in Irenaeus, *Demonstratio* 1 (SC 62, 46–8); Origen, *De principiis* I, 3, 4 (SC 252, 148–53).

39. Tertullian, *Adv. Praxean* 2; 8 (CCL 2, 1160f., 1167f.).

40. Origen, *De principiis* I, 3, 1–8 (SC 252, 142–65).

41. Athanasius, *Epist. ad Serap.* I, 19–25 (PG 26, 573–90); cf. Gregory of Nazianzus, *Oratio* 31, 6 (SC 250, 285–7).

42. On Constantinople cf. A. M. Ritter, *Das Konzil von Konstaninopel und sein Symbol. Studien zur Geschichte und Theologie des 2. Ökumenuschen Konzils*, Forschungen zur Kirchen- und Dogmengeschichte 15, Göttingen 1965; I. Ortiz de Urbina, *Nicée et Constantinople*, Histoire des conciles oecuméniques, ed. G. Dumeige, 1, Paris 1963; W. D. Hauschild, 'Das trinitarische Dogma von 381 als Ergebnis verbindlicher Konsensusbildung', in K. Lehmann and W. Pannenberg (ed.), *Glaubensbekenntnis und Kirchengemeinschaft*, Dialog der Kirchen 1, Freiburg und Göttingen 1982, 13–48.

43. Cf. *COD*, 28.

44. DS 151; ND 13.

45. DS 168–77; ND 306/16–24.

46. Epiphanius, *Ancoratus* 119 (GCS 25, 147–9).

47. DS 150; ND 12.

48. Cf. below, 214ff.

49. On what follows cf. especially Congar, op. cit., 3: 174ff.

50. M. J. Scheeben, *The Mysteries of Christianity*, ET C. J. Vollert, St Louis 1946, 99.

51. Augustine, *De Trinitate* V, 11 (CCL 50, 218ff.).

52. Ibid., VI, 10 (CCL 50, 241ff.); cf. IX 4f. (CCL 50, 297–301).

53. Anselm of Canterbury, *Monologion*, 49ff.

54. Thomas Aquinas, *ST* I, 27, 3f.; 36, 1; *Summa contra Gentiles* IV, 19.

55. Augustine, *De Trinitate* IV, 20 (CCL 50, 195–202); V, 11 and 14 (CCL 50, 218ff., 222f.).

56. Ibid., XV, 17 and 26 (CCL 50A, 501–7, 524–9).

57. Thomas Aquinas, *In I Sent.*, d. 28, q. 1, a. 1; *In III Sent.*, d. 25, q. 1, a. 2.

58. Augustine, *De Trinitate*, VIII, 10 (CCL 50, 290f.); IX, 2 (CCL 50, 294f.).

59. Congar, op. cit., 3: 103–6, 108–14.

60. Richard of St Victor, *De Trinitate* III, 22ff. (ed. J. Ribaillier, 136ff., 202ff.).

61. John Damascene, *De fide orth.* I, 7 (*Die Schriften des Johannes von Damaskus*, ed. B. Kotter, I, Berlin and New York 1973, 16f.), who is quoting Gregory of Nyssa, *Oratio catechetica magna* 2 (PG 45, 17–18c).

62. *De fide orth.* I, 8 (Kotter, 18–31).

63. Ibid., I, 7 (Kotter, 16f.); Gregory of Nyssa, *Oratio catechetica magna* 2 (PG 45, 17–18c).

64. *De fide orth.* I, 8 (Kotter, 18–31).

65. Congar, op. cit. 3: 40f., 49 n. 1.

66. DS 850; ND 321.

67. Congar, op. cit., 3: 25f, 30ff, 35f.

68. Ibid., 3: 32, 39.

69. Tertullian, *Adv. Praxean* 4 (CCL 2, 1162f.).

70. Epiphanius, *Ancoratus* 6 (GCS 25, 12f.).

71. Maximus Confessor, *Opuscula theologica et polemica* (PG 91, 136).

72. DS 188 (?), 284, 470, 485, 490, 527; ND 310.

73. Congar, op. cit., 3, 49ff.

74. DS 805, 850, 853; ND 319, 321, 24. For the contemporary appraisal of this council cf. A. Ganoczy, 'Formale und inhaltliche Aspekte der mittelalterlichen Konzilien als Zeichen kirchlichen Ringens um ein universales Glaubensbekenntnis', in Lehmann and Pannenberg (eds.), op. cit. (n. 42), 49–79.

75. *COD* 65.

76. Congar, op. cit., 3: 57ff.

77. Ibid., 3: 61ff; D. Wendenbourg, *Geist oder Energie? Zur Frage der innergöttlichen Verankerung des christlichen Lebens in der byzantinischen Theologie*, Munich 1980.

78. V. Lossky, *The Mystical Theology of the Eastern Church*, London 1957; 'The Procession of the Holy Spirit in the Orthodox Triadology', *ESQ* 7, 1948, 31–52. Similarly S. Bulgakov, *Le paraclet*, Paris 1946. For a different view: P. Evdokimov, *L'Esprit-Saint dans la tradition orthodoxe*, Paris 1969.

79. V. Bulatov, 'Theses über das Filioque. Von unseren russischen Theologen', *Revue internationale de théologie* 6, 1898, 681–712.

80. Cf. Congar, op. cit., 3: 103ff., 174ff.

81. On the Council of Florence: J. Gill, *Constance et bâle-Florence,* Histoire des conciles oecuméniques, ed. G. Dumeige, 9, Paris 1965, 213ff.; Congar, op. cit., 3: 184ff.

82. DS 850, cf. 1300; ND 321, cf. 322.

83. K. Barth, *Church Dogmatics* I/1, 546–67; cf. I/2, 250.

84. For contemporary ecumenical discussion: L. Vischer (ed.), *Geist Gottes – Geist Christi. Ökumenische Überlegungen zur Filioque-Kontroverse,* Beihefte zur Ökumenischen Rundschau 39, Frankfurt 1981; R. Slenczka, 'Das Filioque in der ökumenischen Diskussion', in Lehmann and Pannenberg (eds.), op. cit. (n. 42), 80–99; Congar, op. cit., 3: 192ff.

85. On recent pneumatology: H. Mühlen, *Der Heilige Geist als Person. Beitrag zur Frage nach der dem Heiligen Geist eigentümlichen Funktion in der Trinität, bei der Inkarnation und im Gnadenbund,* Münsterische Beiträge zur Theologie 26, Münster 1963; id., *Una mystica persona. Die Kirche als das Mysterium der heilsgeschichtlichen Identität des Heiligen Geists in Christus und den Christen: Ein Person in vielen Personen,* Munich – Paderborn – Vienna, ³1968; id., *Die Erneuerung des christlichen Glaubens, Charisma – Geist – Befreiung,* Munich 1974; H. Urs von Balthasar, *Spiritus Creator,* Skizzen zur Theologie 3, Einsiedeln 1967; H. Berkhof, *The Doctrine of the Holy Spirit,* Richmond 1964; W. Dantine, *Der Heilige Geist und der unheilige Geist. Über die Erneuerung der Urteilsfähigkeit,* Stuttgart 1973; C. Heitmann and H. Mühlen (eds.), *Erfahrung und Theologie des Heiligen Geistes,* Hamburg and Munich 1974; E. D. O'Connor, *The Pentecostal Movement in the Catholic Church,* Notre Dame 1971; J. Moltmann, *The Church in the Power of the Spirit: A Contribution to Messianic Ecclesiology,* ET M. Kohl, London and New York 1977; W. Kasper and G. Sauter, *Kirche – Ort des Geistes,* Kleine ökumenische Schriften 8, Freiburg – Basle – Vienna 1976; K. Blaser, *Vorstoss zur Pneumatologie,* Theologische Studien 121, Zürich 1977; J. V. Taylor, *The Go-between God: The Holy Spirit and the Christian Mission,* London and Philadelphia 1973; O. A. Dillschneider, *Geist als Vollender des Glaubens,* Gütersloh 1978; E. Schweizer, *Heiliger Geist,* Themen der Theologie, Erg.-Band, Stuttgart 1978; W. Strolz (ed.), *Vom Geist, den wir brauchen,* Freiburg – Basle – Vienna, 1978; W. Kasper (ed.), *Gegenwart des Geistes. Aspekte der Pneumatologie,* QD 85, Freiburg – Basle – Vienna, 1979; M. Thurian, *Feuer für die Erde. Vom Wirken des Geistes in der Gemeinschaft der Christen,* Freiburg – Basle – Vienna 1979; Y. Congar, *I Believe in the Holy Spirit,* ET David Smith, 3 vols. London and New York 1983; P. J. Rosato, *The Spirit as Lord. The Pneumatology of Karl Barth,* Edinburgh 1981.

86. Thomas Aquinas, *ST* I, 37, 1.

87. Congar, op. cit., 3: 6.

88. H. Urs von Balthasar, 'Der Ubekannte jenseits des Wortes', in *Spiritus Creator* (n. 85), 95–105.

89. Hilary, *De Trinitate* II, 1 (CCL 62, 38).

90. Augustine, *De Trinitate* V, 11 and 14f. (CCL 50, 218ff., 222ff.); VI, 10f (CCL 50, 241–9); XV, 17–21 (CCL 50A, 501–19).

91. Peter Lombard, *I Sent.,* d. 18.

92. Thomas Aquinas, *ST* I, 38.

93. Congar, op. cit., 3: 31, 147f., 150f.

94. K. Barth, *Church Dogmatics* I/2, 242ff.

95. Augustine, *De Trinitate* XV, 17 (CCL 50A, 501–7).

96. Ibid., V, 11 (CCL 50, 218ff.); *In Joannis Evangelium tractatus* 105, 3 (CCL 36, 604f.).

97. Augustine, *De Trinitate* V, 14 (CCL 50, 224).

98. Ibid., V, 15 (CCL 50, 224).

99. Augustine, *Enchiridion* XII, 40 (CCL 46, 72).

100. Cf. H. Urs von Balthasar, 'Der Heilige Geist als Licht', in his *Spiritus Creator* (n. 85), 106–22; W. Kasper, 'Die Kirche als Sakrament des Geistes', in Kasper and Sauter, op. cit. (n. 85), 33f.; Congar, op. cit., 3: 145ff.

101. M. J. Scheeben, *The Mysteries of Christianity* (n. 50), 110ff.

102. Augustine, *De Trinitate* VI, 10 (CCL 50, 241ff.).

103. Cf. H. Schauf, *Die Einwohnung des Heiligen Geistes. Die Lehre von der nicht appropriierten Einwohnung des Heiligen Geistes als Beitrag zur Theologiegeschichte des 19. Jahrhunderts unter besonderer Berücksichtigung der beiden Theologen Carl Passaglia und Clemens Schrader*, Freiburger theologische Studien 59; Freiburg 1941.

104. Thomas Aquinas, *Summa contra Gentiles* IV, 20–2.

105. Vatican II, *Gaudium et spes*, 26, 28, 38, 41, 44.

106. K. Rahner, 'Thoughts on the Possibility of Faith Today', in *Theological Investigations* 5, ET K.-H. Kruger, London and Baltimore 1966, 3–22; 'Christianity and the Non-Christian Religions', ibid., 115–34; 'Anonymous Christians', ibid., 6, ET K.-H. and B. Kruger, London and Baltimore 1969, 390–98; 'Atheism and Implicit Christianity', ibid., 9, ET G. Harrison, London and New York 1972, 145–64; 'Anonymous Christianity and the Missionary Task of the Church', ibid., 12, ET D. Bourke, London and New York 1974, 161–78; 'Observations on the Problem of the "Anonymous Christian" ', ibid., 14, ET D. Bourke, New York 1976, 280–94; 'Anonymous and Explicit Faith', ibid., 16, ET D. Morland, London and New York 1979, 52–59; 'Jesus Christ in the Non-christian Religions', ibid., 17, ET M. Kohl London and New York, 1981, 39–50; 'Missions II: Salvation of the Non-Evangelized', *SacMundi* 4, 79–81.

107. Thomas Aquinas, *Summa contra Gentiles* IV, 21f.

108. Thomas Aquinas, *ST* I-II, 106, 1f.; 108, 1f.

109. Ibid.

110. Ibid., III, 8, 3; cf. M. Seckler, 'Das Haupt aller Menschen. Zur Auslegung eines Thomastextes', in *Virtus politica (FS A. Hufnagel)*, Stuttgart and Bed Canstatt 1974, 104–25.

111. Augustine, *Serm.* 267, 4, PL 38, 1231; Leo XIII, Encyclical *Divinum illud*, in C. Carlen (ed.), *The Papal Encyclicals* 2, Wilmington, NC 1981, 409–17; Pius XII, Encyclical *Mystici corporis*, in C. Carlen (ed.), *The Papal Enclyclicals* 4, 37–63.

112. Irenaeus, *Adv. Haer.* III, 17, 1 (SC 211, 328–31).

PART THREE

Chapter I   Establishment of the Doctrine of the Trinity

1. Recent litature on the doctrine of the Trinity (encyclopedia articles are not listed here, nor are the well-known manuals of dogmatic theology): K. Rahner, 'Remarks on the Dogmatic Treatise "De Trinitate"', in *Theological Investigations* 4, ET K. Smyth, London and Baltimore 1966, 77–102; id., *The Trinity*, ET J.

Donceel, New York 1970; B. Lonergan, *De Deo Trino*, Rome ²1964; J. Daniélou, *La Trinité et le mystère de l'existence*, Paris ²1968; H. Geisser, 'Der Beitrag der Trinitätslere zur Problematik des Redens von Gott', *ZTK* 65, 1968, 231–55; L. Scheffczyk, *Der eine und dreifaltige Gott*, Mainz 1968, F. Bourassa, *Questions de théologie trinitaire*, Rome 1970; E. Fortmann, *The Triune God*, London 1972; M. Durrant, *Theology and Intelligibility: An Examination of the Doctrine that God Is the Last End of Rational Creatures and the Doctrine that God Is Three Persons in One Substance: 'The Doctrine of the Holy Trinity'*, Boston 1975; R. Panikkar, *The Trinity and the Religious Experience of Man. Icon, Person, Mystery*, Maryknoll NY 1973; H. Brunner, *Dreifaltigkeit. Personale Zugänge zum Mysterium*, Einsiedeln 1976; E. Jüngel, *God as the Mystery of the World*, ET Grand Rapids 1982; H. Wipfler, *Grundfragen der Trinitätsspekulation. Die Analogiefrage in der Trinitätstheologie*, Regensburg 1977; J. Moltmann, *The Trinity and the Kingdom: The Doctrine of God*, ET M. Kohl, London and New York 1981; W. Pannenberg, 'Die Subjektivität Gottes und die Trinitätslehre', in his *Grundfragen systematischer Theologie. Gesammelte Aufsätze* 2, Göttingen 1980, 96–111.

2. Cf. K. Rahner, *The Trinity* (n. 1), 10.

3. On the theme of unity: E. Peterson, *Heis Theos. Epigraphische, formgeschichtliche und religionsgeschichtliche Untersuchungen*, Göttingen 1920; L. Oeing-Hanhoff, *Ens et unum convertuntur. Stellung und Gehalt des Grundsatzes in der Philosophie des Hl Thomas von Aquin*, BGPTM, 37/3, Münster 1953; M. Heidegger, *Identity and Difference*, ET J. Stambaugh, New York 1969; K. Rahner, 'Einheit', *LTK* 3, 749–50; H. Volk, 'Die Einheit als theologisches Problem', *MTZ* 12, 1961, 1–13; E. Coreth, 'Einheit und Differenz', in H. Vorgrimler (ed.), *Gott in Welt (FS Karl Rahner)*, 2 vols., Freiburg – Basle – Vienna 1964, 1, 158–87; W. Kern, 'Einheit-in-mannigfaltigkeit. Fragmentarische Überlegungen zur Metaphysik des Geistes', ibid. 1, 207–39; E. Stauffer, 'Heis', *TDNT* 2, 434–42; H. R. Schlette, *Das Eine und das Andere. Studien zur Problematik des Negativen in der Metaphysik Plotins*, Munich 1966; W. Heisenberg, *Der Teil und das Ganze. Gespräche im Umkreis der Atomphysik*, Munich 1969; C. F. von Weizsäcker, *Die Einheit in der Natur*, Munich ²1971; 'Das Eine', *HWP* 2, 361–7; M. Zahn, 'Einheit', *HPG* 1, 320–37.

4. Thomas Aquinas, *De ver* 1, 1; 2, 15; *ST* I, 11, 1.

5. Aristotle, *Metaphysica* IV, 6, 1016b.

6. Cf. ibid.

7. Heraclitus, *Fragm.* 24, in H. Diels and W. Kranz (eds.), *Die Fragmente der Vorsokratiker* 1, Berlin ⁶1951, 178, ET K. Freeman, *Ancilla to the Pre-Socratic Philosophers*, Cambridge, Mass. 1962, 33.

8. On the problem of monotheism in the history of religions: R. Panikkar, *The Trinity and World Religions*, Madras 1970; H. LeSaux, *Sagesse Hindoue, Mystique Chrétienne: Du Vedanta à la Trinité*, Paris 1965.

9. Xenophanes, *Fragm.* 23, in Diels and Kranz (n. 7), 135; ET in Freeman (n. 7), 231.

10. Aristotle, *Metaphysica* XI, 10, 1076a. Cf. E. Peterson, 'Monotheismus als politisches Problem', in *Theologische Traktate*, Munich 1951, 45–147.

11. Cf. H. Kleinknecht, 'Logos', *TDNT* 4, 84f.

12. Aristotle, *Ethica Nicomachea* I, 4, 1096b.

13. Plotinus, *Enneads* VI, 9, 4.

14. Augustine, *Confessiones* XI, 29, 39 (CCL 27, 214f.).

15. On what follows cf. R. Merhlein, 'Drei', *RAC* 4, 269–310.

16. Cf. R. Roques, 'Dionysius Arepagita', *RAC* 3, 1090f.

17. Cf. A. Stuiber, 'Dreieck', *RAC* 4, 310–13.

18. Mehrlein, art. cit., 298–309; C. Delling, 'Treis', *TDNT* 8, 216–25.

19. Mehrlein, art. cit., 280f.

20. On biblical faith in one God cf. E. Stauffer, 'Heis', *TDNT* 2, 434–42; T. C. Vriezen, *An Outline of Old Testament Theology*, ET S. Neuijen, Oxford 1958, 175ff.; A. Deissler, *Die Grundbotschaft des Alten Testaments. Ein theologischer Durchblick*, Freiburg – Basle – Vienna ³1972, 25–31; K. Schelkle, *Theology of the New Testament* 2, ET W. A. Jurgens, Collegeville 1976, 257–61; B. Lang (ed.), *Der einzige Gott. Die Geburt des biblischen Monotheismus*, Munich 1981.

21. Cf. below, 241.

22. Tertullian, *Adv. Marcionem* I, 3 (CCL 1, 443f.).

23. Cf. W. Pannenberg, 'The Appropriation of the Philosophical Concept of God as a Dogmatic Problem of Early Christian Theology', in his *Basic Questions in Theology*, ET G. H. Kehm, 2 vols., Philadelphia and London 1970–71, 2, 119–83.

24. Justin, *Dialogus cum Tryphone* I, 3 (*Corpus Apol.*, 2, 10–17); Tatian, *Oratio adversus Graecos* 14 (PG 6, 836f.); Theophilus of Antioch, *Ad Autolycum* II, 4; 8, 28 (SC 20, 102f., 114–19, 166–9).

25. Cyril of Jerusalem, *Catecheses* 6, 36; 4, 6; 7, 1f.; 17, 2 (PG 33, 601ff., 459ff., 605ff., 969ff.).

26. DS 112; ND 301.

27. DS 2ff., 125, 150; ND 1, 7, 305. Among later magisterial pronouncements that of the Fourth Lateran Council (1215): '*Unus solus est verus Deus* – There is only one true God' (DS 800; ND 19), and that of the First Vatican Council: '*Unum esse Deum verum et vivum* – There is one God, true and living' (DS 3001; ND 327), are especially important.

28. Irenaeus, *Adv. haer.* I, 10, 1 (SC 264, 154–9); II, 1, 1–5 (SC 294, 26–35); Tertullian, *Adv Marcionem* II, 1f. (CCL 1, 475f.); Origen, *Contra Celsum* I, 23 (SC 136, 132–5).

29. Cf. Thomas Aquinas, *ST* I, 11, 3.

30. Cf. below, 393ff.

31. On what follows cf. R. Schulte, 'Die Vorbereitung der Trinitäts-offenbarung', *Mysal* 2, 49–84.

32. C. Westermann, *Genesis* I, Biblischer Kommentar, Altes Testament, I/1, Neukirchen-Vluyn 1974, 199–201.

33. P. Evdokimov, *L'art de l'icône. Théologie de la beauté*, Paris 1972.

34. Cf. below, 249ff.

35. W. Eichrodt, *Theology of the Old Testament*, ET J. A. Baker, 2 vols., London and Philadelphia 1961–67, 2, 23, 27f.

36. Deissler, op. cit. (n. 20), 31.

37. Cf. G. Delling, 'Treis', *TDNT* 8, 216–25; R. Mehrlein, 'Drei', *RAC* 4, 300–10; F. J. Schierse, 'Die neutestamentliche Trinitätsoffenbarung', *Mysal* 2, 85–131; G. Wainwright, *The Trinity in the New Testament*, London 1962; K. H. Schelkle, *Theology of the New Testament* 2 (n. 20), 295–309.

38. Cf. above, 142f., 170ff.

39. F. Lentzen-Deis, *Die Taufe Jesu nach den Synoptikern. Literarkritische*

und gattungsgeschichtliche Untersuchungen, Frankfurter theologische Studien 4, Frankfurt 1970.

40. A. Vögtle, 'Ekklesiologische Auftragsworte des Auferstandenen', in his *Das Evangelium und die Evangelien. Beiträge zur Evangelienforschung*, Düsseldorf 1971, 243–52; id., 'Das christologische und ekklesiologische Anliegen von Mt 28, 18–20', ibid., 253–72.

41. No one before or since has produced anything superior to Augustine's *In Johannis Evangelium tractatus* 104–111 (CCL 36, 601–33). Recent literature: R. Schnackenburg, *The Gospel according to St. John 3*, ET D. Smith and G. A. Kon, New York and London 1982, 167–202; E. Käsemann, *The Testament of Jesus: A Study of the Gospel of John in the Light of Chapter 17*, ET G. Krödel, London and Philadelphia 1968.

42. R. Schnackenburg, *Die Johannisbriefe*, HTKNT 13/3, Freiburg – Basle – Vienna, ²1963, 37–9.

43. O. Cullmann, *Die ersten christlichen Glaubensbekenntnisse*, Theologische Studien 15, Zollikon-Zürich 1949, 45. [There is an ET by J. K. S. Reid: *The Earliest Christian Confessions*, London 1949, but it was not available to me. Tr.]

44. On the history of the theology and dogma of the Trinity (I limit myself to comprehensive presentations and omit studies of details): L. Scheffczyk, 'Lehramtliche Formulierung und Dogmengeschichte der Trinität', *MySal* 1, 146–217; T. de Régnon, *Etudes de théologie positive sur la sainte Trinité*, 3 vols., Paris 1892–8; J. Lebreton, *Histoire du dogme de la Trinité*, 2 vols., Paris, 1927–8, ET of vol. 1 by A. Thorold, *History of the Dogma of the Trinity*, London 1939; G. L. Prestige, *God in Christian Thought*, London ²1952; M. Werner, *The Formation of Christian Dogma: An Historical Study of Its Problem*, ET S. G. F. Brandon, New York 1957; G. Kretschmar, *Studien zur frühchristlichen Trinitätstheologie*, Beiträge zur historischen Theologie 21, Tübingen 1956; C. Andresen, 'Zur Entstehung und Geschichte des trinitarischen Personbegriffs', *ZNW* 52, 1961, 1–39, I. Ortiz de Urbina, *Nicée et Constantinople*, Histore des conciles oecuméniques, ed. G. Dumeige, 1, Paris 1963; A. Adam, *Lehrbuch der Dogmengeschichte* 1, Gütersloh 1965; B. Lohse, *Epochen der Dogmengeschichte*, Stuttgart-Berlin ²1969; B. de Margerie, *La Trinité chrétienne dans l'histoire*, Théologie historique 31, Paris 1975; A. Grillmeier, *Christ in Christian Tradition* 1, ET John Bowden, Oxford and Atlanta, Ga ²1975.

45. Ignatius of Antioch, *Ad Ephesios* 9, 1; 18, 2 (*Patres apostolici*, ed. Funk-Diekamp, 1, 244f., 254–7); *Ad Magnesianos* 13, 1 (ibid., 289); cf. his *Martyrium Polycarpis* (ibid., 420).

46. *1 Clem* 42; 46, 6; 58, 2 (*Die apostolischen Väter*, ed. J. A. Fischer, Darmstadt 1956, 76ff., 82, 98).

47. Athenagoras, *Supplicatio pro Christianis* 12 (TU 4/2, 13f.).

48. Theophilus of Antioch, *Ad Autolycum* II, 15 (SC 20, 138–41); Tertullian, *Adv. Praxean* II, 4; VIII, 7 (CCL 2, 1161, 1168).

49. *Didache* 7, 1 (SC 248, 170f.).

50. Justin, *Apologia I*, 61, 13 (*Corpus Apol.* 1, 166f.).

51. For the history of the creed, in addition to the standard works of F. Kattenbusch, H. Lietzmann, A. von Harnack and J. de Ghellinck, cf. especially J. N. D. Kelly, *Early Christian Creeds*, London and New York ²1960; K. H. Neufeld, *The Earliest Christian Confessions*, Leiden 1963. A first introduction to the history of scholarship is given by J. Quasten, 'Symbolforschung', *LTK* 1, 1210–12.

52. Irenaeus, *Demonstratio* 3; 7 (SC 62, 31–33, 41f.).

53. Ibid., 6 (62, 39f.).

54. DS 10; ND 2.

55. Tertullian, *De baptismo* 6 (CCL 1, 283).

56. Cyprian, *De dominica oratione* 23 (CSEL 3/1, 284f.).

57. Vatican II, *Lumen gentium* 4, ET Flannery, 353.

58. Hilary, *De Trinitate* II, 1 (CCL 62, 38).

59. Augustine, *De Trinitate* XV, 26, 46 (CCL 50A, 525–7).

60. *Didache* 9 (SC 248, 174–9).

61. Justin, *Apologia* I 65; 67 (*Corpus Apol.* 1 178, 184).

62. Hippolytus, *Traditio Apostolica* 4–13, in G. Dix (ed.), *The Treatise on the Apostolic Tradition of St Hippolytus of Rome*, London 1937, 7–9.

63. Cf. Justin, *Apologia* I 67 (*Corpus Apol.* 1, 184–9); Origen, *De oratione* 33 (GCS 2, 401f.); cf. C. Vagaggini, *Theological Dimensions of the Liturgy*, ET L. J. Doyle and W. A. Jurgens, Collegeville 1976, 209f.

64. Cf. J. A. Jungmann, *The Place of Christ in Liturgical Prayer*, ET A. J. Peeler, Staten Island, NY 1965; id., *The Mass of the Roman Rite: Its Origins and Development (Missarum Solemnia)*, ET F. A. Brunner, 2 vols., New York 1951–55, 2, 259ff.

65. On the original meaning of *regula fidei* cf. B. Haeggelund, 'Die Bedeutung der *regual fidei* als Grundlage theologischer Aussagen', *Studia Theologica* 12, 1958, 1–44; J. Quasten, '*Regula fidei*, *LTK* 8, 1102f.

66. Origen, *De principiis*, Praef. 2 (SC, 252, 78f.). After speaking of Jesus Christ as the truth, Origen laments the fact that Christians, though confessing Christ, are at odds over many truths. It is important, therefore, he says, 'to lay down a definite line of thought and unambiguous norms'. Despite all the variations, 'the teaching of the church as handed down in unbroken succession from the apostles is still preserved and continues in the church to this very day; only that, therefore, is to be believed as true which in no way departs from the ecclesial and apostolic truth.' Cf. *De principiis* IV, 2, 2 (SC 268, 300–5).

67. Cf. Augustine, *De Trinitate* I, 1f. (CCL 50, 27ff.), where Augustine explains that for him the faith of the sacred scriptures is the foundation which he intends to expound in agreement with all the available Catholic exegetes of the Old and New Testaments; he then concludes: 'This is likewise my faith, because it is the Catholic faith' (I, 4).

68. On Jewish Christianity cf. especially J. Daniélou, *The Theology of Jewish Christianity*, ET J. A. Baker, London and Chicago 1964; G. Kretschmar, *Studien zur frühchristlichen Trinitätstheologie* (n. 44); J. Barbel, 'Christos Angelos', *Liturgie und Mönchtum* 21, 1957, 71–90; A. Adam, *Lehrbuch der Dogmengeschichte* (n. 44), 1, 127ff.

69. Scattered traces: Tertullian, *De carne Christi* 14 (CCl 2, 899f.); Novatian, *De Trinitate* XVIII, 1022 (CCL 4,44); Origen, *De principiis* I, 3, 4 (SC 252, 148–53); Eusebius, *Praeparatio Evangelii* VII, 14f. (SC 215, 234–7).

70. Cf. above, 178f.

71. This is the kernel of truth in the otherwise monomaniacal thesis of M. Werner, *The Formation of Christian Dogma* (n. 44), according to which Christian dogma arose from an eschatologization of the biblical message.

72. Cf. above, 180f.

73. Cf. n. 44 for literature on the history of the doctrine of the Trinity.

74. On gnosticism cf. above, 180ff.

75. Cf. Irenaeus, *Adv. haer.* I, 1 (SC 264, 28–35); Hippolytus, *Refutatio* VI, 29 (GCS 26, 155–7).

76. Cf. the definition of *emanatio* or *missio* in Irenaeus, *Adv. haer.* II, 13, 6 (SC 294, 118–21); and cf. J. Ratzinger, 'Emanation', *RAC* 4, 1219–28.

77. Irenaeus, *Adv. haer.* IV, 33, 8 (SC 100/2, 818–21).

78. Ibid., I, 10 (SC 264, 154–67).

79. Ibid., II, 28, 6 (SC 294, 282–5).

80. Ibid., II, 13. 4; 28, 5 (SC 294, 116–19, 280–3).

81. On the theory of anakephalaiosis or recapitulation cf. H. Schlier, 'Kephalë', *TDNT* 3, 673–82; W. Staerk, 'Anakephalaiosis', *RAC* 1, 411–14; R. Haubst, 'Anakephalaiosis', *LTK* 1, 466f.; E. Scharl, *Recapitulatio mundi. Die Rekapitulationsbegriff des hl. Irenäus*, Freiburg 1941.

82. Irenaeus, *Adv. haer.* II, 28, 1 (SC 294, 268–71); IV, 9. 1; 20, 4 (SC 100/2, 476–81, 634–7); and elsewhere.

83. Ibid., III, 19, 2; cf. 20, 2 (SC 211, 374–9, 388–93); IV, 20, 4 (SC 100/2, 634–7); V, 16, 2 (SC 153, 216f.).

84. Ibid. III, 8, 3, (SC 211, 94–7); 6, 7; 20, 3; 38, 3 (SC 100/2, 450–5, 632f., 952–7).

85. Ibid., IV, 20, 1 (SC 100/2, 624–7).

86. Tertullian, *De praescriptione* 13, 36; 37 (CCL 1, 197f., 216f., 217f.); *Adv. Marcionem* IV, 5 (CCL 1, 550–52); *Adv. Praxean* II, 1f. (CCL 2, 1160f.).

87. *Adv. Praxean* VIII, 9 (CCL 2, 1167–9).

88. *Apologeticum* XXI, 11 (CCL 1, 124).

89. *Adv. Marcionem* II, 27, 7 (CCL 1, 507).

90. *Adv. Praxean* VIII, 7 (CCL 2, 1168).

91 Ibid., III, 2f. (CCL 2, 1161f.).

92. Ibid., X, 3 (CCL 2, 1169).

93. Ibid., II, 4 (CCL 2, 1161), ET W. A. Jurgens, *The Faith of the Early Fathers* 1, Collegeville 1970, 154. Cf. *De pudicitia* XXI (CCL 2, 1326–8).

94. *Adv. Praxean* XII, 6 (CCL 2, 1173).

95. Ibid., XXV, 1 (CCL 2, 1195).

96. Cf. above, 181.

97. DS 112–15; ND 301–3.

98. Cf above, 216f.

99. Hilary, *De Trinitate* II, 6ff. (CCL 62, 42ff.).

100. Origen, *De principiis*, Praef. 2 (SC 252, 70f.); IV, 2, 2 (SC 268, 300–5).

101 Ibid., I, 1, 1 and 6 (SC 252, 90, 98–105).

102 Ibid., I, 2, 6; 4, 1 (SC 252, 120–5, 166–9); *Contra Celsum* VI, 34, 35 (SC 147, 260–5).

103. *De principiis* I, 6, 2; II, 1, 1 (SC 252, 196–201, 234–7).

104. Ibid., I, 1, 6 (SC 252, 98–105).

105. Ibid., II, 3, 1 (SC 252, 248–51).

106. Ibid., II, 9, 1; 9, 5f. (SC 252, 352–5, 360ff.).

107. Ibid., II, 9, 2; 9, 5f. (SC 252, 354–7, 360ff.).

108. Ibid., I, 6, 1 (SC 252, 194–7).

109. Ibid., II, 10, 1 and 4ff.

110. H. Jonas, *Gnosis und spätantiker Geist* 2/1, Göttingen 1954, 207–10; J. Ratzinger, 'Emanation' (n. 76), 1223.

111. Origen, *De principiis* I, 2, 10 (SC 252, 133–9).

112. Ibid., I, 2, 6 and 9 (SC 252, 120–5, 128–31); IV, 4, 1 (SC 268, 400–5).

113. Ibid., I, 2, 7 (SC 252, 124f.).

114. Ibid., I, 2, 6 (SC 252, 120–5); cf. above 180f.

115. Ibid., I, 2, 2 (SC 252, 112–15).

116. Ibid., I, 2, 10 (SC 252, 132–9); cf. Irenaeus, *Adv. haer.* V, 1, 1 (SC 153, 16–21).

117. Origen, *De principiis* I, 2, 6 (SC 252, 120–5).

118. Ibid., I, 2, 8 (SC 252, 126–9).

119. Ibid., I, 3, 4; 3, 5; 3, 8 (SC 252, 148–53, 152–5, 162–5).

120. Ibid., I, 3, 5 (SC 252, 152–5); cf. *In Joan.* II, 10, 77 (SC 120, 256f.).

121. DS 403–11; ND 401/1, 401/8.

122. Cf. H. Crouzel, 'Die Origenesforschung im zwanzigsten Jahrhundert', in H. Vorgrimler and R. van der Gucht, (eds.), *Bilanz der Theologie im 20. Jahrhundert* 3, Freiburg – Basle – Vienna 1970, 515–21.

123. Cf. above, 181.

124. Cf. above, 183f.

125. Cf. above, 182ff.

126. I. Ortiz de Urbina, *Nicée et Constantinople* (n. 44).

127. Ibid., 82.

128. Ibid., 86–7.

129. Ibid., 75–6.

130. Athanàsius, *Tomus ad Antiochenos* 5 (PG 26, 800f.).

131. Basil, *Ep.* 38 (PG 32, 325–40); *Ep.* 236, 6 (PG 32, 883–6).

132. Id., *Ep.* 38, 4 (PG 32, 329–34); *Ep.* 236, 6 (PG 32, 883–6).

133. Jerome, *Ep.* 15, 4 (PL 22, 357f.); Augustine, *De Trinitate* VII, 4 (CCL 50, 255–60).

134. Basil, *Ep.* 210, 5 (PG 32, 773–8); cf. *Ep.* 214, 4 (PG 32, 789f.); *Ep.* 236, 6 (PG 32, 883–6).

135. *COD* 28.

136. DS 150; ND 12.

137. DS 144.

138. DS 168, 173, 176; ND 306/16, 306/21, 306/24.

139. Cf. W. Kasper, *Jesus the Christ*, ET V. Green, London and New York 1976, 240ff.

140. DS 421; ET in ND 620/1.

141. Ibid.

142. DS 71, 73, 441, 451, 470, 485, 490, 501, 525–32, 542, 566, 568–70, 680 etc.

143. DS 75; ND 16.

144. Tertullian, *Adv. Praxean*, III, 2f. (CCL 2, 1161f.); Origen, *De principiis* I, 2, 10 (SC 252, 132–9).

145. Origen, *De principiis* I, 3, 5 (SC 252, 152–5).

146. Basil, *De spiritu sancto* 16 (SC 17, 173–83).

147. Augustine, *De Trinitate* I, 4, 7; V, 14, 15 (CCL 50, 34–6, 222f.); *Serm.* 213, 6, 6 (PL 33, 968); Basil, ibid.

148. Basil, ibid.: 'When we receive gifts we encounter first the one who distributes them; then we recognize him who is sending them; finally we direct our thoughts

to the origin and source of all blessings. . . . For the sole source is what is works through the Son and completes his action in the Holy Spirit.'

149. Cf. above, 250.

150. Cf. J. Liébaert, 'Eunomios', *LTK* 3, 1182f.

151. Basil, *De spiritu sancto* 18 (SC 17, 191–8); Gregory of Nyssa, *Oratio* 31, 8 (PG 36, 141); John Damascene, *De fide orth.* I, 8 (*Die Schriften des Johannes von Damaskus*, ed. B. Kotter II, Berlin and New York 1973, 18–31).

152. Cf. E. Muhlenberg, *Die Unendlichkeit Gottes bei Gregor von Nyssa*, Göttingen 1966.

153. D. Wendenbourg, *Geist oder Energie? Zur Frage der innergöttlichen Verankerung des christlichen Lebens in der byzantinischen Theologie*, Munich 1980, 24ff.

154. This is Wendenbourg's view; for a different opinion cf. J. Meyendorff, *St. Grégoire Palamas et la mystique orthodoxe*, Paris 1959.

155. Already in Irenaeus, *Adv. haer.* II, 28, 6 and 9 (SC 294, 282–5, 290–3); Hilary, *De Trinitate* II, 9 (CCL 62 46f.); Augustine, *De Trinitate* V, 1 and 9; VII, 4 (CCL 50, 206f., 217, 255–60).

156. Augustine, *De Trinitate* I, 2 and 6 (CCL 50, 31f., 37–44); etc.

157. Ibid., VII, 6 (CCL 50, 261–7); XV, 4 (CCL 50A, 467f.).

158. Ibid., VII, 4 (CCL 50, 255–60).

159. The doctrine of the Trinity as developed by Anselm in *Monologion* 38–65 proceeds entirely from the one spiritual essence of God which finds expression in the essential operations of knowing and willing. As he explains in the Prologue, he intends that 'nothing at all would be argued on scriptural authority', but 'rational necessity would tersely prove' all assertions 'and truth's clarity would openly manifest them' (*Anselm of Canterbury*, ET J. Hopkins and H. Richardson, 4 vols., New York 1974–76, 1, 3).

160. DS 800, cf. 1331; ND 19, 326.

161. Thomas Aquinas, *ST* III, 3, 5.

162. Cf. below, 298.

163. The way had been prepared for this distinction from the time of Augustine. I must agree with J. Auer's cautious judgment: 'God is seen less as the creator who orders everything than as absolute Lord; and numerous specialized studies are still needed before we can say for sure whether this 'absolute Lord' represents a God of irrational arbitrariness or rather the biblical 'Lord of history' ('Nominalismus', *LTK* 7, 1022).

164. *CA* 1; *Schmalkaldische Artikel*, in *BSLK* 414f.

165. The basic formula of the World Council of Churches says: 'The World Council of Churches is a fellowship of churches which confess the Lord Jesus Christ as God and Saviour according to the Scriptures and therefore seek to fulfill together their common calling to the glory of the one God, Father, Son and Holy Spirit' (modified formula adopted at the New Delhi meeting, 1961); cf. W. Theurer, *Die trinitarische Basis des Ökumenischen Rates der Kirchen*, Bergen-Enkheim 1976.

166. Kant's judgment is typical: 'The doctrine of the Trinity, taken literally, has no practical relevance at all', in *The Conflict of the Faculties*, ET M. J. Gregor, New York 1979, 65.

167. F. Schleiermacher, *The Christian Faith*, no. 170, ET H. R. Mackintosh and J. S. Stewart, Edinburgh 1928, reprinted Philadelphia 1976, 741.

Chapter II Exposition of the doctrine of the Trinity

1. Still indispensable: F. C. Baur, *Die christliche Lehre von der Dreieinigkeit und Menschwerdung Gottes in ihrer geschichtlichen Entwicklung* 3, Tübingen 1843; D. F. Strauss, *Die christliche Glaubenslehre in ihrer geschichtlichen Entwicklung und im Kampfe mit der modernen Wissenschaft* 2, Tübingen 1841, reprinted Darmstadt 1973. For recent literature cf. the previous chapter, n. 44.

2. Cf. W. Kasper, *Das Absolute in der Geschichte. Philosophie und Theologie der Geschichte in der Spätphilosophie Schellings*, Mainz 1965, especially 266–84.

3. Hegel, *Vorlesungen über die Philosophie der Religion* (ed. G. Lasson) I, 11. Cf. J. Splett, *Die Trinitätslehre G. W. F. Hegels*, Freiburg and Munich 1965; L. Oeing-Hanhoff, 'Hegels Trinitätslehre', *Theol. Phil.* 52, 1977, 378–407.

4. Hegel, *Vorlesungen* I, 21.

5. Ibid., 36.

6. Ibid., 39f.; cf. 46f.

7. Ibid., 41.

8. Ibid., 40.

9. Ibid., 41f.; etc.

10. Ibid., III, 57, 69, 74, etc.

11. Ibid., 62f., 82f.

12. Ibid., 75.

13. Ibid., 77.

14. DS 3001, 3041; ND 327, 137. Cf. the condemnation of A. Günther, DS 2828–31, and of A. Rosmini, DS 3225.

15. Hegel, *Vorlesungen* III, 72f.

16. Ibid., 64f.; cf. *The Phenomenology of Mind*, ET J. Baillie, rev. and ed. London 1949, 81–2.

17. DS 3024, ET in ND 417.

18. Hegel, *Vorlesungen* III, 85f.

19. Ibid., I, 148.

20. Ibid., III, 74.

21. Ibid., 65f.

22. Ibid., 173f.

23. Ibid., 180, etc.

24. Ibid., 198.

25. L. Feuerbach, 'Principles of the Philosophy of the Future', in Z. Hanfi (ed.), *The Fiery Brook: Selected Writings of Ludwig Feuerbach*, Garden City, NY 1972, 245; *The Essence of Christianity*, ET G. Eliot, London and New York 1957, 65, 232ff.

26. *The Essence of Christianity*, 247–69.   27. Ibid., 251.

28. Cf. E. Jüngel, *God as the Mystery of the World*, Grand Rapids 1982.

29. Vatican II, *Gaudium et spes*, 76.

30. Cf. M. J. Scheeben, *The Mysteries of Christianity*, ET C. Vollert, St. Louis 1946, 25–48.

31. Cf. P. Wenzel, 'Semirationalismus', *LTK* 9, 625f.

32. Cf. below, 272f.

33. Cf. W. Simonis, *Trinität und Vernunft. Untersuchungen zur Möglichkeit einer rationalen Trinitätslehre bei Anselm, Abaelard, den Vatikanern, A. Günther und G. Froschammer*, Frankfurter theologische Studien 12, Frankfurt 1972.

34. Thomas Aquinas, *ST* I, 13, 12 ad 1.

35. Cf. J. E. Kuhn, *Katholische Dogmatik* 2, Tübingen 1857, 502f.

36. Cf. above, 126f.

37. G. Ebeling, 'Profanität und Geheimnis', in his *Wort und Glaube* 2, Tübingen 1969, 196f.; cf. G. Hasenhüttl, *Kritische Dogmatik*, Graz 1979, 26, 36.

38. Cf. above, 127f.

39. Cf. above, 128f.

40. Cf. above, 248f.

41. Tertullian, *De carne Christi* V, 4 (CCL 2, 881); cf. *Apologeticum* 46, 18 (CCL 1, 162).

42. J. E. Kuhn, op. cit., 513.

43. Ibid., 514.

44. Ibid., 520.

45. Cf. above, 234.

46. Vatican II, *Unitatis redintegratio*, 11; cf. U. Valeske, *Hierarchia veritatum. Theologiegeschichtliche Hintergründe und mögliche Konsequenzen eines Himweises im Ökumenismusdekret des II. Vatikanischen Konzils zum zwischenkirchlichen Gespräch*, Munich 1963.

47. DS 3016; ND 132.

48. Ibid., ET in ND 132.

49. Justin, *Dialogus cum Tryphone* 61, 2 (*Corpus Apol.* II, ed. von Otto, 212); Tatian, *Oratio ad Graecos* 5 (PG 6, 813c–818b); Hippolytus, *Ad Noetum* (PG 10, 817c–820a); Tertullian, *Apologeticum* 21 (CCL 1, 122–8).

50. Tatian, ibid.; Athenagoras, *Supplicatio pro Christianis* 24 (TU 4/2, 31ff.); Justin, *Dialogus cum Tryphone* 128 (*Corpus Apol.* II, 458–69); Hippolytus, *Ad Noetum* 10 (PG 10, 817a–818c); Tertullian, *Ad Praxean* 8 (CCL 2, 1167f.).

51. Athanasius, *Expositio fidei* 4 (PG 25, 205c–208a); *De decretis nicaenae synodi* 25 (PG 25, 459c–462c); *De synodis* 52 (PG 26, 785c–788b); *Adv. Arianos* III, 4 (PG 26, 327c–330b).

52. DS 125, 150; ET in ND 7, 12.

53. Tertullian, *Ad Praxean* 8 (CCL 2, 1167f.).

54. Cf. M. J. Schmaus, *Die psychologische Trinitätslehre des hl. Augustinus* Münster 1967², 190ff., 201f.

55. Hilary, *De Trinitate* XI, 11 (CCL 50, 355).

56. Schmaus, op. cit., 195ff.

57. Ibid., 220.

58. Cf. above, 180f.

59. Cf. Schmaus, op. cit., 26ff.

60. Ibid., 195, 230. Recent interpretations: C. Boyer, 'L'image de la Trinité: Synthèse de la pensé augustinienne', *Greg* 27, 1946, 173–99, 333–52; M. Sciaca, 'Trinité et unité de l'esprit', in *Augustinus magister* 1, Paris 1954, 521–33; U. Duchrow, *Sprachverständnis und biblisches Hören bei Augustin*, Hermeneutische Untersuchungen zur Theologie 5, Tübingen 1965; A. Schindler, *Wort und Analogie in Augustins Trinitätslehre*, Hermeneutische Untersuchungen zur Theologie 4, Tübingen 1965.

61. Cf. above, 58, 97f.

62. K. Barth, *Church Dogmatics* I/1, 383–99.

63. DS 3016; ND 132.

64. K. Rahner, 'Remarks on the Dogmatic Treatise "De Trinitate" ', in *Theo-*

logical Investigations 4, ET K. Smyth, London and Baltimore 1966, 87; *The Trinity*, ET J. Donceel, New York and London 1970, 22.

65. K. Barth, *Church Dogmatics* I/1, 548.

66. J. Meyendorff, *Introduction à l'étude de Grégoire Palamas*, Paris 1959, 298.

67. F. Schleiermacher, *The Christian Faith*, no. 172, ET H. R. Mackintosh and J. S. Stewart, Edinburgh 1928, reprinted Philadelphia 1976, 748.

68. F. A. Staudenmaier, *Die christliche Dogmatik* 2, Freiburg 1844, 475.

69. DS 74; ET in ND 16.

70. Cf. W. Kasper, *Jesus the Christ*, ET V. Green, London and New York 1976, 240ff.

71. Cf. H. Achauf, *Die Einwohnung des Heiligen Geistes. Die Lehre von der nichtappropriierten Einwohnung des Heiligen Geistes als Beitrag zur Theologiegeschichte des neunzehnten Jahrhunderts under besonderer Berücksichtigung der beiden Theologen Carl Passaglia und Clemens Schrader*, Freiburger theologische Studien 59, Freiburg 1941.

72. Thus P. Schoonenberg, 'Trinität – der vollendete Bund. Thesen zur Lehre vom dreipersönlichen Gott', *Orientierung* 37, 1973, 115–17.

73. This tendency can be seen in H. Küng, *Does God Exist? An Answer for Today*, ET E. Quinn, New York 1980, 699ff.

74. Cf. Y. Congar, *I Believe in the Holy Spirit* 3. *The River of Life Flows in the East and in the West*, ET David Smith, London and New York 1983, 13ff. Cf. H. Urs von Balthasar, *Theodramatik* 3, Einsiedeln 1980, 297ff.

75. D. Wendenbourg has given convincing proof of this for Athanasius and the Cappadocian theologians in his *Geist oder Energie? Zur Frage der innergöttlichen Verankerung des christlichen Lebens in der byzantinischen Theologie*, Munich 1980, 172–232.

76. Vatican II, *Dei Verbum*, 2.

77. In what follows I shall be attempting a concise summary of the classical doctrine of the Trinity; I shall be restricting myself principally to the concepts of Thomas Aquinas. I am not aiming at a complete presentation of the sometimes very subtle distinctions made but rather at conveying the inner logic and meaning of the doctrine. The most recent presentation of the Scholastic distinctions – a presentation that goes almost to extremes in its subtlety – is B. Lonergan, *De Deo trino* II. *Pars systematica*, Rome 1964. I refer the reader to it, although I do not have the impression that the route of distinction-making will lead us very much further to a deeper insight into the mystery. These distinctions do not seem to me to take us materially beyond the monumental simplicity of Aquinas' *Summa*.

78. Cf. DS 527; ND 310.

79. Thomas Aquinas, *ST* I, 43, 1.

80. Ibid., 43, 2 ad 5.

81. Thus M. J. Scheeben, *The Mysteries of Christianity* (n. 30), 157.

82. DS 150, 525–27, 800, 1330; ND 12, 308–10, 19, 325.

83. Thomas Aquinas, *ST* I, 27, 1.

84. Cf. M. Schmaus, *Katholische dogmatik* 1, Munich ⁶1960, 462f.

85. Cf. above, 184ff., 215ff.

86. Cf. above, 216ff.

87. Albert the Great, *Summa*, tr. 7, q. 31, a. 4.

88. M. J. Scheeben, op. cit., 104 n. 23.

89. Cf. H. Urs von Balthasar, 'Der Heilige Geist als Liebe', in his *Spiritus Creator, Skizzen zur Theologie* 3, Einsiedeln 1967, 106–22.

90. Thomas Aquinas, *ST* I, 28, 1 ad 3.

91. Athanasius, *De synodis* (PG 26, 707–12).

92. Gregory of Nazianzus, *Oratio* 29, 16 (SC 250, 210–13): 'Father' is a name neither of the essence nor of an activity; it is the name of a relation (*schesis*) and shows how the Father is related to the Son and the Son to the Father.' Cf. *Oratio* 31, 14 and 16 (SC 250, 302–5, 306–9); John Damascene, *De fide orth.* I, 8 (*Die Schriften des Johannes von Damaskus*, ed. B. Kotter, II, Berlin and New York 1973, 18–31).

93. Augustine, *De Trinitate* V, 5 (CCL 50, 210f.): 'Therefore while the Father and the Son are distinct, there is no difference in substance. For the determinations 'Father' and 'Son' have to do not with the substance but with relations. This relation, however, is not an accident because it is not changeable.' Cf. VII, 6 (CCL 50, 261–7); VIII, prooem. (CCL 50, 268f.).

94. DS 528ff., 1330; ND 31§, §325.

95. This principle is already recognized by Gregory of Nazianzus, *Oratio* 34 (PG 36, 257a–62d); *Oratio* 20 (SC 270, 37–85, espec. 70–3); *Oratio* 31 (SC 250, 276–343, espec. 282ff.); *Oratio* 41 (PG 36, 427a–52c, espec. 441c), and by Augustine, *De civitate Dei* XI, 10 (CCL 48, 330ff.). It is given its definitive formulation by Anselm of Canterbury, *De processione spiritus sancti* 1, and confirmed by the Council of Florence (DS 1330; ND 325).

96. Thomas Aquinas, *ST* I, 28, 2.

97. On the history of the concept of person: E. Lohse, 'Prosopon', *TDNT* 6, 768–80; S. Schlossmann, *Persona und Prosopon im Recht und im christlichen Dogma* (1906), Darmstadt 1968; H. Rheinfelder, *Das Wort 'Persona'*, Halle 1928; M. Nédoncelle, '*Prosopon et persona* dans l'antiquité classique', *RevSR* 22, 1948, 277–99; A. Halder, A. Grillmeier and H. Erharter, 'Person', *LTK* 8, 287–92 (bibliog.); C. Andresen, 'Zur Entstehung und Geschichte des trinitarischen Personbegriffs', *ZNW* 52, 1961, 1–39; J. Ratzinger, 'Zum Personverständnis in der Theologie', in his *Dogma und Verkündigung*, Munich ³1977, 205–23; H. Köster, 'Hypostasis', *TDNT* 8, 572–89; above all, H. Dörrie, *Hypostasis. Wort- und Bedeutungsgeschichte*, Göttingen 1955; T. de Régnon, *Etudes de théologie positive sur la sainte Trinité* 1, Paris 1892, 129ff., 139ff., 152ff., 167ff., 216ff.; B. Studer, 'Der Person-Begriff in der frühen kirchenamtlichen Trinitätslehre', *Theol. Phil.* 57, 1982, 161–77.

98. Boethius, *Liber de persona et duabus naturis* 3 (PL 64, 1343c–45b); on this definition cf. Thomas Aquinas, *ST* I, 29, 1.

99. Cf. Thomas Aquinas, *ST* I, 29, 1 ad 2; 3 ad 4.

100. Richard of St Victor, *De Trinitate* IV, 22, 24 (ed. J. Ribaillier, 187–90). Duns Scotus in particular adopted this definition and examined it more fully. Cf. J. Duns Scotus, *Ordinatio*, lib. I, dist. 23, q. 1; cf. H. Mühlen, *Sein und Person nach Johannes Duns Scotus. Beiträge zur Metaphysik der Person*, Werl 1954.

101. Thomas Aquinas, *ST* I, 29, 2.

102. Ibid., I, 29, 4: 'Therefore "divine person" signifies a relation as subsisting.'

103. K. Barth, *Church Dogmatics* I/1, 417ff.

104. Anselm of Canterbury, *Monologion* 43; cf. A. Malet, *Personne et amour dans la théologie trinitaire de saint Thomas d'Aquin*, Bibliothéque thomiste 32, Paris 1956, 55f.

105. Thomas Aquinas, *De pot.* 10, 3; cf. *In I Sent.*, d. 23, q. 1, a. 3; cf. A. Malet, op. cit., 71ff.; M. J. Le Guillou, *Das Mysterium des Vaters. Apostolischer Glaube und moderne Gnosis*, Einsiedeln 1974, 110f.
106. John Damascene, *De fide orth.* I, 8 (*Die Schriften...* II, 18–31); Thomas Aquinas, *ST* I, 40, 1–4; 41, 1–6.
107. Cf. T. de Regnon, op. cit. (n. 97), 3/1, 185ff.
108. Thomas Aquinas, *De ver.* 7, 3; *ST* I, 39, 7.
109. Basil, *De spiritu sancto* 18 (SC 17, 191–8).
110. Augustine, *De Trinitate* VI, 7f. (CCL 50, 237f.); cf. DS 367.
111. DS 530; ND 314.
112. Thomas Aquinas, *ST* I, 30, 3.
113. Augustine, *De Trinitate* VII, 4 and 6 (CCL 50, 255–60, 261–7); Thomas Aquinas, *ST* I, 30, 4.
114. Hilary, *De Trinitate* IV (CCL 62, 101–49).
115. T. de Régnon, op. cit. (n. 97), 1, 409ff: A. Deneffe, 'Perichoresis, circumincessio, circuminsessio. Eine terminologische Untersuchung', *ZKT* 47, 1923, 497–532; G. L. Prestige, '*Perichoreo* and *perichoresis* in the Fathers', *JTS* 29, 1928, 242–52.
116. Athenagoras, *Supplicatio pro Christianis* 10, TU 4/2, 10f.; Irenaeus of Lyons, *Adv. haer.* III, 6, 2 (SC 211, 68–71); Dionysius of Rome, DS 145, ND 303; Athanasius, *De decretis nicaenae synodi* 26 (PG 25, 461–6).
117. Hilary, *De Trinitae* III, 4 (CCL 62, 75f.), ET W. A. Jurgens, *The Faith of the Early Fathers* 1, Collegeville 1970, 375.
118. Ibid., IV, 10 (CCL 62, 144f.); cf. VII, 31–2 (CCL 62, 297–300).
119. Augustine, *De Trinitate* IX, 5 (CCL 50, 300f.); cf. VI, 10 (CCL 50, 241ff.).
120. Fulgentius of Ruspe, *De fide ad Petrum seu de regula fidei* 1, 4 (CCL 91A, 713f.).
121. DS 1331; ND 326.
122. Gregory of Nazianzus, *Ep.* 101, 6 (SC 208, 38).
123. John Damascene, *De fide orth.* I, 8 (*Die Schriften...* II, 18–31); III, 5 (ibid., 118f.).
124. Thomas Aquinas, *ST* I, 42, 5.
125. Cf. DS 302; ND 615. This principle is applied to the Trinity in Fulgentius of Ruspe, *Ep.* 14, 9 (CCL 91, 395f.).
126. Cf. DS 302; ND 615.
127. DS 421; ND 620/1.
128. DS 485, 495, 501, 528ff., 542, 546, 805; 1330, etc.; ND 627/1, 311ff., 325.
129. K. Rahner distinguishes betweeen a logical explanation and an ontic explanation. The former simply clarifies the statement or state of affairs in question, i.e., makes it more precise and less liable to misunderstanding; an ontic explanation, however, takes into account a second, different content (e.g. the cause, concrete circumstances, etc.) in order to explain the content which requires clarification. According to Rahner the concept of person provides only a logical explanation of what is originally a statement in revelation. Cf. *The Trinity*, 53.
130. Jerome, *Ep.* 15, 4 (PL 22, 357f.).
131. Augustine, *De Trinitate* V, 9 (CCL 50, 217).
132. Anselm of Canterbury, *Monologion* 79.
133. Thomas Aquinas, *ST* I, 29, 3.

134. Cited by K. Barth, *Church Dogmatics* I/1, 410.

135. J. Locke, *Essay on Human Understanding* II, ch. 27, §9, in *The Works of John Locke*, London 1823, reprinted Aalen 1963, 2, 55.

136. I. Kant, *General Introduction to the Metaphysic of Morals*, ET W. Hastie, in *Kant, Great Books of the Western World* 42, Chicago 1952, 391.

137. K. Barth, *Church Dogmatics* I/1, 412. On this cf. J. Brinktrine, *Die Lehre von Gott* 2, Paderborn 1954; C. Welch, *The Trinity in Contemporary Thought*, London 1954, 190ff.; H. Volk, 'Die Christologie bei Karl Barth und Emil Brunner', in A. Grillmeier and H. Bacht (eds.), *Das Konzil von Chalkedon. Geschichte und Gegenwart* 3, Würzburg 1954, 613–73, esp. 625ff., 634ff.; B. Lonergan, op. cit. (n. 77), 2, 193–6; E. Jüngel, *The Doctrine of the Trinity: God's Being Is in Becoming*, Grand Rapids 1976, 25ff.; B. de Margerie, *La Trinité chrétienne dans l'histoire*, Paris 1975, 289ff.

138. K. Rahner, *The Trinity*, 109ff. On this cf. E. Gutwenger, 'Zur Trinitätslehre von *Mysterium Salutis* II', *ZKT* 90, 1968, 325–8; B. de Margerie, op. cit., 293ff.; H. J. Lauter, 'Die doppelte Aporetik der Trinitätslehre und ihre Überschreitung', *WWeis* 36 1973, 60ff.; F. X. Bantle, 'Person und Personbegriff in der Trinitätslehre Karl Rahners', *MTZ* 30, 1979, 11–24; J. Moltmann, *The Trinity and the Kingdom of God*, ET M. Kohl, London and New York 1981, 144–8.

139. Bonaventure, *De Trinitate* III, 2 and ad 13; Thomas Aquinas, *In I Sent.*, d. 23, q. 1, a. 3; *De pot.* 2, 5 ad 4; 9, 4; 9, 5 ad 23; *ST* I, 30, 4 ad 2; *Compendium theologiae* I, 46.

140. This point was made some time ago with regard to Barth by H. Urs von Balthasar in his *The Theology of Karl Barth*, ET J. Drury, New York 1971. Cf. more recently, with regard to the doctrine of the Trinity, W. Pannenberg, 'Die subjektivität Gottes und die Trinitätslehre', in his *Grundfragen systematischer Theologie. Gesammelte Aufsätze* 2, Göttingen 1980, 96–111. On Barth and Rahner together (but without making a sufficient distinction between the two) cf. J. Moltmann, op. cit. (n. 138), 139–48. Over against the unsophisticated suspicion of tritheism that is attached to Barth and Rahner Moltmann sets the contrasting and equally unsophisticated suspicion of modalism that is attached to his own conception of an open unity in the Trinity. On this point cf. below, n. 183.

141. It is not without significance that K. Barth, *Church Dogmatics* I/1, 414, appeals to the Neo-thomisitc dogmatic theology of F. Diekamp. Cf. F. Diekamp and K. Jüssen, *Katholische Dogmatik nach den Grundsätzen des hl. Thomas* 1, Münster ¹²⁻¹³1958, 329. On this point cf. L. Oeing-Hanhoff, 'Hegels Trinitäts-lehre', *Theol. Phil.* 52, 1977, 399f.

142. B. Lonergan, op. cit., 186–931; cf. Thomas Aquinas, *ST* I, 34, 1 ad 3.

143. Ibid., 193.

144. H. Mühlen, *Der Heilige Geist als Person. Beitrag zur Frage nach der dem Heiligen Geiste eigentümlichen Funktion in der Trinität, bei der Inkarnation und im Gnadenbund*, Münsterische Beiträge zur Theologie 26, Münster, 1963; in addition cf. M. Nédoncelle, *La réciprocité des consciences. Essai sur la nature de la personne*, Paris 1942; B. de Margerie, op. cit. (n. 137), 295ff.; A. Brunner, *Dreifaltigkeit, Personale Zugänge zum Mysterium*, Einsiedeln 1976.

145. Cf. J. G. Fichte, *The Science of Rights*, ET A. E. Kroeger, Philadelphia 1869, reprinted London 1970, §§3f.; *The Destination of Man*, ET P. Sinnett, London 1846, Book 3; *Guide to the Happy Life*, ET W. Smith, in *Fichte: Popular Works*, 2 vols., London 1844–49, Lecture 10; Hegel, *Philosophy of Right*, ET T. M. Knox,

Oxford 1942, §§35f., 48, 57, 71, where it is shown that 'person' concretely includes self-recognition.

146. Cf. B. Langenmeier, *Der dialogische Personalismus in der evangelischen und katholischen Theologie der Gegenwart*, Paderborn 1963; M. Theunissen, *Der Andere. Studien zur Sozialontologie der Gegenwart*, Berlin 1965; B. Casper, *Das dialogische Denken. Eine Untersuchung der religionshilosophischen Bedeutung Franz Rosenzweigs, Ferdinand Ebners and Martin Bubers*, Freiburg – Basle – Vienna 1967; H. H. Schrey, *Dialogisches Denken*, Darmstadt 1970; J. Heinrichs, 'Sein und Intersubjektivität', *Theol. Phil.* 45, 1970, 161ff.

147. Following Lonergan (op. cit., 193), Rahner (*The Trinity*, 107 n. 29) interchanges these two.

148. J. Ratzinger, 'Zum Personverständnis in der Theologie' (n. 97), 206.

149. Ibid., 206ff., 215ff.; cf. his *Introduction to Christianity*, ET J. B. Foster, New York 1970, 128–30.

150. Cf. above, 234ff; 239f.

151. B. Pascal, *Pensées*, fr. 604 (Br 871), ET in A. Krailsheimer, *Pascal's Pensées*, Baltimore 1966, 232.

152. Cf. above, 238ff.

153. Cf. above, 247f.

154. Cf. above, 240f.

155. Tertullian, *Ad Praxean* 3 (CCL 2, 1161f.).

156. Ibid., 10 (CCL 2, 1169f.).

157. Cf. C. Huber, 'Monarchianismus', *LTK* 7, 533f.

158. Aristotle, *Metaphysica* XI, 10, 1076a. Cf. E. Peterson, 'Der Monotheismus als politisches Problem', in *Theologische Traktate*, Munich 1951, 45, 147.

159. Athanasius, *Adv. Arianos* IV, 13–15 (PG 26, 483–90) therefore sees Sabellianism as deriving from Stoicism.

160. Gregory of Nazianzus, *Oratio* 27, 1 (SC 250, 70–73).

161. This has been shown especially by J. A. Möhler, *Athanasius der Grosse und die Kirche seiner Zeit besonders im Kampf mit dem Arianismus*, Mainz 1827, 304ff., where he refers to F. Schleiermacher. Cf. J. Moltmann, *The Trinity and the Kingdom* (n. 140), 129ff.

162. Basil, *Ep.* 226, 4 (PG 32, 849ff.).

163. Basil, *Ep.* 210, 3 (PG 23, 771f.).

164. Basil, *Ep.* 210, 4 (PG 32, 771ff.).

165. Tertullian, *Adv. Praxean* 3, 3f. (CCL 2, 1161f.).

166. Cf. above, 253ff. It is to be noted here that under Stoic influence Tertullian maintained a kind of corporeality in God. Cf. *De carne Christi* 11 (CCL 2, 894f.); *Adv. Praxean* 7 (CCL 2, 1165ff.).

167. Athanasius, *De decretis nicaenae synodi* 11; 22 (PG 25, 433ff, 453ff.).

168. Basil, *De spiritu sancto* 18 (SC 17, 191–8).

169. Basil, *Ep.* 8, 2 (PG 32, 247ff.).

170. Gregory of Nazianzus, *Oratio* 29, 16 (SC 250, 210–13); *Oratio* 31, 9 (SC 250, 290–3).

171. John Damascene, *De fide orth.* I, 8 (*Die Schriften. . .* II, 18–31).

172. Thus J. E. Kuhn, op. cit. (n. 35), 498ff., 545ff.; similarly F. A. Staudenmaier, *Die christliche Dogmatik* 2, Freiburg 1844, 470ff.

173. K. Barth, *Church Dogmatics* I/1, 400.

174. This idea is developed in J. E. Kuhn, op. cit., 558ff, especially in discussion

with Hegel. Cf. W. Pannenberg, 'Die Subjektivität Gottes und die Trinitätslehre' (n. 140), 96–111.

175. Hilary, *De Trinitate* VII, 3 (CCL 62, 261f.), *De synodis* 37; 69 (PL 10, 455f., 526); Peter Chrysologus, *Serm.* 60 (PL 162, 1008f.).

176. DS 125, 150; ND 7, 12.

177. Cf. the condemnation of Roscellinus by the Council of Soissons (1092) and of Gilbert of Poitiers by the Council of Rheims (1148) (DS 745), although it has now been established that the profession of faith directed against Gilbert was not part of the original acts of the council.

178. DS 803; ND 317.

179. DS 528, ET in ND 311.

180 *Catechismus Romanus* II, 2, 10.

181. DS 2697.

182. This theism was represented in philosophy by the Late Idealists Weisse, Fichte, Sengler and others.

183. Cf. J. Moltmann, *The Crucified God: The Cross of Christ as the Foundation and Criticism of Christian Theology*, ET R. A. Wilson and John Bowden, London and New York 1974, 249–52. There is a critical response to Moltmann in W. Pannenberg, 'Die Subjektivität Gottes und die Trinitätslehre' (n. 140), 110 no. 34. The danger of tritheism is even clearer in Moltmann's idea of a social or open Trinity; cf. his *The Trinity and the Kingdom* (n. 138).

184. On tritheistic tendencies in the history of theology cf. M. Schmaus, 'Tritheismus', *LTK* 10, 365f.

185. K. Barth, *Church Dogmatics* I/1, 402f.

186. It was the merit of T. de Régnon, *Etudes de théologie positive sur la sainte Trinité* (n. 97), esp. 1, 335–40, 428–35, to have shown the existence of the two models.

187. Cf., e.g., V. Lossky, *The Mystical Theology of the Eastern Church*, London 1957, 52, 56ff.; S. Bulgakov, *Le Paraclet* Paris 1946, 118.

188. Cf. above, 215f.

189. DS 850; ND 321.

190. A. Malet has brought this out in his *Personne et amour dans la théologie trinitaire de saint Thomas d'Aquin* (n. 104).

191. John Damascene, *De fide orth.* I, 8 (*Die Schriften. . .* II, 18–31).

192. Cf. Malet, op. cit., 14f.

193. Ibid., 55ff.

194. Cf. below, 300ff.

195. Cf. M. J. Le Guillou, *Das Mysterium des Vaters* (n. 105), 104ff.

196. Cf. Malet, op. cit., 37ff.

197. Cf. L. Scheffczyk, 'Die heilsgeschichtliche Trinitätslehre des Rupert von Deutz und ihre dogmatische Bedeutung', in J. Betz and H. Fries (eds.), *Kirche und Überlieferung (FS J. R. Geiselmann)*, Freiburg – Basle – Vienna 1960, 90–118.

198. Cf. Malet, op. cit., 71ff.

199. J. E. Kuhn, op. cit., 553, 572, rightly points this out. On the other hand, Kuhn himself tries rather to carry the Latin and Western approach even further, and he dismisses the Greek approach as insufficiently speculative. In this he is still under the spell of idealism, however firmly he separates himself from Hegel and Günther materially and dogmatically. On this point it is clearer to us today that we need a postidealist and personalist starting point.

200. For what follows cf. K. Barth, *Church Dogmatics*, I/1, 349–83: 'The Root of the Doctrine of the Trinity'. I cannot here discuss Barth's development. The early version of *Church Dogmatics* I/1 in Barth's *Die christliche Dogmatik im Entwurf* 1. *Die Lehre vom Worte Gottes. Prolegomena zur christlichen Dogmatik*, Munich 1927, 126–40, is important.

201. For what follows cf. K. Rahner, *The Trinity*, 80ff.; also 'Remarks on the Dogmatic Treatise "De Trinitate" ', (n. 64), *Foundations of Christian Faith: An Introduction to the Idea of Christianity*. ET W. V. Dych, New York and London 1978, 133–7; 'Trinity, Divine', *SacMundi* 6, 295–303; 'Trinity in Theology', ibid., 6, 303–8; 'Trinity', in K. Rahner and H. Vorgrimler, *Concise Theological Dictionary*, ET R. Strachan, D. Smith, R. Nowell and S. O. Twohy, London and New York ²1981, 513–17; 'Dreifaltigkeitsmystik', *LTK* 3, 563–4. On Rahner's approach cf. G. Lafont, *Peut-on connaître Dieu en Jésus-Christ?* Cogitatio fidei 44, Paris 1969, 172–228; B. van der Heijden, *Karl Rahner. Darlegung und Kritik seiner Grundposition*, Eisiedeln 1973, 424–42; K. Fischer, *Der Mensch als Geheimnis. Die Anthropologie Karl Rahners*, Ökumenische Forschungen II, 5, Freiburg – Basle – Vienna 1974, 337–65; H. Urs von Balthasar, *Theodramatik* 3, Einsiedeln 1980, 298ff.

202. K. Barth, *Church Dogmatics* I/1, 349.

203. Ibid., 351.

204. Ibid., 353.

205. Ibid., 362 and 367.

206. Ibid., 368.

207. Ibid., 381.

208. This is especially clear in his *Die christliche Dogmatik im Entwurf* (n. 200), 140.

209. Thus W. Pannenberg, art cit., (n. 174), 96, in agreement with T. Rendtorff, 'Radikale Autonomie Gottes. Zum Verständnis der Theologie Karl Barths and ihrer Folgen', in *Theorie des Christentums. Historisch-theologische Studien su seiner neuzeitlichen Fassung*, Gütersloh 1972, 161–81.

210. Cf. above, n. 139.

211. K. Rahner, *Foundations of Christian Faith* (n. 201), 116 and elsewhere.

212. Id., *The Trinity*, 88 n. 10.

213. Ibid., 85 n. 7; 100 n. 18; 102 n. 21.

214. Ibid., 83–7.

215. Ibid., 91–8.

216. Ibid., 99–103; *Foundations of Christian Faith*, 136–7.

217. *The Trinity*, 59–60, 83–7.

218. *Foundations of Christian Faith*, 137.

219. Cf. above, 287f.

220. *Worte ins Schweigen*; ET J. Demske, *Encounters with Silence*, Westminster, Md. 1960.

221. Id.,'Current Problems in Christology', *Theological Investigations* 1, ET C. Ernst, London and Baltimore 1961, 157–63, 168–74; 'Dogmatic Reflections on the Knowledge and Self-Consciousness of Christ', in *Theological Investigations* 5, ET K.-H. Kruger, London and Baltimore 1966, 193–215.

222. 'The Position of Christology in the Church between Exegesis and Dogmatics', *Theological Investigations* 11, ET D. Bourke, London and New York 1974, 198–9; for a clear statement", *The Trinity*, 61–3. For this reason the criticism

of B. van der Heijden, *Karl Rahner, Darlegung und Kritik seiner Grundposition* (n. 201), 399H, 435H, seems to point to a real problem but at the same time to interpret Rahner's not entirely clear statement in a certain direction that is itself open to criticism.

233. K. Rahner, 'Christology within an Evolutionary View of the World', *Theological Investigations* 5 (n. 221), 173–88.

224. This finds expression especially in the profound commentary on the prayer which Augustine gives in his *In Joannis Evangelium tractatus*, tract. 107–11 (CCL 36, 613–33). Recent exegesis: R. Bultmann, *The Gospel of John: A Commentary*, ET G. R. Beasley-Murray, R. W. N. Hoare and J. K. Riches, Oxford and Philadelphia 1971, 486–522; W. Thüsing, *Herrlichkeit und Einheit. Eine Auslegung des Hohenpriesterlichen Gebetes Johannes 17*, Die Welt der Bibel 14, Düsseldorf 1972; E. Käsemann, *The Testimony of Jesus: A Study of the Gospel of John in the Light of Chapter 17*, ET G. Krödel, Philadelphia 1968; R. Schnackenburg, *The Gospel according to St. John* 3, ET D. Smith and G. A. Kon, New York 1972, 167–202; S. Schulz, *Das Evangelium nach Johannes*, NTD 4 Göttingen 1972, 213–20.

225. This is the approach taken by J. E. Kuhn, *Katholicsche Dogmatik 2. Die christliche Lehre von der göttlichen Dreifaltigkeit*, Tübingen 1857; cf. A. Brunner, *Dreifaltigkeit. Personale Zugänge zum Mysterium* (n. 144), 23.

226. Cf. above, 167f. This viewpoint is developed especially in J. Moltmann, *The Trinity and the Kingdom* (n. 140).

227. Cf. above, 282f.

228. Augustine, *De Trinitate*, I, 4; etc. (CCL 50, 31); *In Johannis Evangelium tractatus* 105, 3; 107, 6; 111, 3 (CCL 36, 604, 615, 631).

229. Cf. E. Peterson, 'Der Monotheismus als politisches Problem' (n. 158).

230. Ibid., 105.

231. K. Hemmerle, *Thesen zu einer trinitarischen Ontologie*, Einsiedeln 1976, 66ff.

232. Cf. above, 280f.

233. Cf. K. Hemmerle, op. cit., 38ff.

234. The kenotic character of the trinitarian persons as relations has been brought out by H. Urs von Balthasar, 'Mysterium paschale', *Mysal* III/3, 152f., following some modern Russian theologians (especially Soloviev, Turajev and Bulgakov).

235. On this point cf. W. Breuning, 'Stellung der Trinitätslehre', in H. Vorgrimler and R. van der Gucht (eds.), *Bilanz der Theologie im 20. Jahrhundert* 3, Freiburg – Basle – Vienna 1970, 26–8; K. Rahner, 'Trinity in Theology', *SacMundi* 6, 304–5.

236. *A New Catechism: Catholic Faith for Adults*, ET K. Smyth, London and New York 1967, 498–502.

237. K. Rahner, 'Trinity in Theology', *SacMundi* 6, 305.

238. M. Schmaus, *Katholische Dogmatik* 1, Munich ⁵1953.

239. Cf. W. Kasper, 'Christologie und Anthropologie', *TQ* 162, 1982, 202–21.

INDEX OF SUBJECTS

INDEX OF PROPER NAMES

Index of Proper Names
403